ACTEX ACADEMIC SERIES

Models for Quantifying Risk

4th Edition

ROBIN J. CUNNINGHAM, PH.D.
THOMAS N. HERZOG, PH.D., ASA
RICHARD L. LONDON, FSA

ACTEX Publications, Inc.
Winsted, CT

Manufactured in the United States of America

10 9 8 7 6 5 4 3 2 1

Cover design by Christine Phelps

Library of Congress Cataloging-in-Publication Data

Cunningham, Robin J., 1965-
  Models for quantifying risk / Robin J. Cunningham, Thomas N. Herzog, Richard L. London. -- 4th ed.
      p. cm.
  Includes bibliographical references and index.
  ISBN 978-1-56698-819-3 (pbk. : alk. paper) 1. Insurance--Mathematics. 2. Risk management. 3. Financial risk. I. Herzog, Thomas N., 1946- II. London, Richard L. III. Title.
  HG8781.C86 2011
  368'.01--dc23
                              2011034037

ISBN: 978-1-56698-819-3

PREFACE

The analysis and management of financial risk is the fundamental subject matter of the discipline of actuarial science, and is therefore the basic work of the actuary. In order to manage financial risk, by use of insurance schemes or any other risk management technique, the actuary must first have a framework for quantifying the magnitude of the risk itself. This is achieved by using mathematical models that are appropriate for each particular type of risk under consideration. Since risk is, almost by definition, probabilistic, it follows that the appropriate models will also be probabilistic, or stochastic, in nature.

This textbook, appropriately entitled *Models for Quantifying Risk*, addresses the major types of financial risk analyzed by actuaries, and presents a variety of stochastic models for the actuary to use in undertaking this analysis. It is designed to be appropriate for a two-semester university course in basic actuarial science for third-year or fourth-year undergraduate students or entry-level graduate students. It is also intended to be an appropriate text for use by candidates in preparing for Exam MLC of the Society of Actuaries or Exam 3L of the Casualty Actuarial Society.

One way to manage financial risk is to *insure* it, which basically means that a second party, generally an insurance company, is paid a fee to assume the risk from the party initially facing it. Historically the work of actuaries was largely confined to the management of risk within an insurance context, so much so, in fact, that actuaries were thought of as "insurance mathematicians" and actuarial science was thought of as "insurance math." Although the insurance context remains a primary environment for the actuarial management of risk, it is by no means any longer the only one.

However, in recognition of the insurance context as the original setting for actuarial analysis and management of financial risk, we have chosen to make liberal use of insurance terminology and notation to describe many of the risk quantification models presented in this text. The reader should always keep in mind, however, that this frequent reference to an insurance context does not reduce the applicability of the models to risk management situations in which no use of insurance is involved.

The text is written in a manner that assumes each reader has a strong background in calculus, linear algebra, the theory of compound interest, and probability. (A familiarity with statistics is not presumed.)

This edition of the text is organized into three sections. The first, consisting of Chapters 1-4, presents a review of interest theory, probability, Markov Chains, and stochastic simulation, respectively. The content of these chapters is very much needed as background to later material. They are included in the text for readers needing a comprehensive review of the topics. For those requiring an original textbook on any of these topics, we recommend either Broverman [6] or Kellison [16] for interest theory, Hassett and Stewart [12] for probability, Ross [26] for Markov Chains, and Herzog and Lord [13] for simulation.

The second section, made up of Chapters 5-14, addresses the topic of survival-contingent payment models, traditionally referred to as *life contingencies*. The third section, consisting of Chapters 15-17, deals with the topic of models for interest rate risks.

The new material appearing in this edition has been added to the text to meet the new set of learning objectives for Exam MLC, to be effective with the May 2012 administration of the exam. There are several major areas of expanded material:

(1) Part Three (Chapters 15-17) has been added to address the topic of interest rate risk, including an introduction to *variable*, or *interest-sensitive*, insurance and annuities.

(2) The new learning objectives provide that many of the models described in the text should also be presented in the context of multi-state models, using the theory of Markov Chains. Accordingly, we have inserted new Chapter 3 to provide background on Markov Chains, and have then inserted numerous applications of this theory to our actuarial models throughout the text.

(3) In the prior edition of the text, the topic of contingent contract reserves was presented in one large chapter. In the new edition, we have separated the topic into two chapters: Chapter 10 covers net level premium benefit reserves only, and Chapter 11 addresses the accounting notion of reserves as financial liabilities, as well as other policy values, as suggested by the new learning objectives.

(4) Similarly, the topic of multiple decrements is now presented in two chapters: Chapter 13 addresses multiple decrement theory and Chapter 14 presents a number of applications of the theory, many in the context of multi-state models.

(5) Certain actuarial risk models are most efficiently evaluated through simulation, rather than by use of closed form analytic solutions. We have inserted new Chapter 4 to provide theoretical background on the topic of stochastic simulation, and then developed a number of applications of that theory to our actuarial models. Readers who are preparing for SOA Exam MLC should be aware that this topic is *not* covered on that examination. Accordingly we have placed all of the simulation applications in Appendix B in this edition.

(6) A number of minor topics have been deleted from the prior edition, including (a) the central rate of failure, (b) use of the population functions L_x, T_x, and Y_x, and (c) our presentation of Hattendorf's Theorem. Several notational changes have also been made.

The writing team would like to thank a number of people for their contributions to the development of this text.

The original manuscript was thoroughly reviewed by Bryan V. Hearsey, ASA, of Lebanon Valley College and by Esther Portnoy, FSA, of University of Illinois. Portions of the manuscript were also reviewed by Warren R. Luckner, FSA, and his graduate student Luis Gutierrez at University of Nebraska-Lincoln. Kristen S. Moore, ASA, used an earlier draft as a supplemental text in her courses at University of Michigan. Thorough reviews of the original edition were also conducted by James W. Daniel, ASA, of University of Texas, Professor Jacques Labelle, Ph.D., of Université du Québec à Montréal, and a committee appointed by the Society of Actuaries. A number of revisions in the Second Edition were also reviewed by Professors Daniel and Hearsey; Third Edition revisions were reviewed by Professors Samuel A. Broverman, ASA (University of Toronto), Matthew J. Hassett, ASA (Arizona State University), and Warren R. Luckner, FSA (University of Nebraska-Lincoln). All of these academic colleagues made a number of useful comments that have contributed to an improved published text.

The new topics contained in this edition were researched for us by actuaries with considerable experience in their respective fields, and we wish to acknowledge their valuable contributions. They include Ronald Gebhardtsbauer, FSA (Penn State University) for Section 14.5, Ximing Yao, FSA (Hartford Life) for Chapter 16, and Chunhua (Amy) Meng, FSA (Yindga Taihe Life) for Chapter 17.

The new material added to this Fourth Edition was also reviewed by Professor Luckner, as well as by Tracey J. Polsgrove, FSA (John Hancock USA), Link Richardson, FSA (American General Life), Arthur W. Anderson, ASA, EA (The Arthur W. Anderson Group), Cheryl Ann Breindel, FSA (Hartford Life), Douglas J. Jangraw, FSA (Massachusetts Mutual Life), Robert W. Beal, FSA (Milliman Portland), Andrew C. Boyer, FSA (Milliman Windsor), and Matthew Blanchette, FSA (Hartford Life), who also contributed to the Chapter 17 exercises.

Special thanks goes to the students enrolled in Math 287-288 at University of Connecticut during the 2004-05 academic year, where the original text was classroom-tested, and to graduate student Xiumei Song, who developed the computer technology material presented in Appendix A.

Thanks also to the folks at ACTEX Publications, particularly Gail A. Hall, FSA, the project editor, and Marilyn J. Baleshiski, who did the typesetting and graphic arts for all editions. Kathleen H. Borkowski designed the cover for the first two editions, and Christine Phelps did the same for the latter two editions.

Finally, a very special acknowledgment is in order. When the Society of Actuaries published its textbook *Actuarial Mathematics* in the mid-1980s, Professor Geoffrey Crofts, FSA, then at University of Hartford, made the observation that the authors' use of the generic symbol Z as the present value random variable for *all* insurance models and the generic symbol Y as the present value random variable for *all* annuity models was confusing. He suggested that the present value random variable symbols be expanded to identify more characteristics of the models to which each related, following the principle that the present value random variable be notated in a manner consistent with the standard International Actuarial Notation used for its expected value. Thus one should use, for example, $\bar{Z}_{x:\overline{n}|}$ in the case of the continuous endowment insurance model and $_{n|}\ddot{Y}_x$ in the case of the n-year deferred annuity-due model, whose expected values are denoted $\overline{A}_{x:\overline{n}|}$ and $_n|\ddot{a}_x$, respectively. Professor Crofts' notation has been adopted throughout our textbook, and we wish to thank him for suggesting this very useful idea to us.

We wish you good luck with your studies and your exam preparation.

Robin J. Cunningham, FSA   Winsted, Connecticut
San Rafael, California   June 2011

Thomas N. Herzog, ASA
Reston, Virginia

Richard L. London, FSA
Storrs, Connecticut

TABLE OF CONTENTS

PART ONE

REVIEW AND BACKGROUND MATERIAL

The first section of this text presents four sets of mathematical tools, namely interest theory, probability, Markov Chains, and simulation, that will be needed to develop, understand, and analyze the various risk quantification models included later in the text.

With respect to these four tool sets, the text assumes that the reader has already completed a standard university course in each topic, or has otherwise already learned this material at a sufficient level. Accordingly, the presentation of these topics (in Chapters 1, 2, 3, and 4, respectively) will be in the nature of a review.

Note that the mathematical tools of calculus and linear algebra are also deemed to be prerequisite skills for a study of this text, but no specific review of them is included.

CHAPTER ONE

REVIEW OF INTEREST THEORY

Many of the risk quantification models considered in this text are ultimately based on a blend of concepts of probability and the theory of interest. In this chapter we review the basic concepts and notation of interest theory. As stated in the Preface to the text, a prior familiarity with this material is assumed, so that it can be presented as a review without including derivations. Note that only the *compound interest* model is included.

1.1 INTEREST MEASURES

Interest theory usually begins with the concept of the *accumulation function*, denoted $a(t)$, which gives the accumulated value, at time $t \geq 0$, of a unit of money invested at time $t = 0$. Under compound interest, the accumulation function has the exponential form

$$a(t) \;=\; (1+i)^t, \tag{1.1}$$

for $t \geq 0$, where i is a parameter of the function. This is illustrated in Figure 1.1.

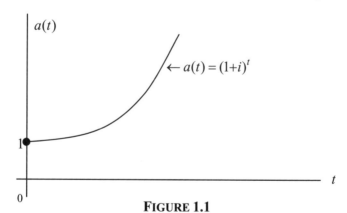

FIGURE 1.1

For the nth time interval, which runs from $t = n-1$ to $t = n$, the *effective rate of interest* is defined as

$$i_n \;=\; \frac{a(n) - a(n-1)}{a(n-1)} \;=\; \frac{(1+i)^n - (1+i)^{n-1}}{(1+i)^{n-1}} \;=\; i. \tag{1.2}$$

Thus we recall that under compound interest the effective periodic interest rate is a constant equal to the parameter in the exponential form of the accumulation function.

For the nth time interval the *effective rate of discount* is defined to be

$$d_n = \frac{a(n) - a(n-1)}{a(n)} = \frac{(1+i)^n - (1+i)^{n-1}}{(1+i)^n} = \frac{i}{1+i} = d. \tag{1.3}$$

Thus we find that the effective periodic discount rate is also a constant, and is a simple function of the parameter of the accumulation function (which is also the effective rate of interest). Solving Equation (1.3) for i we find

$$i = \frac{d}{1-d}. \tag{1.4}$$

The compound interest *discount factor* over one time interval is defined to be

$$v = \frac{1}{1+i}. \tag{1.5}$$

Taking Equations (1.3) and (1.5) together we observe the relationship

$$d = \frac{i}{1+i} = iv. \tag{1.6}$$

Next observe that Equation (1.4) tells us that $d = i(1-d)$ and Equation (1.6) tells us that $d = iv$, so together we have

$$v = 1 - d \tag{1.7}$$

and therefore

$$d = 1 - v. \tag{1.8}$$

This leads to $d = 1 - \frac{1}{1+i}$. Multiplying both sides by $1+i$ then leads to $d + id = 1 + i - 1$, and finally to the relationship

$$id = i - d. \tag{1.9}$$

An instantaneous measure of interest, known as the *force of interest*, is defined by

$$\delta_t = \frac{a'(t)}{a(t)} = \frac{d}{dt} \ln a(t), \tag{1.10a}$$

which, under compound interest, becomes

$$\delta_t = \ln(1+i) = \delta, \tag{1.10b}$$

a constant function of time. Alternatively we can write

$$(1+i) = e^{\delta} \tag{1.11a}$$

and, in light of Equation (1.5),

$$v = e^{-\delta}. \tag{1.11b}$$

Integrating both sides of Equation (1.10a) with respect to t, between the limits 0 to n, results in the relationship

$$a(n) = e^{\int_0^n \delta_t \, dt}. \tag{1.12a}$$

Under compound interest, with $\delta_t = \delta$, a constant, and $a(n) = (1+i)^n$, Equation (1.12a) then becomes

$$(1+i)^n = e^{n\delta}, \tag{1.12b}$$

as already established by Equation (1.11a). Taking the reciprocals of both sides of Equation (1.12b) gives

$$(1+i)^{-n} = v^n = e^{-n\delta}, \tag{1.12c}$$

as already established by Equation (1.11b).

The reader will recall that the *effective period* (also called the *compounding period* or the *conversion period*) for a rate of compound interest (or discount) is a very important parameter. (An effective *annual* rate of 2% is very different from an effective *monthly* rate of 2%.) Thus we always describe an effective rate by both its numerical value and its period of effectiveness. This leads to the notion of the *equivalence of rates* with different effective periods. For example, an effective annual rate of

$$i = (1.02)^{12} - 1 = .26824$$

is equivalent to an effective monthly rate of 2%, and an effective quarterly rate of

$$i = (1.06)^{1/4} - 1 = .01467$$

is equivalent to an effective annual rate of 6%.

For rates with an effective period of less than one year, such as effective monthly, quarterly, or semiannual rates, we have adopted the notational convention of expressing the *annualized value* of the effective periodic rate. This annualized value is called the *nominal annual rate*. Thus, for example, an effective quarterly rate of 2% is stated as a nominal annual rate of 8%, an effective monthly rate of 1% is stated as a nominal annual rate of 12%, and an effective semiannual rate of 5% is stated as a nominal annual rate of 10%. The notation $i^{(4)} = .08$, $i^{(12)} = .12$, and $i^{(2)} = .10$, respectively, is used. Note that the number in the parentheses is the number of compounding (or effective) periods in a year. The same concept of nominal rate notation also applies to effective rates of discount.

1.2 LEVEL ANNUITY FUNCTIONS

In this section we review the terminology and notation used with level payment annuities-certain, evaluated at a constant rate of compound interest per payment period.

1.2.1 IMMEDIATE ANNUITY

A *unit immediate annuity* is one for which the unit payments are made at the *ends* of the respective payment periods, as illustrated in Figure 1.2.

FIGURE 1.2

The *present value* of the annuity, denoted $a_{\overline{n}|}$, is measured at time 0 and is given by

$$a_{\overline{n}|} \;=\; v + v^2 + \cdots + v^n \;=\; \frac{1 - v^n}{i}. \tag{1.13}$$

The *accumulated value* of the annuity, denoted $s_{\overline{n}|}$, is measured at time n and is given by

$$s_{\overline{n}|} \;=\; (1+i)^{n-1} + (1+i)^{n-2} + \cdots + (1+i) + 1 \;=\; \frac{(1+i)^n - 1}{i}. \tag{1.14}$$

From Equations (1.13) and (1.14) together we can see that

$$a_{\overline{n}|} \;=\; v^n \cdot s_{\overline{n}|}, \tag{1.15a}$$

$$s_{\overline{n}|} \;=\; (1+i)^n \cdot a_{\overline{n}|}, \tag{1.15b}$$

and

$$\frac{1}{a_{\overline{n}|}} \;=\; \frac{1}{s_{\overline{n}|}} + i. \tag{1.16}$$

In the limiting case, as $n \to \infty$, we have the notion of the *unit immediate perpetuity*, with present value given by

$$a_{\overline{\infty}|} \;=\; v + v^2 + \cdots \;=\; \frac{1}{i}. \tag{1.17}$$

1.2.2 ANNUITY-DUE

A *unit annuity-due* is one for which the unit payments are made at the *beginnings* of the respective payment periods, as illustrated in Figure 1.3.

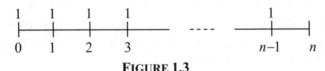

FIGURE 1.3

The present value of the annuity, denoted $\ddot{a}_{\overline{n}|}$, is measured at time 0 and is given by

$$\ddot{a}_{\overline{n}|} \;=\; 1 + v + v^2 + \cdots + v^{n-1} \;=\; \frac{1 - v^n}{d}. \tag{1.18}$$

The accumulated value, denoted $\ddot{s}_{\overline{n}|}$, is measured at time n and is given by

$$\ddot{s}_{\overline{n}|} = (1+i)^n + (1+i)^{n-1} + \cdots + (1+i) = \frac{(1+i)^n - 1}{d}. \tag{1.19}$$

From Equations (1.18) and (1.19) together we can see that

$$\ddot{a}_{\overline{n}|} = v^n \cdot \ddot{s}_{\overline{n}|}, \tag{1.20a}$$

$$\ddot{s}_{\overline{n}|} = (1+i)^n \cdot \ddot{a}_{\overline{n}|}, \tag{1.20b}$$

and

$$\frac{1}{\ddot{a}_{\overline{n}|}} = \frac{1}{\ddot{s}_{\overline{n}|}} + d. \tag{1.21}$$

In the limiting case, as $n \to \infty$, we have the notion of the *unit perpetuity-due*, with present value given by

$$\ddot{a}_{\overline{\infty}|} = 1 + v + v^2 + \cdots = \frac{1}{d}. \tag{1.22}$$

From Equations (1.13) and (1.18) we can see that

$$\ddot{a}_{\overline{n}|} = (1+i) \cdot a_{\overline{n}|} \tag{1.23}$$

and, conversely,

$$a_{\overline{n}|} = v \cdot \ddot{a}_{\overline{n}|}. \tag{1.24}$$

Similarly, from Equations (1.14) and (1.19) we can see that

$$\ddot{s}_{\overline{n}|} = (1+i) \cdot s_{\overline{n}|} \tag{1.25}$$

and, conversely,

$$s_{\overline{n}|} = v \cdot \ddot{s}_{\overline{n}|}. \tag{1.26}$$

1.2.3 CONTINUOUS ANNUITY

Consider the theoretical notion of an annuity paying one unit of money per year, but split into an infinitely large number of payments of infinitely small size each. Clearly the payments are so "close together" that we interpret the unit as being paid *continuously* over the year. Suppose this arrangement continues for n consecutive years.

The present value of this *unit continuous annuity*, denoted $\overline{a}_{\overline{n}|}$, is measured at time 0 and is given by

$$\overline{a}_{\overline{n}|} \;=\; \int_0^n v^t\,dt \;=\; \frac{1-v^n}{\delta}. \tag{1.27}$$

The accumulated value, denoted $\overline{s}_{\overline{n}|}$, is measured at time n and is given by

$$\overline{s}_{\overline{n}|} \;=\; \int_0^n (1+i)^{n-t}\,dt \;=\; \frac{(1+i)^n -1}{\delta}. \tag{1.28}$$

From Equations (1.27) and (1.28) together we can see that

$$\overline{a}_{\overline{n}|} \;=\; v^n \cdot \overline{s}_{\overline{n}|}, \tag{1.29a}$$

$$\overline{s}_{\overline{n}|} \;=\; (1+i)^n \cdot \overline{a}_{\overline{n}|}, \tag{1.29b}$$

and

$$\frac{1}{\overline{a}_{\overline{n}|}} \;=\; \frac{1}{\overline{s}_{\overline{n}|}} + \delta. \tag{1.30}$$

In the limiting case, as $n \to \infty$, we have the notion of the *unit continuous perpetuity*, with present value given by

$$\overline{a}_{\overline{\infty}|} \;=\; \int_0^\infty v^t\,dt \;=\; \frac{1}{\delta}. \tag{1.31}$$

From Equations (1.27), (1.18), and (1.13) together we can see that

$$\overline{a}_{\overline{n}|} \;=\; \frac{d}{\delta} \cdot \ddot{a}_{\overline{n}|} \;=\; \frac{i}{\delta} \cdot a_{\overline{n}|}. \tag{1.32}$$

Similarly, from Equations (1.28), (1.19), and (1.14) together we can see that

$$\overline{s}_{\overline{n}|} \;=\; \frac{d}{\delta} \cdot \ddot{s}_{\overline{n}|} \;=\; \frac{i}{\delta} \cdot s_{\overline{n}|}. \tag{1.33}$$

1.3 NON-LEVEL ANNUITY FUNCTIONS

Often we encounter a sequence of annuity payments that is not level, but that varies in a regular pattern. Here we will consider both arithmetic and geometric patterns of variation.

1.3.1 IMMEDIATE ANNUITIES

Consider the *unit increasing immediate annuity* with the arithmetic pattern of payments illustrated in Figure 1.4.

FIGURE 1.4

The present value of the annuity, denoted $(Ia)_{\overline{n}|}$, is measured at time 0 and is given by

$$(Ia)_{\overline{n}|} \;=\; v + 2v^2 + 3v^3 + \cdots + nv^n \;=\; \frac{\ddot{a}_{\overline{n}|} - nv^n}{i}. \tag{1.34}$$

The accumulated value of this annuity, denoted $(Is)_{\overline{n}|}$, is measured at time n and is given by

$$(Is)_{\overline{n}|} \;=\; (1+i)^{n-1} + 2(1+i)^{n-2} + \cdots + (n-1)(1+i) + n \;=\; \frac{\ddot{s}_{\overline{n}|} - n}{i}. \tag{1.35}$$

From Equations (1.34) and (1.35) together it is clear that

$$(Ia)_{\overline{n}|} \;=\; v^n \cdot (Is)_{\overline{n}|} \tag{1.36a}$$

and

$$(Is)_{\overline{n}|} \;=\; (1+i)^n \cdot (Ia)_{\overline{n}|}. \tag{1.36b}$$

In the limiting case, as $n \to \infty$, we have the notion of the *unit increasing immediate perpetuity*, with present value given by

$$(Ia)_{\overline{\infty}|} \;=\; \frac{1}{id}. \tag{1.37}$$

The *unit decreasing immediate annuity* has the arithmetic payment pattern illustrated in Figure 1.5.

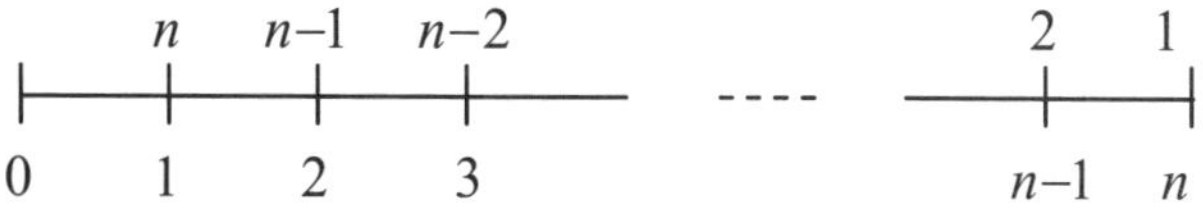

FIGURE 1.5

The present value of this annuity, denoted $(Da)_{\overline{n}|}$, is measured at time 0 and is given by

$$(Da)_{\overline{n}|} \;=\; nv + (n-1)v^2 + (n-2)v^3 + \cdots + 2v^{n-1} + v^n \;=\; \frac{n - a_{\overline{n}|}}{i}. \tag{1.38}$$

The accumulated value of this annuity, denoted $(Ds)_{\overline{n}|}$, is measured at time n and is given by

$$(Ds)_{\overline{n}|} \;=\; n(1+i)^{n-1} + (n-1)(1+i)^{n-2} + \cdots + 2(1+i) + 1 \;=\; \frac{n(1+i)^n - s_{\overline{n}|}}{i}. \tag{1.39}$$

From Equations (1.38) and (1.39) together it is clear that

$$(Da)_{\overline{n}|} \;=\; v^n \cdot (Ds)_{\overline{n}|} \tag{1.40a}$$

and

$$(Ds)_{\overline{n}|} \;=\; (1+i)^n \cdot (Da)_{\overline{n}|}. \tag{1.40b}$$

The notion of a perpetuity does not apply in the decreasing case.

Immediate annuities increasing or decreasing in a *geometric* pattern are handled by first principles. If the initial payment (made at time $t = 1$) is one unit of money, and each subsequent payment is r times the previous payment, then the annuity has a geometrically increasing payment pattern if $r > 1$ and a geometrically decreasing payment pattern if $r < 1$. (If $r = 1$ the annuity is level, as reviewed in Section 1.2.) The immediate geometric annuity is illustrated in Figure 1.6.

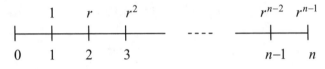

FIGURE 1.6

The present value of this annuity at time 0 is

$$
\begin{aligned}
PV &= v + rv^2 + r^2 v^3 + \cdots + r^{n-2} v^{n-1} + r^{n-1} v^n \\
&= v \left[1 + (rv) + (rv)^2 + \cdots + (rv)^{n-1} \right] = v \left[\frac{1 - (rv)^n}{1 - (rv)} \right].
\end{aligned} \tag{1.41}
$$

The present value will exist for a *geometrically increasing perpetuity* if the growth rate in the payments is less than the interest rate used to discount the future payments (i.e., if $r < 1+i$). Since $r < 1$ in the decreasing case, the present value of the decreasing perpetuity will always exist.

The accumulated value of the annuity at time n is most easily found by the now-familiar relationship $AV = PV(1+i)^n$. Note that we have no standard actuarial symbol for the present and accumulated values of these annuities.

1.3.2 ANNUITIES-DUE

The arithmetic unit increasing, arithmetic unit decreasing, and geometric increasing or decreasing annuities reviewed in Section 1.3.1 all have their annuity-due counterparts, with payments made at the beginnings of the respective periods instead of the ends. The following symbols and formulas should now be well understood:

$$(I\ddot{a})_{\overline{n}|} \;=\; \frac{\ddot{a}_{\overline{n}|} - nv^n}{d} \tag{1.42}$$

$$(I\ddot{s})_{\overline{n}|} \quad = \quad \frac{\ddot{s}_{\overline{n}|} - n}{d} \tag{1.43}$$

$$(D\ddot{a})_{\overline{n}|} \quad = \quad \frac{n - a_{\overline{n}|}}{d} \tag{1.44}$$

$$(D\ddot{s})_{\overline{n}|} \quad = \quad \frac{n(1+i)^n - s_{\overline{n}|}}{d} \tag{1.45}$$

$$(I\ddot{a})_{\overline{\infty}|} \quad = \quad \frac{1}{d^2} \tag{1.46}$$

In all cases the annuity-due function is simply $(1+i)$ times the corresponding immediate annuity function.

In the geometric case, we have the payment pattern illustrated in Figure 1.7.

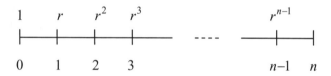

FIGURE 1.7

The present value of this annuity at time 0 is

$$\begin{aligned} PV &= 1 + rv + r^2v^2 + \cdots + r^{n-1}v^{n-1} \\ &= \frac{1-(rv)^n}{1-(rv)} \\ &= \frac{1-\left(\frac{r}{1+i}\right)^n}{1-\left(\frac{r}{1+i}\right)} \\ &= \frac{1-(1+i')^{-n}}{1-(1+i')^{-1}}, \end{aligned} \tag{1.47}$$

which is $\ddot{a}_{\overline{n}|}$ at rate $i' = \frac{1+i}{r} - 1$. The accumulated value at time n is the present value times $(1+i)^n$. Clearly Equations (1.41) and (1.47) together show the now-familiar result that the present value of the annuity-due is always $(1+i)$ times the present value of the corresponding immediate annuity, since both annuities have the same cash flows but each payment is one year earlier under the annuity-due. Again the present value will exist for a perpetuity-due provided $r < 1+i$.

1.3.3 CONTINUOUS ANNUITIES

Now we return to the theoretical notion of an annuity payable continuously, introduced in Section 1.2.3, this time with a non-level payment pattern. We will look at two subcases of this idea.

First we consider the unit increasing annuity, illustrated in the immediate form in Figure 1.4. Instead of making the payments of $1, 2, \cdots, n$ at the ends of each time interval, we think of them as being made continuously over their respective intervals, as illustrated in Figure 1.8.

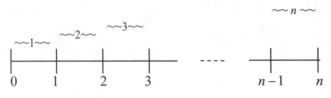

FIGURE 1.8

The present value at time 0 of this step-pattern set of continuous payments can be easily found. We observe that the equivalent value at $t = 1$ of the continuous payment in the first interval only is $\bar{s}_{\overline{1}|}$, the equivalent value at $t = 2$ of the continuous payment in the second interval only is therefore $2 \cdot \bar{s}_{\overline{1}|}$, and so on. The equivalent value at $t = n$ of the continuous payment in the last interval only is $n \cdot \bar{s}_{\overline{1}|}$. Then the present value at time 0 of the entire continuous payment, which is denoted by $(I\bar{a})_{\overline{n}|}$, is

$$(I\bar{a})_{\overline{n}|} = \bar{s}_{\overline{1}|} \cdot v + 2 \cdot \bar{s}_{\overline{1}|} \cdot v^2 + \cdots + n \cdot \bar{s}_{\overline{1}|} \cdot v^n = \bar{s}_{\overline{1}|} \cdot (Ia)_{\overline{n}|}, \tag{1.48a}$$

from Equation (1.34). Since

$$\bar{s}_{\overline{1}|} = \frac{(1+i)^1 - 1}{\delta} = \frac{i}{\delta},$$

Equation (1.48a) is often written as

$$(I\bar{a})_{\overline{n}|} = \frac{i}{\delta} \cdot (Ia)_{\overline{n}|}. \tag{1.48b}$$

The accumulated value at time n then follows as

$$(I\bar{s})_{\overline{n}|} = (1+i)^n \cdot (I\bar{a})_{\overline{n}|} = \frac{i}{\delta} \cdot (Is)_{\overline{n}|}, \tag{1.49}$$

from Equation (1.36b).

Similarly, we can consider the unit decreasing annuity, illustrated in Figure 1.5, in continuous form as well. Here we would have

$$(D\overline{a})_{\overline{n}|} = n \cdot \overline{s}_{\overline{1}|} \cdot v + (n-1) \cdot \overline{s}_{\overline{1}|} \cdot v^2 + \cdots + \overline{s}_{\overline{1}|} \cdot v^n$$

$$= \overline{s}_{\overline{1}|} \cdot (Da)_{\overline{n}|} = \frac{i}{\delta} \cdot (Da)_{\overline{n}|} \tag{1.50}$$

for the present value at time 0, and

$$(D\overline{s})_{\overline{n}|} = \frac{i}{\delta} \cdot (Ds)_{\overline{n}|} \tag{1.51}$$

for the accumulated value at time n.

The second subcase of non-level payment annuities in continuous form is the case for which the payment varies continuously, rather than in the step function pattern considered above.

In general, suppose payment is being made at time t at rate $r(t)$, so that the differential payment made at time t is $r(t) \cdot dt$. The present value at time 0 of this differential payment is then $v^t \cdot r(t) \cdot dt$, and the entire present value is given by

$$PV = \int_0^n r(t) \cdot v^t \, dt. \tag{1.52}$$

Note that we have no standard actuarial symbol for the general case present value. An important special case is the one with $r(t) = t$, so that payment at time t is being made at a rate equal to the time elapsed since time 0. In this case the present value is denoted $(\overline{I}\,\overline{a})_{\overline{n}|}$, and is given by

$$(\overline{I}\,\overline{a})_{\overline{n}|} = \int_0^n t \cdot v^t \, dt = \frac{\overline{a}_{\overline{n}|} - nv^n}{\delta}, \tag{1.53}$$

upon evaluation of the integral using integration by parts. The accumulated value at time n is given by

$$(\overline{I}\,\overline{s})_{\overline{n}|} = \frac{\overline{s}_{\overline{n}|} - n}{\delta}, \tag{1.54}$$

since, in general, the accumulated value is always the present value multiplied by $(1+i)^n$.

1.4 EQUATION OF VALUE

The final item for the reader to review from a prior study of interest theory is the notion of an *equation of value* and its associated *yield rate*.

Suppose we have a series of payments going from Party A to Party B at known points of time, and another series coming back from Party B to Party A at other known points of time. Each series of payments is called a *cash flow*. Note that a cash flow could consist of only one payment. An example of this is illustrated in Figure 1.9.

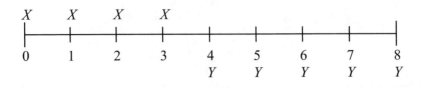

FIGURE 1.9

The cash flow represented by the four X's goes from Party A (say a depositor) to Party B (say a bank) at the times indicated, and the cash flow represented by the five Y's comes back from the bank to the depositor at the times indicated. We can write an equation of value at time 3, for example, as

$$X \cdot s_{\overline{4}|i} \; = \; Y \cdot a_{\overline{5}|i}, \tag{1.55}$$

where i is the periodic effective rate of interest that balances the equation. When viewed as an investment transaction by the depositor, we say that i is the investor's yield rate on the transaction.

Under compound interest it does not matter what point of time is selected at which to write the equation of value; the same value of i will satisfy the equation in any case. Often the choice is made to write the equation as of time 0. Then we would have

$$X + X \cdot v + X \cdot v^2 + X \cdot v^3 \; = \; Y \cdot v^4 + Y \cdot v^5 + Y \cdot v^6 + Y \cdot v^7 + Y \cdot v^8, \tag{1.56}$$

where v is based on effective interest rate i. Finally, it is often common to write the equation of value as

$$X\left[1+v+v^2+v^3\right] - Y\left[v^4+v^5+v^6+v^7+v^8\right] \; = \; 0. \tag{1.57}$$

It is again clear that the same value of i will result from any of Equations (1.55), (1.56), or (1.57). Of course these equations do not lead to closed form expressions for i; rather they must be solved for i numerically using computer software or a sophisticated pocket calculator.

In our work with actuarial models for the quantification of risk throughout this text, we will occasionally encounter the concept of equation of value on either an aggregate or an expected value basis. This review of the equation of value at interest only will help prepare the reader for understanding more complex encounters with the concept when they arise.

CHAPTER TWO

REVIEW OF PROBABILITY

The second basic ingredient for constructing actuarial models for quantifying risk, along with interest theory, is that of basic mathematical probability. Again we are assuming that the reader has completed at least one full semester in calculus-based probability at the university level, so that most of the material contained in this chapter will be somewhat familiar. For several selected topics (see, in particular, Section 2.7), we are less sure that the reader will have this prior familiarity and we will present those topics in greater detail.

Specialized applications of basic probability concepts to various actuarial models are considered throughout the text. Extensions of probability theory that are needed for these specialized applications, which would not normally be covered in a basic probability course, will be introduced as needed in the later chapters.

The most basic concepts of probability are not included in this review; the reader should refer to any standard probability textbook if a review of these concepts is needed.[1] Among the basic concepts not reviewed here are the notion of the probability of an event, negation, union, intersection, mutual exclusion, the general addition rule, conditional probability, independence, the general multiplication rule, the law of total probability, and Bayes' Theorem.

2.1 RANDOM VARIABLES AND THEIR DISTRIBUTIONS

The concept of the *random variable* is the foundation for most of the material presented in this text. Levels of risk can be quantitatively represented by random variables, and understanding the properties of these random variables then allows us to analyze and manage the risk so represented. In this section of this introductory chapter we review basic aspects of random variables and their properties.

2.1.1 DISCRETE RANDOM VARIABLES

A random variable, denoted X, is said to be *discrete* if it can take on only a finite (or countably infinite) number of different values. Each value it can take on is called an *outcome* of the random variable. The set of all possible outcomes is called the *domain*, or *support*, of the random variable.[2] We let x denote a particular value in the domain.

Associated with each value of x is a probability value for the random variable taking on that particular outcome. The probability value is a function of the value of the outcome, denoted

---

[1] For those needing a good probability text, we recommend Hassett and Stewart's *Probability for Risk Management* [12].

[2] Technically, we should say the domain (or support) of the random variable's probability function, but the shorter phrase "domain of the random variable" is often used.

$p(x)$, and is called, appropriately, the *probability function* (PF). That is, $p(x)$ gives the probability of the event $X = x$. (In some textbooks $p(x)$ is called the *probability mass function*.) The set of all probability values constitutes the *distribution* of the random variable. It is necessarily true that

$$\sum_x p(x) = 1, \tag{2.1}$$

where the summation is taken over all values of x in the domain with non-zero probability.

The *expected value* of the random variable, denoted $E[X]$, is a weighted average of all values in the domain, using the associated probability values as weights. Thus we have

$$E[X] = \sum_x x \cdot p(x), \tag{2.2}$$

where the summation is again taken over all values of x with non-zero probability. The expected value is also called the *mean of the random variable* or the *mean of the distribution*. (The expected value exists only if the sum convergence.)

The expected value is a special case of the more general idea of finding the weighted average of a function of the random variable, again using the associated probability values as the weights. If $g(X)$ is any real function of the random variable X, then it can be shown that

$$E[g(X)] = \sum_x g(x) \cdot p(x) \tag{2.3}$$

gives the expected value of the function of the random variable. Note that the mean of the random variable is simply the special case that results when $g(X) = X$.

An important special case is $g(X) = X^k$, and $E[g(X)] = E[X^k]$ is called the kth *moment* of the random variable. (Note that the mean is therefore the *first moment* of the random variable.) Another special case is $g(X) = (X - E[X])^2$, where the expected value of $g(X)$ is called the *variance* of the random variable and is denoted by $Var(X)$. That is,

$$Var(X) = E[(X - E[X])^2] = \sum_x (x - E[X])^2 \cdot p(x). \tag{2.4a}$$

The reader will recall that an equivalent expression for $Var(X)$ is

$$Var(X) = E[X^2] - (E[X])^2, \tag{2.4b}$$

a form often more convenient for calculating $Var(X)$ than is Equation (2.4a). The positive square root of the variance is called the *standard deviation* of X, denoted $SD(X)$.

The moments of a random variable can be generated from a function called, appropriately, the *moment generating function* (MGF), and denoted by $M_X(t)$, provided it exists. It is defined as

$$M_X(t) = E[e^{tX}] = \sum_x e^{tx} \cdot p(x). \tag{2.5}$$

We recognize that this is just another example of finding the expected value of a particular function of the random variable; in this case the function is $g(X) = e^{tX}$. Note that $M_X(t)$ is a function of t, with the subscript X merely reminding us of what the random variable is for which $M_X(t)$ is the MGF.

The reader will recall that the moments are then obtained from the MGF by differentiating $M_X(t)$ with respect to t and evaluating at $t = 0$. The first derivative evaluated at $t = 0$ produces the first moment, the second derivative so evaluated gives the second moment, and so on. In general,

$$E[X^k] = \frac{d^k}{dt^k} M_X(t) \Big|_{t=0} = M_X^{(k)}(0) \tag{2.6}$$

gives the kth moment of the random variable X.

Several other characteristics of the random variable are also important.

The *mode* of the distribution is the value of x at which the greatest amount of probability is located (i.e., the value of x that maximizes $p(x)$). Note that several values of x could be tied for the greatest amount, in which case the distribution would have several modes.

The *cumulative distribution function* (CDF) of the random variable, denoted $F(x)$, gives the accumulated amount of probability at all values of the random variable less than or equal to x. That is,

$$F(x) = Pr(X \le x) = \sum_{y \le x} p(y), \tag{2.7}$$

where the summation is taken over all values of y less than or equal to x.

The value of x for which $F(x) = r$ is called the $100r^{th}$ *percentile* of the distribution. It is the value in the domain of X for which the probability of being less than or equal to that value is r, and the probability of being greater than that value is therefore $1 - r$. In particular, when $r = .50$ we are speaking of the value of x for which half the probability lies below (or at) that value and half lies above that value. The value of x in this case is called the *median* of the distribution.[3]

---

[3] The median (or any other percentile) in a discrete distribution is not always clear. For example, if $p(0) = \frac{1}{3}$ and $p(1) = \frac{2}{3}$, then what is the median? Clearly there is no unique value of x for which $F(x) = .50$. Either we would say the median does not exist, or we would adopt a definition to resolve the question in each case.

2.1.2 CONTINUOUS RANDOM VARIABLES

A random variable is said to be *continuous* if it can take on any value within a defined interval (or the union of several disjoint intervals) on the real number axis. If this set of possible values, again called the domain or support of the random variable,[4] includes all values between, say, a and b, then we would define the domain as $a < x < b$. If the domain were all non-negative real values of x we would write $x \geq 0$, and if it were all real values of x we would write $-\infty < x < \infty$. Note that the defined values of x could be in several disjoint intervals, so the domain would then be the union of these disjoint intervals. For example, the domain could be all x satisfying $a < x < b$ or $c < x < d$.

Associated with each possible value of x is an amount of *probability density*, given as a function of x by the *probability density function* (PDF), denoted by $f(x)$. Together the PDF and the domain define the distribution of the random variable. It is necessarily true that

$$\int_x f(x)\, dx = 1, \tag{2.8}$$

where the integral is taken over all values of x in the domain.

Analogous with the discrete case, we again consider the weighted average of a function of the random variable, which is the expected value of that function, this time using the density as the weight associated with each value of x. Thus is can be shown that

$$E[g(x)] = \int_x g(x) \cdot f(x)\, dx. \tag{2.9}$$

The same special cases apply here as in the discrete case. For $g(X) = X$ we have

$$E[X] = \int_x x \cdot f(x)\, dx \tag{2.10}$$

as the expected value (or first moment) of the random variable. For $g(X) = X^k$ in general we have

$$E[X^k] = \int_x x^k \cdot f(x)\, dx \tag{2.11}$$

as the kth moment. As before, the variance is given by

$$Var(X) = E[(X - E[X])^2] = \int_x (x - E[X])^2 \cdot f(x)\, dx \tag{2.12}$$

and the moment generating function is given by

---

[4] As in the discrete case of Section 2.1.1, the phrase "domain (or support) of the density function of the random variable" is more technically correct, but the briefer phrase "domain of the random variable" is often used.

$$M_X(t) \;=\; E[e^{tX}] \;=\; \int_x e^{tx} \cdot f(x)\,dx. \tag{2.13}$$

The mode of the distribution is the value of x associated with the greatest amount of probability density, so it can be described as the value of x that maximizes the density function. If several values of x have the same maximum density, then the distribution has more than one mode.

As in the discrete case, the cumulative distribution function (CDF) of the random variable X is defined by $F(x) = Pr(X \le x)$. It follows that

$$F(x) \;=\; \int_{-\infty}^{x} f(y)\,dy, \tag{2.14a}$$

and, conversely,

$$f(x) \;=\; \frac{d}{dx} F(x). \tag{2.14b}$$

Just as in the discrete case, the $100r^{th}$ percentile of the distribution is the value of x for which $F(x) = r$, and, in particular, the median of the distribution is the value of x for which $F(x) = .50$.

2.1.3 MIXED RANDOM VARIABLES

On occasion we encounter a random variable that is discrete in one part of its domain and continuous in the rest of the domain. Such random variables are said to have *mixed distributions*. For example, suppose there is a finite probability associated with each of the outcomes $X = a$ and $X = b$, denoted $p(a)$ and $p(b)$, respectively, and a probability density associated with all values of x on the open interval between a and b. Then it would follow that

$$p(a) + \int_a^b f(x)\,dx + p(b) \;=\; 1. \tag{2.15}$$

The kth moment of the mixed random variable X would be found as

$$E[X^k] \;=\; a^k \cdot p(a) + \int_a^b x^k \cdot f(x)\,dx + b^k \cdot p(b). \tag{2.16}$$

Mixed random variables appear quite often in actuarial models, particularly in connection with insurance coverages involving a deductible, or a policy maximum, or both.[5]

2.1.4 MORE ON MOMENTS OF RANDOM VARIABLES

Earlier in this section we reviewed the basic idea of the kth moment of a random variable, denoted by $E[X^k]$. This type of moment is called the kth *raw moment of X*, or the kth *moment about the origin.*

---

[5] These topics are discussed in Kellison and London [17].

By contrast, the quantity $E[(X-\mu)^k]$ is called the kth *central moment of X*, or the kth *moment about the mean*, where $\mu = E[X]$. In particular, the second central moment, denoted by $E[(X-\mu)^2]$, gives the variance of the distribution of X, which is denoted by $Var(X)$ or sometimes by σ^2. Recall that the positive square root of the variance is called the standard deviation, and is denoted by $SD(X)$ or sometimes by σ.

The ratio of the standard deviation to the mean of a random variable is called the *coefficient of variation*, and is denoted by $CV(X)$. Thus we have

$$CV(X) = \frac{\sigma}{\mu}, \tag{2.17}$$

for $\mu \neq 0$. It measures the degree of spread of a random variable relative to its mean.

The *skewness* of a distribution measures its symmetry, or lack thereof. It is defined by

$$\gamma_3 = \frac{E[(X-\mu)^3]}{\sigma^3}, \tag{2.18}$$

the ratio of the third central moment to the cube of the standard deviation. A distribution that is symmetric, such as the normal, will have a skewness measure of zero. A positively skewed distribution will have a right hand tail and a negatively skewed distribution will have a left hand tail.

The extent to which a distribution is peaked or flat is measured by its *kurtosis,* which is defined by

$$\gamma_4 = \frac{E[(X-\mu)^4]}{\sigma^4}, \tag{2.19}$$

the ratio of the fourth central moment to the square of the variance (or the fourth power of the standard deviation). The kurtosis of a normal distribution has a value of 3, so the kurtosis of any other distribution will indicate its degree of peakedness or flatness relative to a normal distribution with equal variance.

It is well known (see Equation (2.4b)) that the second central moment (the variance) is equal to the second raw moment minus the first raw moment (the mean) squared. Similar relationships hold for the higher central moments as well. For example, for the third central moment we have

$$
\begin{aligned}
E[(X-\mu)^3] &= E[X^3 - 3X^2\mu + 3X\mu^2 - \mu^3] \\
&= E[X^3] - 3 \cdot E[X^2] \cdot E[X] + 3 \cdot E[X] \cdot (E[X])^2 - (E[X])^3 \\
&= E[X^3] - 3 \cdot E[X^2] \cdot E[X] + 2(E[X])^3. \tag{2.20}
\end{aligned}
$$

2.2 SURVEY OF PARTICULAR DISCRETE DISTRIBUTIONS

In this section we will review five standard discrete distributions with which the reader should be familiar. They are included here simply as a convenient reference.

2.2.1 THE DISCRETE UNIFORM DISTRIBUTION

If there are n discrete values in the domain of a random variable X, denoted $x_1, x_2, \cdots, x_n$, for which an equal amount of probability is associated with each value, then X is said to have a *discrete uniform distribution*. Its probability function is therefore

$$p(x_i) = \frac{1}{n}, \tag{2.21}$$

for all x_i. Its first moment is

$$E[X] = \sum_{i=1}^{n} x_i \cdot p(x_i) = \frac{1}{n} \cdot \sum_{i=1}^{n} x_i, \tag{2.22a}$$

and its second moment is

$$E[X^2] = \sum_{i=1}^{n} x_i^2 \cdot p(x_i) = \frac{1}{n} \cdot \sum_{i=1}^{n} x_i^2. \tag{2.22b}$$

In the special case where $x_i = i,$ for $i = 1, 2, \cdots, n,$ then we have

$$E[X] = \frac{n+1}{2} \tag{2.23a}$$

and

$$E[X^2] = \frac{(n+1)(2n+1)}{6}, \tag{2.23b}$$

so that

$$Var(X) = E[X^2] - (E[X])^2 = \frac{n^2 - 1}{12}. \tag{2.24}$$

The moment generating function in the special case is

$$M_X(t) = E[e^{tX}] = \frac{e^t(1 - e^{nt})}{n(1 - e^t)}. \tag{2.25}$$

2.2.2 THE BINOMIAL DISTRIBUTION

Recall the binomial (or Bernoulli) model, in which we find the concept of repeated independent trials with each trial ending in either success of failure. The probability of success on a single trial, denoted p, is constant over all trials. The random variable X, denoting the number of successes out of n independent trials, is said to have a *binomial distribution*. The probability function is

$$p(x) = \binom{n}{x} p^x (1-p)^{n-x}, \tag{2.26}$$

for $x = 0,1,2,\cdots,n$, the expected value is

$$E[X] = np, \tag{2.27}$$

the variance is

$$Var(X) = np(1-p), \tag{2.28}$$

and the moment generating function is

$$M_X(t) = (q + pe^t)^n, \tag{2.29}$$

where $q = 1-p$.

2.2.3 THE NEGATIVE BINOMIAL DISTRIBUTION

Note that in the binomial distribution the random variable was the number of successes out of a fixed number of trials, n, where n is a fixed parameter of the distribution. In the *negative binomial distribution* the number of successes, denoted r, is a fixed parameter of the distribution and the random variable X represents the number of failures that occur before the rth success is obtained.[6] The probability function is

$$p(x) = \binom{x+r-1}{r-1} p^r (1-p)^x, \tag{2.30}$$

for $x = 0,1,2,\cdots$, the expected value is

$$E[X] = \frac{rq}{p}, \tag{2.31}$$

the variance is

$$Var(X) = \frac{rq}{p^2}, \tag{2.32}$$

and the moment generating function is

---

[6] Note that if the number of failures, denoted X, is random, then the total number of *trials* needed to obtain r successes, denoted Y, is also random, since we would have $Y = X + r$. Some textbooks (see, for example, Hassett and Stewart [12]), discuss both the "X-meaning" and the "Y-meaning" of the negative binomial distribution.

$$M_X(t) = \left(\frac{p}{1-qe^t}\right)^r, \tag{2.33}$$

where, in all cases, $q = 1-p$.

Note that the description of the negative binomial distribution given here would require that the parameter r be a nonnegative integer. When we consider the important use of the negative binomial random variable as a model for the number of insurance claims, we will see that the requirement of an integer value for r can be relaxed.[7]

2.2.4 THE GEOMETRIC DISTRIBUTION

The *geometric distribution* is simply the special case of the negative binomial with $r = 1$. The random variable, X, now denotes the number of failures that occur before the first success is obtained.[8] Its probability function is

$$p(x) = p(1-p)^x, \tag{2.30a}$$

for $x = 0, 1, 2, \cdots$, the expected value is

$$E[X] = \frac{q}{p}, \tag{2.31a}$$

the variance is

$$Var(X) = \frac{q}{p^2}, \tag{2.32a}$$

and the moment generating function is

$$M_X(t) = \frac{p}{1-qe^t}, \tag{2.33a}$$

where $q = 1-p$ in all cases.

2.2.5 THE POISSON DISTRIBUTION

The *Poisson distribution* is a one-parameter discrete distribution with probability function given by

$$p(x) = \frac{e^{-\lambda}\lambda^x}{x!}, \tag{2.34}$$

for $x = 0, 1, 2, \cdots$, where $\lambda > 0$. Its expected value is

---

[7] See Chapter 3 of Kellison and London [17].

[8] As with the negative binomial, some textbooks define the geometric random variable to be the number of trials, Y, needed to obtain the first success. In that case the probability function is $p(y) = p(1-p)^{y-1}$, for $y = 1, 2, \cdots$.

$$E[X] = \lambda, \tag{2.35}$$

its variance is also

$$Var(X) = \lambda, \tag{2.36}$$

and its moment generating function is

$$M_X(t) = e^{\lambda(e^t - 1)}. \tag{2.37}$$

The Poisson distribution has several delightful properties that make it a convenient one to use in various actuarial and other stochastic applications.

2.3 SURVEY OF PARTICULAR CONTINUOUS DISTRIBUTIONS

In this section we review four standard continuous probability distributions with which the reader should be familiar from a prior study of probability. Additional continuous distributions are introduced later in the text as survival distributions (see Chapter 5).

2.3.1 THE CONTINUOUS UNIFORM DISTRIBUTION

As its name suggests, the *uniform distribution* is characterized by a constant probability density at all points in its domain. If the random variable is defined on the interval $a < X < b$, and if the density function is constant, then it follows that the density function must be

$$f(x) = \frac{1}{b-a}, \tag{2.38}$$

for $a < x < b$. That is, the constant density function is the reciprocal of the length of the interval on which the random variable is defined. The mean of the uniform distribution is

$$E[X] = \frac{a+b}{2}, \tag{2.39}$$

the variance is

$$Var(X) = \frac{(b-a)^2}{12}, \tag{2.40}$$

the moment generating function is

$$M_X(t) = \frac{e^{bt} - e^{at}}{t(b-a)}, \tag{2.41}$$

for $t \neq 0$, and the cumulative distribution function is

$$F(x) = \frac{x-a}{b-a}. \tag{2.42}$$

As a consequence of the constant density function, the median is the same as the mean and there is no mode since all points have the same probability density.

2.3.2 THE NORMAL DISTRIBUTION

The *normal distribution* will have frequent use in our models for quantifying risk. For now the reader should recall that the density function for this distribution is based on the two parameters μ and σ, where $\sigma > 0$, which are also the mean and standard deviation, respectively, of the distribution. Specifically,

$$f(x) = \frac{1}{\sigma \cdot \sqrt{2\pi}} e^{-\frac{1}{2}\left(\frac{x-\mu}{\sigma}\right)^2},$$ (2.43a)

for $-\infty < x < \infty$, where, as mentioned,

$$E[X] = \mu$$ (2.44)

and

$$Var(X) = \sigma^2.$$ (2.45)

The moment generating function is

$$M_X(t) = e^{\mu t + \sigma^2 t^2/2}.$$ (2.46)

An extremely important property of the normal distribution is that any linear transformation of the random variable will also have a normal distribution. In particular, the random variable Z derived from the normal random variable X by the linear transformation

$$Z = \frac{X-\mu}{\sigma}$$ (2.47)

will have a normal distribution with mean

$$E[Z] = \frac{1}{\sigma} \cdot E[X] - \frac{\mu}{\sigma} = 0,$$ (2.48)

since $E[X] = \mu$, and variance

$$Var(Z) = \frac{Var(X)}{\sigma^2} = 1,$$ (2.49)

since $Var(X) = \sigma^2$ and $Var(\mu/\sigma) = 0$. The random variable Z is called the *unit normal random variable* or the *standard normal random variable*. Its probability density function

$$f(x) = \frac{1}{\sqrt{2\pi}} e^{-x^2/2}$$ (2.43b)

does not have a closed form antiderivative, so probability values are not found by analytical integration of $f(x)$. Rather, values of the cumulative distribution function $F_Z(z)$ are determined by approximate integration and stored in a table for look-up as needed. Probability values for the normal random variable X are likewise looked up in the table of standard values after making the appropriate linear transformation. A modern alternative to table look-up is that values can be determined by numerical integration using appropriate computer software or even a pocket calculator.

2.3.3 THE EXPONENTIAL DISTRIBUTION

Another standard continuous distribution with some convenient properties is the one-parameter *exponential distribution*. It is defined over all positive values of x by the density function

$$f(x) = \beta \cdot e^{-\beta x}, \tag{2.50a}$$

for $x > 0$ and $\beta > 0$. The expected value is

$$E[X] = \frac{1}{\beta}, \tag{2.51}$$

the variance is

$$Var(X) = \frac{1}{\beta^2}, \tag{2.52}$$

the moment generating function is

$$M_X(t) = \frac{\beta}{\beta - t}, \tag{2.53}$$

for $t < \beta$, and the cumulative distribution function is

$$F(x) = 1 - e^{-\beta x}. \tag{2.54}$$

(The reader should note that some textbooks prefer the notation

$$f(x) = \frac{1}{\theta} \cdot e^{-x/\theta}, \tag{2.50b}$$

so that $E[X] = \theta, Var(X) = \theta^2$, and $M_X(t) = (1 - \theta t)^{-1}$.)

Properties of the exponential distribution that make it suitable as a survival distribution in certain cases will be explored in Chapter 5.

2.3.4 THE GAMMA DISTRIBUTION

The two-parameter *gamma distribution* is defined by the density function

$$f(x) = \frac{\beta^\alpha}{\Gamma(\alpha)} \cdot x^{\alpha-1} e^{-\beta x}, \tag{2.55}$$

for $x > 0$, $\alpha > 0$, and $\beta > 0$, where $\Gamma(\alpha)$ is the *gamma function* defined by

$$\Gamma(\alpha) = \int_0^\infty x^{\alpha-1} e^{-x}\, dx. \tag{2.56}$$

By substituting $\alpha = 1$ into the gamma density given by Equation (2.55), and noting that $\Gamma(1) = 1$, we obtain the exponential density given by Equation (2.50a). Thus the exponential is a special case of the gamma with $\alpha = 1$. The mean of the gamma distribution is

$$E[X] = \frac{\alpha}{\beta}, \tag{2.57a}$$

the variance is

$$Var(X) = \frac{\alpha}{\beta^2}, \tag{2.57b}$$

and the moment generating function is

$$M_X(t) = \left(\frac{\beta}{\beta-t}\right)^\alpha, \tag{2.57c}$$

for $t < \beta$. The cumulative distribution function is given by

$$F(x) = \int_0^x f(y)\, dy = \frac{\beta^\alpha}{\Gamma(\alpha)} \int_0^x y^{\alpha-1} e^{-\beta y}\, dy. \tag{2.58a}$$

If we let $\beta y = t$, so $y = t / \beta$ and $dy = \frac{1}{\beta} \cdot dt$, then the integral becomes

$$\begin{aligned}
F(x) &= \frac{1}{\Gamma(\alpha)} \int_0^{\beta x} \beta^\alpha \left(\frac{t}{\beta}\right)^{\alpha-1} \cdot e^{-t} \cdot \frac{1}{\beta} \cdot dt \\
&= \frac{1}{\Gamma(\alpha)} \int_0^{\beta x} t^{\alpha-1} e^{-t}\, dt \\
&= \Gamma(\alpha; \beta x),
\end{aligned} \tag{2.58b}$$

where $\Gamma(\alpha; \beta x)$ is the *incomplete gamma function* defined by

$$\Gamma(\alpha; x) = \frac{1}{\Gamma(\alpha)} \int_0^x t^{\alpha-1} e^{-t}\, dt. \tag{2.59}$$

2.4 MULTIVARIATE PROBABILITY

Whenever two or more random variables are involved in the same model we find ourselves dealing with a case of *multivariate probability*. In this section we will review the fundamental aspects of multivariate probability, including the interrelationships among the *joint, marginal*, and *conditional distributions*, in both the discrete and continuous cases.

One of the most important aspects of multivariate probability is the process for finding the unconditional mean and variance of a random variable from the associated conditional means and variances. The formulas relating the unconditional and conditional means and variances are given by the *double expectation theorem*. Although this is a result with which the reader might be familiar from prior study, it has so many important applications in actuarial science that we wish to review it in some detail at this time. We will do this by example, separately for the discrete and continuous cases. An example does not establish the general result, of course; for that purpose the reader is referred to Section 7.4 of Ross [25].

2.4.1 THE DISCRETE CASE

We illustrate the key components of discrete multivariate probability with a numerical example. Suppose the discrete random variable X can assume the values $x = 0, 1, 2$ and the discrete random variable Y can assume the values $y = 1, 2$. Let X and Y have the joint distribution given by the following table, and let $p(x, y)$ denote the joint probability function.

Y \ X	0	1	2
1	.10	.20	.30
2	.10	.10	.20

The marginal distribution of X is given by

$$Pr(X=0) = .10 + .10 = .20,$$

$$Pr(X=1) = .20 + .10 = .30,$$

and

$$Pr(X=2) = .30 + .20 = .50.$$

The moments of X can be calculated directly from the marginal distribution. We have

$$E[X] = (0)(.20) + (1)(.30) + (2)(.50) = 1.30,$$

$$E[X^2] = (0)(.20) + (1)(.30) + (4)(.50) = 2.30,$$

and

$$Var(X) = 2.30 - (1.30)^2 = .61.$$

Now we consider an alternative, but longer (at least this time), way to find $E[X]$ and $Var(X)$. First we find the marginal distribution of Y as

$$Pr(Y=1) = .10+.20+.30 = .60$$

and

$$Pr(Y=2) = .10+.10+.20 = .40.$$

Next we find both conditional distributions for X, one given $Y=1$ and the other given $Y=2$. We have

$$Pr(X=0\,|\,Y=1) = \frac{.10}{.60} = \frac{1}{6},$$

$$Pr(X=1\,|\,Y=1) = \frac{.20}{.60} = \frac{2}{6},$$

and

$$Pr(X=2\,|\,Y=1) = \frac{.30}{.60} = \frac{3}{6}.$$

From this conditional distribution we find the conditional moments of X, given $Y=1$. We have

$$E[X\,|\,Y=1] = (0)\left(\frac{1}{6}\right)+(1)\left(\frac{2}{6}\right)+(2)\left(\frac{3}{6}\right) = \frac{8}{6},$$

$$E[X^2\,|\,Y=1] = (0)\left(\frac{1}{6}\right)+(1)\left(\frac{2}{6}\right)+(4)\left(\frac{3}{6}\right) = \frac{14}{6},$$

and

$$Var(X\,|\,Y=1) = \frac{14}{6}-\left(\frac{8}{6}\right)^2 = \frac{20}{36}.$$

Similarly we find the conditional distribution

$$Pr(X=0\,|\,Y=2) = \frac{.10}{.40} = \frac{1}{4},$$

$$Pr(X=1\,|\,Y=2) = \frac{.10}{.40} = \frac{1}{4},$$

and

$$Pr(X=2\,|\,Y=2) = \frac{.20}{.40} = \frac{2}{4},$$

and its associated conditional moments

$$E[X\,|\,Y=2] = (0)\left(\frac{1}{4}\right)+(1)\left(\frac{1}{4}\right)+(2)\left(\frac{2}{4}\right) = \frac{5}{4},$$

$$E[X^2\,|\,Y=2] = (0)\left(\frac{1}{4}\right)+(1)\left(\frac{1}{4}\right)+(4)\left(\frac{2}{4}\right) = \frac{9}{4},$$

and

$$Var(X\,|\,Y=2) = \frac{9}{4}-\left(\frac{5}{4}\right)^2 = \frac{11}{16}.$$

We now come to the key part of the operation. We recognize that the conditional expected value of X, denoted $E_X[X|Y]$, is a random variable because it is a function of the random variable Y. It can take on the two possible values $\frac{8}{6}$ and $\frac{5}{4}$, and does so with probability .60 and .40, respectively, the probabilities associated with the two possible values of Y. We can find the moments of this random variable as

$$E_Y[E_X[X|Y]] = \left(\frac{8}{6}\right)(.60)+\left(\frac{5}{4}\right)(.40) = \frac{13}{10},$$

$$E_Y[(E_X[X|Y])^2] = \left(\frac{8}{6}\right)^2 \cdot(.60)+\left(\frac{5}{4}\right)^2 \cdot(.40) = \frac{203}{120},$$

and

$$Var_Y(E_X[X|Y]) = \frac{203}{120}-\left(\frac{13}{10}\right)^2 = \frac{1}{600}.$$

Similarly the conditional variance of X given Y, denoted $Var_X(X|Y)$, is a random variable because it too is a function of Y. Its two possible values are $\frac{20}{36}$ and $\frac{11}{16}$, so its expected value is

$$E_Y[Var_X(X|Y)] = \left(\frac{20}{36}\right)(.60)+\left(\frac{11}{16}\right)(.40) = \frac{73}{120}.$$

Finally we observe that

$$E_Y\big[E_X[X|Y]\big] = \frac{13}{10} = E[X],$$

which states that the expected value of the conditional expectation is the unconditional expected value of X. This constitutes the first part of the double expectation theorem. The second part states that

$$E_Y[Var_X(X|Y)]+Var_Y(E_X[X|Y]) = \frac{73}{120}+\frac{1}{600} = \frac{366}{600} = \frac{61}{100} = Var(X),$$

which says that the expected value of the conditional variance plus the variance of the conditional expectation is the unconditional variance of X.

2.4.2 The Continuous Case

Multivariate probability in the continuous case is handled more compactly than in the discrete case. We cannot list all possible pairs of (x,y) in the continuous joint domain; instead we specify the joint density at the point (x,y) in the form of a joint density function denoted $f(x,y)$. Recall that the marginal density of X is then found by integrating the joint density over all values of Y, and the marginal density of Y is found by integrating the joint density over all values of X. The conditional density of X, given Y, is then found by dividing the joint density by the marginal density of Y, and, similarly, the conditional density of Y, given X, is found by dividing the joint density by the marginal density of X. These basic relationships are illustrated in the following example.

Let the continuous random variable X have a uniform distribution on the interval $0 < x < 12$, and let the continuous random variable Y have a conditional distribution, given $X = x$, that is uniform on the interval $0 < y < x$. We seek the unconditional expected value and variance of Y.

We could, of course, proceed by first finding the marginal distribution of Y and then finding the unconditional expected value and variance of Y directly from this marginal distribution. Since X is uniform we have $f_X(x) = \frac{1}{12}$, and since Y is conditionally uniform we have $f_{Y|X}(y|x) = \frac{1}{x}$. Then the joint density is $f(x,y) = \frac{1}{12x}$, and the marginal density of Y is

$$f_Y(y) = \int_y^{12} f(x,y)\, dx = \int_y^{12} \left(\frac{1}{12x}\right) dx = \frac{1}{12}[\ln 12 - \ln y].$$

To then find the first and second moments of Y directly from the marginal density of Y is a bit of a calculus challenge. Instead, we will find the unconditional expected value and variance of Y from its conditional moments by using the double expectation theorem. We have, since Y is conditionally uniform, $E_Y[Y|X] = \frac{X}{2}$ and $Var_Y(Y|X) = \frac{X^2}{12}$. Then, directly from the double expectation theorem, we have

$$E[Y] = E_X\left[E_Y[Y|X]\right] = E_X\left[\frac{X}{2}\right] = \frac{1}{2} \cdot E[X] = 3,$$

since, being uniform on $0 < x < 12$, we have $E[X] = 6$. Similarly,

$$Var(Y) = E_X[Var_Y(Y|X)] + Var_X(E_Y[Y|X])$$
$$= E_X\left[\frac{X^2}{12}\right] + Var_X\left(\frac{X}{2}\right)$$
$$= \frac{1}{12} \cdot E[X^2] + \frac{1}{4} \cdot Var(X) = \left(\frac{1}{12}\right)(48) + \left(\frac{1}{4}\right)(12) = 7,$$

since $Var(X) = 12$ and $E[X^2] = Var(X) + (E[X])^2 = 48$.

In the discrete case example, presented in Section 2.4.1, the unconditional mean and variance were found more easily from the marginal distribution than via the double expectation theorem. In this continuous example, however, the opposite is true; the mean and variance of Y are found more easily via the double expectation theorem than from the marginal distribution of Y. The double expectation theorem will have several applications throughout this text.

CHAPTER THREE

REVIEW OF MARKOV CHAINS

Throughout this text we will present a number of actuarial models in the form of *multi-state models*. The underlying mathematics of multi-state models is that of the *Markov Chain*,[1] which is, in turn, a special case of a *stochastic process*. In this chapter we provide an abbreviated review of several varieties of Markov Chains, to the extent necessary to understand their use in analyzing the multi-state models presented throughout the text. Readers requiring a more thorough study of Markov Chains are referred to Ross [26].

A stochastic process arises when a random variable is indexed over time, with the distribution of that random variable depending on the time at which it is considered. For example, suppose the discrete random variable X can take on only the integer values 1, 2, 3, or 4, but the probability that $X = 3$, for example, depends on time. Because the associated probability values vary over time, even if the domain of $x = \{1, 2, 3, 4\}$ remains fixed, it is necessary to notate the name of the random variable to indicate the time point at which its several probability values are being considered.

There are two sub-cases to consider. If the random variable might be considered at *any* point of time on the real number axis, we denote the random variable at time t by $X(t)$, for $t \geq 0$, and refer to this model as a *continuous-time* stochastic process. On the other hand, if the random variable is considered, or observed, only at the discrete time points $n = 0, 1, 2, \cdots$, then we denote the random variable at time n by X_n, for $n = 0, 1, 2, \cdots$, and refer to the model as a *discrete-time* stochastic process.

A stochastic process can also be classified as *homogeneous* or *non-homogeneous*. Rather than define these terms for stochastic processes in general, we will define them specifically for Markov Chains, the only type of stochastic process considered further in this chapter. The discrete-time process is presented in Section 3.1 and the continuous-time process in Section 3.2.

3.1 DISCRETE-TIME MARKOV CHAINS

For a discrete-time Markov Chain, we begin by defining a model consisting of *m states*, denoted $1, 2, \cdots, m$, where $m \geq 2$. The process moves at random among these states. This is il-

---

[1] Named for the noted Russian mathematician A. A. Markov.

lustrated in the following diagram, with $m = 3$.

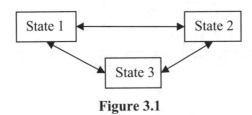

Figure 3.1

The model illustrated in Figure 3.1 involves three states. The arrows indicate that movement is possible from any state to any other state. (When that is so we say that each state *communicates* with each other state.)[2] The random variable X_n takes on the numerical value of the state in which the process is located at time n, for $n = 0, 1, 2, \cdots$, so the possible values of X_n are $\{1, 2, \cdots, m\}$. In other words, if $X_n = i$ we say the process is in State i at time n. In the three-state model of Figure 3.1, the event notated as $X_3 = 2$, for example, is the event that the process is in State 2 at time 3.

The initial state of the process at time 0 must be specified. In nearly all of the applications of Markov Chains to actuarial models presented in this text, the process will begin in State 1, with the meaning of State 1 defined in each case. Thus we would have $X_0 = 1$ in these applications.

3.1.1 TRANSITION PROBABILITIES

The basic building block of a Markov Chain is the conditional probability that the process will be in State j at time $n + 1$, given that it is in State i at time n, including the possibility that $j = i$. For a Markov Chain stochastic process, the probability of being in State j at time $n + 1$ depends *only* on which state the process is in at time n. It does not matter which states the process was in at any times earlier than time n. (For this reason, a Markov Chain is sometimes called a *memoryless* stochastic process.) After moving to a new state, we can completely forget where we were in the past. In fact, it is this property of memorylessness that distinguishes a Markov Chain from more general stochastic processes. In mathematical notation, this conditional probability is written as $Pr[X_{n+1} = j \mid X_n = i]$ and is called a *transition probability*.

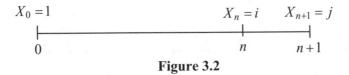

Figure 3.2

If the transition probability of moving from State i to State j remains constant over time (i.e., does not depend on the value of n), the process is said to be *homogeneous*, and if the transition probability varies with n the process is said to be *non-homogeneous*. (The non-homogeneous case is discussed in Section 3.1.5.)

---

[2] In nearly all of the Markov Chain models encountered throughout this text we will find some restrictions on the ability of all states to communicate with each other.

The homogeneous transition probability described above is denoted by p_{ij}, so we have

$$p_{ij} = Pr[X_{n+1} = j \mid X_n = i],$$ (3.1)

where i and j can be any of $1, 2, \cdots, m$, and $n = 0, 1, 2, \cdots$. Because the homogeneous transition probability is constant over time, the value of n need not be included in its notation.

Given that the process is in State i at some discrete time point, it must be in *some* state at the next discrete time point (including possibly State i itself), so it follows that

$$\sum_{j=1}^{m} p_{ij} = 1.$$ (3.2)

If $p_{ii} \neq 0$, then it is possible to remain in State i over the next time interval, whereas $p_{ii} = 0$ would imply that remaining in State i is not possible. (The latter property does not tend to hold in most Markov Chain models encountered in practice.) Further, if $p_{ii} = 1$, then it is not possible to move from State i to another state. In this case we say that State i is an *absorbing state*, a property that we regularly encounter in the models considered later in the text.

The entire set of p_{ij} transition probabilities for all (i, j) is contained in the *transition probability matrix* $\mathbf{P}$, defined as

$$\mathbf{P} = \begin{vmatrix} p_{11} & p_{12} & \cdots & p_{1m} \\ p_{21} & p_{22} & \cdots & p_{2m} \\ \vdots & \vdots & \vdots & \vdots \\ p_{m1} & p_{m2} & \cdots & p_{mm} \end{vmatrix}.$$ (3.3)

For example, consider the transition probability matrix

$$\mathbf{P} = \begin{vmatrix} .80 & .20 & 0 \\ .30 & .60 & .10 \\ 0 & 0 & 1 \end{vmatrix}.$$

The associated Markov Chain has three states, which we call States 1, 2, and 3.[3] The probability of moving from State 2 to State 1, for example, is given by $p_{21} = .30$. The fact that $p_{13} = 0$ tells us that it is not possible to move directly from State 1 to State 3, for some reason. The value $p_{33} = 1$ tells us that State 3 is an absorbing state. Because the process is homogeneous, the same transition probability values apply over all discrete intervals on the time axis.

---

[3] Some textbooks prefer to identify the states in a three-state process as States 0, 1, and 2. The labeling of the states is arbitrary, but we prefer to begin with State 1 so that the notation used in the matrix $\mathbf{P}$ is consistent with that used in matrix algebra. If we begin with State 0, then the upper left entry in matrix $\mathbf{P}$ would be denoted p_{00}, whereas it is usually denoted p_{11} in matrix algebra as the element in the first row and first column.

3.1.2 STATE VECTOR

As described above, at time n the discrete-time Markov Chain process is located in one of m possible states. We denote the probability of the process being in State i at time n by π_{in}, for $i = 1, 2, \cdots, m$, and we represent the set of all such probabilities in a row vector denoted $\boldsymbol{\pi}_n$. That is,

$$\boldsymbol{\pi}_n = (\pi_{1n}, \pi_{2n}, \cdots, \pi_{mn}), \tag{3.4}$$

where

$$\sum_{i=1}^{m} \pi_{in} = 1. \tag{3.5}$$

The vector $\boldsymbol{\pi}_n$ is called the *state vector at time n*. The elements of $\boldsymbol{\pi}_n$ define the *state of the process* at time n by giving the probabilities of the process being in each of the possible states.

Now suppose it is *known* that the process is in State i at time n. Conditional on this knowledge, the value of π_{in} would be 1 and the value of each π_{jn}, for $j \neq i$, would be 0. For example, if a 3-state process is known to be in State 2 at time n, then the time n state vector would be $\boldsymbol{\pi}_n = (0, 1, 0)$.

The time $n+1$ state vector can be determined from the time n state vector as

$$\boldsymbol{\pi}_{n+1} = \boldsymbol{\pi}_n \cdot \mathbf{P}, \tag{3.6a}$$

where $\mathbf{P}$ is the transition probability matrix defined by Equation (3.3). For our 3-state process known to be in State 2 at time n, we have

$$\boldsymbol{\pi}_{n+1} = (0, 1, 0) \cdot \begin{vmatrix} p_{11} & p_{12} & p_{13} \\ p_{21} & p_{22} & p_{23} \\ p_{31} & p_{32} & p_{33} \end{vmatrix} = (p_{21}, p_{22}, p_{23}).$$

This result was to be expected, since the second row of $\mathbf{P}$ gives, in order, the probabilities for being in States 1, 2, 3 at time $n+1$, given that the process is in State 2 at time n.[4]

3.1.3 PROBABILITIES OVER MULTIPLE STEPS

Again consider the 3-state process of Section 3.1.2, known to be in State 2 at time n. What are the probabilities for being in each of States 1, 2, 3 at time $n+2$? These probability values are contained in $\boldsymbol{\pi}_{n+2}$, the time $n+2$ state vector. Since the process is homogeneous, the same set of transition probabilities, contained in the matrix $\mathbf{P}$, apply as the process moves from $n+1$ to $n+2$ as applied when the process moved from n to $n+1$. Thus we have

$$\boldsymbol{\pi}_{n+2} = \boldsymbol{\pi}_{n+1} \cdot \mathbf{P}. \tag{3.6b}$$

---

[4] In this text we presume that the reader has had a standard semester course in linear algebra, and understands basic concepts such as the multiplication of a row vector times a matrix.

Substituting for π_{n+1} from Equation (3.6a) we have

$$\pi_{n+2} = \pi_n \cdot \mathbf{P} \cdot \mathbf{P} = \pi_n \cdot \mathbf{P}^2. \tag{3.6c}$$

With $\pi_n = (0, 1, 0)$ to reflect the known state of the process at time n, we see that the elements in the time $n+2$ state vector are the same as the elements in the second row of the matrix $\mathbf{P}^2 = \mathbf{P} \cdot \mathbf{P}$.

This result is easily generalized from two steps to r steps.

Figure 3.3

To find $_r p_{ij} = Pr[X_{n+r} = j \mid X_n = i]$, the probability that a process known to be in State i at time n will be in State j at time $n+r$ (i.e., after r discrete time intervals), we calculate

$$\pi_{n+r} = \pi_n \cdot \mathbf{P}^r. \tag{3.6d}$$

Since π_n contains the element $\pi_{in} = 1$ and all other elements equal to zero, it follows that the elements of the vector π_{n+r} are the same as those in the ith row of the matrix $\mathbf{P}^r$. The value of $_r p_{ij} = Pr[X_{n+r} = j \mid X_n = i]$ is found in the jth column of the ith row of $\mathbf{P}^r$.

3.1.4 PROPERTIES OF HOMOGENEOUS DISCRETE-TIME MARKOV CHAINS

As a result of having the same set of transition probabilities apply over each successive time interval, the homogeneous model has a number of properties that are mathematically interesting. However, we will find with our presentation of various actuarial models as discrete-time Markov Chains throughout the text that the homogeneous model is not a realistic one to adopt, and we will instead make use of the non-homogeneous model to be described further in Section 3.1.5. Because we will make very little use of the homogeneous model from here on, we will not present its further properties in this chapter. The reader interested in reviewing these properties is referred to Chapter 4 of Ross [26].

3.1.5 THE NON-HOMOGENEOUS DISCRETE-TIME MODEL

All of the results developed thus far are based on the property that the set of transition probabilities, summarized in the matrix $\mathbf{P}$, remains constant over successive steps in the process. Recall that a Markov Chain with this property is said to be homogeneous.

Now we generalize the process to the case where the transition probabilities need not be the same over successive intervals. We let $p_{ij}^{(k)}$, for $k = 0, 1, 2, \cdots$, denote the probability that a process in State i at time k will be in State j at time $k+1$. That is, $p_{ij}^{(k)}$ represents the probability of moving from State i to State j over the $(k+1)^{st}$ discrete time interval of the process. The set of $p_{ij}^{(k)}$ probabilities for all i and j is summarized in the matrix of transition probabilities over the $(k+1)^{st}$ interval, which we denote by $\mathbf{P}^{(k)}$. (Note that, for example, $\mathbf{P}^{(3)}$ denotes the matrix of transition probabilities *over the fourth interval in the process*, whereas $\mathbf{P}^3 = \mathbf{P} \cdot \mathbf{P} \cdot \mathbf{P}$ denotes the matrix of transition probabilities *over any three intervals* in a homogeneous process.) For the multiple-step probability, we define

$$_r p_{ij}^{(n)} = Pr[X_{n+r} = j \mid X_n = i]. \tag{3.7a}$$

A Markov process allowing for different matrices of transition probabilities over different intervals in the process is called a *non-homogeneous* process. It is this version of the Markov Chain that we will use to represent many of the actuarial models encountered later in the text.

In the non-homogeneous case, the state of the process at time n (defined in Section 3.1.2 in the homogeneous case) is given by

$$\boldsymbol{\pi}_n = \boldsymbol{\pi}_0 \cdot \mathbf{P}^{(0)} \cdot \mathbf{P}^{(1)} \cdot \ \cdots \ \cdot \mathbf{P}^{(n-1)}, \tag{3.8}$$

where $\boldsymbol{\pi}_0$ denotes the (known) initial state of the process at time 0, when the process first begins.

For example, we consider a simple two-state model with transition probabilities given by

$$\mathbf{P}^{(0)} = \begin{vmatrix} .60 & .40 \\ .70 & .30 \end{vmatrix}$$

over the first interval of the process, and

$$\mathbf{P}^{(1)} = \begin{vmatrix} .50 & .50 \\ .80 & .20 \end{vmatrix}$$

for the second interval of the process. If the process is known to begin in State 2 at time 0, what is the probability that the process will be in State 1 at time 2?

The desired probability, which we have denoted by $_2 p_{21}^{(0)}$, is given by the element π_{12} in the state vector $\boldsymbol{\pi}_2$. We have

$$\boldsymbol{\pi}_2 = \boldsymbol{\pi}_0 \cdot \mathbf{P}^{(0)} \cdot \mathbf{P}^{(1)}$$

$$= (0,1) \cdot \begin{vmatrix} .60 & .40 \\ .70 & .30 \end{vmatrix} \cdot \begin{vmatrix} .50 & .50 \\ .80 & .20 \end{vmatrix} = (.70, .30) \cdot \begin{vmatrix} .50 & .50 \\ .80 & .20 \end{vmatrix} = (.59, .41),$$

so the answer is $\pi_{12} = {}_2 p_{21}^{(0)} = .59$. Note that here we first multiplied $\boldsymbol{\pi}_0$ times $\mathbf{P}^{(0)}$, and then multiplied the resulting $\boldsymbol{\pi}_1$ vector times $\mathbf{P}^{(1)}$, rather than multiplying $\mathbf{P}^{(0)}$ times $\mathbf{P}^{(1)}$. The answer is the same either way, of course, but with fewer calculations in the approach shown.

The non-homogeneous version of the discrete-time Markov Chain will be used to represent a number of the actuarial models considered throughout this text. The reason why the model needs to be non-homogeneous, rather than homogeneous, will be easily understood as the examples arise.

3.1.6 PROBABILITY OF REMAINING IN STATE i

Consider the general probability value $_r p_{ij}^{(n)}$, given by Equation (3.7a), with $j = i$. In this case we have

$$_r p_{ii}^{(n)} = Pr[X_{n+r} = i \mid X_n = i], \tag{3.7b}$$

and it denotes the probability of the process being in State i at time $n + r$, given that it is in State i at time n. There are two subcases contained in this event, namely that the process *never left* State i between n and $n + r$, or that it did leave State i but returned by time $n + r$.

The first subcase plays a special role later in the text when we represent certain actuarial models in the multi-state context. Because of this, we will find it useful to define the special symbol $_r p_{ii}^{*(n)}$ to denote the probability that a general discrete-time Markov process, known to be in State i at time n, does not leave State i prior to time $n + r$. Since the event of "never leaving" is a subset of the event whose probability is given by $_r p_{ii}^{(n)}$, it follows that

$$_r p_{ii}^{*(n)} \leq {}_r p_{ii}^{(n)}. \tag{3.9}$$

As we shall see later in the text, some models include the feature that State i, once left, can never be reentered. When this restriction holds, then it follows that

$$_r p_{ii}^{*(n)} = {}_r p_{ii}^{(n)}. \tag{3.10}$$

3.2 CONTINUOUS-TIME MARKOV CHAINS

We again consider a model consisting of m states, and let $X(t)$ denote the discrete random variable with possible values $\{1, 2, \cdots, m\}$ that indicates the state in which the process is located at time t, for any $t \geq 0$, so that $X(t) = i$ denotes the event that the process is in State i at time t. The process is said to be a *continuous-time process* because it can be observed at any time t on the real number axis, notwithstanding the fact that $X(t)$ itself is a discrete random variable. As in the discrete-time case, the initial state of the process at time 0 is necessarily known. In nearly all of our applications later in this text, the process will necessarily begin in State 1 at time 0 so we will have $X(0) = 1$.

$$X(0) = 1 \qquad\qquad X(t) = i$$

$$\begin{array}{c} \vdash\!\!\!-\!\!\!-\!\!\!-\!\!\!-\!\!\!-\!\!\!-\!\!\!-\!\!\!+\!\!\!-\!\!\!-\!\!\!-\!\!\! \\ 0 \qquad\qquad\qquad t \end{array}$$

Figure 3.4

Analogous to the non-homogeneous discrete-time probability $_rp_{ij}^{(n)} = Pr[X_{n+r} = j \mid X_n = i]$, the probability that a non-homogeneous process known to be in State i at time n will be in State j after r time intervals, we now consider

$$_rp_{ij}^{(t)} = Pr\big[X(t+r)=j \mid X(t)=i\big], \tag{3.11}$$

the conditional probability that the process will be in State j at time $t+r$, given that it is in State i at time t. To be a continuous-time Markov Chain, the process must possess the memoryless property mentioned for the discrete-time case in Section 3.1.1. That is, the conditional probability of Equation (3.11) depends *only* on being in State i at time t, and does not depend on the path it followed to reach State i nor the length of time it had been in State i prior to time t.

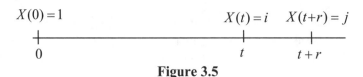

Figure 3.5

Furthermore, if $Pr[X(t+r) = j \mid X(t) = i]$ is independent of t (i.e., it has the same value for all t), and depends only on r, the length of the time interval, we say that the process is *homogeneous*.[5] On the other hand, if this probability value is different for different values of t, then the process is *non-homogeneous*. As with the discrete-time process discussed earlier, we will find that the actuarial models represented as Markov Chains throughout this text will almost invariably be of the non-homogeneous type for reasons that will be apparent at that time.

As mentioned in Section 3.1.6 in the discrete-time case, we also need to distinguish here between $_rp_{ii}^{(t)}$, the probability of being in State i at time $t+r$ for a process known to be in State i at time t, and its subset probability $_rp_{ii}^{*(t)}$, the probability of remaining in State i continuously from time t to time $t+r$.

3.2.1 FORCES OF TRANSITION

For the discrete-time model of Section 3.1, the basic building blocks were the transition probabilities summarized in the matrix **P** (in the homogeneous case) or the sequence of matrices **P**$^{(k)}$ (in the non-homogeneous case). Then all conditional probability values of the form $Pr[X_{n+r}=j \mid X_n=i]$, for all i, j, n, and r, can be determined from the known state vector $\boldsymbol{\pi}_n$ and the appropriate matrices.

For the continuous-time model, with the process observed for all values of t, the basic building blocks are *instantaneous* measures of transition at a point of time, called *forces of transition*.[6] This is a very important point: in the discrete-time case, the process is measured (or observed) only over discrete time intervals, so the event of transition is modeled by probability values over such intervals; in the continuous-time case, the process is measured (or observed) continuously, so the event of transition is modeled by instantaneous rates of transition (which we call forces of transition) rather than by probability values.

---

[5] Some textbooks refer to a continuous-time homogeneous process as a *stationary* process.
[6] These instantaneous measures are analogous to the familiar *force of interest* (see Section 1.1) and the *hazard rate*, or *force of failure*, to be introduced in Section 5.1.4 and used extensively with actuarial models.

In the non-homogeneous case, we denote the function giving the force of transition from State i to State j at time s by $\lambda_{ij}(s)$, where $i \neq j$. That is, for a process known to be in State i at time s, $\lambda_{ij}(s)$ denotes the force of transitioning to State j at that time. Since this force is needed at all values of s, we recognize that $\lambda_{ij}(s)$ is a *force of transition function*. We define

$$\lambda_i(s) = \sum_{j=1}^{i-1} \lambda_{ij}(s) + \sum_{j=i+1}^{m} \lambda_{ij}(s) \qquad (3.12)$$

to be the *total force of transition* out of State i at time s. Note that $\lambda_i(s)$ is the sum of the $\lambda_{ij}(s)$ over all j *except* $j=i$. For completeness, we could define $\lambda_{ii}(s)$ as the *force of remaining* in State i at time s.[7] Then the entire set of $\lambda_{ij}(s)$ forces, including the ones with $j=i$, can be summarized in the *matrix of transition forces* $\mathbf{\Lambda}(s)$, where

$$\mathbf{\Lambda}(s) = \begin{vmatrix} \lambda_{11}(s) & \lambda_{12}(s) & \cdots & \lambda_{1m}(s) \\ \lambda_{21}(s) & \lambda_{22}(s) & \cdots & \lambda_{2m}(s) \\ \vdots & \vdots & \vdots & \vdots \\ \lambda_{m1}(s) & \lambda_{m2}(s) & \cdots & \lambda_{mm}(s) \end{vmatrix}. \qquad (3.13)$$

In the homogeneous case, where $_r p_{ij} = Pr[X(t+r) = j \mid X(t) = i]$ depends only on r and not on t, the force of transition $\lambda_{ij}(s)$ would be a constant function of s, and therefore denoted simply as λ_{ij}. As stated earlier for the discrete-time process, the homogeneous case has many mathematically interesting properties,[8] but is not appropriate for representing the actuarial models considered later in the text. For this reason, we consider only the non-homogeneous case from here on.

3.2.2 FORMULAS FOR $_r p_{ij}^{(t)} = Pr[X(t+r)=j \mid X(t)=i]$

Recall that the non-homogeneous discrete-time process is modeled by the single-interval transition probabilities $p_{ij}^{(n)}$, for $n = 0,1,2,\cdots$, and the general probability value

$$_r p_{ij}^{(n)} = Pr[X_{n+r} = j \mid X_n = i]$$

could be found from those single-interval transition probabilities. In the non-homogeneous continuous-time process, we begin with the force of transition functions $\lambda_{ij}(s)$, for $s > 0$. We now consider the question of how to determine values of

$$_r p_{ij}^{(t)} = Pr[X(t+r)=j \mid X(t)=i]$$

from the set of force of transition functions.

---

[7] The value of $\lambda_{ii}(s)$ is seldom used in the development that follows.

[8] For example, with a constant force of transition in a continuous-time Markov model, the random variable for the waiting time until the next transition would have an exponential distribution. Such a model is discussed in Section 14.4.4.

The derivation of an equation for determining $_r p_{ij}^{(t)}$ starts with an expression for the derivative of $_r p_{ij}^{(t)}$, with respect to r, known as *Kolmogorov's Forward Equation*.[9] This differential equation, which we present without derivation,[10] is

$$\frac{d}{dr} \, _r p_{ij}^{(t)} = \sum_{k \neq j} \left(_r p_{ik}^{(t)} \cdot \lambda_{kj}(t+r) - _r p_{ij}^{(t)} \cdot \lambda_{jk}(t+r) \right). \tag{3.14a}$$

Because the term $_r p_{ij}^{(t)}$ appearing after the minus sign in Equation (3.14a) does not involve k, we can rewrite Equation (3.14a) as

$$\frac{d}{dr} \, _r p_{ij}^{(t)} = \sum_{k \neq j} \left(_r p_{ik}^{(t)} \cdot \lambda_{kj}(t+r) \right) - _r p_{ij}^{(t)} \cdot \lambda_j(t+r), \tag{3.14b}$$

where we have substituted $\lambda_j(t+r)$ for $\sum_{k \neq j} \lambda_{jk}(t+r)$, by Equation (3.11).

For example, consider a three-state model, where all states communicate with each other. If the process is in State $i=1$ at time t, then $_r p_{12}^{(t)}$ is the probability of the process being in State $j=2$ at time $t+r$. In Equation (3.14b), k takes on only the values 1 and 3. We have

$$\frac{d}{dr} \, _r p_{12}^{(t)} = _r p_{11}^{(t)} \cdot \lambda_{12}(t+r) + _r p_{13}^{(t)} \cdot \lambda_{32}(t+r) - _r p_{12}^{(t)} \cdot \lambda_2(t+r). \tag{3.15}$$

For the actuarial models considered in this text, the idea of all states communicating with each other will never hold since there will always be at least one absorbing state. This characteristic will simplify the applicable Kolmogorov equation.

The simplest model, that of one life and one decrement which we encounter first in Chapter 5, has only two states, States 1 and 2. In this model, transition from State 1 to State 2 is possible, but the converse is not. Then with $i=1$ and $j=2$ in Equation (3.14a), k takes on only the value $k=1$ so we have

$$\frac{d}{dr} \, _r p_{12}^{(t)} = _r p_{11}^{(t)} \cdot \lambda_{12}(t+r) - _r p_{12}^{(t)} \cdot \lambda_{21}(t+r)$$

$$= _r p_{11}^{(t)} \cdot \lambda_{12}(t+r), \tag{3.16}$$

since $\lambda_{21}(s) = 0$ for all s. (In Exercise 5-22 the reader is asked to solve this equation for $_n p_{12}^{(t)}$.)

In Section 14.4.2, we encounter a model with States 1, 2, and 3, where transition is possible only from State 1 to State 2, State 1 to State 3, or State 2 to State 3. This means that

---

[9] Named for another great Russian mathematician, A.N. Kolmogorov.

[10] For a derivation of Kolmogorov's Forward Equations in the homogeneous case, see Section 6.4 of Ross [26]; for a derivation in the general, non-homogeneous case, see Section 8.4.1 of Dickson, et al. [8].

$\lambda_{21}(s) = \lambda_{31}(s) = \lambda_{32}(s) = 0$ for all s, and the meaningful values of $_r p_{ij}^{(t)}$ are $_r p_{11}^{(t)}$, $_r p_{12}^{(t)}$, $_r p_{13}^{(t)}$, $_r p_{22}^{(t)}$, and $_r p_{23}^{(t)}$. For $_r p_{12}^{(t)}$, for example, Equation (3.14a) simplifies to

$$\frac{d}{dr} \, _r p_{12}^{(t)} \; = \; _r p_{11}^{(t)} \cdot \lambda_{12}(t+r) - \, _r p_{12}^{(t)} \cdot \lambda_{23}(t+r). \qquad (3.17)$$

We will solve this differential equation for $_n p_{12}^{(t)}$ in Example 14.9, and for other ij combinations in the Chapter 14 exercises.

3.3 PAYMENTS

In nearly all of the actuarial models encountered in this text, we will be interested in the notion of a payment made when the process transitions from one state to another and also the notion of a sequence of payments made while the process remains in a particular state. We first encounter the former idea in Chapter 7 and the latter idea in Chapter 8.

In the discrete case, suppose a payment is to be made at time $n + r$ because the process transitioned from State i to State j during the discrete time interval $(n+r-1, n+r]$. If the process is known to be in State h at time n, then the probability of being in State i at time $n+r-1$ is $_{r-1} p_{hi}^{(n)}$. The conditional probability of being in State j at time $n+r$, given in State i at time $n+r-1$, is $p_{ij}^{(n+r-1)}$. Then the overall probability of payment being made at time $n+r$ is $_{r-1} p_{hi}^{(n)} \cdot p_{ij}^{(n+r-1)}$.

In the continuous case, suppose a payment is to be made at time $t + r$ because the process transitions from State i to State j at precise time $t + r$. If the process is known to be in State h at time t, then the density for transition from State i to State j at time $t + r$ is $_r p_{hi}^{(t)} \cdot \lambda_{ij}(t+r)$.

The second notion of payment made *while in* a particular state, rather than upon transition from one state to another, is easier to formulate. Again assume a discrete process is known to be in State h at time n, and suppose a payment will be made at time $n + r$ if the process is in State i at that time. The probability of this event is simply $_r p_{hi}^{(n)}$, which is therefore the probability of payment.

In the continuous case, again the probability of payment is the same as the probability of being in State i at time $t + r$, given in State h at time t, which is $_r p_{hi}^{(t)}$.

Because the payments are *contingent* on events that are not certain to occur, the value of the payments is determined in a probabilistic, rather than fixed, framework. The meaning of this is explained in the chapters that follow.

CHAPTER FOUR

REVIEW OF STOCHASTIC SIMULATION

In this chapter, we review a number of techniques for using a computer to *imitate*, or *simulate*, a wide range of financial and insurance problems. Such problems, either stochastic or deterministic, typically cannot be solved easily using analytic methods but are readily amenable to stochastic simulation procedures. The term "stochastic" is used to modify simulation in order to emphasize that we are confining our attention to simulation in which values are randomly selected from one or more probability distributions. The term "Monte Carlo" was coined as a synonym for stochastic simulation during U.S. research work on the development of the hydrogen bomb in the years immediately following World War II. Monte Carlo methods were rarely performed prior to the advent of electronic computers. Because tremendous financial resources were expended on the Manhattan Project to develop the atom bomb and the ensuing work on the development of the hydrogen bomb, these projects were some of the first to have such computers. In fact, this explains why much of the early work on random number generators was performed by the scientists working on these two projects. The nearly universal availability of high-speed electronic computers today makes simulation a cheap and effective method for solving a wide variety of complex, practical problems.

The actuarial applications of this technique include (1) model offices of life insurance and annuities, (2) analysis of investment and asset allocation strategies (e.g., bond call properties), (3) asset/liability management, (4) product design and pricing studies, (5) dynamic solvency testing of insurance company (or pension fund) solidity and resilience, (6) collective risk models in general, and (7) aggregate loss distributions in particular.

Various applications of simulation to the models considered in this text are presented in Appendix B.

4.1 THE SIMULATION PROCEDURE

The crucial steps of a simulation are the following:

(1) The construction of an appropriate model.
(2) The design of the experiment.
(3) The repeated generation of *simulated output values* from one (or more) probability distributions.
(4) The analysis of the results.

The focus of this chapter is on the efficient generation of simulated outputs. The other steps, which are heavily dependent on the specific nature of the problem at hand, are illustrated in the applications scattered throughout the remainder of the text. Since the generation of simulated outputs is crucial to any simulation, this chapter contains a discussion of schemes (or algorithms) for the computer generation of them from a number of frequently-used probability distributions. Such generation procedures were used in the past because they produce a large num-number of simulated outputs in a short period of time and do not require much computer storage space, as would a large table of random numbers permanently stored in the computer's memory.

In this text we use the special term *random number*, denoted by u, where $0 \le u < 1$, to refer specifically to a simulated output value from the continuous uniform distribution over the interval [0,1). For convenience, we use the abbreviation $U[0,1)$ to denote this distribution.

When we wish to generate a simulated output value from a distribution other than $U[0,1)$, we normally first generate a random number u from $U[0,1)$ and use it to then generate our desired simulated output value. This two-step process is described in the sections that follow.

4.2 MULTIPLICATIVE CONGRUENTIAL RANDOM NUMBER GENERATORS

A frequently-used type of random number generator is known as a *linear congruential generator*, which was introduced by Lehmer [20]. In order to fully specify an individual linear congruential generator we must select the following four integer-valued parameters:

Parameter Name	Symbol	Restrictions
The modulus	m	$m > 0$
The multiplier	a	$0 \le a < m$
The increment	c	$0 \le c < m$
The starting value	X_0	$0 \le X_0 < m$

The $(n+1)^{st}$ term of the random sequence specified is

$$X_{n+1} \equiv a \cdot X_n + c \quad \mod m. \tag{4.1}$$

In other words, X_{n+1} is the remainder when $(a \cdot X_n + c)$ is divided by m, so the possible values of X_n are $0, 1, \cdots, m-1$. Because such sequences of numbers are in fact deterministic, they are sometimes called *pseudo-random* instead of random.

A *multiplicative congruential generator* is the special case of a linear congruential generator which is obtained when $c = 0$. Because the generation process is a little faster when $c = 0$, and most other desirable features are preserved, many practitioners prefer to use multiplicative congruential generators.

The multiplicative congruential random number generator given by

$$X_{n+1} \equiv 16,807 \cdot X_n \mod 2^{31} - 1, \tag{4.2}$$

where $X_0 = 16,807 = 7^5$ is known as GGL. It was developed by Lewis, Goodman, and Miller [21] at IBM. GGL has a cycle length of $2^{31} - 2 \approx 2$ billion; this is the maximum possible length because, if X_n is ever zero, then all subsequent terms must be zero. Prior to its implementation, this generator successfully passed a wide range of statistical tests as described in Lewis, Goodman, and Miller. GGL is still the random number generator employed as the "?" operator in IBM's version of the APL computer programming language. This generator works well for many problems as noted on page 189 of Knuth [19].

For the initial step in the generation of simulated output values from distributions other than the uniform distribution over [0,1), we generally employ output values (random numbers) drawn from the uniform distribution over [0,1). This is easily accomplished by dividing X_n by m, the modulus of the multiplicative congruential generator.

Unfortunately, there is no all-purpose random number generator, let alone one that is both easy to program and also has a long cycle length. As a consequence, Knuth [19] recommends (see page 189) that "each Monte Carlo" application should be run "at least twice using quite different sources of random numbers, before taking the answers of the program seriously; this will not only give an indication of the stability of the results, it will also guard against the danger of trusting in a generator with hidden deficiencies." Thus the burden is on the analyst to determine the random number generator(s) which are appropriate for the task at hand. The interested reader should see either Herzog and Lord [13] or Knuth [19] for more details about random number generators.

4.3 THE INVERSION METHOD FOR GENERATING SIMULATED OUTPUT VALUES FROM CONTINUOUS DISTRIBUTIONS

In this section, we describe a general method, known as the *inversion method*, for generating simulated random outputs from continuous probability distributions. We illustrate this approach with some examples applying the technique to important distributions. We also include a few clever *ad hoc* techniques that are superior to some of the more general approaches.

Depending on the computer and the programming language being used, the procedures presented here may or may not be the most efficient. For example, one method for generating normal random outputs, the *polar method* (see Section 4.5.1), is thought to be the most efficient for generating such outputs using the APL programming language; however, another method developed by George Marsaglia, known as the *rectangle-wedge-tail method*, is probably the most efficient if the procedure is programmed in machine or assembly language.

Let X denote a continuous random variable with cumulative distribution function $F(x) = Pr(X \le x)$. Since $F(x)$ is a nondecreasing function of x, its inverse function, F^{-1}, may be defined for any value z between 0 and 1 as the smallest x satisfying $F(x) \ge z$. We may write this definition mathematically as

$$F^{-1}(z) = inf\{x \mid F(x) \ge z\}, \tag{4.3}$$

for $0 \le z \le 1$, where $F^{-1}(0) = -\infty$ and $F^{-1}(1)$ may be equal to $+\infty$. This definition of F^{-1} is selected because it always exists.

If the random variable U is uniformly distributed over the interval [0,1), then the continuous random variable

$$X \ = \ F^{-1}(U) \tag{4.4}$$

has cumulative distribution function F. This may be shown as

$$Pr(X \leq x) = Pr\{X \leq F^{-1}[F(x)]\} = Pr\{F^{-1}(U) \leq F^{-1}[F(x)]\}$$
$$= Pr[U \leq F(x)] = F(x).$$

Hence, to generate a simulated value x from the distribution of X, we first draw a random number u from the uniform distribution over $[0,1)$ and then set $x = F^{-1}(u)$. The inversion method is illustrated in Figure 4.1 below and in the examples which follow.

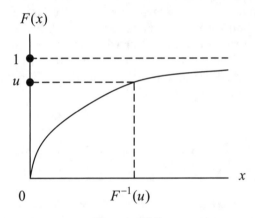

FIGURE 4.1

If $F^{-1}(u)$ is easily calculated, as illustrated in Sections 4.3.1 and 4.3.2, then this is perhaps the easiest way to generate simulated output values of the random variable X. Most of the other methods are designed for situations where it is not easy (or even possible) to calculate $F^{-1}(u)$ directly.[1]

4.3.1 THE EXPONENTIAL DISTRIBUTION

If we let

$$u \ = \ F(x) \ = \ 1 - e^{-\beta x}, \tag{4.5a}$$

and solve for x, we obtain

$$x \ = \ F^{-1}(u) \ = \ \frac{-\ln(1-u)}{\beta}. \tag{4.5b}$$

In order to generate a simulated value x from the exponential distribution with multiplicative parameter β, we proceed as follows:

---

[1] If $x = F^{-1}(u)$ does not exist in closed form, we can still generally solve the equation $u = F(x)$ iteratively for x given the uniform output value u. This would be true even if $F(x)$ does not exist in closed form (as, for example, with the normal distribution), because we can iteratively solve the equation $u = \int_{-\infty}^{x} f(y)\,dy$.

Step 1: Draw a random number u from the $U[0,1)$ distribution.

Step 2: Set $x = F^{-1}(u) = \dfrac{-\ln(1-u)}{\beta}$.

Note that if U is uniformly distributed over $[0,1)$, then so is $1-U$; a slightly faster generation method is obtained by setting $x = \dfrac{-\ln u}{\beta}$ in Step 2.

4.3.2 THE PARETO DISTRIBUTION

Consider the density function

$$f(x) = \frac{\alpha \cdot \theta^{\alpha}}{(x+\theta)^{\alpha+1}}, \tag{4.6a}$$

where $x > 0, \theta > 0$, and $\alpha > 0$. Now we have

$$u = F(x) = 1 - \frac{\theta^{\alpha}}{(x+\theta)^{\alpha}}, \tag{4.6b}$$

which implies that

$$x = F^{-1}(u) = \frac{\theta}{(1-u)^{1/\alpha}} - \theta. \tag{4.6c}$$

Then we can generate a random number u from the $U[0,1)$ distribution, and use Equation (4.6c) to generate a simulated output value of x from the Pareto distribution.

4.3.3 ADDITIONAL CONTINUOUS DISTRIBUTIONS

Suppose the random variable X has a cumulative distribution function given by

$$F(x) = 1 - \frac{1}{1 + \exp\left(\frac{x-1}{2}\right)},$$

for $-\infty < x < \infty$, and suppose the random number $u = .40$ is generated from the $U[0,1)$ distribution. We can then use the inversion method to determine a simulated value of the random variable X.

We first need to solve $u = F(x)$ for $x = F^{-1}(u)$. We have

$$1 + \exp\left(\frac{x-1}{2}\right) = \frac{1}{1-u},$$

so

$$\frac{x-1}{2} = \ln\left(\frac{1}{1-u} - 1\right) = \ln\left(\frac{u}{1-u}\right),$$

and finally $x = 1 + 2 \cdot \ln\left(\dfrac{u}{1-u}\right)$. Since the random number is $u = .40$, the simulated value of x will be

$$x = 1 + 2 \cdot \ln\left(\frac{.40}{.60}\right) = .18907.$$

4.4 THE TABLE LOOK-UP METHOD FOR DISCRETE PROBABILITY DISTRIBUTIONS

The *table look-up method* may be considered to be the discrete analog of the inversion method. However, with the table look-up method we do not need to know the mathematical distributional form.

Let X be a discrete random variable having positive probability at the points $x_1, x_2, \cdots$. The probability function is

$$p(x_i) = Pr(X = x_i),$$

where the probabilities $p(x_i)$ satisfy the condition that $p(x_i) > 0$ for all i, and

$$\sum_{i=1}^{\infty} p(x_i) = 1.$$

Without loss of generality we can assume that $x_1 < x_2 < \cdots$. The table look-up method proceeds by the following steps. First we select a random number u from the $U[0,1)$ distribution. Then we set

$$x = x_1 \quad \text{if} \quad 0 \le u < p(x_1) \tag{4.7a}$$

or

$$x = x_j \quad \text{if} \quad \sum_{i=1}^{j-1} p(x_i) \le u < \sum_{i=1}^{j} p(x_i). \tag{4.7b}$$

Going in order through the x_i's is a brute-force approach that suffers from a possibly high expected number of comparisons, as mentioned below. If computational speed is an issue (which, with today's computing power, would occur only for a very large number of x_i's), then the expected number of comparisons could be reduced substantially either by employing a smart search algorithm (*e.g.*, successive bisections) or applying appropriate ad hoc procedures as illustrated later in this section. We note that the average number of comparisons is $\sum_{i=1}^{\infty} i \cdot p(x_i)$. The table look-up method works best if the cumulating sums of probabilities reduce to a simple expression, as in the geometric distribution discussed below.

4.4.1 THE DISCRETE UNIFORM DISTRIBUTION

Let $p(x) = \frac{1}{b-a}$, where $x = a, a+1, \cdots, b-1$, and $a < b$. Then if u is a random number from $U[0,1)$, we set

$$x = a + \lfloor (b-a)u \rfloor, \tag{4.8}$$

where $\lfloor y \rfloor$ denotes the largest integer less than or equal to y.

4.4.2 THE BERNOULLI DISTRIBUTION

Let $p(0) = 1-p$ and $p(1) = p$. Then if u is a random number from $U[0,1)$, we set

$$x = 0 \quad \text{if} \quad u < 1-p \tag{4.9a}$$

or

$$x = 1 \quad \text{if} \quad u \geq 1-p. \tag{4.9b}$$

4.4.3 THE BINOMIAL DISTRIBUTION

Table Look-Up for the Binomial Distribution

One procedure for simulating output values from a binomial distribution using the table look-up method is as follows. Let the binomial cumulative distribution function be

$$F(k) = \sum_{j=0}^{k} \binom{n}{j} p^j (1-p)^{n-j}, \tag{4.10}$$

for $k = 0,1,\ldots,n$, with the obvious extension between integer points. A value, s, may be generated by first generating a random number u from $U[0,1)$, and then setting s equal to zero if $u < F(0)$ or else setting s equal to r, where r satisfies

$$F(r-1) \leq u < F(r). \tag{4.11}$$

Note that this is a brute force type of strategy.

Modified Table Look-Up for the Binomial Distribution

For this distribution, $p(0) = (1-p)^n$ and $\frac{p(k+1)}{p(k)} = \frac{(n-k)p}{(k+1)(1-p)}$ (see Section 2.2.2), so we have the recursion expression

$$Pr(K = k+1) = Pr(K = k) \cdot \frac{(n-k)p}{(k+1)(1-p)}. \tag{4.12}$$

This is an acceleration strategy, as opposed to the brute-force strategy of the table look-up method described above. The algorithm for this process follows the following steps:

Step 1 (Initialization): Define $C = \frac{p}{1-p}$, set the initial value of the counter at $K = 0$, set the initial value of $PR = Pr(K{=}0) = (1{-}p)^n$, and set the initial value of the cumulative sum at $CS = PR$.

Step 2: Generate a value u from $U[0,1)$.

Step 3: If $u < CS$, output K and stop.

Step 4 (Apply recursive formula): Set

$$PR = PR \cdot C \frac{n-K}{K+1}.$$

Step 5: Set $CS = CS + PR$ and $K = K{+}1$.

Step 6: Return to Step 3.

We note two other methods for simulating output values from a binomial distribution. Because each binomial random variable may be considered to be a sum of Bernoulli random variables, one approach is to use convolutions as discussed in Section 4.2 of Herzog and Lord [13]. The second is the normal approximation that we describe next.

Normal Approximation to the Binomial Distribution

The normal approximation to the binomial distribution is generally assumed to apply if either (1) $np > 10$ and $p > .50$, or (2) $n(1{-}p) > 10$ and $p < .50$. In this case, we employ the statistic

$$Z = \frac{K - np + .50}{\sqrt{np(1{-}p)}}, \tag{4.13}$$

which is asymptotically distributed as a standard normal random variable. Thus we can simulate a standard normal variable, Z, according to the strategy of Section 4.5 and then solve the above equation for K.

4.4.4 THE NEGATIVE BINOMIAL DISTRIBUTION

We discuss here two approaches to use with the negative binomial distribution. A third approach, the *convolution approach*, is described in Section 4.2 of Herzog and Lord [13].

Modified Table Look-Up Approach (with recursion)

For this distribution we have $p(0) = p^r$ and $\frac{p(x+1)}{p(x)} = \frac{(x+r)(1-p)}{x+1}$ (see Section 2.2.3). We can use the recursion relationship

$$Pr(X = x{+}1) = Pr(X = x) \cdot \frac{(x+r)(1-p)}{x+1}. \tag{4.14}$$

The algorithm for this is as follows:

Step 1 (Initialization): Set the initial value of the counter at $X = 0$, set the initial value of $PR = Pr(X=0) = p^r$, and set the initial value of the cumulative sum $CS = PR$.

Step 2: Generate a value u from $U[0,1)$.

Step 3: If $u \le CS$, output X and stop.

Step 4 (Apply recursive formula): Set

$$PR = PR \cdot \frac{(X+r)(1-p)}{X+1}.$$

Step 5: Set $CS = CS+PR$ and $X = X+1$.

Step 6: Return to Step 3.

The expected number of iterations of Steps 3-6 required to simulate one value from this distribution using this algorithm is $\frac{1+r(1-p)}{p}$.

Tossing a Biased Coin Approach[2]

We use the following algorithm to execute this event simulation approach:

Step 1 (Initialization): Set the initial counter values at $X = 0$ and $R = 0$.

Step 2: Generate a value u from the uniform distribution over $[0,1)$.

Step 3: If $u \ge 1-p$, go to Step 7.

Step 4: Set $R = R+1$.

Step 5: If $R = r$, output X and stop.

Step 6: Go to Step 2.

Step 7: Set $X = X+1$.

Step 8: Return to Step 2.

This approach is relatively inefficient. We might use it only if it were the only available strategy.

4.4.5 THE POISSON DISTRIBUTION

Modified Table Look-Up

Here we have $p(0) = e^{-\lambda}$ and $\frac{p(k+1)}{p(k)} = \frac{\lambda}{k+1}$ (see Section 2.2.5), leading to the recursion

---

[2] This procedure should be employed only when r is a positive integer.

$$Pr(K = k+1) = Pr(K = k) \cdot \frac{\lambda}{k+1}. \tag{4.15}$$

The algorithm for this is as follows:

Step 1 (Initialization): Set the initial value of the counter at $K = 0$, set the initial value of $PR = Pr(K=0) = e^{-\lambda}$, and set the initial value of the cumulative sum $CS = PR$.

Step 2: Generate a value u from $U[0,1)$.

Step 3: If $u < CS$, output K and stop.

Step 4 (Apply recursive formula): Set

$$PR = PR \cdot \frac{\lambda}{K+1}.$$

Step 5: Set $CS = CS + PR$ and $K = K+1$.

Step 6: Return to Step 3.

Normal Approximation to the Poisson Distribution

Another simulation approach is to use a normal approximation. This pertains if the Poisson mean, λ, is large, such as, for example, $\lambda > 10$. In this case we employ the statistic

$$Z = \frac{K - \lambda + .50}{\sqrt{\lambda}}, \tag{4.16}$$

which is asymptotically distributed as a standard normal random variable. We can draw standard normal variates Z according to the strategy of Section 4.5, and then solve the above equation for K.

Exponential Interarrival Time Approach

Another simulation approach is based on the fact that if the time intervals between events have independent exponential distributions, each with mean $\frac{1}{\lambda}$, then the number of events, X, occurring in each unit interval of time has a Poisson distribution with parameter (mean) λ.[3]

Let $T_1, T_2, \cdots$, be a sequence of independent random variables, each of which has an exponential distribution with parameter λ. Then X is determined from the relationship

$$\sum_{i=0}^{X} T_i \le 1 < \sum_{i=0}^{X+1} T_i, \tag{4.17a}$$

---

[3] See, for example, Chapter 8 of Hassett and Stewart [12].

where $T_0 = 0$. In other words, exactly X events occur within a single unit interval of time. As shown in Section 4.3.1, if U_i is uniformly distributed over [0,1), then

$$T_i = -\frac{1}{\lambda} \cdot \ln U_i. \qquad (4.18)$$

Thus we may rewrite the previous inequality as

$$\sum_{i=0}^{X} -\frac{1}{\lambda} \cdot \ln U_i \leq 1 < \sum_{i=0}^{X+1} -\frac{1}{\lambda} \cdot \ln U_i, \qquad (4.17b)$$

or, multiplying by $-\lambda$, as

$$\sum_{i=0}^{X} \ln U_i > -\lambda \geq \sum_{i=0}^{X+1} \ln U_i, \qquad (4.17c)$$

or, finally, as

$$\prod_{i=0}^{X} U_i > e^{-\lambda} \geq \prod_{i=0}^{X+1} U_i. \qquad (4.17d)$$

Output values from a Poisson distribution with mean λ can be generated by using the following algorithm.

Step 1 (Initialization): Set the counter at $K = 0$ and set the initial cumulative product at $CPROD = 1$.

Step 2: Generate a value u from $U[0,1)$.

Step 3: Update the cumulative product as $CPROD = u \cdot CPROD$.

Step 4: If $CPROD < e^{-\lambda}$, output K and stop; otherwise go to Step 5.

Step 5: $K = K+1$

Step 6: Return to Step 2.

As an example, suppose we wish to simulate a single output value from a Poisson distribution with mean 3. A random number generator produces the following sequence of random numbers from $U[0,1)$:

Position in Sequence (i)	Random Number (u_i)
1	.70
2	.30
3	.70
4	.50
5	.10

To determine the simulated Poisson output value, we first note that $e^{-3} = .0498$. The simulated Poisson output value will be the smallest integer x that satisfies

$$\prod_{i=1}^{x+1} u_i \leq .0498.$$

The given random numbers lead to the following set of cumulative products:

x	$\prod_{i=1}^{x+1} u_i$
0	.70
1	$(.70)(.30) = .21$
2	$(.70)(.30)(.70) = (.21)(.70) = .147$
3	$(.70)(.30)(.70)(.50) = (.147)(.50) = .0735$
4	$(.70)(.30)(.70)(.50)(.10) = (.0735)(.10) = .00735$

We need to go to the product of the first five values of u_i before the cumulative product becomes less than .0498, so the simulated Poisson distribution value is $x = 4$.

4.4.6 APPLICATIONS OF THE MATERIAL OF SECTION 4.4

The material discussed in Section 4.4 has a wide range of applications. The binomial, Poisson, and negative binomial are often used to model the frequency of loss among groups of insureds. (See Chapter 3 of Kellison and London [17].) In a case study involving home equity conversion mortgages (see Chapter 11 of Herzog and Lord [13]), the authors assume that the mortality experience of the insureds can be modeled as a Bernoulli trial.

4.5 METHODS FOR GENERATING SIMULATED NORMAL DISTRIBUTION VALUES

In this section we present two methods for generating simulated normal distribution values.

4.5.1 THE POLAR METHOD

Our first method for simulating normal output values is the *polar method*, which produces a pair of output values x_1 and x_2, drawn independently from the standard normal distribution. Here we inscribe a circle (of radius 1, centered at the origin of a two-dimensional Cartesian coordinate system) within a square and accept only those values falling inside the circle.

To perform the polar method, we first generate two random numbers, u_1 and u_2, from $U[0,1]$. Then we compute

$$v_i = 2 \cdot u_i - 1,$$

for $i = 1, 2,$ and form the ordered pair (v_1, v_2), where v_1 and v_2 represent output values drawn independently from the uniform distribution over $[-1, 1)$.

If (v_1, v_2) is in the interior of the unit circle defined in the first paragraph, we then compute x_1 and x_2 as

$$x_1 = v_1 \cdot \sqrt{(-2 \cdot \ln s)/s} \qquad (4.18a)$$

and

$$x_2 = v_2 \cdot \sqrt{(-2 \ln s)/s}, \qquad (4.18b)$$

where the square of the radius is $s = v_1^2 + v_2^2$. x_1 and x_2 are the desired standard normal output values. If (v_1, v_2) is outside the unit circle, we generate another pair of random numbers and repeat the above procedure.

The polar method is quite efficient for generating simulated normal outcomes in a programming language such as APL, in which the operations of natural logarithm and raise to an arbitrary power are essentially part of the language. However, if the programming is to be done in machine language or assembly language, then the rectangle-wedge-tail method described on pages 123-128 of Knuth [19] will be more efficient than the polar method and should be employed instead.

4.5.2 THE BOX-MULLER METHOD

A second method for simulating standard normal output values is the *Box-Muller method*.[4] Under this method, we first obtain two random numbers u_1 and u_2 from $U[0,1)$. We then produce a pair of independent simulated values from the standard normal distribution as

$$x_1 = \sqrt{-2 \cdot \ln u_1} \cdot \cos(2\pi u_2) \qquad (4.19a)$$

and

$$x_2 = \sqrt{-2 \cdot \ln u_1} \cdot \sin(2\pi u_2). \qquad (4.19b)$$

As an example, if $u_1 = .823$ and $u_2 = .317$, then $x_1 = -.2551$ and $x_2 = .5697$ represent a pair of independent output values drawn from the standard normal distribution.

---

[4] The original presentation is found in Box and Muller [5] . The technique is also described in Ross [25] .

PART TWO

MODELS FOR
SURVIVAL-CONTINGENT RISKS

The second section of the text addresses traditional contingent payment models where payments are dependent on the continued survival (or failure to survive) of a defined entity. This entire subject has traditionally been known as *life contingencies*, since the payment(s) were contingent on the continued life (or death) of a designated person. In this textbook the subject is treated in a more general fashion, where "survival" can just as easily mean the continuation of a labor strike, the functioning of a mechanical device (often called *reliability theory*), or the regular payment of scheduled coupons under a corporate bond.

Discrete functions numerically evaluated from a discrete survival model (i.e., a life table) are emphasized, since they represent most of the practical problems encountered by actuaries. The more abstract continuous functions are also considered, frequently for their interesting mathematical behavior. A random variable approach is employed along with a deterministic approach when that view is useful to broaden the reader's understanding.

In addition, the traditional actuarial models considered in this section can be presented as multi-state models, which are based on discrete-time or continuous-time Markov Chains. The background theory of Markov Chains was presented in Chapter 3.

The survival model is presented in Chapters 5 and 6, in both its parametric and tabular contexts.

The standard set of single-life, single-decrement actuarial topics is covered in Chapters 7-11: contingent payment models (with emphasis on their standard insurance applications), contingent annuities (life annuities), annual funding schemes (annual premiums), including their m^{thly} and continuous variations, and contingent contract reserves, now presented in two chapters. Extensions to the multi-status cases of joint and last-survivor are presented in Chapter 12 and multiple decrement models are covered in Chapters 13 and 14.

A discussion of using Microsoft Excel to calculate actuarial values from a life table is presented in Appendix A.

Standard actuarial notation is employed throughout this section.

CHAPTER FIVE

SURVIVAL MODELS
(CONTINUOUS PARAMETRIC CONTEXT)

A *survival model* is simply a probability distribution for a particular type of random variable. Thus the general theory of probability, as reviewed in Chapter 2, is fully applicable here. However the particular history of the survival model random variable is such that specific terminology and notation has developed, particularly in an actuarial context. In this chapter (and the next) the reader will see this specialized terminology and notation, and recognize that it is *only* the terminology and notation that is new; the underlying probability theory is the same as that applying to any other continuous random variable and its distribution.

In actuarial science, the survival distribution is frequently summarized in tabular form, which is called a *life table*.[1] Because the life table form is so prevalent in actuarial work, we will devote a full chapter to it in this textbook (see Chapter 6).

5.1 THE AGE-AT-FAILURE RANDOM VARIABLE

We begin our study of survival distributions by defining the generic concept of *failure*. In any situation involving a survival model, there will be a defined entity and an associated concept of *survival*, and hence of failure, of that entity.[2] Here are some examples of entities and their associated random variables.

(1)   The operating lifetime of a light bulb. The bulb is said to survive as long as it keeps burning, and fails at the instant it burns out.

(2)   The duration of labor/management harmony. The state of harmony continues to survive as long as regular work schedules are met, and fails at the time a strike is called. (Conversely, we could model the duration of a strike, where the strike survives until it is settled and workers return to the job. The settlement event constitutes the failure of the strike status.)

(3)   The lifetime of a new-born person. The person survives until death occurs, which constitutes the failure of the human entity. This will be the most common example considered in this text.

Let T_0 denote the continuous random variable for the age of the entity at the instant it fails.

---

[1] Alternatively, the tabular model is also called a *mortality table*.

[2] Another term for failure is *decrement*. If an entity has a particular status, such as survival, then failure to retain that status is often described as being *decremented* from that status. This terminology is particularly useful in the context of multiple decrements, which we encounter in Chapters 13 and 14.

We assume that the entity exists at age 0, so the domain of the random variable T_0 is $T_0 > 0$. We refer to T_0 as the *age-at-failure* random variable. We will consider the terms "failure" and "death" to be synonymous, so we will also refer to T_0 as the *age-at-death* random variable.[3]

It is easy to see that the numerical value of the age at failure is the same as the *length of time* that survival lasts until failure occurs, since the variable begins at age 0, so we can also refer to T_0 as the *time-to-failure* random variable. (If failure occurs at exact *age t*, then *t* is also the time until failure occurs.)

Later (see Section 5.3) we will consider the case where the entity of interest is known to have survived to some age $x > 0$. Then the time-to-failure random variable, to be denoted by T_x, will not be identical to the age-at-failure random variable T_0, although they will be related to each other by $T_0 = x + T_x$. When dealing with this more general case we will do our thinking in terms of the time-to-failure random variable.

5.1.1 THE CUMULATIVE DISTRIBUTION FUNCTION OF T_0

For the age-at-failure random variable T_0, we denote its CDF by

$$F_0(t) = Pr(T_0 \leq t), \tag{5.1}$$

for $t \geq 0$.[4] We have already noted, however, that $T_0 = 0$ is not possible, so we will always consider that $F_0(0) = 0$. We observe that $F_0(t)$ gives the probability that failure will occur prior to (or at) precise age *t* for our entity known to exist at age 0. In actuarial notation, this probability is denoted by $_t q_0$, so we have

$$_t q_0 = F_0(t) = Pr(T_0 \leq t). \tag{5.2}$$

5.1.2 THE SURVIVAL DISTRIBUTION FUNCTION OF T_0

The *survival distribution function* (SDF) for the survival random variable T_0 is denoted by $S_0(t)$, and is defined by

$$S_0(t) = 1 - F_0(t) = Pr(T_0 > t), \tag{5.3}$$

for $t \geq 0$. Since we take $F_0(0) = 0$, it follows that we will always take $S_0(0) = 1$. The SDF gives the probability that the age at failure exceeds *t*, which is the same as the probability that the entity known to exist at age 0 will survive to age *t*. Since the notion of infinite survival is unrealistic, we consider that

---

[3] In practice, age-at-failure is often used for inanimate objects, such as light bulbs or labor strikes, and age-at-death is used for animate entities, such as laboratory animals or human persons under an insurance arrangement.

[4] In probability theory, it is customary to subscript the CDF symbol with the name of the random variable, which suggests the notation $F_{T_0}(t)$ in this case. With the name of the random variable understood to be T_0 in this section, we prefer the notation $F_0(t)$ to avoid the awkwardness of subscripting a subscript.

$$\lim_{t \to \infty} S_0(t) = 0 \tag{5.4a}$$

and

$$\lim_{t \to \infty} F_0(t) = 1. \tag{5.4b}$$

In actuarial notation, the probability represented by $S_0(t)$ is denoted $_t p_0$, so we have

$$_t p_0 = S_0(t) = Pr(T_0 > t). \tag{5.5}$$

In probability textbooks in general, the CDF is given greater emphasis than is the SDF. (Some textbooks do not even define the SDF at all.) But when we are dealing with an age-at-failure random variable, and its associated distribution, the SDF will receive greater attention.

EXAMPLE 5.1

Use both the CDF and the SDF to express the probability that an entity known to exist at age 0 will fail between the ages of 10 and 20.

SOLUTION

We seek the probability that T_0 will take on a value between 10 and 20. In terms of the CDF we have

$$Pr(10 < T_0 \leq 20) = F_0(20) - F_0(10).$$

Since $S_0(t) = 1 - F_0(t)$, then we also have

$$Pr(10 < T_0 \leq 20) = S_0(10) - S_0(20). \qquad \square$$

5.1.3 THE PROBABILITY DENSITY FUNCTION OF T_0

For a continuous random variable in general, the *probability density function* (PDF) is defined as the derivative of the CDF. Thus we have here

$$f_0(t) = \frac{d}{dt} F_0(t) = -\frac{d}{dt} S_0(t), \tag{5.6}$$

for $t > 0$. Consequently,

$$F_0(t) = \int_0^t f_0(y) \, dy \tag{5.7}$$

and

$$S_0(t) = \int_t^\infty f_0(y) \, dy. \tag{5.8}$$

Of course it must be true that

$$\int_0^\infty f_0(y)\,dy = 1. \tag{5.9}$$

Although we have given mathematical definitions of $f_0(t)$, it will be useful to describe $f_0(t)$ more fully in the context of the age-at-failure random variable. Whereas $F_0(t)$ and $S_0(t)$ are probabilities that relate to certain *time intervals*, $f_0(t)$ relates to a *point of time*, and is not a probability. It is the density of failure *at* age t, and is therefore an *instantaneous* measure, as opposed to an interval measure.

It is important to recognize that $f_0(t)$ is the *unconditional* density of failure at age t. By this we mean that it is the density of failure at age t given *only* that the entity existed at $t = 0$. The significance of this point will become clearer in the next subsection.

5.1.4 THE HAZARD RATE FUNCTION OF T_0

Recall that the PDF of T_0, $f_0(t)$, is the *unconditional* density of failure at age t. We now define a *conditional* density of failure at age t, with such density conditional on survival to age t. This conditional instantaneous measure of failure at age t, given survival to age t, is called the *hazard rate* at age t, or the *hazard rate function* (HRF) when viewed as a function of t. (In some textbooks the hazard rate is called the *failure rate*.) It will be denoted by $\lambda_0(t)$.

In general, if a conditional measure is multiplied by the probability of obtaining the conditioning event, then the corresponding unconditional measure will result. Specifically,

(Conditional density of failure at age t, given survival to age t)
× (Probability of survival to age t)
= (Unconditional density of failure at age t).

Symbolically this states that

$$\lambda_0(t) \cdot S_0(t) = f_0(t), \tag{5.10}$$

or

$$\lambda_0(t) = \frac{f_0(t)}{S_0(t)}. \tag{5.11}$$

Equations (5.11) and (5.6) give formal definitions of the HRF and the PDF, respectively, of the age-at-failure random variable. Along with the definitions it is also important to have a clear understanding of the *conceptual meanings* of $\lambda_0(t)$ and $f_0(t)$. They are both instantaneous measures of the density of failure at age t; they differ from each other in that $\lambda_0(t)$ is conditional on survival to age t, whereas $f_0(t)$ is unconditional (i.e., given only existence at age 0).

In the actuarial context of survival models for animate objects, including human persons, failure means death, or mortality, and the hazard rate is normally called the *force of mortality*. We will discuss the actuarial context further in Section 5.1.6 and in Chapter 6.

Some important mathematical consequences follow directly from Equation (5.11). Since $f_0(t) = -\frac{d}{dt} S_0(t)$, it follows that

$$\lambda_0(t) = \frac{-\frac{d}{dt} S_0(t)}{S_0(t)} = -\frac{d}{dt} \ln S_0(t). \tag{5.12}$$

Integrating, we have

$$\int_0^t \lambda_0(y) \, dy = -\ln S_0(t), \tag{5.13}$$

or

$$S_0(t) = \exp\left[-\int_0^t \lambda_0(y) \, dy\right]. \tag{5.14}$$

The *cumulative hazard function* (CHF) is defined to be

$$\Lambda_0(t) = \int_0^t \lambda_0(y) \, dy = -\ln S_0(t), \tag{5.15}$$

so that

$$S_0(t) = e^{-\Lambda_0(t)}. \tag{5.16}$$

EXAMPLE 5.2

An age-at-failure random variable has a distribution defined by

$$F_0(t) = 1 - .10(100-t)^{1/2},$$

for $0 \leq t \leq 100$. Find (a) the PDF and (b) the HRF for this random variable.

SOLUTION

(a) The PDF is given by

$$f_0(t) = \frac{d}{dt} F_0(t) = -(.10)(.50)(100-t)^{-1/2} \cdot (-1) = .05(100-t)^{-1/2}.$$

(b) The HRF is given by

$$\lambda_0(t) = \frac{f_0(t)}{S_0(t)} = \frac{.05(100-t)^{-1/2}}{.10(100-t)^{1/2}} = .50(100-t)^{-1}. \qquad \square$$

5.1.5 THE MOMENTS OF THE AGE-AT-FAILURE RANDOM VARIABLE T_0

The first moment of a continuous random variable defined on $[0,\infty)$ is given by

$$E[T_0] = \int_0^\infty t \cdot f_0(t)\, dt, \tag{5.17}$$

if the integral exists, and otherwise the first moment is undefined. Integration by parts yields the alternative formula

$$E[T_0] = \int_0^\infty S_0(t)\, dx, \tag{5.18}$$

provided $\lim_{t\to\infty} t \cdot S_0(t) = 0$, a form which is frequently used to find the first moment of an age-at-failure random variable.

The second moment of T_0 is given by

$$E\left[T_0^2\right] = \int_0^\infty t^2 \cdot f_0(t)\, dt, \tag{5.19}$$

if the integral exists, so the variance of T_0 can be found from

$$Var(T_0) = E\left[T_0^2\right] - \left\{E[T_0]\right\}^2. \tag{5.20}$$

Specific expressions can be developed for the moments of T_0 for specific forms of $f_0(t)$. This will be pursued in the following section.

Another property of the age-at-failure random variable that is of interest is its *median* value. We recall that the median of a continuous random variable is the value for which there is a 50% chance that the random variable will exceed (and thus also not exceed) that value. Mathematically, y is the median of T_0 if

$$Pr(T_0 > y) = Pr(T_0 \le y) = \frac{1}{2}, \tag{5.21}$$

so that $S_0(y) = F_0(y) = \frac{1}{2}$.

5.1.6 ACTUARIAL SURVIVAL MODELS

When the age-at-failure random variable is considered in an actuarial context, special symbols are used for some of the concepts defined in this section. The hazard rate, now called the force of mortality, is denoted by μ_t, rather than $\lambda_0(t)$. Thus we have

$$\mu_t = \frac{-\frac{d}{dt} S_0(t)}{S_0(t)} = -\frac{d}{dt} \ln S_0(t). \qquad (5.22)$$

It is customary to denote the first moment of T_0 by $\overset{\circ}{e}_0$. Thus we have

$$\overset{\circ}{e}_0 = E[T_0] = \int_0^\infty t \cdot f_0(t) \, dt. \qquad (5.23)$$

Since $\overset{\circ}{e}_0$ is the unconditional expected value of T_0, given only alive at $t = 0$, it is called the *complete expectation of life at birth.*[5]

We recognize that the moments of T_0 given above are all unconditional. Conditional moments, and other conditional measures, are defined in Section 5.3, and the standard actuarial notation for them is reviewed in Chapter 6.

EXAMPLE 5.3

For the distribution of Example 5.2, find (a) $E[T_0]$ and (b) the median of the distribution.

SOLUTION

(a) The expected value is given by Equation (5.18) as

$$E[T_0] = \int_0^{100} .10(100-t)^{1/2} \, dt$$

$$= -\left(\frac{2}{3}\right)(.10)(100-t)^{3/2}\Big|_0^{100} = \left(\frac{2}{3}\right)(.10)(100)^{3/2} = \frac{200}{3}.$$

(b) The median is the value of y satisfying $S_0(y) = .10(100-y)^{1/2} = .50$, which solves for $y = 75$. ◻

5.2 EXAMPLES OF PARAMETRIC SURVIVAL MODELS

In this section we explore several non-negative continuous probability distributions that are candidates for serving as survival models. In practice, some distributions fit better than others to the empirical evidence of the shape of a survival distribution, so we will comment on each distribution we present regarding its suitability as a survival model.

5.2.1 THE UNIFORM DISTRIBUTION

The continuous uniform distribution, defined in Section 2.3.1, is a simple two-parameter distribution with a constant PDF. The parameters of the distribution are the limits of the interval

---

[5] The significance of the adjective "complete" will become clearer when we consider an alternative measure of the expectation of life in Sections 5.3.6 and 6.3.4.

on the real number axis over which it is defined, and its PDF is the reciprocal of that interval length. Thus if a generic random variable X is defined over the interval $[a,b]$, then $f_X(x) = \frac{1}{b-a}$, for $a \leq x \leq b$, and $f_X(x) = 0$ elsewhere.

For the special case of the age-at-failure random variable, $a = 0$ so b is the length of the interval, as well as the greatest value of t for which $f_0(t) > 0$. When the uniform distribution is used as a survival model, the Greek ω is frequently used for this parameter, so the distribution is defined by

$$f_0(t) = \frac{1}{\omega}, \tag{5.24}$$

for $0 < t \leq \omega$. The following properties of the uniform distribution easily follow, and should be verified by the reader:

$$F_0(t) = \int_0^t f_0(y)\,dy = \frac{t}{\omega} \tag{5.25}$$

$$S_0(t) = 1 - F_0(t) = \int_t^\omega f_0(y)\,dy = \frac{\omega - t}{\omega} \tag{5.26}$$

$$\lambda_0(t) = \frac{f_0(t)}{S_0(t)} = \frac{1}{\omega - t} \tag{5.27}$$

$$E[T_0] = \int_0^\omega t \cdot f_0(t)\,dt = \frac{\omega}{2} \tag{5.28}$$

$$Var(T_0) = E\left[T_0^2\right] - \left\{E[T_0]\right\}^2 = \frac{\omega^2}{12} \tag{5.29}$$

The uniform distribution, as a survival model, is not appropriate over a broad range of age, at least as a model for *human* survival. It is of historical interest, however, to note that it was the first continuous probability distribution to be suggested for that purpose, in 1724, by Abraham de Moivre. As a result, actuarial literature and exams often refer to the uniform distribution as "de Moivre's law."

The major use of this distribution is over short ranges of time (or age). We will explore this use of the uniform distribution quite thoroughly in Section 6.5.1.

5.2.2 THE EXPONENTIAL DISTRIBUTION

This very popular one-parameter distribution (see Section 2.3.3) is defined by its SDF to be

$$S_0(t) = e^{-\lambda t}, \tag{5.30}$$

for $t > 0$ and $\lambda > 0$. It then follows that the PDF is

$$f_0(t) = -\frac{d}{dt} S_0(t) = \lambda \cdot e^{-\lambda t}, \tag{5.31}$$

so that the HRF is

$$\lambda_0(t) = \frac{f_0(t)}{S_0(t)} = \lambda, \tag{5.32}$$

a constant. In the actuarial context, where the hazard rate is generally called the force of mortality, the exponential distribution is referred to as the *constant force distribution*.

The exponential distribution, with its property of a constant hazard rate, is frequently used in reliability engineering as a survival model for inanimate objects such as machine parts. Like the uniform distribution, however, it is not appropriate as a model for human survival over a broad range, but might be used over short intervals, such as one year, due to its mathematical simplicity. This will be explored in Section 6.5.2.

5.2.3 THE GOMPERTZ DISTRIBUTION

This distribution was suggested as a model for human survival by Gompertz [10] in 1825. The distribution is usually defined by its force of mortality as

$$\mu_t = Bc^t, \tag{5.33}$$

for $t > 0$, $B > 0$, and $c > 1$. Then the SDF is given by

$$S_0(t) = \exp\left[-\int_0^t Bc^y \, dy\right] = \exp\left[\frac{B}{\ln c}(1-c^t)\right]. \tag{5.34}$$

The PDF is given by $\mu_t \cdot S_0(t)$, and is clearly not a very convenient mathematical form. A closed-form expression for the mean of the distribution, $E[T_0]$, does not exist, but the mean can be approximated by numerical integration with a large finite upper limit replacing the actual upper limit of infinity.

5.2.4 THE MAKEHAM DISTRIBUTION

In 1860 Makeham [23] modified the Gompertz distribution by taking the force of mortality to be

$$\mu_t = A + Bc^t, \tag{5.35}$$

for $t > 0$, $B > 0$, $c > 1$, and $A > -B$. Makeham was suggesting that part of the hazard at any age is independent of the age itself, so a constant was added to the Gompertz force of mortality.

The SDF for this distribution is given by

$$S_0(t) = \exp\left[-\int_0^t (A+Bc^y)\,dy\right] = \exp\left[\frac{B}{\ln c}(1-c^t) - At\right].\tag{5.36}$$

Again it is clear that the PDF for this distribution is not mathematically tractable. As with the Gompertz distribution, there is no closed-form expression for $E[T_0]$, although it can also be approximated by numerical integration.[6]

5.2.5 SUMMARY OF PARAMETRIC SURVIVAL MODELS

We have briefly explored four distributions here: two (uniform and exponential) which are mathematically simple, and two (Gompertz and Makeham) which are not. For many illustrations, where we wish to avoid mathematical complexity, we will use the uniform or the exponential for illustrative purposes only, not necessarily suggesting that they are applicable in practice. The exponential has been applied in many situations not involving healthy human lives, and has been widely used in those situations.

5.3 THE TIME-TO-FAILURE RANDOM VARIABLE

In Section 5.1 we defined a continuous random variable, denoted T_0, which measured the length of time from age 0 until failure occurs. Now we turn to the case where our entity of interest is known to have survived to age x, where $x > 0$, and we wish to consider the random variable for the *additional* time that the entity might survive beyond age x. We denote this random variable by T_x, and note that its domain is $T_x > 0$. We define the random variable T_x to be the *time-to-failure* random variable for an entity known to be alive (i.e., known to have not yet failed) at age x. We will use the notation (x) to denote the entity known to be alive at age x.[7]

If T_x is the random time-to-failure for an entity alive at age x, it follows that the age-at-failure will be T_x more than age x, so we have the relationship $T_0 = x + T_x$ between our two basic random variables. This is illustrated in the following figure.

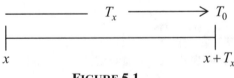

FIGURE 5.1

Rather than develop separate distributions for T_x for each different value of x, we will simply calculate probability values for T_x from the distribution of T_0. (An exception to this will be explored in Section 5.4.)

---

[6] A generalization of the Makeham distribution is presented in Exercise 5-10.
[7] The time until failure of (x) can also be called the future lifetime of (x), so T_x is therefore often called the *future lifetime* random variable for the entity (x).

5.3.1 THE SURVIVAL DISTRIBUTION FUNCTION OF T_x

For an entity known to be alive at age x, which we denote by (x), the probability of surviving an additional t time units[8] is denoted by $_t p_x$ in actuarial notation. In probability terminology, we note that this is simply the *conditional* probability of failure beyond age $x+t$, given survival to age x (hence failure beyond age x). Thus we have

$$
\begin{aligned}
_t p_x &= Pr(T_x > t) \\
&= Pr(T_0 > x+t \mid T_0 > x).
\end{aligned}
$$

(5.37)

Recall from basic probability theory that the conditional probability $Pr(E \mid F)$ is defined to be

$$Pr(E \mid F) = \frac{Pr(E \cap F)}{Pr(F)},$$

(5.38)

where $Pr(E \cap F)$ denotes the probability that both events E and F occur. In our example, E is the event $T_0 > x+t$ and F is the event $T_0 > x$. But if $T_0 > x+t$, then $T_0 > x$ necessarily, so the intersection of these two events is simply the event $T_0 > x+t$. Thus we have

$$
\begin{aligned}
_t p_x &= S_x(t)^{\,9} \\
&= Pr(T_x > t) \\
&= Pr(T_0 > x+t \mid T_0 > x) \\
&= \frac{Pr(T_0 > x+t)}{Pr(T_0 > x)} \\
&= \frac{S_0(x+t)}{S_0(x)}.
\end{aligned}
$$

(5.39)

5.3.2 THE CUMULATIVE DISTRIBUTION FUNCTION OF T_x

We denote the CDF of the random variable T_x by $F_x(t)$ in probability notation and by $_t q_x$ in actuarial notation. It gives the conditional probability that failure occurs not later than age $x+t$, given survival to age x. Thus we have

---

[8] In the case of human persons under life insurance arrangements, time will normally be measured in years. For inanimate objects, such as light bulbs or mechanical devices operating under test conditions, time might be measured in hours.

[9] As with the random variable T_0 defined earlier, the notational convention in probability theory would be to write the SDF symbol as $S_{T_x}(t)$. To avoid subscripting a subscript, we use the simpler $S_x(t)$. This notational principle will hold for the CDF, PDF, and HRF as well.

$$_t q_x = F_x(t) = Pr(T_x \leq t)$$

$$= Pr(T_0 \leq x+t \mid T_0 > x)$$

$$= 1 - Pr(T_0 > x+t \mid T_0 > x)$$

$$= 1 - \frac{S_0(x+t)}{S_0(x)}, \tag{5.40}$$

where we use Equation (5.39) to express $Pr(T_0 > x+t \mid T_0 > x)$ in terms of $S_0(x)$, the SDF of the age-at-failure random variable T_0. We can easily write Equation (5.40) in terms of $F_0(x)$. We have

$$_t q_x = 1 - \frac{1 - F_0(x+t)}{1 - F_0(x)} = \frac{F_0(x+t) - F_0(x)}{1 - F_0(x)}. \tag{5.41}$$

Since the CDF and SDF are complements of each other, then it follows that $_t p_x = 1 - {}_t q_x$ and vice versa.

In the special case of $t = 1$, the notational convention is to suppress the t part of the symbol. Thus the probability of (x) surviving one additional year beyond age x is given by

$$p_x = Pr(T_0 > x+1 \mid T_0 > x) = \frac{S_0(x+1)}{S_0(x)}, \tag{5.42}$$

and the complementary probability that (x) will fail within the year following age x is given by

$$q_x = 1 - p_x = Pr(T_0 \leq x+1 \mid T_0 > x) = \frac{F_0(x+1) - F_0(x)}{1 - F_0(x)}. \tag{5.43}$$

5.3.3 THE PROBABILITY DENSITY FUNCTION OF T_x

The PDF of the time-to-failure (or future lifetime) random variable T_x, denoted $f_x(t)$, gives the conditional density for failure at time t for an entity known to be alive at age x. Thus we can say that it gives the conditional density for failure at age $x+t$, given survival to age x. It is given by

$$f_x(t) = \frac{d}{dt} F_x(t) = -\frac{d}{dt} S_x(t)$$

$$= -\frac{d}{dt} \frac{S_0(x+t)}{S_0(x)}$$

$$= \frac{f_0(x+t)}{S_0(x)}, \tag{5.44}$$

since $f_0(x+t) = -\frac{d}{dt} S_0(x+t)$.

5.3.4 THE HAZARD RATE FUNCTION OF T_x

Recall that the HRF of T_0, denoted $\lambda_0(t)$, is itself a conditional measure, conditional on survival to age t. Therefore the hazard rate at age $x+t$ for (x), which we might denote by $\lambda_x(t \mid T_0 > x)$, is the same concept as $\lambda_0(x+t)$ itself. The condition of survival to age $x+t$ supercedes the condition of survival to age x.

Considering together Equation (5.44) and Equation (5.10), with x replaced by $x+t$, we can express the PDF of T_x in terms of the distribution of T_0 as

$$f_x(t) = \frac{f_0(x+t)}{S_0(x)} = \frac{S_0(x+t) \cdot \lambda_0(x+t)}{S_0(x)}. \tag{5.45}$$

In the actuarial context and notation, where the hazard rate is called the force of mortality and denoted by μ_t, we have

$$f_x(t) = {}_t p_x \cdot \mu_{x+t}, \tag{5.46}$$

by using Equation (5.39) to substitute ${}_t p_x$ for $\frac{S_0(x+t)}{S_0(x)}$.

5.3.5 MOMENTS OF THE FUTURE LIFETIME RANDOM VARIABLE T_x

The expected value of T_x, given alive at age x, is called the *complete expectation of life at age x*,[10] or the *expected future lifetime at age x*, and is denoted by $\overset{o}{e}_x$. Recall that the age-at-failure random variable T_0 and the time-to-failure (or future lifetime) random variable T_x are related by $T_0 = T_x + x$, so $T_x = T_0 - x$. Thus we have

$$\overset{o}{e}_x = E[T_x \mid T_0 > x] = E[T_0 - x \mid T_0 > x] = E[T_0 \mid T_0 > x] - x. \tag{5.47}$$

Equation (5.47) makes the point that the expected future lifetime of (x) is the excess of the conditional expected age at failure, $E[T_0 \mid T_0 > x]$, over the value of x itself. It can be calculated from the conditional PDF of T_0 as

$$\overset{o}{e}_x = \int_0^\infty t \cdot f_0(x+t \mid T_0 > x)\, dt. \tag{5.48a}$$

Using Equation (5.44) this can be written as

$$\overset{o}{e}_x = \int_0^\infty t \cdot \frac{f_0(x+t)}{S_0(x)} dt = \frac{1}{S_0(x)} \int_0^\infty t \cdot f_0(x+t) dt. \tag{5.48b}$$

---

[10] See footnote 5.

Next, recall from Equation (5.18) that integration by parts on Equation (5.48b) leads to

$$\overset{o}{e}_x = \frac{1}{S_0(x)} \int_0^\infty S_0(x+t)dt, \tag{5.48c}$$

and finally to

$$\overset{o}{e}_x = \int_0^\infty \frac{S_0(x+t)}{S_0(x)} dt = \int_0^\infty {}_t p_x dt, \tag{5.48d}$$

by use of Equation (5.39). As we will see in Chapter 6, Equation (5.48d) is a common way to define, and eventually calculate, $\overset{o}{e}_x$.

Finally, since the age at failure, given alive at age x, is the future lifetime, given alive at age x, plus x itself, then it follows that

$$Var(T_0 \,|\, T_0 > x) = Var(T_x \,|\, T_0 > x), \tag{5.49}$$

since x is a constant. To calculate $Var(T_0 \,|\, T_0 > x)$ we first calculate

$$E[T_0 \,|\, T_0 > x] = \int_x^\infty y \cdot f_0(y \,|\, T_0 > x) \, dy \tag{5.50}$$

and

$$E\left[T_0^2 \,|\, T_0 > x\right] = \int_x^\infty y^2 \cdot f_0(y \,|\, X > x) \, dy, \tag{5.51}$$

provided the two expectations exist. Then the variance of the age at failure and also of the time to failure is given by

$$Var(T_0 \,|\, T_0 > x) = Var(T_x \,|\, T_0 > x) = E\left[T_0^2 \,|\, T_0 > x\right] - \left\{E[T_0 \,|\, T_0 > x]\right\}^2. \tag{5.52}$$

EXAMPLE 5.4

For the distribution of Example 5.2, find each of (a) ${}_{20}p_{36}$, (b) $f_{36}(t)$, and (c) $\overset{o}{e}_{36}$.

SOLUTION

(a) From Equation (5.39) we have

$$_{20}p_{36} = \frac{S_0(56)}{S_0(36)} = \frac{(100-56)^{1/2}}{(100-36)^{1/2}} = .82916.$$

(b) From Equation (5.44) we have

$$f_{36}(t) = \frac{f_0(36+t)}{S_0(36)} = \frac{.05(100-36-t)^{-1/2}}{.10(100-36)^{1/2}} = \frac{.0625}{(64-t)^{1/2}},$$

where we use the result of part (a) of Example 5.2 to find $f_0(36+t)$.

(c) In general we have

$$_t p_{36} = \frac{S_0(36+t)}{S_0(36)} = .125(64-t)^{1/2}.$$

Then from Equation (5.48d) we find

$$\overset{o}{e}_{36} = .125 \int_0^{64} (64-t)^{1/2} \, dt = \frac{128}{3}. \qquad \square$$

5.3.6 DISCRETE TIME-TO-FAILURE RANDOM VARIABLES

In this section we present two different, but closely related, discrete random variables. The first, which we denote by K_x, is the *curtate duration at failure* random variable. It is defined to be the integral part of T_x, the future lifetime of (x). The second, which we denote by K_x^*, is the *time interval of failure* random variable. Both random variables are illustrated in Figure 5.2.

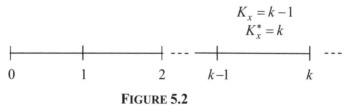

FIGURE 5.2

Consider the kth time interval, which we denote by $(k-1, k]$ to suggest that the precise time point k is included in the kth interval and the precise time point $k-1$ is included in the $(k-1)^{st}$ interval. If failure occurs in the kth interval, including the special case of $T_x = k$, then $K_x^* = k$ but $K_x = k-1$, the greatest integer in T_x. Then it follows that, in general,

$$K_x^* = K_x + 1. \qquad (5.53)$$

In particular, if failure occurs in the first time interval following age x, then we have $K_x^* = 1$ but $K_x = 0$. The probability function of K_x^* is

$$Pr(K_x^* = k) = Pr(k-1 < T_x \le k) \qquad (5.54a)$$
$$= Pr(x+k-1 < T_0 \le x+k \,|\, T_0 > x), \qquad (5.54b)$$

for $k = 1, 2, \cdots$, and is denoted by $_{k-1|}q_x$ in actuarial notation. The probability function of K_x is

$$Pr(K_x = k) \; = \; Pr(k < T_x \le k+1) \tag{5.55a}$$
$$= \; Pr(x+k < T_0 \le x+k+1 \,|\, T_0 > x), \tag{5.55b}$$

for $k = 0, 1, 2, \cdots$, and is denoted by $_{k|}q_x$ in actuarial notation.

The moments of K_x and K_x^* are all conditional on survival to age x, denoted by $T_0 > x$. The expected value of K_x is given by

$$E[K_x \,|\, T_0 > x] \; = \; \sum_{k=0}^{\infty} k \cdot {}_{k|}q_x. \tag{5.56a}$$

It is denoted by e_x in actuarial notation, and is called the *curtate expectation of life at age x*.[11] The expected value of K_x^* is given by

$$E[K_x^* \,|\, T_0 > x] \; = \; \sum_{k=1}^{\infty} k \cdot {}_{k-1|}q_x. \tag{5.56b}$$

From Equation (5.53) it is clear that

$$E[K_x^* \,|\, T_0 > x] \; = \; E[K_x \,|\, T_0 > x] + 1 \; = \; e_x + 1 \tag{6.57a}$$

and

$$Var(K_x^* \,|\, T_0 > x) \; = \; Var(K_x \,|\, T_0 > x), \tag{5.57b}$$

since K_x and K_x^* differ only by an additive constant. This common variance would be found by first finding either

$$E[K_x^2 \,|\, T_0 > x] \; = \; \sum_{k=0}^{\infty} k^2 \cdot {}_{k|}q_x \tag{5.58a}$$

or

$$E[K_x^{*\,2} \,|\, T_0 > x] \; = \; \sum_{k=1}^{\infty} k^2 \cdot {}_{k-1|}q_x. \tag{5.58b}$$

Next we define the continuous random variable R_x to represent the fractional part of the time interval lived through in the interval of failure for an entity alive at age x. This is illustrated in Figure 5.3.

---

[11]Note the similarity of $e_x = E[K_x \,|\, T_0 > x]$ to $\overset{\circ}{e}_x = E[T_x \,|\, T_0 > x]$, defined by Equation (5.47). Recall that the latter is called the *complete* expectation of life at age x whereas the former is called the *curtate* expectation.

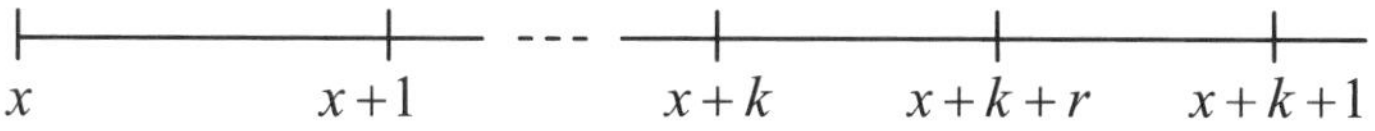

FIGURE 5.3

If failure occurs at time r, where $0 < r \leq 1$, within year $k+1$, then we have $K_x = k$, $R_x = r$, and $T_x = k+r$. In general we have

$$T_x = K_x + R_x.\,^{12} \tag{5.59a}$$

Note that, in the case described in Figure 5.3, the time-interval-of-failure random variable is $K_x^* = k+1$, so the general relationship is

$$T_x = K_x^* - 1 + R_x. \tag{5.59b}$$

5.4 SELECT SURVIVAL MODELS

Recall that $_tp_x$, defined in terms of the survival model $S_0(t)$ by Equation (5.39), is a conditional probability, where the given condition is simply that survival to age x has occurred. No other information beyond the basic fact of survival to age x is presumed.

In the life insurance context, a person being issued life insurance coverage at age x is certainly known to be alive at age x. But additional information is also available about this person as a result of the underwriting and selection process (see Chapter 4) that people seeking insurance would undergo. Therefore the probability of surviving on from age x to age $x+t$ for such a person would logically be different (likely greater) than the comparable probability for a person known only to have survived to age x. The probability of surviving from age x to age $x+t$ for a person *underwritten and selected for insurance at age x* is denoted by $_tp_{[x]}$, to distinguish it from $_tp_x$.

The survival probability $_tp_{[x]}$ can be represented in survival distribution form. We consider that the selection event defines time $t = 0$, and the age at selection, denoted $[x]$, is merely an identifying characteristic of the person whose survival distribution we are considering. We denote such a survival distribution by $S_{[x]}(t;x)$, and denote the random variable for length of survival by $T_{[x]}$ in this case. The identifying characteristic $[x]$, the age of the person at selection, is called a *concomitant variable*. Note that since age x corresponds to time $t = 0$, then $_tp_{[x]}$ is an unconditional probability whereas $_tp_x$ is a conditional probability.

The *select survival model* $S_{[x]}(t;x)$, in parametric form, would be a function of the two variables t and x. In actuarial practice, select models are generally presented in tabular form as a *select life table*. This is explored further in Section 6.6.

---

[12] We will further discuss the relationship of the random variables T_x, K_x, K_x^*, and R_x in Section 6.5.1.

EXAMPLE 5.5

Find, in terms of $S_{[x]}(t;x)$, the probability that an entity selected at age x, and known to be alive at age $x+10$, will fail before age $x+20$.

SOLUTION

We seek the probability of failure prior to age $x+20$, given survival to age $x+10$, which is denoted by $_{10}q_{[x]+10}$ in standard actuarial notation. It is equal to

$$1 - Pr(survival\ to\ x{+}20\,|\,survival\ to\ x{+}10) \quad = \quad 1 - {_{10}}p_{[x]+10}.$$

When the conditional probability $_{10}p_{[x]+10}$ is multiplied by the probability of the conditioning event, which is $S_{[x]}(10;x)$, the result is the unconditional probability of survival to $x+20$, which is $S_{[x]}(20;x)$. Thus we have

$$_{10}q_{[x]+10} = 1 - {_{10}}p_{[x]+10}$$

$$= 1 - \frac{S_{[x]}(20;x)}{S_{[x]}(10;x)}. \qquad \square$$

5.5 MULTI-STATE MODEL INTERPRETATION

The survival model presented in this chapter can be represented as a simple, two-state, continuous-time Markov model, where State 1 is continued survival and State 2 is failure (or death).[13] It is clear that the process must begin in State 1 and equally clear that State 2 is an absorbing state. Therefore there can be only one transition, from State 1 to State 2, over the entire process. The model is represented by the following diagram.

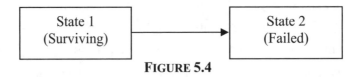

| State 1 (Surviving) | | State 2 (Failed) |

FIGURE 5.4

The arrow in Figure 5.4 reminds us that transition from State 2 back to State 1 is not possible.

Because the process cannot reenter State 1 once it has left it, it follows that the event of being in State 1 at time $t+r$, given in State 1 at time t, can occur *only* if the process never leaves State 1 over that time interval. Then it follows that $_{r}p_{11}^{*(t)} = {_{r}}p_{11}^{(t)}$, as defined in Section 3.2.

---

[13] In Chapter 6 we will represent the survival model as a discrete-time Markov model.

To show the correspondence of the multi-state model notation, defined in Chapter 3, with the actuarial notation, defined in this chapter, suppose we have a person alive at age x at time t. The person constitutes the model; since the person is known to be alive, the model is known to be in State 1. Then the probability of still being in State 1 at time $t+r$ is given by

$$_r p_x = {}_r p_{11}^{*(t)} = {}_r p_{11}^{(t)}. \tag{5.60}$$

The probability of failure before time $t+r$, given survival to time t, is given by

$$_r q_x = {}_r p_{12}^{(t)}. \tag{5.61}$$

The force of transition from State 1 to State 2 at time s, denoted by $\lambda_{12}(s)$ in Section 3.2.1, is also $\lambda_1(s)$, the total force of transition out of State 1 since State 2 is the only state to which the process can move. Note that $\lambda_{21}(s) = 0$ for all s. In actuarial notation, the force of transition $\lambda_{12}(s)$ is called the force of failure, or the force of mortality, and is denoted simply by $\lambda(s)$ or sometimes by μ_s.

The Kolmogorov Forward Equation, given by Equation (3.14b), simplifies considerably when applied to this two-state survival model.

EXAMPLE 5.6

Solve the Kolmogorov differential equation for $_r p_{11}^{(t)}$, and translate the result into standard actuarial notation.

SOLUTION

In this case, where $j = i = 1$, the index k in Equation (3.14b) takes on only the value $k = 2$, since $k \neq j = 1$. We have

$$\frac{d}{dr} {}_r p_{11}^{(t)} = {}_r p_{12}^{(t)} \cdot \lambda_{21}(t+r) - {}_r p_{11}^{(t)} \cdot \lambda_1(t+r).$$

But $\lambda_{21}(t+r) = 0$, so this equation reduces to

$$\frac{d}{dr} {}_r p_{11}^{(t)} = - {}_r p_{11}^{(t)} \cdot \lambda_1(t+r).$$

Dividing both sides by $_r p_{11}^{(t)}$ we have

$$\frac{\frac{d}{dr} {}_r p_{11}^{(t)}}{{}_r p_{11}^{(t)}} = \frac{d}{dr} \ln {}_r p_{11}^{(t)} = -\lambda_1(t+r),$$

or

$$d \ln {}_r p_{11}^{(t)} = -\lambda_1(t+r)\, dr.$$

Integrating both sides from $r = 0$ to $r = n$, we have

$$\int_0^n d \ln {}_r p_{11}^{(t)} = \int_0^n -\lambda_1(t+r)\, dr$$

or

$$\ln {}_r p_{11}^{(t)} \Big|_0^n = \int_0^n -\lambda_1(t+r)\, dr$$

or

$$\ln\left(\frac{{}_n p_{11}^{(t)}}{{}_0 p_{11}^{(t)}}\right) = -\int_0^n \lambda_1(t+r)\, dr$$

or

$${}_n p_{11}^{(t)} = e^{-\int_0^n \lambda_1(t+r)\, dr}, \tag{5.62a}$$

since ${}_0 p_{11}^{(t)} = 1$. State 1 is the surviving state, so ${}_n p_{11}^{(t)}$ represents the probability that a process (person) alive at age x at time t will be still alive at time $t+n$, which we call ${}_n p_x$ in actuarial notation. Also, in actuarial notation, our process (person) is age $x+r$ at time $t+r$, so we would use the notation μ_{x+r} in place of the multi-state model symbol $\lambda_1(t+r)$. Then Equation (5.62a) would be written as

$${}_n p_x = e^{-\int_0^n \mu_{x+r}\, dr}, \tag{5.62b}$$

an expression we will encounter frequently later in the text. ❑

We can similarly solve Kolmogorov's differential equation for ${}_r p_{12}^{(t)}$, the probability of being failed (i.e., of being in State 2) at time $t+r$, given alive (i.e., being in State 1) at age x at time t. (The actuarial symbol for this probability is ${}_r q_x$.) The details of this are left to the reader as Exercise 5-22.

Finally, we observe that if the underlying survival model is exponential, so that the force of transition function $\lambda_{12}(s)$ is a constant, say λ, then we have a homogeneous Markov model, and the Kolmogorov differential equation is even more easily solved for ${}_r p_{11}^{(t)}$ or ${}_r p_{12}^{(t)}$. The details of this are left to the reader as Exercises 5-24 and 5-25.

5.6 EXERCISES

5.1 The Age-at-Failure Random Variable

5-1   The hazard rate of a survival distribution is a linear function, $\lambda_0(t) = a + bt$,   where $a > 0$ and $b > 0$. Find each of the following:

(a) $S_0(t)$ (b) $f_0(t)$ (c) The mode of the distribution

5-2 Let a survival distribution be defined by $S_0(t) = at^2 + b$, for $0 < t \leq k$. If the expected value of T_0 is 60, find the median of T_0.

5-3 Explain why the hazard rate $\lambda_0(t) = e^{-rt}$, where $r > 0$, is not appropriate for a survival distribution.

5-4 Which of the following could serve as a survival model, for $t > 0$? If not, why not?

(a) $S_0(t) = e^{[t - .70(2^t - 1)]}$

(b) $S_0(t) = (1+t)^{-2}$

(c) $S_0(t) = e^{-t^2}$

5.2 Examples of Parametric Survival Models

5-5 If T_0 is uniformly distributed over $(0, 2)$, find $Var(T_0)$.

5-6 Let X_1 and X_2 be independent generic random variables (i.e., not necessarily age-at-failure random variables). Define the new random variables $Y = \min(X_1, X_2)$ and $Z = \max(X_1, X_2)$.

(a) Show that $S_Y(y)$ is the product of the SDF's of X_1 and X_2.

(b) Show that $F_Z(z)$ is the product of the CDF's of X_1 and X_2.

(c) Show that if X_1 and X_2 both have exponential distributions, then Y also has an exponential distribution, but Z does not.

5-7 Let the independent generic random variables X_1 and X_2 both have exponential distributions, with parameters λ_1 and λ_2, respectively, where $\lambda_1 > \lambda_2$. Let Y and Z be as defined in Exercise 5-6. Given that $S_Y(2) = .24$ and $S_Z(2) = .86$, find the value of λ_1.

5-8 $_m|q_0 = S_0(m) - S_0(m+1)$ is the probability that an entity existing at age 0 will fail between $t = m$ and $t = m+1$. Determine whether $_m|q_0$ is an increasing, decreasing, or constant function of m for each of the following distributions:

(a) Uniform

(b) Exponential

(c) $f_0(t) = .00125t$, for $0 \leq t \leq 40$

5-9   Given that $\lambda_0(t) = k \cdot t^n$ and $\lambda_0(22) = 1.26$, where 22 is the median age of the distribution, find the value of n. (A model with this hazard rate is called a *Weibull distribution*.)

5-10   The *generalized Makeham distribution* is defined by its force of mortality as

$$\mu_t = p_1(t) + e^{p_2(t)},$$

where $p_1(t)$ and $p_2(t)$ are polynomials in t. Show that the Gomperz distribution, given by Equation (5.33), and the Makeham distribution, given by Equation (5.35), are special cases of the generalized distribution.

5.3 The Time-to-Failure Random Variable

5-11   Given that T_0 has a uniform distribution and that $\overset{\circ}{e}_{16} = 42$, find $Var(T_{16})$.

5-12   Given that $S_0(t) = \frac{9000 - 10t - t^2}{9000}$, for $0 < t \le 90$, find the value of $q_{50} - \mu_{50}$.

5-13   Given that $\mu_t = kt$, for all $t > 0$, and $_{10}p_{35} = .81$, find the value of $_{20}p_{40}$.

5-14   Given that $S_0(t) = (1 - \frac{t}{\omega})^r$, for $0 < t < \omega$ and $r > 0$, and that $\mu_y = .10$ and $\overset{\circ}{e}_y = 8.75$ for some $0 < y < \omega$, find the value of r.

5-15   Given that $\lambda_0(t) = (80 - t)^{-1/2}$, for $0 < t < 80$, find the median of the distribution of T_{20}.

5-16   Given that $S_0(t) = \frac{\sqrt{k^2 - t}}{k}$, for $0 < t \le k^2$ and $k > 0$, and that $\overset{\circ}{e}_{40} = 2 \cdot \overset{\circ}{e}_{80}$, find the value of $\overset{\circ}{e}_{60}$.

5-17   Given that $S_0(t) = 1 - (.01t)^2$, for $0 < t \le 100$, find the expected future lifetime at the median age of the distribution.

5.4 Select Survival Models

5-18   A select survival distribution is defined by $S_{[x]}(t; x) = \left(1 - \frac{t}{40 - x}\right)$, for $0 \le x < 40$ and $0 < t < 40 - x$. Find each of the following:

(a) $_4p_{[30]}$ (b) $\overset{\circ}{e}_{[30]}$ (c) $\mu_{[20]+t}$

5-19   A select survival model is defined by $\lambda_{[x]}(t;x) = B \cdot r^t \cdot c^{x+t}$. Show that the select survival function is of the form

$$S_{[x]}(t;x) = \exp\left[\frac{B}{\ln r + \ln c}\left(c^x - r^t c^{x+t}\right)\right].$$

5.5 Multi-State Model Interpretation

5-20   Consider an entity age 0 at time $t = 0$, with age-at-failure random variable T_0 as defined in Section 5.1. Consider also the continuous-time Markov process $X(t)$ as defined in Section 5.6, with $X(0) = 1$. Define the random variable T_0 in terms of the Markov process $X(t)$.

5-21   Consider an entity age x at time $t = 0$, with time-to-failure random variable T_x as defined in Section 5.3. Consider also the continuous-time Markov process $X(t)$, with $X(0) = 1$. Define the random variable T_x in terms of the Markov process $X(t)$.

5-22   (a) Solve Kolmogorov's differential equation for ${}_n p_{12}^{(t)}$.
       (b) Translate the result into standard actuarial notation.

5-23   Give a formula in multi-state model notation for the expected time spent in State 1, given a continuous-time Markov survival process for an entity known to be in State 1 at age x at time $t = 0$.

5-24   Solve Kolmogorov's differential equation for ${}_n p_{11}^{(t)}$ for a homogeneous Markov survival model, with constant force of transition function $\lambda_{12}(s) = \lambda_1(s) = \lambda$.

5-25   Repeat Exercise 5-24 to solve for ${}_n p_{12}^{(t)}$.

CHAPTER SIX

THE LIFE TABLE
(DISCRETE TABULAR CONTEXT)

In this chapter we describe the nature of the traditional life table, showing that it can have all the properties of the survival models described in Chapter 5. When a survival model is presented in the life table format, it is customary to use notation and terminology which differ somewhat from that presented in Chapter 5. A major objective of this chapter will be to show clearly the correspondence between notation used in the probability model and that used in the life table model.

The reader should realize that life tables were developed by actuaries independently from (and a century earlier than) the development of the statistical theory of survival models as probability distributions[1]. For this reason, traditional life table notation and terminology will not tend to reveal the stochastic nature of the model as clearly as is done by the probability model in Chapter 5. By showing the correspondence of the life table symbols to those of the probability model, we intend to correct this.

6.1 DEFINITION OF THE LIFE TABLE

The life table can be defined as a table of numerical values of $S_0(x)$ for certain values of x (which we now prefer to use instead of t). Table 6.1 illustrates such a table.

TABLE 6.1

x	0	1	2	3	4	$\cdots$	109	110
$S_0(x)$	1.00000	.97408	.97259	.97160	.97082	$\cdots$	.00001	.00000

Typically a complete life table shows values of $S_0(x)$ for all integral values of x, $x = 0,1,\ldots$. Since $S_0(x)$ is represented by these values, it is clear that a practical upper limit on x must be adopted beyond which values of $S_0(x)$ are taken to be zero. Traditionally, ω is used for the smallest value of x for which $S_0(x)=0$. Then $S_0(\omega-1)>0$, but $S_0(\omega)=0$. In Table 6.1, $\omega=110$.

From Table 6.1, we can calculate the conditional probabilities represented by $_np_x$ and $_nq_x$ for integral x and n. However, these are the *only* functions that can be determined from the tabular model. Functions such as $f_0(x)$, $\lambda_0(x)$, and $\overset{\circ}{e}_x$ cannot be determined from the tabular model unless we expand the model by adopting assumed values for $S_0(x)$ between adjacent integers. We will pursue this in Section 6.6.

---

[1] The first modern life table, called the Breslau Table, dates from 1693 and is attributed to Edmund Halley [11] of Halley's Comet fame.

EXAMPLE 6.1

From Table 6.1, calculate (a) the probability that a life age 0 will fail before age 3; (b) the probability that a life age 1 will survive to age 4.

SOLUTION

(a) This is given directly by $F_0(3) = 1 - S_0(3) = .02840$.

(b) This conditional probability is given by $_3p_1 = \frac{S_0(4)}{S_0(1)} = .99665$. ☐

6.2 THE TRADITIONAL FORM OF THE LIFE TABLE

The tabular survival model was developed by the early actuaries many years ago. The history of this model is reported throughout actuarial literature, and a brief summary of this history is presented by Dobson [9].

Traditionally, the tabular survival model differs from Table 6.1 in two respects. Rather than presenting decimal values of $S_0(x)$, it is usual to multiply these values by, say, 100,000, and thereby present the $S_0(x)$ values as integers. Secondly, since these integers are not probabilities (which $S_0(x)$ values are), the column heading is changed from $S_0(x)$ to ℓ_x, where ℓ stands for *number living*, or *number of lives*. In this way the tabular survival model became known as the *life table*.

Since $S_0(0) = 1$, then ℓ_0 is the same as the constant multiple which transforms all $S_0(x)$ into ℓ_x. This constant is called the *radix* of the table. Formally,

$$\ell_x = \ell_0 \cdot S_0(x). \tag{6.1}$$

Using a radix of 100,000, we transform Table 6.1 into Table 6.1a.

TABLE 6.1a

x	0	1	2	3	4	$\cdots$	109	110
ℓ_x	100,000	97,408	97,259	97,160	97,082	$\cdots$	1	0

The basic advantage of the traditional form of the life table is its susceptibility to interpretation. If we view $\ell_0 = 100,000$ as a hypothetical cohort group of newborn lives, or other new entities such as lightbulbs, electronic devices, or laboratory animals, then each value of ℓ_x represents the survivors of that group to age x, according to the model. This is a convenient, deterministic, interpretation of the model. Of course, since $\ell_x = \ell_0 \cdot S_0(x)$, and $S_0(x)$ is a probability, then ℓ_x is really the *expected number* of survivors to age x out of an original group of ℓ_0 new entities. This connection between $S_0(x)$ and ℓ_x is also given in Chapter 1 of Jordan [15].

Although the basic representation of the tabular survival model is in terms of the values of ℓ_x, it is customary for the table to also show the value of several other functions derived from ℓ_x. We define

$$d_x = \ell_x - \ell_{x+1}, \tag{6.2}$$

or, more generally,

$$_n d_x = \ell_x - \ell_{x+n}. \tag{6.3}$$

Since ℓ_x represents the size of the cohort at age x, and ℓ_{x+n} is the number of them still surviving at age $x+n$, then clearly $_n d_x$ gives the number who fail (or die) between ages x and $x+n$. (This portrayal of number dying explains the frequent historical reference to these models as *mortality tables*.) Furthermore,

$$q_x = \frac{d_x}{\ell_x}, \tag{6.4}$$

or, more generally,

$$_n q_x = \frac{_n d_x}{\ell_x} \tag{6.5}$$

gives the conditional probability of failure, given alive at age x. Finally, we have

$$_n p_x = 1 - _n q_x = \frac{\ell_x - _n d_x}{\ell_x} = \frac{\ell_{x+n}}{\ell_x} \tag{6.6}$$

as the conditional probability of surviving to age $x+n$, given alive at age x. With $n=1$, we have the special case

$$p_x = \frac{\ell_{x+1}}{\ell_x}. \tag{6.7}$$

Recall that the conditional probabilities $_n p_x$ and $_n q_x$ were defined in Section 5.3 in terms of $S_0(x)$. The consistency of those definitions with the ones presented in this section is easily seen since ℓ_x is simply $\ell_0 \cdot S_0(x)$. We redefined $_n p_x$ and $_n q_x$ in terms of ℓ_x here simply to complete our description of the life table form of the survival model.

EXAMPLE 6.2

From Table 6.1a, find (a) the number who fail between ages 2 and 4; (b) the probability that a life age 1 will survive to age 4.

Solution

(a) This is given by $_2d_2 = \ell_2 - \ell_4 = 177$.

(b) This is given by $_3p_1 = \frac{\ell_4}{\ell_1} = .99665$. (Compare with part (b) of Example 6.1.) ☐

6.3 Other Functions Derived from ℓ_x

Although a life table only presents values of ℓ_x for certain (say, integral) values of x, we wish to adopt the view that the ℓ_x function which produces these values is a continuous and differentiable function. In other words, we assume that a continuous and differentiable ℓ_x function *exists*, but only certain values of it are presented in the survival model. The reason we make this assumption is that there are several other important functions that can be derived from ℓ_x if ℓ_x is continuous and differentiable.

If values of ℓ_x are known only at integral x, the question of how to *evaluate* these additional functions then arises, and the usual way to accomplish this evaluation is to make an assumption about the form of ℓ_x between adjacent integral values of x.

In this section we will derive these several new functions from ℓ_x symbolically, assuming ℓ_x to be continuous and differentiable. In Section 6.6 we will discuss three common distribution assumptions, and show how they allow us to evaluate the functions of this section from a table of ℓ_x values at integral x only. We will also interpret these distribution assumptions in terms of both ℓ_x and $S_0(x)$.

6.3.1 The Force of Failure

The derivative of ℓ_x can be interpreted as the absolute instantaneous annual rate of change of ℓ_x. Since ℓ_x represents the number of survivors at age x, then the derivative, which is the annual rate at which ℓ_x is changing, gives the annual rate at which failures are occurring at age x. This derivative is negative since ℓ_x is a decreasing function. To obtain the absolute magnitude of this instantaneous rate of failure, we will use the negative of the derivative. Finally, since the magnitude of the derivative depends on the size of ℓ_x itself, we obtain the *relative instantaneous rate of failure* by dividing the negative derivative of ℓ_x by ℓ_x itself. Thus we have

$$\mu_x = \frac{-\frac{d}{dx}\ell_x}{\ell_x}, \tag{6.8}$$

which we call the *force of failure* (or *force of mortality*) at age x. Since $\ell_x = \ell_0 \cdot S_0(x)$, we see that Equation (6.8) is the same as

$$\lambda(x) = \frac{-\frac{d}{dx}S_0(x)}{S_0(x)} = \frac{f_0(x)}{S_0(x)}. \tag{6.9}$$

Thus the hazard rate and the force of failure are identical.

If we multiply both sides of Equation (5.14) by ℓ_0 and substitute μ_y for $\lambda_0(y)$, we obtain

$$\ell_x = \ell_0 \cdot S_0(x) = \ell_0 \cdot \exp\left[-\int_0^x \mu_y \, dy\right]. \tag{6.10}$$

In the life table context, $S_0(x) = {}_xp_0 = \exp[-\int_0^x \mu_y \, dy]$ can be interpreted as a decremental factor that reduces the initial cohort of size ℓ_0 to size ℓ_x at age x.

By a simple variable change we can write Equation (6.8) as

$$\mu_{x+t} = \frac{-\frac{d}{dt}\ell_{x+t}}{\ell_{x+t}}, \tag{6.8a}$$

a form in which the force of failure will frequently be expressed.

EXAMPLE 6.3

Show that the force of failure, μ_x, is the limiting value of the probability of failure over an interval divided by the interval length (in years), as the interval length approaches zero.

SOLUTION

Consider first a one-year interval, with $q_x = \frac{d_x}{\ell_x}$. Then consider a half-year interval with $\frac{{}_{1/2}q_x}{1/2} = \frac{\ell_x - \ell_{x+1/2}}{1/2 \cdot \ell_x}$. Now, in general, consider $\frac{{}_{\Delta x}q_x}{\Delta x} = \frac{\ell_x - \ell_{x+\Delta x}}{\Delta x \cdot \ell_x}$, and show that $\lim_{\Delta x \to 0} \frac{{}_{\Delta x}q_x}{\Delta x} = \mu_x$.
We have

$$\lim_{\Delta x \to 0}\left[\frac{\ell_x - \ell_{x+\Delta x}}{\Delta x \cdot \ell_x}\right] = \frac{1}{\ell_x} \cdot \lim_{\Delta x \to 0}\left[\frac{\ell_x - \ell_{x+\Delta x}}{\Delta x}\right] = \frac{1}{\ell_x}\left[-\frac{d}{dx}\ell_x\right] = \mu_x,$$

by Equation (6.8). ◻

6.3.2 THE PROBABILITY DENSITY FUNCTION OF T_0

With the force of failure, which is the same as the hazard rate, now defined, the next function to develop from ℓ_x is the PDF of the age-at-failure random variable T_0 (Remember that we wish to show that the life table is a representation of the distribution of this random variable.)

From Equation (5.10) we have $f_0(x) = \lambda_0(x) \cdot S_0(x)$. In the life table context, $\lambda_0(x) = \mu_x$ and $S_0(x) = \frac{\ell_x}{\ell_0}$. Thus we have, for $x \geq 0$,

$$f_0(x) = \mu_x \left(\frac{\ell_x}{\ell_0} \right) = {}_xp_0\mu_x. \tag{6.11}$$

Also, from Equation (6.8), $\frac{d}{dx}\ell_x = -\ell_x\mu_x$. Dividing both sides by ℓ_0 gives

$$\frac{d}{dx}\,{}_xp_0 = -{}_xp_0\mu_x. \tag{6.12}$$

EXAMPLE 6.4

Show that $\int_0^\infty f_0(x)\,dx = 1$.

SOLUTION

Since $f_0(x) = {}_xp_0\mu_x$, we have $\int_0^\infty {}_xp_0\mu_x\,dx = -{}_xp_0\,\big|_0^\infty$, from Equation (6.12). Thus we have ${}_0p_0 - {}_\infty p_0 = 1$, since ${}_0p_0 = 1$ and ${}_\infty p_0 = 0$. ❑

With the PDF in hand, we can now find $E[T_0]$, which we recall is denoted by $\overset{\text{o}}{e}_0$. (Throughout this and the following section, all expectations are assumed to exist.) We have

$$\overset{\text{o}}{e}_0 = E[T_0] = \int_0^\infty x \cdot f_0(x)\,dx = \int_0^\infty x \cdot {}_xp_0\mu_x\,dx. \tag{6.13}$$

Integration by parts produces the alternative formula

$$\overset{\text{o}}{e}_0 = E[T_0] = \int_0^\infty {}_xp_0\,dx = \frac{1}{\ell_0} \cdot \int_0^\infty \ell_x\,dx. \tag{6.14}$$

The second moment of T_0 is found from

$$E[T_0^2] = \int_0^\infty x^2 \cdot {}_xp_0\mu_x\,dx. \tag{6.15a}$$

Integration by parts produces

$$E[T_0^2] = 2\int_0^\infty x \cdot {}_xp_0\,dx = \frac{2}{\ell_0} \cdot \int_0^\infty x \cdot \ell_x\,dx. \tag{6.15b}$$

Then the variance of T_0 is given by

$$Var(T_0) = E[T_0^2] - \{E[T_0]\}^2 = \frac{2}{\ell_0} \cdot \int_0^\infty x \cdot \ell_x \, dx - \left(\frac{1}{\ell_0} \cdot \int_0^\infty \ell_x \, dx \right)^2. \tag{6.16}$$

6.3.3 Conditional Probabilities and Densities

We have already discussed the conditional probabilities $_np_x$ and $_nq_x$ in terms of both $S_0(x)$ and ℓ_x.

Another conditional probability of some interest is denoted by $_{n|m}q_x$. It represents the probability that an entity known to be alive at age x will fail between ages $x+n$ and $x+n+m$. In terms of the probability notation of Chapter 5, $_{n|m}q_x = Pr[(x+n) < T_0 \leq (x+n+m) \,|\, T_0 > x]$. This can also be expressed as the probability that an entity age x will survive n years, but then fail within the next m years. This way of stating the probability suggests that we can write

$$_{n|m}q_x = {_np_x} \cdot {_m q_{x+n}}. \tag{6.17}$$

Here $_m q_{x+n}$ is the conditional probability of failing between ages $x+n$ and $x+n+m$, given alive at age $x+n$. In turn, $_np_x$ is the conditional probability of surviving to age $x+n$, given alive at age x. Their product gives the probability of failing between ages $x+n$ and $x+n+m$, given alive at age x. In terms of ℓ_x, we have, from Equations (6.6) and (6.5),

$$_{n|m}q_x = \frac{\ell_{x+n}}{\ell_x} \cdot \frac{_m d_{x+n}}{\ell_{x+n}} = \frac{_m d_{x+n}}{\ell_x}. \tag{6.18a}$$

When $m=1$ we use the notation

$$_{n|}q_x = \frac{d_{x+n}}{\ell_x}. \tag{6.18b}$$

Recall that $_{n|}q_x$ was defined in Section 5.3.6 as $Pr(K_x = n)$ or $Pr(K_x^* = n+1)$, the probability that an entity alive at age x would fail in the $(n+1)^{st}$ year.

Example 6.5

Show that $_{n|m}q_x = {_np_x} - {_{n+m}p_x}$, and give an interpretation of this result.

Solution

Since, from Equation (6.3), $_m d_{x+n} = \ell_{x+n} - \ell_{x+n+m}$, then Equation (6.18a) becomes $_{n|m}q_x = \frac{\ell_{x+n} - \ell_{x+n+m}}{\ell_x} = {_np_x} - {_{n+m}p_x}$. Since $_np_x$ is the probability of surviving to age $x+n$, we can think of it as containing the probability of surviving to any age beyond $x+n$. If we remove from $_np_x$ the probability of surviving to $x+n+m$, which is $_{n+m}p_x$, we have the probability of surviving to $x+n$, but not to $x+n+m$, which is $_{n|m}q_x$. ❑

Next we wish to explore the conditional PDF for death at age y, given alive at age x, where $y > x$. From Equation (5.44) we know this conditional PDF is $f_0(y \mid T_0 > x) = \frac{f_0(y)}{S_0(x)}$. Now from Equation (6.11) we have $f_0(y) = \frac{1}{\ell_0} \cdot \ell_y \mu_y$, and from Equation (6.1) we have $S_0(x) = \frac{\ell_x}{\ell_0}$. Thus

$$f_0(y \mid T_0 > x) = \frac{\ell_y \mu_y}{\ell_x} = _{y-x}p_x \mu_y. \tag{6.19a}$$

Letting $t = y-x$, so $y = x+t$, we have

$$f_0(x+t \mid T_0 > x) = _tp_x \mu_{x+t}, \tag{6.19b}$$

the conditional PDF of the random variable for the length of future lifetime of an entity alive at age x. This conditional PDF is a very useful function for developing other results.

If both numerator and denominator on the right side of Equation (6.8a) are divided by ℓ_x, we obtain

$$\mu_{x+t} = \frac{-\frac{d}{dt} \, _tp_x}{_tp_x}, \tag{6.20}$$

which is equivalent to

$$\frac{d}{dt} \, _tp_x = -_tp_x \mu_{x+t}. \tag{6.21}$$

The expected future lifetime of an entity alive at age x is given by

$$\overset{\circ}{e}_x = E[T_x] = \int_0^\infty t \cdot _tp_x \mu_{x+t} \, dt = \int_0^\infty \, _tp_x \, dt, \tag{6.22}$$

by evaluating the first integral using integration by parts. The second moment of T_x is

$$E[T_x^2] = \int_0^\infty t^2 \cdot _tp_x \mu_{x+t} \, dt = 2\int_0^\infty t \cdot _tp_x \, dt, \tag{6.23}$$

again by using integration by parts on the first integral, so its variance is

$$Var(T_x) = E[T_x^2] - \{E[T_x]\}^2 = 2\int_0^\infty t \cdot _tp_x \, dt - \left(\int_0^\infty \, _tp_x \, dt\right)^2. \tag{6.24}$$

The concept of complete expectation of future lifetime can be restricted to a temporary period. We let $\overset{\circ}{e}_{x:\overline{n}|}$ denote the expected future lifetime for an entity alive at age x *over the next n years only.* It is given by

$$\overset{\circ}{e}_{x:\overline{n}|} = \int_0^n {}_tp_x \, dt = \frac{1}{\ell_x}\int_0^n \ell_{x+t} \, dt. \tag{6.25}$$

EXAMPLE 6.6

A survival model is defined by $\ell_x = \frac{10,000}{(x+1)^3}$, for $x \geq 0$. Determine $Var(T_0 \,|\, T_0 > x)$, where T_0 is the age-at-failure random variable.

SOLUTION

We recognize that the age-at-failure random variable T_0 and the future lifetime random variable T_x are related by $T_0 = x+T_x$, where x is a constant. Thus, $Var(T_0\,|\,T_0 > x) = Var(T_x\,|\,T_0 > x)$. To use Equation (6.24), we first find

$$_tp_x = \frac{\ell_{x+t}}{\ell_x} = \frac{(x+1)^3}{(x+t+1)^3}.$$

Then

$$E[T_x] = \int_0^\infty {}_tp_x \, dt = (x+1)^3 \cdot \int_0^\infty (x+t+1)^{-3} \, dt = \frac{x+1}{2}$$

and

$$E[T_x^2] = 2\int_0^\infty t \cdot {}_tp_x \, dt = 2(x+1)^3 \cdot \int_0^\infty t(x+t+1)^{-3} \, dt = (x+1)^2,$$

so

$$Var(T_x\,|\,T_0 > x) = (x+1)^2 - \left(\frac{x+1}{2}\right)^2 = \frac{3(x+1)^2}{4}. \qquad \square$$

6.3.4 THE CURTATE EXPECTATION OF LIFE

Recall the concept of the *curtate expectation of life at age x*, defined in Section 5.3.6 as $e_x = E[K_x\,|\,T_0 > x]$. Now we return to the e_x concept and present it in the context of the life table model. If we define e_x as the expected (or average) number of *whole years of future lifetime* for an entity in the ℓ_x group, then it is given by

$$e_x = \frac{1}{\ell_x}\sum_{y=x+1}^\infty \ell_y = \frac{1}{\ell_x}\sum_{k=1}^\infty \ell_{x+k} = \sum_{k=1}^\infty {}_kp_x. \tag{6.26}$$

If we make the reasonable assumption that an entity survives approximately one-half year in the year of failure, then we see that $\overset{o}{e}_x$ exceeds e_x by that half-year. Thus

$$\overset{o}{e}_x \approx e_x + \frac{1}{2}.^2 \tag{6.27}$$

The temporary curtate expectation of life at age x, denoted $e_{x:\overline{n}|}$, can also be defined. We have

$$e_{x:\overline{n}|} = \frac{1}{\ell_x} \sum_{k=1}^{n} \ell_{x+k} = \sum_{k=1}^{n} {}_k p_x, \tag{6.28}$$

and note that this represents the expected (or average) number of whole years lived over the interval $(x, x+n]$ by an entity in the ℓ_x group.

EXAMPLE 6.7

Show that the stochastic definition of e_x given in Section 5.3.6 and the life table definition given by Equation (6.26) are the same.

SOLUTION

In Section 5.3.6 we defined e_x as

$$e_x = E[K_x \,|\, T_0 > x]$$

$$= \sum_{k=1}^{\infty} k \cdot Pr(K_x = k)$$

$$= \sum_{k=1}^{\infty} k \cdot {}_{k|}q_x$$

$$= \sum_{k=1}^{\infty} k({}_k p_x - {}_{k+1}p_x)$$

$$= 1(p_x - {}_2 p_x) + 2({}_2 p_x - {}_3 p_x) + \cdots$$

$$= p_x + {}_2 p_x + \cdots,$$

which is the right side of Equation (6.26). ❏

---

[2] See Section 6.6.1, where we show that this result is exact under a particular assumption.

6.4 SUMMARY OF CONCEPTS AND NOTATION

Thus far we have been striving for an understanding of the nature and properties of survival models, both in the notation of the probability model of Chapter 5 and the life table model of Chapter 6. At this point we summarize the concepts developed thus far, and give the standard formulas or symbols for them in the notation of both chapters. (See Table 6.2 on page 96.)

6.5 MULTI-STATE MODEL INTERPRETATION

Recall the formulation of the two-state survival model as a multi-state model in Section 5.5 and illustrated in Figure 5.4. In Section 5.5 we analyzed the parametric survival model as a continuous-time Markov model; in this section we view the tabular survival model as a discrete-time Markov model.

The basic properties of this two-state model remain as described in Section 5.5. These include the notion that State 1 cannot be reentered once left, and that State 2 is an absorbing state. Consequently we have $_r p_{11}^{*(n)} = _r p_{11}^{(n)}$, as established by Equation (3.9b).

Consider that we have an entity that is surviving (i.e., in State 1) at age x at time 0, so that $X_0 = 1$. Then the event of being in State 1 at time 1 is the same as the event of surviving from age x to age $x+1$, so their probabilities are the same. That is,

$$p_{11}^{(0)} = Pr[X_1 = 1 | X_0 = 1] = p_x. \tag{6.29a}$$

Similarly,

$$p_{12}^{(0)} = Pr[X_1 = 2 | X_0 = 1] = q_x, \tag{6.29b}$$

where the right side of each equation writes the probability in standard actuarial notation. Then the matrix of transition probabilities for the first interval is

$$\mathbf{P}^{(0)} = \begin{vmatrix} p_{11}^{(0)} & p_{12}^{(0)} \\ 0 & 1 \end{vmatrix} = \begin{vmatrix} p_x & q_x \\ 0 & 1 \end{vmatrix}. \tag{6.30}$$

For the discrete time interval from time 1 to time 2, we similarly have

$$p_{11}^{(1)} = Pr[X_2 = 1 | X_1 = 1] = p_{x+1}, \tag{6.31a}$$

$$p_{12}^{(1)} = Pr[X_2 = 2 | X_1 = 1] = q_{x+1}, \tag{6.31b}$$

and

$$\mathbf{P}^{(1)} = \begin{vmatrix} p_{11}^{(1)} & p_{12}^{(1)} \\ 0 & 1 \end{vmatrix} = \begin{vmatrix} p_{x+1} & q_{x+1} \\ 0 & 1 \end{vmatrix}. \tag{6.32}$$

TABLE 6.2

Concept	Chapter 5 Formulas	Chapter 6 Formulas
1. Unconditional probability of survival from age 0 to age x	$S_0(x)$	$_x p_0 = \dfrac{\ell_x}{\ell_0}$
2. Unconditional probability of failure not later than age x	$F_0(x)$	$_x q_0 = \dfrac{\ell_0 - \ell_x}{\ell_0}$
3. Conditional probability of survival from age x to age $x+n$	$\dfrac{S_0(x+n)}{S_0(x)}$	$_n p_x = \dfrac{\ell_{x+n}}{\ell_x}$
4. Conditional probability of failure before age $x+n$, given alive at age x	$\dfrac{S_0(x) - S_0(x+n)}{S_0(x)}$	$_n q_x = \dfrac{\ell_x - \ell_{x+n}}{\ell_x}$ $= \dfrac{_n d_x}{\ell_x}$
5. Hazard rate (force of failure) at exact age x	$\lambda_0(x) = \dfrac{-\frac{d}{dx} S_0(x)}{S_0(x)}$ $= -\dfrac{d}{dx} \ln S_0(x)$	$\mu_x = \dfrac{-\frac{d}{dx} \ell_x}{\ell_x}$ $= -\dfrac{d}{dx} \ln \ell_x$
6. Unconditional density function for failure at exact age x	$f_0(x) = \dfrac{d}{dx} F_0(x)$ $= -\dfrac{d}{dx} S_0(x)$	$_x p_0 \mu_x = -\dfrac{d}{dx}\, _x p_0$
7. Unconditional expectation of future lifetime at birth	$E[T_0] = \int_0^\infty x \cdot f_0(x)\, dx$ $= \int_0^\infty S_0(x)\, dx$	$\overset{\circ}{e}_0 = \int_0^\infty x \cdot {}_x p_0 \mu_x\, dx$ $= \int_0^\infty {}_x p_0\, dx$
8. Unconditional variance of future lifetime at birth	$Var(T_0) = \int_0^\infty x^2 \cdot f_0(x)\, dx$ $- \{E[T_0]\}^2$	$\int_0^\infty x^2 \cdot {}_x p_0 \mu_x\, dx - (\overset{\circ}{e}_0)^2$ (no specific symbol)
9. Conditional density function for failure at age y, given alive at age x, where $y > x$	$f_0(y \mid T_0 > x) = \dfrac{f_0(y)}{S_0(x)}$	$_{y-x} p_x \mu_y = {}_t p_x \mu_{x+t}$, where $t = y-x$
10. Conditional expectation of future lifetime at age x	$E[T_0 - x \mid T_0 > x] = E[T_x \mid T_0 > x]$ $= \int_0^\infty t \cdot f_0(x+t \mid T_0 > x)\, dt$ $= \int_0^\infty \dfrac{S_0(x+t)}{S_0(x)}\, dt$	$\overset{\circ}{e}_x = \int_0^\infty t \cdot {}_t p_x \mu_{x+t}\, dt$ $= \int_0^\infty {}_t p_x\, dt$
11. Conditional variance of future lifetime at age x	$Var(T_x \mid T_0 > x) = Var(T_0 \mid T_0 > x)^*$ $= \int_0^\infty t^2 \cdot f_0(x+t \mid T_0 > x)\, dt$ $- \{E[T_x \mid T_0 > x]\}^2$	$\int_0^\infty t^2 \cdot {}_t p_x \mu_{x+t}\, dt - (\overset{\circ}{e}_x)^2$ (no specific symbol)

*Variance of future lifetime and variance of age at failure are equal, since $T_x = T_0 - x$, and x is a constant.

When the discrete-time Markov process is used to represent the tabular survival model, it should be clear that the model is non-homogeneous.

Since the process necessarily begins in State 1, it follows that the initial state vector is $\boldsymbol{\pi}_0 = (1, 0)$. At time n in general, the state vector $\boldsymbol{\pi}_n$ contains the two probability values

$$_n p_{11}^{(0)} = {}_n p_x$$

and

$$_n p_{12}^{(0)} = {}_n q_x,$$

and is given by

$$\boldsymbol{\pi}_n = (1, 0) \cdot \begin{vmatrix} p_x & q_x \\ 0 & 1 \end{vmatrix} \cdot \begin{vmatrix} p_{x+1} & q_{x+1} \\ 0 & 1 \end{vmatrix} \cdot \dots \cdot \begin{vmatrix} p_{x+n-1} & q_{x+n-1} \\ 0 & 1 \end{vmatrix}. \tag{6.33}$$

EXAMPLE 6.8

Develop expressions for the elements in the state vector $\boldsymbol{\pi}_3$, using standard actuarial notation.

SOLUTION

The two elements in the state vector $\boldsymbol{\pi}_3$ are $\pi_{13} = {}_3 p_x$ and $\pi_{23} = {}_3 q_x$. (Recall from Section 3.1.2 that π_{in} is the probability of being in State i at time n.) We have

$$\boldsymbol{\pi}_3 = (1, 0) \cdot \begin{vmatrix} p_x & q_x \\ 0 & 1 \end{vmatrix} \cdot \begin{vmatrix} p_{x+1} & q_{x+1} \\ 0 & 1 \end{vmatrix} \cdot \begin{vmatrix} p_{x+2} & q_{x+2} \\ 0 & 1 \end{vmatrix}$$

$$= (p_x, q_x) \cdot \begin{vmatrix} p_{x+1} & q_{x+1} \\ 0 & 1 \end{vmatrix} \cdot \begin{vmatrix} p_{x+2} & q_{x+2} \\ 0 & 1 \end{vmatrix}$$

$$= (p_x \cdot p_{x+1}, q_x + p_x \cdot q_{x+1}) \cdot \begin{vmatrix} p_{x+2} & q_{x+2} \\ 0 & 1 \end{vmatrix}$$

$$= (p_x \cdot p_{x+1} \cdot p_{x+2}, \; q_x + p_x \cdot q_{x+1} + p_x \cdot p_{x+1} \cdot q_{x+2}).$$

Then we have

$$\pi_{13} = {}_3 p_x = p_x \cdot p_{x+1} \cdot p_{x+2}$$

and

$$\pi_{23} = {}_3 q_x = q_x + p_x \cdot q_{x+1} + p_x \cdot p_{x+1} \cdot q_{x+2},$$

as already developed earlier in this chapter. ❑

Further analysis of the tabular survival model as a discrete-time Markov process will be pursued in the exercises (see Exercises 6-18 through 6-20).

6.6 METHODS FOR NON-INTEGRAL AGES

A review of the functions that we have developed, and summarized in Table 6.2, shows that not many of them can be numerically determined from a life table that gives values of ℓ_x only for integral x. Actually, only the probability function $_np_x$ (and its complement $_nq_x$) for integral x and n can be so determined. (Note that $_xp_0$ and $_xq_0$, for integral x, are special cases of $_np_x$ and $_nq_x$.)

The determination of all other functions requires that values of ℓ_{x+t} be available for all t, $0 < t < 1$. This is obtained in the life table model by assuming that ℓ_{x+t} has a certain mathematical form between x and $x+1$. This assumed form for ℓ_{x+t} will be differentiable on the open interval $0 < t < 1$, but not at $t = 0$ or $t = 1$.

The ability to determine ℓ_{x+t} numerically for any t, $0 < t < 1$, will allow us to calculate probabilities of the form $_tp_x$ and its complement $_tq_x$ for all t. The differentiability of ℓ_{x+t} will allow us to evaluate μ_{x+t}, and hence the conditional density function $f_x(t\,|\,T_0 > x) = {}_tp_x\mu_{x+t}$, for all t on the open interval $0 < t < 1$. The integrability of ℓ_{x+t} will allow us to calculate $\overset{\circ}{e}_x$ and the conditional variance of future lifetime (or age at failure), $Var(T_0\,|\,T_0 > x)$.

We should not lose sight of the fact that we are assuming a mathematical form for ℓ_{x+t} *only* between x and $x+1$, not for the entire domain of x; the latter case would return us to the continuous parametric models described in Chapter 5. We will also see that each particular mathematical function that we assume for ℓ_{x+t} will correspond to a certain interpolation method.

To recapitulate, we assume that we have a life table with numerical values of ℓ_x given for all integral x. We then assume a mathematical form for ℓ_{x+t}, $0 \le t \le 1$, and show how to calculate, from the given life table, values of $_tp_x$ and $\overset{\circ}{e}_x$. (The function $Var(T_0\,|\,T_0 > x)$ can also be evaluated, but with greater difficulty.) We will now pursue three different assumptions of a mathematical form for ℓ_{x+t}.

6.6.1 LINEAR FORM FOR ℓ_{x+t}

If ℓ_{x+t} is a linear function between x and $x+1$, then it is of the form $a+bt$. To provide continuity for ℓ_{x+t}, we require, at $t = 0$, that $\ell_x = a$, and at $t = 1$, that $\ell_{x+1} = a+b$, so that $b = \ell_{x+1} - a$, or $b = \ell_{x+1} - \ell_x = -d_x$. Thus we have

$$\ell_{x+t} = \ell_x - t \cdot d_x. \tag{6.34a}$$

An alternate form is to use $\ell_x - \ell_{x+1}$ in place of d_x, obtaining

$$\ell_{x+t} = \ell_x - t(\ell_x - \ell_{x+1}) = t \cdot \ell_{x+1} + (1-t) \cdot \ell_x. \tag{6.34b}$$

Both Equations (6.34a) and (6.34b) reveal that the linear assumption for ℓ_{x+t} means we are determining values of ℓ_{x+t} from ℓ_x and ℓ_{x+1} by *linear interpolation*.

The determination of other functions follows from Equation (6.34a). We have

$$_t p_x = \frac{\ell_{x+t}}{\ell_x} = 1 - t \cdot \frac{d_x}{\ell_x} = 1 - t \cdot q_x, \tag{6.35}$$

and

$$_t q_x = 1 - _t p_x = t \cdot q_x. \tag{6.36}$$

We also have

$$\mu_{x+t} = \frac{-\frac{d}{dt} \ell_{x+t}}{\ell_{x+t}} = \frac{d_x}{\ell_x - t \cdot d_x} = \frac{q_x}{1 - t \cdot q_x}, \tag{6.37}$$

which, when multiplied by Equation (6.35), leads to the convenient result

$$f_x(t \,|\, T_0 > x) = _t p_x \mu_{x+t} = q_x, \tag{6.38}$$

for $0 < t < 1$. Note that μ_{x+t}, and hence $f_x(t \,|\, T_0 > x)$, are not defined at $t = 0$ and $t = 1$ since ℓ_{x+t} is not differentiable there.

We can find $\overset{o}{e}_x = E[T_x]$ from Equation (6.22) as

$$\begin{aligned}
\overset{o}{e}_x &= \int_0^\infty {_t p_x}\ dt \\
&= \sum_{r=0}^{\infty} {_r p_x} \int_0^1 {_s p_{x+r}}\ ds \\
&= \sum_{r=0}^{\infty} {_r p_x} \int_0^1 (1 - s \cdot q_{x+r})\ ds \\
&= \sum_{r=0}^{\infty} {_r p_x} \left(1 - \tfrac{1}{2} \cdot q_{x+r}\right) \\
&= \sum_{r=0}^{\infty} \left({_r p_x} - \tfrac{1}{2} \cdot {_r|\, q_x}\right) \\
&= 1 + e_x - \frac{1}{2} = e_x + \frac{1}{2}, \tag{6.39}
\end{aligned}$$

which we developed intuitively in Equation (6.27).

EXAMPLE 6.9

The function $_{r|h}q_x = {}_rp_x \cdot {}_hq_{x+r}$ denotes the probability that an entity alive at age x will fail between ages $x+r$ and $x+r+h$, where $r>0$, $h>0$, and $r+h<1$. Show that

$$_{r|h}q_x = h \cdot q_x, \tag{6.40}$$

under the linear form for ℓ_{x+t}.

SOLUTION

$$_{r|h}q_x = \frac{\ell_{x+r} - \ell_{x+r+h}}{\ell_x}$$

$$= \frac{(\ell_x - r \cdot d_x) - (\ell_x - (r+h)d_x)}{\ell_x} = \frac{h \cdot d_x}{\ell_x} = h \cdot q_x. \qquad \square$$

Turning to the question of the associated probability distribution over the interval $(x, x+1]$, we note that the PDF for time of failure within the interval is a constant, and the CDF, which is $_tq_x$, is a linear function. This shows that the random variable T_x has a uniform distribution over $(x, x+1]$. Furthermore, the linear nature of Equation (6.34a) shows that ℓ_{x+t} decreases uniformly (i.e., entities are failing uniformly) over the interval. For these reasons, this linear assumption for ℓ_{x+t} has traditionally been called the *uniform distribution of failures* or *uniform distribution of deaths* assumption, which is commonly referred to as UDD.

Recall the relationship among the random variables T_x, K_x and R_x, given by Equation (5.59a), and refer to Figure 5.3 shown in Section 5.3.6. Consider the event that an entity alive at age x fails between ages $x+k$ and $x+k+r$, which we denote by $(k < T_x \le k+r)$. This event can also be stated as the event of failure in the $(k+1)^{st}$ interval *and* in the first r of that interval. Then in terms of probabilities we have

$$Pr(k < T_x \le k+r) = Pr(K_x = k \cap R_x \le r). \tag{6.41}$$

In actuarial notation this is written as $_kp_x \cdot {}_rq_{x+k}$, where x and $x+k$ are integers. Using Equation (6.36) we can substitute $r \cdot q_{x+k}$ for $_rq_{x+k}$, so we find

$$Pr(K_x = k \cap R_x \le r) = {}_kp_x \cdot r \cdot q_{x+k} = {}_{k|}q_x \cdot r. \tag{6.42a}$$

But we know that $Pr(K_x = k) = {}_{k|}q_x$, and, because R_x has a continuous uniform distribution on the interval $(0, 1]$, then $Pr(R_x \le r) = r$. Therefore we can write Equation (6.42a) as

$$Pr(K_x = k \cap R_x \le r) = Pr(K_x = k) \cdot Pr(R_x \le r), \tag{6.42b}$$

showing that the random variables K_x and R_x are independent under the UDD assumption. A similar argument can be used to show the independence of K_x^* and R_x as well.

Without question the UDD assumption is extremely useful for making calculations from the life table. No doubt the ability to analyze the assumption in terms of the uniform (or even) distribution pattern of the occurring failures, along with the mathematical simplicity afforded by the constant PDF, are the major reasons for this assumption's popularity.

6.6.2 EXPONENTIAL FORM FOR ℓ_{x+t}

If ℓ_{x+t} is an exponential function between x and $x+1$, then it is of the form $\ell_{x+t} = a \cdot b^t$. To assure continuity, at $t = 0$ we have $\ell_x = a$ and at $t = 1$ we have $\ell_{x+1} = ab$, so that $b = \frac{\ell_{x+1}}{a} = \frac{\ell_{x+1}}{\ell_x}$. Thus we have

$$\ell_{x+t} = \ell_x \left(\frac{\ell_{x+1}}{\ell_x} \right)^t = (\ell_{x+1})^t \cdot (\ell_x)^{1-t}, \tag{6.43a}$$

which shows that the exponential assumption for ℓ_{x+t} allows us to determine values of ℓ_{x+t} from values of ℓ_x and ℓ_{x+1} by *exponential interpolation*. (Note the similarity of Equations (6.43a) and (6.34b).) An alternative form of Equation (6.43a), which results from substituting $\ell_{x+1} = \ell_x \cdot p_x$, is

$$\ell_{x+t} = \ell_x (p_x)^t. \tag{6.43b}$$

The determination of other functions follows from Equation (6.43a) or (6.43b). Thus

$$_t p_x = \frac{\ell_{x+t}}{\ell_x} = (p_x)^t, \tag{6.44}$$

and

$$_t q_x = 1 - _t p_x = 1 - (p_x)^t = 1 - (1 - q_x)^t, \tag{6.45}$$

We also have

$$\mu_{x+t} = \frac{-\frac{d}{dt}\ell_{x+t}}{\ell_{x+t}} = \frac{-\ell_x (p_x)^t \cdot \ln p_x}{\ell_x (p_x)^t} = -\ln p_x, \tag{6.46}$$

a constant, for $0 < t < 1$. Thus we have the useful result that if ℓ_{x+t} is exponential, then the force of failure, μ_{x+t}, is constant over $(x, x+1)$. We call this constant force μ_x^*. Then Equation (6.46), which says $\mu_x^* = -\ln p_x$, can be rearranged to read

$$p_x = e^{-\mu_x^*}, \tag{6.47}$$

from which Equation (6.44) becomes

$$_tp_x = e^{-t \cdot \mu_x^*}. \tag{6.48}$$

The conditional PDF is then found by multiplying Equations (6.48) and (6.46), obtaining

$$f_x(t \mid T_0 > x) = {}_tp_x\mu_{x+t} = \mu_x^* \cdot e^{-t \cdot \mu_x^*}. \tag{6.49}$$

The PDF of T_x, given by Equation (6.49), and its SDF, given by Equation (6.48), clearly show us that T_x has an exponential distribution over $(x, x+1]$. (Recall from Section 5.2.2 that this distribution has a constant hazard rate, which is the same as the force of failure.) This constant force of failure has led to this assumption being traditionally called the *constant force assumption*.

Of course this μ_x^* is the constant value of μ_{x+t}, $0 < t < 1$. For the interval $(x+1, x+2)$ we have a different constant force, namely $\mu_{x+1}^* = -\ln p_{x+1}$. Then it can be shown (see Exercise 6-32) that

$$\overset{o}{e}_x = \frac{1}{\ell_x} \cdot \sum_{y=x}^{\infty} \frac{d_y}{\mu_y^*}. \tag{6.50}$$

6.6.3 HYPERBOLIC FORM FOR ℓ_{x+t}

Historically, textbooks on actuarial mathematics have included a third method for non-integral ages, namely the assumption that ℓ_{x+t} is a hyperbolic function between x and $x+1$. A hyperbolic function is a reciprocal linear function of the form $\ell_{x+t} = (a+bt)^{-1}$, so we have $\ell_x = \frac{1}{a}$ and $\ell_{x+1} = \frac{1}{a+b}$. From this we find

$$\frac{1}{\ell_{x+t}} = t \cdot \frac{1}{\ell_{x+1}} + (1-t) \cdot \frac{1}{\ell_x}, \tag{6.51}$$

showing that we can find values of ℓ_{x+t} by linear interpolation between the reciprocals of ℓ_x and ℓ_{x+1}. (Linear interpolation on the reciprocal of a function is called *harmonic interpolation* on the function itself.) From Equation (6.51) we can find

$$(_tp_x)^{-1} = \frac{\ell_x}{\ell_{x+t}} = t \cdot \frac{\ell_x}{\ell_{x+1}} + (1-t) \cdot \frac{\ell_x}{\ell_x} = \frac{t}{p_x} + (1-t) = \frac{t + (1-t) \cdot p_x}{p_x},$$

so that

$$_tp_x = \frac{p_x}{t + (1-t) \cdot p_x} = \frac{1 - q_x}{1 - (1-t) \cdot q_x} \tag{6.52}$$

and therefore

$$_t q_x = 1 - {_t p_x} = \frac{t \cdot q_x}{1 - (1-t) \cdot q_x}. \tag{6.53}$$

Using Equation (6.52) we can then find

$$\mu_{x+t} = \frac{-\frac{d}{dt} {_t p_x}}{{_t p_x}} = \frac{(1-q_x) \cdot q_x}{[1-(1-t) \cdot q_x]^2} \div \frac{1-q_x}{1-(1-t) \cdot q_x} = \frac{q_x}{1-(1-t) \cdot q_x}, \tag{6.54}$$

for $0 < t < 1$, which is a decreasing function of t. It can also be shown (see Exercise 6-33) that

$$_{1-t} q_{x+t} = (1-t) \cdot q_x. \tag{6.55}$$

In the past, the traditional actuarial approach to survival model estimation utilized a method that frequently involved functions of the form $_{1-t} q_{x+t}$, which could be simplified to $(1-t) \cdot q_x$ under the hyperbolic assumption. This approach to estimation work is no longer commonly used, so this major use of the hyperbolic assumption no longer exists. Today we might view it as being primarily of historical interest.

The Italian actuary Gaetano Balducci made major use of the hyperbolic distribution in several of his writings, such as [1] and [2]. Although he did not originate the use of this assumption, it has come to be called the *Balducci assumption*, or Balducci distribution.

EXAMPLE 6.10

In a certain life table, $\ell_x = 1000$ and $\ell_{x+1} = 900$. Evaluate $\mu_{x+1/4}$ under each of the UDD, constant force, and hyperbolic assumptions.

SOLUTION

From the given values we find $q_x = .10$ and $p_x = .90$. Then under UDD we have

$$\mu_{x+1/4} = \frac{.10}{.975} = .10256.$$

Under constant force we have

$$\mu_{x+1/4} = \mu_x^* = -\ln p_x = .10536.$$

Under hyperbolic we have

$$\mu_{x+1/4} = \frac{.10}{.925} = .10811. \qquad \square$$

6.6.4 SUMMARY

Table 6.3 summarizes most of the results developed in this section. Further analysis of these assumptions is given by Batten [3], and Mereu [24] gives a presentation of the use of these assumptions in actuarial calculations.

TABLE 6.3

Function	Linear (UDD)	Exponential (Constant Force)	Hyperbolic (Balducci)
ℓ_{x+t}	$t \cdot \ell_{x+1} + (1-t) \cdot \ell_x$	$(\ell_{x+1})^t \cdot (\ell_x)^{1-t}$	$\left(\dfrac{t}{\ell_{x+1}} + \dfrac{1-t}{\ell_x} \right)^{-1}$
$_t p_x$	$1 - t \cdot q_x$	$(p_x)^t = e^{-\mu t}$	$\dfrac{1-q_x}{1-(1-t)\cdot q_x}$
$_t q_x$	$t \cdot q_x$	$1 - (1-q_x)^t$	$\dfrac{t\cdot q_x}{1-(1-t)\cdot q_x}$
μ_{x+t}	$\dfrac{q_x}{1-t\cdot q_x}$	$\mu = -\ln p_x$	$\dfrac{q_x}{1-(1-t)\cdot q_x}$
$_t p_x \mu_{x+t}$	q_x	$\mu \cdot e^{-\mu t}$	$\dfrac{q_x(1-q_x)}{[1-(1-t)\cdot q_x]^2}$

6.7 SELECT LIFE TABLES

In this section we consider life tables developed from the select survival distribution defined in Section 5.4 as $S_{[x]}(t;x)$, for $t \geq 0$.

It is easy to see that a life table based on this SDF is completely parallel to one based on $S_0(x)$. Thus we begin with a radix which represents a hypothetical cohort of lives selected at age x, which we call $\ell_{[x]}$. Then subsequent values are developed from

$$\ell_{[x]+t} = \ell_{[x]} \cdot S_{[x]}(t;x). \tag{6.56}$$

If values of $\ell_{[x]+t}$ are specified for all integral t, the resulting select life table (for age at selection x) can then be used to obtain other values, just as we did for the aggregate life table earlier in this chapter. It is important to specify the age at selection in the symbols for the functions derived from a select table. For example, if selection is at age x, the conditional probability of failure between ages $x+7$ and $x+10$, for an entity known to be alive at age $x+5$, is given by

$$_{2|3}q_{[x]+5} = \frac{\ell_{[x]+7} - \ell_{[x]+10}}{\ell_{[x]+5}}. \tag{6.57}$$

Select life tables do not normally extend to all values of t in a manner that is unique to the selection age. For example, consider two entities, one selected at age 20 and now age 30 ($t=10$), and the other selected at age 21 and now age 30 ($t=9$). Their conditional probabilities of survival for another n years are $_nP_{[20]+10} = \frac{\ell_{[20]+10+n}}{\ell_{[20]+10}}$ and $_nP_{[21]+9} = \frac{\ell_{[21]+9+n}}{\ell_{[21]+9}}$, respectively. If we believe that selection no longer has an effect on failure at these durations, then the two probabilities should have the same value, denoted by $\frac{\ell_{30+n}}{\ell_{30}}$. A life table with this characteristic is called a *select and ultimate table*.

The first step in developing a select and ultimate table is to determine the length of the *select period*, the time over which selection is assumed to have an effect on failure. Although there is evidence that effects of selection can persist for many years, published tables will seldom show a select period greater than 15 years. For illustration in this text, however, we will assume only a four-year select period. This means that for entities four and more years beyond selection, failure is a function of attained age only.

Suppose $[x]$ is the youngest age at selection in the table which we wish to construct. Then we select a radix, $\ell_{[x]}$, and generate

$$\ell_{[x]+t} = \ell_{[x]} \cdot S_{[x]}(t;x), \tag{6.58a}$$

for $t = 1, 2, 3$, and

$$\ell_{x+t} = \ell_{[x]} \cdot S_{[x]}(t;x), \tag{6.58b}$$

for $t \geq 4$. Instead of arranging these values of $\ell_{[x]+t}$ and ℓ_{x+t} in a column, as in our earlier Table 6.1a, we arrange them in the row-and-column format shown in Table 6.4.

TABLE 6.4

$\ell_{[x]}$	$\ell_{[x]+1}$	$\ell_{[x]+2}$	$\ell_{[x]+3}$	ℓ_{x+4}
				ℓ_{x+5}
				ℓ_{x+6}
				$\vdots$
				$\vdots$

Next, consider age at selection $[x+1]$. If a radix, $\ell_{[x+1]}$, were arbitrarily chosen, then we would generate

$$\ell_{[x+1]+t} = \ell_{[x+1]} \cdot S_{[x+1]}(t;x+1), \tag{6.59a}$$

for $t = 1, 2, 3$, and

$$\ell_{x+1+t} = \ell_{[x+1]} \cdot S_{[x+1]}(t;x+1), \tag{6.59b}$$

for $t \geq 4$. But the basic idea of the select and ultimate table is that the same values of ℓ_{x+t}, for $t \geq 5$, should be common to the cohorts $\ell_{[x]}$ and $\ell_{[x+1]}$. Thus $\ell_{[x+1]}$ must be chosen so that $\ell_{[x+1]} \cdot S_{[x+1]}(4; x+1)$ produces the same ℓ_{x+5} as was produced by $\ell_{[x]} \cdot S_{[x]}(5; x)$. This is easily accomplished by taking

$$\ell_{[x+1]} = \frac{\ell_{x+5}}{S_{[x+1]}(4; x+1)}. \tag{6.60}$$

Then $\ell_{[x+1]+1}, \ell_{[x+1]+2},$ and $\ell_{[x+1]+3}$ can be found from this $\ell_{[x+1]}$ by using Equation (6.59a). Note that values of $S_{[x+1]}(t; x+1)$ for $t > 4$ are not utilized once it has been decided to use a four-year select period.

Similarly, $\ell_{[x+2]}$ would be found from the already established value of ℓ_{x+6} by

$$\ell_{[x+2]} = \frac{\ell_{x+6}}{S_{[x+2]}(4; x+2)}, \tag{6.61}$$

and then values of $\ell_{[x+2]+t}$, for $t = 1, 2, 3,$ are found from

$$\ell_{[x+2]+t} = \ell_{[x+2]} \cdot S_{[x+2]}(t; x+2). \tag{6.62}$$

The complete select and ultimate table is in the format of Table 6.5, where we assume age 20 is the youngest age at selection.

TABLE 6.5

$[x]$	$\ell_{[x]}$	$\ell_{[x]+1}$	$\ell_{[x]+2}$	$\ell_{[x]+3}$	ℓ_{x+4}	$x+4$
[20]	$\ell_{[20]}$	$\ell_{[20]+1}$	$\ell_{[20]+2}$	$\ell_{[20]+3}$	ℓ_{24}	24
[21]	$\ell_{[21]}$	$\ell_{[21]+2}$	$\ell_{[21]+2}$	$\ell_{[21]+3}$	ℓ_{25}	25
[22]	$\ell_{[22]}$	$\ell_{[22]+1}$	$\ell_{[22]+2}$	$\ell_{[22]+3}$	ℓ_{26}	26
⋮	⋮	⋮	⋮	⋮	⋮	⋮
⋮	⋮	⋮	⋮	⋮	⋮	⋮

EXAMPLE 6.11

Express the conditional probabilities (a) $_{2|4}q_{[20]+1}$ and (b) $_{2|4}q_{[22]+3}$ in terms of ℓ functions, assuming a 4-year select period.

SOLUTION

(a) This is the probability of failure between ages 23 and 27 for an entity age 21, selected at age 20. The number of such failures, from Table 6.5, is $\ell_{[20]+3} - \ell_{27}$, so the desired

probability is $\dfrac{\ell_{[20]+3} - \ell_{27}}{\ell_{[20]+1}}$.

(b) Here we seek the probability of failure between ages 27 and 31 for an entity age 25, selected at age 22. For this entity, age 27 is already beyond the select period, so the probability is $\dfrac{\ell_{27} - \ell_{31}}{\ell_{[22]+3}}$. ☐

6.8 LIFE TABLE SUMMARY

This chapter has described, in great detail, the generic life table, which is the most fundamental model supporting the actuarial determination of financial values associated with life insurance and pension plans. Although all life tables are basically of the same form, they may vary considerably with respect to their numerical values, their applicability, and the experience data upon which they are based.

All life tables arise from statistical studies of experience data.[3] Logically, a life table developed for the purpose of pricing life insurance should be based on data derived from life insurance experience. Similarly, a life table used for annuity calculations should be based on data derived from the survival experience of annuitants, a pension life table should be based on the survival experience of pensioners, and so on.

Life insurance coverage is available through *individual* insurance policies, which is the focus of most of the discussion throughout this text, and also through *group* insurance coverage generally provided by an employer. Under group insurance coverage, the degree of screening of individual participants for healthiness is considerably less than under individual insurance coverage.[4] Consequently, the survival patterns of persons insured under individual policies versus those insured under group coverages would be expected to differ. It logically follows that life tables used for group insurance should be based on group insurance experience and those used for individual insurance should be based on individual insurance experience.

Within individual insurance, it is common to use different life tables to calculate premiums (see Chapter 9) from those used to calculate reserves (see Chapters 10 and 11). A major concern in determining premiums is that of *competitiveness* in the marketplace, whereas a major concern in determining reserves is that of *adequacy*. Consequently, tables used for calculating reserves (also called *valuation*) might be more conservative than those used for pricing.

By definition, tables based on experience data reflect recent historical patterns of survival and failure. If such tables are used to determine contract values that apply in the future, it is inherently being assumed that past and future survival patterns will be the same. If future improvements in medicine and other factors influencing survival occur, which is likely, then tables based on historical data will be overly conservative for life insurance, but may be significantly inappropriate for life annuities. To address this possibility, actuaries frequently apply survival-improvement projections to tables based on historical data for use with annuity calculations.

---

[3] The statistical estimation procedures used to construct life tables are described in several textbooks, including Batten [3], London [22],and Kellison and London [17], and are covered on Society of Actuaries Exam C.

[4] The screening of proposed insured persons for healthiness, and other elements of insurability, is referred to as *underwriting*.

Experience data consistently shows that females live longer than males, so separate tables for the genders have traditionally been used. For political reasons, however, it has become common practice in recent years to use the same table, referred to as a *unisex table*, for both genders. Of course, a unisex table should be estimated from historical data derived from a group that includes both genders.

A very special life table, not related to insurance or pension applications, is the *population life table* which is naturally based on the survival experience of the population of a nation or a political subdivision thereof. This topic belongs to the general field of demography (see, for example, Brown [7]). In general, mortality rates derived from general population experience will exceed those derived from insurance or annuity experience.

In Section 6.7 we explored the concept of the select and ultimate life table. When such a model is derived from experience data, the select portion of the table would be estimated from the survival experience during the first k years of insurance coverage (where k is the length of the select period), and the ultimate portion would be estimated from survival experience beyond the first k years. A life table estimated from *all* years of experience, without regard to duration since selection, is called an *aggregate table*.

6.9 EXERCISES

6.1 Definition of the Life Table
6.2 The Traditional Form of the Life Table

6-1   A life table is defined by the following values of p_x:

x	p_x
0	.90
1	.80
2	.60
3	.30
4	.00

(a) Find the corresponding values of $S_0(x)$, for
$x = 0,1,2,3,4,5.$

(b) Derive a life table showing the values of ℓ_x and d_x, using a radix of 10,000.

(c) What is the value of ω in this table?

(d) Verify that $\displaystyle\sum_{x=0}^{\omega-1} d_x = \ell_0.$

6-2   From the life table developed in Exercise 6-1, calculate each of the following:

(a) $_3d_0$ (b) $_2q_1$ (c) $_3p_1$ (d) $_3q_2$

6-3   The unconditional probability of failure between ages x and $x+1$, given only alive at age 0, is denoted by $_x|q_0$.

     (a) Define $_x|q_0$ in terms of $S_0(x)$ and ℓ_x.

     (b) Show that $\displaystyle\sum_{x=0}^{\omega-1} {}_x|q_0 = 1$.

6-4   A survival model is defined by $S_0(x) = \frac{c-x}{c+x}$, for $0 \leq x \leq c$. A life table is then developed from this SDF using a radix of 100,000. In the resulting life table, $\ell_{35} = 44,000$.

     (a) Find the value of ω in the life table.

     (b) Find the probability of surviving from birth to age 60.

     (c) Find the probability that a life age 10 will fail between age 30 and age 45.

6.3 Other Functions Derived from ℓ_x
6.4 Summary of Concepts and Notation

6-5   Given that

$$\mu_x = \frac{2}{x+1} + \frac{2}{100-x},$$

for $0 \leq x < 100$, find the number of failures which occur between ages 1 and 4 in a life table with a radix of 10,000.

6-6   Find each of the following derivatives:

     (a) $\dfrac{\partial}{\partial t}\, {}_tp_x$

     (b) $\dfrac{\partial}{\partial x}\, {}_tp_x$

6-7   A simple approximation for the derivative of ℓ_x is $\frac{\ell_{x+1}-\ell_{x-1}}{2}$. Use this approximation to determine a value for μ_2 from the life table shown in Table 6.1a.

6-8   Given that $\mu_x = k + e^{2x}$, for $x \geq 0$, and that $_{.40}p_0 = .50$, find the value of k.

6-9   Given that

$$\ell_x = 2500(64-.80x)^{1/3},$$

for $0 \le x \le 80,$ find each of the following:

(a) $f_0(x)$

(b) $E[T_0]$

(c) $Var(T_0)$

6-10   Given that $\overset{\circ}{e}_0 = 25$ and $\ell_x = \omega - x,$ for $0 \le x \le \omega,$ find the value of $Var(T_{10}).$

6-11   Given that $_1|q_{x+1} = .095,$ $_2|q_{x+1} = .171,$ and $q_{x+3} = .200,$ find the value of $q_{x+1} + q_{x+2}.$

6-12   For the ℓ_x function given in Exercise 6-9, find $\overset{\circ}{e}_{70}$ and the variance of future lifetime for a person age 70.

6-13   A survival model follows a uniform distribution with limiting age $\omega = 100.$ It is estimated that a certain medical breakthrough will increase the value of $\overset{\circ}{e}_{30}$ by 4 years. Assuming the survival model is still uniform after the medical breakthrough, find the new limiting age of the model.

6-14   Given that $\mu_x = .04$ for $0 < x \le 40,$ and $\mu_x = .05$ for $x > 40,$ find the value of $\overset{\circ}{e}_{25:\overline{25|}}.$

6-15   Show that $e_x = p_x(1+e_{x+1}).$

6-16   Let e_x be the curtate expectation of life at age x according to a certain life table, and let e'_x be the same concept according to a second life table. For all x it is known that $\frac{1+e_x}{1+e'_x} = 1+k,$ where k is a constant. Show that $q'_x = q_x + \frac{k}{1+e_{x+1}}.$

6-17   Use Equation (6.20) to show that $_t p_x = e^{-\int_0^t \mu_{x+r}\, dr}.$

6.5 Multi-State Model Interpretation

6-18   Use Table 6.1 (or Table 6.1a) to calculate p_x and q_x, for $x = 0, 1, 2, 3$. Then define the state vector π_4 in terms of π_0 and $\mathbf{P}^{(k)}$, for $k = 0, 1, 2, 3$, and show that $\pi_4 = (.97082, .02918)$.

6-19   Consider a tabular survival model for an inanimate object (such as a light bulb) for which the probability of continued survival over each successive discrete time interval, say, p, is the same regardless of the attained age of the object, so that the survival model can be represented by a homogeneous discrete-time Markov model with $X_0 = 1$. (Assume that the object, once failed, remains failed forever.) Define each of the following mulit-state model concepts.

(a) $Pr[X_7 = 2 \mid X_6 = 1]$
(b)   The homogeneous transition matrix $\mathbf{P}$.
(c)   The state vector at time n, π_n.

6-20   For the homogeneous model of Exercise 6-25, find the expected whole number of time intervals that the object will survive.

6.6 Methods for Non-Integral Ages

6-21   Which of the following relationships are correct under the linear assumption for ℓ_{x+t}, for $0 < t < 1$?

(a) $_{1/2}q_x < {}_{1/2}q_{x+1/2}$
(b) $_t q_x = {}_{1-t}p_x \cdot {}_t q_{x+1-t}$
(c) $\mu_{x+t} > {}_t q_x$

6-22   Given the UDD assumption and the value $\mu_{45.5} = .50$, find the value of $\overset{o}{e}_{45:\overline{1}|}$.

6-23   Given the UDD assumption and the values $q_{70} = .040$ and $q_{71} = .044$, find the value of $\overset{o}{e}_{70:\overline{1.5}|}$.

6-24   Given the UDD assumption and the values $\mu_{80.5} = .0202$, $\mu_{81.5} = .0408$, and $\mu_{82.5} = .0619$, find the value of $_2 q_{80.5}$.

6-25 Show that linear interpolation on the log of a function is the same as exponential interpolation on the function itself.

6-26 Given that $\ell_x = 1000(100-x)^{1/2}$, for $0 \le x \le 100$, calculate the exact value of $\mu_{36.25}$, and compare it with the value obtained from each of the linear, exponential, and hyperbolic assumptions. (Round the value of ℓ_{37} to the nearer integer.)

6-27 Let μ_{x+k} denote a constant force of mortality for the age interval $(x+k, x+k+1)$. Find the value of $\overset{o}{e}_{x:\overline{3}|}$, the expected number of years to be lived over the next three years by a life age x, given the following data:

k	$e^{-\mu_{x+k}}$	$\dfrac{1-e^{-\mu_{x+k}}}{\mu_{x+k}}$
0	.9512	.9754
1	.9493	.9744
2	.9465	.9730

6-28 Find the median of future lifetime for an entity age 50, under each of the (a) uniform and (b) exponential assumptions, given the following excerpt from a life table:

x	ℓ_x
50	80,000
74	42,693
75	40,280
76	37,480

6-29 The following excerpt from a life table shows values of ℓ_x at non-integral ages calculated under the linear assumption. If the values of ℓ_x at integral ages are retained, but the values at non-integral ages are recalculated under the exponential assumption, find the recalculated value of $\ell_{97.5}$.

x	ℓ_x
95.0	1,000
95.5	800
96.0	600
96.5	480
97.0	---
97.5	288
98.0	---

6-30   Each individual in a population is subject to a constant force of mortality, where that constant force is itself a random variable distributed uniformly over the interval (0, 2). Find the probability that an individual drawn at random from the population will fail within one year.

6-31   Show that

$$Var(T_x \mid T_0 > x) = Var(K_x \mid T_0 > x) + \frac{1}{12},$$

under the UDD assumption.

6-32   Derive Equation (6.50).

6-33   Derive Equation (6.55).

6.7 Select Life Tables

6-34   For a select and ultimate table with a four-year select period, show that

$$\overset{o}{e}_{[20]} = \overset{o}{e}_{[20]:\overline{4}|} + {}_4p_{[20]} \cdot \overset{o}{e}_{24}.$$

6-35   A select and ultimate table with a three-year select period begins at selection age 0. Given the following values, find the radix $\ell_{[0]}$.

$\ell_6 = 90,000$

$q_{[0]} = \dfrac{1}{6}$

${}_5p_{[1]} = \dfrac{4}{5}$

$d_x = 5,000$ for all $x \geq 3$

${}_3p_{[0]+1} = \dfrac{9}{10} \cdot {}_3p_{[1]}$

6-36   Given the following excerpt from a select and ultimate table with a two-year select period, and assuming UDD between integral ages, find the value of ${}_{.90}q_{[60]+.60}$.

x	$\ell_{[x]}$	$\ell_{[x]+1}$	ℓ_{x+2}	$x+2$
60	80,625	79,954	78,839	62
61	79,137	78,402	77,252	63
62	77,575	76,770	75,578	64

6-37 Given the following excerpt from a select and ultimate table with a three-year select period, find the probability that a person selected on 01/01/Z, and known to be alive at exact age 61 on 01/01/Z+1, will still be alive on 01/01/Z+6.

x	$q_{[x]}$	$q_{[x]+1}$	$q_{[x]+2}$	q_{x+3}	$x+3$
60	.09	.11	.13	.15	63
61	.10	.12	.14	.16	64
62	.11	.13	.15	.17	65
63	.12	.14	.16	.18	66
64	.13	.15	.17	.19	67

CHAPTER SEVEN

CONTINGENT PAYMENT MODELS (INSURANCE MODELS)

In this chapter we address the concept of models for a single payment arising from the occurrence of a defined random event. This description, and the mathematics that follows, is intended to be very general.

A particular random event is defined. If, and when, that event occurs, a single payment of predetermined amount is paid as a consequence of the occurrence of the event. A wide variety of examples can be cited, including the following:

(1)   I will pay you $10.00 the next time your favorite football team wins a game.

(2)   The outstanding balance of a loan becomes payable if the borrower defaults on the loan.

(3)   The face amount of a life insurance policy becomes payable upon the death of the person insured under the policy.

Note what is common to all three examples: a payment is made due to the occurrence of a defined random event. The payments are *contingent* on the occurrence of the associated events. Models representing such payments are collectively referred to as *contingent payment models*. In those cases where a financial loss results from the occurrence of the event, and the loss is reimbursed (in whole or in part) by another party, then we say the loss is *insured*. The party reimbursing the loss is an *insurer*, and the model describing the reimbursement arrangement is an *insurance model*.

Note that the mathematics of a contingent payment model does not depend on whether or not the loss is insured. Thus we use *contingent payment model* as the more general concept, and *insurance model* as a special case. The meaning of this will become clearer as the mathematics unfolds throughout the chapter.

7.1 DISCRETE STOCHASTIC MODELS

A common feature of the contingent payment models presented in this text is that the associated random event occurs at some *point in time* (if indeed it occurs at all). Furthermore, in many actuarial applications, the random event of interest is the *failure* of some defined *status* to continue to exist. In the examples presented at the beginning of this chapter, (1) the event of winning a game represents the "failure" of the continuation of a losing streak, (2) the event of default represents the failure of the loan to continue to be in good standing, and (3) the event of death represents the failure of the continued survival of the person insured under the policy. In this section of the chapter we develop the mathematics of contingent payment models wherein the time of failure of the status of interest is observed to occur in some finite time interval.

7.1.1 THE DISCRETE RANDOM VARIABLES FOR TIME OF FAILURE

Recall the two discrete random variables defined in Section 5.3.6, namely K_x for the *curtate duration at failure* and K_x^* for the *time interval of failure*, so that $K_x^* = K_x + 1$. We think of x as an *identifying characteristic* of the status of interest as of time 0. A common example of this will be that x denotes the age of the status at that time. Thus, in the life insurance example, K_x will denote the curtate duration at failure and K_x^* will denote the time interval of failure for a person (the "status") who is age x at time 0, the time at which the insurance is issued. This is further pursued in Section 7.1.4.

7.1.2 THE PRESENT VALUE RANDOM VARIABLE

Suppose a unit of money is payable at the *end* of the time interval in which failure occurs. Then if failure occurs in the interval $(k-1, k]$, a unit is paid at time k. Assuming a constant rate of compound interest throughout the model, the present value at time 0 of this payment is denoted by v^k. But the time of payment is a random variable, so the present value of payment is likewise a random variable, which we denote by Z_x.

If failure occurs in $(k-1, k]$, with payment at time k, then $K_x = k-1$ and $K_x^* = k$. Then the present value random variable Z_x can be defined as either

$$Z_x = v^{K_x + 1},$$
(7.1a)

for $K_x = 0, 1, 2, \cdots$, or as

$$Z_x = v^{K_x^*},$$
(7.1b)

for $K_x^* = 1, 2, 3, \cdots$. Although Z_x can be defined using either K_x or K_x^*, the definition using K_x^* is the more convenient one. Since K_x denotes the duration at the *beginning* of the failure interval, but the payment is at the *end* of that interval, then the exponent of v needs to be $K_x + 1$. We will use the more convenient K_x^* definition throughout this section.[1]

The expected value (or first moment) of the random variable Z_x is denoted by A_x. Thus we have

$$A_x = E[Z_x] = \sum_{k=1}^{\infty} v^k \cdot Pr(K_x^* = k),$$
(7.2)

a case of finding the expected value of a function of the discrete random variable K_x^*. (See Equation 2.3 in Section 2.1.1.) The second moment of Z_x is denoted by ^2A_x, and is given by

---

[1] Other texts choose to define Z_x in terms of K_x. See, for example, Bowers, et al. [4] or Dickson, et al. [8].

$$^2A_x = E[Z_x^2] = \sum_{k=1}^{\infty} (v^k)^2 \cdot Pr(K_x^* = k). \qquad (7.3)$$

Recall from the theory of compound interest (see Section 1.1) that the discount factor v is related to the force of interest δ by $v = e^{-\delta}$. If we let $v' = v^2$, then it follows that $v' = (e^{-\delta})^2 = e^{-2\delta}$. In Equation (7.3) we can substitute $(v^k)^2 = v^{2k} = (v^2)^k = (v')^k$, so that Equation (7.3) becomes

$$^2A_x = E[Z_x^2] = \sum_{k=1}^{\infty} (v')^k \cdot Pr(K_x^* = k). \qquad (7.4)$$

This shows that ^2A_x is the same kind of function as is A_x, except that it is calculated at a force of interest that is double the force of interest used to calculate A_x. Recall also from compound interest theory that if $\delta' = 2\delta$, then $1 + i' = e^{\delta'} = e^{2\delta} = (e^{\delta})^2 = (1+i)^2$, so that $i' = (1+i)^2 - 1$. Thus if interest rate i is used to calculate A_x, then ^2A_x is calculated at rate $i' = (1+i)^2 - 1 = 2i + i^2$, but not $i' = 2i$. It is important to remember that ^2A_x is calculated at double the *force of interest*, not double the *effective rate of interest*.

The variance of the present value random variable Z_x is then given by

$$Var(Z_x) = {}^2A_x - A_x^2. \qquad (7.5)$$

Because K_x^* is discrete, then $Z_x = v^{K_x^*}$ is also discrete, so the full distribution of Z_x can be tabulated from the distribution of K_x^*. Having the full distribution enables us to find the median (or any other percentile) of the random variable Z_x. This is illustrated in part (c) of the following example.

EXAMPLE 7.1

A payment of $10.00 will be made at the end of the week during which a family's supply of laundry detergent runs out. The family's usage of detergent is variable, so the week of exhaustion of the supply is a random variable K, with the following distribution:

k	$Pr(K=k)$ [2]
1	.20
2	.30
3	.20
4	.15
5	.15

Let $Z = 10v^K$ denote the present value of payment random variable. Find (a) the mean,

---

[2] It is not possible for the supply to last more than five weeks.

(b) the variance, and (c) the median of Z, using an interest rate of $i = .01,$ effective per week.

SOLUTION

(a) By Equation (7.2) the mean of Z is

$$E[Z] = \sum_{k=1}^{5} 10v^k \cdot Pr(K=k)$$

$$= 10\left[\frac{.20}{1.01} + \frac{.30}{(1.01)^2} + \frac{.20}{(1.01)^3} + \frac{.15}{(1.01)^4} + \frac{.15}{(1.01)^5}\right] = 9.73094.$$

(b) First we find $i' = (1.01)^2 - 1 = .0201.$ Then from Equation (7.3) we have

$$E[Z^2] = \sum_{k=1}^{5} \left(10v^k\right)^2 \cdot Pr(K=k)$$

$$= 100\sum_{k=1}^{5} (v')^k \cdot Pr(K=k)$$

$$= 100\left[\frac{.20}{1.0201} + \frac{.30}{(1.0201)^2} + \frac{.20}{(1.0201)^3} + \frac{.15}{(1.0201)^4} + \frac{.15}{(1.0201)^5}\right] = 94.70782.$$

Then $Var(Z) = 94.70782 - (9.73094)^2 = .01663.$

(c) The five possible values of $Z = 10v^K$ follow from the five possible values of K itself. The complete distribution of Z is as follows:

k	$z = 10v^k$	$Pr(Z=z)$
5	9.51466	.15
4	9.60980	.15
3	9.70591	.20
2	9.80296	.30
1	9.90099	.20

We take the median of Z to be the smallest value m for which

$$Pr(Z \leq m) = .50. \tag{7.6}$$

In this case the median is $z = 9.70591,$ since $Pr(Z \leq 9.70591) = .50.$ (Note that the median of a discrete random variable is not always so easy to define as it is in this case. See Footnote 3 on page 17.) ◻

7.1.3 MODIFICATIONS OF THE PRESENT VALUE RANDOM VARIABLE

Equations (7.1a) and (7.1b) define the present value random variable in the case where payment is made at the end of the time interval of failure, with no restriction as to when that might be. In this section we consider three alternatives to that model.

For our first alternative, consider the case where payment is made at the end of the interval of failure *only if* failure occurs *within* the first n time intervals, i.e., only if $K_x^* \leq n$. We denote the present value random variable in this case by $Z_{x:\overline{n}|}^1$. (The reasoning behind this choice will be explained in Section 7.1.4.) From the description of the case, it follows that

$$Z_{x:\overline{n}|}^1 = \begin{cases} v^{K_x^*} & \text{for } K_x^* \leq n, \\ 0 & \text{for } K_x^* > n \end{cases}, \tag{7.7}$$

since there is no payment if $K_x^* > n$.

Analogous to the case of the random variable Z_x presented in Section 7.1.2, we can define the first moment of $Z_{x:\overline{n}|}^1$ to be

$$A_{x:\overline{n}|}^1 = E\left[Z_{x:\overline{n}|}^1\right] = \sum_{k=1}^{n} v^k \cdot Pr(K_x^* = k), \tag{7.8}$$

and the second moment to be

$$^2A_{x:\overline{n}|}^1 = E\left[Z_{x:\overline{n}|}^{1\,2}\right] = \sum_{k=1}^{n} (v')^k \cdot Pr(K_x^* = k), \tag{7.9}$$

where, again, $v' = v^2$ which means $i' = (1+i)^2 - 1$ and $\delta' = 2\delta$. Then the variance of $Z_{x:\overline{n}|}^1$ is

$$Var\left(Z_{x:\overline{n}|}^1\right) = {}^2A_{x:\overline{n}|}^1 - A_{x:\overline{n}|}^{1\,2}. \tag{7.10}$$

EXAMPLE 7.2

For the model of Example 7.1, find the first and second moments of the present value of payment random variable if payment is made only for failure of the detergent supply *within the first three weeks*.

SOLUTION

The first moment is

$$E[Z] = \sum_{k=1}^{3} 10v^k \cdot Pr(K=k) = 10\left[\frac{.20}{1.01} + \frac{.30}{(1.01)^2} + \frac{.20}{(1.01)^3}\right] = 6.86227.$$

The second moment is

$$E[Z^2] = \sum_{k=1}^{3} \left(10v^k\right)^2 \cdot Pr(K=k)$$

$$= 100\left[\frac{.20}{1.0201} + \frac{.30}{(1.0201)^2} + \frac{.20}{(1.0201)^3}\right]$$

$$= 67.27624. \qquad\qquad \square$$

Our second alternative is the flip side of the first. Here we consider the case where payment is made at the end of the interval of failure *only if* failure occurs *after* the first n time intervals, *i.e.*, only if $K_x^* > n$. The present value random variable in this case is denoted by $_n|Z_x$, a choice to be explained in Section 7.1.4. Then we have

$$_n|Z_x = \begin{cases} 0 & \text{for } K_x^* \le n, \\ v^{K_x^*} & \text{for } K_x^* > n, \end{cases} \tag{7.11}$$

since there is no payment if $K_x^* \le n$.

The first moment of $_n|Z_x$ is given by

$$_n|A_x = E[_n|Z_x] = \sum_{k=n+1}^{\infty} v^k \cdot Pr(K_x^* = k), \tag{7.12}$$

the second moment is given by

$$^2_n|A_x = E[_n|Z_x{}^2] = \sum_{k=n+1}^{\infty} (v')^k \cdot Pr(K_x^* = k), \tag{7.13}$$

and the variance is given by

$$Var(_n|Z_x) = {}^2_n|A_x - {}_n|A_x{}^2. \tag{7.14}$$

Taking Equations (7.7) and (7.11) together, it is clear that

$$Z_x = Z^1_{x:\overline{n}|} + {}_n|Z_x, \tag{7.15}$$

so that

$$A_x = E[Z_x] = E\left[Z^1_{x:\overline{n}|}\right] + E[_n|Z_x] = A^1_{x:\overline{n}|} + {}_n|A_x. \tag{7.16}$$

This is also clear by considering Equations (7.2), (7.8), and (7.12). Similarly, by considering Equations (7.4), (7.9), and (7.13), it is clear that

$$^2A_x = {}^2A^1_{x:\overline{n}|} + {}^2_n|A_x. \tag{7.17}$$

This may appear surprising at first, because Equation (7.15) shows us that

$$Z_x^{\,2} = Z_{x:\overline{n}|}^{1}{}^2 + {}_n|Z_x^{\,2} + 2 \cdot Z_{x:\overline{n}|}^{1} \cdot {}_n|Z_x.$$

However Equations (7.7) and (7.11) show us that for any value of K_x^* one of $Z_{x:\overline{n}|}^1$ or ${}_n|Z_x$ is zero, so it follows that

$$Z_{x:\overline{n}|}^{1} \cdot {}_n|Z_x = 0$$

for all K_x^*. Thus we have

$$Z_x^{\,2} = Z_{x:\overline{n}|}^{1}{}^2 + {}_n|Z_x^{\,2}$$

for all K_x^*, and Equation (7.17) follows.

Clearly $Z_{x:\overline{n}|}^1$ and ${}_n|Z_x$ are not independent, so again from Equation (7.15) we have

$$Var(Z_x) = Var\left(Z_{x:\overline{n}|}^{1}\right) + Var\left({}_n|Z_x\right) + 2 \cdot Cov\left(Z_{x:\overline{n}|}^{1}, {}_n|Z_x\right). \qquad (7.18)$$

With the three variances given by Equations (7.5), (7.10), and (7.14), respectively, we can solve for

$$Cov\left(Z_{x:\overline{n}|}^{1}, {}_n|Z_x\right) = \frac{1}{2}\left(A_{x:\overline{n}|}^{1}{}^2 + {}_n|A_x^{\,2} - A_x^{\,2}\right). \qquad (7.19a)$$

This result can be obtained in another way. Recall that

$$Cov(U,V) = E[U \cdot V] - E[U] \cdot E[V],$$

where here $U = Z_{x:\overline{n}|}^1$ and $V = {}_n|Z_x$. But we know that $U \cdot V = 0$ so $E[U \cdot V] = 0$. Thus we have

$$Cov\left(Z_{x:\overline{n}|}^{1}, {}_n|Z_x\right) = -A_{x:\overline{n}|}^{1} \cdot {}_n|A_x. \qquad (7.19b)$$

With the help of Equation (7.16) we can easily see that the right hand sides of Equations (7.19a) and (7.19b) are equal. (The details of this are left to the reader as Exercise 7-2.)

EXAMPLE 7.3

For the model of Example 7.1, find the first and second moments of the present value of payment random variable if payment is made only for failure of the detergent supply *after the first three weeks*.

SOLUTION

The first moment is

$$E[Z] = \sum_{k=4}^{5} 10v^k \cdot Pr(K=k) = 10\left[\frac{.15}{(1.01)^4} + \frac{.15}{(1.01)^5}\right] = 2.86867.$$

The second moment is

$$E[Z^2] = \sum_{k=4}^{5} \left(10v^k\right)^2 \cdot Pr(K=k) = 100\left[\frac{.15}{(1.0201)^4} + \frac{.15}{(1.0201)^5}\right] = 27.43158. \qquad \square$$

(Note that the results in Examples 7.2 and 7.3 sum to the corresponding results in Example 7.1, as expected from Equations (7.16) and (7.17).)

For our third alternative, consider the case where payment is made at precise time n *if and only if* failure occurs *after* the first n time intervals, i.e., only if $K_x^* > n$. The present value random variable in this case is denoted by $Z_{x:\overline{n}|}^{\;1}$, and we have

$$Z_{x:\overline{n}|}^{\;1} = \begin{cases} 0 & \text{for } K_x^* \le n \\ v^n & \text{for } K_x^* > n \end{cases}. \tag{7.20}$$

It is important to note the similarity, and the important difference, between $Z_{x:\overline{n}|}^{\;1}$ and $_n|Z_x$, as defined by Equation (7.11). In both cases a payment is made only if $K_x^* > n$. The distinction is that for $Z_{x:\overline{n}|}^{\;1}$ the payment is made at time n, whereas for $_n|Z_x$ it is made at time K_x^* itself, the end of the interval during which failure occurs.

The first moment of $Z_{x:\overline{n}|}^{\;1}$ is given by

$$A_{x:\overline{n}|}^{\;1} = E\left[Z_{x:\overline{n}|}^{\;1}\right] = v^n \cdot Pr(K_x^* > n), \tag{7.21}$$

the second moment is given by

$$^2A_{x:\overline{n}|}^{\;1} = E\left[Z_{x:\overline{n}|}^{\;1\,2}\right] = (v')^n \cdot Pr(K_x^* > n), \tag{7.22}$$

where, once again, $v' = v^2$ follows from $\delta' = 2\delta$, and the variance is given by

$$Var\left(Z_{x:\overline{n}|}^{\;1}\right) = {}^2A_{x:\overline{n}|}^{\;1} - A_{x:\overline{n}|}^{\;1\,2}. \tag{7.23}$$

An interesting special case is created by combining the first and third alternatives, with features similar to what we found when we combined the first and second alternatives in Equation (7.15). The combination of the first and third alternatives has its meaning primarily within the context of life insurance, so we will defer this until the next section.

EXAMPLE 7.4

For the model of Example 7.1, calculate the values of $A_{x:\overline{3}|}^{1}$ and $^{2}A_{x:\overline{3}|}^{1}$.

SOLUTION

From Example 7.1 we find $Pr(K > 3) = .30,$ so we have

$$A_{x:\overline{3}|}^{1} = v^3 \cdot Pr(K > 3) = \frac{.30}{(1.01)^3} = .29117$$

and

$$^{2}A_{x:\overline{3}|}^{1} = (v')^3 \cdot Pr(K > 3) = \frac{.30}{(1.0201)^3} = .28261. \qquad \square$$

7.1.4 APPLICATION TO LIFE INSURANCE

The models, mathematics, and notation developed thus far in Section 7.1 have their origins in actuarial science, with particular reference to life insurance. In this text we prefer to develop the theory in as general a setting as possible, and then show how the theory is adapted to various applications. With life insurance as a very important one of these applications, we have chosen to use the standard life insurance notation as much as possible even in the general cases. In this section we describe the terminology used when the general models are applied in the context of life insurance.

Let the identifying characteristic of the status whose failure occurs in the kth time interval, denoted by x, represent the attained age of a person being issued life insurance at time 0. It is customary to presume that x is an integer. Then the time line diagram of Figure 5.2 can be replaced by the age line diagram of Figure 7.1.

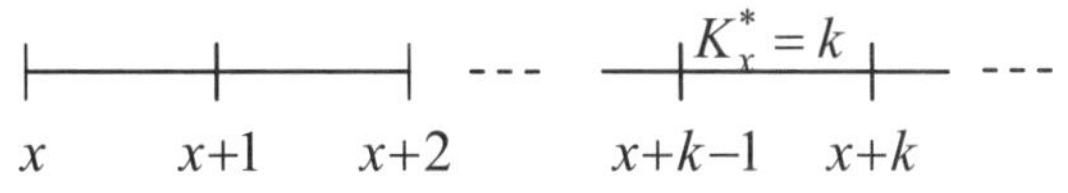

FIGURE 7.1

The present value random variable Z_x, defined by Equation (7.1b) for $K_x^* = 1, 2, \cdots$, represents the present value of a unit payment made at the end of the time interval in which the insured person dies, regardless of when that may be. In the life insurance context, time will be measured in years. Thus we refer to Z_x as the present value random variable for a *whole life insurance, of unit payment, made at the end of the year of death*. Since payment will be made regardless of when death occurs, the insurance coverage is for the *whole of life*, which explains the name *whole life insurance*.

The expected value of Z_x, denoted A_x, is called the *expected present value* (EPV) of a whole life insurance. (Other texts use the phrase *actuarial present value* (APV).) A_x is also called the *net single premium* (NSP) for a unit whole life insurance, a term whose meaning will be more fully explained in Section 7.2.

The present value random variable $Z^1_{x:\overline{n}|}$ is the random variable for an *n-year temporary insurance*, also called an *n-year term insurance*, since the insurance coverage is limited to the first n years (from age x to age $x+n$) only. Its expected value, denoted $A^1_{x:\overline{n}|}$, is called the EPV, or APV, or NSP for a unit n-year term insurance.

The present value random variable $_n|Z_x$ is the random variable for an *n-year deferred insurance*, since the insurance coverage is deferred for n years after age x and is effective only from age $x+n$ onward. Its expected value, denoted $_n|A_x$, is called the EPV, or APV, or NSP for a unit n-year deferred insurance.

The present value random variable $Z_{x:\overline{n}|}^{\ \ 1}$ is the random variable for an *n-year pure endowment*, since the benefit is paid (or *endowed*) to the insured if survival to age $x+n$ occurs. (Note that the condition $K^*_x > n$ implies failure (death) after time n, or age $x+n$, so that survival to age $x+n$ has occurred.) Its expected value, $A_{x:\overline{n}|}^{\ \ 1}$, is called the EPV, or APV, or NSP for a unit n-year pure endowment. An alternative symbol for $A_{x:\overline{n}|}^{\ \ 1}$ is $_nE_x$, which we will often use in this text.

We now consider the special case, mentioned at the end of Section 7.1.3, that results from combining the n-year term insurance model, defined by Equation (7.7), with the n-year pure endowment model, defined by Equation (7.20). Letting $Z_{x:\overline{n}|}$ denote the present value random variable for the combined model, we have

$$Z_{x:\overline{n}|} = \begin{cases} v^{K^*_x} & \text{for } K^*_x \le n \\ v^n & \text{for } K^*_x > n \end{cases}. \tag{7.24}$$

It is clear that

$$Z_{x:\overline{n}|} = Z^1_{x:\overline{n}|} + Z_{x:\overline{n}|}^{\ \ 1}, \tag{7.25}$$

with expected value given by

$$A_{x:\overline{n}|} = A^1_{x:\overline{n}|} + A_{x:\overline{n}|}^{\ \ 1}, \tag{7.26}$$

and, since $Z^1_{x:\overline{n}|} \cdot Z_{x:\overline{n}|}^{\ \ 1} = 0$ for all K^*_x, then

$$Z_{x:\overline{n}|}^{\ \ 2} = Z^1_{x:\overline{n}|}{}^2 + Z_{x:\overline{n}|}^{\ \ 1\ 2} \tag{7.27}$$

as well, so that

$$^2A_{x:\overline{n}|} = {}^2A^1_{x:\overline{n}|} + {}^2A_{x:\overline{n}|}^{\ \ 1} \tag{7.28}$$

gives the second moment of $Z_{x:\overline{n}|}$.

In the context of life insurance this combination is called an *n-year endowment insurance*, and its expected value $A_{x:\overline{n}|}$ is the EPV, or APV, or NSP for a *n*-year endowment insurance.

The insurance pays its unit benefit at the end of the year of death, if death occurs within the first *n* years, or at the end of *n* years if death has not occurred.

It is clear that $Z^1_{x:\overline{n}|}$ and $Z_{x:\overline{n}|}^{1}$ are not independent random variables, so we have

$$Var\left(Z_{x:\overline{n}|}\right) = Var\left(Z^1_{x:\overline{n}|}\right) + Var\left(Z_{x:\overline{n}|}^{1}\right) + 2 \cdot Cov\left(Z^1_{x:\overline{n}|}, Z_{x:\overline{n}|}^{1}\right).$$

Since $Z^1_{x:\overline{n}|} \cdot Z_{x:\overline{n}|}^{1} = 0$ for all K_x, then $E\left[Z^1_{x:\overline{n}|} \cdot Z_{x:\overline{n}|}^{1}\right] = 0$ as well, so the covariance is given by

$$Cov\left(Z^1_{x:\overline{n}|}, Z_{x:\overline{n}|}^{1}\right) = -E\left[Z^1_{x:\overline{n}|}\right] \cdot E\left[Z_{x:\overline{n}|}^{1}\right] = -A^1_{x:\overline{n}|} \cdot A_{x:\overline{n}|}^{1}. \qquad (7.29)$$

Finally, we can explain the notational devices used in this section.

In the symbol $Z^1_{x:\overline{n}|}$, the first subscript (x) denotes the age of the person insured as of time 0 and the second subscript $(\overline{n}|)$ denotes the length of the term during which failure (death) must occur in order that payment be made. The "upper one" over the x indicates that the life (x) must fail *before* the *n*-year term fails. Conversely, the symbol $Z_{x:\overline{n}|}^{1}$ is used to show that the *n*-year term must fail *before* the life (x) fails in order for the benefit to be paid.

The combination of $Z^1_{x:\overline{n}|}$ and $Z_{x:\overline{n}|}^{1}$ into $Z_{x:\overline{n}|}$, the *n*-year endowment insurance, represents a situation where the benefit is paid upon the *first* failure between the life (x) and the *n*-year term, whichever it may be. Hence there is no required order of failure, so there is no "upper one." Such situations are called *joint status* situations, and will be further explored in Chapter 12.

Example 7.5

For the model of Example 7.1, calculate (a) $A_{x:\overline{3}|}$, (b) $^2A_{x:\overline{3}|}$, and (c) $Cov\left(Z^1_{x:\overline{3}|}, Z_{x:\overline{3}|}^{1}\right)$.

SOLUTION

(a) From Equation (7.26) we have

$$A_{x:\overline{3}|} = A^1_{x:\overline{3}|} + A_{x:\overline{3}|}^{1} = .68623 + .29117 = .97740.$$

(b) From Equation (7.27) we have

$$^2A_{x:\overline{3}|} = {}^2A^1_{x:\overline{3}|} + {}^2A_{x:\overline{3}|}^{1} = .67276 + .28261 = .95537.$$

(c) From Equation (7.29) we have

$$Cov\left(Z^1_{x:\overline{3}|}, Z_{x:\overline{3}|}^{\ 1}\right) = -A^1_{x:\overline{3}|} \cdot A_{x:\overline{3}|}^{\ 1} = -(.68623)(.29117) = -.19980. \qquad \square$$

7.2 GROUP DETERMINISTIC APPROACH

In this section we will develop the same models as we did in Section 7.1, but from a different perspective that will add to our understanding of the models.

Consider the life table model described in Chapter 6. Recall that ℓ_x denotes the number of entities (in this case, persons) in the survivorship group when all are age x. Suppose all ℓ_x persons purchase a whole life insurance of unit benefit, with each person paying amount X to purchase the insurance. Then we have an initial fund of $X \cdot \ell_x$ dollars at time 0.

According to the life table model, d_x persons fail (die) in the age interval $(x, x+1]$, d_{x+1} fail in the age interval $(x+1, x+2]$, and so on, until all have failed. Since each insurance pays a unit benefit, then the sequence $d_x, d_{x+1}, d_{x+2}, \ldots$ represents the sequence of payments made under the insurances in total. This is represented in Figure 7.2.

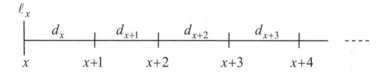

FIGURE 7.2

All payments are made at the end of the year of failure. The total present value at time 0 (age x) of all the payments is

$$v \cdot d_x + v^2 \cdot d_{x+1} + v^3 \cdot d_{x+2} + \cdots,$$

which is set equal to the initial fund. That is,

$$X \cdot \ell_x = v \cdot d_x + v^2 \cdot d_{x+1} + v^3 \cdot d_{x+2} + \cdots. \qquad (7.30)$$

If we divide both sides of Equation (7.30) by ℓ_x we obtain

$$X = v \cdot \frac{d_x}{\ell_x} + v^2 \cdot \frac{d_{x+1}}{\ell_x} + v^3 \cdot \frac{d_{x+2}}{\ell_x} + \cdots, \qquad (7.31a)$$

where X represents each person's share of the total present value of all the benefit payments. Thus X can be interpreted as the price, or *premium*, each of the ℓ_x persons should pay for the insurance coverage, and is called the *net single premium* (NSP) for the whole life insurance.

Finally we observe that the general term in Equation (7.31a), namely $\frac{d_{x+t}}{\ell_x}$, can be regarded as the probability that the life (x) fails in the age interval $(x+t, x+t+1]$, which, from Equation (6.18b), is denoted $_{t|}q_x$. Thus we have

$$X = \sum_{t=0}^{\infty} v^{t+1} \cdot _{t|}q_x = \sum_{t=1}^{\infty} v^t \cdot _{t-1|}q_x. \qquad (7.31b)$$

But $_{t-1|}q_x$, the probability that failure occurs between ages $x+t-1$ and $x+t$ is the same as the probability that failure occurs in the tth year, which was denoted earlier by $Pr(K_x = t)$. Thus the right hand sides of Equations (7.2) and (7.31b) are the same, so $X = A_x$.

This is a very important result. The net single premium per life in the group deterministic approach of this section is the same as the expected present value of the benefit in the stochastic approach of Section 7.1. Although either approach can be used to find A_x, the stochastic approach is the more useful one for us to consider since it also allows us to explore the second moment, variance, and percentiles of the random variable Z_x.

The group deterministic approach applies to the other models presented in Section 7.1 as well. The simplest is the pure endowment model. If ℓ_x persons each pay X to purchase an n-year pure endowment, the initial fund at time 0 (age x) is of size $X \cdot \ell_x$. But this must represent the present value of the ℓ_{x+n} dollars paid out at time n, one dollar to each of the ℓ_{x+n} survivors. Thus we have

$$X \cdot \ell_x = v^n \cdot \ell_{x+n},$$

which becomes, upon division by ℓ_x,

$$X = v^n \cdot \frac{\ell_{x+n}}{\ell_x} = v^n \cdot _n p_x, \qquad (7.32)$$

where $_n p_x = \frac{\ell_{x+n}}{\ell_x}$ is defined by Equation (6.6). But $_n p_x$ is the probability of survival to age $x+n$, so $_n p_x = Pr(K_x > n)$. Therefore the right hand sides of Equations (7.21) and (7.32) are the same, so $X = A_{x:\overline{n}|}^{\ 1} = _n E_x$.

The group interpretation can also be used to derive $A_{x:\overline{n}|}^1$, $_{n|}A_x$, and $A_{x:\overline{n}|}$. These derivations are totally parallel to the two cases presented here and are therefore left as exercises. Note that if the several insurance APVs are calculated from a select table, the subscript x in the APV symbol would be replaced by $[x]$.

EXAMPLE 7.6

Convert the probability distribution of Example 7.1 into a life table model, using a radix of $\ell_0 = 100$. Then repeat the calculation of part (a) of Example 7.1.

SOLUTION

Using standard life table notation from Chapter 6 we obtain the following result:

x	$_x|q_0$	d_x	ℓ_x	p_x	q_x
0	.20	20	100	.800	.200
1	.30	30	80	.625	.375
2	.20	20	50	.600	.400
3	.15	15	30	.500	.500
4	.15	15	15	.000	1.000

Note that $_x|q_0 = Pr(K^* = x+1)$, the probability that the entity of interest fails in the $(x+1)^{st}$ interval. Note also that $\ell_5 = 0$, so $p_4 = 0$ and $q_4 = 1$.

The point of this example is to show that the net single premium found by the group deterministic approach is the same as the actuarial present value found by the stochastic (i.e., random variable) approach. Here we have

$$NSP = \frac{10}{\ell_0}\left[v \cdot d_0 + v^2 \cdot d_1 + \cdots + v^5 \cdot d_4\right] = \frac{10}{\ell_0}\left[\frac{20}{1.01} + \frac{30}{(1.01)^2} + \cdots + \frac{15}{(1.01)^5}\right] = 9.73094,$$

which agrees with the result of part (a) of Example 7.1. ❑

7.3 CONTINUOUS STOCHASTIC MODELS

Four of the five models discussed in Sections 7.1 and 7.2 have continuous counterparts, which we will develop in this section.

7.3.1 THE CONTINUOUS RANDOM VARIABLE FOR TIME TO FAILURE

Let the continuous random variable T denote the *point of time of failure* for the status of interest, so that $T = t$, for $t > 0$, denotes the event of failure at precise time t, as shown in Figure 7.3.

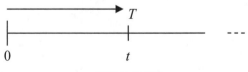

FIGURE 7.3

Let $f(t)$ denote the probability density function (PDF) of the random variable T. Since failure must eventually occur at some time, then

$$\int_0^\infty f(t)\,dt \;=\; 1. \tag{7.33}$$

We again use the subscript x to denote an identifying characteristic of the status of interest, such as the age of the status (possibly, person) at time 0. Then T_x is called the *future lifetime random variable* for the person age x at time 0, as already defined in Section 5.3.[3]

7.3.2 THE PRESENT VALUE RANDOM VARIABLE

If a unit of money is payable at time t as a result of failure at time t, then the present value random variable (in the continuous case), which we denote by $\overline{Z}_x$, is

$$\overline{Z}_x \;=\; v^{T_x}, \tag{7.34}$$

for $T_x > 0$. The expected value of $\overline{Z}_x$, denoted $\overline{A}_x$, is given by

$$\overline{A}_x \;=\; E[\overline{Z}_x] \;=\; \int_0^\infty v^t \cdot f(t)\,dt \;=\; \int_0^\infty v^t \cdot {}_tp_x\mu_{x+t}\,dt, \tag{7.35}$$

where ${}_tp_x\mu_{x+t}$ is the PDF of T_x (see Equation (6.19b)).

In a manner completely parallel to the discrete case of Section 7.1, the second moment of $\overline{Z}_x$, denoted ${}^2\overline{A}_x$, is given by

$$ {}^2\overline{A}_x \;=\; E[\overline{Z}_x{}^2] \;=\; \int_0^\infty (v')^t \cdot {}_tp_x\mu_{x+t}\,dt, \tag{7.36}$$

where, once again, $v' = v^2$ which follows from $\delta' = 2\delta$. The variance of $\overline{Z}_x$ is then

$$Var(\overline{Z}_x) \;=\; {}^2\overline{A}_x - \overline{A}_x{}^2. \tag{7.37}$$

EXAMPLE 7.7

A continuously-operating air conditioning unit has an exponential lifetime distribution with mean 4 years. When the unit fails it must be replaced at a cost of $1000.00, which we consider to be a unit of money. Let $\overline{Z}$ denote the present value random variable for the unit payment made at the time point of failure. Using an effective annual interest rate of 5%, calculate each of (a) $E[\overline{Z}]$, (b) $Var(\overline{Z})$, and (c) the 90th percentile of the distribution of $\overline{Z}$.

SOLUTION

(a) The PDF of T is $f(t) = .25e^{-.25t}$. The force of interest associated with $i = .05$ is $\delta = \ln(1.05) = .04879$, so we have $v^t = (1+i)^{-t} = e^{-\delta t}$ and $(v')^t = (1+i')^{-t} = e^{-\delta't} = e^{-2\delta t}$.

---

[3] Some texts (see, for example, Bowers et al. [4]) use the notation $T(x)$ instead of T_x for this random variable.

Then

$$E[\bar{Z}] = \int_0^\infty e^{-\delta t} \cdot f(t)\, dt = .25\int_0^\infty e^{-(.04879+.25)t}\, dt = \frac{.25}{.04879+.25} = .83670.$$

(b) $\displaystyle E[\bar{Z}^2] = \int_0^\infty e^{-2\delta t} \cdot f(t)\, dt = .25\int_0^\infty e^{-(.09758+.25)t}\, dt = \frac{.25}{.09758+.25} = .71925.$

Then we have $Var(\bar{Z}) = .71925 - (.83670)^2 = .01918.$

(c) Let p denote the 90th percentile of $\bar{Z}$. Then we have

$$Pr(\bar{Z} \le p) = Pr\left(T \ge \frac{-\ln p}{\delta}\right) = .90.$$

Since T has an exponential distribution, then

$$Pr\left(T \ge \frac{-\ln p}{\delta}\right) = e^{-.25(-\ln p/\delta)},$$

so we have $e^{-.25(-\ln p/.04879)} = e^{5.124(\ln p)} = p^{5.124} = .90,$ which solves for $p = .97965.$ [4] ❑

7.3.3 MODIFICATIONS OF THE PRESENT VALUE RANDOM VARIABLE

The random variables $\bar{Z}^1_{x:\overline{n}|}$ and $_n|\bar{Z}_x$ are defined as the continuous counterparts to $Z^1_{x:\overline{n}|}$ and $_n|Z_x$. Their first moments, second moments, and variances are found in a similar manner, and these are all left as exercises for the reader.

Note, however, that the pure endowment random variable $Z_{x:\overline{n}|}^{1}$ does not have a continuous counterpart, since the payment is made at time n for failure after time n, whether denoted by $K_x > n$ or $T_x > n$. Then the continuous version of the n-year endowment insurance model is

$$\bar{Z}_{x:\overline{n}|} = \bar{Z}^1_{x:\overline{n}|} + Z_{x:\overline{n}|}^{1}, \tag{7.38a}$$

with expected value given by

$$\bar{A}_{x:\overline{n}|} = \bar{A}^1_{x:\overline{n}|} + A_{x:\overline{n}|}^{1}. \tag{7.38b}$$

7.3.4 APPLICATIONS TO LIFE INSURANCE

Under the continuous model the benefit is paid at the precise time point of failure. In the insurance context, this is referred to as *benefit payable at the moment of death* or sometimes called *immediate payment of claims*.

---

[4] The 90th percentile of $\bar{Z} = e^{-\delta T}$ corresponds to the 10th percentile of T, denoted by t. We easily solve $1 - e^{-.25t} = .10$ for $t = .42144.$ Then $p = e^{-\delta t} = e^{-(.04879)(.42144)} = .97965.$

Clearly the payment of insurance benefits at the precise moment of death cannot be done in practice, but neither is it true that insurance benefits are delayed until the end of the year of death. Thus neither the Z_x nor $\bar{Z}_x$ models are completely correct in practice, but both are used to evaluate (at least approximately) insurance arrangements.

A compromise between the end-of-year-of-death and moment-of-death models would be one in which the benefit is paid at the end of the mth of the year of death, such as paid at the end of the quarter of death $(m = 4)$. We let J_x denote the random variable for the m^{thly} time interval in which failure (death) occurs. Then the event $J_x = j$ denotes failure in the jth m^{thly} time interval, and the present value of a unit paid at the end of this interval is v^j, where the interest rate upon which v^j is based is effective over $1/m$ of a year. The random variable for the present value of payment, which we denote by $Z_x^{(m)}$, is

$$Z_x^{(m)} = v^{J_x}, \qquad (7.39)$$

for $j_x = 1, 2, \ldots$, with expected value given by

$$A_x^{(m)} = E[Z_x^{(m)}] = \sum_{j=1}^{\infty} v^j \cdot Pr(J_x = j), \qquad (7.40a)$$

and variance given by

$$Var(Z_x^{(m)}) = {}^2A_x^{(m)} - A_x^{(m)\,2}. \qquad (7.40b)$$

The m^{thly} counterpart to the annual recursion formula given in Exercise 7-6 would be

$$A_x^{(m)} = v^{1/m} \cdot {}_{1/m}q_x + v^{1/m} \cdot {}_{1/m}p_x \cdot A_{x+1/m}^{(m)}. \qquad (7.40c)$$

If $A_x^{(m)}$ is evaluated from a tabular survival model (life table) showing values of $\ell_x = \ell_0 \cdot S_0(x)$ only for integral (annual) values of x, then we will have to use approximate methods. We will pursue this in Section 7.5. The random variable $Z_x^{(m)}$ and its expected value $A_x^{(m)}$ will arise again in Chapter 8 when we discuss contingent annuities payable at m^{thly} intervals.

7.3.5 CONTINUOUS FUNCTIONS EVALUATED FROM PARAMETRIC SURVIVAL MODELS

In this section we consider the evaluation of continuous functions directly from a parametric survival model. Only the exponential and continuous uniform distributions are considered here, since they are sufficiently simple mathematically to allow for easy determination of results. We repeat the observations made in Sections 5.2.1 and 5.2.2 that these distributions are not at all appropriate as models for human survival over the full life span. In this section the contingent payment models depending on the concept of survival should be viewed as applying to entities for which the presumed survival distributions are realistic. An example of this was presented in Example 7.7.

The properties of the exponential distribution are described in Section 2.3.3 in general, and again in Section 5.2.2 in the context of its use as a survival model. Starting with Equation (5.30) which defines the exponential survival function as $S_0(x) = e^{-\lambda x}$, we then easily find

$$_t p_x = \frac{S_0(x+t)}{S_0(x)} = e^{-\lambda t}, \tag{7.41}$$

$$\mu_{x+t} = \lambda_0(x+t) = \lambda, \tag{7.42}$$

which is a constant, and

$$_t p_x \mu_{x+t} = \lambda \cdot e^{-\lambda t}. \tag{7.43}$$

With these building blocks we can easily find expressions for the basic continuous contingent functions defined earlier in this chapter. The continuous function $\bar{A}_x$ (see Section 7.3.2) is

$$\bar{A}_x = \int_0^\infty v^t \cdot {_t p_x} \mu_{x+t} \, dt = \lambda \int_0^\infty e^{-\delta t} \cdot e^{-\lambda t} \, dt = \frac{\lambda}{\delta + \lambda}. \tag{7.44}$$

The pure endowment function $_n E_x$ evaluated under an exponential distribution is

$$_n E_x = v^n \cdot {_n p_x} = e^{-n\delta} \cdot e^{-\lambda n} = e^{-(\delta + \lambda)n}. \tag{7.45}$$

Then expressions for other continuous insurance models can be obtained from the whole life function given by Equation (7.44) by using the various identities developed earlier in the chapter.

EXAMPLE 7.8

Evaluate $\bar{A}_{x:\overline{n}|}$ under the exponential distribution.

SOLUTION

Recall that

$$\begin{aligned}
\bar{A}_{x:\overline{n}|} &= \bar{A}^1_{x:\overline{n}|} + {_n E_x} \\
&= \bar{A}_x - {_n|}\bar{A}_x + {_n E_x} \\
&= \bar{A}_x - {_n E_x} \cdot \bar{A}_{x+n} + {_n E_x} \\
&= \bar{A}_x + {_n E_x}\left(1 - \bar{A}_{x+n}\right) \\
&= \frac{\lambda}{\delta + \lambda} + e^{-(\delta+\lambda)n}\left(1 - \frac{\lambda}{\delta+\lambda}\right) = \frac{\lambda + \delta \cdot e^{-(\delta+\lambda)n}}{\delta + \lambda},
\end{aligned}$$

under the exponential distribution.   ❑

The basic properties of the continuous uniform distribution are presented in Section 2.3.1 and again in Section 5.2.1 in the context of a survival model. Starting with Equation (5.26) for the SDF as $S_0(x) = \frac{\omega - x}{\omega}$, we then find

$$
_t p_x = \frac{S_0(x+t)}{S_0(x)} = \frac{\omega - x - t}{\omega - x}, \tag{7.46}
$$

$$
\mu_{x+t} = \lambda_0(x+t) = \frac{1}{\omega - x - t}, \tag{7.47}
$$

and

$$
_t p_x \mu_{x+t} = \frac{1}{\omega - x}, \tag{7.48}
$$

which is a constant. The basic continuous contingent payment functions then follow from these building blocks. For example, the continuous whole life insurance APV would be

$$
\bar{A}_x = \int_0^{\omega - x} v^t \cdot {}_t p_x \mu_{x+t} \, dt
$$

$$
= \frac{1}{\omega - x} \int_0^{\omega - x} v^t \, dt
$$

$$
= \frac{\bar{a}_{\overline{\omega - x}|}}{\omega - x} \tag{7.49a}
$$

$$
= \frac{1 - v^{\omega - x}}{\delta(\omega - x)}. \tag{7.49b}
$$

7.4 CONTINGENT PAYMENT MODELS WITH VARYING PAYMENTS

The expected present value of payment formula, given by Equation (7.2), can be generalized to incorporate the case of non-level, or varying, contingent payment. Let the contingent benefit payment be denoted by b_k for failure in the kth time interval, with payment made at time k, and let B_x denote, in general, a present value of payment random variable with varying payment for an entity of interest with identifying characteristic x. Then the actuarial present value is given by

$$
E[B_x] = \sum_{k=1}^{\infty} b_k \cdot v^k \cdot Pr(K_x^* = k) \tag{7.50}
$$

in the whole life case. (Note that $B_x = Z_x$ in the special case where $b_k = 1$ for all k.)

Another special case arises if $b_k = k$ for all k. In this case the APV, which we denote by $(IA)_x$, is given by

$$
(IA)_x = E[B_x] = \sum_{k=1}^{\infty} k \cdot v^k \cdot Pr(K_x^* = k). \tag{7.51}
$$

In the life insurance context, we define the APV for an n-year unit *increasing term insurance* to be

$$(IA)^1_{x:\overline{n}|} = \sum_{k=1}^n k \cdot v^k \cdot Pr(K_x^* = k) \qquad (7.52)$$

and the APV for an n-year unit *decreasing term insurance* to be

$$(DA)^1_{x:\overline{n}|} = \sum_{k=1}^n (n-k+1) \cdot v^k \cdot Pr(K_x^* = k). \qquad (7.53)$$

EXAMPLE 7.9

Calculate $(IA)_x$ and $(DA)^1_{x:\overline{3}|}$ for the probability model of Example 7.1.

SOLUTION

From Equation (7.51) we have

$$(IA)_x = 1 \cdot v \cdot Pr(K_x^* = 1) + 2 \cdot v^2 \cdot Pr(K_x^* = 2) + \cdots + 5 \cdot v^5 \cdot Pr(K_x^* = 5)$$
$$= \frac{(1)(.20)}{1.01} + \frac{(2)(.30)}{(1.01)^2} + \frac{(3)(.20)}{(1.01)^3} + \frac{(4)(.15)}{(1.01)^4} + \frac{(5)(.15)}{(1.01)^5} = 2.65874.$$

From Equation (7.53) we have

$$(DA)^1_{x:\overline{3}|} = 3 \cdot v \cdot Pr(K_x^* = 1) + 2 \cdot v^2 \cdot Pr(K_x^* = 2) + 1 \cdot v^3 \cdot Pr(K_x^* = 3)$$
$$= \frac{(3)(.20)}{1.01} + \frac{(2)(.30)}{(1.01)^2} + \frac{(1)(.20)}{(1.01)^3} = 1.37636. \qquad \square$$

We can also consider the continuous case (that is, the immediate payment of claims) with non-level benefit. Let the contingent benefit payment be b_t for failure at time t, and payable at precise time t, and let $\overline{B}_x$ denote the present value of payment random variable. Then the APV is given by

$$E[\overline{B}_x] = \int_0^\infty b_t \cdot v^t \cdot f(t)\, dt. \qquad (7.54)$$

In particular, let $b_t = t$ for all t. Then the APV, which we denote by $(\overline{I}\,\overline{A})_x$ is given by

$$(\overline{I}\,\overline{A})_x = \int_0^\infty t \cdot v^t \cdot f(t)\, dt$$
$$= \int_0^\infty t \cdot v^t \cdot {}_tp_x \mu_{x+t}\, dt. \qquad (7.55)$$

Another model of interest is the piece-wise continuous model with benefit paid at the instant of failure, but with benefit amount changing only at the end of the interval. In this case we have $b_t = \lfloor t+1 \rfloor$, the greatest integer less than $t+1$. Thus the benefit is 1 for failure at time t for

$0 < t \le 1, 2$ for failure at time t for $1 < t \le 2,$ and so on. The APV in this case is given by

$$(I\overline{A})_x = \int_0^\infty \lfloor t+1 \rfloor \cdot v^t \cdot {}_t p_x \mu_{x+t} \; dt. \tag{7.56}$$

For n-year increasing term insurance we have

$$(\overline{I}\,\overline{A})^1_{x:\overline{n}|} = \int_0^n t \cdot v^t \cdot {}_t p_x \mu_{x+t} \; dt \tag{7.57}$$

in the fully continuous model and

$$(I\overline{A})^1_{x:\overline{n}|} = \int_0^n \lfloor t+1 \rfloor \cdot v^t \cdot {}_t p_x \mu_{x+t} \; dt \tag{7.58}$$

in the piece-wise continuous model. For n-year decreasing term insurance the formulas are

$$(\overline{D}\overline{A})^1_{x:\overline{n}|} = \int_0^n (n-t) \cdot v^t \cdot {}_t p_x \mu_{x+t} \; dt \tag{7.59}$$

in the fully continuous case and

$$(D\overline{A})^1_{x:\overline{n}|} = \int_0^n \lfloor n+1-t \rfloor \cdot v^t \cdot {}_t p_x \mu_{x+t} \; dt \tag{7.60}$$

in the piece-wise continuous case.

7.5 CONTINUOUS AND m^{thly} FUNCTIONS APPROXIMATED FROM THE LIFE TABLE

For many contingent models, including insurance models dependent on human survival, a mathematically convenient parametric survival model that sufficiently closely represents the human survival distribution might not be known to us. Consequently, we will adopt an approach of evaluating continuous contingent model functions from the discrete life table by imposing an additional assumption on the discrete model.

Recall the discussion of the *uniform distribution of deaths* (UDD) assumption defined and illustrated in Section 6.6.1. In this section we will now show how to evaluate continuous and m^{thly} functions from the discrete life table by imposing the UDD assumption on each separate annual age interval $(x, x+1)$.

7.5.1 CONTINUOUS CONTINGENT PAYMENT MODELS

Consider first the n-year term insurance model with immediate payment of claims, with expected value given by Exercise 7-16(b), and consider the special case with $n=1$. The expected value of the present value random variable $\overline{Z}^1_{x:\overline{1}|}$ is denoted by $\overline{A}^1_{x:\overline{1}|}$, and is given by

$$\overline{A}^1_{x:\overline{1}|} = \int_0^1 v^t \cdot {}_tp_x\mu_{x+t}\,dt. \tag{7.61}$$

From Equation (6.38) we know that ${}_tp_x\mu_{x+t} = q_x$ under the UDD assumption over the interval $(x,x+1)$. Substituting into Equation (7.61) we have

$$\overline{A}^1_{x:\overline{1}|} = q_x\int_0^1 v^t\,dt, \tag{7.62}$$

since q_x is constant with respect to t. The integral evaluates to

$$-\frac{v^t}{\delta}\Big|_0^1 = \frac{1-v}{\delta} = \frac{d}{\delta} = \frac{iv}{\delta},$$

so Equation (7.62) becomes

$$\overline{A}^1_{x:\overline{1}|} = \frac{i}{\delta}\cdot v\cdot q_x = \frac{i}{\delta}\cdot A^1_{x:\overline{1}|}, \tag{7.63}$$

since

$$v\cdot q_x = v\cdot Pr(K_x^* = 1)$$
$$= E\left[Z^1_{x:\overline{1}|}\right]$$
$$= A^1_{x:\overline{1}|}$$

by Equation (7.8).

The result given by Equation (7.63) is very important, and extends to other contingent payment models. For n-year term insurance in general we have, from Exercise 7-16(b),

$$\overline{A}^1_{x:\overline{n}|} = \int_0^n v^t\cdot {}_tp_x\mu_{x+t}\,dt$$
$$= \sum_{k=0}^{n-1}\int_k^{k+1} v^t\cdot {}_tp_x\mu_{x+t}\,dt$$
$$= \sum_{k=0}^{n-1}\int_0^1 v^{s+k}\cdot {}_{s+k}p_x\mu_{x+s+k}\,ds$$
$$= \sum_{k=0}^{n-1} v^k\cdot {}_kp_x\int_0^1 v^s\cdot {}_sp_{x+k}\mu_{x+k+s}\,ds$$
$$= \sum_{k=0}^{n-1} v^k\cdot {}_kp_x\cdot \overline{A}^1_{x+k:\overline{1}|}. \tag{7.64a}$$

By imposing the UDD assumption on each interval $(x+k,\,x+k+1)$ separately, we have

$$\overline{A}^1_{x+k:\overline{1}|} = \frac{i}{\delta}\cdot A^1_{x+k:\overline{1}|}$$

as given by Equation (7.63). Then Equation (7.64a) becomes

$$\overline{A}^1_{x:\overline{n}|} = \frac{i}{\delta} \sum_{k=0}^{n-1} v^k \cdot {}_kp_x \cdot A^1_{x+k:\overline{1}|}$$

$$= \frac{i}{\delta} \sum_{k=0}^{n-1} v^k \cdot {}_kp_x \cdot v \cdot q_{x+k}$$

$$= \frac{i}{\delta} \sum_{k=0}^{n-1} v^{k+1} \cdot {}_{k|}q_x$$

$$= \frac{i}{\delta} \sum_{k=1}^{n} v^k \cdot {}_{k-1|}q_x$$

$$= \frac{i}{\delta} \sum_{k=1}^{n} v^k \cdot Pr(K_x = k) = \frac{i}{\delta} \cdot A^1_{x:\overline{n}|}, \qquad (7.64b)$$

from Equation (7.8).

Letting $n \to \infty$ in Equation (7.64b) leads immediately to a similar relationship for the continuous whole life model evaluated under UDD, namely

$$\overline{A}_x = \frac{i}{\delta} \cdot A_x. \qquad (7.65)$$

Furthermore, since

$$_n|\overline{A}_x = \overline{A}_x - \overline{A}^1_{x:\overline{n}|}$$

(see Exercise 7-17(c)), then we have

$$_n|\overline{A}_x = \overline{A}_x - \overline{A}^1_{x:\overline{n}|}$$

$$= \frac{i}{\delta} \left(A_x - A^1_{x:\overline{n}|} \right)$$

$$= \frac{i}{\delta} \cdot {}_n|A_x, \qquad (7.66)$$

from Equation (7.16).

Finally, from Equation (7.38b) we have

$$\overline{A}_{x:\overline{n}|} = \overline{A}^1_{x:\overline{n}|} + A_{x:\overline{n}|}^{1} = \frac{i}{\delta} \cdot A^1_{x:\overline{n}|} + A_{x:\overline{n}|}^{1}. \qquad (7.67)$$

(It is important to note that since there is no continuous counterpart to the discrete $A_{x:\overline{n}|}^{1}$, then it is *not* true that $\overline{A}_{x:\overline{n}|} = \frac{i}{\delta} \cdot A_{x:\overline{n}|}$.)

Finally, any of the continuous functions based on the doubled force of interest, such as $^2\overline{A}_x$, can be evaluated from the corresponding discrete function under the UDD assumption as

$$^2\overline{A}_x = \frac{i'}{\delta'} \cdot {}^2A_x = \frac{(1+i)^2 - 1}{2\delta} \cdot {}^2A_x. \tag{7.68}$$

An alternative to using UDD is to simply assume that failure benefits are paid in the middle of the discrete interval used in the life table. In the annual case this suggests that we take

$$\overline{A}_x = (1+i)^{1/2} \cdot A_x, \tag{7.69}$$

since A_x assumes payment at the end of the year. (Another approximation for $\overline{A}_x$ is given in Exercise 8-46(b).)

7.5.2 m^{thly} CONTINGENT PAYMENT MODELS

Our discussion of m^{thly} contingent functions will parallel the discussion of continuous functions in Section 7.5.1. Indeed m^{thly} functions represent a generalization of continuous functions, or, conversely, continuous functions represent a special case of m^{thly} functions, namely the limiting case as $m \to \infty$.

As we did with the continuous models of Section 7.5.1, we begin with the function $A\overset{(m)}{\underset{x:\overline{1}|}{1}}$, the

APV for one-year term insurance with contingent benefit paid at the end of the mth of failure. We have

$$A\overset{(m)}{\underset{x:\overline{1}|}{1}} = \sum_{r=0}^{m-1} v^{(r+1)/m} \cdot {}_{r/m}p_x \cdot {}_{1/m}q_{x+r/m}. \tag{7.70}$$

To evaluate this function under the UDD assumption, we recall from Example 6.9 that

$${}_{r/m}p_x \cdot {}_{1/m}q_{x+r/m} = \frac{1}{m} \cdot q_x.$$

Then Equation (7.70) simplifies to

$$A\overset{(m)}{\underset{x:\overline{1}|}{1}} = \frac{1}{m} \cdot q_x \sum_{r=0}^{m-1} v^{(r+1)/m}$$

$$= q_x \cdot a_{\overline{1}|}^{(m)}$$

$$= \frac{d}{i^{(m)}} \cdot q_x$$

$$= \frac{i}{i^{(m)}} \cdot v \cdot q_x = \frac{i}{i^{(m)}} \cdot A\overset{1}{\underset{x:\overline{1}|}{}}. \tag{7.71}$$

Note the consistency of Equations (7.63) and (7.71), since

$$\overline{A}^1_{x:\overline{1}|} = \lim_{m \to \infty} A^{(m)1}_{x:\overline{1}|} = \lim_{m \to \infty} \frac{i}{i^{(m)}} \cdot A^1_{x:\overline{1}|} = \frac{i}{\delta} \cdot A^1_{x:\overline{1}|}.$$

Then in a manner totally parallel with the continuous cases of Section 7.5.1 we have

$$A^{(m)1}_{x:\overline{n}|} = \frac{i}{i^{(m)}} \cdot A^1_{x:\overline{n}|} \tag{7.72}$$

for n-year term insurance,

$$A^{(m)}_x = \frac{i}{i^{(m)}} \cdot A_x \tag{7.73}$$

for whole life insurance,

$$_n|A^{(m)}_x = \frac{i}{i^{(m)}} \cdot {}_n|A_x \tag{7.74}$$

for deferred insurance, and

$$A^{(m)}_{x:\overline{n}|} = \frac{i}{i^{(m)}} \cdot A^1_{x:\overline{n}|} + A_{x:\frac{1}{n}|} \tag{7.75}$$

for endowment insurance, since only the term insurance component has the m^{thly} nature.

The m^{thly} counterpart to Equation (7.69) would be

$$A^{(m)}_x = (1+i)^{(m-1)/2m} \cdot A_x, \tag{7.76}$$

to reflect the payment being made $\frac{m-1}{2m}$ of a year earlier than the end of the year, on average.

7.6 MULTI-STATE MODEL REPRESENTATION

In Section 5.5 we represented the parametric survival model as a continuous-time Markov Chain, and in Section 6.5 we represented the tabular survival model as a discrete-time Markov Chain. We now return to those representations and express the discrete and continuous contingent payment models of this chapter in the multi-state model context. It is important to note that no new results are introduced here; we will only be expressing various actuarial present values in multi-state model, rather than standard actuarial, notation.

7.6.1 DISCRETE MODELS

The whole life contingent payment model makes a payment at time k if failure occurs in the kth time interval, with probability $_{k-1}p_x \cdot q_{x+k-1}$, for an entity alive at age x at time 0. In the context of our two-state discrete-time Markov model, we say that payment is made at time k if transition from State 1 (survival) to State 2 (failure) occurs in the kth time interval, for an entity known to be in State 1 at age x at time 0. In the notation of Section 6.5, the probability of this is $_{k-1}p_{11}^{(0)} \cdot p_{12}^{(k-1)}$.

There is no existing standardized multi-state model notation for the APV symbol itself, in the case of a payment made upon transition from State i to State j. With standard actuarial notation already established, we see no need to define a second symbol for the same concept.[5] Thus we write

$$A_x = \sum_{k=1}^{\infty} v^k \cdot {_{k-1}p_{11}^{(0)}} \cdot p_{12}^{(k-1)}, \qquad (7.77)$$

where the probability values in Equation (7.77) are understood to be appropriate for an entity age x at time 0.

The general case addresses the APV for a payment made upon the first transition from a specific State i to a specific State j, for a process known to have begun in State h at time 0. If the transition occurs in the kth time interval, with payment at time k, then the process must not have been in State j at time $k-1$. This means that $i \neq j$. For a process that begins in State h at time 0, the probability of being in State i at time $k-1$ is $_{k-1}p_{hi}^{(0)}$, where $i = h$ is possible. The probability of transitioning from State i to State j in the kth time interval is $p_{ij}^{(k-1)}$. Then this APV is given by

$$APV = \sum_{k=1}^{\infty} v^k \cdot {_{k-1}p_{hi}^{(0)}} \cdot p_{ij}^{(k-1)}. \qquad (7.78)$$

Equation (7.77) is a special case of Equation (7.78) with $i = h = 1$ and $j = 2$.

If the payment is made for transition into State j from *any* other state (except State j itself, of course), then the probability of payment at time k is $\sum_{i \neq j} {_{k-1}p_{hi}^{(0)}} \cdot p_{ij}^{(k-1)}$ and the APV is

$$APV = \sum_{k=1}^{\infty} v^k \cdot \left(\sum_{i \neq j} {_{k-1}p_{hi}^{(0)}} \cdot p_{ij}^{(k-1)} \right). \qquad (7.79)$$

The APVs for other discrete contingent payment models developed in Section 7.1, now expressed in multi-state model notation, are considered in Exercise 7-32.

7.6.2 CONTINUOUS MODELS

In the continuous whole life contingent payment model, a payment is made at the precise time of failure. In the multi-state context, we would say that payment is made at the precise time of transition from State 1 to State 2, for an entity known to be in State 1 at age x at time 0.

---

[5] Other texts (see, for example, Dickson, et al. [8] do choose to define special multi-state model APV symbols to correspond to the standardized actuarial ones.

In Section 5.5 we denoted the probability of surviving in State 1 from time 0 to time r by $_r p_{11}^{(0)} = {}_r p_{11}^{*(0)}$, and the force of transition from State 1 to State 2 at time r by $\lambda_{12}(r)$. Then the APV for a continuous whole life contingent payment model is given by

$$\overline{A}_x = \int_0^\infty v^r \cdot {}_r p_{11}^{(0)} \cdot \lambda_{12}(r)\, dr, \tag{7.80}$$

where, as before, the probability and force functions in Equation (7.80) are understood to be appropriate for an entity age x at time 0.

For the general continuous case, consider a payment made at time r for transition into State j from *any* other state. Now the probability of being in State i at time r, for a process known to have begun in State h, is $_r p_{hi}^{(0)}$, and the force of transition to State j at time r is $\lambda_{ij}(r)$. Then the APV is

$$APV = \int_0^\infty v^r \cdot \left(\sum_{i \neq j} {}_r p_{hi}^{(0)} \cdot \lambda_{ij}(r) \right) dr. \tag{7.81}$$

If the payment is made only upon transition from a specific State i to the named State j, then the APV is

$$APV = \int_0^\infty v^r \cdot {}_r p_{hi}^{(0)} \cdot \lambda_{ij}(r)\, dr. \tag{7.82}$$

Equation (7.80) is the special case of Equation (7.82) with $i = h = 1$ and $j = 2$.

APVs for other continuous contingent payment models developed in Section 7.3 are pursued in Exercise 7-33.

7.6.3 EXTENSION TO MODELS WITH VARYING PAYMENTS

The discrete and continuous models considered above can be generalized to those with a payment amount that depends on the interval of failure (in the discrete case) or the precise time of failure (in the continuous case). No new concepts are involved beyond those introduced in Section 7.4. Writing APVs with varying payments in terms of multi-state model notation is pursued in Exercise 7-34.

7.7 MISCELLANEOUS EXAMPLES

In this final section we present several examples to illustrate additional applications of the material presented in the chapter. No new concepts are introduced in these examples; all of the examples can be worked by applying the understanding developed throughout the chapter.

EXAMPLE 7.10

It is instructive to determine the change to a particular actuarial function if the value of one parameter underlying that function is changed. For example, consider the increasing whole life insurance with net single premium given by Equation (7.51). Suppose the NSP for such an insurance issued to (80) is $(IA)_{80} = 4$, based on $q_{80} = .10$ and $v = .925$. Find the value of $(IA)_{80}$ if q_{80} is changed to .20, with all other q_x values unchanged.

SOLUTION

We can write

$$(IA)_{80} = v \cdot q_{80} + v \cdot p_{80} \cdot APV_{81},$$

where APV_{81} is the actuarial present value at age 81 of all future benefits. We are given that

$$4 = (.925)(.10) + (.925)(.90) APV_{81},$$

from which we find

$$APV_{81} = \frac{4 - (.925)(.10)}{(.925)(.90)} = 4.69369.$$

Since only q_{80} is changed, the value of APV_{81} is not affected. Then the revised value of $(IA)_{80}$ is

$$(IA)_{80} = (.925)(.20) + (.925)(.80)(4.69369) = 3.65833. \qquad \square$$

EXAMPLE 7.11

An important application of the results developed for individual contingent payment contracts is to investigate the aggregate outcome for a group of such contracts. Here it is customary to assume independence among the individual risks and employ the normal approximation for the sum of random variables. As an example of this, consider a group of 100 persons, all age x, each of whom contribute an amount k to a fund. A failure benefit of 1000 is paid to each person at the end of the year of failure. What does the amount k need to be in order that the fund will be able to make all the promised benefit payments with 95% probability, given the values $A_x = .06$ and $^2A_x = .01$?

SOLUTION

The initial fund is $100k$. We want the random variable for present value of all benefits to be less than $100k$ with probability .95. We let

$$Z_{Agg} = Z_1 + Z_2 + \cdots + Z_{100}$$

denote the aggregate present value random variable, where Z_i denotes the present value random variable for the ith individual risk. Assuming independence, we have

$$E[Z_{Agg}] = 100 \cdot E[Z_i] = (100)(1000)(.06) = 6000$$

and

$$Var(Z_{Agg}) = 100 \cdot Var(Z_i) = (100)\left[(1000)^2(.01) - ((1000)(.06))^2\right] = 640,000$$

so $SD(Z_{Agg}) = 800$. Then, assuming that Z_{Agg} is approximately normal, we have

$$Pr(Z_{Agg} < 100k) = Pr\left(Z < \frac{100k - 6000}{800}\right) = .95,$$

so

$$\frac{100k - 6000}{800} = 1.645,$$

which solves for $k = 73.16$. ☐

EXAMPLE 7.12

Another interesting variation arises with a contingent payment contract whose benefit amount includes the return of the net single premium itself, with or without interest, along with a fixed benefit amount. For example, suppose a whole life insurance pays a fixed benefit of 1 plus the NSP with interest at $\delta = .08,$ payable at the exact time of failure. Calculate the NSP assuming an exponential distribution for T_x with $\lambda = .04$ and interest at $\delta = .16$. (Note that the interest rate used to find the present value of benefit is not the same as the rate used to accumulate the NSP as a failure benefit.)

SOLUTION

The benefit amount is non-level, so this is a special case of the model represented by Equation (7.54). In this case we have

$$
\begin{aligned}
E[\bar{B}_x] = NSP &= \int_0^\infty b_t \cdot v^t \cdot {}_t p_x \mu_{x+t} \, dt \\
&= \int_0^\infty (1 + NSP \cdot e^{.08t}) \cdot e^{-.16t} \cdot e^{-.04t} (.04) \, dt \\
&= .04 \int_0^\infty e^{-.20t} \, dt + .04 NSP \int_0^\infty e^{-.12t} \, dt \\
&= (.04)\left(\frac{1}{.20}\right) + (.04 NSP)\left(\frac{1}{.12}\right).
\end{aligned}
$$

Solving for NSP we have $NSP\left(1 - \frac{.04}{.12}\right) = \frac{.04}{.20}$, which gives us $NSP = .30$. Note that, without the return-of-premium feature, the NSP would be $\frac{.04}{.20} = .20$, so the return feature increases the NSP by 50%. ☐

7.8 EXERCISES

7.1 Discrete Stochastic Models

7-1 Derive Equation (7.19a).

7-2 Show that the right hand sides of Equations (7.19a) and (7.19b) are equal.

7-3 For the model of Example 7.1, calculate $Cov(Z^1_{x:\overline{3}|}, {}_3|Z_x)$.

7-4 A 2-year discrete term insurance is issued to (x) at interest rate $i = 0$. Given $q_x = .50$ and $Var(Z^1_{x:\overline{2}|}) = .1771$, calculate q_{x+1}.

7-5 A one-year endowment insurance issued to (x) pays b at the end of the year if (x) fails in $(x, x+1]$ and pays e at the end of the year if (x) survives to $x+1$. Let $Z^*_{x:\overline{1}|}$ denote the present value of benefit for this insurance. Show that $Var(Z^*_{x:\overline{1}|}) = v^2(b-e)^2 \cdot p_x \cdot q_x$.

7-6 Show that $A_x = v \cdot q_x + v \cdot p_x \cdot A_{x+1}$.

7-7 Calculate the value of $Var(Z_{51})$, given the following values:

$$A_{51} - A_{50} = .004 \qquad\qquad i = .02$$
$${}^2A_{51} - {}^2A_{50} = .005 \qquad\qquad p_{50} = .98$$

7-8 Let Z_1 denote the present value random variable for a 25-year term insurance of amount 7, and let Z_2 denote the present value random variable for a 10-year term insurance of amount 4 that is deferred for 25 years. Calculate the value of $Var(Z_1 + Z_2)$, given the following values:

$$E[Z_1] = 2.80 \qquad\qquad Var(Z_1) = 5.76$$
$$E[Z_2] = 0.12 \qquad\qquad Var(Z_2) = 0.10$$

7-9 Let $Z = 1000Z_{x:\overline{n}|}$ denote the present value random variable for an n-year endowment insurance of amount 1000. Calculate the value of $Var(Z)$, given the following values:

$$ {}^2A_x = .2196 \qquad\qquad A_{x:\overline{n}|} = .7896$$
$$ {}^2A_{x+n} = .2836 \qquad\qquad {}^2A^{\,1}_{x:\overline{n}|} = .5649$$

7-10   A special ten-year endowment insurance pays 1000 for survival to time 10, or a benefit at the end of the year of failure, whichever occurs first. Let Z_1 denote the present value random variable for this insurance if the failure benefit is $1000 \cdot {}_{10}E_x$, let Z_2 denote the present value random variable if the failure benefit is $750 \cdot {}_{10}E_x$, and let Z_3 denote the present value random variable if the failure benefit is $500 \cdot {}_{10}E_x$. Given also that $A_{x:\overline{10|}} = .57$ and $\frac{E[Z_1]}{E[Z_2]} = 1.005$, calculate the value of $E[Z_3]$.

7.2 Group Deterministic Approach

7-11   Show that $_n|A_x = {}_nE_x \cdot A_{x+n}$.

7-12   Use the group deterministic approach to interpret each of the following expected present value functions as net single premiums.

(a) $A^1_{x:\overline{n|}}$

(b) $_n|A_x$

(c) $A_{x:\overline{n|}}$

7-13   Calculate A_{77}, given that $A_{76} = .800$, $v \cdot p_{76} = .90$, and $i = .03$.

7-14   A special n-year endowment contract, with net single premium of 600, pays 1000 for survival to time n but pays only the net single premium for failure before time n. Given that $A_{x:\overline{n|}} = .80$, find the value of $_nE_x$.

7.3 Continuous Stochastic Models

7-15   A benefit of 50 is paid at the precise time of failure t. The PDF of T_x, the random variable for time of failure, is given by

$$f_x(t) = \begin{cases} \frac{t}{5000} & \text{for } 0 < t \le 100 \\ 0 & \text{otherwise} \end{cases}$$

Find the APV of the benefit using force of interest $\delta = .10$.

7-16   (a) Define random variable $\overline{Z}^1_{x:\overline{n|}}$ by reference to Equation (7.7).

(b) Give expressions for the first and second moments of $\overline{Z}^1_{x:\overline{n|}}$.

7-17 (a) Define random variable $_n|\overline{Z}_x$ by reference to Equation (7.11).

(b) Give expressions for the first and second moments of $_n|\overline{Z}_x$.

(c) Show that $_n|\overline{A}_x + \overline{A}^1_{x:\overline{n}|} = \overline{A}_x$.

7-18 The random variable $_n|\overline{Z}_x$ has a mixed distribution. If the future lifetime random variable T_x has PDF given by $(110-t)^{-1}$, describe the discrete part of the mixed distribution of $_{20}|\overline{Z}_{40}$.

7-19 Calculate the value of $Var(\overline{Z}_{x:\overline{n}|})$, given the following values:

$$E[\overline{Z}^1_{x:\overline{n}|}] = .23 \qquad v^n = .20 \qquad Var(\overline{Z}^1_{x:\overline{n}|}) = .08 \qquad _n p_x = .50$$

7-20 Find an expression for $Var(\overline{Z}_x)$ when the age-at-failure random variable X has an exponential distribution with parameter λ.

7-21 Find an expression for $_n|\overline{A}_x$ when the age-at-failure random variable X has an exponential distribution with parameter λ.

7-22 Let the age-at-failure random variable X have a uniform distribution with $\omega = 110$. Let $f_Z(z)$ denote the PDF of the random variable $\overline{Z}_{40}$. Calculate the value of $f_Z(.80)$, given also that $\delta = .05$.

7-23 Let $M_{T_x}(r)$ denote the moment generating function of the random variable T_x. Show that $\overline{A}_x = M_{T_x}(-\delta)$.

7.4 Contingent Payment Models with Varying Payments

7-24 Let $\overline{B}_x$ denote the present value random variable for a continuously increasing contingent payment contract with benefit $b_t = 1 + .10t$ for failure at time t. Given also that $v^t = (1+.10t)^{-2}$ and the PDF of T_x, the random variable for time of failure, is given by $f_x(t) = .02$ for $0 \le t \le 50$, find the variance of $\overline{B}_x$.

7-25 (a) Show that $(IA)_x = A_x + {}_1E_x \cdot (IA)_{x+1}$.

(b) Calculate the value of $(IA)_{36}$, given the following values:

$$(IA)_{35} = 3.711 \qquad A_{35:\overline{1}|} = .9434 \qquad A_{35} = .1300 \qquad p_{35} = .9964$$

7-26 A student loan of amount 10,000 is amortized over 20 years by continuous payment at $\delta = .08$. The loan is subject to default at constant force of default $\lambda = .01$. A government agency guarantees the outstanding balance of the loan in case of default. Using force of interest .05, calculate the APV of the guarantee.

7-27 A special 10-year endowment contract, with failure benefit paid at the end of the year of failure, has an increasing failure benefit of amount $b_k = (1.06)^{k-1}$ for failure in the kth year and a unit pure endowment benefit paid for survival to time 10. The age-at-failure random variable X is uniformly distributed with $\omega = 100$, and the interest rate is $i = .06$. Let $Z^*_{30:\overline{10}|}$ denote the present value random variable for this contingent contract, issued to a person age 30. Find each of the following.

(a) $Pr[Z^*_{30:\overline{10}|} = (1.06)^{-1}]$

(b) $E[Z^*_{30:\overline{10}|}]$

(c) $Var(Z^*_{30:\overline{10}|})$

7.5 Continuous and m^{thly} Functions Approximated from the Life Table

7-28 Assuming failures are uniformly distributed over each interval $(x, x+1)$, calculate the value of A_{35} given the following values:

$$i = .05 \qquad q_{35} = .01 \qquad \overline{A}_{36} = .185$$

7-29 Assuming failures are uniformly distributed over each interval $(x, x+1)$, calculate the value of $\overline{A}^1_{x:\overline{2}|}$ given the following values:

$$i = .10 \qquad q_x = .05 \qquad q_{x+1} = .08$$

7-30 Assuming failures are uniformly distributed over each interval $(x, x+1)$, calculate the value of ${}^2\overline{A}^1_{x:\overline{2}|}$ given the following values:

$$i = .12 \qquad q_x = .10 \qquad q_{x+1} = .20$$

7-31   Assuming failures are uniformly distributed over each interval $(x, x+1)$, show that

$$\frac{(I\bar{A})_x - (\bar{I}\bar{A})_x}{\bar{A}_x} = \frac{1}{d} - \frac{1}{\delta}.$$

7.6 Multi-State Model Representation

7-32   Using the multi-state model notation defined earlier, give APV formulas for each of the following discrete contingent payment models.

(a) n-year pure endowment

(b) n-year term insurance

(c) n-year deferred insurance

7-33   Using the multi-state model notation defined earlier, give APV formulas for each of the following continuous contingent payment models.

(a) n-year term insurance

(b) n-year deferred insurance

7-34   Using the multi-state model notation defined earlier, give APV formulas for each of the following contingent payment models with varying payments.

(a) The increasing insurance whose APV is given by $(IA)_x$ in standard actuarial notation

(b) The increasing insurance whose APV is given by $(IA)^1_{x:\overline{n}|}$ in standard actuarial notation

(c) The increasing insurance whose APV is given by $(\bar{I}\bar{A})_x$ in standard actuarial notation

(d) The decreasing insurance whose APV is given by $(\bar{D}\bar{A})^1_{x:\overline{n}|}$ in standard actuarial notation

Chapter Eight

Contingent Annuity Models
(Life Annuities)

In this chapter we consider annuity models under which the making of each scheduled payment is *contingent* upon some random event. The reader will note a degree of similarity in notation and terminology with our discussion of interest-only annuities in Chapter 1. In fact, interest-only annuities can be viewed as special cases of contingent annuities where the scheduled payments are made with probability 1. In other words, the making of the payments is not contingent on any probabilistic event.

Generally the random event upon which each payment is contingent is the continued *survival* of a defined entity of interest, such as the continued survival of an identified person. (In this case, contingent annuities are called *life annuities*.) Other examples of contingent annuities could be a sequence of costs incurred (due to lost revenue) as long as a labor strike continues, or a sequence of coupon payments made as long as a particular corporate bond remains in good standing.

Contingent annuities are closely related to the contingent payment models of Chapter 7. In the prior chapter, a *single payment* is made at the time of the *failure* of the entity of interest; in this chapter, a *sequence of payments* is made during the *continued survival* of the entity of interest, up until the failure occurs.

There are many contingent annuity models we wish to present in this chapter, and the reader will need to go over this material several times in order to grasp all the different cases. To help with this sorting task, we will start with an overview of the contents of the chapter.

First, we can separate all contingent annuity models in two groups according to whether the payments in the sequence are level or non-level. Most of our attention will be given to the level payment case, presented in Sections 8.1 - 8.4. Our somewhat abbreviated presentation of the non-level case will all be contained in Section 8.5.

Level payment contingent annuities will be discussed in both discrete and continuous contexts. In the discrete case, we further distinguish between annuities with annual payments and those with payments scheduled more frequently than annual, say m times per year, such as annuities with scheduled (albeit contingent) monthly payments ($m = 12$).

Furthermore, discrete payment annuities, whether annual or m^{thly}, can be of either the immediate type (payments made at ends of payment periods) or the due type (payments made at beginnings of payment periods), as described in Section 1.2.

Within all three categories of discrete annual, discrete m^{thly}, and continuous we will define three different contingent annuity models, namely the whole life, temporary, and deferred whole life models. (The significance of these model names will become clearer as the discussion unfolds.) Furthermore, we will present several different approaches to defining and analyzing these models.

The whole life model, in the annual immediate, annual due, and continuous cases, is presented in Section 8.1, the temporary model, in the same three cases, is presented in Section 8.2, and the deferred whole life model, again in the same three cases, is presented in Section 8.3. (Recall that continuous annuity models do not have both immediate and due cases.) The m^{thly} case, both immediate and due, is presented in Section 8.4.

8.1 WHOLE LIFE ANNUITY MODELS

In nearly all cases, discrete contingent annuity models are evaluated from a discrete survival model (life table), such as that presented in Chapter 6 of this text. Here we assume that time is measured in years in the life table, so a contingent annuity with annual payments can be directly evaluated from the table. In this section we will present the whole life model, in each of the immediate, due, and continuous cases, and will analyze the model from several perspectives.

8.1.1 THE IMMEDIATE CASE

We begin by recalling the n-year pure endowment model with present value random variable $Z_{x:\overline{n}|}^{1}$ defined by Equation (7.20), and expected present value (or actuarial present value) denoted by $A_{x:\overline{n}|}^{1}$ or $_nE_x$. Suppose we have a status with identifying characteristic (x) as of time 0, such as a person alive at time 0 at age x, and a sequence of unit payments scheduled to be made at the end of each year *as long as the status continues to survive*. Such a model is called a *whole life* contingent immediate annuity model, since the payment sequence will continue for the *whole of life* of the status of interest. It is easy to see that this arrangement is merely a series of t-year pure endowments for $t = 1, 2, \ldots$. If we let Y_x denote the present value random variable for this model, then we have

$$Y_x = \sum_{t=1}^{\infty} Z_{x:\overline{t}|}^{1}. \tag{8.1}$$

The expected value of the present value random variable Y_x is denoted a_x, so we have

$$a_x = E[Y_x] = \sum_{t=1}^{\infty} E\left[Z_{x:\overline{t}|}^{1} \right] = \sum_{t=1}^{\infty} A_{x:\overline{t}|}^{1} = \sum_{t=1}^{\infty} {}_tE_x, \tag{8.2a}$$

by using results and notation developed in Chapter 7. Furthermore, since $Pr(K_x^* > t) = {}_tp_x$, then from Equation (7.21) we have $A_{x:\overline{t}|}^{1} = v^t \cdot {}_tp_x$ so that Equation (8.2a) can also be written as

$$a_x = \sum_{t=1}^{\infty} v^t \cdot {}_tp_x. \tag{8.2b}$$

As in the case of single contingent payment models in Chapter 7, we refer to the expected value of the contingent annuity present value random variable as, interchangeably, the expected present value (EPV), or the actuarial present value (APV), or the net single premium (NSP).

This model has a group deterministic interpretation, similar to that presented for the whole life insurance in Section 7.2. Suppose ℓ_x persons each purchase a whole life annuity with unit payments at the end of each year, with each person paying amount X to purchase the annuity. Then we have an initial fund of $X \cdot \ell_x$ dollars at time 0. According to the life table model, ℓ_{x+1} persons survive to the end of the first year, ℓ_{x+2} survive to the end of the second year, and so on, until there are no more survivors. Then the sequence $\ell_{x+1}, \ell_{x+2}, \dots$ represents the sequence of payments made under the annuities in total. This is illustrated in the following figure.

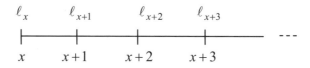

FIGURE 8.1

The total present value at time 0 (age x) of all annuity payments made is

$$v \cdot \ell_{x+1} + v^2 \cdot \ell_{x+2} + v^3 \cdot \ell_{x+3} + \cdots,$$

which is set equal to the initial fund. That is,

$$X \cdot \ell_x \;=\; v \cdot \ell_{x+1} + v^2 \cdot \ell_{x+2} + v^3 \cdot \ell_{x+3} + \cdots. \tag{8.3}$$

If we divide both sides of Equation (8.3) by ℓ_x we obtain

$$X \;=\; v \cdot \frac{\ell_{x+1}}{\ell_x} + v^2 \cdot \frac{\ell_{x+2}}{\ell_x} + v^3 \cdot \frac{\ell_{x+3}}{\ell_x} + \cdots, \tag{8.4a}$$

where X represents each person's share of the total present value of all annuity payments made. Thus X is the *net single premium* that each of the ℓ_x persons should pay to purchase the annuity. But the general term in Equation (8.4a), namely $\frac{\ell_{x+t}}{\ell_x}$, is simply $_tp_x$, the probability of survival to time t. Thus we have

$$X \;=\; \sum_{t=1}^{\infty} v^t \cdot {_tp_x}, \tag{8.4b}$$

already identified as the EPV of the annuity by Equation (8.2b). Thus we have established that the expected value of the present value random variable (EPV) and the net single premium (NSP) are the same.

EXAMPLE 8.1

Using the annual interest rate $i = .05$ and the life table values $\ell_{95} = 100$, $\ell_{96} = 70$, $\ell_{97} = 40$, $\ell_{98} = 20$, $\ell_{99} = 4$, and $\ell_{100} = 0$, determine the value of a_{95}.

SOLUTION

Using either the EPV approach of Equation (8.2b) or the NSP approach of Equation (8.4a) we have

$$a_{95} = \left(\frac{1}{1.05}\right)\left(\frac{70}{100}\right) + \left(\frac{1}{1.05}\right)^2\left(\frac{40}{100}\right) + \left(\frac{1}{1.05}\right)^3\left(\frac{20}{100}\right) + \left(\frac{1}{1.05}\right)^4\left(\frac{4}{100}\right)$$

$$= .6667 + .3628 + .1728 + .0329 = 1.2352. \qquad \square$$

There is another, very important, random variable approach to understanding the whole life contingent annuity. If the status of interest fails in the kth time interval, denoted by the event $K_x^* = k$, then exactly $k-1$ annuity payments are made, since no payment would be made at time k (age $x+k$). This is represented in the following diagram.

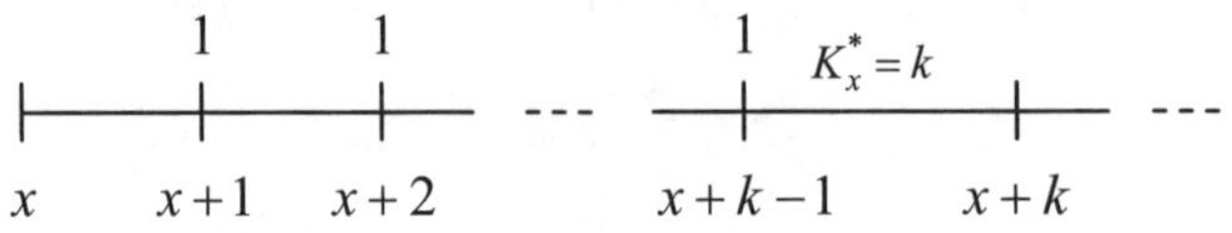

FIGURE 8.2

Thus if $K_x^* = k$ the present value of the annuity is $a_{\overline{k-1}|}$, so, in general, the present value is a random variable denoted by $Y_x = a_{\overline{K_x^*-1}|}$.[1] The expected value of this present value random variable is then

$$E[Y_x] = E\left[a_{\overline{K_x^*-1}|}\right] = \sum_{k=1}^{\infty} a_{\overline{k-1}|} \cdot Pr(K_x^* = k) = \sum_{k=1}^{\infty} \frac{1-v^{k-1}}{i} \cdot {}_{k-1|}q_x, \qquad (8.5a)$$

using Equation (1.13) for $a_{\overline{k-1}|}$ and the actuarial notation ${}_{k-1|}q_x$ to represent $Pr(K_x^* = k)$. Then by using ${}_{k-1|}q_x = {}_{k-1}p_x - {}_kp_x$ (see Example 6.5), we have

$$E[Y_x] = \frac{1}{i}\sum_{k=1}^{\infty}\left[{}_{k-1|}q_x - v^{k-1}({}_{k-1}p_x - {}_kp_x)\right]$$

$$= \frac{1}{i}\left[\sum_{k=1}^{\infty} {}_{k-1|}q_x - \sum_{k=1}^{\infty} v^{k-1} \cdot {}_{k-1}p_x + (1+i)\sum_{k=1}^{\infty} v^k \cdot {}_kp_x\right].$$

---

[1] In terms of the curtate-duration-at-failure random variable K_x, we would have $Y_x = a_{\overline{K_x}|}$.

(Note that we want the third summand to involve v^k, so we must factor $1+i=v^{-1}$ outside the summation.) The first summation clearly evaluates to 1 (since (x) must fail sometime), the second summation evaluates to $1+a_x$ (from Equation (8.2b) and the fact that $_0p_x=1$), and the third summation evaluates to $(1+i)a_x$, again from Equation (8.2b). Thus we have

$$E[Y_x] = \frac{1}{i}\left[1-(1+a_x)+(1+i)a_x\right] = a_x, \tag{8.5b}$$

as already established by Equation (8.2a).

This random variable approach to the whole life contingent annuity is particularly useful in finding higher moments of the present value random variable Y_x. First we note that

$$Y_x = a_{\overline{K_x^*-1}|} = \frac{1}{i}\left[1-v^{K_x^*-1}\right] = \frac{1}{i}\left[1-(1+i)\cdot v^{K_x^*}\right] = \frac{1}{i}\left[1-(1+i)\cdot Z_x\right], \tag{8.6}$$

where $Z_x = v^{K_x^*}$ is defined by Equation (7.1b). We can now use this relationship between the random variables Y_x and Z_x to find the variance of Y_x. We have

$$Var(Y_x) = Var\left[\frac{1-(1+i)\cdot Z_x}{i}\right] = \frac{(1+i)^2 \cdot Var(Z_x)}{i^2} = \frac{Var(Z_x)}{d^2}, \tag{8.7a}$$

since $d=\frac{i}{1+i}$. Then using Equation (7.5) for $Var(Z_x)$ we have

$$Var(Y_x) = \frac{{}^2A_x - A_x^2}{d^2}, \tag{8.7b}$$

where A_x and ${}^2A_x$ are defined in Section 7.1.2.

The relationship between Y_x and Z_x can also be used to develop other relationships between insurance and annuity functions, as shown in the following example and also in the exercises.

EXAMPLE 8.2

Show that $A_x = v - d \cdot a_x$.

SOLUTION

Taking the expectation in Equation (8.6) we obtain

$$a_x = E[Y_x] = E\left[\frac{1-(1+i)\cdot Z_x}{i}\right] = \frac{1-(1+i)\cdot A_x}{i} = \frac{v-A_x}{d}.$$

Rearrangement yields the requested identity. ◻

EXAMPLE 8.3

Using the values given in Example 8.1, find $Var(Y_{95})$.

SOLUTION

Recall that $\delta' = 2\delta$ implies $i' = (1+i)^2 - 1$, so with $i = .05$ we have $i' = (1.05)^2 - 1 = .1025$. Furthermore, $v' = (1+i')^{-1} = (1.05)^{-2} = .90702$ and $d' = i'v' = .09297$. Calculating the annuity APV at rate i' we find

$$
{}^2 a_{95} = \left(\frac{1}{1.1025}\right)\left(\frac{70}{100}\right) + \left(\frac{1}{1.1025}\right)^2\left(\frac{40}{100}\right) + \left(\frac{1}{1.1025}\right)^3\left(\frac{20}{100}\right) + \left(\frac{1}{1.1025}\right)^4\left(\frac{4}{100}\right)\,{}^2
$$

$$
= .6349 + .3291 + .1492 + .0271 = 1.1403.
$$

Using the identity derived in Example 8.2 and the value of a_{95} from Example 8.1, we find

$$
A_{95} = (1.05)^{-1} - \left(\frac{.05}{1.05}\right)(1.2352) = .8936
$$

and using the values developed above we find

$$
{}^2 A_{95} = (1.1025)^{-1} - \left(\frac{.1025}{1.1025}\right)(1.1403) = .8010.
$$

Finally we find

$$
Var(Y_{95}) = \frac{{}^2 A_{95} - A_{95}{}^2}{d^2} = \frac{.8010 - (.8936)^2}{\left(\frac{.05}{1.05}\right)^2} = 1.0933. \qquad \square
$$

8.1.2 THE DUE CASE

In this section we will essentially repeat the presentation given in Section 8.1.1, but this time with contingent payments made at the *beginning* of each year instead of the end of each year. Recall from Chapter 1 that such annuities are called *annuities-due*. Because the mathematics is totally parallel to that used in Section 8.1.1, we can present it here in a more streamlined fashion.

In the annuity-due case, the whole life contingent annuity model is the same as in the immediate case, except that payments are scheduled at the beginning of each year instead of the end. Since the status (x) is known to exist at time 0, then the payment scheduled at time 0 (age x) is certain to be made. Thus we have the same series of contingent payments as in the immediate

---

[2] The symbol ${}^2 a_x$ denotes the APV calculated at double the force of interest, so that ${}^2 a_x$ is related to a_x in the same manner as ${}^2 A_x$ is related to A_x. Note, however, that ${}^2 A_x$ is also the second moment of Z_x, but ${}^2 a_x$ is *not* the second moment of Y_x.

case, plus the certain payment of 1 at time 0. If we let $\ddot{Y}_x$ denote the present value random variable in the annuity-due case, then we have

$$\ddot{Y}_x = 1 + Y_x = 1 + \sum_{t=1}^{\infty} Z_{x:t|}^{\;1}. \qquad (8.8)$$

Then the expected value of $\ddot{Y}_x$, denoted $\ddot{a}_x$, is easily found as

$$\begin{aligned} \ddot{a}_x &= E[\ddot{Y}_x] = 1 + E[Y_x] \\ &= 1 + \sum_{t=1}^{\infty} {}_tE_x \\ &= \sum_{t=0}^{\infty} {}_tE_x \\ &= \sum_{t=0}^{\infty} v^t \cdot {}_tp_x, \end{aligned} \qquad (8.9)$$

where we note that ${}_0E_x = v^0 \cdot {}_0p_x = 1$. Furthermore, since $E[Y_x] = a_x$ we have the important relationship

$$\ddot{a}_x = a_x + 1. \qquad (8.10)$$

Again we note that $\ddot{a}_x = E[\ddot{Y}_x]$ is called the EPV or APV or NSP for the whole life contingent annuity-due.

The group deterministic interpretation is parallel to that in the immediate case, except that there will be a payment of ℓ_x dollars at time 0 (age x) itself. Thus we would modify Equation (8.3) to read

$$X \cdot \ell_x = \ell_x + v \cdot \ell_{x+1} + v^2 \cdot \ell_{x+2} + \cdots \qquad (8.11)$$

and Equation (8.4a) to read

$$X = \frac{\ell_x}{\ell_x} + v \cdot \frac{\ell_{x+1}}{\ell_x} + v^2 \cdot \frac{\ell_{x+2}}{\ell_x} + \cdots. \qquad (8.12a)$$

Substituting ${}_tp_x$ for $\frac{\ell_{x+t}}{\ell_x}$, for $t = 1, 2, \ldots$, and $v^0 \cdot {}_0p_x = 1$ for $\frac{\ell_x}{\ell_x}$, we reach

$$X = \sum_{t=0}^{\infty} v^t \cdot {}_tp_x, \qquad (8.12b)$$

showing again that the NSP and the EPV are the same.

With respect to the random variable approach in the case of the annuity-due, we note that if failure occurs in the kth time interval, as indicated by the event $K_x^* = k$, then exactly k annuity payments are made since a payment is made at the beginning of the kth year itself (at age $x+k-1$). This is illustrated in the following diagram.

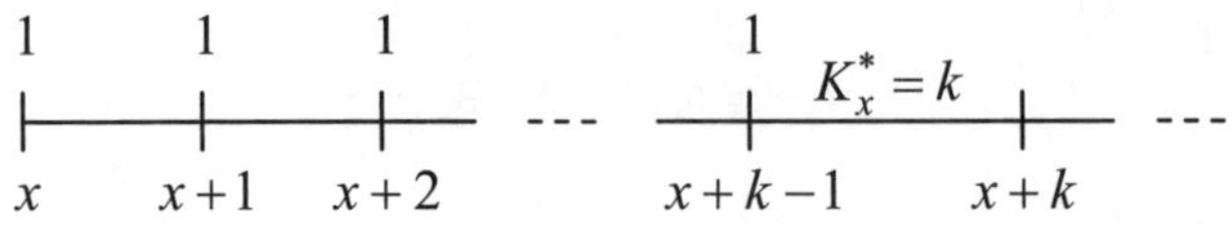

FIGURE 8.3

Then, in general, the present value is a random variable denoted by

$$\ddot{Y}_x = \ddot{a}_{\overline{K_x^*}|} = \frac{1-v^{K_x^*}}{d}, \qquad (8.13)$$

with expected value given by

$$E[\ddot{Y}_x] = E\left[\ddot{a}_{\overline{K_x^*}|}\right] = \sum_{k=1}^{\infty} \ddot{a}_{\overline{k}|} \cdot Pr(K_x^*=k). \qquad (8.14)$$

In steps parallel to those taken in Section 8.1.1 to show that the right side of Equation (8.5a) reduced to a_x, we can similarly show that the right side of Equation (8.14) reduces to $\ddot{a}_x$. The details are left to the reader as Exercise 8-9.

Since $\ddot{Y}_x = 1+Y_x$, it follows immediately that

$$Var(\ddot{Y}_x) = Var(Y_x) = \frac{Var(Z_x)}{d^2} = \frac{{}^2A_x - A_x^2}{d^2}, \qquad (8.15)$$

as established by Equation (8.7b).

EXAMPLE 8.4

Use Equation (8.13) to derive the useful relationship $A_x = 1 - d \cdot \ddot{a}_x$.

SOLUTION

Equation (8.13) can be rearranged as

$$v^{K_x^*} = Z_x = 1 - d \cdot \ddot{Y}_x.$$

Taking the expectation yields the desired relationship. ❑

---

[3] In terms of the curtate-duration-at-failure random variable K_x, we would have $\ddot{Y}_x = \ddot{a}_{\overline{K_x+1}|}$.

8.1.3 THE CONTINUOUS CASE

In this section we return to the abstract notion of continuous payment, introduced in Section 1.2.3 in the case of interest-only annuities. Although continuous payment annuities cannot exist in practice, there is some theoretical value in studying them. Furthermore, continuous annuities might be considered good approximations to annuities payable very frequently, such as weekly or even monthly.

For the continuous case, we return to the future lifetime random variable T_x, defined in Section 7.3.1, in place of the time interval of failure random variable K_x^* used thus far in this chapter. If failure occurs at precise time t, which is measured in years and denoted by the event $T_x = t$, for the status of interest with identifying characteristic (x) at time 0, then continuous annuity payment (at an annual rate of 1 unit of money) will be made for exactly t years. The present value of this continuous annuity is $\bar{a}_{\overline{t}|}$, so, in general, the present value is a random variable which we denote by

$$\bar{Y}_x = \bar{a}_{\overline{T_x}|} = \frac{1 - v^{T_x}}{\delta}. \tag{8.16}$$

The expected value of this present value random variable, denoted $\bar{a}_x$, is given by

$$\bar{a}_x = E[\bar{Y}_x] = E\left[\bar{a}_{\overline{T_x}|}\right] = \int_0^\infty \bar{a}_{\overline{t}|} \cdot f_x(t)\, dt, \tag{8.17a}$$

where $f_x(t)$ is the probability density function of the random variable T_x. Recall from Section 5.3 that this PDF is given by $f_x(t) = {}_t p_x \cdot \mu_{x+t}$. (See Equation 5.46.) Then we can write Equation (8.17a) as

$$\bar{a}_x = \int_0^\infty \bar{a}_{\overline{t}|} \cdot {}_t p_x \mu_{x+t}\, dt. \tag{8.17b}$$

We evaluate the integral using integration by parts to obtain

$$\int_0^\infty \bar{a}_{\overline{t}|} \left| \begin{array}{c} {}_t p_x \mu_{x+t}\, dt \\ \hline v^t\, dt \end{array} \right| \begin{array}{c} \\ -{}_t p_x \end{array} = -\bar{a}_{\overline{t}|} \cdot {}_t p_x \bigg|_0^\infty + \int_0^\infty v^t \cdot {}_t p_x\, dt = \int_0^\infty v^t \cdot {}_t p_x\, dt,$$

since $\bar{a}_{\overline{t}|} \cdot {}_t p_x \big|_0^\infty$ is 0 at both the upper and lower limits. Thus we have

$$\bar{a}_x = \int_0^\infty v^t \cdot {}_t p_x\, dt, \tag{8.17c}$$

a convenient form for evaluating $\bar{a}_x$ from some parametric survival models with known conditional survival function ${}_t p_x = \frac{S_0(x+t)}{S_0(x)}$. This is illustrated in the following example.

EXAMPLE 8.5

Evaluate $\bar{a}_x$ from an exponential survival model.

SOLUTION

We know that $_t p_x = e^{-\mu t}$ under an exponential survival model. Furthermore we know that $v^t = e^{-\delta t}$, so we have

$$\bar{a}_x = \int_0^\infty e^{-\delta t} \cdot e^{-\mu t}\, dt = \frac{e^{-(\mu+\delta)t}}{-(\mu+\delta)}\bigg|_0^\infty = \frac{1}{\mu+\delta}. \qquad \square$$

In most practical cases we will not have a convenient parametric survival model from which to evaluate $\bar{a}_x$. Instead it will be evaluated approximately from a discrete survival model in life table form. We will explore this in Section 8.4.4 and the exercises.

Returning to the random variable $\bar{Y}_x$, we observe that it is closely related to the random variable $\bar{Z}_x = v^{T_x}$ defined by Equation (7.34). We have

$$\bar{Y}_x = \bar{a}_{\overline{T_x}|} = \frac{1-v^{T_x}}{\delta} = \frac{1-\bar{Z}_x}{\delta}, \qquad (8.18a)$$

which we can also write as

$$\bar{Z}_x + \delta \cdot \bar{Y}_x = 1. \qquad (8.18b)$$

Equation (8.18a) enables us to easily find the variance of $\bar{Y}_x$ as

$$Var(\bar{Y}_x) = Var\left(\frac{1-\bar{Z}_x}{\delta}\right) = \frac{Var(\bar{Z}_x)}{\delta^2} = \frac{^2\bar{A}_x - \bar{A}_x^{\,2}}{\delta^2} \qquad (8.19)$$

from Equation (7.37).

The relationship between $\bar{Y}_x$ and $\bar{Z}_x$ can be used to develop other relationships between continuous insurance and annuity functions, which will be pursued in the exercises.

8.2 TEMPORARY ANNUITY MODELS

As the name implies, temporary contingent annuities are payable as long as the status of interest continues to survive, but not beyond a predetermined temporary period such as n years.

8.2.1 THE IMMEDIATE CASE

The *immediate n-year temporary annuity*, payable to a status with identifying characteristic (x) at time 0, will make a payment at the end of each year for n years at the most, provided the status continues to survive. If we let $Y_{x:\overline{n}|}$ denote the present value random variable for this model, then in terms of a series of t-year pure endowments we have

$$Y_{x:\overline{n}|} = \sum_{t=1}^{n} Z_{x:\overline{t}|}^{1} . \tag{8.20}$$

The expected value of this present value random variable (EPV) is denoted $a_{x:\overline{n}|}$, and is given by

$$a_{x:\overline{n}|} = E\left[Y_{x:\overline{n}|}\right]$$

$$= \sum_{t=1}^{n} E\left[Z_{x:\overline{t}|}^{1}\right]$$

$$= \sum_{t=1}^{n} A_{x:\overline{t}|}^{1} = \sum_{t=1}^{n} {}_{t}E_{x} = \sum_{t=1}^{n} v^{t} \cdot {}_{t}p_{x}, \tag{8.21}$$

using results developed earlier in the text.

The group deterministic interpretation for the temporary immediate annuity is the same as that presented for the whole life immediate annuity in Section 8.1.1, except that all series are finite with final term involving ℓ_{x+n}. The derivation is left to the reader as Exercise 8-20.

To analyze the random variable approach to the temporary immediate annuity, consider the following diagram.

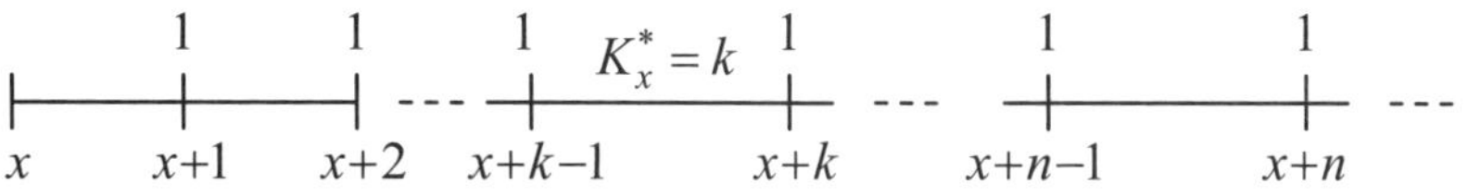

FIGURE 8.4

If failure occurs in the kth time interval, where $k \leq n$, then $k-1$ payments are made, with the last payment made at the end of the interval preceding the interval of failure, so the present value of payments will be $a_{\overline{k-1}|}$. But if failure occurs after age $x+n$, so that $K_{x}^{*} > n$, then n payments will be made and the present value of payments will be $a_{\overline{n}|}$. Therefore the present value random variable $Y_{x:\overline{n}|}$ is defined as

$$Y_{x:\overline{n}|} = \begin{cases} a_{\overline{K_{x}^{*}-1}|} & \text{for } K_{x}^{*} \leq n \\ a_{\overline{n}|} & \text{for } K_{x}^{*} > n \end{cases}, \tag{8.22}$$

with expected value given by

$$E\left[Y_{x:\overline{n}|}\right] = \sum_{k=1}^{n} a_{\overline{k-1}|} \cdot Pr(K_{x}^{*} = k) + \sum_{k=n+1}^{\infty} a_{\overline{n}|} \cdot Pr(K_{x}^{*} = k). \tag{8.23}$$

As we did for the whole life model in Section 8.1.1, we now want to show that the right side of Equation (8.23) reduces to $a_{x:\overline{n}|}$, as defined by Equation (8.21). The details are left to the reader as Exercise 8-21.

Finding the variance of $Y_{\overline{x:n}|}$ directly from its definition is a bit of a challenge. Consequently we defer this task to Section 8.2.2.

Recall from Chapter 1 that the n-payment immediate interest-only annuity has present value given by $a_{\overline{n}|}$ and accumulated value given by $s_{\overline{n}|} = a_{\overline{n}|} \cdot (1+i)^n$ (see Equation (1.15b)). In contingent immediate annuities we have the analogous concept of the *actuarial accumulated value* (AAV), which is denoted by $s_{x:\overline{n}|}$ and is related to the actuarial present value (APV) $a_{x:\overline{n}|}$ by

$$s_{x:\overline{n}|} = a_{x:\overline{n}|} \cdot \frac{1}{{}_nE_x} = a_{x:\overline{n}|} \cdot \frac{1}{v^n {}_nP_x} = a_{x:\overline{n}|} \cdot \frac{(1+i)^n \cdot \ell_x}{\ell_{x+n}}. \tag{8.24}$$

To get some understanding of what $s_{x:\overline{n}|}$ represents, we will make use of our group deterministic interpretation. Consider the following diagram, where each ℓ_{x+t} value represents the number of survivors at age $x+t$.

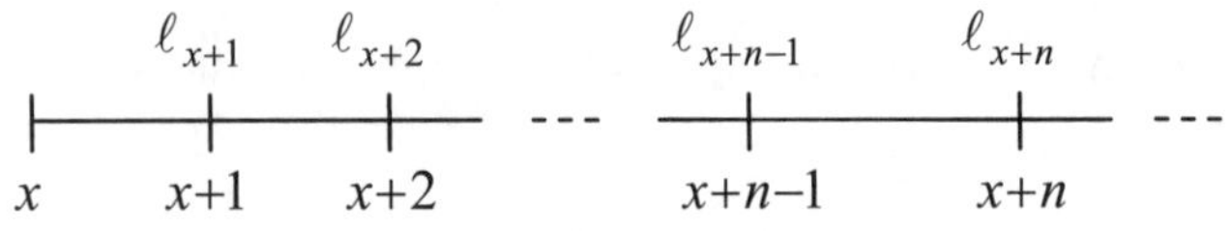

FIGURE 8.5

Suppose each of the ℓ_{x+1} survivors deposits one unit of money in a fund at time $t=1$, each of the ℓ_{x+2} survivors do the same at time $t=2$, and so on, with each of the ℓ_{x+n} survivors doing the same at time $t=n$. Suppose the fund accumulates at compound interest rate i, and the total accumulated fund is then distributed equally among the ℓ_{x+n} survivors at time n. The share of each of the ℓ_{x+n} survivors would then be

$$
\begin{aligned}
X &= \frac{\ell_{x+1}(1+i)^{n-1} + \ell_{x+2}(1+i)^{n-2} + \cdots + \ell_{x+n}}{\ell_{x+n}} \\[2mm]
&= \frac{(1+i)^n \cdot \ell_x}{\ell_{x+n}} \left[\frac{\ell_{x+1}(1+i)^{n-1} + \ell_{x+2}(1+i)^{n-2} + \cdots + \ell_{x+n}}{(1+i)^n \cdot \ell_x} \right] \\[2mm]
&= \frac{(1+i)^n \cdot \ell_x}{\ell_{x+n}} \left[\frac{v \cdot \ell_{x+1} + v^2 \cdot \ell_{x+2} + \cdots + v^n \cdot \ell_{x+n}}{\ell_x} \right] \\[2mm]
&= \frac{(1+i)^n \cdot \ell_x}{\ell_{x+n}} \left[v \cdot p_x + v^2 \cdot {}_2p_x + \cdots + v^n \cdot {}_np_x \right] = \frac{(1+i)^n \cdot \ell_x}{\ell_{x+n}} \cdot a_{x:\overline{n}|},
\end{aligned}
$$

from Equation (8.21). This establishes Equation (8.24).

EXAMPLE 8.6

An investor wishes to purchase a 10-year corporate bond with annual coupons of $40.00 each. The investor estimates that each year there is a 2% chance that the bond will default and no further coupons would be paid. At a yield rate of $i = .06$, find the expected present value of the coupons.

SOLUTION

If the coupons were certain to be paid, the present value would be $40a_{\overline{10}|.06} = 294.40$. By introducing the default consideration, we now have a 10-year temporary contingent annuity with probability of survival to time t given by $_tp_x = (.98)^t$. Then the expected present value of the coupons is

$$EPV = 40\sum_{t=1}^{10} v^t \cdot {}_tp_x = 40\sum_{t=1}^{10}\left(\frac{.98}{1.06}\right)^t = 40\left(\frac{.98}{1.06}\right)\left[\frac{1-\left(\frac{.98}{1.06}\right)^{10}}{1-\left(\frac{.98}{1.06}\right)}\right] = 266.44. \qquad \square$$

8.2.2 THE DUE CASE

If contingent payments are made at the beginning of each year instead of the end, but for n years at the most and contingent on the continued survival of (x), then we have the *n-year temporary annuity-due* model. It can be analyzed in a manner totally parallel to the immediate annuity case.

The present value random variable is denoted $\ddot{Y}_{x:\overline{n}|}$ and is given as a series of pure endowments by

$$\ddot{Y}_{x:\overline{n}|} = \sum_{t=0}^{n-1} Z_{x:\overline{t}|}^{\,1}. \tag{8.25}$$

The expected value of $\ddot{Y}_{x:\overline{n}|}$, denoted $\ddot{a}_{x:\overline{n}|}$, is then given by

$$\ddot{a}_{x:\overline{n}|} = E\left[\ddot{Y}_{x:\overline{n}|}\right] = \sum_{t=0}^{n-1} E\left[Z_{x:\overline{t}|}^{\,1}\right]$$

$$= \sum_{t=0}^{n-1} {}_tE_x = \sum_{t=0}^{n-1} v^t \cdot {}_tp_x. \tag{8.26}$$

Comparing Equations (8.20) and (8.25) it is easy to see that $\ddot{Y}_{x:\overline{n}|}$ is related to $Y_{x:\overline{n}|}$ by

$$\ddot{Y}_{x:\overline{n}|} = Y_{x:\overline{n}|} + 1 - Z_{x:\overline{n}|}^{\,1}, \tag{8.27}$$

since $Z_{x:\overline{0}|}^{\,1} = 1$. Then it follows that

$$\ddot{a}_{x:\overline{n}|} = E\left[\ddot{Y}_{x:\overline{n}|}\right] = E\left[Y_{x:\overline{n}|}+1-Z_{x:\overline{n}|}^{\;1}\right] = a_{x:\overline{n}|}+1-\,_{n}E_{x}. \qquad (8.28)$$

(Note the similarity of Equation (8.28) to the interest-only relationship $\ddot{a}_{\overline{n}|} = a_{\overline{n}|}+1-v^{n}$.)

The group deterministic interpretation for the temporary annuity-due is left to the reader as Exercise 8-22.

For the random variable approach in the annuity-due case we have

$$\ddot{Y}_{x:\overline{n}|} = \begin{cases} \ddot{a}_{\overline{K_{x}^{*}|}} & \text{for} \;\; K_{x}^{*} \le n \\ \ddot{a}_{\overline{n}|} & \text{for} \;\; K_{x}^{*} > n \end{cases}, \qquad (8.29a)$$

with expected value given by

$$E\left[\ddot{Y}_{x:\overline{n}|}\right] = \sum_{k=1}^{n} \ddot{a}_{\overline{k}|} \cdot Pr(K_{x}^{*}=k) + \sum_{k=n+1}^{\infty} \ddot{a}_{\overline{n}|} \cdot Pr(K_{x}^{*}=k). \qquad (8.30)$$

As with the temporary immediate annuity case, we can show that the right side of Equation (8.30) reduces to $\ddot{a}_{x:\overline{n}|}$, as defined by Equation (8.26). The details are left as Exercise 8-23.

By writing Equation (8.29a) as

$$\ddot{Y}_{x:\overline{n}|} = \begin{cases} \dfrac{1-v^{K_{x}^{*}}}{d} & \text{for} \;\; K_{x}^{*} \le n \\ \dfrac{1-v^{n}}{d} & \text{for} \;\; K_{x}^{*} > n \end{cases}, \qquad (8.29b)$$

it then follows that

$$\ddot{Y}_{x:\overline{n}|} = \frac{1-Z_{x:\overline{n}|}}{d}, \qquad (8.31)$$

where

$$Z_{x:\overline{n}|} = \begin{cases} v^{K_{x}^{*}} & \text{for} \;\; K_{x}^{*} \le n \\ v^{n} & \text{for} \;\; K_{x}^{*} > n \end{cases}$$

was given by Equation (7.24). Taking the expectation in Equation (8.31) we obtain

$$\ddot{a}_{x:\overline{n}|} = E\left[\ddot{Y}_{x:\overline{n}|}\right] = \frac{1-E\left[Z_{x:\overline{n}|}\right]}{d} = \frac{1-A_{x:\overline{n}|}}{d}, \qquad (8.32a)$$

which is often stated as

$$A_{x:\overline{n}|} = 1-d \cdot \ddot{a}_{x:\overline{n}|}. \qquad (8.32b)$$

Taking the variance in Equation (8.31) we find

$$Var\left(\ddot{Y}_{x:\overline{n}|}\right) = \frac{Var\left(Z_{x:\overline{n}|}\right)}{d^2} = \frac{{}^2A_{x:\overline{n}|} - A_{x:\overline{n}|}^2}{d^2}. \tag{8.33}$$

Returning now to the temporary immediate case, we see that

$$Y_{x:\overline{n}|} = \ddot{Y}_{x:\overline{n+1}|} - 1 \tag{8.34}$$

(see Exercise 8-24), where $Y_{x:\overline{n}|}$ is defined by Equation (8.20) and $\ddot{Y}_{x:\overline{n+1}|}$ is defined by Equation (8.25). Therefore $Var(Y_{x:\overline{n}|}) = Var(\ddot{Y}_{x:\overline{n+1}|})$, so $Var(Y_{x:\overline{n}|})$ can be found from Equation (8.33) with n replaced by $n+1$.

Finally, the actuarial accumulated value in the annuity-due case is denoted by $\ddot{s}_{x:\overline{n}|}$ and is given by

$$\ddot{s}_{x:\overline{n}|} = \ddot{a}_{x:\overline{n}|} \cdot \frac{1}{{}_nE_x} = \frac{(1+i)^n \cdot \ell_x}{\ell_{x+n}} \cdot \ddot{a}_{x:\overline{n}|}. \tag{8.35}$$

The derivation by the group deterministic interpretation is left as Exercise 8-25.

EXAMPLE 8.7

Find the variance of the present value random variable for the 5-year temporary annuity-due model, given the following information:

$$\ddot{a}_{x:\overline{5}|.05} = 4.13038$$

$$\ddot{a}_{x:\overline{5}|.1025} = 3.79209$$

SOLUTION

First we use Equation (8.32b) to calculate

$$A_{x:\overline{5}|} = 1 - \left(\frac{.05}{1.05}\right)(4.13038) = .80331$$

and

$${}^2A_{x:\overline{5}|} = 1 - \left(\frac{.1025}{1.1025}\right)(3.79209) = .64744.$$

Then from Equation (8.33) we find

$$Var\left(\ddot{Y}_{x:\overline{5}|}\right) = \frac{.64744-(.80331)^2}{\left(\frac{.05}{1.05}\right)^2} = .94067.$$ ☐

8.2.3 THE CONTINUOUS CASE

As with the whole life continuous model in Section 8.1.3, we return to the future lifetime random variable T_x in place of the time interval of failure random variable K_x^* used thus far in this section. We consider that annuity payment is made continuously at annual rate 1 up to the time of failure of status (x), but for n years at the most. Then if $T_x = t$, for $t \le n$, the present value of payment is $\overline{a}_{\overline{t}|}$. If $T_x = t$ for $t > n$, then the present value of payment is $\overline{a}_{\overline{n}|}$. Together we have

$$\overline{Y}_{x:\overline{n}|} = \begin{cases} \overline{a}_{\overline{T_x}|} & \text{for } T_x \le n \\ \overline{a}_{\overline{n}|} & \text{for } T_x > n \end{cases}. \tag{8.36}$$

The expected value of the continuous present value random variable, denoted $\overline{a}_{x:\overline{n}|}$, is therefore

$$\overline{a}_{x:\overline{n}|} = E\left[\overline{Y}_{x:\overline{n}|}\right] = \int_0^n \overline{a}_{\overline{t}|} \cdot {}_tp_x\mu_{x+t}\, dt + \overline{a}_{\overline{n}|} \cdot Pr(T_x > n). \tag{8.37a}$$

Substituting $\overline{a}_{\overline{t}|} = (1-v^t)/\delta$ and $Pr(T_x > n) = {}_np_x$, we have

$$\overline{a}_{x:\overline{n}|} = \frac{1}{\delta}\left[\int_0^n (1-v^t) \cdot {}_tp_x\mu_{x+t}\, dt + (1-v^n) \cdot {}_np_x\right]$$

$$= \frac{1}{\delta}\left[{}_np_x - v^n \cdot {}_np_x + \int_0^n {}_tp_x\mu_{x+t}\, dt - \int_0^n v^t \cdot {}_tp_x\mu_{x+t}\, dt\right].$$

The first integral inside the bracket evaluates to

$${}_nq_x = 1 - {}_np_x$$

and the second integral evaluates (using integration by parts) to

$$1 - v^n \cdot {}_np_x - \delta\int_0^n v^t \cdot {}_tp_x\, dt.$$

Substituting we have

$$\overline{a}_{x:\overline{n}|} = \frac{1}{\delta}\left[{}_np_x - v^n \cdot {}_np_x + 1 - {}_np_x - 1 + v^n \cdot {}_np_x + \delta\int_0^n v^t \cdot {}_tp_x\, dt\right] = \int_0^n v^t \cdot {}_tp_x\, dt, \tag{8.37b}$$

a convenient form for $\overline{a}_{x:\overline{n}|}$ that is analogous to Equation (8.17c) for the whole life case.

We recall from Equation (7.38a) and the exercises associated with Section 7.3.3 that

$$\bar{Z}_{x:\overline{n}|} = \bar{Z}^1_{x:\overline{n}|} + Z_{x:\overline{n}|}^{1} = \begin{cases} v^{T_x} & \text{for } T_x \leq n \\ v^n & \text{for } T_x > n \end{cases}.$$

Comparing this with Equation (8.36) for $\bar{Y}_{x:\overline{n}|}$ we observe that

$$\bar{Y}_{x:\overline{n}|} = \frac{1 - \bar{Z}_{x:\overline{n}|}}{\delta}. \tag{8.38}$$

Taking the expectation in Equation (8.38) we obtain

$$\bar{a}_{x:\overline{n}|} = E\left[\bar{Y}_{x:\overline{n}|}\right] = \frac{1 - E\left[\bar{Z}_{x:\overline{n}|}\right]}{\delta} = \frac{1 - \bar{A}_{x:\overline{n}|}}{\delta}, \tag{8.39a}$$

which is often stated as

$$\bar{A}_{x:\overline{n}|} = 1 - \delta \cdot \bar{a}_{x:\overline{n}|}. \tag{8.39b}$$

Taking the variance in Equation (8.38) we find

$$Var\left(\bar{Y}_{x:\overline{n}|}\right) = \frac{Var\left(\bar{Z}_{x:\overline{n}|}\right)}{\delta^2} = \frac{{}^2\bar{A}_{x:\overline{n}|} - \bar{A}_{x:\overline{n}|}^2}{\delta^2}. \tag{8.40}$$

Finally, the actuarial accumulated value in the continuous case is denoted by $\bar{s}_{x:\overline{n}|}$ and is given by

$$\begin{aligned}
\bar{s}_{x:\overline{n}|} &= \bar{a}_{x:\overline{n}|} \cdot \frac{1}{{}_nE_x} \\
&= \frac{(1+i)^n \cdot \ell_x}{\ell_{x+n}} \int_0^n v^t \cdot {}_tp_x \, dt \\
&= \int_0^n (1+i)^{n-t} \cdot \frac{\ell_{x+t}}{\ell_{x+n}} \, dt \\
&= \int_0^n \frac{(1+i)^{n-t}}{{}_{n-t}p_{x+t}} \, dt. \tag{8.41}
\end{aligned}$$

EXAMPLE 8.8

Show that

$$\frac{\partial}{\partial x} \bar{a}_{x:\overline{n}|} = \bar{a}_{x:\overline{n}|}(\mu_x + \delta) - (1 - {}_nE_x).$$

SOLUTION

Working from Equation (8.37b) we have

$$\frac{\partial}{\partial x}\,\bar{a}_{x:\overline{n}|} = \frac{\partial}{\partial x}\int_0^n v^t \cdot {}_t p_x\,dt = \int_0^n v^t \cdot \frac{\partial}{\partial x}\,{}_t p_x\,dt$$

$$= \int_0^n v^t\left[{}_t p_x(\mu_x - \mu_{x+t})\right]dt = \mu_x \cdot \bar{a}_{x:\overline{n}|} - \bar{A}^{1}_{x:\overline{n}|}.$$

Then we use Equation (8.39b) to substitute

$$\bar{A}^{1}_{x:\overline{n}|} = \bar{A}_{x:\overline{n}|} - {}_n E_x = 1 - \delta \cdot \bar{a}_{x:\overline{n}|} - {}_n E_x,$$

obtaining

$$\frac{\partial}{\partial x}\,\bar{a}_{x:\overline{n}|} = \mu_x \cdot \bar{a}_{x:\overline{n}|} - 1 + \delta \cdot \bar{a}_{x:\overline{n}|} + {}_n E_x.$$

Rearrangement yields the desired result. ❑

8.3 DEFERRED WHOLE LIFE ANNUITY MODELS

In this section we consider contingent annuities that make no payments for the first n years, and then make payments in the $(n+1)^{st}$ and subsequent years provided the status (x) has not yet failed. Once begun, payments then continue as long as the status continues to survive. We consider the same three cases of immediate, due, and continuous as in prior sections.

8.3.1 THE IMMEDIATE CASE

Payments under the *immediate n-year deferred whole life annuity* are illustrated in the following diagram.

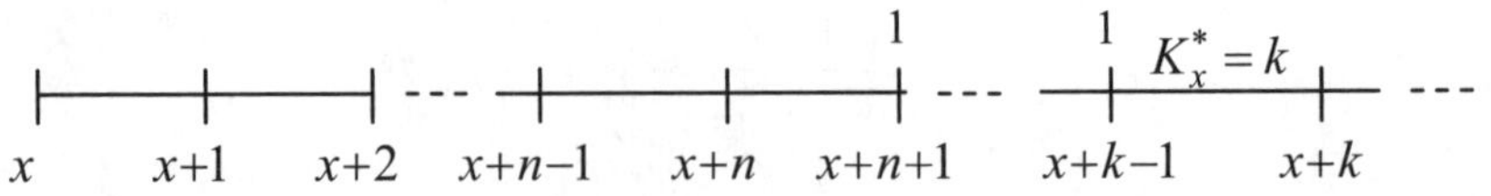

FIGURE 8.6

Note that the first payment is at time $t = n+1$, provided (x) has not yet failed. The payments are deferred for n years, so the first payment is for the $(n+1)^{st}$ year. Since the annuity is immediate, the first payment is therefore at $t = n+1$. The last payment is at the end of the year preceding the year of failure, provided failure does not occur so early that payment never begins at all.

It is clear from Figure 8.6 that the present value random variable for this model, which we denote by ${}_n|Y_x$, is given by

$$_n|Y_x = \sum_{t=n+1}^{\infty} Z_{x:t|}^{\;\;1},$$

(8.42)

in terms of a series of pure endowments. It is also easy to see from Figures 8.4 and 8.6 that the temporary annuity provides payments over the first n years and the deferred annuity provides payments after the first n years, contingent on the survival of (x) in all cases, of course. Together these two models provide the same payments as the whole life model of Section 8.1. Therefore it follows that

$$Y_x = Y_{x:n|} + {}_n|Y_x$$

(8.43a)

or

$$_n|Y_x = Y_x - Y_{x:n|}.$$

(8.43b)

Then the expected present value of the immediate deferred model is

$$_n|a_x = E[_n|Y_x] = E[Y_x - Y_{x:n|}] = a_x - a_{x:n|} = \sum_{t=n+1}^{\infty} v^t \cdot {}_tp_x,$$

(8.44)

using results developed earlier in the chapter.

Using the change of variable $s = t-n$, so that $t = s+n$, we can rewrite Equation (8.44) as

$$_n|a_x = \sum_{s=1}^{\infty} v^{s+n} \cdot {}_{s+n}p_x = v^n \cdot {}_np_x \sum_{s=1}^{\infty} v^s \cdot {}_sp_{x+n} = {}_nE_x \cdot a_{x+n}.$$

(8.45)

EXAMPLE 8.9

Use Equation (8.43b) to show that

$$_n|Y_x = \begin{cases} 0 & \text{for } K_x^* \leq n \\ v^n \cdot a_{\overline{K_x^*-n-1|}} & \text{for } K_x^* > n \end{cases}.$$

(8.46)

SOLUTION

Since $_n|Y_x = Y_x - Y_{x:n|}$, then for $K_x^* \leq n$ we have $_n|Y_x = a_{\overline{K_x^*-1|}} - a_{\overline{K_x^*-1|}} = 0$, and for $K_x^* > n$ we have $_n|Y_x = a_{\overline{K_x^*-1|}} - a_{\overline{n|}} = v^n \cdot a_{\overline{K_x^*-n-1|}}$, as required. ◻

From Equation (8.46) we can write

$$_n|a_x = E[_n|Y_x] = \sum_{k=n+1}^{\infty} v^n \cdot a_{\overline{k-n-1|}} \cdot Pr(K_x^*=k),$$

(8.47)

and can show that the right side of Equation (8.47) reduces to the right side of Equation (8.45). The details are left as Exercise 8-30.

8.3.2 THE DUE CASE

For the *n-year deferred whole life annuity-due*, the first payment is at $t = n$, provided (x) has survived to that point. The present value random variable is

$$_{n|}\ddot{Y}_x = \sum_{t=n}^{\infty} Z_{x:\overline{t}|}^{1}, \tag{8.48a}$$

with expected value given by

$$_{n|}\ddot{a}_x = E\left[_{n|}\ddot{Y}_x\right] = \sum_{t=n}^{\infty} E\left[Z_{x:\overline{t}|}^{1}\right] = \sum_{t=n}^{\infty} v^t \cdot {_tp_x}. \tag{8.48b}$$

It should be clear that

$$_{n|}\ddot{Y}_x = \ddot{Y}_x - \ddot{Y}_{x:\overline{n}|}, \tag{8.49}$$

so that

$$_{n|}\ddot{a}_x = \ddot{a}_x - \ddot{a}_{x:\overline{n}|}. \tag{8.50}$$

EXAMPLE 8.10

Show that $\quad _{n|}\ddot{a}_x = {_nE_x} \cdot \ddot{a}_{x+n}.$

SOLUTION

If we let $s = t-n$, so that $t = s+n$, in Equation (8.48b) we have

$$_{n|}\ddot{a}_x = \sum_{s=0}^{\infty} v^{s+n} \cdot {_{s+n}p_x} = v^n \cdot {_np_x} \sum_{s=0}^{\infty} v^s \cdot {_sp_{x+n}} = {_nE_x} \cdot \ddot{a}_{x+n}, \tag{8.51}$$

as required. □

8.3.3 THE CONTINUOUS CASE

If failure occurs at time $T_x = t$, for $t > n$, then continuous payment (at annual rate 1) will be made from time n to time t. The present value of this payment stream at $t = 0$ is $v^n \cdot \overline{a}_{\overline{t-n}|}$. (If failure is at time $T_x = t$ for $t \leq n$, no payment is made.) Then the present value random variable is

$$_{n|}\overline{Y}_x = \begin{cases} 0 & \text{for } T_x \leq n \\ v^n \cdot \overline{a}_{\overline{T_x-n}|} & \text{for } T_x > n, \end{cases} \tag{8.52a}$$

with expected value given by

$$_{n|}\overline{a}_x = E\left[_{n|}\overline{Y}_x\right] = \int_n^{\infty} v^n \cdot \overline{a}_{\overline{t-n}|} \cdot {_tp_x}\mu_{x+t} \, dt. \tag{8.52b}$$

Using the variable change $s = t-n$, so that $t = s+n$, we have

$$_{n|}\bar{a}_x = \int_0^\infty v^n \cdot \bar{a}_{\overline{s}|} \cdot {}_{s+n}p_x \mu_{x+s+n} \, ds = v^n \cdot {}_np_x \int_0^\infty \bar{a}_{\overline{s}|} \cdot {}_sp_{x+n}\mu_{x+n+s} \, ds = {}_nE_x \cdot \bar{a}_{x+n}, \quad (8.53)$$

from Equation (8.17a).

Returning to Equation (8.52b) we can write

$$\begin{aligned}
_{n|}\bar{a}_x &= \frac{1}{\delta}\int_n^\infty v^n(1-v^{t-n}) \cdot {}_tp_x\mu_{x+t} \, dt \\
&= \frac{1}{\delta}\left[v^n \int_n^\infty {}_tp_x\mu_{x+t} \, dt - \int_n^\infty v^t \cdot {}_tp_x\mu_{x+t} \, dt\right] \\
&= \frac{1}{\delta}\left[v^n \cdot {}_np_x - v^n \cdot {}_np_x + \delta\int_n^\infty v^t \cdot {}_tp_x \, dt\right] \\
&= \int_n^\infty v^t \cdot {}_tp_x \, dt,
\end{aligned} \quad (8.54)$$

from the now-familiar integration by parts technique. It is clear that

$$_{n|}\bar{Y}_x = \bar{Y}_x - \bar{Y}_{x:\overline{n}|} \quad (8.55)$$

so that

$$_{n|}\bar{a}_x = \bar{a}_x - \bar{a}_{x:\overline{n}|} \quad (8.56)$$

upon taking the expectation in Equation (8.55).

To find the variance of the continuous deferred annuity present value random variable $_{n|}\bar{Y}_x$, we first find its second moment. We have

$$\begin{aligned}
E\left[_{n|}\bar{Y}_x^{\,2}\right] &= \int_n^\infty v^{2n} \cdot \left(\bar{a}_{\overline{t-n}|}\right)^2 \cdot {}_tp_x\mu_{x+t} \, dt \\
&= \int_0^\infty v^{2n} \cdot \left(\bar{a}_{\overline{s}|}\right)^2 \cdot {}_{s+n}p_x\mu_{x+s+n} \, ds = \frac{v^{2n} \cdot {}_np_x}{\delta^2}\int_0^\infty (1-v^s)^2 \cdot {}_sp_{x+n}\mu_{x+n+s} \, ds.
\end{aligned}$$

Now we use integration by parts to evaluate the integral. We have

$$\int_0^\infty \left.\frac{(1-v^s)^2}{2(1-v^s)\cdot\delta v^s}\right|_{-\,{}_sp_{x+n}}^{{}_sp_{x+n}\mu_{x+n+s}\,ds} = -(1-v^s)^2 \cdot {}_sp_{x+n}\Big|_0^\infty + 2\delta\int_0^\infty (v^s - v^{2s}) \cdot {}_sp_{x+n} \, ds\,.$$

The first term is zero at both limits, so we have

$$E\left[_{n|}\bar{Y}_x^{\,2}\right] = \frac{v^{2n} \cdot {}_np_x}{\delta^2}\left[2\delta\int_0^\infty (v^s - v^{2s}) \cdot {}_sp_{x+n} \, ds\right] = \frac{2}{\delta} \cdot v^{2n} \cdot {}_np_x(\bar{a}_{x+n} - {}^2\bar{a}_{x+n}).$$

(The observation made in Footnote 2 on page 154 applies here in the continuous case as well.) Then the variance of $_{n|}\bar{Y}_x$ is given by

$$Var\left(_{n|}\overline{Y}_x\right) = E\left[_{n|}\overline{Y}_x^2\right] - \left(E\left[_{n|}\overline{Y}_x\right]\right)^2 = \frac{2}{\delta} \cdot v^{2n} \cdot {}_np_x\left(\overline{a}_{x+n} - {}^2\overline{a}_{x+n}\right) - \left(_{n|}\overline{a}_x\right)^2. \quad (8.57)$$

EXAMPLE 8.11

Show that $\frac{\partial}{\partial n} \, _{n|}\overline{a}_x = -\,_nE_x.$

SOLUTION

Working from Equation (8.54) we have

$$\frac{\partial}{\partial n} \, _{n|}\overline{a}_x = \frac{\partial}{\partial n}\int_n^\infty v^t \cdot {}_tp_x \, dt = -v^n \cdot {}_np_x = -\,_nE_x,$$

by the fundamental theorem of calculus. ❑

8.4 CONTINGENT ANNUITIES PAYABLE m^{thly}

In this section we consider the case of contingent annuities with payments made more often than once per year, such as semiannually, quarterly, or monthly. In general we consider payments made m^{thly}. Note that the special case of $m = 1$ returns the general model to the annual model described earlier in this chapter.

When payments are made m^{thly} the standard actuarial convention and notation considers a unit annual payment, but paid m times within the year so that each actual payment is of size $1/m$. Note that payments, being contingent on the continued survival of the status of interest, can cease somewhere within a year, and not just at a year-end point.

As in prior sections of this chapter, we will consider both the immediate annuity and annuity-due cases, and all three of the whole life, temporary, and deferred whole life models.

8.4.1 THE IMMEDIATE CASE

The immediate whole life m^{thly} contingent annuity pays an amount $1/m$ at the end of each $(1/m)^{th}$ of a year, provided the status (x) continues to survive. This is illustrated in the following diagram specifically for $m = 4$.

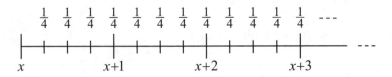

FIGURE 8.7

Generalizing from the annual payment cases presented earlier in the chapter, it is clear that the actuarial present value of the annuity, which we denote by $a_x^{(m)}$, is given by

$$a_x^{(m)} = \frac{1}{m} \cdot \sum_{t=1}^{\infty} v^{t/m} \cdot {}_{t/m} p_x. \tag{8.58}$$

Remember that the base symbol for the APV, $a_x^{(m)}$ in this case, represents a payment amount of one unit per year, but payable m^{thly} within the year, so that each actual payment is amount $1/m$.

For the temporary m^{thly} immediate annuity, payment is made at one unit per year for n years at the most, but payable m^{thly} within the year. The APV is denoted by $a_{x:n|}^{(m)}$, and is given by

$$a_{x:n|}^{(m)} = \frac{1}{m} \cdot \sum_{t=1}^{mn} v^{t/m} \cdot {}_{t/m} p_x. \tag{8.59}$$

Note that the final payment (contingent on survival) is made at time $t = n$ years, or $t = mn$ m^{ths} of a year. As before, the actuarial accumulated value is

$$s_{x:n|}^{(m)} = a_{x:n|}^{(m)} \cdot \frac{1}{{}_n E_x}. \tag{8.60}$$

The n-year deferred whole life contingent m^{thly} immediate annuity would make its first payment at the end of the first m^{th} following the n-year deferral period, contingent on the survival of (x), of course. Its actuarial present value would therefore be

$$_n| a_x^{(m)} = \frac{1}{m} \cdot \sum_{t=mn+1}^{\infty} v^{t/m} \cdot {}_{t/m} p_x. \tag{8.61}$$

8.4.2 THE DUE CASE

In the whole life m^{thly} annuity-due case, the first payment of $1/m$ is made at time 0 (age x) itself, and is made with probability 1 since the status (x) is known to exist at that time. For the temporary m^{thly} annuity-due, the final payment (contingent on the survival of (x), of course) is at the beginning of the final m^{th} in the nth year. For the deferred m^{thly} annuity-due, the first payment is at time n, the beginning of the first m^{th} following the deferral period. Thus the APV's in the annuity-due case are

$$\ddot{a}_x^{(m)} = \frac{1}{m} \cdot \sum_{t=0}^{\infty} v^{t/m} \cdot {}_{t/m} p_x, \tag{8.62}$$

$$\ddot{a}_{x:n|}^{(m)} = \frac{1}{m} \cdot \sum_{t=0}^{mn-1} v^{t/m} \cdot {}_{t/m} p_x, \tag{8.63}$$

and

$$_n| \ddot{a}_x^{(m)} = \frac{1}{m} \cdot \sum_{t=mn}^{\infty} v^{t/m} \cdot {}_{t/m} p_x, \tag{8.64}$$

for the whole life, temporary, and deferred whole life models, respectively. As before, the actuarial accumulated value of the temporary m^{thly} annuity-due is

$$\ddot{s}^{(m)}_{x:\overline{n}|} = \ddot{a}^{(m)}_{x:\overline{n}|} \cdot \frac{1}{{}_nE_x}. \tag{8.65}$$

An analogous set of identities to those developed in the annual payment case exist in the m^{thly} payment case as well, such as

$$_n|a^{(m)}_x = {}_nE_x \cdot a^{(m)}_{x+n}, \tag{8.66}$$

$$_n|\ddot{a}^{(m)}_x = {}_nE_x \cdot \ddot{a}^{(m)}_{x+n}, \tag{8.67}$$

$$a^{(m)}_x = a^{(m)}_{x:\overline{n}|} + {}_n|a^{(m)}_x, \tag{8.68}$$

and

$$\ddot{a}^{(m)}_x = \ddot{a}^{(m)}_{x:\overline{n}|} + {}_n|\ddot{a}^{(m)}_x. \tag{8.69}$$

It should also be clear that

$$\ddot{a}^{(m)}_x = a^{(m)}_x + \frac{1}{m}. \tag{8.70}$$

8.4.3 RANDOM VARIABLE ANALYSIS

Contingent m^{thly} annuity models can be analyzed in a random variable framework totally parallel to that presented for the annual payment cases. Recall the random variable J_x defined in Section 7.3.4 as the m^{thly} time interval in which the status of interest fails. Then the event $J_x = j$ denotes failure in the jth m^{thly} time interval. In this case, $(j-1)$ m^{thly} payments are made under an immediate annuity and j m^{thly} payments are made under an annuity-due, and the present value of the payments is then $(1/m) \cdot a_{\overline{j-1}|}$ or $(1/m) \cdot \ddot{a}_{\overline{j}|}$, respectively. Note that the interest rate contained in $a_{\overline{j-1}|}$ and $\ddot{a}_{\overline{j}|}$ is effective over $(1/m)^{th}$ of a year.

Proceeding in a manner totally parallel to the annual payment case, we define, in the immediate case, the present value random variable

$$Y^{(m)}_x = \frac{1}{m} \cdot a_{\overline{J_x-1}|} = \frac{1}{m}\left(\frac{1-v^{J_x-1}}{i},\right) \tag{8.71}$$

where i is an effective m^{thly} interest rate, with expected value

$$a^{(m)}_x = E\left[Y^{(m)}_x\right] = \frac{1}{m} \cdot \sum_{j=1}^{\infty} \frac{1-v^{j-1}}{i} \cdot Pr(J_x=j). \tag{8.72}$$

Note that

$$Y_x^{(m)} = \frac{1}{m}\left(\frac{1-(1+i)\cdot v^{J_x}}{i}\right) = \left(\frac{1}{m}\right)\left(\frac{1}{i}\right)\left[1-(1+i)\cdot Z_x^{(m)}\right], \tag{8.73}$$

where $Z_x^{(m)}$ is defined by Equation (7.39), with expected value

$$a_x^{(m)} = E\left[Y_x^{(m)}\right] = \left(\frac{1}{m}\right)\left(\frac{1}{i}\right)\left[1-(1+i)\cdot A_x^{(m)}\right] \tag{8.74}$$

and variance

$$Var\left(Y_x^{(m)}\right) = Var\left[\frac{1-(1+i)\cdot Z_x^{(m)}}{m\cdot i}\right] = \frac{(1+i)^2\cdot Var\left(Z_x^{(m)}\right)}{m^2\cdot i^2} = \frac{Var\left(Z_x^{(m)}\right)}{m^2\cdot d^2},$$

where d is the effective m^{thly} discount rate so that $m\cdot d$ is the nominal annual discount rate $d^{(m)}$. Thus we can write the variance of $Y_x^{(m)}$ as

$$Var\left(Y_x^{(m)}\right) = \frac{Var\left(Z_x^{(m)}\right)}{\left(d^{(m)}\right)^2} = \frac{{}^2A_x^{(m)} - A_x^{(m)\,2}}{\left(d^{(m)}\right)^2}. \tag{8.75}$$

Note the similarity of Equation (8.72) to Equation (8.5a), of Equation (8.73) to Equation (8.6), of Equation (8.74) to Example 8.2, and of Equation (8.75) to Equation (8.7b).

In the annuity-due case the present value random variable is

$$\ddot{Y}_x^{(m)} = \frac{1}{m}\cdot\ddot{a}_{\overline{J_x}|} = Y_x^{(m)} + \frac{1}{m}, \tag{8.76}$$

from which, by taking expectations, we verify that

$$\ddot{a}_x^{(m)} = a_x^{(m)} + \frac{1}{m}, \tag{8.70}$$

and also that

$$Var\left(\ddot{Y}_x^{(m)}\right) = Var\left(Y_x^{(m)}\right),$$

as given by Equation (8.75).

8.4.4 NUMERICAL EVALUATION IN THE m^{thly} AND CONTINUOUS CASES

If annuity functions are being evaluated from a parametric survival model, then it is no more difficult to evaluate the m^{thly} functions than to evaluate the annual functions, since $_r p_x$ can be calculated for fractional as well as integral values of r. The challenge arises when we seek to evaluate the m^{thly} functions from a life table showing values of $_r p_x$ only for integral values of r. In this case we must resort to an approximate approach. Two such approximations are presented in this section.

As we did in Section 7.5.2 for the m^{thly} contingent payment models, we will first show how to approximate m^{thly} contingent annuity functions from a life table under the UDD assumption.

Along with the identities $A_x = 1 - d \cdot \ddot{a}_x$ (in the discrete annual case) and $\overline{A}_x = 1 - \delta \cdot \overline{a}_x$ (in the continuous case), we also have

$$A_x^{(m)} = 1 - d^{(m)} \cdot \ddot{a}_x^{(m)} \tag{8.77}$$

in the discrete m^{thly} case. Then we can obtain the UDD-based approximation for the APV of the m^{thly} whole life annuity-due as

$$
\begin{aligned}
\ddot{a}_x^{(m)} &= \frac{1 - A_x^{(m)}}{d^{(m)}} \\
&= \frac{1 - \frac{i}{i^{(m)}} \cdot A_x}{d^{(m)}} \\
&= \frac{1 - \frac{i}{i^{(m)}}(1 - d \cdot \ddot{a}_x)}{d^{(m)}} \\
&= \frac{1}{d^{(m)}}\left(1 - \frac{i}{i^{(m)}}\right) + \frac{id}{i^{(m)}d^{(m)}} \cdot \ddot{a}_x \\
&= \frac{id}{i^{(m)}d^{(m)}} \cdot \ddot{a}_x - \frac{i - i^{(m)}}{i^{(m)}d^{(m)}}.
\end{aligned}
\tag{8.78}
$$

The UDD-based approximations for $_n|\ddot{a}_x^{(m)}$, $\ddot{a}_{x:\overline{n}|}^{(m)}$, and $\ddot{s}_{x:\overline{n}|}^{(m)}$ are found from Equation (8.78) by utilizing relationships established earlier, and are left as Exercise 8-38.

UDD-based approximations for the m^{thly} immediate annuities can be found by first expressing the m^{thly} immediate annuity functions in terms of the corresponding m^{thly} annuity-due functions and then substituting the UDD-based approximations for the m^{thly} annuity-due functions. These are left as Exercise 8-39.

The continuous annuity functions are limiting cases of the corresponding m^{thly} functions as $m \to \infty$, so the UDD-based approximations for the continuous functions follow from the approximations for the corresponding m^{thly} functions. This is pursued in Exercise 8-40.

An alternative to the UDD-based approximations is supplied by the Woolhouse formula, which expresses the sum of a function over m^{thly} steps in terms of the sum of the function over unit steps plus adjustment terms.[4]

Consider a continuous function $g(t)$ for which a number of successive derivatives exist. The Woolhouse formula states that

---

[4] The original presentation is found in Woolhouse [27]. The formula is also derived in standard textbooks on numerical analysis.

$$\sum_{t=1}^{\infty} g(t/m) = m\left[\sum_{t=1}^{\infty} g(t) - \frac{m-1}{2m} \cdot g(t)\Big|_0^{\infty} - \frac{m^2-1}{12m^2} \cdot g'(t)\Big|_0^{\infty} + \cdots\right], \quad (8.79)$$

where $g'(t)$ denotes the first derivative of $g(t)$.

To apply this formula to m^{thly} annuity functions, we let $g(t) = v^t \cdot {}_tp_x$ so that

$$\begin{aligned} g'(t) &= \frac{d}{dt}\left(v^t \cdot {}_tp_x\right) \\ &= v^t \cdot \frac{d}{dt}\,{}_tp_x + {}_tp_x \cdot \frac{d}{dt}v^t \\ &= v^t\left(-\,{}_tp_x\mu_{x+t}\right) + {}_tp_x\left(-\delta \cdot v^t\right) \\ &= -v^t \cdot {}_tp_x\left(\mu_{x+t} + \delta\right). \end{aligned} \quad (8.80)$$

Then

$$g(t)\Big|_0^{\infty} = v^t \cdot {}_tp_x\Big|_0^{\infty} = 0 - 1 = -1$$

and

$$g'(t)\Big|_0^{\infty} = -v^t \cdot {}_tp_x\left(\mu_{x+t} + \delta\right)\Big|_0^{\infty} = 0 - \left[-\left(\mu_x + \delta\right)\right] = \mu_x + \delta,$$

so we have

$$\sum_{t=1}^{\infty} v^{t/m} \cdot {}_{t/m}p_x = m\left[\sum_{t=1}^{\infty} v^t \cdot {}_tp_x + \frac{m-1}{2m} - \frac{m^2-1}{12m^2}\left(\mu_x + \delta\right) + \cdots\right] \quad (8.81a)$$

or

$$\frac{1}{m} \cdot \sum_{t=1}^{\infty} v^{t/m} \cdot {}_{t/m}p_x = \sum_{t=1}^{\infty} v^t \cdot {}_tp_x + \frac{m-1}{2m} - \frac{m^2-1}{12m^2}\left(\mu_x + \delta\right) + \cdots, \quad (8.81b)$$

which, by Equations (8.58) and (8.2b), gives

$$a_x^{(m)} = a_x + \frac{m-1}{2m} - \frac{m^2-1}{12m^2}\left(\mu_x + \delta\right) + \cdots. \quad (8.81c)$$

We show the application of the Woolhouse formula only as far as three terms, since, in practice, it is seldom applied using more than three terms. In fact, historically the formula has often been applied using only two terms, so that

$$a_x^{(m)} \approx a_x + \frac{m-1}{2m} \quad (8.82a)$$

and

$$\ddot{a}_x^{(m)} = a_x^{(m)} + \frac{1}{m}$$

$$\approx a_x + \frac{m-1}{2m} + \frac{1}{m}$$

$$\approx \ddot{a}_x - 1 + \frac{m-1}{2m} + \frac{1}{m}$$

$$\approx \ddot{a}_x - \frac{m-1}{2m}. \tag{8.82b}$$

From Equation (8.81c) we can find the Woolhouse three-term approximations for $_n|a_x^{(m)}, a_{x:n}^{(m)}$, and $s_{x:n}^{(m)}$ (see Exercise 8-41). Similarly, from Equation (8.81c) we can find the Woolhouse three-term approximation for $\ddot{a}_x^{(m)}$, and then those for $_n|\ddot{a}_x^{(m)}, \ddot{a}_{x:n}^{(m)}$, and $\ddot{s}_{x:n}^{(m)}$ (see Exercise 8-42). Finally, from Equations (8.82a) and (8.82b) we can find the Woolhouse two-term approximations for $_n|\ddot{a}_x^{(m)}, \ddot{a}_{x:n}^{(m)}, \ddot{s}_{x:n}^{(m)}, _n|a_x^{(m)}, a_{x:n}^{(m)}$, and $s_{x:n}^{(m)}$ (see Exercise (8-43).

In light of the relationship previously established between m^{thly} annuities and insurances, we can develop Woolhouse approximations for $A_x^{(m)}$ and $\overline{A}_x$. This is pursued in Exercise 8-46.

8.5 NON-LEVEL PAYMENT ANNUITY FUNCTIONS

The level immediate annuity APVs given by Equation (8.2b) in the whole life case and Equation (8.21) in the temporary case can be modified to incorporate the case of non-level payment. If the payment made at time t is denoted by r_t, then we have, in general,

$$APV = \sum_{t=1}^{\infty} r_t \cdot v^t \cdot _t p_x \tag{8.83}$$

in the whole life case and

$$APV = \sum_{t=1}^{n} r_t \cdot v^t \cdot _t p_x \tag{8.84}$$

in the n-year temporary case. In particular if $r_t = t$, so the payment sequence is increasing, we have

$$(Ia)_x = \sum_{t=1}^{\infty} t \cdot v^t \cdot _t p_x \tag{8.85}$$

and

$$(Ia)_{x:n} = \sum_{t=1}^{n} t \cdot v^t \cdot _t p_x. \tag{8.86}$$

(Note the notational similarity with the interest-only increasing annuity defined by Equation (1.34).)

The unit decreasing n-year temporary immediate contingent annuity has APV given by

$$(Da)_{x:\overline{n}|} = \sum_{t=1}^{n} (n+1-t) \cdot v^t \cdot {}_t p_x. \tag{8.87}$$

The comparable expressions in the annuity-due case would be

$$(I\ddot{a})_x = \sum_{t=0}^{\infty} (t+1) \cdot v^t \cdot {}_t p_x, \tag{8.88}$$

$$(I\ddot{a})_{x:\overline{n}|} = \sum_{t=0}^{n-1} (t+1) \cdot v^t \cdot {}_t p_x, \tag{8.89}$$

and

$$(D\ddot{a})_{x:\overline{n}|} = \sum_{t=0}^{n-1} (n-t) \cdot v^t \cdot {}_t p_x. \tag{8.90}$$

In the case of continuous payment, with payment made at rate $r(t)$ at time t, we would have

$$APV = \int_0^{\infty} r(t) \cdot v^t \cdot {}_t p_x \, dt \tag{8.91}$$

in the whole life case and

$$APV = \int_0^{n} r(t) \cdot v^t \cdot {}_t p_x \, dt \tag{8.92}$$

in the n-year temporary case. In particular, if $r(t) = t$ we have the increasing continuous models with

$$(\overline{I}\,\overline{a})_x = \int_0^{\infty} t \cdot v^t \cdot {}_t p_x \, dt \tag{8.93}$$

in the whole life case and

$$(\overline{I}\,\overline{a})_{x:\overline{n}|} = \int_0^{n} t \cdot v^t \cdot {}_t p_x \, dt \tag{8.94}$$

in the n-year temporary case. If $r(t) = n-t$ we have the decreasing n-year temporary case with

$$(\overline{D}\overline{a})_{x:\overline{n}|} = \int_0^{n} (n-t) \cdot v^t \cdot {}_t p_x \, dt. \tag{8.95}$$

8.6 MULTI-STATE MODEL REPRESENTATION

We return to the idea presented earlier whereby we represent the survival model as a simple, two-state Markov model, where State 1 denotes survival and State 2 denotes failure. The life annuity presented in this chapter can now be described as a sequence of payments made while the process remains in State 1.

As with the insurance models of Chapter 7, we emphasize that no new concepts arise here; we will merely write annuity APVs using multi-state model notation rather than standard actuarial notation.[5]

In the discrete case, a payment is made at time k if the process, known to have started in State 1 at time 0 for an entity age x, is still in State 1. The probability of this is $_k p_{11}^{(0)}$. Then the APV for a whole life annuity-due is

$$\ddot{a}_x = \sum_{k=0}^{\infty} v^k \cdot {_k p_{11}^{(0)}}, \tag{8.96}$$

where $_k p_{11}^{(0)} = {_k p_x}$. In the continuous case, the probability of still being in State 1 at time r is $_r p_{11}^{(0)}$, and the APV for a whole life continuous annuity is

$$\bar{a}_x = \int_0^{\infty} v^r \cdot {_r p_{11}^{(0)}} \, dr, \tag{8.97}$$

where $_r p_{11}^{(0)} = {_r p_x}$ and the usual assumption is made that the entity is known to begin in State 1 at age x at time 0.

The general case addresses payments made while in State i for a process known to have begun in State h at time 0, where $i = h$ is possible. Then the probability of payment at discrete time k is $_k p_{hi}^{(0)}$, and the APV is

$$APV = \sum_{k=0}^{\infty} v^k \cdot {_k p_{hi}^{(0)}} \tag{8.98}$$

for an annuity-due. Note that $_0 p_{hi}^{(0)} = 1$ if $i = h$ and $_0 p_{hi}^{(0)} = 0$ if $i \neq h$. In the continuous case we have

$$APV = \int_0^{\infty} v^r \cdot {_r p_{hi}^{(0)}} \, dr. \tag{8.99}$$

Note that Equation (8.96) is the special case of Equation (8.98), and Equation (8.97) is the special case of Equation (8.99), with $i = h = 1$ in both cases.

---

[5] As in Chapter 7, we see no need to create a new symbol for the APV itself.

8.7 MISCELLANEOUS EXAMPLES

In this section we continue the practice, begun in Section 7.7, of presenting several additional applications of the theory developed in this chapter.

EXAMPLE 8.12

It is useful to determine the probability that a present value random variable will exceed its own expected value. Consider the present value random variable $\bar{Y}_x = \bar{a}_{\overline{T_x}|}$, where T_x has an exponential distribution with parameter $\lambda = .06$ and interest is at $\delta = .04$. Find

$$Pr(\bar{Y}_x > E[\bar{Y}_x]).$$

SOLUTION

We know that $E[\bar{Y}_x] = \bar{a}_x = \frac{1}{\lambda + \delta} = 10$ in this case. Then

$$
\begin{aligned}
Pr(\bar{Y}_x > 10) &= Pr\left(\frac{1 - v^{T_x}}{.04} > 10\right) \\
&= Pr(1 - v^{T_x} > .40) \\
&= Pr(v^{T_x} < .60) \\
&= Pr(T_x \cdot \ln v < \ln .60) \\
&= Pr(T_x \cdot -\delta < -.51083) \\
&= Pr\left(T_x > \frac{.51083}{\delta}\right) \\
&= Pr(T_x > 12.77075).
\end{aligned}
$$

Since T_x is exponential, then

$$Pr(T_x > 12.77075) = e^{-12.77075(.06)} = .46475. \qquad \square$$

EXAMPLE 8.13

The idea introduced in Example 7.11 of investigating the aggregate outcome for a group of contracts is continued here in the case of annuities. A fund is established to pay continuous whole life annuities to 100 independent lives all age x at annual payment rate 10,000. Using the normal approximation, determine the initial size of the fund such that all payments can be made with probability .90, given the values $\bar{A}_x = .40$, $^2\bar{A}_x = .25$, and $\delta = .06$.

SOLUTION

Let F denote the initial fund and let $\bar{Y}_{Agg}$ denote the present value random variable for the aggregate annuity payments. We seek $Pr(\bar{Y}_{Agg} \leq F)$. We have

$$\overline{Y}_{Agg} = \overline{Y}_1 + \overline{Y}_2 + \cdots + \overline{Y}_{100},$$

where $\overline{Y}_i = 10,000\overline{Y}_x$. Then

$$E[\overline{Y}_{Agg}] = 100 \cdot E[\overline{Y}_i] = (100)(10,000) \cdot E[\overline{Y}_x]$$

$$= 1,000,000\left(\frac{1-\overline{A}_x}{\delta}\right)$$

$$= 1,000,000\left(\frac{1-.40}{.06}\right) = 10,000,000.$$

Similarly, because the $\overline{Y}_i$'s are independent, we have

$$Var(\overline{Y}_{Agg}) = 100 \cdot Var(\overline{Y}_i)$$

$$= (100)(10,000)^2\left(\frac{^2\overline{A}_x - \overline{A}_x^2}{\delta^2}\right)$$

$$= (100)(10,000)^2\left(\frac{.25-.16}{.0036}\right) = 2.5\times10^{11},$$

and therefore $SD(\overline{Y}_{Agg}) = \sqrt{Var(\overline{Y}_{Agg})} = 500,000$. Then, assuming that $\overline{Y}_{Agg}$ is approximately normal, we have

$$Pr(\overline{Y}_{Agg} \leq F) = Pr\left(Z \leq \frac{F-10,000,000}{500,000}\right) = .90,$$

which tells us that

$$\frac{F-10,000,000}{500,000} = 1.282,$$

and therefore $F = (1.282)(500,000)+10,000,000 = 10,641,000.$ ❐

EXAMPLE 8.14

An important annuity form is one for which the first n years of payments are guaranteed to be made, with all payments after the first n years made only if the annuitant continues to survive. Such annuities are referred to as *n-year certain and continuous*, meaning that the payments can continue after the first n years. (This phrase is used even though the payments are not being made continuously.)[6] Consider a person age 40 who wins 10,000 in a lottery and elects to receive payments of P at the beginning of each year for 10 years certain and continuous thereafter for life. Calculate P, given the values $A_{40} = .30$, $A_{50} = .35$, $A^1_{40:\overline{10|}} = .09$, and $i = .04$.

---

[6] The phrase *n-year certain and life* is also used to describe this annuity. Its standard actuarial symbol is defined in Section 12.2.

SOLUTION

The guaranteed payments constitute an annuity-certain and the non-guaranteed payments constitute a deferred whole life annuity. The equation of value is

$$10,000 = P(\ddot{a}_{\overline{10|}} + {}_{10|}\ddot{a}_{40}) = P(\ddot{a}_{\overline{10|}} + {}_{10}E_{40} \cdot \ddot{a}_{50}).$$

To calculate ${}_{10}E_{40}$, note that

$$A_{40} - A^1_{40:\overline{10|}} = .21 = {}_{10}E_{40} \cdot A_{50},$$

so ${}_{10}E_{40} = \frac{.21}{.35} = .60$. We also have

$$\ddot{a}_{50} = \frac{1 - A_{50}}{d} = \frac{1 - .35}{.04/1.04} = 16.90,$$

and

$$\ddot{a}_{\overline{10|}} = \frac{1 - (1.04)^{-10}}{.04/1.04} = 8.43533.$$

Then

$$P = \frac{10,000}{8.43533 + (.60)(16.90)} = 538.35.$$ ❑

EXAMPLE 8.15

We observe that an insurance contract will result in a loss to the insurer if failure occurs early, and, conversely, an annuity contract will result in a loss if failure occurs late. Then a contract that pays both annuity benefits and a failure benefit on the same life has the property of offsetting risks, as measured by the variance of the present value random variable. Consider a whole life annuity paying 12,000 at the beginning of each year to (x), combined with a failure benefit of B paid at the end of the year of failure. Using a discount rate of $d = .08$, determine the value of B that will minimize the variance of the present value random variable for the contract.

SOLUTION

Let X denote the present value random variable for the contract. We have

$$X = 12,000\ddot{Y}_x + B \cdot Z_x$$

$$= 12,000\left(\frac{1 - Z_x}{d}\right) + B \cdot Z_x$$

$$= \left(B - \frac{12,000}{d}\right) \cdot Z_x + \frac{12,000}{d},$$

so

$$Var(X) = \left(B - \frac{12,000}{d}\right)^2 \cdot Var(Z_x).$$

To find the value of B that minimizes $Var(X)$, we take

$$\frac{d}{dB} Var(X) = 2(B-150,000) \cdot Var(Z_x),$$

since $Var(Z_x)$ is a constant with respect to B. Equating to zero we easily find $B = 150,000$. (Note that this value of B minimizes the variance at $Var(X) = 0$, making the combined contract risk-free to the insurer.) ❑

8.8 EXERCISES

8.1 Whole Life Annuity Models

8-1   Derive the identity $i \cdot a_x + (1+i)A_x = 1$.

8-2   Use a group deterministic interpretation to show that $\sum_{t=1}^{\infty} \ell_{x+t} \cdot A_{x+t} = \ell_x \cdot a_x$.

8-3   Show that $a_x = v \cdot p_x (1+a_{x+1})$. (Note that when $i = 0$ this equation reduces to that shown in Exercise 6-15.)

8-4   Calculate the value of $Var(\ddot{Y}_x)$, given the values $\ddot{a}_x = 10$, $^2\ddot{a}_x = 6$, and $i = \frac{1}{24}$.

8-5   Show that $A_x = v \cdot \ddot{a}_x - a_x$.

8-6   Show that $\ddot{a}_x = 1 + v \cdot p_x \cdot \ddot{a}_{x+1}$.

8-7   After calculating the value of $\ddot{a}_x$ at interest rate $i = .05$, a student discovers that the value of p_{x+1} is larger by .03 than the value used in the initial calculation. Find the amount by which the value of $\ddot{a}_x$ is increased when the correct value of p_{x+1} is used, given the following values used in the initial calculation:

$$q_x = .01 \qquad\qquad q_{x+1} = .05 \qquad\qquad \ddot{a}_{x+1} = 6.951$$

8-8   A whole life annuity product pays the contract holder 12,000 at the beginning of each year. It is suggested that a death benefit, payable at the end of the year of death, be added to the product. Find the size of the death benefit that will minimize the variance of the present value random variable of the new product, given $d = .08$.

8-9   Show that the right side of Equation (8.14) reduces to $\ddot{a}_x$, as defined by Equation (8.9).

8-10   Use Equation (8.18) to derive the useful relationship $\overline{A}_x = 1 - \delta \cdot \overline{a}_x$.

8-11   Show that $\frac{d}{dx} \overline{a}_x = \overline{a}_x(\mu_x + \delta) - 1$.

8-12   Show that if the age-at-failure random variable has a uniform distribution with parameter ω, then the expected value of $\overline{Y}_x$ is given by

$$E[\overline{Y}_x] = \frac{(\omega - x) - \overline{a}_{\overline{\omega - x}|}}{\delta(\omega - x)}.$$

8-13   Find the value of $\overline{A}_x$, given the following values:

$$\overline{a}_x = 10 \qquad\qquad {}^2\overline{a}_x = 7.375 \qquad\qquad Var(\overline{a}_{\overline{T_x}|}) = 50$$

8-14   Given that $Var(\overline{a}_{\overline{T_x}|}) = \frac{100}{9}$, $\delta = 4k$, and $\mu_{x+t} = k$ for all t, find the value of k.

8-15   If $\delta = .03$ and $\mu_{x+t} = .025$ for all t, calculate the probability that $\overline{Y}_x = \overline{a}_{\overline{T_x}|}$ will exceed 20.

8-16   Show that

$$Cov(\overline{Y}_x, \overline{Z}_x) = \frac{\overline{A}_x^{\,2} - {}^2\overline{A}_x}{\delta}.$$

8-17 $\overline{a}_x$ is calculated using force of failure μ_{x+t} and force of interest δ. $\overline{a}_x^{\,*}$ is calculated using force of failure μ_{x+t}^{*} and force of interest δ^{*}. Given that $\delta^{*} = 3\delta$ and $\overline{a}_x^{\,*} = \overline{a}_x$ for all x, show that $\mu_{x+t}^{*} = \mu_{x+t} - 2\delta$.

8-18   A group of persons all age x is made up of 50% females and 50% males. Find the value of $Var(\overline{Y}_x)$ for a person chosen at random from the group, given $\delta = .10$ and the following values:

	Female	Male
$E[\overline{Z}_x]$	0.09	0.15
$Var(\overline{Y}_x)$	4.00	5.00

8.2 Temporary Annuity Models

8-19 Show that $i \cdot a_{x:n|} + i \cdot A^1_{x:n|} + A_{x:n|} = 1$.

8-20 Repeat the group deterministic demonstration, presented in Section 8.1.1 for the whole life case, to show that the APV and the NSP for the temporary immediate annuity are equal.

8-21 Show that the right side of Equation (8.23) reduces to $a_{x:n|}$, as defined by Equation (8.21).

8-22 Repeat Exercise 8-20 to show that the APV and the NSP for the temporary annuity-due are equal.

8-23 Show that the right side of Equation (8.30) reduces to $\ddot{a}_{x:n|}$, as defined by Equation (8.26).

8-24 Derive Equation (8.34).

8-25 Repeat the group deterministic demonstration, presented in Section 8.2.1 for the temporary immediate case, to derive Equation (8.35) for the actuarial accumulated value in the annuity-due case.

8-26 Calculate the value of $\ddot{a}_{x:4|}$, given the following values:

k	$\ddot{a}_{k|}$	$_{k-1|}q_x$
1	1.00	.33
2	1.93	.24
3	2.80	.16
4	3.62	.11

8-27 Calculate the value of $Var(\ddot{Y}_{x:3|})$, given $_tp_x = (.90)^t$ for $t \geq 0$ and the following values of $\ddot{Y}_{x:3|}$, for given values of K^*_x, the random variable for the interval of failure of (x):

K^*_x	$\ddot{Y}_{x:3|}$
1	1.00
2	1.87
3	2.62

8-28   Show that $Var(\overline{Y}_{x:\overline{n}|})$ in terms of annuity functions is given by

$$Var(\overline{Y}_{x:\overline{n}|}) = \frac{2}{\delta}(\overline{a}_{x:\overline{n}|} - {}^2\overline{a}_{x:\overline{n}|}) - \overline{a}_{x:\overline{n}|}^2.$$

8-29   Show that $\int_0^n \overline{a}_{\overline{t}|} \cdot {}_tp_x\mu_{x+t} \, dt = \overline{a}_{x:\overline{n}|} - {}_np_x \cdot \overline{a}_{\overline{n}|}.$

8.3 Deferred Whole Life Annuity Models

8-30   Show that the right side of Equation (8.47) reduces to ${}_n|a_x$, as defined by Equation (8.45).

8-31   Show that

$${}_n|\ddot{Y}_x = \begin{cases} 0 & \text{for } K_x^* \le n \\ v^n \cdot \ddot{a}_{\overline{K_x^*-n}|} & \text{for } K_x^* > n \end{cases}.$$

Then show that $E[{}_n|\ddot{Y}_x] = {}_nE_x \cdot \ddot{a}_{x+n} = {}_n|\ddot{a}_x.$

8-32   Let S denote the number of annuity payments actually made under a unit 5-year deferred whole life annuity-due. Find the value of $Pr(S > 5|\ddot{a}_x)$, given the following values:

$$\ddot{a}_{x:\overline{5}|} = 4.542 \qquad\qquad i = .04 \qquad\qquad \mu_{x+t} = .01, \quad \text{for all } t$$

8-33   A 30-year unit deferred whole life annuity-due is issued to (35), with the extra feature that the net single premium is refunded without interest if (35) dies during the deferred period. Calculate the net single premium, given the following values:

$$\ddot{a}_{65} = 9.90 \qquad\qquad A_{35:\overline{30}|} = .21 \qquad\qquad A_{35:\overline{30}|}^1 = .07$$

8-34   A present value random variable $\overline{Y}$ is defined by

$$\overline{Y} = \begin{cases} \overline{a}_{\overline{n}|} & \text{for } T_x \le n \\ \overline{a}_{\overline{T_x}|} & \text{for } T_x > n \end{cases}.$$

Show that $E[\overline{Y}] = \overline{a}_{\overline{n}|} + {}_n|\overline{a}_x.$

8.4 Contingent Annuities Payable m^{thly}

8-35   Derive each of Equations (8.66) through (8.70).

8-36   (a)   Show that $\ddot{a}_{x:\overline{n}|}^{(m)} = a_{x:\overline{n}|}^{(m)} + \frac{1}{m}(1 - {}_nE_x)$.

           (b)   Show that ${}_n|\ddot{a}_x^{(m)} = {}_n|a_x^{(m)} + \frac{1}{m} \cdot {}_nE_x$.

8-37   Derive Equation (8.77).

8-38   Derive the following UDD-based approximations.

           (a) ${}_n|\ddot{a}_x^{(m)} \approx \dfrac{id}{i^{(m)}d^{(m)}} \cdot {}_n|\ddot{a}_x - \dfrac{i - i^{(m)}}{i^{(m)}d^{(m)}} \cdot {}_nE_x$

           (b) $\ddot{a}_{x:\overline{n}|}^{(m)} \approx \dfrac{id}{i^{(m)}d^{(m)}} \cdot \ddot{a}_{x:\overline{n}|} - \dfrac{i - i^{(m)}}{i^{(m)}d^{(m)}}(1 - {}_nE_x)$

           (c) $\ddot{s}_{x:\overline{n}|}^{(m)} \approx \dfrac{id}{i^{(m)}d^{(m)}} \cdot \ddot{s}_{x:\overline{n}|} - \dfrac{i - i^{(m)}}{i^{(m)}d^{(m)}}\left(\dfrac{1}{{}_nE_x} - 1\right)$

8-39   Derive the following UDD-based approximations.

           (a) $a_x^{(m)} \approx \dfrac{id}{i^{(m)}d^{(m)}} \cdot a_x + \dfrac{d^{(m)} - d}{i^{(m)}d^{(m)}}$

           (b) ${}_n|a_x^{(m)} \approx \dfrac{id}{i^{(m)}d^{(m)}} \cdot {}_n|a_x + \dfrac{d^{(m)} - d}{i^{(m)}d^{(m)}} \cdot {}_nE_x$

           (c) $a_{x:\overline{n}|}^{(m)} \approx \dfrac{id}{i^{(m)}d^{(m)}} \cdot a_{x:\overline{n}|} + \dfrac{d^{(m)} - d}{i^{(m)}d^{(m)}}(1 - {}_nE_x)$

           (d) $s_{x:\overline{n}|}^{(m)} \approx \dfrac{id}{i^{(m)}d^{(m)}} \cdot s_{x:\overline{n}|} + \dfrac{d^{(m)} - d}{i^{(m)}d^{(m)}}\left(\dfrac{1}{{}_nE_x} - 1\right)$

8-40   (a)   By taking the limit as $m \to \infty$ in Equation (8.78), derive the UDD-based approximation

$$\overline{a}_x \approx \dfrac{id}{\delta^2} \cdot \ddot{a}_x - \dfrac{i - \delta}{\delta^2}.$$

           (b)   By taking the limit as $m \to \infty$ in Exercise 8-39(a), derive the alternative UDD-based approximation

$$\overline{a}_x \approx \dfrac{id}{\delta^2} \cdot a_x + \dfrac{\delta - d}{\delta^2}.$$

           (c)   Show that the right sides in parts (a) and (b) are equal.

8-41   Derive the following Woolhouse three-term approximations.

(a) $_n|a_x^{(m)} \approx {}_n|a_x + {}_nE_x\left[\dfrac{m-1}{2m} - \dfrac{m^2-1}{12m^2}(\mu_{x+n}+\delta)\right]$

(b) $a_{x:n|}^{(m)} \approx a_{x:n|} + \dfrac{m-1}{2m}(1-{}_nE_x) - \dfrac{m^2-1}{12m^2}\left[\mu_x - {}_nE_x\cdot\mu_{x+n} + \delta(1-{}_nE_x)\right]$

(c) $s_{x:n|}^{(m)} \approx s_{x:n|} + \dfrac{m-1}{2m}\left(\dfrac{1}{{}_nE_x}-1\right) - \dfrac{m^2-1}{12m^2}\left[\dfrac{\mu_x}{{}_nE_x} - \mu_{x+n} + \delta\left(\dfrac{1}{{}_nE_x}-1\right)\right]$

8-42   Derive the following Woolhouse three-term approximations.

(a) $\ddot{a}_x^{(m)} \approx \ddot{a}_x - \dfrac{m-1}{2m} - \dfrac{m^2-1}{12m^2}(\mu_x+\delta)$

(b) $_n|\ddot{a}_x^{(m)} \approx {}_n|\ddot{a}_x - {}_nE_x\left[\dfrac{m-1}{2m} + \dfrac{m^2-1}{12m^2}(\mu_{x+n}+\delta)\right]$

(c) $\ddot{a}_{x:n|}^{(m)} \approx \ddot{a}_{x:n|} - \dfrac{m-1}{2m}(1-{}_nE_x) - \dfrac{m^2-1}{12m^2}\left[\mu_x - {}_nE_x\cdot\mu_{x+n} + \delta(1-{}_nE_x)\right]$

(d) $\ddot{s}_{x:n|}^{(m)} \approx \ddot{s}_{x:n|} - \dfrac{m-1}{2m}\left(\dfrac{1}{{}_nE_x}-1\right) - \dfrac{m^2-1}{12m^2}\left[\dfrac{\mu_x}{{}_nE_x} - \mu_{x+n} + \delta\left(\dfrac{1}{{}_nE_x}-1\right)\right]$

8-43   Derive the following Woolhouse two-term approximations.

(a) $_n|\ddot{a}_x^{(m)} \approx {}_n|\ddot{a}_x - \dfrac{m-1}{2m}\cdot{}_nE_x$

(b) $\ddot{a}_{x:n|}^{(m)} \approx \ddot{a}_{x:n|} - \dfrac{m-1}{2m}(1-{}_nE_x)$

(c) $\ddot{s}_{x:n|}^{(m)} \approx \ddot{s}_{x:n|} - \dfrac{m-1}{2m}\left(\dfrac{1}{{}_nE_x}-1\right)$

(d) $_n|a_x^{(m)} \approx {}_n|a_x + \dfrac{m-1}{2m}\cdot{}_nE_x$

(e) $a_{x:n|}^{(m)} \approx a_{x:n|} + \dfrac{m-1}{2m}(1-{}_nE_x)$

(f) $s_{x:n|}^{(m)} \approx s_{x:n|} + \dfrac{m-1}{2m}\left(\dfrac{1}{{}_nE_x}-1\right)$

8-44   Show that the approximations given by Equations (8.82a) and (8.82b), applied to continuous annuity models, lead to

$$\overline{a}_x \approx \ddot{a}_x - \dfrac{1}{2} = a_x + \dfrac{1}{2}.$$

8-45   Show that, under the UDD assumption,

$$\bar{A}_x = \frac{i}{\delta} - \frac{(i-d)\ddot{a}_x}{\delta}.$$

8-46   Derive the following Woolhouse three-term approximations.

(a) $\bar{a}_x \approx \ddot{a}_x - \frac{1}{2} - \frac{1}{12}(\mu_x+\delta) = a_x + \frac{1}{2} - \frac{1}{12}(\mu_x+\delta)$

(b) $\bar{A}_x = 1 - \delta\left[\ddot{a}_x - \frac{1}{2} - \frac{1}{12}(\mu_x+\delta)\right]$

8.5 Non-Level Payment Annuity Functions

8-47   Calculate the probability that the present value of payments actually made under a unit 3-year temporary increasing annuity-due will exceed the APV of the annuity contract, given the following values:

$$p_x = .80 \qquad p_{x+1} = .75 \qquad p_{x+2} = .50 \qquad v = .90$$

8-48   An increasing temporary annuity-due pays 2 in the first year, 3 in the second year, and 4 in the third year. Using the values given in Exercise 8-47, calculate the variance of the present value random variable for this annuity.

8-49   (a) Show that
$$(IA)_x = \ddot{a}_x - d \cdot (I\ddot{a})_x.$$

(b)   Show that
$$(\bar{I}\bar{A})_x = \bar{a}_x - \delta \cdot (\bar{I}\bar{a})_x.$$

8.6 Multi-State Model Representation

8-50   Using the multi-state model notation defined in Section 8.6 and earlier, give APV formulas for each of the following.

(a)   Whole life immediate annuity

(b) n-year temporary annuity-due

(c) n-year deferred immediate annuity

(d) n-year temporary continuous annuity

CHAPTER NINE

FUNDING PLANS FOR CONTINGENT CONTRACTS (ANNUAL PREMIUMS)

Suppose a small mining company wishes to operate only one mine at a time. While still working a particular mine, it begins to look ahead to the next time it will need to explore for a new mining location when the current mine is no longer productive. The company wishes to accumulate, out of current revenue, a fund to finance these future exploration costs. From past experience the company has a good idea of how much will be needed, but does not know *when* the future exploration costs will arise.

Similarly, an insurance company that has sold a whole life insurance contract to a person age x at issue of the contract knows how much will be needed to pay the eventual death benefit under the contract, but does not know *when* the death benefit cost will occur.

How should these businesses go about the task of *funding* these eventual costs?

Suppose the uncertainty regarding time of future payment did not exist. That is, suppose we know that we will need amount X at time k, and we wish to fund this eventual need by accumulating deposits of size P each made at the beginning of each time interval from now (which we denote as time 0) until time k.

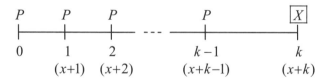

FIGURE 9.1

If the deposits will earn effective interest rate i per period, then we might determine P so that the accumulated fund at time k will provide exactly the needed amount X. Thus we have

$$P \cdot \ddot{s}_{\overline{k}|i} = X,$$ (9.1a)

which we can also write as

$$P \cdot \ddot{a}_{\overline{k}|i} = X \cdot v^k.$$ (9.1b)

Equation (9.1b) defines the periodic deposit by equating the present value of the funding scheme to the present value of the amount to be needed at time k, where each present value is taken at interest only.

With contingent payment models, including insurance contracts, the time at which amount X is needed is stochastic rather than fixed. The analogy to Equation (9.1b) is that the periodic funding payment is found by equating the *actuarial present value* (APV) of the funding scheme to the APV of the contingent payment. Funding payments determined in this manner are said to satisfy the *equivalence principle*.[1]

9.1 ANNUAL FUNDING SCHEMES FOR CONTINGENT PAYMENT MODELS

In this section we consider funding schemes for various types of contingent contracts, wherein the funding pattern is represented by a series of discrete annual funding payments.

9.1.1 DISCRETE CONTINGENT PAYMENT MODELS

Consider the whole life contingent payment model, as developed in Section 7.1, under which a payment of X will be made at time k if the status of interest, which we denote by (x), fails in the interval $(k-1, k]$. If this contingent payment is funded under the equivalence principle, then the periodic funding payment P is determined from

$$P \cdot \ddot{a}_x = X \cdot A_x, \tag{9.2}$$

where $X \cdot A_x$ is the APV of the contingent payment and $P \cdot \ddot{a}_x$ is the APV of the funding scheme. Note that funding payments are made at the *beginning* of each time interval including the beginning of the interval of failure.

To define the standard actuarial terminology and notation for contingent payment funding schemes, we consider the eventual contingent payment to be of unit amount. For a whole life contingent model, with time measured in years, the periodic funding payment is denoted by P_x. Thus we have

$$P_x \cdot \ddot{a}_x = A_x \tag{9.3a}$$

or

$$P_x = \frac{A_x}{\ddot{a}_x}, \tag{9.3b}$$

from which P_x can be calculated from values of A_x and $\ddot{a}_x$ defined in Chapters 7 and 8, respectively.

Using the identity $A_x = 1 - d \cdot \ddot{a}_x$ (see Example 8.4), we can write

$$P_x = \frac{1 - d \cdot \ddot{a}_x}{\ddot{a}_x} = \frac{1}{\ddot{a}_x} - d, \tag{9.4}$$

which allows us to calculate the funding payment from the contingent annuity APV only.

---

[1] See Section 9.3 for an alternative method of determining funding payments. The notion of analyzing the adequacy of funding payments by simulation is considered in Appendix B.

For any of the n-year term insurance, n-year pure endowment, or n-year endowment insurance models, the contingent payment will be made at time n at the latest (if, in fact, ever made at all). Clearly it would not be reasonable to fund one of these contingent benefits *beyond* time n, the point at which the benefit either has already been paid or it has become clear that the benefit will never be paid. Of course funding does not extend beyond the time of failure of (x) in any case. This suggests that the APV of the funding scheme for these n-year contracts is represented by the temporary n-year annuity-due. Thus we have

$$P^1_{x:\overline{n}|} = \frac{A^1_{x:\overline{n}|}}{\ddot{a}_{x:\overline{n}|}} \tag{9.5}$$

for the n-year term insurance model,

$$P_{x:\overline{n}|}{}^1 = \frac{A_{x:\overline{n}|}{}^1}{\ddot{a}_{x:\overline{n}|}} \tag{9.6}$$

for the n-year pure endowment model, and

$$P_{x:\overline{n}|} = \frac{A_{x:\overline{n}|}}{\ddot{a}_{x:\overline{n}|}} \tag{9.7a}$$

for the n-year endowment insurance model. If we substitute for $A_{x:\overline{n}|}$ using Equation (7.26), we then have

$$P_{x:\overline{n}|} = P^1_{x:\overline{n}|} + P_{x:\overline{n}|}{}^1. \tag{9.7b}$$

Note the notational principle used to define the symbol for the annual funding payment: in the above cases the annual funding payment symbol is the same as the APV symbol, with A replaced by P.

In the life insurance context, annual funding payments are called *annual premiums*. To clarify that these funding payments provide *only* for the contingent benefit payment, and not for such things as profit margins or expenses of operation, they are referred to as *net annual premiums* or *benefit annual premiums*.[2] Recall from Chapter 7 that the APV of the benefit payment is also called the *net single premium* (NSP). Thus we see that a contingent benefit could be funded by a net single premium, which is the APV of the contingent benefit, or by a sequence of net annual premiums whose APV is equal to the APV of the benefit and therefore equal to the NSP.[3]

We have established that funding should not extend beyond the occurrence of the contingent event that triggers the payment, nor beyond the duration of a contract with a maximum term. However it is possible to plan the funding scheme over a *shorter* period than the term of the contract. In general, if the funding scheme is confined to the first t years of a contract, where

---

[2] The issue of adjusting net premiums to cover expenses and profit margins will be addressed in Section 9.6.

[3] In certain property/casualty insurance arrangements, the term *pure premium* is used in place of net premium.

$t < n$ in the case of n-year contracts and $t < \infty$ in the case of whole life contracts, then the APV of the funding scheme is given by $P \cdot \ddot{a}_{x:\overline{t}|}$. Such funding schemes are referred to as *limited payment funding patterns* and the resulting net premium is called the *limited payment net premium* or the *t-pay net premium*.

The standard actuarial notation for all limited payment net premiums involves the use of a pre-subscript t on the basic P symbol. Thus we have, for example,

$$_t P_x = \frac{A_x}{\ddot{a}_{x:\overline{t}|}} \tag{9.8a}$$

for limited payment whole life (or *t*-pay whole life),

$$_t P^1_{x:\overline{n}|} = \frac{A^1_{x:\overline{n}|}}{\ddot{a}_{x:\overline{t}|}} \tag{9.8b}$$

for limited payment *n*-year term insurance,

$$_t P_{x:\overline{n}|}^{1} = \frac{A_{x:\overline{n}|}^{1}}{\ddot{a}_{x:\overline{t}|}} \tag{9.8c}$$

for limited payment *n*-year pure endowment, and

$$_t P_{x:\overline{n}|} = \frac{A_{x:\overline{n}|}}{\ddot{a}_{x:\overline{t}|}} \tag{9.8d}$$

for *t*-pay *n*-year endowment insurance. Note that $t < n$ in Equations (9.8b), (9.8c), and (9.8d).

In the special case of *n*-year deferred insurance, as defined in Section 7.1, if the funding scheme continues until the failure of (x) the net premium is defined by

$$P\left(_n|A_x\right) = \frac{_n|A_x}{\ddot{a}_x}, \tag{9.9a}$$

and if the funding is limited to the first t years (contingent on the survival of (x), of course) the net premium is defined by

$$_t P\left(_n|A_x\right) = \frac{_n|A_x}{\ddot{a}_{x:\overline{t}|}}, \tag{9.9b}$$

where logically $t \le n$.

EXAMPLE 9.1

A special 10-year contingent contract issued to (30) will pay a unit benefit at the end of the year of failure, if failure occurs during the 10-year period, or will refund the net annual premiums paid if (30) survives to the end of the 10-year period. Calculate the net annual premium, using the equivalence principle, given the following values:

$$A_{30:\overline{10}|} = .60 \qquad A^{1}_{30:\overline{10}|} = .47 \qquad d = .05$$

SOLUTION

Under the equivalence principle we equate the APV of the funding scheme to the APV of the contingent benefits. Let P denote the net level annual premium. We have

$$P \cdot \ddot{a}_{30:\overline{10}|} = A^{1}_{30:\overline{10}|} + 10P \cdot A^{1}_{30:\overline{10}|}.$$

Then

$$P = \frac{A^{1}_{30:\overline{10}|}}{\ddot{a}_{30:\overline{10}|} - 10 A^{1}_{30:\overline{10}|}},$$

where

$$A^{1}_{30:\overline{10}|} = A_{30:\overline{10}|} - A^{1}_{30:\overline{10}|} = .60 - .47 = .13$$

and

$$\ddot{a}_{30:\overline{10}|} = \frac{1 - A_{30:\overline{10}|}}{d} = \frac{1 - .60}{.05} = 8.$$

Then

$$P = \frac{.13}{8 - (10)(.47)} = .03939. \qquad \square$$

9.1.2 CONTINUOUS CONTINGENT PAYMENT MODELS

Recall the continuous contingent payment models developed in Section 7.3, which are referred to as *immediate payment of claims models* in the life insurance context. Here we consider such contingent payment contracts funded by net annual premiums that have been determined by the equivalence principle. The notation for the net annual premium is different from that defined in Section 9.1.1 to reveal the immediate payment of claims feature. Here we have

$$P(\overline{A}_x) = \frac{\overline{A}_x}{\ddot{a}_x} \qquad (9.10a)$$

for the whole life model,

$$P(\overline{A}^{1}_{x:\overline{n}|}) = \frac{\overline{A}^{1}_{x:\overline{n}|}}{\ddot{a}_{x:\overline{n}|}} \qquad (9.10b)$$

for the n-year term insurance model, and

$$P\left(\overline{A}_{x:\overline{n}|}\right) = \frac{\overline{A}_{x:\overline{n}|}}{\ddot{a}_{x:\overline{n}|}} \qquad (9.10c)$$

for the n-year endowment insurance model. (Recall that there is no continuous version of the pure endowment model with APV given by $A_{x:\overline{n}|}^{1} = {}_nE_x$.) If these immediate payment of claims models are funded by t-year limited payment plans, then each P symbol carries the pre-subscript t and each $\ddot{a}$ function in the denominator is replaced by $\ddot{a}_{x:\overline{t}|}$, where $t < n$.[4]

The net annual premiums in this section can be evaluated from a life table by approximating the continuous functions in the numerator under the UDD assumption, as described in Section 7.5.1.

9.1.3 Contingent Annuity Models

An n-year deferred contingent annuity contract, with net single premium given by ${}_{n|}a_x$ in the immediate case, ${}_{n|}\ddot{a}_x$ in the due case, and ${}_{n|}\overline{a}_x$ in the continuous case, is often funded by annual premiums paid over the n-year deferred period, subject to the continued survival of (x), of course. The net annual premiums are defined by

$$P\left({}_{n|}a_x\right) = \frac{{}_{n|}a_x}{\ddot{a}_{x:\overline{n}|}}, \qquad (9.11a)$$

$$P\left({}_{n|}\ddot{a}_x\right) = \frac{{}_{n|}\ddot{a}_x}{\ddot{a}_{x:\overline{n}|}}, \qquad (9.11b)$$

and

$$P\left({}_{n|}\overline{a}_x\right) = \frac{{}_{n|}\overline{a}_x}{\ddot{a}_{x:\overline{n}|}}, \qquad (9.11c)$$

respectively.

The annual premiums defined by Equations (9.11a), (9.11b), and (9.11c) provide *only* for the deferred annuity payments, which are made only if (x) survives through the n-year deferred period. This implies that no benefit is paid, and premiums are therefore forfeited, in the case of failure during the deferred period. In practice this is not the case, and a failure benefit is paid in the event of failure during the deferred period. Suppose the deferred period failure benefit is the return of net annual premiums paid, with interest at the same rate i as is used to discount the benefit back to issue, and the unit annuity payments begin at age $x + n$. What would the net annual premium be in this case?

---

[4] Some textbooks refer to these net annual premiums for immediate payment of claims models as *semicontinuous net premiums* or *semicontinuous benefit premiums*. When the premium is paid annually, and the benefit is paid at the end of the year of failure (as in Section 9.1.1), some texts refer to the premium as a *fully discrete* annual premium.

If the net annual premium is P, then the failure benefit is $P \cdot \ddot{s}_{\overline{1}|}$ for failure in the first year, $P \cdot \ddot{s}_{\overline{2}|}$ for failure in the second year, and so on. The equation of value is therefore

$$P \cdot \ddot{a}_{x:\overline{n}|} = {}_n|\ddot{a}_x + \sum_{t=1}^{n} P \cdot \ddot{s}_{\overline{t}|} \cdot v^t \cdot {}_{t-1}|q_x,$$

for an n-year deferred annuity-due. The summation term is evaluated as

$$P \sum_{t=1}^{n} \ddot{s}_{\overline{t}|} \cdot v^t \cdot {}_{t-1}|q_x = \frac{P}{d} \sum_{t=1}^{n} [(1+i)^t - 1] \cdot v^t \cdot {}_{t-1}|q_x$$

$$= \frac{P}{d} \left[\sum_{t=1}^{n} {}_{t-1}|q_x - \sum_{t=1}^{n} v^t \cdot {}_{t-1}|q_x \right]$$

$$= \frac{P}{d} \left[{}_n q_x - A^1_{x:\overline{n}|} \right]$$

$$= \frac{P}{d} \left[1 - {}_n p_x - (1 - d \cdot \ddot{a}_{x+n} - {}_n E_x) \right]$$

$$= P \cdot \ddot{a}_{x:\overline{n}|} + \frac{P}{d} \left({}_n E_x - {}_n p_x \right).$$

Recall that ${}_n E_x = v^n \cdot {}_n p_x$, so ${}_n p_x = {}_n E_x \cdot (1+i)^n$. Substituting for ${}_n p_x$ in the last line of the summation evaluation yields

$$P \cdot \ddot{a}_{x:\overline{n}|} - \frac{P}{d} [(1+i)^n - 1] \cdot {}_n E_x.$$

Then the equation of value becomes

$$P \cdot \ddot{a}_{x:\overline{n}|} = {}_n|\ddot{a}_x + P \cdot \ddot{a}_{x:\overline{n}|} - P \cdot \ddot{s}_{\overline{n}|} \cdot {}_n E_x,$$

which leads to

$$P \cdot \ddot{s}_{\overline{n}|} \cdot {}_n E_x = {}_n|\ddot{a}_x$$

and finally to

$$P = \frac{1}{\ddot{s}_{\overline{n}|}} \cdot \frac{1}{{}_n E_x} \cdot {}_n|\ddot{a}_x = \frac{\ddot{a}_{x+n}}{\ddot{s}_{\overline{n}|}}, \qquad (9.12)$$

since ${}_n|\ddot{a}_x = {}_n E_x \cdot \ddot{a}_{x+n}$. This result shows that the premium in this case is the amount that accumulates, at interest only, to the amount needed at the start of the benefit period, which is $\ddot{a}_{x+n}$.[5] Because the premium is an interest-only function, and does not depend on the survival/failure rates, we say there is no cost of insurance under such a contract. We will later encounter deferred annuities that do involve a cost of insurance.

---

[5] We will derive this result again in Chapter 10 using reserves (see Example 10.5).

9.1.4 NON-LEVEL PREMIUM CONTRACTS

Contingent payment contracts can be funded by a non-level sequence of net premiums. To find the sequence of net premiums under the equivalence principle would require that the net premiums in the sequence bear a known relationship to each other, for otherwise the equivalence principle relationship would contain several unknowns.

For example, suppose a 5-year increasing term insurance contract, with benefit $1000k$ for failure in the kth year, for $k = 1, 2, 3, 4, 5$, is funded by a net premium sequence of P, $2P$, $3P$, $4P$, $5P$, paid at the beginning of each year. Then the equivalence principle states that

$$P \cdot (I\ddot{a})_{x:\overline{5}|} = 1000(IA)^1_{x:\overline{5}|},$$

where the two increasing functions are defined by Equations (8.89) and (7.52), respectively.

EXAMPLE 9.2

A whole life contingent contract, with benefit paid at the end of the year of failure, pays a benefit of 1 for failure in the first year and a benefit increasing by 4% per year for failure thereafter. The net premium increases by 4% per year as well. Using a 4% interest rate, find an expression for the initial net premium.

SOLUTION

The APV of the premium stream is

$$P_1[1 + (1.04) \cdot v \cdot p_x + (1.04)^2 \cdot v^2 \cdot {}_2p_x + \cdots] = P_1(1 + p_x + {}_2p_x + \cdots) = P_1(1 + e_x),$$

where P_1 denotes the initial net premium. The APV of the benefit is

$$\sum_{k=1}^{\infty} b_k \cdot v^k \cdot {}_{k-1}|q_x = \sum_{k=1}^{\infty} (1.04)^{k-1} \cdot v^k \cdot {}_{k-1}|q_x = v \sum_{k=1}^{\infty} {}_{k-1}|q_x = v,$$

since $\sum_{k=1}^{\infty} {}_{k-1}|q_x = 1$. Then by the equivalence principle we have

$$P_1 = \frac{v}{1 + e_x}. \qquad \square$$

9.2 RANDOM VARIABLE ANALYSIS

The topic of determining annual funding payments for contingent contracts can be approached in a stochastic manner, building on the discussion and results presented in Chapters 7 and 8. Suppose a unit payment will be made at time k if the status of interest (x) fails in the kth time interval, and this contingent payment arrangement is funded by payments of P

at the beginning of each time interval until failure occurs. This familiar model is illustrated in the following figure.

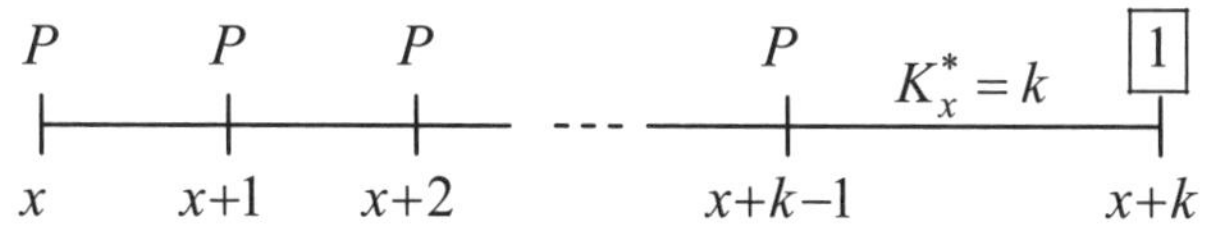

FIGURE 9.2

If the payment is made at time k, then v^k is the present value of the payment, and $P \cdot \ddot{a}_{\overline{k}|}$ is the present value of the associated income. The excess of v^k over $P \cdot \ddot{a}_{\overline{k}|}$ would represent the *present value of the loss* occurring under this arrangement if, specifically, $K_x^* = k$. In general, we let L_x denote the random variable for the present value of loss in this whole life contingent payment model. Then we have

$$L_x = v^{K_x^*} - P \cdot \ddot{a}_{\overline{K_x^*}|} = Z_x - P \cdot \ddot{Y}_x, \tag{9.13}$$

using notation defined in Chapters 7 and 8. Note that L_x could turn out to be either positive or negative, with a negative loss interpreted as a gain under the arrangement.

The expected value of L_x is given by

$$E[L_x] = E[Z_x - P \cdot \ddot{Y}_x] = A_x - P \cdot \ddot{a}_x. \tag{9.14}$$

If we adopt the rule that the annual premium will be selected so that $E[L_x] = 0$, then we have $E[L_x] = A_x - P \cdot \ddot{a}_x = 0$, which leads to

$$P = \frac{A_x}{\ddot{a}_x} = P_x, \tag{9.15}$$

as already defined by Equation (9.3b). Thus we see that determining the net premium by setting the expected value of the present value of loss equal to zero is identical to the equivalence principle used throughout Section 9.1. This is true for all of the contingent payment models we have defined, not just for the whole life model illustrated here.

Recall that

$$\ddot{Y}_x = \ddot{a}_{\overline{K_x^*}|} = \frac{1 - v^{K_x^*}}{d} = \frac{1 - Z_x}{d},$$

so we can write the present value of loss random variable as

$$L_x = Z_x - P \cdot \ddot{Y}_x = Z_x - P\left(\frac{1 - Z_x}{d}\right) = Z_x\left(1 + \frac{P}{d}\right) - \frac{P}{d}. \tag{9.16}$$

Equation (9.16) enables us to find the variance of L_x. Since the variance of the constant P/d is zero, then we have

$$Var(L_x) = Var\left[Z_x\left(1+\frac{P}{d}\right)\right] = \left(1+\frac{P}{d}\right)^2 \cdot Var(Z_x)$$

$$= \left(1+\frac{P}{d}\right)^2 \cdot \left(^2A_x - A_x^2\right), \qquad (9.17a)$$

by using Equation (7.5) for the variance of Z_x. In the special case of net premium determined by the equivalence principle, which implies $E[L_x] = 0$, we have $P = P_x$. Then Equation (9.17a) can be written as

$$Var(L_x) = \left(1+\frac{P_x}{d}\right)^2 \cdot \left(^2A_x - A_x^2\right)$$

$$= \left(\frac{P_x+d}{d}\right)^2 \cdot \left(^2A_x - A_x^2\right)$$

$$= \left(\frac{1}{d\cdot\ddot{a}_x}\right)^2 \cdot \left(^2A_x - A_x^2\right), \qquad (9.17b)$$

from Equation (9.4).

If $E[L_x] = 0$ it follows that $Var(L_x) = E[L_x^2]$. For the discrete whole life contingent payment model, with $P = P_x$ under the equivalence principle, we have

$$L_x^2 = \left[Z_x\left(1+\frac{P_x}{d}\right) - \frac{P_x}{d}\right]^2. \qquad (9.18)$$

It can then be shown that $E[L_x^2]$, with L_x^2 given by Equation (9.18), reduces to the expression for $Var(L_x)$ given by Equation (9.17b). The details are left as Exercise 9-9.

Example 9.3

Let $L = L_{x:\overline{2}|}^1$ denote the present value of loss random variable for a two-year term insurance with unit benefit paid at the end of the year of failure, and net annual premium determined by the equivalence principle. Given the values $q_x = .10$, $q_{x+1} = .20$, and $v = .90$, calculate the value of $Var(L)$.

Solution

The net annual premium is

$$P_{x:\overline{2}|}^1 = \frac{A_{x:\overline{2}|}^1}{\ddot{a}_{x:\overline{2}|}} = \frac{v\cdot q_x + v^2 \cdot p_x \cdot q_{x+1}}{1+v\cdot p_x} = \frac{(.90)(.10)+(.90)^2(.90)(.20)}{1+(.90)(.90)} = .13027.$$

If failure occurs in the first year, which happens with probability .10, one premium will have been paid, and the present value of loss will be

$$v - P^1_{x:\overline{2|}} = .90 - .13027 = .76973.$$

If failure occurs in the second year, which happens with probability $(.90)(.20) = .18$, two premiums will have been paid, and the present value of loss will be

$$v^2 - P^1_{x:\overline{2|}} - v \cdot P^1_{x:\overline{2|}} = (.90)^2 - .13027 - .13027(.90) = .56249.$$

If failure does not occur in the first two years at all, which happens with probability $(.90)(.80) = .72$, two premiums *but no benefit* will have been paid, and the present value of loss will be

$$0 - P^1_{x:\overline{2|}} - v \cdot P^1_{x:\overline{2|}} = -.24751.$$

Since $E[L] = 0$, by the equivalence principle, then we have

$$Var(L) = E[L^2]$$
$$= (.76973)^2(.10) + (.56249)^2(.18) + (-.24751)^2(.72) = .16030. \qquad \square$$

We can observe from Example 9.3 that the insurer sustains a loss on this particular contract if failure occurs in either of the two contract years, which happens with probability .28, and enjoys a gain if failure does not occur, which happens with probability .72. Although the expected loss (and hence the expected gain) is zero, we see that the probability of gain exceeds the probability of loss.

This notion of gain or loss on a single contract can be explored for contracts that are more extensive than the simple two-year term insurance of Example 9.3. Consider a unit discrete whole life contract issued at age 40, with net annual premium determined by the equivalence principle using the life table of Appendix A and 6% interest. The life table gives the value $A_{40} = .12401$, so we have

$$\ddot{a}_{40} = \frac{1 - A_{40}}{d} = \frac{1 - .12401}{.06/1.06} = 15.47582,$$

and therefore

$$P_{40} = \frac{A_{40}}{\ddot{a}_{40}} = \frac{.12401}{15.47582} = .00801.$$

Then we can calculate the possible values of L_{40} as follows:

If $K^*_x = 1$, then

$$L_{40} = v - P_{40} = .93539;$$

if $K_x^* = 2$, then

$$L_{40} = v^2 - P_{40} \cdot \ddot{a}_{\overline{2}|} = .87443;$$

$$\vdots$$

if $K_x^* = 35$, then

$$L_{40} = v^{35} - P_{40} \cdot \ddot{a}_{\overline{35}|} = .00701;$$

if $K_x^* = 36$, then

$$L_{40} = v^{36} - P_{40} \cdot \ddot{a}_{\overline{36}|} = -.00140.$$

This shows us that the insurer sustains a loss on this contract if failure occurs within the first 35 years, and enjoys a gain if failure occurs in the 36th or later year. Then the probability of gain, from Table A.2, is $_{35}p_{40} = \frac{69,287}{97,033} = .71406$, and the probability of loss is .28594, notwithstanding that the expected gain (and therefore expected loss) is zero.

Note that the gain/loss analysis presented here is on a *net premium basis*. We will revisit this issue in Section 9.6 where we consider the gain/loss on a *gross premium basis*.

The variance of L can be found for other than the whole life contingent payment model, as illustrated in the following example.

EXAMPLE 9.4

Find the variance of the present value of loss random variable for an *n*-year endowment model, with net premium determined by the equivalence principle.

SOLUTION

The loss random variable is

$$L_{x:\overline{n}|} = Z_{x:\overline{n}|} - P_{x:\overline{n}|} \cdot \ddot{Y}_{x:\overline{n}|}, \tag{9.19a}$$

where $Z_{x:\overline{n}|}$ is given by Equation (7.24) and $\ddot{Y}_{x:\overline{n}|}$ is given by Equation (8.29a). But from Equation (8.31) we know that

$$\ddot{Y}_{x:\overline{n}|} = \frac{1 - Z_{x:\overline{n}|}}{d},$$

so we can write

$$L_{x:\overline{n}|} = Z_{x:\overline{n}|}\left(1 + \frac{P_{x:\overline{n}|}}{d}\right) - \frac{P_{x:\overline{n}|}}{d}. \tag{9.19b}$$

Then the variance of $L_{x:\overline{n}|}$ follows directly as

$$Var\left(L_{x:\overline{n}|}\right) = \left(1+\frac{P_{x:\overline{n}|}}{d}\right)^2 \cdot Var\left(Z_{x:\overline{n}|}\right) = \left(1+\frac{P_{x:\overline{n}|}}{d}\right)^2 \cdot \left({}^2A_{x:\overline{n}|} - A_{x:\overline{n}|}{}^2\right). \qquad (9.20)$$

□

9.3 THE PERCENTILE PREMIUM PRINCIPLE

As an alternative to determining net annual premiums by the equivalence principle, we might select the premium such that the probability of a positive loss is less than some tolerance limit. For example, let us find the net premium for a unit discrete whole life insurance issued to (40) such that $Pr(L_{40} > 0) < .25$, where L_{40} is the loss at issue random variable defined in Section 9.2, assuming $i = .05$ and a uniform distribution of future lifetime with $\omega = 110$.

First we recall that

$$L_{40} = Z_{40} - P \cdot \ddot{Y}_{40} = Z_{40}\left(1+\frac{P}{d}\right) - \frac{P}{d},$$

so

$$Pr(L_{40} = 0) = Pr\left[v^{K_x^*}\left(1+\frac{P}{d}\right) = \frac{P}{d}\right]. \qquad (9.21)$$

The future lifetime random variable T_{40} has a uniform distribution over the interval $(0,70)$, so the 25th percentile of the distribution of T_{40} is at $t = 17.50$. Therefore the premium is set so that $L_{40} = 0$ for failure in the 18th year, which is denoted by $K_x^* = 18$. That is,

$$v^{18}\left(1+\frac{P}{d}\right) = \frac{P}{d},$$

which solves for

$$P = \frac{d \cdot v^{18}}{1 - v^{18}} = \frac{1}{\ddot{s}_{\overline{18}|.05}} = .03385.$$

Note that, at this premium rate, if failure occurs earlier than the 18th year a positive loss will result and if failure occurs later than the 18th year the loss will be negative. If the premium rate is higher than .03385, then $Pr(L_{40} > 0)$ is even smaller than .25. Premiums determined by this method are called *percentile premiums* (the 25th percentile premium in this case).

The above application of the percentile premium principle was done with respect to a single contract. In practice, the insurer is less likely to be concerned with the probability of gain/loss on a single contract, and more likely to examine the probability of gain/loss on a block of similar policies. This is explored in the following example.

EXAMPLE 9.5

Continuing the concept explored in Examples 7.11 and 8.13, we will now investigate the aggregate outcome for a group of annual premium contracts. Consider the present value of loss random variable for a discrete whole life insurance, introduced in Section 9.2, with net annual premium $P = .025$. (Note that the premium has not necessarily been determined by the equivalence principle.) Using the normal approximation, determine the minimum number of contracts to be issued to independent lives all age x so that the probability of a positive loss on the collection of contracts does not exceed .05, given the values $A_x = .24905$, $^2A_x = .09476$, and $i = .06$.

SOLUTION

The aggregate loss at issue is

$$L_{Agg} = L_1 + L_2 + \cdots + L_n,$$

where n, the number of contracts to be issued, is the value we seek. The criterion for determining n is

$$Pr(L_{Agg} > 0) \le .05.$$

Recall (see Section 9.2) that

$$L_i = Z_x - P \cdot \ddot{Y}_x$$
$$= \left(1 + \frac{P}{d}\right) \cdot Z_x - \frac{P}{d}$$
$$= \left(1 + \frac{.025}{.06/1.06}\right) \cdot Z_x - \frac{.025}{.06/1.06}.$$

Then
$$E[L_i] = 1.44167 A_x - .44167$$
$$= (1.44167)(.24905) - .44167 = -.08262$$

and
$$Var(L_i) = (1.44167)^2 \cdot (^2A_x - A_x^2)$$
$$= (1.44167)^2 \cdot [.09476 - (.24905)^2] = .06803.$$

Then
$$E[L_{Agg}] = n \cdot E[L_i] = -.08262n$$

and
$$Var(L_{Agg}) = n \cdot Var(L_i) = .06803n,$$

so $SD(L_{Agg}) = \sqrt{Var(L_{Agg})} = .26084\sqrt{n}$. Then, assuming that L_{Agg} is approximately normal, we have

$$Pr(L_{Agg} > 0) = Pr\left(Z > \frac{0 - (-.08262n)}{.26084\sqrt{n}}\right) = .05,$$

which tells us that

$$1.645 = \frac{0-(-.08262n)}{.26084\sqrt{n}} = \frac{.08262n}{.26084\sqrt{n}}.$$

This leads to

$$.42907\sqrt{n} = .08262n,$$

which solves for $n = 26.97$, or $n = 27$. ◻

The same analysis as in Example 9.5 could be used to determine the net annual premium, with the value of n given. This is pursued in Exercise 9-13. Note how the premium in the $n = 100$ case is lower than in the $n = 27$ case. This illustrates the notion of how the mortality risk is diversified over the group of contracts. The risk declines as the size of the group increases.

9.4 CONTINUOUS PAYMENT FUNDING SCHEMES

In this section we consider a funding scheme for a contingent payment model wherein the funding payments are made continuously. As we have noted before, the notion of continuous payment is totally abstract and does not occur in practice, but the mathematics of continuous payment models is sufficiently interesting to merit at least a brief study. We will consider in detail only the whole life model; the extension to certain other models by analogous steps will be clear.

9.4.1 DISCRETE CONTINGENT PAYMENT MODELS

If a unit contingent payment is made at the end of the time interval of failure, its APV is given by A_x. If the funding payment, which we also call the net annual premium, is made continuously at annual rate P, then the APV of the funding scheme is $P \cdot \bar{a}_x$. Equating the two APV's gives the net continuous annual premium rate, which is denoted by $\bar{P}_x$. Thus we have

$$\bar{P}_x = \frac{A_x}{\bar{a}_x}. \tag{9.22a}$$

By similar reasoning we obtain

$$\bar{P}^1_{x:\overline{n}|} = \frac{A^1_{x:\overline{n}|}}{\bar{a}_{x:\overline{n}|}} \tag{9.22b}$$

for n-year term insurance with continuous premium,

$$\bar{P}_{x:\overline{n}|}^{1} = \frac{A_{x:\overline{n}|}^{1}}{\bar{a}_{x:\overline{n}|}} \tag{9.22c}$$

for n-year pure endowment with continuous premium,

$$\bar{P}_{x:\overline{n}|} = \frac{A_{x:\overline{n}|}}{\bar{a}_{x:\overline{n}|}} \qquad (9.22d)$$

for n-year endowment insurance with continuous premium, and

$$\bar{P}(_n|A_x) = \frac{_n|A_x}{\bar{a}_{x:\overline{n}|}} \qquad (9.22e)$$

for n-year deferred insurance with continuous premium paid during the deferred period as long as (x) continues to survive.

The net annual premiums in this section can be evaluated from a life table by approximating the continuous annuity functions in the denominator under one of the two assumptions described in Section 8.4.4 and its associated exercises.

9.4.2 CONTINUOUS CONTINGENT PAYMENT MODELS

Of greater theoretical interest than the Section 9.4.1 models involving continuous funding but benefit payment at the end of the interval of failure would be those with continuous funding and benefit payment at the precise time point of failure. (Recall that in the insurance context this is referred to as immediate payment of claims.[6]) The annual premium rate for the whole life model in this case is denoted by $\bar{P}(\bar{A}_x)$. By the now-familiar equivalence principle we have

$$\bar{A}_x = \bar{P}(\bar{A}_x) \cdot \bar{a}_x \qquad (9.23a)$$

or

$$\bar{P}(\bar{A}_x) = \frac{\bar{A}_x}{\bar{a}_x}. \qquad (9.23b)$$

Using the result of Exercise 8-10 we can write

$$\bar{P}(\bar{A}_x) = \frac{1 - \delta \cdot \bar{a}_x}{\bar{a}_x} = \frac{1}{\bar{a}_x} - \delta, \qquad (9.24a)$$

or

$$\frac{1}{\bar{a}_x} = \bar{P}(\bar{A}_x) + \delta. \qquad (9.24b)$$

EXAMPLE 9.6

If the age-at-failure random variable has an exponential distribution with mean $\frac{1}{\lambda}$, show that $\bar{P}(\bar{A}_x) = \lambda$.

---

[6] In some texts these models of continuous funding coupled with immediate payment of claims are called *fully continuous premium models*.

SOLUTION

From Equation (7.44) we have $\bar{A}_x = \frac{\lambda}{\lambda+\delta}$, where δ is the force of interest, and from Example 8.5 we have $\bar{a}_x = \frac{1}{\lambda+\delta}$. Then

$$\bar{P}(\bar{A}_x) \;=\; \frac{\lambda}{\lambda+\delta} \div \frac{1}{\lambda+\delta} \;=\; \lambda. \qquad\qquad \square$$

The stochastic approach, using the present value of loss random variable, extends nicely to these continuous funding models. By analogy to the discrete case presented in Section 9.2 we define the present value of loss to be

$$\bar{L}(\bar{A}_x) \;=\; v^{T_x} - \bar{P} \cdot \bar{a}_{\overline{T_x}|} \qquad\qquad (9.25a)$$

for an arbitrary continuous premium rate. But under the equivalence principle, which implies $E\big[\bar{L}(\bar{A}_x)\big] = 0$, we have $\bar{P} = \bar{P}(\bar{A}_x)$ as already defined by Equation (9.23b). Thus we have

$$
\begin{aligned}
\bar{L}(\bar{A}_x) &= v^{T_x} - \bar{P}(\bar{A}_x) \cdot \bar{a}_{\overline{T_x}|} \\
&= \bar{Z}_x - \bar{P}(\bar{A}_x) \cdot \bar{Y}_x \\
&= \bar{Z}_x - \bar{P}(\bar{A}_x) \cdot \left(\frac{1-\bar{Z}_x}{\delta} \right) \\
&= \bar{Z}_x \left(1 + \frac{\bar{P}(\bar{A}_x)}{\delta} \right) - \frac{\bar{P}(\bar{A}_x)}{\delta},
\end{aligned}
\qquad (9.25b)
$$

which leads directly to

$$
\begin{aligned}
Var\big[\bar{L}(\bar{A}_x)\big] &= \left(1 + \frac{\bar{P}(\bar{A}_x)}{\delta} \right)^2 \cdot Var(\bar{Z}_x) \\
&= \left(1 + \frac{\bar{P}(\bar{A}_x)}{\delta} \right)^2 \cdot \left({}^2\bar{A}_x - \bar{A}_x^{\,2} \right) \\
&= \left(\frac{1}{\delta \cdot \bar{a}_x} \right)^2 \cdot \left({}^2\bar{A}_x - \bar{A}_x^{\,2} \right),
\end{aligned}
\qquad (9.26a)
$$

by use of Equation (9.24b). Then using the result of Exercise 8-10 we also have

$$Var\big[\bar{L}(\bar{A}_x)\big] \;=\; \frac{{}^2\bar{A}_x - \bar{A}_x^{\,2}}{(1-\bar{A}_x)^2}. \qquad\qquad (9.26b)$$

EXAMPLE 9.7

Let $L = \bar{L}(\bar{A}_x)$ denote the present value of loss random variable under a fully continuous whole life model with continuous annual premium rate determined by the equivalence principle. Let $L*$ denote the present value of loss random variable under a similar model with continuous annual premium rate .05. Find the value of $Var(L*)$, given the following values:

$$Var(L) = .25 \qquad \overline{A}_x = .40 \qquad \delta = .06$$

SOLUTION

From Equation (9.25a) we have

$$L = \overline{Z}_x - P \cdot \overline{Y}_x = \overline{Z}_x - P\left(\frac{1-\overline{Z}_x}{\delta}\right) = \overline{Z}_x\left(1+\frac{P}{\delta}\right) - \frac{P}{\delta}.$$

When the premium rate is determined from the equivalence principle, we have

$$P = \frac{\overline{A}_x}{\overline{a}_x} = \frac{.40}{\frac{1-.40}{.06}} = .04.$$

Then the variance is

$$Var(L) = \left(1+\frac{P}{\delta}\right)^2 \cdot Var(\overline{Z}_x) = \left(1+\frac{.04}{.06}\right)^2 \cdot Var(\overline{Z}_x) = .25,$$

which solves for $Var(\overline{Z}_x) = .09$. Similarly,

$$Var(L*) = \left(1+\frac{P*}{\delta}\right)^2 \cdot Var(\overline{Z}_x) = \left(1+\frac{.05}{.06}\right)^2 (.09) = .3025. \qquad \square$$

9.5 FUNDING SCHEMES WITH m^{thly} PAYMENTS

In many applications, such as with insurance contracts, periodic funding payments are made at m^{thly} intervals within the year, such as semiannually, quarterly, or monthly. In general, if funding payments are made m times within a year, at the beginning of each mth of the year, the annual rate of funding will be denoted by the symbol $P^{(m)}$, with additional notation to identify the particular model being funded. It is important to remember that $P^{(m)}$ denotes the *annual funding rate*, with funding payments made m times within the year, so that each actual funding payment is $\frac{P^{(m)}}{m}$. In the insurance context, $P^{(m)}$ is called a *true fractional premium*.

As before, the annual funding rate will be determined by the equivalence principle, with the actuarial present value of the funding scheme found by using the m^{thly} annuity-due function developed in Section 8.4.2. Thus we would have

$$P_x^{(m)} = \frac{A_x}{\ddot{a}_x^{(m)}} \qquad (9.27a)$$

for the whole life contingent payment model with m^{thly} funding,

$$\overset{(m)}{P^1_{\overline{x:n|}}} = \frac{A^1_{\overline{x:n|}}}{\ddot{a}^{(m)}_{\overline{x:n|}}}$$ (9.27b)

for the n-year term insurance model,

$$\overset{(m)}{P_{\overline{x:n|}}^{\ 1}} = \frac{A_{\overline{x:n|}}^{\ 1}}{\ddot{a}^{(m)}_{\overline{x:n|}}}$$ (9.27c)

for the n-year pure endowment model,

$$P^{(m)}_{\overline{x:n|}} = \frac{A_{\overline{x:n|}}}{\ddot{a}^{(m)}_{\overline{x:n|}}}$$ (9.27d)

for the n-year endowment insurance model, and

$$P^{(m)}({}_n|a_x) = \frac{{}_n|a_x}{\ddot{a}^{(m)}_{\overline{x:n|}}}$$ (9.27e)

for the n-year deferred immediate annuity model.

Under the immediate payment of claims models, where the contingent payment is made at the moment of failure rather than the end of the interval of failure, the APV in the numerator of the premium formula is replaced by its continuous counterpart and the premium symbol is adjusted as well. We would have

$$P^{(m)}\left(\overline{A}_x\right) = \frac{\overline{A}_x}{\ddot{a}^{(m)}_x}$$ (9.28a)

for the whole life model,

$$P^{(m)}\left(\overline{A}^1_{\overline{x:n|}}\right) = \frac{\overline{A}^1_{\overline{x:n|}}}{\ddot{a}^{(m)}_{\overline{x:n|}}}$$ (9.28b)

for the n-year term insurance model, and

$$P^{(m)}\left(\overline{A}_{\overline{x:n|}}\right) = \frac{\overline{A}_{\overline{x:n|}}}{\ddot{a}^{(m)}_{\overline{x:n|}}}$$ (9.28c)

for the n-year endowment insurance model.

If the funding scheme is limited to t years, where $t < n$, then the APV of the m^{thly} annuity in the denominator of the premium formula becomes $\ddot{a}^{(m)}_{x:\overline{t}|}$ and the premium symbol is adjusted to include the pre-subscript t as in the Equation (9.8) set. For example, for t-pay n-year term insurance with immediate payment of claims we would have

$$_t P^{(m)} \left(\overline{A}^1_{x:\overline{n}|} \right) = \frac{\overline{A}^1_{x:\overline{n}|}}{\ddot{a}^{(m)}_{x:\overline{t}|}}. \tag{9.29}$$

The numerical calculation of m^{thly} funding payments follows directly from the approximate calculation of the associated m^{thly} annuity-due in the denominator of the premium formula. The details of such calculations are presented in Section 8.4.4 and its associated exercises.

9.6 FUNDING PLANS INCORPORATING EXPENSES

Recall the observation made earlier in this chapter that the annual funding payments determined by the equivalence principle, which we called net annual premiums in the life insurance context, provide only for the contingent benefit payment. In practice, of course, the price of an insurance (or other contingent payment) product must be set higher than the net premium in order to generate revenue to pay expenses of operation and the contingent benefit payments, as well as providing a profit margin to the insurer. The total annual premium charged for an insurance product is called the *gross annual premium* or the *contract premium*. A premium determined to cover benefits and expenses, but not profit, is called the *expense-augmented premium*.

It is a simple matter to extend the equivalence principle to incorporate expenses and therefore to calculate expense-augmented premiums. For ease of illustration we assume that the expenses allocated to a particular contingent contract are fixed costs known in advance. Then the *expense-augmented equivalence principle* states that the APV of the expense-augmented funding scheme equals the APV of the benefit payment plus the APV of the expense charges allocated to the contract.

For illustration we assume that expense charges allocated to a contract are of the following four types:

(1) A percentage of the gross premium itself.

(2) A fixed amount per unit of benefit payment.

(3) A fixed (or percentage of benefit) amount incurred when the benefit payment is made.

(4) A fixed amount for the contract itself, regardless of benefit amount.

The analysis of corporate operational expenses leading to the determination of expense charges to be included in the price of each product is a complex issue that will vary according to the type of business under discussion. In any case the mechanics of this expense analysis are beyond the scope of this text.

We will, however, illustrate the four types of expense charges listed above under a typical life insurance policy, since the pricing of life insurance is a common example of this type of actuarial analysis.

Percent of premium expenses arise as commissions paid to sales agents and state premium taxes. It is customary for sales commissions to be larger for the first several years of a contract and then smaller in later years. The premium tax is likely to be level over all years.

The amount per unit of insurance might be expected to cover such things as underwriting (i.e., risk classification) expense, policy issue expenses, and subsequent policy maintenance expenses. Again it would be customary for these per unit expenses to be higher in the first year than in subsequent years of the policy. In our illustration we will consider the unit of insurance to be $1000.

The expense associated with making the benefit payment, called the *settlement expense*, is a one-time charge incurred at the same time as the benefit is paid. Therefore it can be introduced into the gross premium calculation by simply adding it to the benefit payment amount.

Since premiums need to be calculated per unit of benefit, such as per $1000, it is convenient to convert the fixed amount per policy expenses to the fixed amount per unit of insurance type by assuming an average policy size.[7] We illustrate the above discussion with the following example.

EXAMPLE 9.8

Assume that all per policy expenses have been converted to the per $1000 of benefit type. Assume a whole life insurance contract issued to (x), with the following expenses: 75% of the first premium and 10% of all premiums thereafter; $10 at the beginning of the first year and $2 at the beginning of each year thereafter; $20 settlement expense. Find an expression for the expense-augmented premium of a $1000 benefit contract.

SOLUTION

If we let G denote the expense-augmented premium, then the APV of the premium income is $G \cdot \ddot{a}_x$. The APV of the percent of premium expense charges is $.75G + .10G \cdot a_x$, since the 10% charge is incurred at the beginning of each year after the first only if the contract is still in force. The APV of the fixed per $1000 of benefit expense charges is $10 + 2a_x$, by the same reasoning. The APV of the settlement expense is $20A_x$, since it is incurred at the same time as the benefit payment. Of course the APV of the benefit payment itself is $1000A_x$. Then the equivalence principle states that

$$G \cdot \ddot{a}_x = .75G + .10G \cdot a_x + 10 + 2a_x + 1020A_x$$

so

---

[7] An alternative approach is to determine an annual policy fee that is independent of policy size. Actuaries who specialize in life insurance pricing will study this issue far more deeply than the introductory level presented here. In particular, they will explore this issue of policy fee determination and the important topic of expense analysis mentioned earlier.

$$G = \frac{1020A_x + 10 + 2a_x}{\ddot{a}_x - .75 - .10a_x}.$$

Since $\ddot{a}_x = a_x + 1$, this can also be written as

$$G = \frac{1020A_x + 8 + 2\ddot{a}_x}{.90\ddot{a}_x - .65}. \qquad \square$$

Recall the present value of payment random variable Z_x, defined in Section 7.1.2, and the present value of an immediate contingent unit payment stream random variable Y_x, as defined in Section 8.1.1. We can use Z_x and Y_x to now define a *present value of expenses random variable*, which we denote by H_x. The definition of H_x will depend on the specific pattern of expenses in each case. For the contract described in Example 9.8, for example, it would be defined as

$$H_x = (.75G + 10) + (.10G + 2) \cdot Y_x + 20Z_x, \qquad (9.30)$$

which the reader is asked to verify in Exercise 9-27.

Recall the whole life present value of loss random variable L_x, defined by Equation (9.13). We can now define an *expense-augmented present value of loss random variable*, which we denote by L_x^G, as the excess of the present value of benefits and expenses over the present value of expense-augmented premiums. For the whole life contract described in Example 9.8, we have

$$L_x^G = 1000Z_x + H_x - G \cdot \ddot{Y}_x, \qquad (9.31)$$

where H_x is defined by Equation (9.30), which the reader is asked to verify in Exercise 9-28.

The expense-augmented equivalence principle applied to determine the expense-augmented premium would then solve for G such that $E[L_x^G] = 0$. For the contract of Example 9.8 we have

$$\begin{aligned} L_x^G &= 1000Z_x + H_x - G \cdot \ddot{Y}_x \\ &= 1020Z_x + (.75G + 10) + (.10G + 2) \cdot Y_x - G \cdot \ddot{Y}_x. \end{aligned}$$

Then

$$E[L_x^G] = 1020A_x + (.75G + 10) + (.10G + 2) \cdot a_x - G \cdot \ddot{a}_x = 0$$

implies

$$G \cdot \ddot{a}_x = .75G + .10G \cdot a_x + 10 + 2a_x + 1020A_x,$$

as already established in Example 9.8.

9.7 MISCELLANEOUS EXAMPLES

EXAMPLE 9.9

In Example 7.12 we considered a contingent payment contract with failure benefit including a return of the net *single* premium with interest. Now we consider the case where the failure benefit includes a return of the net *annual* premiums, this time without interest. For a discrete whole life insurance issued to (35), the failure benefit is 1000 plus the return of net annual premiums without interest. Calculate the net annual premium for this contract, given the values $A_{35} = .42898$, $(IA)_{35} = 6.16761$, and $i = .05$.

SOLUTION

If the net annual premium is P, then the benefit is $1000 + P$ for failure in the first year, $1000 + 2P$ for failure in the second year, and so on. Then the equation of value is

$$P \cdot \ddot{a}_{35} = 1000 A_{35} + P \cdot (IA)_{35},$$

where

$$\ddot{a}_{35} = \frac{1 - A_{35}}{d} = \frac{1 - .42898}{.05 / 1.05} = 11.99142.$$

Then we have

$$P = \frac{1000 A_{35}}{\ddot{a}_{35} - (IA)_{35}}$$

$$= \frac{(1000)(.42898)}{11.99142 - 6.16761} = 73.66. \qquad \square$$

EXAMPLE 9.10

We know that if the annual benefit premium is determined by the equivalence principle, then the expected value of the loss at issue random variable is zero. Here we consider the case where the premium is determined from a selected survival model, but the contingent contract is issued on a risk with an elevated failure probability in a particular year. Suppose an insurance of 1000 is issued to (60) at the standard premium rate, but this person is expected to experience a first-year failure probability that is ten times the standard value, with all other probabilities at the standard rates. Find the expected loss at issue in this case, given the values $i = .06$, $A_{60} = .36933$, $A_{61} = .38300$, and $q_{60} = .01376$.

SOLUTION

The original benefit premium is

$$1000 P_{60} = \frac{1000 A_{60}}{\ddot{a}_{60}} = \frac{369.33}{11.14184} = 33.15,$$

where

$$\ddot{a}_{60} = \frac{1 - A_{60}}{d} = \frac{.63067}{.06/1.06} = 11.14184.$$

For this particular insured the loss at issue is

$$L = 1000 Z'_{60} - 33.15 \ddot{Y}'_{60},$$

where Z'_{60} and $\ddot{Y}'_{60}$ denote the present value random variables based on $q'_{60} = 10 \cdot q_{60} = .13760$.

Then

$$E[L] = 1000 A'_{60} - 33.15 \ddot{a}'_{60},$$

where

$$A'_{60} = v \cdot q'_{60} + v \cdot p'_{60} \cdot A_{61} = \frac{.13760}{1.06} + \frac{.86240}{1.06}(.38300) = .44141,$$

so

$$\ddot{a}'_{60} = \frac{1 - A'_{60}}{d} = \frac{.55859}{.06/1.06} = 9.86840.$$

Finally

$$E[L] = (1000)(.44141) - (33.15)(9.86840) = 114.27. \qquad \square$$

Example 9.11

A life insurance policy generally includes a clause stating that if the age of the insured is misstated at issue, but later discovered, the benefit under the contract will be adjusted, as of issue, to whatever amount the premium actually paid would purchase at the correct age. Consider a discrete three-year term insurance of 1000 issued to an applicant whose stated age is 30. During the third year the insurer discovers that the applicant was actually age 31 at issue. Calculate the amount of the adjusted benefit, given the values $q_{30} = .01$, $q_{31} = .02$, $q_{32} = .03$, $q_{33} = .04$, and $i = .04$.

Solution

The calculated premium, assuming issue age 30, is

$$P = \frac{1000\left[\frac{.01}{1.04} + \frac{(.99)(.02)}{(1.04)^2} + \frac{(.99)(.98)(.03)}{(1.04)^3}\right]}{1 + \frac{.99}{1.04} + \frac{(.99)(.98)}{(1.04)^2}} = 18.88300.$$

Using the correct issue age of 31, with a benefit of amount X and net premium of 18.88300, the equation of value is

$$18.88300\left[1 + \frac{.98}{1.04} + \frac{(.98)(.97)}{(1.04)^2}\right] = X\left[\frac{.02}{1.04} + \frac{(.98)(.03)}{(1.04)^2} + \frac{(.98)(.97)(.04)}{(1.04)^3}\right],$$

which solves for

$$X = \frac{(18.88300)(2.82119)}{.08022} = 664.10. \qquad \square$$

EXAMPLE 9.12

In Examples 7.10 and 9.10 we explored the effect on various actuarial functions of changing one particular value of q_x. Now we consider the effect on the net annual premium if we modify the underlying force of mortality. Suppose an impaired life is subject to a force of mortality given by $\mu'_x = \mu_x + c$, where $c > 0$ is a constant and μ_x is the standard force of mortality. How will the net annual premium for a five-year term insurance issued on the impaired life compare with the standard net annual premium?

SOLUTION

For the impaired life we have

$$_t p'_x = e^{-\int_0^t \mu'_{x+r}\, dr}$$

$$= e^{-\int_0^t \mu_{x+r}\, dr} \cdot e^{-\int_0^t c\, dr}$$

$$= {}_t p_x \cdot e^{-ct},$$

where $_t p_x$ is based on standard mortality. Then

$$\ddot{a}'_{x:\overline{5}|} = \sum_{t=0}^4 v^t \cdot {}_t p'_x = \sum_{t=0}^4 e^{-\delta t} \cdot e^{-ct} \cdot {}_t p_x = \sum_{t=0}^4 e^{-\delta' t} \cdot {}_t p_x,$$

where $\delta' = \delta + c$. Thus we see that the annuity function for the impaired life can be calculated the same as the standard annuity function but at the higher interest rate. To illustrate, let $c = .002$ and $i = .06$ (so that $\delta = \ln(1.06) = .05827$). Let the standard survival probabilities be $p_x = .99105$, $_2 p_x = .98143$, $_3 p_x = .97107$, $_4 p_x = .95994$, and $_5 p_x = .94800$. Then the standard annuity function is

$$\ddot{a}_{x:\overline{5}|} = 1 + \frac{.99105}{1.06} + \frac{.98143}{(1.06)^2} + \frac{.97107}{(1.06)^3} + \frac{.95994}{(1.06)^4}$$

$$= 1 + .93495 + .87347 + .81533 + .76036 = 4.38411.$$

Then we have

$$A^1_{x:\overline{5}|} = 1 - d \cdot \ddot{a}_{x:\overline{5}|} - {}_5E_x$$

$$= 1 - \left(\frac{.06}{1.06}\right)(4.38411) - \frac{.94800}{(1.06)^5}$$

$$= 1 - .24816 - .70840 = .04344,$$

and therefore

$$P^1_{x:\overline{5}|} = \frac{.04344}{4.38411} = .00991.$$

Now we let $\delta' = \delta + c = .06027$, so $1 + i' = e^{\delta'} = e^{.06027} = 1.06212$. Then the impaired life annuity function is

$$\ddot{a}'_{x:\overline{5}|} = 1 + \frac{.99105}{1.06212} + \frac{.98143}{(1.06212)^2} + \frac{.97107}{(1.06212)^3} + \frac{.95994}{(1.06212)^4}$$

$$= 1 + .93309 + .86999 + .81046 + .75431 = 4.36785.$$

Then

$$A'^1_{x:\overline{5}|} = 1 - \left(\frac{.06}{1.06}\right)(4.36785) - \frac{.94800}{(1.06212)^5}$$

$$= 1 - .24724 - .70136 = .05140,$$

and therefore

$$P'^1_{x:\overline{5}|} = \frac{.05140}{4.36785} = .01177. \qquad \square$$

9.8 EXERCISES

9.1 Annual Funding Schemes for Contingent Payment Models

9-1   Show that

$$P_{x:\overline{n}|} = \frac{1}{\ddot{a}_{x:\overline{n}|}} - d.$$

9-2   Show that

$$_t P^1_{x:\overline{n}|} = P^1_{x:\overline{t}|} + P^{\ 1}_{x:\overline{t}|} \cdot A^{\ 1}_{x+t:\overline{n-t}|}.$$

9-3   A 10-pay limited-payment whole life contract issued to (30) pays a benefit at the end of the year of failure of amount 1000 plus a refund of all net level premiums paid, without interest. Show that the net level annual premium, determined by the equivalence principle, is

$$P = \frac{1000 A_{30}}{\ddot{a}_{30:\overline{10}|} - (IA)^1_{30:\overline{10}|} - 10 \cdot {}_{10|}A_{30}}.$$

9-4   A whole life contingent contract issued to (75) pays 1000 at the end of the interval of failure. The net premium paid at the beginning of the kth year is $P_k = P_1(1+i)^{k-1}$. The interest rate is 5% and the age-at-failure random variable has a uniform distribution with $\omega = 105$. Using the equivalence principle, find the value of P_1.

9-5   A 40-year-old home buyer takes out a 25-year mortgage of 100,000 at interest rate 5%, and purchases a 25-year decreasing term insurance contract with a death benefit that will exactly pay off the mortgage at the end of the year of death of the borrower. Calculate the net level annual premium for the term insurance, given the following values:

$$\ddot{a}_{40:\overline{25}|} = 14 \qquad\qquad {}_{25}p_{40} = .80$$

9-6   Calculate the value of $1000P(\overline{A}_{x:\overline{n}|})$, assuming UDD over each interval $(x, x+1)$ and the following values:

$$\overline{A}_{x:\overline{n}|} = .804 \qquad\qquad {}_nE_x = .600 \qquad\qquad i = .04$$

9-7   A 10-year deferred annuity-due with annual payment 10,000 is issued to (55), with net annual premiums paid during the deferred period. In addition to the annuity payments, the contract also provides for the return of all net premiums paid, without interest, if death occurs during the deferred period. Find the net level annual premium, given the following values:

$$\ddot{a}_{55:\overline{10}|} = 8 \qquad\quad \ddot{a}_{55} = 12 \qquad\quad (IA)^1_{55:\overline{10}|} = 2.50$$

9-8   Show that

$$\ddot{s}_{x:\overline{n}|} = \frac{1}{P_{x:\overline{n}|}^1}.$$

9.2 Random Variable Analysis

9-9   Show that $E[L_x{}^2]$, where $L_x{}^2$ is defined by Equation (9.18), simplifies to the expression for $Var(L_x)$ given by Equation (9.17b).

9-10   Recall that $E[L_x]=0$ only if the net premium is determined by the equivalence principle. Find the value of $E[L_{49}]$, given the following values:

$$A_{49} = .29224 \qquad\qquad Var(L_{49}) = .10$$
$$^2A_{49} = .11723 \qquad\qquad i = .05$$

9-11   For a unit whole life insurance, let L_x denote the present value of loss random variable when the premium is chosen such that $E[L_x]=0$, and let L_x^* denote the present value of loss random variable when the premium is chosen such that $E[L_x^*] = -.20$. Given that $Var(L_x) = .30$, find the value of $Var(L_x^*)$.

9-12   Let π denote the annual premium for a whole life contingent contract of benefit amount 10,000 issued to (30), and let $L(\pi)$ denote the present value of loss random variable for this contract. The interest rate is $i=.06$. Find the smallest value of π such that $Pr[L(\pi) > 0] < .50$, given the following values from the life table survival model to which (30) is subject:

$$\ell_{30} = 9,501,382 \qquad \ell_{77} = 4,828,285 \qquad \ell_{78} = 4,530,476$$

9.3 The Percentile Premium Principle

9-13   Rework Example 9.5 to solve for the net annual premium so that the probability of a positive loss on a collection of 100 identical and independent contracts does not exceed .05.

9-14   Rework Example 9.5 with $P=.024$ and $n=100$ to find the probability of a positive loss on the collection of contracts.

9.4 Continuous Payment Funding Schemes

9-15   Find the value of $1000[\overline{P}(\overline{A}_x) - P_x]$, given the following values:

$$_k|q_x = \frac{.90^{k+1}}{9} \text{ for } k = 0,1,2,\ldots \qquad \mu_{x+t} = \mu, \text{ for all } t \qquad i = .08$$

9-16 A fully continuous whole life model has an increasing benefit function of amount $b_t = (1+i)^t$ for failure at time t. If the premium is determined by the equivalence principle, show that the present value of loss random variable is

$$\overline{L}(\overline{A}_x) = \frac{\overline{Z}_x - \overline{A}_x}{1 - \overline{A}_x}.$$

9-17 If the force of interest is δ and the force of failure is $\lambda(x) = \lambda$ for all x, show that $Var[\overline{L}(\overline{A}_x)] = \frac{\lambda}{\lambda + 2\delta}$, with continuous premium rate determined by the equivalence principle.

9-18 Let L denote the present value of loss random variable under a fully continuous whole life model with continuous annual premium rate determined by the equivalence principle. Let L^* denote the present value of loss random variable under a similar model with continuous annual premium rate $\frac{4}{3}$ times the rate in L. Find the sum of the expected value and standard deviation of L^*, given the following values:

$$Var(L) = .5652 \qquad \overline{a}_x = 5 \qquad \delta = .08$$

9-19 Let L denote the present value of loss random variable under a fully continuous whole life model with continuous annual premium rate .09, and with a benefit of 2 paid at the precise instant of failure. Given that $\delta = .06$ and $\mu_{x+t} = .04$ for all t, find the value of $Var(L)$.

9-20 Let L denote the present value of loss random variable under a fully continuous whole life model with continuous annual premium rate determined by the equivalence principle. Find the value of $\overline{P}(\overline{A}_x)$, given the following values:

$$\frac{Var(\overline{Z}_x)}{Var(L)} = .36 \qquad \overline{a}_x = 10$$

9-21 Let L denote the present value of loss random variable under a fully continuous whole life contract issued to (40), with continuous annual premium rate determined by the equivalence principle. The applicable survival model is uniform with $\omega = 100$. Given also that $\delta = .02$ and $^2\overline{A}_{40} = .379$, find the value of $Var(L)$.

9-22 Show that $\overline{P}(\overline{A}_x) = \frac{\delta \cdot \overline{A}_x}{1 - \overline{A}_x}$.

9-23 Find the CDF of $\overline{L}(\overline{A}_x)$, as defined by Equation (9.25a), if T_x has an exponential distribution with mean $\frac{1}{\lambda}$.

9.5 Funding Schemes with m^{thly} Payments

9-24   A 10-year term insurance issued to (30) for amount 10,000 has benefit paid at the end of the year of failure. Level true fractional premiums are determined under the equivalence principle and the UDD assumption. Calculate the difference (accurate to two decimals) between the annual premium rates if premiums are paid monthly versus semiannually, given the following values:

$$A^1_{30:\overline{10}|} = .015 \quad \ddot{a}_{30:\overline{10}|} = 8 \quad {}_{10}E_{30} = .604 \quad i = .05$$

9.6 Funding Plans Incorporating Expenses

9-25   A special endowment contract issued to (25) pays a pure endowment of 150,000 for survival to age 65, and a refund of all gross annual premiums paid, with interest, at the end of the year of failure, for failure before age 65. The gross annual premium is 1.20 times the net level annual premium. Calculate the net level annual premium, given the values $P_{25:\overline{40}|} = .008$, ${}_{40}p_{25} = .80$, and $i = .06$.

9-26   Consider a 20-pay unit discrete whole life insurance, with expense factors of a flat amount .02 each year, plus an additional .05 in the first year only, plus 3% of each premium paid. Find the expense-augmented annual premium for this contract, given the values $\ddot{a}_x = 20$, $\ddot{a}_{x:\overline{20}|} = 10$, and $d = .04$.

9-27   Verify Equation (9.30).

9-28   Verify Equation (9.31).

CHAPTER TEN

CONTINGENT CONTRACT RESERVES (NET LEVEL PREMIUM BENEFIT RESERVES)

We introduce the very important concept of reserves under contingent contracts by returning to the simple funding arrangement presented at the beginning of Chapter 9. Recall that the periodic funding payment was determined such that the present value at time 0 (at interest only) of the funding scheme was equal to the present value at time 0 of the payment needed at time k.

Now we consider time t, where $0 < t < k$, and analyze the status of our funding arrangement at that time. (For convenience we assume that both t and k are integers.) This is illustrated in Figure 10.1, where the payments denoted by P have been made and those denoted by (P) are scheduled but have not yet been made.

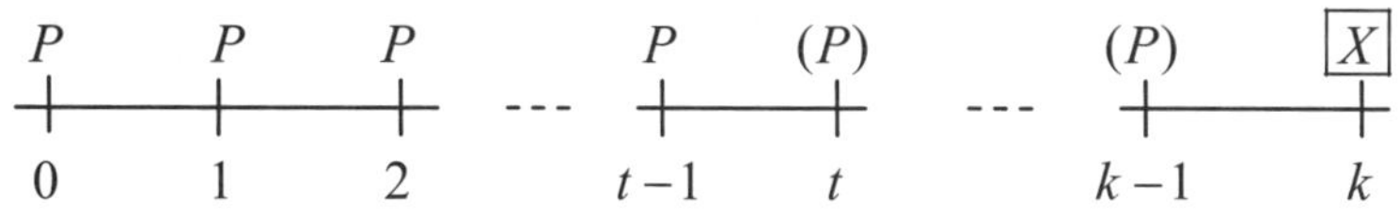

FIGURE 10.1

If we multiply both sides of Equation (9.1b) by $(1+i)^t$ we obtain

$$P \cdot \ddot{a}_{\overline{k}|i}(1+i)^t = X \cdot v^{k-t}, \tag{10.1a}$$

which equates the value at time t of the funding scheme to the value at time t of the future payment being funded. But the value at time t of the funding scheme can be separated into the value of the payments already made and the value of those yet to be made. When we do this, Equation (10.1a) becomes

$$P \cdot \ddot{s}_{\overline{t}|i} + P \cdot \ddot{a}_{\overline{k-t}|i} = X \cdot v^{k-t}, \tag{10.1b}$$

where $t < k$, or

$$P \cdot \ddot{s}_{\overline{t}|i} = X \cdot v^{k-t} - P \cdot \ddot{a}_{\overline{k-t}|i}. \tag{10.1c}$$

The left side of Equation (10.1c) gives the balance at time t of the fund being accumulated to provide the needed amount X at time k, and therefore represents the *financial status of the funding arrangement* as of time t. The right side of Equation (10.1c) represents the same concept and quantity, of course, but expresses the status of the funding arrangement as the excess of the present value of the future needed payment over the present value of the future funding payments yet to be made.

In general, we refer to the financial status of a funding arrangement as the *reserve* associated with that funding arrangement. Note that the reserve is measured at the *end* of the tth time interval, *just before* the funding payment for the $(t+1)^{st}$ interval is made. For this reason we refer to the reserve as a *terminal reserve*.[1] Note also that the reserve is different for different values of t, so we view the reserve as a function of t. In general we will use the symbol $_tV$ to denote the tth *terminal reserve* of a funding plan, with additional notation to describe the nature of the arrangement being funded.

(Viewing the reserve as the financial status of a funding arrangement is only applicable from the perspective of the party funding the future payment, not the party receiving the funding payments. The latter's perspective is explained more fully in the next chapter.)

With contingent payment models, including insurance contracts, the future time k at which amount X is paid out is stochastic rather than fixed and the future funding stream is stochastic as well. The analogy to the right side of Equation (10.1c) is that the reserve in the contingent payment case will be found as the excess of the APV of the future contingent payment over the APV of the future funding stream. In light of this use of *future* activity only, we say the reserve is determined by the *prospective method*.[2]

In the insurance context, the contingent payment is called the *benefit* under the insurance contract and the funding payments are called the *benefit premiums*. Therefore the general idea of the tth terminal benefit reserve, determined by the prospective method, under an insurance contract can be expressed as

$$_tV = (APV\ of\ future\ benefits) - (APV\ of\ future\ benefit\ premiums). \qquad (10.2)$$

In the sections that follow, we will analyze the terminal benefit reserve concept for various types of contingent contracts. Because the tth reserve is fundamentally just the status of the funding scheme at duration t of the contingent contract, the format of this chapter will closely follow that of Chapter 9 where the funding payments themselves were defined. Furthermore, we will be assuming that the benefit premium used in the funding scheme has been determined by the equivalence principle, and the same interest rate and life table that were used to determine the premium in the first place are also used to determine the benefit reserves.

In Chapter 9 (see page 191) it was mentioned that benefit premiums are also called net premiums. Then if a level benefit premium, or level net premium, has been determined by the equivalence principle, and used to calculate a benefit reserve according to Equation (10.2), the resulting benefit reserve is called the *net level premium benefit reserve*; we will refer to such reserves as *NLP reserves*.

Chapter 10 is concerned with NLP terminal reserves only. We wish to emphasize that the NLP terminal reserve is simply a mathematical function of the insurance contract. Its practical significance is somewhat limited; this will become clearer when we consider other important types of reserves, and other contract values, in Chapters 11 and 14.

---

[1] An alternative measure of the funding status, called the *initial reserve*, will arise in Section 10.1.3.

[2] The alternative, of determining the reserve at duration t from *past* activity only, is called the *retrospective method*, and will be introduced in Section 10.1.2. This will be the contingent payment analogy to the left side of Equation (10.1c).

10.1 NLP RESERVES FOR CONTINGENT PAYMENT MODELS WITH ANNUAL PAYMENT FUNDING

In this section we consider NLP reserves for various types of contingent payment models being funded by a series of discrete level annual premiums, as identified in Section 9.1. We will also analyze the reserve from the random variable perspective introduced in Section 9.2. Throughout Sections 10.1.1 - 10.1.5, we will be assuming that the single contingent payment is made at the end of the time interval (e.g., year) of failure. The alternative case of immediate payment of claims is treated in Section 10.1.6, and the case of contingent annuities is treated in Section 10.1.7.

Note that t is necessarily an integer throughout this section. This restriction is then relaxed for the fully continuous models of Section 10.2.

10.1.1 NLP RESERVES BY THE PROSPECTIVE METHOD

The following diagram provides an orientation for much of the discussion in this section.

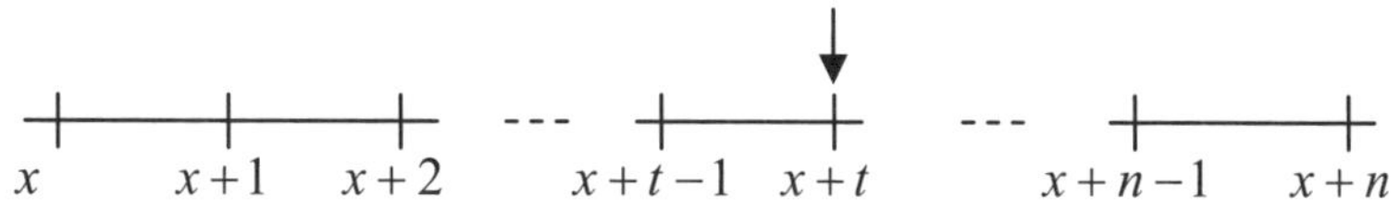

FIGURE 10.2

Consider the unit whole life contingent payment contract, with benefit payable at the end of the year in which the status of interest (x) fails, being funded by discrete level annual premiums of P_x paid at the beginning of each year. Given that the contract is still in effect at duration t (i.e., given that (x) has not yet failed at time t), the tth NLP terminal reserve by the prospective method is given by Equation (10.2) as

$$_tV_x = A_{x+t} - P_x \cdot \ddot{a}_{x+t}. \tag{10.3}$$

For n-year term insurance, with $t < n$, we have

$$_tV^1_{x:\overline{n}|} = A^1_{x+t:\overline{n-t}|} - P^1_{x:\overline{n}|} \cdot \ddot{a}_{x+t:\overline{n-t}|}, \tag{10.4}$$

for n-year pure endowment we have

$$_tV_{x:\overline{n}|}^{1} = A_{x+t:\overline{n-t}|}^{1} - P_{x:\overline{n}|}^{1} \cdot \ddot{a}_{x+t:\overline{n-t}|}, \tag{10.5}$$

and for n-year endowment insurance we have

$$_tV_{x:\overline{n}|} = A_{x+t:\overline{n-t}|} - P_{x:\overline{n}|} \cdot \ddot{a}_{x+t:\overline{n-t}|}. \tag{10.6}$$

All of Equations (10.4), (10.5) and (10.6) presume $t < n$. For $t = n$ the term insurance NLP reserve is $_nV^1_{x:\overline{n}|} = 0$, because the contract has expired without value. In the case of both pure endowment and endowment insurance we have $_nV\frac{1}{x:n|} = _nV_{x:n|} = 1$, because the contract matures at duration n for the amount of the unit endowment benefit.

In the case of limited payment funding patterns, such as h-pay whole life, we have

$$^h_tV_x = A_{x+t} - _hP_x \cdot \ddot{a}_{x+t:\overline{h-t}|}, \tag{10.7a}$$

for $t < h$, since the future premium stream continues only to the hth year.[3]

For $t \geq h$ there are no future premiums so the prospective NLP reserve is simply

$$^h_tV_x = A_{x+t}. \tag{10.7b}$$

Prospective NLP reserve expressions for other types of contingent payment contracts with limited payment funding patterns will be pursued in the exercises.

In the special case of the n-year deferred insurance defined in Section 7.1.3, the prospective NLP reserve expression will depend on the duration of the funding scheme. For example, if the funding is limited to the first n years (i.e., the deferred period), then we have

$$^n_tV(_n|A_x) = _{n-t}|A_{x+t} - _nP(_n|A_x) \cdot \ddot{a}_{x+t:\overline{n-t}|}, \tag{10.8a}$$

for $t < n$, and

$$^n_tV(_n|A_x) = A_{x+t}, \tag{10.8b}$$

for $t \geq n$. NLP reserve expressions resulting from other assumptions about the funding pattern will be pursued in the exercises.

EXAMPLE 10.1

Find the value of $_{n-1}V_{x:n|}$, given $A_{x:n|} = .20$ and $d = .08$.

SOLUTION

Prospectively we have

$$_{n-1}V_{x:n|} = A_{x+n-1:\overline{1}|} - P_{x:n|} \cdot \ddot{a}_{x+n-1:\overline{1}|}.$$

But $A_{x+n-1:\overline{1}|} = v$, since payment is certain at age $x+n$ under the endowment contract, and $\ddot{a}_{x+n-1:\overline{1}|} = 1$, so we have

$$_{n-1}V_{x:n|} = v - P_{x:n|}.$$

---

[3] Note the notational rules. The parameter for number of premiums, h, occupies the pre-subscript position in the premium symbol $_hP_x$. But that position is reserved for the duration in the NLP reserve symbol, so the number-of-premiums parameter h is moved to the pre-superscript position in $^h_tV_x$.

Recall that

$$P_{x:\overline{n}|} = \frac{A_{x:\overline{n}|}}{\ddot{a}_{x:\overline{n}|}} = \frac{A_{x:\overline{n}|}}{\frac{1 - A_{x:\overline{n}|}}{d}} = \frac{.20}{\frac{.80}{.08}} = .02.$$

Then

$$_{n-1}V_{x:\overline{n}|} = (1-.08)-.02 = .90. \qquad \square$$

10.1.2 NLP RESERVES BY THE RETROSPECTIVE METHOD

As mentioned in the introductory section of this chapter, we can develop an expression for the NLP terminal reserve at duration t by considering only the past activity in the interval $(x, x+t]$, which we refer to as the *retrospective method*. For the whole life contingent payment model, we begin with the equivalence relationship between benefits and premiums stated as of time 0 and given by Equation (9.3a). Then we focus our attention at time t, and assume the contract is still in force at that time. We can separate the APV of the contingent annuity into the part addressing payments over the first t years and the part addressing payments after the first t years. From Equation (8.50) and Example 8.10 we have

$$\ddot{a}_x = \ddot{a}_{x:\overline{t}|} + {}_t|\ddot{a}_x = \ddot{a}_{x:\overline{t}|} + {}_tE_x \cdot \ddot{a}_{x+t}. \qquad (10.9)$$

Similarly, we can separate the APV of the contingent benefit payment into the part addressing payment if the contingent event occurs within the first t years and the part addressing payment if the contingent event occurs after the first t years. From Equation (7.16) and Exercise 7-11 we have

$$A_x = A^1_{x:\overline{t}|} + {}_t|A_x = A^1_{x:\overline{t}|} + {}_tE_x \cdot A_{x+t}. \qquad (10.10)$$

Now we use Equations (10.9) and (10.10) to substitute for $\ddot{a}_x$ and A_x, respectively, in Equation (9.3a) to obtain

$$P_x (\ddot{a}_{x:\overline{t}|} + {}_tE_x \cdot \ddot{a}_{x+t}) = A^1_{x:\overline{t}|} + {}_tE_x \cdot A_{x+t}$$

or

$$P_x \cdot \ddot{a}_{x:\overline{t}|} - A^1_{x:\overline{t}|} = {}_tE_x \left(A_{x+t} - P_x \cdot \ddot{a}_{x+t} \right)$$

or

$$\left(P_x \cdot \ddot{a}_{x:\overline{t}|} - A^1_{x:\overline{t}|} \right) \cdot \frac{1}{{}_tE_x} = A_{x+t} - P_x \cdot \ddot{a}_{x+t}. \qquad (10.11a)$$

Recall from Equation (8.35) that

$$\ddot{s}_{x:\overline{t}|} = \ddot{a}_{x:\overline{t}|} \cdot \frac{1}{{}_tE_x}$$

gives the accumulated actuarial value of the temporary annuity-due. Finally we define

$$_{t}k_{x} = A^{1}_{x:t|} \cdot \frac{1}{_{t}E_{x}} \qquad (10.12)$$

to be the *accumulated cost of insurance* over the age interval $(x, x+t]$. Substituting in Equation (10.11a) we have

$$P_{x} \cdot \ddot{s}_{x:t|} - {}_{t}k_{x} = A_{x+t} - P_{x} \cdot \ddot{a}_{x+t}. \qquad (10.11b)$$

We recognize the right side of Equation (10.11b) as $_{t}V_{x}$ by the prospective method, so the left side must be $_{t}V_{x}$ as well. Thus we have

$$_{t}V_{x} = P_{x} \cdot \ddot{s}_{x:t|} - {}_{t}k_{x} \qquad (10.11c)$$

as the tth retrospective reserve for the whole life contingent payment model.

EXAMPLE 10.2

Find the value of $P^{1}_{x:n|}$, given $P_{x} = .090$, $_{n}V_{x} = .563$, and $P_{x:n|}^{1} = .00864$.

SOLUTION

Because the value of $P_{x:n|}^{1}$ is given, and the value of the term insurance premium $P^{1}_{x:n|}$ is sought, the retrospective view of the NLP reserve is suggested. We have

$$
\begin{aligned}
_{n}V_{x} &= P_{x} \cdot \ddot{s}_{x:n|} - {}_{n}k_{x} \\
&= P_{x}\left(\frac{\ddot{a}_{x:n|}}{_{n}E_{x}}\right) - \frac{A^{1}_{x:n|}}{_{n}E_{x}} \\
&= P_{x}\left(\frac{\ddot{a}_{x:n|}}{_{n}E_{x}}\right) - \frac{P^{1}_{x:n|} \cdot \ddot{a}_{x:n|}}{_{n}E_{x}} \\
&= P_{x}\left(\frac{1}{P_{x:n|}^{1}}\right) - \frac{P^{1}_{x:n|}}{P_{x:n|}^{1}}.
\end{aligned}
$$

(See Exercise 9-8.) Then we have

$$_{n}V_{x} = \frac{.090}{.00864} - \frac{P^{1}_{x:n|}}{.00864} = .563,$$

which solves for $P^{1}_{x:n|} = .08514$. ◻

We need to get a better understanding about what $_t k_x$ actually represents, and we can do this by returning to the deterministic group approach used several times in Chapters 7 and 8. Consider the following diagram, which is an extension of Figure 7.2.

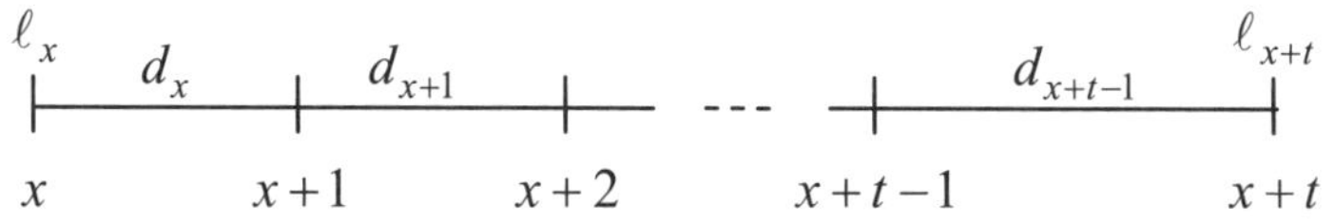

FIGURE 10.3

The sequence $d_x, d_{x+1}, \ldots, d_{x+t-1}$ represents the sequence of payments made if each of ℓ_x persons purchases a whole life insurance of unit benefit at age x. The accumulated value at time t (age $x+t$) of the benefit payments is

$$d_x(1+i)^{t-1} + d_{x+1}(1+i)^{t-2} + \cdots + d_{x+t-1},$$

since all payments are made at the end of the interval of failure. There are ℓ_{x+t} survivors in the group at time t. Each survivor's share of this accumulated value of benefit payments is called the *accumulated cost of insurance* and is given by

$$
\begin{aligned}
_t k_x &= \frac{d_x(1+i)^{t-1} + d_{x+1}(1+i)^{t-2} + \cdots + d_{x+t-1}}{\ell_{x+t}} \\
&= \frac{\ell_x}{\ell_{x+t}} \left[\frac{d_x(1+i)^{t-1} + d_{x+1}(1+i)^{t-2} + \cdots + d_{x+t-1}}{\ell_x} \right] \\
&= \frac{(1+i)^t}{_t p_x} \left[\frac{v \cdot d_x + v^2 \cdot d_{x+1} + \cdots + v^t \cdot d_{x+t-1}}{\ell_x} \right] = \frac{1}{_t E_x} \cdot A^1_{x:\overline{t}|},
\end{aligned}
$$

as established by Equation (10.12).

Retrospective NLP reserve expressions for other types of contingent payment models will be developed in the exercises.

10.1.3 Additional NLP Terminal Reserve Expressions

Starting with the basic prospective reserve expression given by Equation (10.3) for the whole life contingent payment model, we can develop several additional expressions for the tth NLP terminal reserve under that model. We have

$$_t V_x = A_{x+t} - P_x \cdot \ddot{a}_{x+t} = (1 - d \cdot \ddot{a}_{x+t}) - P_x \cdot \ddot{a}_{x+t} = 1 - (P_x + d) \cdot \ddot{a}_{x+t} \qquad (10.13)$$

by using the result of Example 8.4. Then substituting for $(P_x + d)$ from Equation (9.4) we have the elegant formula

$$_t V_x = 1 - \frac{\ddot{a}_{x+t}}{\ddot{a}_x}, \qquad (10.14)$$

which expresses the NLP reserve in terms of contingent annuity values.

If we substitute for $\ddot{a}_{x+t}$ in Equation (10.13) by again using Equation (9.4) we obtain

$$_tV_x = 1 - \frac{P_x + d}{P_{x+t} + d} = \frac{P_{x+t} - P_x}{P_{x+t} + d}, \tag{10.15}$$

which expresses the NLP reserve in terms of net annual premium values. Conversely, if we substitute $\frac{1 - A_x}{d}$ for $\ddot{a}_x$ and $\frac{1 - A_{x+t}}{d}$ for $\ddot{a}_{x+t}$ in Equation (10.14), we obtain

$$_tV_x = 1 - \frac{1 - A_{x+t}}{1 - A_x} = \frac{A_{x+t} - A_x}{1 - A_x}, \tag{10.16}$$

which expresses the NLP reserve in terms of net single premium values. By substituting $P_{x+t} \cdot \ddot{a}_{x+t}$ for A_{x+t} in Equation (10.13) we obtain

$$_tV_x = P_{x+t} \cdot \ddot{a}_{x+t} - P_x \cdot \ddot{a}_{x+t} = (P_{x+t} - P_x) \cdot \ddot{a}_{x+t}, \tag{10.17}$$

which is called the *premium difference formula*.

Another expression results if we substitute for $\ddot{a}_{x+t}$ in Equation (10.13) using

$$\ddot{a}_{x+t} = \frac{A_{x+t}}{P_{x+t}},$$

which itself comes from Equation (9.3a) with x replaced by $x+t$. Then Equation (10.13) becomes

$$_tV_x = A_{x+t} - P_x\left(\frac{A_{x+t}}{P_{x+t}}\right) = \left(1 - \frac{P_x}{P_{x+t}}\right) \cdot A_{x+t}. \tag{10.18}$$

Equation (10.18) has an important interpretation. If a whole life insurance contract were issued at age $x+t$, then a level annual benefit premium of P_{x+t} would be sufficient to fund the future unit contingent benefit payment. But instead the contract was issued at age x, with level annual benefit premium of P_x (where $P_x < P_{x+t}$), so the future premium stream of P_x each will fund a future contingent payment of size $\frac{P_x}{P_{x+t}} < 1$. The remainder of the future contingent payment, which is $1 - \frac{P_x}{P_{x+t}}$, must be funded by the NLP reserve at time t, so the reserve has to be the expected present value of a benefit of that size, which is stated by Equation (10.18). The amount of future benefit funded by the NLP reserve is called the *amount of reduced paid-up insurance*, because this amount of benefit is "paid up" at duration t even if no future premiums are paid. (See also Section 14.3.2.)

NLP reserve expressions similar to those given by Equations (10.13) through (10.18) for the whole life model can also be developed for the endowment insurance model. This is pursued in Exercise 10-5.

10.1.4 RANDOM VARIABLE ANALYSIS

Recall that the present value of loss random variable defined by Equation (9.13) measures the present value of loss at time 0. (Recall that the value of P resulting from setting $E[L_x] = 0$ is the same as the value of P produced by the equivalence principle.) Now suppose the contingent contract is still in effect at time t, which means that the status of interest has not yet failed at time t. This means we are given that $K_x^* > t$. Then conditional on $K_x^* > t$ we can write the present value of future loss at time t as $v^{k-t} - P \cdot \ddot{a}_{\overline{k-t}|}$ for failure occurring in the kth time interval, where $k > t$. In general we would have

$$ {}_tL_x = v^{K_x^* - t} - P_x \cdot \ddot{a}_{\overline{K_x^* - t}|} \tag{10.19a} $$

$$ = Z_{x+t} - P_x \cdot \ddot{Y}_{x+t} \tag{10.19b} $$

as the present value of loss random variable measured at time t, given $K_x^* > t$.[4] This is illustrated in the following figure.

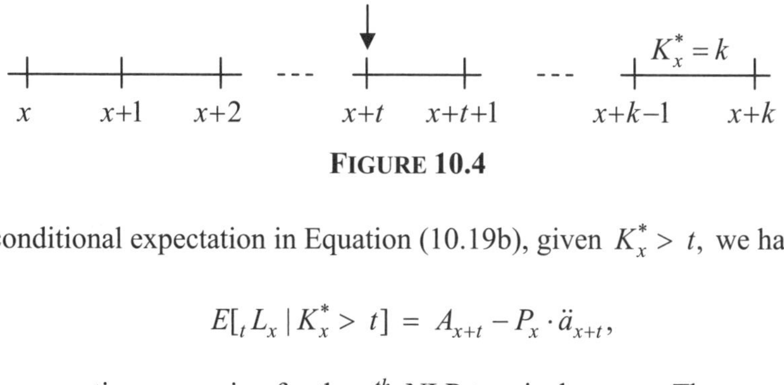

FIGURE 10.4

Taking the conditional expectation in Equation (10.19b), given $K_x^* > t$, we have

$$ E[{}_tL_x \mid K_x^* > t] = A_{x+t} - P_x \cdot \ddot{a}_{x+t}, \tag{10.20} $$

which is the prospective expression for the tth NLP terminal reserve. Thus we conclude that if the level funding payment is determined by the equivalence principle, then the NLP terminal reserve is given by the conditional expected value of the present value of loss random variable measured at time t.

The conditional variance of the present value of loss random variable ${}_tL_x$ is found in the same way we found $Var({}_0L_x)$ in Section 9.2 (see Equations (9.17a) and (9.17b)), producing

$$ Var\left({}_tL_x \mid K_x^* > t\right) = \left(1 + \frac{P_x}{d}\right)^2 \cdot \left({}^2A_{x+t} - A_{x+t}{}^2\right). \tag{10.21} $$

The parallel development of the expected value and variance of ${}_tL_{x:\overline{n}|}$ is left as Exercise 10-8.

---

[4] The definition of ${}_tL_x$ suggests that the simpler L_x of Equation (9.13) should now be written as ${}_0L_x$.

EXAMPLE 10.3

Let $_2L = 1000 \cdot {}_2L^1_{x:\overline{4}|}$ denote the present value of loss random variable at duration 2 for a 4-year term insurance of amount 1000 issued to (x), given $K^*_x > 2$. Find the value of $Var(_2L)$, given the following values:

$$P^1_{x:\overline{4}|} = .12 \qquad q_{x+2} = .12 \qquad q_{x+3} = .13 \qquad i = 0$$

SOLUTION

Note that $v = 1$ since $i = 0$. We will use P in place of $1000P^1_{x:\overline{4}|}$ for notational convenience. $_2L$ assumes the value $1000 - P = 880$ if failure occurs in $(x+2, x+3]$, which event happens with probability .12, and $_2L$ assumes the value $1000 - 2P = 760$ if failure occurs in $(x+3, x+4]$, which happens with probability $(.88)(.13) = .1144$. If survival to age $x+4$ occurs, which happens with probability $(.88)(.87) = .7656$, then $_2L$ assumes the value $0 - 2P = -240$. (Note that $_2L$ is defined conditional on $K^*_x > 2$.) Then we find

$$E[_2L|K^*_x > 2] = (880)(.12) + (760)(.1144) + (-240)(.7656) = 8.80$$

and

$$E[_2L^2|K^*_x > 2] = (880)^2(.12) + (760)^2(.1144) + (-240)^2(.7656) = 203,104$$

and therefore

$$Var(_2L|K^*_x > 2) = 203,104 - (8.80)^2 = 203,026.56. \qquad \square$$

10.1.5 NLP RESERVES FOR CONTINGENT CONTRACTS WITH IMMEDIATE PAYMENT OF CLAIMS

Recall the continuous contingent payment models developed in Section 7.3, which we also refer to as immediate payment of claims models. The annual funding payments for such models were considered in Section 9.1.2. Prospective expressions for the tth NLP terminal reserve for such models are parallel to those developed earlier in this section for models with benefit paid at the end of the year of failure.[5] Thus, for example, we have

$$_tV(\overline{A}_x) = \overline{A}_{x+t} - P(\overline{A}_x) \cdot \ddot{a}_{x+t} \tag{10.22}$$

for the whole life model,

$$_tV(\overline{A}^1_{x:\overline{n}|}) = \overline{A}^1_{x+t:\overline{n-t}|} - P(\overline{A}^1_{x:\overline{n}|}) \cdot \ddot{a}_{x+t:\overline{n-t}|} \tag{10.23}$$

for the n-year term insurance model, and

---

[5] Just as the level annual premiums for immediate payment of claims models are sometimes called semicontinuous net premiums, just so the associated NLP reserves are sometimes called *semicontinuous benefit reserves*.

$$_tV\left(\overline{A}_{x:\overline{n}|}\right) = \overline{A}_{x+t:\overline{n-t}|} - P\left(\overline{A}_{x:\overline{n}|}\right)\cdot\ddot{a}_{x+t:\overline{n-t}|} \tag{10.24}$$

for the n-year endowment insurance model. If the contract involves a limited funding pattern over the first h years only, then the tth NLP reserve for an n-year term insurance with immediate payment of claims is given by

$$_t^hV\left(\overline{A}_{x:\overline{n}|}^1\right) = \overline{A}_{x+t:\overline{n-t}|}^1 - _hP\left(\overline{A}_{x:\overline{n}|}^1\right)\cdot\ddot{a}_{x+t:\overline{h-t}|} \tag{10.25a}$$

for $t < h < n$, and

$$_t^hV\left(\overline{A}_{x:\overline{n}|}^1\right) = \overline{A}_{x+t:\overline{n-t}|}^1 \tag{10.25b}$$

for $h < t < n$.

The retrospective reserve expression for the whole life model is

$$_tV\left(\overline{A}_x\right) = P\left(\overline{A}_x\right)\cdot\ddot{s}_{x:\overline{t}|} - _t\overline{k}_x, \tag{10.26}$$

where

$$_t\overline{k}_x = \overline{A}_{x:\overline{t}|}^1 \cdot \frac{1}{_tE_x}. \tag{10.27}$$

Other NLP terminal reserve expressions for contracts with immediate payment of claims are developed in the exercises. The NLP reserve expressions in this section can be evaluated from a life table by using the UDD assumption to evaluate the various $\overline{A}$ functions.

10.1.6 NLP RESERVES FOR CONTINGENT ANNUITY MODELS

If an n-year deferred contingent annuity-due contract is funded by level annual premiums over the deferred period, then the tth NLP terminal reserve, for $t < n$, is given by

$$_tV\left(_n|\ddot{a}_x\right) = _{n-t}|\ddot{a}_{x+t} - P\left(_n|\ddot{a}_x\right)\cdot\ddot{a}_{x+t:\overline{n-t}|}, \tag{10.28}$$

since the future benefit is still a deferred annuity-due (deferred for $n-t$ years) and $n-t$ level annual funding payments still remain to be made. The level benefit premium $P\left(_n|\ddot{a}_x\right)$ is defined by Equation (9.11b).

10.2 RECURSIVE RELATIONSHIPS FOR DISCRETE MODELS WITH ANNUAL PREMIUMS

Additional understanding of the NLP reserve concept can be obtained by examining how the reserve evolves from one duration to the next. We will again make use of the group deterministic interpretation as the easiest way to present these ideas for the first time, and then move to a stochastic presentation of the same concepts. We will use the generic symbols P (for the level annual benefit premium) and $_tV$ (for the NLP terminal benefit reserve at integral duration t), since the presentation here is applicable to any of the whole life, term, or endowment insurance models, including the h-pay limited-payment models provided $t < h$. We also assume a unit contingent payment benefit.[6]

We focus on the single year of age from $x+t$ to $x+t+1$, which is the $(t+1)^{st}$ year of the contingent payment contract. This is illustrated in the following figure.

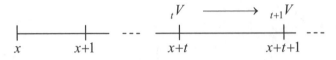

FIGURE 10.5

We will find it useful to begin with the group deterministic approach considered in Section 7.2 and several places in Chapter 8. Suppose ℓ_x persons each purchase an identical unit benefit contingent contract with level annual benefit premium P. At the end of the tth year there are ℓ_{x+t} persons alive (and hence ℓ_{x+t} contracts in force). Each contract carries an NLP terminal reserve of size $_tV$ at that time, so the total aggregate reserve fund is $\ell_{x+t} \cdot {_tV}$. At the beginning of the $(t+1)^{st}$ year each person pays a premium of P, so the aggregate fund becomes

$$\ell_{x+t}(_tV+P) = \ell_{x+t} \cdot {_{t+1}I}, \tag{10.29}$$

where $_{t+1}I = {_tV}+P$ is called the $(t+1)^{st}$ *initial reserve* for the contingent contract. This aggregate initial reserve fund then earns interest at rate i, and therefore grows to amount $\ell_{x+t}(_tV+P)(1+i)$ by the end of the $(t+1)^{st}$ year. During that year d_{x+t} contracts fail and ℓ_{x+t+1} contracts survive. The aggregate fund at time $t+1$ must be sufficient to pay the unit contingent benefit to each of the d_{x+t} that fail and establish the $(t+1)^{st}$ NLP terminal reserve for the ℓ_{x+t+1} that survive. Thus we have

$$\ell_{x+t}(_tV+P)(1+i) = d_{x+t} + \ell_{x+t+1} \cdot {_{t+1}V}. \tag{10.30a}$$

If we divide both sides of Equation (10.30a) by ℓ_{x+t}, we obtain

$$(_tV+P)(1+i) = q_{x+t} + p_{x+t} \cdot {_{t+1}V}, \tag{10.30b}$$

which expresses the same idea as Equation (10.30a), but on an expected value basis for one particular contingent contract rather than on an aggregate deterministic basis for a collection of similar contingent contracts. If we multiply both sides of Equation (10.30b) by v we obtain

$$_tV+P = v \cdot q_{x+t} + v \cdot p_{x+t} \cdot {_{t+1}V}, \tag{10.30c}$$

---

[6] In Section 11.3 we generalize this development to the case with non-level premiums and/or benefits.

which expresses the initial NLP reserve as an expected present value by considering the two possible uses of the initial reserve at year end, depending on whether the contract fails (with probability q_{x+t}) or survives (with probability p_{x+t}). Next we subtract $_tV$ from both sides of Equation (10.30c) and multiply it by $p_{x+t} + q_{x+t} = 1$, obtaining

$$P = v \cdot q_{x+t} + v \cdot p_{x+t} \cdot {}_{t+1}V - {}_tV(p_{x+t} + q_{x+t}) = (v - {}_tV) \cdot q_{x+t} + (v \cdot {}_{t+1}V - {}_tV) \cdot p_{x+t}. \quad (10.30d)$$

Equation (10.30d) expresses the net level benefit premium as an expected present value by considering the two possible roles it could play at year end, namely providing the excess of the present value of benefit over the existing NLP reserve (if the contract fails) or the excess of the present value of the new $(t+1)^{st}$ NLP reserve over the existing reserve (if the contract survives).

Finally, substituting $1 - q_{x+t}$ for p_{x+t} in Equation (10.30b) and rearranging we have

$$_{t+1}V = (_tV + P)(1+i) - q_{x+t}(1 - {}_{t+1}V). \quad (10.30e)$$

The excess of the unit benefit over the NLP terminal reserve, $1 - {}_{t+1}V$, is called the *net amount at risk*. This is a cost to the insurer at time $t+1$ if the contract fails in $(t, t+1]$, which happens with probability q_{x+t}, so the product $q_{x+t}(1 - {}_{t+1}V)$ is called the *expected cost of insurance based on the net amount at risk*.

EXAMPLE 10.4

For a whole life contract with net level annual premiums issued to (x), the NLP initial reserve for year t is 200 and the net amount at risk for year t is 1295. Find the NLP terminal reserve for year $t-1$, given the following values:

$$\ddot{a}_x = 16.20 \qquad q_{x+t-1} = .00386 \qquad i = .05$$

SOLUTION

Note that the amount of the contingent benefit, B, is not given. Adapting Equation (10.30e) to this problem we have

$$_tV = (_{t-1}V + P)(1+i) - q_{x+t-1}(B - {}_tV) = (200)(1.05) - (.00386)(1295) = 205,$$

so the amount of the benefit is $B = 1295 + 205 = 1500$. Then we can find the net level premium as

$$P = 1500\left(\frac{A_x}{\ddot{a}_x}\right) = 1500\left(\frac{1 - \frac{.05}{1.05}(16.20)}{16.20}\right) = 21.16,$$

and finally we can find

$$_{t-1}V = 200 - 21.16 = 178.84. \qquad \qquad \Box$$

Example 10.5

Contingent payment contracts sometimes contain a refund of premium feature, with or without interest. Consider an n-year deferred annuity-due issued to (x), with net level annual premiums paid during the deferred period. The contract includes a benefit of return of net level premiums paid, with interest at rate i, for failure during the deferred period. The net level premium and the NLP reserves are also calculated at rate i. Find expressions for the net level annual premium and the tth NLP terminal reserve, for $t \le n$.

Solution

The problem is best approached using the recursive relationship of this section. Since $_0V = 0$ we have

$$P(1+i) = q_x[P(1+i)] + p_x \cdot {_1V}$$

or

$$P(1+i) \cdot (1-q_x) = p_x \cdot {_1V},$$

so $_1V = P(1+i)$. Thus we see that the first NLP reserve is the same as the failure benefit in the first year, namely the first premium with interest.

Similarly, we have

$$({_1V}+P)(1+i) = q_{x+1}(P \cdot \ddot{s}_{\overline{2}|}) + p_{x+1} \cdot {_2V}.$$

But

$$({_1V}+P)(1+i) = [P(1+i)+P](1+i) = P \cdot \ddot{s}_{\overline{2}|},$$

so we have

$$P \cdot \ddot{s}_{\overline{2}|} \cdot (1-q_{x+1}) = p_{x+1} \cdot {_2V},$$

so $_2V = P \cdot \ddot{s}_{\overline{2}|}$. Continuing in this way we can see that $_tV = P \cdot \ddot{s}_{\overline{t}|}$ for all $t \le n$. But, prospectively, $_nV = \ddot{a}_{x+n}$, so we find $P = \dfrac{\ddot{a}_{x+n}}{\ddot{s}_{\overline{n}|}}$. ☐

Thus we see that if the failure benefit is the return of net premiums with interest at the same rate as that used for premium and reserve calculation, then the NLP reserve is the same as the failure benefit. (Recall that we developed this result for the net annual premium only in Section 9.1.3.) When the failure benefit is the reserve, then there is no cost of insurance under the contract, since each contract provides its own failure benefit. In effect, the mortality risk has been transferred from the insurer to the insured.

Examples 10.4 (for insurance) and 10.5 (for annuities) illustrate the basic mathematics of universal life insurance and deferred variable annuities, respectively. Because these contracts typically involve non-level premiums, we will defer our introduction of them to Chapter 11 (see Sections 11.5 and 11.6).

10.3 NLP RESERVES FOR CONTINGENT PAYMENT MODELS WITH CONTINUOUS PAYMENT FUNDING

Here we return to the concept of funding contingent payment contracts with continuous funding payments, as introduced in Section 9.3. We repeat the observation made in Section 9.3 that this notion is an abstract one, but with some interesting mathematics that justifies a brief study of it. We will consider in detail only the whole life model.

10.3.1 DISCRETE WHOLE LIFE CONTINGENT PAYMENT MODELS

Consider the discrete whole life contingent payment model with continuous funding at annual rate $\overline{P}_x$, as defined by Equation (9.20a). (Recall that the payment model is called discrete because the contingent payment is made at the end of the discrete interval (generally year) of failure, notwithstanding that the funding scheme is continuous.) If the contract has not yet failed at time t, then the tth NLP terminal reserve is given by the prospective method as

$$_t \overline{V}_x = A_{x+t} - \overline{P}_x \cdot \overline{a}_{x+t}.$$ (10.31)

If the continuous funding scheme is limited to the first h years of the contract, then we have

$$_t^h \overline{V}_x = A_{x+t} - {_h}\overline{P}_x \cdot \overline{a}_{x+t:\overline{h-t}|}$$ (10.32a)

if $t < h$, and

$$_t^h \overline{V}_x = A_{x+t}$$ (10.32b)

if $t \geq h$, since there are no future funding payments beyond duration h.

The retrospective NLP reserve is given by

$$_t \overline{V}_x = \overline{P}_x \cdot \overline{s}_{x:\overline{t}|} - {_t}k_x,$$ (10.33)

which differs from the annual premium case given by Equation (10.11c) in that the accumulation of past premium occurs continuously. The continuous actuarial accumulated value, denoted $\overline{s}_{x:\overline{t}|}$, is defined by Equation (8.41).

The NLP reserve expressions in this section can be evaluated from a life table by using the UDD-based approximations or the Woolhouse approximations described in Chapter 8, to evaluate the various continuous annuity functions.

10.3.2 CONTINUOUS WHOLE LIFE CONTINGENT PAYMENT MODELS

Next we consider the whole life model with both continuous funding and immediate payment of claims, as introduced in Section 9.3.2, with annual premium rate denoted by $\overline{P}(\overline{A}_x)$. Recall that such models are sometimes called fully continuous premium models.

By now the reader should understand the principles used to write various NLP reserve expressions. For this model the NLP reserve at duration t is given prospectively as

$$_t\overline{V}(\overline{A}_x) = \overline{A}_{x+t} - \overline{P}(\overline{A}_x) \cdot \overline{a}_{x+t} \tag{10.34}$$

and retrospectively as

$$_t\overline{V}(\overline{A}_x) = \overline{P}(\overline{A}_x) \cdot \overline{s}_{x:\bar{t}|} - _t\overline{k}_x, \tag{10.35}$$

where the continuous version of the accumulated cost of insurance, denoted $_t\overline{k}_x$, is defined by Equation (10.27).

Additional expressions for the reserve in the fully continuous case, analogous to those presented in Section 10.1.3 in the discrete case, can be developed by steps parallel to those used in Section 10.1.3. Accordingly we will present only a sample of results here, and then invite the reader to derive the continuous version of the rest of the Section 10.1.3 results in the exercises.

Analogous to Equation (10.13) we now have

$$_t\overline{V}(\overline{A}_x) = 1 - \left[\overline{P}(\overline{A}_x) + \delta\right] \cdot \overline{a}_{x+t}, \tag{10.36}$$

analogous to Equation (10.14) we now have

$$_t\overline{V}(\overline{A}_x) = 1 - \frac{\overline{a}_{x+t}}{\overline{a}_x}, \tag{10.37}$$

and analogous to Equation (10.17) we now have

$$_t\overline{V}(\overline{A}_x) = \left[\overline{P}(\overline{A}_{x+t}) - \overline{P}(\overline{A}_x)\right] \cdot \overline{a}_{x+t}. \tag{10.38}$$

In the fully continuous case, the NLP reserve is defined for all real values of t, rather than being restricted to integral t only. Strictly speaking, $_t\overline{V}(\overline{A}_x)$ should be called a "terminal" reserve only for integral t. Since $_t\overline{V}(\overline{A}_x)$ is defined for *all* t, we do not refer to it as a terminal reserve.

EXAMPLE 10.7

Show that

$$\frac{d}{dt} _t\overline{V}(\overline{A}_x) = \frac{\overline{A}_{x+t} - \overline{a}_{x+t} \cdot \mu_{x+t}}{\overline{a}_x}.$$

SOLUTION

Using Equation (10.37) we have

$$\frac{d}{dt} _t\overline{V}(\overline{A}_x) = \frac{d}{dt}\left(1 - \frac{\overline{a}_{x+t}}{\overline{a}_x}\right) = -\frac{1}{\overline{a}_x} \cdot \frac{d}{dt}\overline{a}_{x+t} = -\frac{\overline{a}_{x+t}(\mu_{x+t} + \delta) - 1}{\overline{a}_x},$$

using the result from Exercise 8-11. Then we have

$$\frac{d}{dt}{}_t\overline{V}(\overline{A}_x) = \frac{1-\delta\cdot\overline{a}_{x+t}-\overline{a}_{x+t}\cdot\mu_{x+t}}{\overline{a}_x} = \frac{\overline{A}_{x+t}-\overline{a}_{x+t}\cdot\mu_{x+t}}{\overline{a}_x},$$

as required.   ❑

For this fully continuous whole life model, the analogy to the discrete model recursion formula, given in Section 10.2, would be in the form of a differential equation. Using the group deterministic approach of Section 10.2, we observe that the aggregate reserve fund at time t is $\ell_{x+t}\cdot{}_t\overline{V}(\overline{A}_x)$, for all $t>0$. Due to its continuous nature, this aggregate fund is increasing at time t at rate $\ell_{x+t}\cdot\overline{P}(\overline{A}_x)$, from the arrival of premium income; it also is increasing at time t at rate $\delta\cdot\ell_{x+t}\cdot{}_t\overline{V}(\overline{A}_x)$, from interest earnings (assuming a constant rate of interest); and it is decreasing at time t at rate $\ell_{x+t}\cdot\mu_{x+t}$, from unit benefits paid to those failing at time t. Then the total rate of change of the aggregate reserve fund at time t is

$$\ell_{x+t}\cdot\overline{P}(\overline{A}_x)+\delta\cdot\ell_{x+t}\cdot{}_t\overline{V}(\overline{A}_x)-\ell_{x+t}\cdot\mu_{x+t}.$$

Since the rate of change is given by the derivative, we can write

$$\frac{d}{dt}\left(\ell_{x+t}\cdot{}_t\overline{V}(\overline{A}_x)\right)=\ell_{x+t}\cdot\overline{P}(\overline{A}_x)+\delta\cdot\ell_{x+t}\cdot{}_t\overline{V}(\overline{A}_x)-\ell_{x+t}\cdot\mu_{x+t}. \tag{10.39}$$

To solve this differential equation,[7] we transpose the term involving δ to the left side and multiply both sides by the integrating factor v^t to obtain

$$v^t\cdot\frac{d}{dt}\left(\ell_{x+t}\cdot{}_t\overline{V}(\overline{A}_x)\right)-\delta\cdot v^t\left(\ell_{x+t}\cdot{}_t\overline{V}(\overline{A}_x)\right) = v^t\cdot\ell_{x+t}\left(\overline{P}(\overline{A}_x)-\mu_{x+t}\right). \tag{10.40}$$

Next, recall from interest theory that

$$\frac{d}{dt}v^t = v^t\cdot\ln v = -\delta\cdot v^t.$$

Then using the product rule for differentiation, we recognize the left side of Equation (10.40) as

$$\frac{d}{dt}\left(v^t\cdot\ell_{x+t}\cdot{}_t\overline{V}(\overline{A}_x)\right) = v^t\cdot\frac{d}{dt}\left(\ell_{x+t}\cdot{}_t\overline{V}(\overline{A}_x)\right)+\left(\ell_{x+t}\cdot{}_t\overline{V}(\overline{A}_x)\right)\cdot\frac{d}{dt}v^t,$$

so we have

$$\frac{d}{dt}\left(v^t\cdot\ell_{x+t}\cdot{}_t\overline{V}(\overline{A}_x)\right) = v^t\cdot\ell_{x+t}\left(\overline{P}(\overline{A}_x)-\mu_{x+t}\right). \tag{10.41}$$

---

[7] Equation (10.39) is known as Thiele's Equation in the actuarial literature. We encounter it here in the simplified case of a net level premium rate and a fixed unit failure benefit. We will encounter Thiele's Equation again in Chapter 11 in a more general single-decrement setting, and again in Section 14.4.5 in a multiple-decrement setting.

Now we integrate both sides of Equation (10.41) from $t = 0$ to $t = n$, obtaining

$$\int_0^n d\left(v^t \cdot \ell_{x+t} \cdot {}_t\overline{V}(\overline{A}_x)\right) = \int_0^n v^t \cdot \ell_{x+t} \left(\overline{P}(\overline{A}_x) - \mu_{x+t}\right) dt. \tag{10.42}$$

Since ${}_0\overline{V}(\overline{A}_x) = 0$, the left side of Equation (10.42) evaluates to $v^n \cdot \ell_{x+n} \cdot {}_n\overline{V}(\overline{A}_x)$. We divide both sides by ℓ_x to obtain

$$v^n \cdot {}_n p_x \cdot {}_n\overline{V}(\overline{A}_x) = \overline{P}(\overline{A}_x) \cdot \int_0^n v^t \cdot {}_t p_x \, dt - \int_0^n v^t \cdot {}_t p_x \mu_{x+t} \, dt = \overline{P}(\overline{A}_x) \cdot \overline{a}_{x:\overline{n}|} - \overline{A}^1_{x:\overline{n}|}. \tag{10.43}$$

Finally, dividing both sides of Equation (10.43) by ${}_n E_x = v^n \cdot {}_n p_x$ we have

$$_n\overline{V}(\overline{A}_x) = \overline{P}(\overline{A}_x) \cdot \overline{s}_{x:\overline{n}|} - {}_n\overline{k}_x,$$

the retrospective NLP reserve expression given by Equation (10.35).

10.3.3 RANDOM VARIABLE ANALYSIS

Recall the present value of loss random variable defined in the fully continuous case by Equation (9.25a). Recall also that under the equivalence principle we have $E[\overline{L}(\overline{A}_x)] = 0$ and $P = \overline{P}(\overline{A}_x)$. Then given that $T_x > t$, so the contingent contract is still in effect at time t, the present value of loss random variable at time t is given by

$$_t\overline{L}(\overline{A}_x) = v^{T_x - t} - \overline{P}(\overline{A}_x) \cdot \overline{a}_{\overline{T_x - t}|} \tag{10.44a}$$

$$= \overline{Z}_{x+t} - \overline{P}(\overline{A}_x) \cdot \overline{Y}_{x+t}. \tag{10.44b}$$

Taking the conditional expectation of Equation (10.44b) we find

$$E\left[{}_t\overline{L}(\overline{A}_x) \middle| T_x > t\right] = \overline{A}_{x+t} - \overline{P}(\overline{A}_x) \cdot \overline{a}_{x+t}, \tag{10.45}$$

which is the prospective expression for the NLP benefit reserve at time t in the fully continuous case. Thus we find that, just as in the discrete case of Section 10.1.4, if the continuous funding rate is determined by the equivalence principle, the NLP benefit reserve is the conditional expected value of the present value of loss random variable measured at time t.

The variance of ${}_t\overline{L}(\overline{A}_x)$ is found from Equation (10.44b) in the same way we found $Var[\overline{L}(\overline{A}_x)]$ in Section 9.4.2, producing

$$Var\left[{}_t\overline{L}(\overline{A}_x) \middle| T_x > t\right] = \left(\frac{1}{\delta \cdot \overline{a}_x}\right)^2 \cdot \left({}^2\overline{A}_{x+t} - \overline{A}_{x+t}^2\right) \tag{10.46a}$$

$$= \frac{{}^2\overline{A}_{x+t} - \overline{A}_{x+t}^2}{(1 - \overline{A}_x)^2}. \tag{10.46b}$$

In this section we have presented only the expected value and variance of the random variable $_t\overline{L}(\overline{A}_x)$, conditional on $T_x > t$ in both cases. For a more extensive exploration of this random variable, including the development of both its CDF and PDF, the reader is referred to Section 7.2 of Bowers, *et al.* [4].

10.4 NLP RESERVES FOR CONTINGENT PAYMENT MODELS WITH m^{thly} PAYMENT FUNDING

Suppose periodic funding payments are made at m^{thly} intervals within the year, at annual premium rates defined in Section 9.4. Since the NLP reserve at duration t is merely the status of the funding scheme at that time, then expressions for the prospective NLP reserve follow directly from those for the associated premium rate. Here we assume that t is an integer, so the reserve is being measured at annual intervals.

For the whole life contingent payment model with m^{thly} funding, the tth NLP terminal reserve is given prospectively by

$$_tV_x^{(m)} = A_{x+t} - P_x^{(m)} \cdot \ddot{a}_{x+t}^{(m)}. \tag{10.47a}$$

For the n-year term insurance model we have

$$_tV_{x:\overline{n}|}^{1(m)} = A_{x+t:\overline{n-t}|}^{1} - P_{x:\overline{n}|}^{1(m)} \cdot \ddot{a}_{x+t:\overline{n-t}|}^{(m)}, \tag{10.47b}$$

for the n-year pure endowment model we have

$$_tV_{x:\overline{n}|}^{(m)\,1} = A_{x+t:\overline{n-t}|}^{1} - P_{x:\overline{n}|}^{1(m)} \cdot \ddot{a}_{x+t:\overline{n-t}|}^{(m)}, \tag{10.47c}$$

and for the n-year endowment insurance model we have

$$_tV_{x:\overline{n}|}^{(m)} = A_{x+t:\overline{n-t}|} - P_{x:\overline{n}|}^{(m)} \cdot \ddot{a}_{x+t:\overline{n-t}|}^{(m)}. \tag{10.47d}$$

Note that $t < n$ in all three of these n-year models. Similarly, for the n-year deferred immediate contingent annuity model we have

$$_tV^{(m)}(_n|a_x) = _{n-t}|a_{x+t} - P^{(m)}(_n|a_x) \cdot \ddot{a}_{x+t:\overline{n-t}|}^{(m)}, \tag{10.47e}$$

for $t < n$. The premium rates appearing in Equations (10.47a) through (10.47e) are defined by Equations (9.27a) through (9.27e), respectively.

Under the whole life model with immediate payment of claims, with premium rate defined by Equation (9.28a), the prospective reserve is given by

$$\,_tV^{(m)}(\overline{A}_x) \;=\; \overline{A}_{x+t} - P^{(m)}(\overline{A}_x)\cdot \ddot{a}^{(m)}_{x+t}. \tag{10.48}$$

Retrospective NLP reserve expressions are also easily written by analogy to other cases already discussed. Thus we would have

$$\,_tV^{(m)}_x \;=\; P^{(m)}_x \cdot \ddot{s}^{(m)}_{x:\overline{t}|} - \,_tk_x \tag{10.49a}$$

for the whole life model with m^{thly} premiums and

$$\,_tV^{(m)}_{x:\overline{n}|} \;=\; P^{(m)}_{x:\overline{n}|} \cdot \ddot{s}^{(m)}_{x:\overline{t}|} - \,_tk_x \tag{10.49b}$$

for the n-year endowment insurance model.

As with the continuous payment funding cases of Section 10.2, the NLP reserve expressions in this section can be evaluated from a life table by using one of the approximation methods presented in Chapter 8 for the m^{thly} annuities.

EXAMPLE 10.8

Show that, under the assumption of UDD over each interval $(x, x+1)$,

$$\,_tV^{(m)}_x \;=\; \left[1 + \frac{i - i^{(m)}}{i^{(m)}d^{(m)}} \cdot P^{(m)}_x\right]\cdot \,_tV_x. \tag{10.50}$$

SOLUTION

Starting with Equation (10.47a) we have

$$\,_tV^{(m)}_x \;=\; A_{x+t} - P^{(m)}_x \cdot \ddot{a}^{(m)}_{x+t}.$$

Substituting for A_{x+t} from Equation (10.3) and for $\ddot{a}^{(m)}_{x+t}$ from Equation (8.78) we have

$$\,_tV^{(m)}_x \;=\; \,_tV_x + P_x\cdot \ddot{a}_{x+t} - P^{(m)}_x\left[\frac{id}{i^{(m)}d^{(m)}}\cdot \ddot{a}_{x+t} - \frac{i - i^{(m)}}{i^{(m)}d^{(m)}}\right].$$

For convenience of notation, let $\alpha(m) = \frac{id}{i^{(m)}d^{(m)}}$ and $\beta(m) = \frac{i - i^{(m)}}{i^{(m)}d^{(m)}}$. Then we have

$$\,_tV^{(m)}_x \;=\; \,_tV_x + \beta(m)\cdot P^{(m)}_x - \ddot{a}_{x+t}\left[\alpha(m)\cdot P^{(m)}_x - P_x\right].$$

Next recall that $P_x = \frac{A_x}{\ddot{a}_x}$ and $P^{(m)}_x = \frac{A_x}{\ddot{a}^{(m)}_x}$, so $P_x = P^{(m)}_x\cdot \frac{\ddot{a}^{(m)}_x}{\ddot{a}_x}$. Substituting this for P_x we have

$$_tV_x^{(m)} = {}_tV_x + \beta(m) \cdot P_x^{(m)} - \ddot{a}_{x+t} \cdot P_x^{(m)} \left[\alpha(m) - \frac{\ddot{a}_x^{(m)}}{\ddot{a}_x} \right].$$

Since $\ddot{a}_x^{(m)} = \alpha(m) \cdot \ddot{a}_x - \beta(m)$, the last term becomes $\frac{\ddot{a}_{x+t}}{\ddot{a}_x} \cdot P_x^{(m)} \cdot \beta(m)$, which leads finally to

$$_tV_x^{(m)} = {}_tV_x + \beta(m) \cdot P_x^{(m)} \left(1 - \frac{\ddot{a}_{x+t}}{\ddot{a}_x} \right) = \left[1 + \beta(m) \cdot P_x^{(m)} \right] \cdot {}_tV_x,$$

as required.   □

10.5 MULTI-STATE MODEL REPRESENTATION

In Chapters 9 and 10 we have defined notation and formulas used to express net premiums and net level premium reserves in standard actuarial notation for a variety of contingent payment contract models. All such formulas evolved from the notation used for insurance and annuity models as presented in Chapters 7 and 8, respectively.

Similarly, we can express net premiums and net level premium reserves in multi-state model notation, using the notation defined for the insurance and annuity models in Sections 7.6 and 8.6, respectively. This is pursued in Exercises 10-27 and 10-28.

10.6 MISCELLANEOUS EXAMPLES

EXAMPLE 10.9

In earlier examples we considered insurance contracts where the failure benefit was a return of premiums paid, or where the failure benefit was simply the benefit reserve. Now we explore the case where the failure benefit is a fixed amount *plus* the benefit reserve. Consider a discrete single premium 20-year term insurance, with failure benefit of 1000 plus the terminal benefit reserve. Calculate the net single premium for this contract, given the values $i = .07$ and $q_{x+t} = .03$, for $t \geq 0$.

SOLUTION

This type of question is best approached by the recursive relationships of Section 10.2. In general we have

$$(_tV + P)(1+i) = B \cdot q_{x+t} + {}_{t+1}V \cdot p_{x+t}.$$

When, as in this case, $B = 1000 + {}_{t+1}V$, the right side simplifies to

$$(1000 + {}_{t+1}V) \cdot q_{x+t} + {}_{t+1}V \cdot p_{x+t} = 1000 q_{x+t} + {}_{t+1}V,$$

since $q_{x+t} + p_{x+t} = 1$. Also, in this case, only the first year recursion relationship includes a premium term. Thus, with $_0V = 0$, we have

$$P(1+i) = 1000q_x + {_1V}$$

or

$$_1V = P(1+i) - 1000q_x.$$

Then, recursively, we find

$$\begin{aligned} _2V &= {_1V}(1+i) - 1000q_{x+1} \\ &= [P(1+i) - 1000q_x](1+i) - 1000q_{x+1} \\ &= P(1+i)^2 - 1000[q_x(1+i) + q_{x+1}], \end{aligned}$$

and eventually

$$_{20}V = P(1+i)^{20} - 1000[q_x(1+i)^{19} + q_{x+1}(1+i)^{18} + \cdots + q_{x+19}] = P(1+i)^{20} - (1000)(.03) \cdot s_{\overline{20}|i},$$

since $q_x = q_{x+1} = \cdots = q_{x+19} = .03$. But we also know that $_{20}V = 0$, so

$$P = \frac{(1000)(.03) \cdot s_{\overline{20}|.07}}{(1.07)^{20}} = 317.82. \qquad \square$$

EXAMPLE 10.10

The NLP benefit reserve plays an important role in cases where changes to an existing contract are proposed. For example, consider a discrete whole life insurance of 1000 issued to (40). At age 50 the insured elects an option to continue the coverage as written, but to shorten the future premium-paying period to only ten more years. (Clearly this will result in an increased premium rate.) Find the revised level annual premium, given the values $A_{40} = .16132$, $A_{50} = .24905$, $\ddot{a}_{50:\overline{10}|} = 7.57362$, and $i = .06$.

SOLUTION

The reserve at duration 10 will be the same under both the original arrangement and the new arrangement. Since the APV of future benefit is the same in both cases, then the APV of future premiums must also be the same. If P' denotes the revised premium, then we have

$$P' \cdot \ddot{a}_{50:\overline{10}|} = 1000 P_{40} \cdot \ddot{a}_{50}.$$

We find

$$\ddot{a}_{40} = \frac{1 - A_{40}}{d} = \frac{1 - .16132}{.06 / 1.06} = 14.81668,$$

$$\ddot{a}_{50} = \frac{1-A_{50}}{d} = \frac{1-.24905}{.06/1.06} = 13.26678,$$

and

$$1000P_{40} = \frac{1000A_{40}}{\ddot{a}_{40}} = \frac{161.32}{14.81668} = 10.88773.$$

Then

$$P' = \frac{1000P_{40} \cdot \ddot{a}_{50}}{\ddot{a}_{50:\overline{10|}}}$$

$$= \frac{(10.88773)(13.26678)}{7.57362} = 19.07. \qquad \square$$

EXAMPLE 10.11

Insight into the NLP reserve concept can be gained by recognizing that a reserve builds up in the early years of a contract because the level annual premium paid each year exceeds the annual cost of insurance. Prospectively the reserve is needed because annual premiums in the future are less than the annual cost of insurance in those years. If the (unlevel) annual premium were exactly equal to the cost of insurance each year, no reserve would develop and none would be needed. Consider a discrete whole life insurance of 1000 issued to (40), wherein the level annual benefit premium is P in each of the first 20 years, followed by unlevel premiums of $1000 \cdot v \cdot q_x$ at age x each year thereafter. Calculate P, given the values $\ddot{a}_{40} = 14.8166$, $\ddot{a}_{60} = 11.1459$, $_{20}E_{40} = .27414$, and $i = .06$.

SOLUTION

Since each unlevel premium is the annual cost of insurance after age 60, then there is no reserve. This means that P is the annual premium for 20-year term insurance of 1000, or $P = 1000P^1_{40:\overline{20|}}$. To calculate P we first find

$$\ddot{a}_{40:\overline{20|}} = \ddot{a}_{40} - _{20}E_{40} \cdot \ddot{a}_{60} = (14.8166) - (.27414)(11.1459) = 11.7611$$

and

$$A^1_{40:\overline{20|}} = 1 - d \cdot \ddot{a}_{40:\overline{20|}} - _{20}E_{40} = 1 - \frac{.06}{1.06}(11.7611) - .27414 = .06014,$$

so

$$P = 1000P^1_{40:\overline{20|}} = \frac{1000A^1_{40:\overline{20|}}}{\ddot{a}_{40:\overline{20|}}} = \frac{60.14}{11.7611} = 5.11. \qquad \square$$

EXAMPLE 10.12

The matter of a modified parameter in one particular year, already explored in Examples 7.10 and 9.11, can arise in connection with reserves as well. Consider a unit discrete whole life insurance issued to (x), with non-level premiums. The insured is expected to experience a higher than standard failure probability at age $x+19$ only. The benefit premium for the 20th contract year is higher than the standard annual premium P_x by .01, but all benefit reserves on this contract are identical to those on a standard whole life contract with level premiums. Calculate the excess of q'_{x+19}, the rate experienced by this insured, over the standard rate q_{x+19}, given the values $_{20}V_x = .427$ and $i = .03$.

SOLUTION

Recursively, for a standard policy, we have

$$(_{19}V_x + P_x)(1.03) = q_{x+19} + p_{x+19} \cdot {}_{20}V_x,$$

and for this particular substandard policy we have

$$(_{19}V'_x + P_x + .01)(1.03) = q'_{x+19} + p'_{x+19} \cdot {}_{20}V'_x.$$

But $_{19}V'_x = {}_{19}V_x$ and $_{20}V'_x = {}_{20}V_x$. Subtracting the first equation from the second we find

$$(.01)(1.03) = (q'_{x+19} - q_{x+19}) + {}_{20}V_x \cdot (p'_{x+19} - p_{x+19}) = (q'_{x+19} - q_{x+19})(1 - {}_{20}V_x),$$

so

$$q'_{x+19} - q_{x+19} = \frac{(.01)(1.03)}{1 - .427} = .01798. \qquad \square$$

EXAMPLE 10.13

Consider a 5-year discrete unit endowment insurance issued to (50). Using the life table given in Appendix A and interest rate $i = .06$, the net level benefit premium is .16902. (The reader should verify this calculation.) Suppose 100,000 identical contracts are issued. Then if the premium assumptions are realized (i.e., if 6% interest is earned and the survival pattern follows the table exactly), the aggregate NLP reserve fund at time $t = 5$ should be the exact amount needed to pay the unit pure endowment benefit to each survivor at that time. Show that this is so.

SOLUTION

We use the recursive method for determining reserves. The calculations are shown in the following table:

t	Survivors $(2)_t = (2)_{t-1} - (4)_{t-1}$	Premiums $(3)_t = .16902(2)_t$	Failures $(4)_t = (2)_t \cdot q_{50+t}$	NLP Reserve Fund $(5)_t = [(5)_{t-1} + (3)_t](1.06) - (4)_t$
0	100,000	16,902	356	17,560
1	99,644	16,842	392	36,074
2	99,252	16,776	431	55,590
3	98,821	16,703	469	76,162
4	98,352	16,623	512	97,840
5	97,840			

Thus we see that there are 97,840 survivors at age 55, and the aggregate NLP reserve fund holds the exact amount needed to pay the unit pure endowment benefit to the survivors, as expected.

10.7 EXERCISES

10.1 Reserves for Contingent Payment Models with Annual Payment Funding

10-1 Write prospective NLP reserve expressions for the following:

(a) ${}_t^h V_{x:\overline{n}|}^1$ (b) ${}_t^h V_{x:\overline{n}|}$

10-2 Write the prospective NLP reserve expression for an h-pay n-year deferred insurance, where $h < n$.

10-3 Calculate ${}_{20}V_{45,}$ given the following values:

$$P_{45} = .014 \qquad P_{45:\overline{20}|} = .030 \qquad P_{45:\overline{20}|}^{\,1} = .022$$

10-4 Write retrospective NLP reserve expressions for the following:

(a) ${}_tV_{x:\overline{n}|}^1$, for $t < n$ (c) ${}_tV_{x:\overline{n}|}^{\,1}$, for $t < n$

(b) ${}_tV_{x:\overline{n}|}$, for $t < n$ (d) ${}_t^h V_x$, for $t > h$

10-5 Derive each of the following expressions for ${}_tV_{x:\overline{n}|}$, for $t < n$.

(a) $1 - (P_{x:\overline{n}|} + d) \cdot \ddot{a}_{x+t:\overline{n-t}|}$ (d) $\dfrac{A_{x+t:\overline{n-t}|} - A_{x:\overline{n}|}}{1 - A_{x:\overline{n}|}}$

(b) $1 - \dfrac{\ddot{a}_{x+t:\overline{n-t}|}}{\ddot{a}_{x:\overline{n}|}}$ (e) $(P_{x+t:\overline{n-t}|} - P_{x:\overline{n}|}) \cdot \ddot{a}_{x+t:\overline{n-t}|}$

(c) $\dfrac{P_{x+t:\overline{n-t}|} - P_{x:\overline{n}|}}{P_{x+t:\overline{n-t}|} + d}$ (f) $A_{x+t:\overline{n-t}|}\left(1 - \dfrac{P_{x:\overline{n}|}}{P_{x+t:\overline{n-t}|}}\right)$

10-6 Calculate the value of $1000({}_2V_{x:\overline{3}|} - {}_1V_{x:\overline{3}|})$, given the following values:

$$P_{x:\overline{3}|} = .33251 \qquad i = .06 \qquad \ell_x = 100 \qquad \ell_{x+1} = 90$$

10-7   Let $_{10}V$ denote the benefit reserve at duration 10 for a modified whole life insurance contract issued to (x) that pays nothing for failure in the first year and 5000, paid at the end of the year of failure, for failure after the first year. Net level benefit premiums, determined by the equivalence principle, are payable for the life of the contract. Calculate the value of $_{10}V$, given the following values:

$$_{10}V_x = .20 \qquad \ddot{a}_x = 5 \qquad q_x = .05 \qquad v = .90$$

10-8   Consider the n-year endowment contract, with benefit premium determined by the equivalence principle.

(a) Define the random variable for the present value of loss at duration t, denoted by $_tL_{x:\overline{n}|}$, where $t < n$.

(b) Give an expression for the conditional expected value of $_tL_{x:\overline{n}|}$, given $K_x > t$.

(c) Give an expression for the conditional variance of $_tL_{x:\overline{n}|}$, given $K_x > t$.

10-9   A 2-year term insurance of amount 400 is issued to (x), with benefit premium determined by the equivalence principle. Find the probability that the loss at issue is less than 190, given the following values:

$$P^1_{x:\overline{2}|} = .185825 \qquad {}_1V^1_{x:\overline{2}|} = .04145 \qquad i = .10$$

10-10   Show that $_t\overline{k}_x = \frac{i}{\delta} \cdot {}_tk_x$, under the assumption of UDD over each separate interval $(x+j, x+j+1)$, for $j = 0,1,\ldots,t-1$.

10-11   Derive the reserve formula

$$_tV(\overline{A}_x) \;=\; [P(\overline{A}_{x+t}) - P(\overline{A}_x)] \cdot \ddot{a}_{x+t}.$$

10-12   A single-premium 10-year temporary continuous contingent annuity, with unit annual benefit rate, is issued to (80). The applicable survival model is uniform with $\omega = 100$. Given $\delta = \frac{1}{15}$, find the value of $Var(_5L)$.

10.2 Recursive Relationships for Discrete Models with Annual Premiums

10-13   A contingent contract issued to (35) has a benefit of 2500 for failure in the 10th year. The interest rate is $i = .10$. The net annual premium is P. Given that $_9V + P = {}_{10}V = 500$, find the value of q_{44}.

10-14 Calculate p_{38}, given the following values:

$$_{23}^{20}V_{15} = .585 \qquad _{24}^{20}V_{15} = .600 \qquad i = .04$$

10-15 A 10-pay whole life contract of amount 1000 is issued to (x). The net annual premium is 32.88 and the NLP benefit reserve at the end of year 9 is 322.87. Given $i = .06$ and $q_{x+9} = .01262$, find the value of P_{x+10}.

10-16 A 10-year deferred annuity-due issued to (x) includes a failure benefit during the deferred period that is a refund of the net single premium with interest at the same rate i used to calculate the premium. The terminal reserve at the end of year 9 is 15.238 and the interest rate is $i = .05$. Calculate the net single premium.

10-17 A single premium 25-year deferred annuity-due, with unit annual benefit, is issued to (40). The applicable survival model is uniform with $\omega = 100$. The interest rate is $i = .05$. The single premium is refunded with interest at 5% at the end of the year of failure if failure occurs during the deferred period. Find the value of the benefit reserve at duration 20.

10-18 Beginning with Equation (10.30b), derive the Fackler recursive reserve formula

$$_{t+1}V = \frac{_tV + P}{_1E_{x+t}} - \frac{A_{x+t:\overline{1}|}^{1}}{_1E_{x+t}}.$$

10.3 Reserves for Contingent Payment Models with Continuous Payment Funding

10-19 Derive each of the following expressions for $_tV(\overline{A}_x)$.

(a) $\dfrac{\overline{A}_{x+t} - \overline{A}_x}{1 - \overline{A}_x}$

(b) $\left(1 - \dfrac{\overline{P}(\overline{A}_x)}{\overline{P}(\overline{A}_{x+t})}\right) \cdot \overline{A}_{x+t}$

10-20 Let $_0\overline{L}(\overline{A}_x)$ denote the present value of loss at issue for a fully continuous whole life contract issued to (x). Find the value of $_{20}\overline{V}(\overline{A}_x)$, given the following values:

$$Var[_0\overline{L}(\overline{A}_x)] = .20 \qquad ^2\overline{A}_x = .30 \qquad \overline{A}_{x+20} = .70$$

10-21 Calculate $\overline{a}_{x+t}$, given the following values:

$$_t\overline{V}(\overline{A}_x) = .1000 \qquad \overline{P}(\overline{A}_x) = .0105 \qquad \delta = .03$$

10-22   If the survival model is uniform with $\omega = 100$ and the interest rate is $i = .05$, calculate the value of $_{10}\bar{V}(\bar{A}_{40})$.

10-23   If the survival model is exponential with failure rate λ and the force of interest is δ, calculate the value of $_t\bar{V}(\bar{A}_x)$. Explain the logic behind the result.

10-24   Equation (10.39) gives Thiele's differential equation in the context of the aggregate reserve fund. From it, derive the result

$$\frac{d}{dt}\,_t\bar{V}(\bar{A}_x) \;=\; \bar{P}(\bar{A}_x) + \delta \cdot \,_t\bar{V}(\bar{A}_x) - \mu_{x+t}\big(1 - \,_t\bar{V}(\bar{A}_x)\big),$$

which is Thiele's differential equation in the context of a single whole life policy.

10.4   Reserves for Contingent Payment Models with m^{thly} Payment Funding

10-25   Assuming UDD over each interval $(x, x+1)$, calculate (accurate to two decimals) the value of $1000(_5V_{35}^{(4)} - _5V_{35})$, given the following values:

$$_5V_{35} = .04471 \qquad A_{35} = .17092 \qquad i = .05$$

10-26   Instead of approximating $\ddot{a}_x^{(m)}$ using UDD, use the Woolhouse approximation given by Equation (8.82b). Find the value of $_4V_x^{(2)}$ accurate to five decimal places, given the values $\ddot{a}_x = 20$, $_4V_x = .06$, and $d = .026$.

10.5 Multi-State Model Representation

10-27   Using the multi-state model notation defined earlier, give the prospective formula for the reserve represented by $_{20}V_{30}$ in standard actuarial notation.

10-28   Using the multi-state model notation defined earlier, give the prospective formula for the reserve represented by $_{10}V_{30:\overline{20}|}^{1}$ in standard actuarial notation.

CHAPTER ELEVEN

CONTINGENT CONTRACT RESERVES (RESERVES AS FINANCIAL LIABILITIES)

In Chapter 10 we presented an extensive analysis of the concept of net level premium benefit reserves, pointing out that the NLP benefit reserve is a mathematical function of the contingent contract under consideration. In this chapter we describe several reserve concepts beyond that of the NLP benefit reserve.

A basic new idea in this chapter is the recognition that the contingent contract reserve constitutes a *financial liability* for the institution, such as a life insurer, that has issued the contingent contract.[1] When a contingent contract, such as a life insurance policy, provides for a benefit payment at some unknown time in the future, with the benefit funded by annual premium payments, the premiums paid in the early contract years exceed the cost of coverage in those years. The fund accumulated as a result of this cannot be considered profit to the insurer; its value must be retained *as an accounting liability* and eventually used to pay the contingent benefit when it arises.

Along with its role on the liability side of the balance sheet, the contract reserve plays an important role in the determination of annual net income.

Consider a whole life insurance contract with annual gross premium G and associated expense amount E_t in the tth contract year. If the reserve concept were ignored, the stream of annual contributions to net income would be $G - E_t$ in the tth year, for each year that the failure benefit is not paid, and $G - E_n - B$ if the benefit is paid in the nth year. This stream of small positive contributions to net income each year, along with the large negative contribution in the year of failure, does not represent an appropriate accounting for the contract. It represents, in effect, a reported income stream generated by cash accounting.

When the reserve concept is recognized, the contribution to net income each year is reduced by the increase in reserve for that year. Then the stream of (usually positive) contributions to net income is $G - E_1 - {}_1V$ in the first year and $G - E_t - ({}_tV - {}_{t-1}V)$ in the tth year in general. If failure occurs in the nth year, the benefit is paid and the reserve is released so the contribution to net income is $G - E_n - (B - {}_{n-1}V)$, which is generally negative. By reporting the annual reserve increase as an expense item, the pattern of annual contributions to net income has been placed on an accrual, rather than cash, accounting basis.

---

[1] We assume here that the reader has had (at least) a one-semester university course in financial accounting, and understands such basic accounting concepts as assets, liabilities, and net worth, and the summary accounting reports of income statement and balance sheet.

In Chapter 10 we developed formulas for determining this accounting liability under the assumption that it would be defined as the NLP benefit reserve, using the net benefit premium developed by the equivalence principle. In practice, the financial liability held by the insurer, and reported on its balance sheet, is not normally the NLP benefit reserve. In this chapter we develop several alternatives to NLP benefit reserves that might be calculated by the insurer and held as the financial liability associated with a particular contingent contract. These alternatives include modified benefit reserves (in Section 11.1), benefit reserves at non-integral durations of the contingent contract (in Section 11.2), benefit reserves using non-level benefit premiums (in Section 11.3), and reserves incorporating expenses (in Section 11.4).

An insurer is likely to determine reserves of more than one type for use in more than one set of financial statements. Statements produced for the insurance regulatory authorities have traditionally used modified benefit reserves.[2] Statements produced for internal company management purposes are more likely to use expense-augmented reserves (see Section 11.4). Still a third set of financial reports, meeting requirements set by the applicable taxing authority, might be maintained for income tax purposes.

At the time of this writing, the insurance industry and its regulators in the United States are discussing a new concept known as *principle-based reserving*. The basic idea is that reserves would be principles-driven, rather than formula-driven, and each insurer would set its contingent contract reserves at levels appropriate for that company, rather than have such levels prescribed by the regulators. To guard against the possibility of insurers setting their reserve levels too low, a mechanism for testing the reserves for adequacy (likely by stochastic simulation) would be established.

Similar considerations apply to the question of how much *surplus* should be retained by an insurer, versus the alternative of paying larger dividends to shareholders or policyholders. This is a basic corporate accounting issue, rather than a contingent contract issue, and is not discussed further in this text.

We also use the reserve concept as a useful setting in which to introduce two special contracts, namely universal life insurance (in Section 11.5) and variable annuities (in Section 11.6).

11.1 Modified Benefit Reserves

Consider a contingent contract with level annual gross premium (or contract premium) G, as described in Section 9.6. If the level benefit premium P is used to provide cost of coverage and reserve accumulation, as discussed throughout Chapter 10, then it follows that the level amount $G - P$ is available each year to cover expenses of operation and a contribution to profit. In reality, for the type of contingent contracts considered in this text, such as insurance policies, the pattern of expenses each year is not level. Expenses are much greater in the first year, due to the cost of underwriting and issuing the contract, plus the practice of paying a larger commission to the sales agent in the first year.

---

[2] In the United States, the business of insurance is regulated by the states. Each state has a Commissioner of Insurance, and the several commissioners work together through the National Association of Insurance Commissioners (NAIC). The regulatory financial reporting and reserving requirements are specified by the NAIC.

11.1.1 RESERVE MODIFICATION IN GENERAL

To address this, we consider that a *smaller* portion of the gross premium be used for cost of coverage plus reserve accumulation in the first year, with a *larger* portion used in subsequent years, than would be the case under the NLP reserve system. To quantify this idea, let α denote the benefit premium in the first year and β denote the benefit premium in all years after the first (also called the *renewal* years), where $\alpha < P < G$ and $P < \beta < G$. Then the amount available for expenses and profit is $G - \alpha$ in the first year and $G - \beta$ in all subsequent years. The *modified benefit reserve* at the end of the first year for a unit insurance can be calculated from Equation (10.30b), using α in place of P and $_0V = 0$, obtaining

$$\alpha(1+i) = q_x + p_x \cdot {_1V^M} \tag{11.1a}$$

or

$$_1V^M = \frac{\alpha(1+i) - q_x}{p_x}. \tag{11.1b}$$

Then for a contract still in force at duration t, for $t \geq 1$, the modified benefit reserve can be calculated prospectively as

$$_tV^M = (APV\ of\ future\ benefits) \\ - (APV\ of\ future\ modified\ benefit\ premiums). \tag{11.2}$$

The modified benefit premiums α and β are determined at issue so that the APV of all modified benefit premiums will equal the APV of future benefits. Of course this will also be the APV of the net level benefit premiums, so we have

$$\alpha + \beta \cdot a_x = P_x \cdot \ddot{a}_x \tag{11.3a}$$

for a whole life contract, and

$$\alpha + \beta \cdot a_{x:\overline{n-1}|} = P \cdot \ddot{a}_{x:\overline{n}|} \tag{11.3b}$$

for a contract with premium paying period limited to n years.

It is also possible to use modified benefit premiums over only the first k years of a contract, where $k < n$. In this case, α is used in the first year, β is used in years 2 through k, and the net level benefit premium P is used in all years thereafter. Then Equation (11.3b) would be altered to read

$$\alpha + \beta \cdot a_{x:\overline{k-1}|} = P \cdot \ddot{a}_{x:\overline{k}|}, \tag{11.3c}$$

which is the more general case.

The solution of Equation (11.3c) for α and β is not unique, of course, so it follows that either α or β (or possibly the quantity $\beta - \alpha$) must be defined in each specific case. This is illustrated in the examples and exercises that follow.

EXAMPLE 11.1

Show that

$$\beta = P + \frac{\beta - \alpha}{\ddot{a}_{x:\overline{k}|}}. \tag{11.4}$$

SOLUTION

In Equation (11.3c) we substitute the identity

$$a_{x:\overline{k-1}|} = \ddot{a}_{x:\overline{k}|} - 1,$$

obtaining

$$\alpha + \beta\left(\ddot{a}_{x:\overline{k}|} - 1\right) = P \cdot \ddot{a}_{x:\overline{k}|}$$

or

$$(\beta - P) \cdot \ddot{a}_{x:\overline{k}|} = \beta - \alpha,$$

from which the desired formula immediately follows. (Equation (11.4) is useful in cases where the modified reserve system is defined by specifying the excess of β over α.) ❏

A theoretical fully continuous whole life contract funded by a continuous net level benefit premium $\overline{P}(\overline{A}_x)$ will generate fully continuous NLP reserves, denoted by $_t\overline{V}(\overline{A}_x)$, as described in Section 10.3.2. If such a contract were to use modified continuous premiums in lieu of the level $\overline{P}(\overline{A}_x)$, then modified fully continuous reserves would result. In this case, the discrete modified premium structure of α in the first year and β in the renewal years, described earlier in this section, would be replaced by a continuous premium rate of $\overline{\alpha}(r)$ at time r, increasing continuously to a level benefit premium rate of $\overline{\beta}$ after some defined length of time. This notion is further explored in Exercise 11-2.

11.1.2 FULL PRELIMINARY TERM MODIFIED RESERVES

Many specific modified reserve systems have been defined over the years.[3] In this section we consider one special case of modified reserves.

As a minimum, we consider that the first year modified benefit premium α should be no less than the cost of insurance coverage in the first year. For a unit insurance contract, this would be $v \cdot q_x = A^1_{x:\overline{1}|}$, which is also denoted by c_x in the actuarial literature. If β is then

---

[3] The details of these systems are beyond the scope of this introductory text. Actuarial readers eventually specializing in life insurance reserving (also called *valuation*) will study these methods in detail at a later time. In particular, the reader will learn the importance of the *Commissioners Reserve Valuation Method* (CRVM).

the renewal modified benefit premium for the remainder of the premium-paying period n, then we have

$$\alpha^F = v \cdot q_x = c_x \tag{11.5a}$$

and

$$\beta^F = \frac{P \cdot \ddot{a}_{x:\overline{n}|} - c_x}{a_{x:\overline{n-1}|}}, \tag{11.5b}$$

from Equation (11.3b). This modified reserve system is called the *full preliminary term* (FPT) *method*, which explains the use of the superscript F on α and β.

EXAMPLE 11.2

Show that for a whole life unit insurance issued at age x, under the FPT reserving method, the first year terminal reserve is $_1V^F = 0$ and the renewal modified benefit premium is $\beta^F = P_{x+1}$.

SOLUTION

The first result follows from Equation (10.30b) with $P = \alpha^F = v \cdot q_x$ and $_0V = 0$. We have

$$\alpha^F (1+i) = q_x + p_x \cdot {_1V^F},$$

or

$$v \cdot q_x (1+i) = q_x = q_x + p_x \cdot {_1V^F},$$

from which the result $_1V^F = 0$ follows since $p_x \neq 0$. Then from Equation (11.3a) we have

$$\alpha^F + \beta^F \cdot a_x = P_x \cdot \ddot{a}_x = A_x.$$

Substituting $\alpha^F = v \cdot q_x$ we have

$$\beta^F \cdot a_x = A_x - v \cdot q_x$$

or

$$\beta^F (v \cdot p_x \cdot \ddot{a}_{x+1}) = v \cdot p_x \cdot A_{x+1},$$

from which the result $\beta^F = P_{x+1}$ follows. ❑

The results of Example 11.2 can be generalized to other insurance coverages. Since the first year FPT reserve is zero and the modified renewal benefit premium is the same as the net level benefit premium at the attained age, then an insurance contract known to be in force at duration $t = 1$ (age $x+1$) will have FPT reserves that are the same as the NLP reserves for a similar contract issued at one age higher with one year less to run. This idea is further explored in Exercise 11-3.

A natural extension of the FPT method is the *two-year full preliminary term method*, whereby the modified benefit premiums are $\alpha_1 = c_x$ in the first year, $\alpha_2 = c_{x+1}$ in the second year, and β in all years after the second. This method is further explored in Exercise 11-4.

Example 11.2 and Exercise 11-4 show that when the net premium for a particular year equals the cost of insurance for that year, the terminal benefit reserve is zero. This shows us that long-term insurance coverage could be provided by a sequence of one-year term insurances, and no terminal benefit reserve would ever develop. This is a basic characteristic of a contract of universal life insurance, which we explore in Section 11.5.

11.1.3 Deficiency Reserves

On rare occasion, it might turn out that $\beta > G$ (i.e., that the modified benefit premium exceeds the gross premium). In that case, G is used in place of β in the prospective reserve formula. The excess of the reserve using G over the reserve using β is called a *deficiency reserve*.

11.1.4 Negative Reserves

Another unusual situation would arise if, at any duration t, the APV of future modified benefit premiums was to exceed the APV of future benefits, which would produce a *negative reserve*. Since the reserve represents a liability that the insurer eventually owes to the insured, a negative reserve would suggest a liability that the insured eventually owes to the insurer. But the insured could terminate the contract at any time, and escape paying this accrued liability. In light of this, insurers take care to avoid the kind of policy structure that could create a negative reserve.

11.2 Benefit Reserves at Fractional Durations

In Chapter 10, and thus far in this chapter, all the discussion regarding reserves for contingent contracts with annual payment funding had assumed the parameter t to be an integer, so that the reserve was being measured at the end of the tth contract year. (For contracts with continuous payment funding, on the other hand, the reserve is defined for all values of t on the real number axis.) Now in this section we address the practical issue of defining the benefit reserve at a non-integral duration for annual payment funding contracts, as illustrated in the following figure.

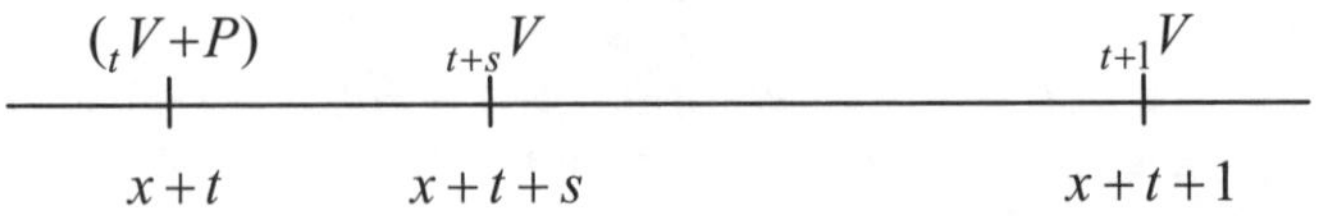

$$({}_tV+P) \qquad\qquad {}_{t+s}V \qquad\qquad\qquad {}_{t+1}V$$

$$x+t \qquad\qquad x+t+s \qquad\qquad\qquad x+t+1$$

Figure 11.1

Using the basic prospective approach, we can write the fractional duration reserve ${}_{t+s}V$ as the actuarial present value of future benefits (APVB) minus the actuarial present value of future premiums (APVP) as of duration $t+s$. We have

$$_{t+s}V = v^{1-s} \cdot {}_{1-s}q_{x+t+s} + v^{1-s} \cdot {}_{1-s}p_{x+t+s} \cdot APVB_{t+1} - v^{1-s} \cdot {}_{1-s}p_{x+t+s} \cdot APVP_{t+1}$$
$$= v^{1-s} \cdot {}_{1-s}q_{x+t+s} + v^{1-s} \cdot {}_{1-s}p_{x+t+s} \cdot {}_{t+1}V. \tag{11.6}$$

Now we multiply both sides of Equation (11.6) by $v^s \cdot {}_s p_{x+t}$, obtaining

$$v^s \cdot {}_s p_{x+t} \cdot {}_{t+s}V = v \cdot {}_{s|1-s}q_{x+t} + v \cdot p_{x+t} \cdot {}_{t+1}V. \tag{11.7}$$

Next we take Equation (10.30c), rewrite it as $v = \frac{{}_tV + P - v \cdot p_{x+t} \cdot {}_{t+1}V}{q_{x+t}}$, and substitute the right side for the first value of v on the right side of Equation (11.7), obtaining

$$v^s \cdot {}_s p_{x+t} \cdot {}_{t+s}V = ({}_tV + P)\left(\frac{{}_{s|1-s}q_{x+t}}{q_{x+t}}\right) + (v \cdot p_{x+t} \cdot {}_{t+1}V)\left(1 - \frac{{}_{s|1-s}q_{x+t}}{q_{x+t}}\right). \tag{11.8}$$

Equation (11.8) shows us that the expected present value at duration t of the fractional duration reserve $_{t+s}V$ is a weighted average of the initial reserve $({}_tV + P)$ and the expected present value of the terminal reserve $_{t+1}V$, with weights r and $1 - r$, respectively, where

$$r = \frac{{}_{s|1-s}q_{x+t}}{q_{x+t}}. \tag{11.9}$$

Next we evaluate r under the UDD assumption over the age interval $(x+t, x+t+1)$, obtaining $r = 1 - s$ (see Exercise 11-5), which allows us to write

$$v^s \cdot {}_s p_{x+t} \cdot {}_{t+s}V = ({}_tV + P)(1-s) + (v \cdot p_{x+t} \cdot {}_{t+1}V)(s). \tag{11.10}$$

A more intuitive approach to the fractional duration reserve is suggested by the graph shown in Figure 11.2.

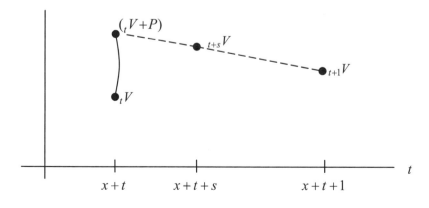

Figure 11.2

In practice the reserve at fractional duration $t+s$ is often found by linear interpolation between the initial reserve $(_tV+P)$ and the terminal reserve $_{t+1}V$, producing

$$_{t+s}V = (_tV+P)(1-s)+(_{t+1}V)(s). \tag{11.11}$$

Equation (11.11) is reached from Equation (11.10) by assuming that $i=q_{x+t}=0$ over the interval $(x+t, x+t+1)$. Finally, we can write Equation (11.11) as

$$_{t+s}V = (_tV)(1-s)+(_{t+1}V)(s)+(P)(1-s). \tag{11.12}$$

In Equation (11.12), the interpolated reserve $(1-s)(_tV)+(s)(_{t+1}V)$ is called the *mid-terminal reserve factor* and the final term is called the *unearned premium reserve*. In particular, when $s=\frac{1}{2}$ the interim reserve $_{t+1/2}V$ is called the *mean reserve*.

The development of $_{t+s}V^{(m)}$, the fractional duration reserve for a contingent contract funded by m^{thly} premiums, is a bit more complex, and is not pursued in this text. The interested reader is referred to pages 240-241 of Bowers, et al. [4] or pages 112-113 of Jordan [15].

11.3 GENERALIZATION TO NON-LEVEL BENEFITS AND BENEFIT PREMIUMS

In this section we consider cases where the benefit payment and/or the funding payment stream are not level. Clearly the level models considered earlier are special cases of the more general non-level models considered in this section.

11.3.1 DISCRETE MODELS

Let the benefit payment for failure in the kth year, payable at the end of that year, be denoted by b_k, and let the benefit premium for the kth year, payable at the beginning of that year, be denoted by P_k. This is illustrated in the following diagram.

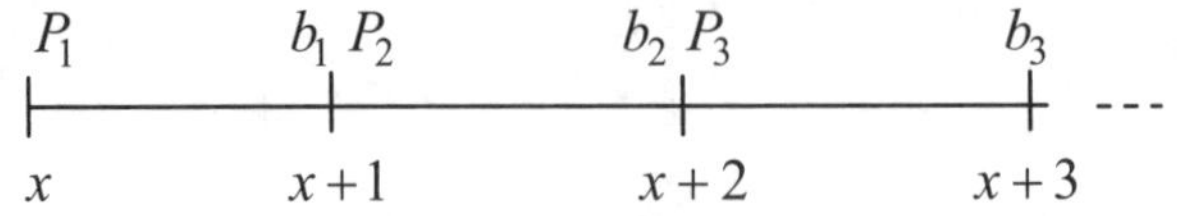

FIGURE 11.3

Then the APV of benefit for a whole life model is given by Equation (7.50) as

$$APVB = \sum_{k=1}^{\infty} b_k \cdot v^k \cdot Pr(K_x^* = k) = \sum_{k=1}^{\infty} b_k \cdot v^k \cdot {}_{k-1}p_x \cdot q_{x+k-1}. \tag{11.13a}$$

Similarly, the APV of the benefit premium stream is given by an adaptation of Equation (8.83) as

$$APVP = \sum_{k=0}^{\infty} P_{k+1} \cdot v^k \cdot {}_k p_x.$$ (11.13b)

We then use the basic equivalence principle at time 0 to write

$$\sum_{k=1}^{\infty} b_k \cdot v^k \cdot {}_{k-1} p_x \cdot q_{x+k-1} = \sum_{k=0}^{\infty} P_{k+1} \cdot v^k \cdot {}_k p_x.$$ (11.14)

Of course there is no unique solution to Equation (11.14) for the sequence of benefit premiums, given the sequence of benefit payment amounts. In practice we might solve for the $\{P_k\}$ sequence by establishing a relationship among the terms in the sequence. For example, we might let the benefit premium sequence vary in a geometric pattern with $P_k = P_1(1+r)^{k-1}$, where $r > 0$ provides a pattern of increasing premiums, $r < 0$ provides a pattern of decreasing premiums, and $r = 0$ provides a pattern of level premiums as in Chapter 9.

Once the sequence of benefit premiums is established, the terminal benefit reserve at integral duration t, given that the contract has not yet failed, is easily written by again invoking the equivalence principle. By the prospective method we have

$$_tV = \sum_{k=1}^{\infty} b_{t+k} \cdot v^k \cdot {}_{k-1} p_{x+t} \cdot q_{x+t+k-1} - \sum_{k=0}^{\infty} P_{t+k+1} \cdot v^k \cdot {}_k p_{x+t}.$$ (11.15)

In Exercise 11-7 the reader will be asked to write the general retrospective formula. Note that the other formulas for the whole life case, presented in Section 10.1.3, do not extend to the general case. We can, however, easily adapt the recursive relationships, presented in Section 10.2 in the level benefit and level premium case, to the general case. Focusing on the $(t+1)^{st}$ contract year (see Figure 10.5), with benefit premium P_{t+1} paid at the beginning of the year and benefit b_{t+1} paid at the end of the year if failure occurs in that year, Equation (10.30a) now becomes

$$\ell_{x+t}(_tV + P_{t+1})(1+i) = b_{t+1} \cdot d_{x+t} + \ell_{x+t+1} \cdot {}_{t+1}V,$$ (11.16a)

Equation (10.30b) now becomes

$$(_tV + P_{t+1})(1+i) = b_{t+1} \cdot q_{x+t} + p_{x+t} \cdot {}_{t+1}V,$$ (11.16b)

and Equation (10.30e) now becomes

$$_{t+1}V = (_tV + P_{t+1})(1+i) - q_{x+t}(b_{t+1} - {}_{t+1}V),$$ (11.16e)

where $b_{t+1} - {}_{t+1}V$ is the net amount at risk for the $(t+1)^{st}$ year.

The derivation of Equation (10.30c) by the use of random variables in the level benefit and level premium case is also easily extended to derive its counterpart in the general case, which would be

$$_tV + P_{t+1} = v \cdot b_{t+1} \cdot q_{x+t} + v \cdot p_{x+t} \cdot {}_{t+1}V.$$ (11.16c)

EXAMPLE 11.3

A 20-year endowment contract issued to (55) has a decreasing failure benefit, paid at the end of the year of failure, of $b_k = (21-k)$ for failure in the kth year and a pure endowment benefit of 1. The annual benefit premium is level. Find the value of $_{11}V$, given the following values:

$$_{10}V = 5.00 \qquad _{19}V = .60 \qquad q_{65} = .10 \qquad i = .08$$

SOLUTION

First we look at the last year, where we have

$$(_{19}V + P)(1+i) = b_{20} \cdot q_{74} + 1 \cdot p_{74},$$

under the endowment insurance. But $b_{20} = 1$, so we have

$$(.60 + P)(1.08) = 1$$

which solves for $P = .32592$. Then we look at the eleventh year, where we have

$$(_{10}V + P)(1+i) = b_{11} \cdot q_{65} + _{11}V \cdot p_{65},$$

or

$$(5.00 + .32592)(1.08) = (10)(.10) + _{11}V(.90),$$

which solves for $_{11}V = 5.28$. ☐

11.3.2 CONTINUOUS MODELS

In the fully continuous general whole life model, with payment of benefit amount b_r for failure at precise time r and benefit premium at rate $\bar{P}(r)$ at time r, the prospective reserve at time t, given that the contract has not yet failed at that time, is given by

$$_t\bar{V} = \int_0^\infty b_{t+s} \cdot v^s \cdot {}_sp_{x+t}\mu_{x+t+s} \, ds - \int_0^\infty \bar{P}(t+s) \cdot v^s \cdot {}_sp_{x+t} \, ds. \tag{11.17}$$

Similarly, the retrospective reserve at time t would be

$$_t\bar{V} = \int_0^t \bar{P}(r) \cdot \frac{1}{_{t-r}E_{x+r}} \, dr - \int_0^t b_r \cdot \mu_{x+r} \cdot \frac{1}{_{t-r}E_{x+r}} \, dr. \tag{11.18}$$

EXAMPLE 11.4

A fully continuous whole life contract issued to (65) has continuous level net premiums. The survival model is exponential with hazard rate .02 and the force of interest is .04. The failure benefit rate is $b_t = 1000e^{.04t}$ for failure at time $t > 0$. Given that survival to duration 2 has occurred, calculate the value of $_2\overline{V}$.

SOLUTION

The continuous premium rate $\overline{P}$ is found as

$$\overline{P} \cdot \overline{a}_{65} = \int_0^\infty b_t \cdot v^t \cdot {}_t p_{65} \mu_{65+t} \, dt$$

$$= (1000)(.02) \int_0^\infty e^{.04t} \cdot e^{-.04t} \cdot e^{-.02t} \, dt = 1000.$$

Under the exponential survival model the value of $\overline{a}_{65}$ is $\frac{1}{\lambda + \delta} = \frac{1}{.06}$, so the premium rate is $\overline{P} = 60$. At duration $t = 2$ the APV of future premium is $\overline{P} \cdot \overline{a}_{67}$, which is still 1000 under this survival model. The APV of future benefit at $t = 2$ is given by

$$\int_0^\infty b_{s+2} \cdot v^s \cdot {}_s p_{67} \mu_{67+s} \, ds = (1000)(.02) \int_0^\infty e^{.04(s+2)} \cdot e^{-.04s} \cdot e^{-.02s} \, ds$$

$$= 20e^{.08} \int_0^\infty e^{-.02s} \, ds$$

$$= \frac{20e^{.08}}{.02} = 1083.29.$$

Then the reserve, by the prospective method, is

$$_2\overline{V} = 1083.29 - 1000.00 = 83.29. \qquad \square$$

The analysis at the end of Section 10.3.2 involving Thiele's differential equation can be modified to apply to the fully continuous general whole life model with benefit amount b_r and benefit premium rate $\overline{P}(r)$. In the general case, the aggregate reserve fund at time t is $\ell_{x+t} \cdot {}_t\overline{V}$ and its total rate of change at time t is

$$\ell_{x+t} \cdot \overline{P}(t) + \delta \cdot \ell_{x+t} \cdot {}_t\overline{V} - b_t \cdot \ell_{x+t} \cdot \mu_{x+t},$$

which is the derivative of the aggregate reserve fund. Then the general form of the differential equation, analogous to Equation (10.39) in Section 10.3.2, is

$$\frac{d}{dt}\left(\ell_{x+t} \cdot {}_t\overline{V}\right) = \ell_{x+t} \cdot \overline{P}(t) + \delta \cdot \ell_{x+t} \cdot {}_t\overline{V} - b_t \cdot \ell_{x+t} \cdot \mu_{x+t}. \qquad (11.19)$$

The differential equation is solved by steps parallel to those used in Section 10.3.2 for the level-premium, level-benefit case, to reach the general retrospective reserve expression given by Equation (11.18). The details are left for the reader as Exercise 11-12.

11.4 Incorporation of Expenses

Recall that all reserve expressions developed in Chapter 10 and thus far in this chapter are for *benefit reserves* only, by which we mean that they are based on benefit premiums (also called net premiums). In Section 9.6 we saw how to incorporate expense factors into an expense-augmented equivalence principle to determine expense-augmented funding payments.

It is now a simple matter to include the expense factors, along with the expense-augmented premium, to determine *expense-augmented reserves*. (When profit margins are also included in the premium, the resulting reserves are referred to as *gross premium reserves*.) The general prospective formula for the tth benefit reserve, given by Equation (10.2), is now modified to read

$$_tV^G = (APV \ of \ future \ benefits \ and \ expenses)$$
$$- (APV \ of \ future \ expense\text{-}augmented \ premiums), \qquad (11.20)$$

where the symbol $_tV^G$ denotes the tth expense-augmented reserve. This is illustrated in the following example.

Example 11.5

Give an expression for the tth prospective expense-augmented reserve for the whole life contract described in Example 9.8.

Solution

At duration t, given that the contingent contract is still in effect, the APV of the future expense-augmented premium income is $G \cdot \ddot{a}_{x+t}$, where G is defined in Example 9.8. The APV of the future percent of premium expense charges is $.10G \cdot \ddot{a}_{x+t}$, and the APV of the future fixed per \$1000 of benefit expense charges is $2\ddot{a}_{x+t}$. The APV of the benefit payment itself plus the settlement expense together is $1020A_{x+t}$. Thus we have

$$_tV^G = 1020A_{x+t} + (.10G+2)\ddot{a}_{x+t} - G \cdot \ddot{a}_{x+t} = 1020A_{x+t} - (.90G-2)\ddot{a}_{x+t}. \qquad \square$$

Returning to Section 9.6, we can separate the amount of the level benefit premium P from the expense-augmented premium G. The remainder of G represents the amount of annual premium needed to fund the expenses of administering the contract. In other words, we define

$$EP = G - P \qquad (11.21)$$

to be the annual *expense premium* for the contract.

The notion of separating the expense-augmented premium into benefit premium and expense premium components naturally extends to the reserve. As already covered extensively in

Chapter 10, the prospective benefit reserve is the APV of future benefits minus the APV of future benefit premiums. Similarly we define the tth prospective *expense reserve* to be

$$_tV^E = (APV \text{ of future expenses}) \\ -(APV \text{ of future expense premiums}). \tag{11.22}$$

It should be clear that

$$_tV^G = {}_tV + {}_tV^E. \tag{11.23}$$

EXAMPLE 11.6

Give an expression for the tth prospective expense reserve for the whole life contract described in Example 9.8.

SOLUTION

First we find the level expense premium as

$$EP \cdot \ddot{a}_x = .75G + .10G \cdot a_x + 10 + 2a_x + 20A_x,$$

where G is defined in Example 9.8. Then the expense reserve is

$$_tV^E = 20A_{x+t} + (.10G+2)\ddot{a}_{x+t} - EP \cdot \ddot{a}_{x+t}. \qquad \square$$

Recall how the concept of the present value of loss (at issue) random variable, L_x, introduced in Section 9.2, was easily extended to the present value of loss (at duration t) random variable, $_tL_x$, defined in Section 10.1.4. In the same way, the expense-augmented present value of loss (at issue) random variable, L_x^G, defined in Section 9.6, is easily extended to the expense-augmented present value of loss (at duration t) random variable, which we denote by $_tL_x^G$. This is pursued in Exercise 11-15.

Recall that we expanded Equation (10.30b), which had presumed level benefit premiums and a level failure benefit, into Equation (11.16b), which generalized Equation (10.30b) for non-level benefits and benefit premium. Now we generalize further to include expenses.

Let G_t denote the expense-augmented premium for the tth contract year, r_t denote the percent-of-premium expense factor for that year, e_t denote the fixed expense for that year, and s_t denote the settlement expense associated with a benefit paid at the end of the tth contract year. Then Equation (11.16b) is generalized to

$$[_tV + G_{t+1}(1-r_{t+1}) - e_{t+1}](1+i_{t+1}) = (b_{t+1}+s_{t+1}) \cdot q_{x+t} + p_{x+t} \cdot {}_{t+1}V. \tag{11.24}$$

Note that Equation (11.24) allows for the reserve interest rate to also vary by contract year, for maximum generality. In many applications, i_{t+1} will be set as a constant.

11.5 INTRODUCTION TO UNIVERSAL LIFE INSURANCE

The *universal life insurance* (UL) product entered the life insurance market in the early 1980s. The intent of the new product was to provide a great degree of flexibility for individual insureds. It allows for a combination of insurance protection and investment growth, and permits the insured to place relative emphasis on one or the other. Many variations on the basic universal life idea exist, and some of these are discussed in Chapter 16.

In this chapter we confine our attention to the basic mechanics of the contracts. There are two sub-cases, which we present in the following two subsections.

11.5.1 UNIVERSAL LIFE WITH VARIABLE FAILURE BENEFIT

In this version a contract of insurance, either term or whole life, is issued with a *fixed face amount* of failure benefit, which we denote by B. At the beginning of the tth year,[4] the insured makes a contribution of amount G_t.[5] The insurer deducts the contractual expense charges from the contribution. For simplicity we assume a percent-of-contribution expense factor r_t and fixed expense amount e_t for the tth year. Then the net contribution invested in the contract is $G_t(1-r_t)-e_t$ at the beginning of the tth year.

The failure benefit of amount B is funded as one-year term insurance. Then for a contract issued at age x, or at select age $[x]$, the first year's cost of insurance is $v_1 \cdot q_x \cdot B$ at the beginning of the year. The remainder of the net contribution, after deducting the cost of insurance, then earns interest at rate i_1 to the end of the first year. The accumulated value at that time is called the *account value* at time 1, which we denote by AV_1. Then we have

$$AV_1 = [G_1(1-r_1)-e_1 - v_1 \cdot q_x \cdot B](1+i_1), \qquad (11.25a)$$

which is positive provided the net contribution exceeds the cost of insurance.

If failure occurs in the first year, the face amount benefit of B is provided by the one-year term insurance coverage. The account value AV_1 is released to the insured, since the contract is completed, so the total failure benefit is $B + AV_1$. (This explains why the failure benefit is variable although the face amount is fixed.)

If failure does not occur in the first year, the process is repeated, producing an account value at the end of the second year of

$$AV_2 = [AV_1 + G_2(1-r_2)-e_2 - v_2 \cdot q_{x+1} \cdot B](1+i_2). \qquad (11.25b)$$

In general, for the $(t+1)^{st}$ year we have

---

[4] Time could be measured in years, quarters, months, or even shorter intervals. For convenience here we will assume the annual case, with extension to shorter intervals easy to see.

[5] Because the insured has considerable choice in the amount of each payment, we prefer to refer to the payments as *contributions*, rather than *premiums*.

$$AV_{t+1} = [AV_t + G_{t+1}(1-r_{t+1}) - e_{t+1} - v_{t+1} \cdot q_{x+t} \cdot B](1+i_{t+1}), \qquad (11.25c)$$

so the total failure benefit would be $B + AV_{t+1}$ for failure in the $(t+1)^{st}$ year. The process of updating the account value is called *account value roll forward*. Note that if the process is carried out on, say, a monthly basis, with monthly contributions, the failure rate q_{x+t} must be available at monthly ages. (See Exercise 11-17.)

Note that no terminal reserve need be held for the face amount failure benefit, since it is provided by a sequence of one-year (or one-interval) term insurances. Since the account value is also paid at failure, it, or a function of it, would be held as a financial liability by the insurer.[6]

EXAMPLE 11.7

Consider a universal life contract issued to (30), with a face amount of 100,000. The percent-of-contribution expense factors are $r_1 = .75$ in the first year and $r_t = .10$ in all subsequent years; the fixed expense amount is $e_1 = 100$ in the first year and $e_t = 20$ in all subsequent years. The interest rate is fixed at 3%, failure rates are given in Appendix A, and the insured makes an annual contribution of 5,000. Calculate the account value at the end of each of the first five years.

SOLUTION

The calculations are shown in Table 11.1.

TABLE 11.1

Year t	Prior Year Account Value Plus Net Contribution $AV_{t-1} + G_t(1-r_t) - e_t$	Cost of Insurance $100{,}000 v \cdot q_{x+t-1}$	End-of-Year Account Value
1	$5{,}000(.25) - 100$ $= 1{,}150.00$	$\dfrac{(100{,}000)(.00076)}{1.03} = 73.79$	$(1{,}150.00 - 73.79)(1.03)$ $= 1{,}108.50$
2	$1{,}108.50 + 5{,}000(.90) - 20$ $= 5{,}588.50$	$\dfrac{(100{,}000)(.00081)}{1.03} = 78.64$	$(5{,}588.50 - 78.64)(1.03)$ $= 5{,}675.16$
3	$5{,}675.16 + 5{,}000(.90) - 20$ $= 10{,}155.16$	$\dfrac{(100{,}000)(.00085)}{1.03} = 82.52$	$(10{,}115.16 - 82.52)(1.03)$ $= 10{,}333.61$
4	$10{,}333.61 + 5{,}000(.90) - 20$ $= 14{,}813.61$	$\dfrac{(100{,}000)(.00090)}{1.03} = 87.38$	$(14{,}813.61 - 87.38)(1.03)$ $= 15{,}168.02$
5	$15{,}168.02 + 5{,}000(.90) - 20$ $= 19{,}648.02$	$\dfrac{(100{,}000)(.00095)}{1.03} = 92.23$	$(19{,}648.02 - 92.23)(1.03)$ $= 20{,}142.46$

❑

---

[6] In Section 14.3.4, after we introduce the concept of multiple decrements, we will discuss the right of the insured to surrender the contract for its account value, or a function of it.

Because the annual contribution in Example 11.7 is considerably in excess of the annual expenses plus cost of insurance, the account value continues to increase. Note that it would be possible to make reduced contributions, or even to make no contribution at all, in certain years without impairing the contract as long as the account value is sufficient to provide the annual cost of insurance. Of course the account value, and hence the total failure benefit, would decline if no contributions are made.

We discuss the notion of a surrender benefit under these contracts in Section 14.3.4, and other, more advanced, aspects of them in Chapter 16.

11.5.2 UNIVERSAL LIFE WITH FIXED FAILURE BENEFIT

If the total failure benefit is to be fixed at face amount B, then the amount of one-year term insurance to be purchased each year is the excess of B over the year-end account value. Then when failure occurs, the one-year term insurance benefit plus the released account value together provide a total failure benefit of B. The amount of one-year term insurance purchased is called the *net amount at risk* (NAR). In this case Equation (11.25c) is modified to read

$$AV_{t+1} = [AV_t + G_{t+1}(1-r_{t+1}) - e_{t+1} - v_{t+1} \cdot q_{x+t}(B - AV_{t+1})](1+i_{t+1}), \qquad (11.26a)$$

or

$$AV_{t+1} = [AV_t + G_{t+1}(1-r_{t+1}) - e_{t+1}](1+i_{t+1}) - q_{x+t}(B - AV_{t+1}), \qquad (11.26b)$$

which is analogous to Equation (10.30e). Then

$$AV_{t+1} = \frac{[AV_t + G_{t+1}(1-r_{t+1}) - e_{t+1}](1+i_{t+1}) - q_{x+t} \cdot B}{p_{x+t}}. \qquad (11.27)$$

In practice the cost of insurance is sometimes calculated in a way that is slightly different from the theoretically correct way shown in Equation (11.26a). This is explored in Exercise 11-18.

EXAMPLE 11.8

Repeat Example 11.7, except that the total failure benefit is to remain fixed at 100,000.

SOLUTION

From Equation (11.27) we have

$$AV_1 = \frac{[5,000(.25) - 100](1.03) - (.00076)(100,000)}{.99924} = 1,109.34,$$

$$AV_2 = \frac{[1,109.34 + 5,000(.90) - 20](1.03) - (.00081)(100,000)}{.99919} = 5,680.62,$$

$$AV_3 = \frac{[5,680.62 + 5,000(.90) - 20](1.03) - (.00085)(100,000)}{.99915} = 10,389.27,$$

$$AV_4 = \frac{[10,389.27 + 5,000(.90) - 20](1.03) - (.00090)(100,000)}{.99910} = 15,239.06,$$

and

$$AV_5 = \frac{[15,239.06 + 5,000(.90) - 20](1.03) - (.00095)(100,000)}{.99905} = 20,234.86. \qquad \square$$

We observe that the account values are larger here than in Example 11.7, which is to be expected since a smaller total failure benefit is being provided by the same level of contribution. Again no terminal reserve is required for the one-year term insurance, but the insurer must hold the account value, or a function of it, as a financial liability.

As with the variable failure benefit contract of Section 11.5.1, several variations of the contract described in this section exist in practice. We will pursue this further in Chapter 16.

11.6 INTRODUCTION TO DEFERRED VARIABLE ANNUITIES

The basic mathematics underlying the *deferred variable annuity* was suggested by Example 10.5. First we recall from Section 9.1.3 that a deferred annuity with no failure benefit during the deferred period, so that premiums paid would be forfeited in the case of failure during the deferred period, is not a product actually sold. We then learned in Example 10.5 that if the failure benefit is the reserve at the end of the year of failure, the reserve is merely the accumulation of the net premiums paid.

We now generalize this notion in a similar manner as we did in Section 11.5 for life insurance. Suppose the annuitant makes a contribution of amount G_t at the beginning of the tth contract year, from which an expense charge of $r_t \cdot G_t + e_t$ is deducted. The net contribution then earns interest at rate i_t. If the failure benefit is simply the year-end account value, then such account value is simply the accumulation of the net contributions with interest. There is no other cost of insurance. This means that

$$AV_{t+1} = [AV_t + G_{t+1}(1 - r_{t+1}) - e_{t+1}](1 + i_{t+1}). \tag{11.28}$$

Then if the annuitant survives to duration n, and begins receiving annuity payments at that time, the account value AV_n acts as a net single premium to provide the benefits. If the annuitant is age $x + n$ at time n, and selects a level monthly annuity-due at that time, the monthly annuity payment would be

$$P = \frac{AV_n}{12 \cdot \ddot{a}_{x+n}^{(12)}}. \tag{11.29}$$

As with the insurance contracts of Section 11.5, there are additional important features of the deferred variable annuity yet to discuss. In Section 14.3.5, with the concept of multiple decrements already introduced, we discuss surrender benefits under these contracts. In Chapter 17 we present more advanced aspects of the variable annuity contract.

11.7 EXERCISES

11.1 Modified Benefit Reserves

11-1   If benefit premiums are modified for the entire premium paying period of n years, show each of the following:

(a) $_tV_{x:\overline{n}|}^{NLP} - _tV_{x:\overline{n}|}^{M} = (\beta-P)\cdot\ddot{a}_{x+t:\overline{n-t}|}$

(b) $_tV_{x:\overline{n}|}^{M} = 1-(\beta+d)\cdot\ddot{a}_{x+t:\overline{n-t}|}$

11-2   Consider a fully continuous unit whole life insurance issued at age x, under which modified continuous reserves accumulate using modified benefit premium rate $\overline{\alpha}(r)$ at time r, for $0<r\le5$, and modified benefit premium rate $\overline{\beta}$ at time $r\ge5$. The premium rate $\overline{\alpha}(r)$ is defined as $\overline{\alpha}(0)=.25\overline{\beta}$, increasing linearly to $\overline{\alpha}(5)=\overline{\beta}$. Show that

$$\overline{\beta} = \frac{\overline{A}_x}{\overline{a}_x -.75\overline{a}_{x:\overline{5}|}+.15(\overline{Ia})_{x:\overline{5}|}}.$$

11-3   For an h-pay, n-year unit endowment insurance issued at age x, with reserves calculated by the FPT method, show that

$$_t^hV_{x:\overline{n}|}^{FPT} = {}_{t-1}^{h-1}V_{x+1:\overline{n-1}|}^{NLP},$$

where $t<h<n$.

11-4   As an extension of Example 11.2, show that, under the two-year FPT reserving method, $_1V^F = {}_2V^F = 0$ and $\beta = P_{x+2}$.

11.2 Benefit Reserves at Fractional Durations

11-5   Show that the expression for r given in Equation (11.9) reduces to $r=1-s$ under the UDD assumption.

11-6   Show that the tth year mean reserve for a unit insurance can be written as

$$_{t-1/2}V = \frac{1}{2}\big[(1+v\cdot p_{x+t-1})\cdot {}_tV +v\cdot q_{x+t-1}\big].$$

11.3 Generalization to Non-Level Benefits and Premiums

11-7 Write the general retrospective formula which is the counterpart to the prospective formula given by Equation (11.15).

11-8 A 3-year term insurance issued to (x) has a decreasing failure benefit, paid at the end of the year of failure. The interest rate is $i = .06$. Calculate the initial reserve for the second year, given the following values:

$$b_1 = 200 \qquad b_2 = 150 \qquad b_3 = 100$$
$$q_x = .03 \qquad q_{x+1} = .06 \qquad q_{x+2} = .09$$

11-9 A 2-year endowment contract issued to (x) has a failure benefit of 1000 plus the reserve at the end of the year of failure and a pure endowment benefit of 1000. Given that $i = .10$, $q_x = .10$, and $q_{x+1} = .11$, calculate the net level benefit premium.

11-10 A whole life contract issued to (40) pays a benefit, at the end of the year of failure, of b_k for failure in the kth year. The net premium P is equal to P_{20}, and the benefit reserves satisfy $_tV = {}_tV_{20}$, for $t = 0,1,\ldots,19$. Furthermore, $q_{40+k} = q_{20+k} + .01$, for $k = 0,1,\ldots,19$. Given that $_{11}V_{20} = .08154$ and $q_{30} = .008427$, calculate b_{11}.

11-11 A continuously decreasing 25-year term insurance issued to (40) has benefit rate $b_t = 1000\overline{a}_{\overline{25-t|}}$ for failure at time t. The continuous net premium rate is $\overline{P} = 200$. Given also that $i = .05$ and $\overline{A}_{50:\overline{15|}} = .60$, find the benefit reserve at time $t = 10$.

11-12 Solve Thiele's differential equation, given by Equation (11.19), to reach the retrospective reserve expression given by Equation (11.18).

11.4 Incorporation of Expenses

11-13 For the 20-pay whole life insurance described in Exercise 9-26, find the expense-augmented reserve at (a) duration 10 and (b) duration 20, given the additional values $\ddot{a}_{x+10} = 16.5$, $\ddot{a}_{x+20} = 12.5$, and $\ddot{a}_{x+10:\overline{10|}} = 7$.

11-14 Show that $_tV = {}_tV^G - {}_tV^E$, where $_tV^G$ is given in Example 11.5 and $_tV^E$ is given in Example 11.6.

11-15   We now define $_tL_x^G$ as the expense-augmented present value of prospective loss measured at time t, given that $K_x^* > t$ (i.e., the contract has not yet failed at time t). For the whole life contract described in Example 9.8, show that

$$E\left[_tL_x^G \mid K_x^* > t\right] = {_tV^G},$$

the expense-augmented reserve, as determined in Example 11.5.

11-16   Consider the expense-augmented premium recursion relationship given by Equation (11.24). Suppose the premium is paid continuously at annual rate $\bar{G}_t$ at time t, and fixed expenses are paid continuously at annual rate $\bar{e}_t$ at time t. State Thiele's differential equation in this general case including expenses.

11.5 Introduction to Universal Life Insurance

11-17   The account value roll forward process under a universal life contract is often done on a monthly basis. Suppose the contract in Example 11.7 receives *annual* contributions of 5000, earns interest at $i^{(12)} = .03$, assesses expense charges at 50% of contribution plus 10 per month, and estimates monthly mortality rates at $1/12$ the corresponding annual rate. Calculate the account values at the ends of each of the first three months.

11-18   In practice, the net amount at risk under a universal life contract paying a failure benefit fixed at amount B is often defined as the excess of B over the prior period ending account value plus the current period net contribution before deducting fixed expenses. The cost of insurance is then defined as the mortality rate times the net amount at risk, without the discount factor. Rework Example 11.8 under these definitions of NAR and COI.

11.6 Introduction to Deferred Variable Annuities

11-19   A five-year deferred variable annuity is issued to (60) who makes annual contributions of 5,000 each. The percent-of-contribution expense rate is 60% in the first year and 10% in subsequent years. There is an annual expense charge of 2% of the prior year's account value, assessed at the beginning of each year. For convenience, assume the interest rate credited to the account is constant at 8%, and the failure benefit is the account value. At age 65 the account value is used to purchase an annual annuity-due based on 6% interest and the survival model of Appendix A. Calculate the annual annuity payment.

Chapter Twelve

Models Dependent on Multiple Survivals (Multi-Life Models)

All the discussion to this point in the text has focused on the complementary concepts of survival and failure of a single entity, such as a single person under a life insurance policy or a life annuity. We consistently referred to the entity whose survival was being observed as our *status of interest*, and we defined what constituted survival (and therefore failure) in each particular case. This generic approach to the concept of survival will be continued in this chapter.

We now consider the case where the status of interest is itself made up of two or more entities, such as two separate individual lives. In actuarial science such models are said to involve multiple lives and are known as *multi-life models*. We will develop the theory of multi-life models in the two-life case first, and then show how it is easily extended to more than two lives.

We will also need to distinguish whether the two individual lives comprising a multi-life status have independent or dependent future lifetimes. The assumption of independence will simplify our work to some extent, and is presumed wherever needed throughout the chapter. Independence is not presumed for the discussion in Sections 12.5 and 12.6.

12.1 The Joint-Life Model

A *joint-life status* is one for which survival of the status requires the survival of *all* (or *both*, in the two-life case) of the individual members making up the status. Accordingly, the status fails upon the *first* failure of its component members.

12.1.1 The Time-to-Failure Random Variable for a Joint-Life Status

Consider a two-life joint status, made up of lives that are ages x and y as of time 0. We use the notation (xy) to denote such a status,[1] and we use T_{xy} to denote the random variable for the future lifetime (or time-to-failure) of the status. From the definition of failure it is clear that T_{xy} will be the *smaller* of the individual future lifetimes denoted by T_x and T_y. That is,

$$T_{xy} = \min(T_x, T_y). \tag{12.1}$$

Our analysis of the future lifetime random variable T_{xy} will parallel that for the individual life T_x presented in Section 5.3. Indeed, by using the generic concept of a status or entity, the two cases of T_{xy} and T_x are really the same except for the different notation.

---

[1] If numerical ages are used instead of the letters x and y, such as if $x = 20$ and $y = 25$, for example, the status is denoted (20:25). The colon would also be used to denote the status $(x+n : y+n)$.

12.1.2 THE SURVIVAL DISTRIBUTION FUNCTION OF T_{xy}

We begin our analysis of the random variable T_{xy} with its SDF, given by

$$S_{xy}(t) = Pr(T_{xy} > t) \tag{12.2}$$

and denoted by $_tp_{xy}$ in standard actuarial notation. Since survival of the status itself requires the survival of both component members of the status, then assuming independence of the individual lifetimes we have

$$_tp_{xy} = {_tp_x} \cdot {_tp_y}, \tag{12.3}$$

which is the bridge between joint-life and individual life functions. Equation (12.3) will allow us to evaluate many joint-life functions from a single-life tabular survival model.

12.1.3 THE CUMULATIVE DISTRIBUTION FUNCTION OF T_{xy}

The CDF of T_{xy} is given by

$$F_{xy}(t) = 1 - S_{xy}(t) = Pr(T_{xy} \leq t), \tag{12.4}$$

and is denoted by $_tq_{xy}$ in actuarial notation. It follows that

$$_tq_{xy} = 1 - {_tp_{xy}} \tag{12.5a}$$

for all t. If the individual lifetimes are independent, then we can write

$$\begin{aligned} _tq_{xy} &= 1 - {_tp_x} \cdot {_tp_y} \\ &= 1 - (1 - {_tq_x})(1 - {_tq_y}) = {_tq_x} + {_tq_y} - {_tq_x} \cdot {_tq_y}. \end{aligned} \tag{12.5b}$$

Equation (12.5b) illustrates a very basic concept in probability. $_tq_{xy}$ denotes the probability that the joint status fails before (or at) time t, which occurs if either or both of the individual lives fail before (or at) time t. Since the events $(T_x \leq t)$ and $(T_y \leq t)$ are not mutually exclusive, the probability of the union event, which is $_tq_{xy}$, is given by the general addition rule reflected in Equation (12.5b).

As in the individual life case discussed earlier in the text, the pre-subscript t is suppressed in the special case of $t = 1$. Thus we have

$$p_{xy} = S_{xy}(1) = Pr(T_{xy} > 1) \tag{12.6a}$$

and

$$q_{xy} = 1 - p_{xy} = F_{xy}(1) = Pr(T_{xy} \leq 1). \tag{12.6b}$$

EXAMPLE 12.1

If T_x and T_y are independent, and each is uniformly distributed over each year of age separately, show that, for $0 < t < 1$,

$$_tq_{xy} = t \cdot q_x(1-t \cdot q_y) + t \cdot q_y(1-t \cdot q_x) + t^2 \cdot q_x \cdot q_y.$$

SOLUTION

With independent lifetimes we have, from Equation (12.5b),

$$_tq_{xy} = {}_tq_x + {}_tq_y - {}_tq_x \cdot {}_tq_y.$$

Under UDD this becomes

$$
\begin{aligned}
_tq_{xy} &= t \cdot q_x + t \cdot q_y - t^2 \cdot q_x \cdot q_y \\
&= t \cdot q_x - t^2 \cdot q_x \cdot q_y + t \cdot q_y - t^2 \cdot q_x \cdot q_y + t^2 \cdot q_x \cdot q_y \\
&= t \cdot q_x(1-t \cdot q_y) + t \cdot q_y(1-t \cdot q_x) + t^2 \cdot q_x \cdot q_y,
\end{aligned}
$$

as required. ❑

12.1.4 THE PROBABILITY DENSITY FUNCTION OF T_{xy}

The PDF of T_{xy} is defined by

$$f_{xy}(t) = \frac{d}{dt}F_{xy}(t) = -\frac{d}{dt}S_{xy}(t). \qquad (12.7)$$

In the special case of independence, we have

$$
\begin{aligned}
f_{xy}(t) &= -\frac{d}{dt}S_{xy}(t) \\
&= -\frac{d}{dt}({}_tp_x \cdot {}_tp_y) \\
&= -\left({}_tp_x \cdot \frac{d}{dt}{}_tp_y + {}_tp_y \cdot \frac{d}{dt}{}_tp_x\right) \\
&= -[{}_tp_x(-{}_tp_y\mu_{y+t}) + {}_tp_y(-{}_tp_x\mu_{x+t})] \\
&= {}_tp_x \cdot {}_tp_y\mu_{y+t} + {}_tp_y \cdot {}_tp_x\mu_{x+t} \\
&= {}_tp_{xy}(\mu_{x+t} + \mu_{y+t}), \qquad (12.8)
\end{aligned}
$$

where we have used Equation (6.21) for $\frac{d}{dt}{}_tp_x$ and $\frac{d}{dt}{}_tp_y$.

12.1.5 The Hazard Rate Function of T_{xy}

Recall that a hazard rate function (HRF) measures the conditional instantaneous rate of failure at precise time t, given survival to time t. For individual lives in a life insurance context we refer to the hazard rate as the *force of mortality*; in the context of a joint status it is more appropriate to view the hazard rate as a *force of failure* rather than a force of mortality. Regardless of the terminology used, the HRF is defined as

$$\lambda_{xy}(t) = \frac{f_{xy}(t)}{S_{xy}(t)}. \tag{12.9a}$$

In the special case of independent lives we have

$$\lambda_{xy}(t) = \frac{{}_tp_{xy}(\mu_{x+t}+\mu_{y+t})}{{}_tp_{xy}} = \mu_{x+t} + \mu_{y+t}. \tag{12.9b}$$

In standard actuarial notation the HRF is denoted by $\mu_{x+t:y+t}$,[2] so we have

$$\mu_{x+t:y+t} = \mu_{x+t} + \mu_{y+t}. \tag{12.9c}$$

This shows that the force of failure acting on the joint status is the sum of the forces of failure (or forces of mortality) acting on the individual components (lives) in the case of independent lives.

12.1.6 Conditional Probabilities

The conditional failure probability, denoted by ${}_{n|}q_x$ in the single-life case, has its counterpart in the joint-life case. We define

$${}_{n|}q_{xy} = Pr(n < T_{xy} \le n+1), \tag{12.10}$$

the probability that the time of failure of the joint status occurs in the $(n+1)^{st}$ time interval.[3] Since failure of the status occurs with the first failure of the individual components, then ${}_{n|}q_{xy}$ denotes the probability that the first failure occurs in the $(n+1)^{st}$ interval. Thus we have

$${}_{n|}q_{xy} = {}_np_{xy} - {}_{n+1}p_{xy} \tag{12.11a}$$

$$= {}_np_{xy}(1-p_{x+n:y+n})$$

$$= {}_np_{xy} \cdot q_{x+n:y+n}. \tag{12.11b}$$

---

[2] Note that the joint status HRF is a function of t, with the identifying characteristics of its component members (x) and (y) fixed at time $t = 0$. To reinforce the idea that the joint status HRF is a function of t only, some texts prefer the notation $\mu_{xy}(t)$. (See, for example, Section 9.3 of Bowers, *et al.* [4] .)

[3] Recall the discrete random variable K_x^*, defined in Chapter 5 as the time interval of failure for the status (x). If we now define K_{xy}^* as the random variable for the interval of failure of the joint status (xy), we have ${}_{n|}q_{xy} = Pr(K_{xy}^* = n+1)$.

In the case of independent lives we can evaluate $_n|q_{xy}$ from the life table using

$$_n|q_{xy} = {}_nP_x \cdot {}_nP_y - {}_{n+1}P_x \cdot {}_{n+1}P_y. \tag{12.12}$$

EXAMPLE 12.2

If T_x and T_y are independent, calculate the value of $_2|q_{xy}$ given the following values:

$$q_x = .08 \qquad q_{x+1} = .09 \qquad q_{x+2} = .10$$
$$q_y = .10 \qquad q_{y+1} = .15 \qquad q_{y+2} = .20$$

SOLUTION

$_2|q_{xy}$ denotes the probability that the joint-life status fails in the third year, which is also denoted by $Pr(K_{xy}^* = 3)$. Here we have

$$
\begin{aligned}
_2|q_{xy} &= {}_2P_{xy} \cdot q_{x+2:y+2} \\
&= {}_2P_x \cdot {}_2P_y (1 - P_{x+2} \cdot P_{y+2}) \\
&= (.92)(.91)(.90)(.85)[1 - (.90)(.80)] = .17932. \qquad \square
\end{aligned}
$$

12.1.7 MOMENTS OF T_{xy}

The expected value of T_{xy} gives the complete expectation of future "lifetime" of the joint status. It is denoted by $\overset{o}{e}_{xy}$ in actuarial notation and defined by

$$\overset{o}{e}_{xy} = E[T_{xy}] = \int_0^\infty t \cdot f_{xy}(t)\, dt \tag{12.13a}$$

$$= \int_0^\infty {}_tP_{xy}\, dt, \tag{12.13b}$$

the joint status counterpart to Equation (5.48d). The second moment is given by

$$E[T_{xy}^2] = \int_0^\infty t^2 \cdot f_{xy}(t)\, dt, \tag{12.14}$$

and the variance of T_{xy} follows as

$$Var(T_{xy}) = E[T_{xy}^2] - \left(E[T_{xy}]\right)^2. \tag{12.15}$$

Similarly, we can define the *curate expectation of future lifetime for the joint status*, the counterpart to the single-life function of Section 6.3.4, as

$$e_{xy} = \sum_{k=1}^\infty {}_kP_{xy} \tag{12.16}$$

and the temporary curtate lifetime as

$$e_{\overline{xy:n}} = \sum_{k=1}^{n} {}_k p_{xy}. \tag{12.17}$$

Note that $e_{\overline{xy:n}}$ represents the average number of whole years of survival within the next n years for the joint status (xy).

EXAMPLE 12.3

Let T_x and T_y be independent time-to-failure random variables, each with exponential distributions with hazard rates λ_x and λ_y, respectively. Find an expression for $\overset{o}{e}_{xy}$.

SOLUTION

We know that ${}_t p_x = e^{-t \cdot \lambda_x}$ and ${}_t p_y = e^{-t \cdot \lambda_y}$, so under independence we have

$${}_t p_{xy} = {}_t p_x \cdot {}_t p_y = e^{-t(\lambda_x + \lambda_y)}.$$

This shows us that T_{xy} has an exponential distribution with hazard rate $\lambda = \lambda_x + \lambda_y$, so

$$\overset{o}{e}_{xy} = E[T_{xy}] = \frac{1}{\lambda_x + \lambda_y}. \qquad \qquad \Box$$

12.2 THE LAST-SURVIVOR MODEL

A *last-survivor status* is one for which survival of the status requires the survival of any one (or more) of its component members. That is, the status is said to survive as long as *at least one* of its members survives, so that it fails only when *all* of its members have failed. Then the time of failure of the status is the time of the *last* failure among its components, or the *second* failure in the two-life case. Note that the n-year certain and continuous annuity, defined in Example 8.14, is a special case of a last-survivor status, since the annuity pays until the second failure out of (40) and $\overline{10}$. The APV of this annuity is denoted $\ddot{a}_{\overline{40:\overline{10}}}$ in actuarial notation.

12.2.1 THE TIME-TO-FAILURE RANDOM VARIABLE
FOR A LAST-SURVIVOR STATUS

For a two-life last-survivor status composed of the individual lives (x) and (y), we denote the status itself by $(\overline{xy})$ and the random variable for the future lifetime of the status by $T_{\overline{xy}}$. Since the status fails on the last failure, then $T_{\overline{xy}}$ will be the *larger* of the individual future lifetimes T_x and T_y. That is

$$T_{\overline{xy}} = \max(T_x, T_y). \tag{12.18}$$

12.2.2 FUNCTIONS OF THE RANDOM VARIABLE $T_{\overline{xy}}$

If T_x and T_y are independent, then it follows that the CDF of $T_{\overline{xy}}$ is

$$F_{\overline{xy}}(t) = Pr(T_{\overline{xy}} \le t) = F_x(t) \cdot F_y(t). \tag{12.19a}$$

In actuarial notation we would write

$$_tq_{\overline{xy}} = {}_tq_x \cdot {}_tq_y. \tag{12.19b}$$

The SDF of $T_{\overline{xy}}$ can then be found as

$$S_{\overline{xy}}(t) = Pr(T_{\overline{xy}} > t) = 1 - F_{\overline{xy}}(t). \tag{12.20a}$$

In actuarial notation, again presuming the independence of T_x and T_y, we have

$$\begin{aligned}
_tp_{\overline{xy}} &= 1 - {}_tq_{\overline{xy}} \\
&= 1 - {}_tq_x \cdot {}_tq_y \\
&= 1 - (1 - {}_tp_x)(1 - {}_tp_y) \\
&= {}_tp_x + {}_tp_y - {}_tp_x \cdot {}_tp_y \\
&= {}_tp_x + {}_tp_y - {}_tp_{xy}.
\end{aligned} \tag{12.20b}$$

Equation (12.20b) is very important, as it allows us to express last-survivor survival probabilities in terms of single-life and joint-life functions, so we will be able to evaluate last-survivor functions from a single-life survival model or life table. Although Equation (12.20b) was derived here assuming the independence of T_x and T_y, the identity is also true for dependent lifetimes T_x and T_y, as we shall see in Section 12.2.3.

The PDF of $T_{\overline{xy}}$ is then found from the SDF as

$$\begin{aligned}
f_{\overline{xy}}(t) &= -\frac{d}{dt} S_{\overline{xy}}(t) \\
&= -\frac{d}{dt}({}_tp_x + {}_tp_y - {}_tp_{xy}) \\
&= {}_tp_x\mu_{x+t} + {}_tp_y\mu_{y+t} - {}_tp_{xy}\mu_{x+t:y+t},
\end{aligned} \tag{12.21}$$

and the HRF follows as

$$\lambda_{\overline{xy}}(t) = \frac{f_{\overline{xy}}(t)}{S_{\overline{xy}}(t)} = \frac{{}_tp_x\mu_{x+t} + {}_tp_y\mu_{y+t} - {}_tp_{xy}\mu_{x+t:y+t}}{{}_tp_x + {}_tp_y - {}_tp_{xy}}. \tag{12.22}$$

The conditional probability for failure of the status in the $(n+1)^{st}$ time interval is

$$\begin{aligned}
{}_n|q_{\overline{xy}} &= Pr(n < T_{\overline{xy}} \le n+1) \\
&= {}_nP_{\overline{xy}} - {}_{n+1}P_{\overline{xy}} \\
&= ({}_nP_x + {}_nP_y - {}_nP_{xy}) - ({}_{n+1}P_x + {}_{n+1}P_y - {}_{n+1}P_{xy}) \\
&= {}_n|q_x + {}_n|q_y - {}_n|q_{xy}.
\end{aligned} \tag{12.23}$$

As with the joint-life function (see Footnote 3), we can define $K_{\overline{xy}}^*$ as the random variable for the interval of failure of the last-survivor status $(\overline{xy})$, so we have

$$_n|q_{\overline{xy}} = Pr(K_{\overline{xy}}^* = n+1). \tag{12.24}$$

EXAMPLE 12.4

Find the probability that the second failure out of independent lives (x) and (y) occurs in the fifth year, given the following values:

$$_4P_x = .85 \qquad _4P_y = .68 \qquad _5P_x = .81 \qquad _5P_y = .60$$

SOLUTION

We seek the value of

$$_4|q_{\overline{xy}} = {}_4P_{\overline{xy}} - {}_5P_{\overline{xy}}.$$

Due to independence we have

$$_4P_{\overline{xy}} = .85 + .68 - (.85)(.68) = .952$$

and

$$_5P_{\overline{xy}} = .81 + .60 - (.81)(.60) = .924.$$

Then

$$_4|q_{\overline{xy}} = .952 - .924 = .028. \qquad \square$$

The expected value of $T_{\overline{xy}}$ gives the complete expectation of future lifetime for the last-survivor status. We have

$$\overset{o}{e}_{\overline{xy}} = E[T_{\overline{xy}}] = \int_0^\infty t \cdot f_{\overline{xy}}(t)\, dt = \int_0^\infty {}_tP_{\overline{xy}}\, dt. \tag{12.25a}$$

Then using Equation (12.20b) for ${}_tP_{\overline{xy}}$ we have

$$\overset{o}{e}_{\overline{xy}} = \overset{o}{e}_x + \overset{o}{e}_y - \overset{o}{e}_{xy}. \tag{12.25b}$$

The corresponding curtate expectation is

$$e_{\overline{xy}} = \sum_{k=1}^{\infty} {}_k p_{\overline{xy}} = e_x + e_y - e_{xy} \tag{12.26}$$

and the temporary curtate expectation is

$$e_{\overline{xy}:\overline{n}|} = \sum_{k=1}^{n} {}_k p_{\overline{xy}} = e_{x:\overline{n}|} + e_{y:\overline{n}|} - e_{xy:\overline{n}|}. \tag{12.27}$$

EXAMPLE 12.5

Calculate $\overset{\circ}{e}_{\overline{50:60}}$, given that T_{50} and T_{60} are independent and each follows a survival distribution given by $\lambda(x) = \frac{1}{100-x}$, for $0 < x < 100$.

SOLUTION

We recognize the given survival model to be uniform with $\omega = 100$, so we have ${}_t p_{50} = \frac{50-t}{50}$, for $0 \le t \le 50$, ${}_t p_{60} = \frac{40-t}{40}$, for $0 \le t \le 40$, and ${}_t p_{50:60} = \left(\frac{50-t}{50}\right)\left(\frac{40-t}{40}\right)$, for

$0 \le t \le 40$. We also know that $\overset{\circ}{e}_{50} = 25$ and $\overset{\circ}{e}_{60} = 20$. We find $\overset{\circ}{e}_{50:60}$ from

$$\begin{aligned}
\overset{\circ}{e}_{50:60} &= \int_0^{40} {}_t p_{50:60} \, dt \\
&= \frac{1}{2000} \int_0^{40} (50-t)(40-t) \, dt \\
&= \frac{1}{2000}\left(2000t - 45t^2 + \tfrac{1}{3}t^3\right)\Big|_0^{40} = 14.67.
\end{aligned}$$

Then

$$\overset{\circ}{e}_{\overline{50:60}} = 25 + 20 - 14.67 = 30.33. \qquad \square$$

12.2.3 RELATIONSHIPS BETWEEN T_{xy} AND $T_{\overline{xy}}$

Recall that T_{xy} is the time of the first failure between (x) and (y), and $T_{\overline{xy}}$ is the time of the second failure. Then it follows that T_{xy} is one of T_x or T_y and $T_{\overline{xy}}$ is necessarily the other one. Without knowing which one is which, it will still follow that

$$T_{xy} + T_{\overline{xy}} = T_x + T_y \tag{12.28a}$$

and

$$T_{xy} \cdot T_{\overline{xy}} = T_x \cdot T_y. \tag{12.28b}$$

From Equation (12.28a) we have

$$T_{\overline{xy}} = T_x + T_y - T_{xy},$$ (12.29)

which, upon taking expectations, leads directly to Equation (12.25b). By similar reasoning we have

$$_t p_{xy} + {_t p_{\overline{xy}}} = {_t p_x} + {_t p_y},$$ (12.30)

from which Equation (12.20b) follows without assuming independence.

Even if T_x and T_y are independent, it should be clear that T_{xy} and $T_{\overline{xy}}$ are not. We can use Equation (12.28b), along with other earlier results, to find the covariance of T_{xy} and $T_{\overline{xy}}$. We have

$$Cov(T_{xy}, T_{\overline{xy}}) = E[T_{xy} \cdot T_{\overline{xy}}] - E[T_{xy}] \cdot E[T_{\overline{xy}}] = E[T_x \cdot T_y] - E[T_{xy}] \cdot E[T_x + T_y - T_{xy}],$$

by use of Equations (12.28b) and (12.29). But if T_x and T_y are independent, then

$$E[T_x \cdot T_y] = E[T_x] \cdot E[T_y],$$

so we have

$$\begin{aligned}
Cov(T_{xy}, T_{\overline{xy}}) &= E[T_x] \cdot E[T_y] - E[T_{xy}] \cdot \left(E[T_x] + E[T_y] - E[T_{xy}] \right) \\
&= \overset{o}{e}_x \cdot \overset{o}{e}_y - \overset{o}{e}_{xy} \left(\overset{o}{e}_x + \overset{o}{e}_y - \overset{o}{e}_{xy} \right) \\
&= \overset{o}{e}_x \cdot \overset{o}{e}_y - \overset{o}{e}_x \cdot \overset{o}{e}_{xy} - \overset{o}{e}_y \cdot \overset{o}{e}_{xy} + \overset{o}{e}_{xy}{}^2 \\
&= \left(\overset{o}{e}_x - \overset{o}{e}_{xy} \right) \left(\overset{o}{e}_y - \overset{o}{e}_{xy} \right).
\end{aligned}$$ (12.31)

Note that this covariance is always positive.

12.3 CONTINGENT PROBABILITY FUNCTIONS

For two individual statuses (x) and (y), we might be interested in the probability that (x) will fail before (y) fails. A probability for an event addressing order of failures is called a *contingent probability*. The event that (x) fails before (y) is represented by the event $T_x < T_y$. If T_x and T_y are independent, then we have

$$Pr(T_x < T_y) = \int_0^{\infty} f_x(t) \cdot S_y(t) \, dt,$$ (12.32a)

since if (x) fails at time t the event $T_x < T_y$ is satisfied if (y) has not yet failed at that time, the probability of which is $S_y(t)$. In actuarial notation we have

$$Pr(T_x < T_y) = {}_\infty q^1_{xy} = \int_0^\infty {}_t p_x \mu_{x+t} \cdot {}_t p_y \, dt = \int_0^\infty {}_t p_{xy} \mu_{x+t} \, dt. \tag{12.32b}$$

The "upper one" in ${}_\infty q^1_{xy}$ is used to denote order of failure ((x) must fail before (y) to satisfy the event), which we saw earlier in the symbol $Z^1_{x:\overline{n}|}$ (see Section 7.1). The pre-subscript ∞ indicates that the event is satisfied if (x) fails before (y) within unlimited time. The probability that (x) fails before (y) and within n years is therefore given by

$$_n q^1_{xy} = \int_0^n {}_t p_{xy} \mu_{x+t} \, dt. \tag{12.33a}$$

Similarly we would have

$$_n q^{\;1}_{xy} = \int_0^n {}_t p_{xy} \mu_{y+t} \, dt. \tag{12.33b}$$

EXAMPLE 12.6

Show that

$$_n q^1_{xy} + {}_n q^{\;1}_{xy} = {}_n q_{xy}.$$

SOLUTION

The result is intuitive. $_n q^1_{xy}$ represents the probability that the first failure occurs before time n and it is (x), and $_n q^{\;1}_{xy}$ is the same probability with the first failure being (y). Together they represent the probability that the first failure occurs before time n, which is $_n q_{xy}$. Mathematically, using Equations (12.33a) and (12.33b) we have

$$_n q^1_{xy} + {}_n q^{\;1}_{xy} = \int_0^n {}_t p_{xy} \mu_{x+t} \, dt + \int_0^n {}_t p_{xy} \mu_{y+t} \, dt$$

$$= \int_0^n {}_t p_{xy} (\mu_{x+t} + \mu_{y+t}) \, dt = \int_0^n {}_t p_{xy} \mu_{x+t:y+t} \, dt = {}_n q_{xy}. \qquad \square$$

The event that (x) fails *after* (y) is represented by $T_x > T_y$, and we have

$$Pr(T_x > T_y) = \int_0^\infty f_x(t) \cdot F_y(t) \, dt, \tag{12.34a}$$

since if (x) fails at time t the event $T_x > T_y$ requires that (y) has already failed at that time, the probability of which is $F_y(t)$. In actuarial notation we have

$$Pr(T_x > T_y) = {}_{\infty}q^2_{xy} = \int_0^{\infty} {}_t p_x \mu_{x+t} (1 - {}_t p_y)\, dt$$

$$= \int_0^{\infty} {}_t p_x \mu_{x+t}\, dt - \int_0^{\infty} {}_t p_{xy} \mu_{x+t}\, dt = 1 - {}_{\infty}q^1_{xy}, \qquad (12.34b)$$

as expected. The probability that (x) fails after (y) and within n years is then

$${}_n q^2_{xy} = \int_0^n {}_t p_x \mu_{x+t} (1 - {}_t p_y)\, dt = {}_n q_x - {}_n q^1_{xy}. \qquad (12.35)$$

EXAMPLE 12.7

Show that

$${}_n q^2_{xy} + {}_n q^{\,2}_{xy} = {}_n q_{\overline{xy}}.$$

SOLUTION

Again the result is intuitive. Mathematically we have

$${}_n q^2_{xy} + {}_n q^{\,2}_{xy} = \int_0^n {}_t p_x \mu_{x+t} (1 - {}_t p_y)\, dt + \int_0^n {}_t p_y \mu_{y+t} (1 - {}_t p_x)\, dt$$

$$= \int_0^n \Big[{}_t p_x \mu_{x+t} + {}_t p_y \mu_{y+t} - {}_t p_{xy} (\mu_{x+t} + \mu_{y+t}) \Big] dt = {}_n q_x + {}_n q_y - {}_n q_{xy} = {}_n q_{\overline{xy}},$$

since $\mu_{x+t} + \mu_{y+t} = \mu_{x+t:y+t}$. $\qquad\qquad\square$

12.4 CONTINGENT CONTRACTS INVOLVING MULTI-LIFE STATUSES

All the material presented in Chapters 7 - 11 concerning contingent payment models and contingent annuities, including their funding and reserving plans, is applicable to the two-life statuses (joint and last-survivor) defined in this chapter. Indeed, the presentation throughout Chapters 7 - 11 was made in general terms to facilitate its extension to the multi-life case. Thus the general concept of a status with identifying characteristic x now can represent the joint-life status (xy) or the last-survivor status $(\overline{xy})$. Throughout this section we assume the independence of T_x and T_y when needed.

It is therefore unnecessary to duplicate the entire presentation in the earlier chapters simply substituting (xy) or $(\overline{xy})$ for (x). Rather we will list only a very small selection of the relationships we developed earlier, now recast in joint or last-survivor notation, to illustrate this point.

12.4.1 CONTINGENT PAYMENT MODELS (CHAPTER 7 MODELS)

If K^*_{xy} denotes the random variable for the time interval in which the joint status (xy) fails, then

$$Z_{xy} = v^{K_{xy}^*} \tag{12.36}$$

denotes the random variable for the present value of a unit paid at the end of that interval. Further,

$$A_{xy} = E[Z_{xy}] = \sum_{k=1}^{\infty} v^k \cdot {}_{k-1|}q_{xy} \tag{12.37}$$

denotes the first moment of Z_{xy} and

$$^2A_{xy} = E[Z_{xy}{}^2] = \sum_{k=1}^{\infty} (v^k)^2 \cdot {}_{k-1|}q_{xy} \tag{12.38}$$

denotes its second moment, from which the variance follows.

The extension to joint-life term insurance, deferred insurance, pure endowment, and endowment insurance all follow directly from their Chapter 7 counterparts.

Similar remarks hold for continuous contingent payment models. We define

$$\overline{Z}_{xy} = v^{T_{xy}} \tag{12.39}$$

as the random variable for the present value of a unit paid at the precise time of failure of (xy), with

$$\overline{A}_{xy} = E[\overline{Z}_{xy}] = \int_0^{\infty} v^t \cdot {}_t p_{xy} \mu_{x+t:y+t} \, dt \tag{12.40}$$

and

$$^2\overline{A}_{xy} = E[\overline{Z}_{xy}{}^2] = \int_0^{\infty} (v^t)^2 \cdot {}_t p_{xy} \mu_{x+t:y+t} \, dt \tag{12.41}$$

as its first and second moments.

The same definitions apply for the last-survivor status, with some notational adjustments. We have, for example,

$$A_{\overline{xy}} = E[Z_{\overline{xy}}] = \sum_{k=1}^{\infty} v^k \cdot {}_{k-1|}q_{\overline{xy}}. \tag{12.42a}$$

Substituting for ${}_{k-1|}q_{\overline{xy}}$ from Equation (12.23) we then have

$$A_{\overline{xy}} = A_x + A_y - A_{xy}. \tag{12.42b}$$

In the case of the continuous function we have

$$\overline{A}_{\overline{xy}} = E[\overline{Z}_{\overline{xy}}] = \int_0^\infty v^t \cdot f_{\overline{xy}}(t)\, dt$$

$$= \int_0^\infty v^t (\, _tp_x\mu_{x+t} + \, _tp_y\mu_{y+t} - \, _tp_{xy}\mu_{x+t:y+t})\, dt$$

$$= \overline{A}_x + \overline{A}_y - \overline{A}_{xy}, \tag{12.42c}$$

using Equation (12.21) for the PDF of $T_{\overline{xy}}$.

12.4.2 CONTINGENT ANNUITY MODELS (CHAPTER 8 MODELS)

We can again substitute the joint-life status (xy) or the last-survivor status $(\overline{xy})$ for the generic status of interest (x) used in Chapter 8 to define annuities payable as long as a joint-life or last-survivor status continues to survive. As in Chapter 8, such annuities can be paid as immediate, due, or continuous. We would have, for example,

$$a_{xy} = \sum_{k=1}^{\infty} v^k \cdot \, _kp_{xy}, \tag{12.43}$$

$$\ddot{a}_{\overline{xy}} = \sum_{k=0}^{\infty} v^k \cdot \, _kp_{\overline{xy}}, \tag{12.44}$$

$$\overline{a}_{xy:\overline{n}|} = \int_0^n v^t \cdot \, _tp_{xy}\, dt \tag{12.45}$$

and

$$\ddot{s}_{\overline{xy}:\overline{n}|} = \ddot{a}_{\overline{xy}:\overline{n}|} \cdot \frac{1}{_nE_{\overline{xy}}}, \tag{12.46}$$

where

$$_nE_{\overline{xy}} = v^n \cdot \, _np_{\overline{xy}} = \, _nE_x + \, _nE_y - \, _nE_{xy}. \tag{12.47}$$

The relationship between insurance and annuity functions, presented in Chapter 8, will also hold in the multi-life cases. We would have, for example,

$$A_{xy} = 1 - d \cdot \ddot{a}_{xy} \tag{12.48}$$

and

$$\overline{A}_{\overline{xy}} = 1 - \delta \cdot \overline{a}_{\overline{xy}}. \tag{12.49}$$

12.4.3 ANNUAL PREMIUMS AND RESERVES

The annual benefit premium for a whole life joint-life insurance of unit amount is given by the equivalence principle as

$$P_{xy} = \frac{A_{xy}}{\ddot{a}_{xy}}. \tag{12.50}$$

Note that since the contingent benefit pays on the first failure, the funding scheme should stop at the first failure as well. In the case of a last-survivor status, we have

$$P_{\overline{xy}} = \frac{A_{\overline{xy}}}{\ddot{a}_{\overline{xy}}} \tag{12.51}$$

if the funding continues until the second failure at which point the benefit is paid.

EXAMPLE 12.8

A contingent contract pays a benefit of amount b at the end of the year of the second failure of independent lives (x) and (y). The net annual premium is 110 paid at the beginning of each year while both (x) and (y) survive and 40 per year after the first failure. Find the value of b, given the following values:

$$A_{xy} = .80 \qquad \ddot{a}_x = 8 \qquad \ddot{a}_y = 7 \qquad d = .05$$

SOLUTION

The APV of the benefit is $b \cdot A_{\overline{xy}}$. The APV of the premium stream is

$$110\ddot{a}_{xy} + 40(\ddot{a}_{\overline{xy}} - \ddot{a}_{xy}).$$

By the equivalence principle we have

$$b(A_x + A_y - A_{xy}) = 40\ddot{a}_x + 40\ddot{a}_y + 30\ddot{a}_{xy}$$

or

$$b[1 - (.05)(8) + 1 - (.05)(7) - .80] = (40)(8) + (40)(7) + (30)\left(\frac{1 - .80}{.05}\right),$$

which solves for $b = 1600$. ❑

Benefit terminal reserves can easily be defined by the prospective method. For the joint-life insurance we have

$$_tV_{xy} = A_{x+t:y+t} - P_{xy} \cdot \ddot{a}_{x+t:y+t} \tag{12.52}$$

if the status has not yet failed as of time t. For the last-survivor status, a bit more care is needed. Although the status $(\overline{xy})$ has not yet failed at time t, it is possible that one of its component members may have already failed. Thus there are three cases for the reserve at duration t, namely

$$_tV_{\overline{xy}} = A_{\overline{x+t:y+t}} - P_{\overline{xy}} \cdot \ddot{a}_{\overline{x+t:y+t}} \tag{12.53a}$$

if both components (x) and (y) still survive,

$$_tV_{\overline{xy}} = A_{x+t} - P_{\overline{xy}} \cdot \ddot{a}_{x+t} \tag{12.53b}$$

if (y) has already failed and only (x) survives, or

$$_tV_{\overline{xy}} = A_{y+t} - P_{\overline{xy}} \cdot \ddot{a}_{y+t} \tag{12.53c}$$

if (x) has already failed and only (y) survives.

12.4.4 Reversionary Annuities

A special type of two-life annuity is one that pays only after one of the lives has failed, and then for as long as the other continues to survive. Such annuities are called *reversionary annuities*.

If payment is made to the status (y), provided it has not failed, but only after the failure of the status (x), then the total condition for payment at time k is that (x) has failed but (y) has not. The probability of this is

$$_kq_x \cdot {}_kp_y = {}_kp_y(1-{}_kp_x) = {}_kp_y - {}_kp_{xy}, \tag{12.54}$$

so the actuarial present value of a reversionary annuity payable under such circumstances would be

$$a_{x|y} = \sum_{k=1}^{\infty} v^k({}_kp_y - {}_kp_{xy}) = a_y - a_{xy}. \tag{12.55}$$

The result is intuitive. a_y represents the APV of payment made for the lifetime of (y), and a_{xy} is the APV of payment made for the joint lifetime of (xy). We can read Equation (12.55) as providing payment as long as (y) survives, but taking it away while (x) also survives, with the net effect being payment made while (y) survives but after the failure of (x).

If the payment is made for n years at most, with the requirement that (y) has failed but (x) has not, the APV would be

$$a_{y|x:\overline{n}|} = \sum_{k=1}^{n} v^k \cdot {}_kp_x \cdot {}_kq_y$$

$$= \sum_{k=1}^{n} v^k({}_kp_x - {}_kp_{xy}) = a_{x:\overline{n}|} - a_{xy:\overline{n}|}. \tag{12.56}$$

In the continuous case we have

$$\overline{a}_{x|y} = \int_0^{\infty} v^t \cdot {}_tp_y \cdot {}_tq_x \, dt$$

$$= \int_0^{\infty} v^t({}_tp_y - {}_tp_{xy}) \, dt = \overline{a}_y - \overline{a}_{xy}. \tag{12.57}$$

If a reversionary annuity is funded by annual premiums, the length of the premium-paying period would be the joint lifetime, since upon failure of the joint status either payments begin or the contract expires without value. If payments are to be made to (x) after the failure of (y), then use of the equivalence principle leads to the annual benefit premium

$$P(a_{y|x}) = \frac{a_{y|x}}{\ddot{a}_{xy}} = \frac{a_x - a_{xy}}{\ddot{a}_{xy}}. \tag{12.58}$$

The benefit reserve at duration t would again depend on what combination of (x) and (y) still survive. If both are alive, the reversionary annuity contract is still in premium-paying status so the reserve is

$$_tV(a_{y|x}) = a_{y+t|x+t} - P(a_{y|x}) \cdot \ddot{a}_{x+t:y+t}. \tag{12.59a}$$

If (x) only is alive the contract is beyond the premium-paying period and in payout status, so the reserve is simply

$$_tV(a_{y|x}) = a_{x+t}. \tag{12.59b}$$

If (y) only is alive, no payment will ever be made so the contract has expired and the reserve is zero.

EXAMPLE 12.9

Show that $a_{\overline{xy}} = a_{x|y} + a_{y|x} + a_{xy}$.

SOLUTION

The result is intuitive. $a_{x|y}$ represents payments made if (y) is alive but (x) is not, $a_{y|x}$ represents payments made if (x) is alive but (y) is not, and a_{xy} represents payments made if both are alive. The three cases are mutually exclusive. Together they provide payments if either (x) or (y) is alive, which is represented by $a_{\overline{xy}}$. Mathematically,

$$\begin{aligned} a_{x|y} + a_{y|x} + a_{xy} &= a_y - a_{xy} + a_x - a_{xy} + a_{xy} \\ &= a_x + a_y - a_{xy} \\ &= a_{\overline{xy}}, \end{aligned}$$

as required. ❑

12.4.5 CONTINGENT INSURANCE FUNCTIONS

A *contingent insurance* is one for which payment of the unit benefit depends on the order of failure among its component members. The insurance functions follow from the probability functions introduced in Section 12.3. Here we consider only insurances with immediate payment of claims.

A contingent insurance benefit paid at the failure of (x) only if (x) fails *before* (y) has APV given by

$$\overline{A}_{xy}^1 = \int_0^\infty v^t \cdot {}_tp_{xy}\mu_{x+t}\, dt. \tag{12.60}$$

If the benefit is paid at the failure of (x) only if (x) fails *after* (y), the APV is

$$\overline{A}_{xy}^2 = \int_0^\infty v^t \cdot {}_tp_x\mu_{x+t}(1- {}_tp_y)\, dt = \overline{A}_x - \overline{A}_{xy}^1. \tag{12.61}$$

EXAMPLE 12.10

Show that
$$\overline{A}_{xy}^1 + \overline{A}_{xy}^{\ 1} = \overline{A}_{xy}$$
and
$$\overline{A}_{xy}^2 + \overline{A}_{xy}^{\ 2} = \overline{A}_{\overline{xy}}.$$

SOLUTION

$$\overline{A}_{xy}^1 + \overline{A}_{xy}^{\ 1} = \int_0^\infty v^t \cdot {}_tp_{xy}\mu_{x+t}\, dt + \int_0^\infty v^t \cdot {}_tp_{xy}\mu_{y+t}\, dt$$

$$= \int_0^\infty v^t \cdot {}_tp_{xy}\mu_{x+t:y+t}\, dt = \overline{A}_{xy}$$

$$\overline{A}_{xy}^2 + \overline{A}_{xy}^{\ 2} = \left(\overline{A}_x - \overline{A}_{xy}^1\right) + \left(\overline{A}_y - \overline{A}_{xy}^{\ 1}\right)$$

$$= \overline{A}_x + \overline{A}_y - \left(\overline{A}_{xy}^1 - \overline{A}_{xy}^{\ 1}\right)$$

$$= \overline{A}_x + \overline{A}_y - \overline{A}_{xy} = \overline{A}_{\overline{xy}} \qquad \square$$

12.5 MULTI-STATE MODEL REPRESENTATION

The multi-life models presented thus far in this chapter can be easily represented as multi-state models. We illustrate this idea in the two-life case, with extension to three or more lives being apparent.

12.5.1 THE GENERAL MODEL

Consider two persons alive at ages x and y, respectively, at time t. The model is in State 1 as long as both lives continue to survive. Since both lives are surviving at time t, it follows that the process begins in State 1 at that time. The model is illustrated in Figure 12.1 on the following page.

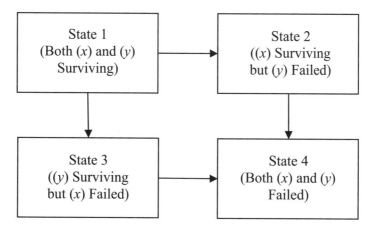

FIGURE 12.1

Since the only decrement is failure, or death, it follows that any state, once left, cannot be reentered. Therefore the event of being in State 1 at time $t+r$, given in State 1 at time t, is the same as the event of never leaving State 1 over that time interval.

Similarly, the event of being in State i, for $i = 2$ or 3, at any time after entering that state is the same as the event of never leaving that state once it has been entered. Note that transition from State 2 to State 3, or from State 3 to State 2, is not possible.

Clearly State 4 is an absorbing state, which can never be left once it has been entered. We also assume, in this model, that the simultaneous failure of (x) and (y) is not possible, so direct transition from State 1 to State 4 cannot occur.[4]

12.5.2 THE JOINT-LIFE MODEL

By definition, the joint-life status continues to survive as long as the process is in State 1, and fails when the process transitions to either State 2 or State 3. For a discrete process known to be in State 1 at time n, the probability of being in State 1 at time $n+r$ is

$$Pr[X_{n+r} = 1 \mid X_n = 1] = {}_r p_{11}^{(n)} = {}_r p_{11}^{*(n)}, \tag{12.62a}$$

and for a continuous process known to be in State 1 at time t, the probability of being in State 1 at time $t+r$ is

$$Pr[X(t+r) = 1 \mid X(t) = 1] = {}_r p_{11}^{(t)} = {}_r p_{11}^{*(t)}. \tag{12.62b}$$

In the single-life case, for a person alive (i.e., in State 1) at age x at discrete time n (or continuous time t), the probability of being in State 1 at discrete time $n+r$ (or continuous time $t+r$) is ${}_r p_x$ in all cases. That is,

---

[4] This restriction is relaxed in Section 12.8.

$$_r p_x = {_r p_{11}^{(n)}} = {_r p_{11}^{*(n)}} = {_r p_{11}^{(t)}} = {_r p_{11}^{*(t)}}. \tag{12.63a}$$

In the multi-life case, assuming independence of (x) and (y), the corresponding probability is $_r p_{xy} = {_r p_x} \cdot {_r p_y}$. That is,

$$_r p_{xy} = {_r p_x} \cdot {_r p_y} = {_r p_{11}^{(n)}} = {_r p_{11}^{*(n)}} = {_r p_{11}^{(t)}} = {_r p_{11}^{*(t)}}. \tag{12.63b}$$

For the joint-life model, we can write the APVs for annuities and insurances in multi-state model notation by analogy to the single-life model as presented in Section 8.6 (for annuities) and Section 7.6 (for insurances). Two examples of this are presented in Example 12.11, with others left to the exercises (see Exercise 12-18).

Example 12.11

Write the APVs for (a) the joint-life annuity-due and (b) the continuous joint-life insurance in multi-state model notation.

Solution

(a) For two persons alive at ages x and y, respectively, at time 0, the APV of a unit annuity-due, by analogy to Equation (8.96), is

$$\ddot{a}_{xy} = \sum_{k=0}^{\infty} v^k \cdot {_k p_{11}^{(0)}}, \tag{12.64}$$

where $_k p_{11}^{(0)} = {_k p_{xy}} = {_k p_x} \cdot {_k p_y}$, if (x) and (y) are independent.

(b) The unit continuous joint-life insurance is payable at the instant of transition from State 1 to State 2 *or* from State 1 to State 3. These events are mutually exclusive, so the APV, by analogy to Equation (7.80), is

$$\bar{A}_{xy} = \int_0^{\infty} v^r \cdot {_r p_{11}^{(0)}} \left(\lambda_{12}(r) + \lambda_{13}(r) \right) dr, \tag{12.65}$$

where $_r p_{11}^{(0)}$ is defined in part (a), $\lambda_{12}(r) = \mu_{y+r}$, and $\lambda_{13}(r) = \mu_{x+r}$. □

12.5.3 Reversionary Annuities

Recall from Section 12.4.4 that the reversionary annuity with APV given by $a_{y|x}$ is payable to (x) after the failure of (y). In the multi-state model context, such an annuity is payable if the process is in State 2. Then we would write

$$a_{y|x} = \sum_{k=1}^{\infty} v^k \cdot {}_k p_{12}^{(0)}, \qquad (12.66)$$

where ${}_k p_{12}^{(0)} = {}_k p_x \cdot {}_k q_y = {}_k p_x - {}_k p_{xy}$. The APV for a reversionary annuity payable to (y) after the failure of (x) follows by symmetry. (See Exercise 12-19.)

12.5.4 CONTINGENT INSURANCE FUNCTIONS

The continuous contingent insurance with APV given in standard actuarial notation by $\overline{A}_{xy}^1$ is payable at the instant of transition from State 1 to State 3 in the multi-state model context. The one with APV given by $\overline{A}_{xy}^2$ is payable at the instant of transition from State 2 to State 4. The reader is asked to write the APVs for these, and other, contingent insurances in multi-state model notation in Exercise 12-20.

12.5.5 THE LAST-SURVIVOR MODEL

The last-survivor status continues to exist while *any* of its component members survive, so, in the multi-state model context, the status is surviving while the process is in any of States 1, 2, or 3, and the status fails when the process transitions to State 4 from either State 2 or State 3. APVs for last-survivor functions can be written in multi-state model notation by analogy to APVs developed earlier. This is illustrated in the following example and in Exercise 12-21.

EXAMPLE 12.12

For two lives known to be surviving at time 0 at ages x and y, write the APVs for (a) the last-survivor immediate annuity and (b) the last-survivor continuous whole life insurance.

SOLUTION

(a) The annuity is payable at the end of each year while either (or both) of (x) and (y) survive, which means the process is in any one of States 1, 2, or 3. These events are mutually exclusive, so the APV is

$$a_{\overline{xy}} = \sum_{r=1}^{\infty} v^r \left({}_r p_{11}^{(0)} + {}_r p_{12}^{(0)} + {}_r p_{13}^{(0)} \right), \qquad (12.67a)$$

where ${}_r p_{11}^{(0)} = {}_r p_x \cdot {}_r p_y$, ${}_r p_{12}^{(0)} = {}_r p_x \cdot {}_r q_y$, and ${}_r p_{13}^{(0)} = {}_r p_y \cdot {}_r q_x$, assuming independence of (x) and (y).

(b) The insurance is payable at the instant of the second failure, with APV denoted by $\overline{A}_{\overline{xy}}$.

In the multi-state model context, it is payable at the instant of transition from State 2 to State 4 or from State 3 to State 4. The APV is

$$\overline{A}_{\overline{xy}} = \int_0^\infty v^r \left({}_r p_{12}^{(0)} \cdot \lambda_{24}(r) + {}_r p_{13}^{(0)} \cdot \lambda_{34}(r) \right) dr, \qquad (12.67b)$$

where ${}_r p_{12}^{(0)} = {}_r p_x \cdot {}_r q_y$, ${}_r p_{13}^{(0)} = {}_r p_y \cdot {}_r q_x$, $\lambda_{24}(r) = \mu_{x+r}$, and $\lambda_{34}(r) = \mu_{y+r}$. $\quad\square$

12.5.6 SOLVING THE KOLMOGOROV FORWARD EQUATION

In this section we consider the Kolmogorov differential equation presented in Section 3.2.2 as it applies to the multi-life model of Section 12.5.1. As shown by the arrows in Figure 12.1, not all transitions between states are possible, so the only non-zero forces of transition are $\lambda_{12}(s)$, $\lambda_{13}(s)$, $\lambda_{24}(s)$, and $\lambda_{34}(s)$.

Suppose (x) and (y) are both alive at those ages at general time t, so that the process is in State 1. Then ${}_r p_{11}^{(t)}$ denotes the probability that the process is still in State 1 (i.e., both are still surviving) at time $t+r$, and ${}_r p_{12}^{(t)}$ denotes the probability that the process is in State 2 (i.e., (x) is surviving but (y) has failed) at time $t+r$. (Note that ${}_r p_{13}^{(t)}$ is the same as ${}_r p_{12}^{(t)}$, with the roles of (x) and (y) reversed.)

If the process is in State 2 at time t, then both ${}_r p_{22}^{(t)}$ and ${}_r p_{24}^{(t)}$ denote concepts of interest to us. (Note that ${}_r p_{21}^{(t)} = {}_r p_{23}^{(t)} = 0$.) Furthermore, both ${}_r p_{33}^{(t)}$ and ${}_r p_{34}^{(t)}$ are also concepts of interest, but they are the same as ${}_r p_{22}^{(t)}$ and ${}_r p_{24}^{(t)}$, respectively, with the roles of (x) and (y) reversed.

It is clear that, for a process in State 4 at time t, ${}_r p_{41}^{(t)} = {}_r p_{42}^{(t)} = {}_r p_{43}^{(t)} = 0$ and ${}_r p_{44}^{(t)} = 1$ for all r.

The above analysis suggests that we need solve the Kolmogorov equation only for ${}_n p_{11}^{(t)}$, ${}_n p_{12}^{(t)}$, ${}_n p_{22}^{(t)}$, and ${}_n p_{24}^{(t)}$. We do this for ${}_n p_{12}^{(t)}$ in the following example, and defer the others three cases to Exercises 12-22 and 12-23.

EXAMPLE 12.13

The symbol ${}_n p_{12}^{(t)}$ denotes the probability that a process in State 1 at time t will be in State 2 at time $t+n$, where State 1 means both (x) and (y) are alive at those ages. To be in State 2 at time $t+n$ requires that (y) fails in, and (x) survives over, the interval $(t,t+n]$. (In actuarial notation this is denoted by ${}_n p_x \cdot {}_n q_y$, assuming that (x) and (y) are independent lives.) Show that the Kolmogorov equation can be solved for this result.

SOLUTION

In Equation (3.14a), $i=1$ and $j=2$ so k takes on the values 1, 3, 4 in the summation. Then we have

$$\frac{d}{dr} {}_r p_{12}^{(t)} = {}_r p_{11}^{(t)} \cdot \lambda_{12}(t+r) - {}_r p_{12}^{(t)} \cdot \lambda_{21}(t+r) \qquad \text{(at } k=1)$$

$$+ {}_r p_{13}^{(t)} \cdot \lambda_{32}(t+r) - {}_r p_{12}^{(t)} \cdot \lambda_{23}(t+r) \qquad \text{(at } k=3)$$

$$+ {}_r p_{14}^{(t)} \cdot \lambda_{42}(t+r) - {}_r p_{12}^{(t)} \cdot \lambda_{24}(t+r) \qquad \text{(at } k=4)$$

$$= {}_r p_{11}^{(t)} \cdot \lambda_{12}(t+r) - {}_r p_{12}^{(t)} \cdot \lambda_{24}(t+r),$$

since $\lambda_{21}(s) = \lambda_{32}(s) = \lambda_{23}(s) = \lambda_{42}(s) = 0$ for all s. Then integrating from $r=0$ to $r=n$ we have

$$\int_0^n d \, {}_r p_{12}^{(t)} = \int_0^n {}_r p_{11}^{(t)} \cdot \lambda_{12}(t+r) \, dr - \int_0^n {}_r p_{12}^{(t)} \cdot \lambda_{24}(t+r) \, dr.$$

The left side integrates to ${}_n p_{12}^{(t)}$, as expected, since ${}_0 p_{12}^{(t)} = 0$. The right side is more easily understood when written in actuarial notation. We have

$$\int_0^n {}_r p_{xy} \cdot \mu_{y+r} \, dr - \int_0^n {}_r p_x \cdot {}_r q_y \cdot \mu_{x+r} \, dr,$$

since $\lambda_{12}(t+r)$ is the force of failure for (y) at age $y+r$ and $\lambda_{24}(t+r)$ is the force of failure for (x) at age $x+r$. We can represent both integrals in contingent probability notation, from Section 12.3, obtaining the result

$${}_n p_{12}^{(t)} = {}_n q_{xy}^1 - {}_n q_{xy}^2.$$

But ${}_n q_{xy}^2 = {}_n q_x - {}_n q_{xy}^1$, so we can write our result as

$${}_n p_{12}^{(t)} = {}_n q_{xy}^1 - ({}_n q_x - {}_n q_{xy}^1)$$

$$= {}_n q_{xy} - {}_n q_x$$

$$= 1 - {}_n p_x \cdot {}_n p_y - 1 + {}_n p_x = {}_n p_x - {}_n p_x \cdot {}_n p_y = {}_n p_x (1 - {}_n p_y) = {}_n p_x \cdot {}_n q_y,$$

as requested. ◻

12.6 GENERAL RANDOM VARIABLE ANALYSIS

Consider again the case of two individual lives (x) and (y), with time-to-failure (or future lifetime) random variables T_x and T_y, respectively. When T_x and T_y are independent, we have seen how all discrete multi-life functions can ultimately be evaluated from a single-life survival model, usually in life table form. But how do we evaluate multi-life functions if independence does not hold?

In theory we can proceed according to the general rules regarding the joint distribution of two random variables, as presented in a basic probability course and reviewed in Section 2.4 of this text. We presume that we are given a joint density function of the random variables T_x and T_y, denoted by $f_{x,y}(t_x,t_y)$, for $t_x > 0$ and $t_y > 0$, where T_x and T_y are not necessarily independent.[5] From the joint density function we can then determine all other desired functions.

12.6.1 MARGINAL DISTRIBUTIONS OF T_x AND T_y

We can find the marginal densities of T_x and T_y by integrating the joint density function across the opposite variable. Thus we have

$$f_x(t_x) = \int_{t_y} f_{x,y}(t_x,t_y)\, dt_y \qquad (12.68a)$$

and

$$f_y(t_y) = \int_{t_x} f_{x,y}(t_x,t_y)\, dt_x. \qquad (12.68b)$$

From the separate marginal distributions we can evaluate any probability or other single-life function as described in earlier chapters.

12.6.2 THE COVARIANCE OF T_x AND T_y

From the joint PDF of T_x and T_y we can find

$$E[T_x \cdot T_y] = \int_0^\infty \int_0^\infty t_x t_y \cdot f_{x,y}(t_x,t_y)\, dt_x\, dt_y. \qquad (12.69)$$

Then from the separate marginal PDF's of T_x and T_y we find $E[T_x]$ and $E[T_y]$, and therefore

$$Cov(T_x,T_y) = E[T_x \cdot T_y] - E[T_x] \cdot E[T_y]. \qquad (12.70)$$

EXAMPLE 12.14

An electronic device relies on two essential components, denoted (x) and (y), for its operation. The joint density function of the lifetimes of (x) and (y), measured in months, is

$$f_{x,y}(t_x,t_y) = \frac{t_x + t_y}{27},$$

for $0 < t_x < 3$ and $0 < t_y < 3$.

---

[5] The case where T_x and T_y *are* independent will be contained within the general analysis as a special case.

(a) Show that T_x and T_y are not independent.

(b) Find the correlation coefficient of T_x and T_y.

SOLUTION

First we find the marginal density of T_x as

$$f_x(t_x) = \int_0^3 f_{x,y}(t_x, t_y)\, dt_y$$

$$= \int_0^3 (t_x + t_y)\, dt_y = \frac{1}{27}\left(t_x t_y + \frac{1}{2}t_y^2\right)\bigg|_0^3 = \frac{1}{27}\left(3t_x + \frac{9}{2}\right) = \frac{2t_x + 3}{18},$$

for $0 < t_x < 3$. By the symmetry of the joint PDF it follows that

$$f_y(t_y) = \frac{2t_y + 3}{18},$$

for $0 < t_y < 3$. Next we find

$$E[T_x] = \int_0^3 t_x \cdot f_x(t_x)\, dt_x = \frac{1}{18}\int_0^3 (2t_x^2 + 3t_x)\, dt_x = \frac{1}{18}\left(\frac{2}{3}t_x^3 + \frac{3}{2}t_x^2\right)\bigg|_0^3 = 1.75$$

and

$$E[T_x^2] = \int_0^3 t_x^2 \cdot f_x(t_x)\, dt_x = \frac{1}{18}\int_0^3 (2t_x^3 + 3t_x^2)\, dt_x = \frac{1}{18}\left(\frac{1}{2}t_x^4 + t_x^3\right)\bigg|_0^3 = 3.75,$$

so

$$Var(T_x) = 3.75 - (1.75)^2 = .6875.$$

Again by symmetry the same values apply to T_y. Directly from the joint PDF we find

$$E[T_x \cdot T_y] = \int_0^3\int_0^3 t_x t_y \cdot f_{x,y}(t_x, t_y)\, dt_x\, dt_y$$

$$= \frac{1}{27}\int_0^3\int_0^3 (t_x^2 t_y + t_x t_y^2)\, dt_x\, dt_y$$

$$= \frac{1}{27}\int_0^3\left(\frac{1}{3}t_x^3 t_y + \frac{1}{2}t_x^2 t_y^2\right)\bigg|_0^3 dt_y$$

$$= \frac{1}{27}\int_0^3\left(9t_y + 4.5t_y^2\right) dt_y$$

$$= \frac{1}{27}\left(4.5t_y^2 + 1.5t_y^3\right)\bigg|_0^3 = 3.$$

(a) We observe that

$$f_x(t_x) \cdot f_y(t_y) \neq f_{x,y}(t_x,t_y),$$

so T_x and T_y are not independent.

(b) From the results developed above we find

$$Cov(T_x,T_y) = 3 - (1.75)(1.75) = -.0625$$

and therefore

$$\rho_{T_x,T_y} = \frac{Cov(T_x,T_y)}{\sqrt{Var(T_x) \cdot Var(T_y)}} = \frac{-.0625}{\sqrt{(.6875)^2}} = -.09091. \qquad \Box$$

12.6.3 OTHER JOINT FUNCTIONS OF T_x AND T_y

If the individual domains of T_x and T_y are both all positive values, then their joint domain will be the entire first quadrant, as illustrated in the following figure.

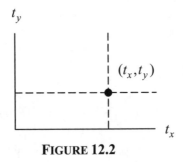

FIGURE 12.2

The joint CDF of T_x and T_y is given by

$$F_{x,y}(t_x,t_y) = Pr(T_x \le t_x \cap T_y \le t_y) = \int_0^{t_y} \int_0^{t_x} f_{x,y}(r,s)\, dr\, ds \qquad (12.71)$$

for $t_x > 0$ and $t_y > 0$, and $F_{x,y}(t_x,t_y) = 0$ for any other values of t_x and/or t_y. For example, consider the case where $t_x < 0$ and $t_y > 0$, so the point (t_x,t_y) lies in the second quadrant. Since the joint CDF represents $Pr(T_x \le t_x \cap T_y \le t_y)$, it is easy to see that the joint CDF is zero, since the event $T_x \le t_x$ cannot occur. Similar reasoning applies to a point (t_x,t_y) lying in the third or fourth quadrants.

If the joint domain of T_x and T_y does not cover the entire first quadrant, the joint CDF can be non-zero in portions of the first quadrant where the joint PDF is zero. This is illustrated in the following example.

EXAMPLE 12.15

Find the joint CDF for the joint distribution of Example 12.14.

SOLUTION

Consider the following figure:

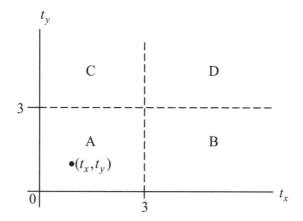

FIGURE 12.3

The joint PDF is non-zero only within Region A of the first quadrant. Within Region A the joint CDF of T_x and T_y is given by

$$
\begin{aligned}
F_{x,y}(t_x,t_y) &= \int_0^{t_y}\int_0^{t_x} f_{x,y}(r,s)\,dr\,ds \\
&= \frac{1}{27}\int_0^{t_y}\int_0^{t_x}(r+s)\,dr\,ds \\
&= \frac{1}{27}\int_0^{t_y}\left(\frac{1}{2}r^2+rs\right)\Big|_0^{t_x}\,ds \\
&= \frac{1}{27}\int_0^{t_y}\left(\frac{1}{2}t_x^2 + t_x s\right)ds \\
&= \frac{1}{27}\left(\frac{1}{2}t_x^2 s + \frac{1}{2}t_x s^2\right)\Big|_0^{t_y} = \frac{t_x^2 t_y + t_x t_y^2}{54},
\end{aligned}
$$

for $0 < t_x < 3$ and $0 < t_y < 3$. For a point (t_x,t_y) in Region B, the event $T_x \le t_x$ is certain to occur, since $t_x > 3$ in Region B. Therefore the joint CDF, which is $Pr(T_x \le t_x \cap T_y \le t_y)$, is the same as $Pr(T_y \leq t_y)$ since $Pr(T_x \leq t_x) = 1$. Then we see that

$$F_{x,y}(t_x, t_y) \equiv F_y(t_y)$$

for $t_x > 3$ and $0 < t_y < 3$. By similar reasoning, for any point in Region C we have

$$F_{x,y}(t_x, t_y) \equiv F_x(t_x)$$

for $0 < t_x < 3$ and $t_y > 3$. In Region D both events $T_x \leq t_x$ and $T_y \leq t_y$ are certain to occur so we have

$$F_{x,y}(t_x, t_y) \equiv 1$$

for $t_x > 3$ and $t_y > 3$. ❑

The joint SDF of T_x and T_y is given by

$$S_{x,y}(t_x, t_y) = Pr\left(T_x > t_x \cap T_y > t_y\right) = \int_{t_y}^{\infty} \int_{t_x}^{\infty} f_{x,y}(r, s)\, dr\, ds, \qquad (12.72)$$

for $t_x > 0$ and $t_y > 0$. For a (t_x, t_y) point in the second quadrant, the event $T_x > t_x$ is certain to occur so $Pr(T_x > t_x \cap T_y > t_y)$ is the same as $Pr(T_y > t_y) = S_{T_y}(t_y)$. Similar reasoning for a (t_x, t_y) point in the fourth quadrant shows that $Pr(T_x > t_x \cap T_y > t_y)$ is the same as $Pr(T_x > t_x) = S_{T_x}(t_x)$. In the third quadrant, both events $T_x > t_x$ and $T_y > t_y$ are certain to occur so $S_{x,y}(t_x, t_y) = 1$ for $t_x < 0$ and $t_y < 0$.

12.6.4 JOINT AND LAST-SURVIVOR STATUS FUNCTIONS

If the general joint SDF of T_x and T_y is evaluated at a common point, say $t_x = t_y = n$, then we have

$$S_{x,y}(n, n) = Pr\left(T_x > n \cap T_y > n\right) = Pr(T_{xy} > n) = {}_n p_{xy}, \qquad (12.73)$$

in actuarial notation. Therefore all joint life functions presented in Section 12.1 can be evaluated from the general joint SDF of T_x and T_y. Note that the relationship ${}_n p_{xy} = {}_n p_x \cdot {}_n p_y$ will generally hold only if T_x and T_y are independent.

EXAMPLE 12.16

Suppose the device described in Example 12.14 fails upon the first failure of its two essential components. Find the probability that the device fails during its first month of operation.

SOLUTION

Since the device fails on the *first* failure of its components, then the two components form a joint status. We seek the probability value given by $q_{xy} = 1 - p_{xy}$. The joint SDF of T_x and T_y in Example 12.14 is given by

$$S_{x,y}(t_x, t_y) = \frac{1}{27} \int_{t_y}^{3} \int_{t_x}^{3} (r+s) \, dr \, ds,$$

so the joint status probability p_{xy} is given by

$$\begin{aligned} p_{xy} &= S_{x,y}(1,1) = \frac{1}{27} \int_{1}^{3} \int_{1}^{3} (r+s) \, dr \, ds \\ &= \frac{1}{27} \int_{1}^{3} \left(\frac{1}{2} r^2 + rs \right) \bigg|_{1}^{3} ds \\ &= \frac{1}{27} \int_{1}^{3} (4 + 2s) \, ds \\ &= \frac{1}{27} \left(4s + s^2 \right) \bigg|_{1}^{3} = \frac{16}{27}. \end{aligned}$$

Finally the desired probability is

$$q_{xy} = 1 - p_{xy} = 1 - \frac{16}{27} = \frac{11}{27}. \qquad \square$$

If the general joint CDF of T_x and T_y is evaluated at the common point $t_x = t_y = n$, then we have

$$F_{x,y}(n,n) = Pr\left(T_x \leq n \cap T_y \leq n \right) = Pr(T_{\overline{xy}} \leq n) = {}_n q_{\overline{xy}},$$

in actuarial notation. Thus we see that both the joint and last-survivor distributions can be determined from the general joint distribution of T_x and T_y, where we find the SDF of the joint status from the joint SDF of T_x and T_y and we find the CDF of the last-survivor status from the joint CDF of T_x and T_y.

12.7 COMMON SHOCK – A MODEL FOR LIFETIME DEPENDENCY

A natural example of two lives (x) and (y) having dependent lifetimes might be a married couple or a pair of business partners who travel together, or are otherwise exposed to a common hazard factor, on a regular basis. We refer to this common hazard as a *common shock*.

To analyze the common shock model, we begin by hypothesizing that (x) is subject to a hazard rate, or force of failure, denoted μ_{x+t}^{*}, that takes into account only failure forces operating at time t that are specific to (x) and not to (y). Similarly, μ_{y+t}^* denotes failure forces operating at time t that are applicable to (y) but not to (x). With regard only to the failure forces represented by μ_{x+t}^* and μ_{y+t}^*, we consider that (x) and (y) have independent survival patterns because of the nature of the hazard factors included in μ_{x+t}^* and μ_{y+t}^*.

Next we assume that the common hazard, or common shock, to which both (x) and (y) are subject can be represented by a constant (over time) hazard function, which we denote by $\mu_t^c = \lambda$. We assume that the hazard forces unique to (x), reflected in μ_{x+t}^*, and the hazard forces reflected in the common shock hazard function μ_t^c are non-overlapping, so the total force of failure to which (x) is subject is given by

$$\mu_{x+t} = \mu_{x+t}^* + \mu_t^c = \mu_{x+t}^* + \lambda. \tag{12.74a}$$

Similarly, the force of failure to which (y) is subject is given by

$$\mu_{y+t} = \mu_{y+t}^* + \mu_t^c = \mu_{y+t}^* + \lambda. \tag{12.74b}$$

The total force of failure operating on the joint-life status (xy) is given by

$$\mu_{x+t:y+t} = \mu_{x+t}^* + \mu_{y+t}^* + \lambda. \tag{12.75}$$

The three forces are additive because each represents hazard factors that are disjoint from each other. Furthermore, the total joint force of failure contains only one λ (not two) since failure of either (x) or (y) due to the common shock constitutes failure of the joint-life status.

The joint-life survival function in the common shock model can then be found from the joint-life force of failure. We have

$$
\begin{aligned}
{}_tp_{xy} &= e^{-\int_0^t \mu_{x+r:y+r}\, dr} \\
&= e^{-\int_0^t (\mu_{x+r}^* + \mu_{y+r}^* + \lambda)\, dr} \\
&= e^{-\int_0^t \mu_{x+r}^*\, dr} \cdot e^{-\int_0^t \mu_{y+r}^*\, dr} \cdot e^{-\int_0^t \lambda\, dr} \\
&= {}_tp_x^* \cdot {}_tp_y^* \cdot e^{-\lambda t}.
\end{aligned}
\tag{12.76}
$$

Note that ${}_tp_x^*$ is not the same as ${}_tp_x$, since the latter survival probability takes into account the common shock hazard factors but the former does not.

There is an alternative, and equivalent, way to develop the common shock model. Let T_x^* and T_y^* denote the future lifetime random variables for (x) and (y), respectively, without regard for the common shock hazard factors. Consistent with the discussion above, we assume that T_x^* and T_y^* are independent. Let S denote the future lifetime of either (x) or (y) with regard to the common shock hazard factors only, where S is independent of both T_x^* and T_y^*. Then it follows that the overall lifetime random variable for (x) is given by

$$T_x = \min(T_x^*, S), \tag{12.77a}$$

and similarly the overall future lifetime random variable for (y) is given by

$$T_y = \min(T_y^*, S). \tag{12.77b}$$

Note that whereas T_x^* and T_y^* are independent, T_x and T_y are *not* independent since they both involve the common shock hazard factors and depend on the common future lifetime random variable S.

Since T_x^* and S are independent, however, it follows that the SDF of T_x is the product of the SDF's of T_x^* and S. That is,

$$_t p_x = S_x(t) = S_{x*}(t) \cdot S_S(t) = {}_t p_x^* \cdot e^{-\lambda t}, \tag{12.78a}$$

where $S_S(t) = e^{-\lambda t}$ since the random variable S has a constant hazard rate and therefore an exponential distribution. Similarly, the SDF of T_y is given by

$$_t p_y = S_y(t) = S_{y*}(t) \cdot S_S(t) = {}_t p_y^* \cdot e^{-\lambda t}. \tag{12.78b}$$

We observe that $_t p_{xy}$, given by Equation (12.76), is *not* equal to the product of $_t p_x$ and $_t p_y$, given by Equations (12.78a) and (12.78b), respectively, which shows that T_x and T_y are not independent random variables.

EXAMPLE 12.17

A convenient way to illustrate the common shock model is to assume that both T_x^* and T_y^* have exponential distributions, and therefore constant hazard rates λ_x and λ_y, respectively. Under this assumption, find an expression for the APV of a last-survivor whole life insurance, with benefit paid at the moment of failure of the status.

SOLUTION

The overall force of failure for (x) is then $\mu_{x+t} = \lambda_x + \lambda$, where λ denotes the hazard of the common shock, and the overall force of failure for (y) is $\mu_{y+t} = \lambda_y + \lambda$. The force of failure for the joint-life status (xy) is $\mu_{x+t:y+t} = \lambda_x + \lambda_y + \lambda$. Using results developed in Chapter 7, we then have

$$\overline{A}_x = \frac{\lambda_x + \lambda}{\lambda_x + \lambda + \delta},$$

$$\overline{A}_y = \frac{\lambda_y + \lambda}{\lambda_y + \lambda + \delta},$$

and

$$\overline{A}_{xy} = \frac{\lambda_x + \lambda_y + \lambda}{\lambda_x + \lambda_y + \lambda + \delta},$$

and $\overline{A}_{\overline{xy}}$ then follows as $\overline{A}_x + \overline{A}_y - \overline{A}_{xy}$. □

Because of the common hazard factor, such as travel accidents, there is a non-zero probability of simultaneous failure of (x) and (y). When represented as a multi-state model, the earlier Figure 12.1 is modified as shown in Figure 12.4.

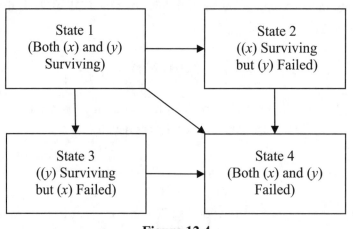

Figure 12.4

The only change in this model from our Figure 12.1 model is that $\lambda_{14}(s)$, the force of transition function for transition directly from State 1 to State 4 is now non-zero. This means that the probability value

$$_r p_{14}^{(t)} = Pr[X(t+r) = 4 \mid X(t) = 1]$$

can be satisfied by direct transition from State 1 to State 4. In the Figure 12.1 model, $_r p_{14}^{(t)}$ could be satisfied only by transition from State 1 to State 2 to State 4 or by transition from State 1 to State 3 to State 4.

12.8 EXERCISES

12.1 The Joint-Life Model

12-1 Show that

$$q_{xy} = q_x + p_x \cdot q_y,$$

assuming independence of the individual lifetimes T_x and T_y.

12-2 Let T_x and T_y be independent future lifetime random variables. Given $q_x = .080$, $q_y = .004$, $_tp_x = 1 - t^2 \cdot q_x$, and $_tp_y = 1 - t^2 \cdot q_y$, both for $0 \le t \le 1$, evaluate the PDF of T_{xy} at $t = .50$.

12-3 Two microwave models, denoted Type I and Type II, follow survival models defined by $\mu_x^I = \ln 1.25$, for $x > 0$, and $\mu_x^{II} = \frac{1}{9-x}$, for $0 < x < 9$, respectively. Given that both models are currently two years old, and that they have independent lifetimes, find the probability that the first failure will occur between ages 3 and 6.

12-4 At all ages greater than 50, the force of failure for smokers is double that for non-smokers. Suppose the age-at-failure random variable for nonsmokers has a uniform distribution with $\omega = 75$. If (65) and (55) have independent lifetimes, where (65) is a nonsmoker and (55) is a smoker, find the value of $\overset{o}{e}_{65:55}$.

12-5 Let T_x and T_y be independent future lifetime random variables, each with an exponential distribution with mean 20. Find the value of $Var(T_{xy})$.

12.2 The Last-Survivor Model

12-6 Let T_{80} and T_{85} be independent random variables with uniform distributions with $\omega = 100$. Find the probability that the second failure occurs within five years.

12-7 Derive each of the following identities. Which of them require an assumption of the independence of T_x and T_y?

(a) $_tq_{\overline{xy}} = {}_tq_x + {}_tq_y - {}_tq_{xy}$

(b) $f_{T_{\overline{xy}}}(t) = {}_tq_x \cdot {}_tp_y \mu_{y+t} + {}_tq_y \cdot {}_tp_x \mu_{x+t}$

(c) $_n|q_{\overline{xy}} = {}_nq_x \cdot {}_n|q_y + {}_nq_y \cdot {}_n|q_x + {}_n|q_x \cdot {}_n|q_y$

12-8   If T_x and T_y are independent, and each is uniformly distributed over each year of age separately, show that

$$18\left(_{1/3}q_{xy}\right) - 12\left(_{1/2}q_{xy}\right) \;=\; q_{\overline{xy}}.$$

12-9   For independent lives (x) and (y), the force of failure is constant over each year of age. Find the value of $_{.75}p_{\overline{x+.25:y+.25}}$, given that $q_x = .08$ and $q_y = .06$.

12-10   For the model of Exercise 12-5, find the value of $Cov(T_{xy}, T_{\overline{xy}})$.

12.3 Contingent Probability Functions

12-11   Coffee Maker I follows a survival model defined by $\mu_x^I = \frac{1.80}{9-x}$, for $0 < x < 9$, and Coffee Maker II follows a survival model defined by $\mu_x^{II} = \frac{1.50}{9-x}$, for $0 < x < 9$. The two coffee makers have independent lifetimes. Find the probability that Coffee Maker I fails before Coffee Maker II.

12.4 Contingent Contracts Involving Multi-Life Statuses

12-12   Let Z denote the present value random variable for a contingent contract that pays a unit benefit at the end of the year of the first failure between (x) and (y), and another unit benefit at the end of the year of the second failure. Find the value of $E[Z]$, given the values $a_x = 9$, $a_y = 13$, and $i = .04$.

12-13   Let Y denote the present value random variable for a contingent annuity-due with unit payment made during the first 15 years if at least one of (x) and (y) survive, but made after the first 15 years only if exactly one of (x) and (y) survive. Find the value of $E[Y]$, given the following values:

$$\ddot{a}_x = 9.80 \qquad \ddot{a}_y = 11.60 \qquad \ddot{a}_{xy} = 7.60 \qquad _{15}|\ddot{a}_{xy} = 3.70$$

12-14   Let K_{xy}^* denote the year of failure of the joint-life status (xy). Find the value of the discount rate d, given the values $\ddot{a}_{xy} = 10$, $^2\ddot{a}_{xy} = 7$, and $Var(\ddot{a}_{\overline{K_{xy}^*|}}) = 27$.

12-15   Two lives (x) and (y) have independent and identically distributed future lifetimes. Given the values $P_x = P_y = .10$, $P_{\overline{xy}} = .06$, and $d = .06$, find the value of P_{xy}.

12-16 A discrete unit benefit contingent contract is issued to the last-survivor status $(\overline{xx})$, where the two future lifetime random variables T_x are independent. The contract is funded by discrete net annual premiums, which are reduced by 25% after the first failure. Find the value of the initial net annual premium, under the equivalence principle, given the values $A_x = .40$, $A_{xx} = .55$, and $\ddot{a}_x = 10.00$.

12-17 A continuous two-life annuity has actuarial present value 1180. The annuity pays at annual rate 100 while both (x) and (y) survive, 70 while (x) survives after the failure of (y), and 50 while (y) survives after the failure of (x). Find the value of $\overline{a}_{\overline{xy}}$, given that $\overline{a}_x = 12$ and $\overline{a}_y = 10$.

12.5 Multi-State Model Representation

12-18 Using the multi-state model notation defined earlier, give formulas for each of the following joint-life functions.

(a) $\overline{a}_{xy:\overline{n}|}$ (b) P_{xy} (c) $A_{xy:\overline{n}|}$ (d) $\overline{P}(\overline{A}\,{}^1_{xy:\overline{n}|})$

12-19 Using the model shown in Figure 12.1, give the formula for $a_{x|y}$ in multi-state model notation.

12-20 Using the multi-state model notation defined earlier, give formulas for each of the following continuous contingent insurance functions.

(a) $\overline{A}\,{}^1_{xy}$ (b) $\overline{A}\,{}^1_{xy}$ (c) $\overline{A}\,{}^2_{xy}$ (d) $\overline{A}\,{}^2_{xy}$

12-21 Using the multi-state model notation defined earlier, give formulas for each of the following last-survival functions.

(a) $\overline{a}_{\overline{xy}}$ (b) $\ddot{a}_{\overline{xy}:\overline{n}|}$ (c) $A\,{}^1_{\overline{xy}:\overline{n}|}$ (d) $_{n|}\overline{A}_{\overline{xy}}$

12-22 For two persons alive at ages x and y at time t, solve the Kolmogorov differential equation for $_np_{11}^{(t)}$, writing the result in standard actuarial notation.

12-23 For a person alive at age x at time t, with (y) failed, solve the Kolmogorov differential equation for (a) $_np_{22}^{(t)}$ and (b) $_np_{24}^{(t)}$, writing the results in standard actuarial notation.

12.6 General Random Variable Analysis

12-24   Consider the joint density function of T_x and T_y given by

$$f_{x,y}(t_x,t_y) = \frac{4}{(1+t_x+2t_y)^3},$$

for $t_x > 0$ and $t_y > 0$. Show that T_x and T_y are not independent.

12-25   For the survival model of Exercise 12-24, find $S_x(t)$, the marginal survival function of T_x.

12-26   For the survival model of Exercise 12-24, evaluate $F_{x,y}(1,2)$.

12-27   For the survival model of Exercise 12-24, evaluate $S_{x,y}(1,2)$.

12-28   For the survival model of Exercise 12-24, find an expression for $_n p_{xy}$.

12-29   For the survival model of Exercise 12-24, find an expression for $_n q_{\overline{xy}}$.

12.7   Common Shock – A Model for Lifetime Dependency

12-30   The APV for a last-survivor whole life insurance on $(\overline{xy})$, with unit benefit paid at the instant of failure of the status, was calculated assuming independent future life-times for (x) and (y) with constant hazard rate .06 for each. It is now discovered that although the total hazard rate of .06 is correct, the two lifetimes are not inde-pendent since each includes a common shock hazard factor with constant force .02. The force of interest used in the calculation is $\delta = .05$. Calculate the increase in the APV that results from recognition of the common shock element.

12-31   Lives (x) and (y) have independent future lifetime exponential random variables T_x^* and T_y^* with respect to risk factors unique to (x) and (y), respectively. As well, both (x) and (y) are subject to a constant common hazard rate $\lambda = .01$. Given that $p_x = .96$ and $p_y = .97$, calculate the value of $_5 p_{xy}$.

12-32   For two persons alive at ages x and y at time t, show that the Kolmogorov differen-tial equation for $_r p_{14}^{(t)}$ solves for

$$_n p_{14}^{(t)} = {}_n q_{\overline{xy}} + \lambda \cdot \overset{\circ}{e}_{xy},$$

where λ is the constant common shock hazard described in Section 12.7.

CHAPTER THIRTEEN

MULTIPLE-DECREMENT MODELS (THEORY)

For most of this text we have considered models with payments contingent on the occurrence of a particular concept of failure for a specified entity of interest. In this chapter we consider models in which the entity of interest faces multiple types of failure. Each type of failure is called a *decrement*. In earlier chapters, the entity of interest faced only one type of decrement, such as the death of (x) under a life insurance arrangement. Such models are therefore called *single-decrement models*. In this chapter, with simultaneous exposure to multiple concepts of failure, we refer to the models as *multiple-decrement models*.

For example, consider a group insurance plan provided by an employer. At time $t = 0$, some number of employees begin coverage under the plan. Over time the number of covered employees will decrease due to death, retirement, disability, or changing jobs. Each of these reasons for leaving the group is a different cause of failure, or a different decrement. To accurately model the costs of such plans we require models that take into account both the time and cause of decrement.

Throughout this chapter we will refer back to formulas and derivations from the single-decrement models developed earlier.

There are many applications of multiple-decrement theory, and we present several of them in Chapter 14. As we shall see then, the multi-state formulation illustrated earlier with various single-decrement models will be particularly useful.

13.1 DISCRETE MULTIPLE-DECREMENT MODELS

Without losing generality, we will introduce our multiple-decrement models in a life insurance context. Consider a closed group of 1000 insureds with annual premium life insurance policies. Each year these insureds can leave the group by one of two decrements, either death or withdrawal, but not both. We will refer to death as Cause 1 and withdrawal as Cause 2. We begin by defining several additional actuarial symbols.[1]

We let $q_x^{(j)}$ denote the probability that (x) fails in the next year of age due to Cause j, for $j = 1, 2$. Since the causes are mutually exclusive, then the probability that (x) fails in the next year due to *any* cause, denoted by $q_x^{(\tau)}$, is given by

$$q_x^{(\tau)} = q_x^{(1)} + q_x^{(2)}. \tag{13.1a}$$

---

[1] Note that the deterministic (life table) view of Chapter 6 is being taken here.

In general, if there are m distinct causes of decrement, we have

$$q_x^{(\tau)} = \sum_{j=1}^{m} q_x^{(j)}. \tag{13.1b}$$

The probability that (x) does not fail in the next year at all is given by

$$p_x^{(\tau)} = 1 - q_x^{(\tau)}. \tag{13.2}$$

We let $d_x^{(j)}$ denote the number of people in the group at age x who will fail (i.e., be decremented from the group) before age $x+1$ due to Cause j, and $d_x^{(\tau)}$ denote the total number of failures for all causes combined. Clearly we have

$$d_x^{(\tau)} = \sum_{j=1}^{m} d_x^{(j)}. \tag{13.3}$$

More generally, the number who fail due to Cause j over the n-year interval $(x, x+n]$ is denoted by $_n d_x^{(j)}$, the number who fail for all causes combined is denoted $_n d_x^{(\tau)}$, the probability of failure due to Cause j over $(x, x+n]$ is denoted $_n q_x^{(j)}$, the probability of failure due to any cause over $(x, x+n]$ is denoted $_n q_x^{(\tau)}$, and the probability of surviving all causes of failure over $(x, x+n]$ is denoted $_n p_x^{(\tau)}$. Note that

$$_n d_x^{(j)} = \sum_{t=0}^{n-1} d_{x+t}^{(j)} \tag{13.4}$$

and

$$_n d_x^{(\tau)} \quad \sum_{j=1}^{m} {}_n d_x^{(j)}. \tag{13.5a}$$

Dividing both sides of Equation (13.5a) by the number of survivors in the group at age x, which we denote by $\ell_x^{(\tau)}$, gives

$$_n q_x^{(\tau)} = \sum_{j=1}^{m} {}_n q_x^{(j)}. \tag{13.5b}$$

Finally, we let $\ell_x^{(j)}$ denote the number in the group at age x who eventually fail due to Cause j at some time after age x. Since each person fails due to only one cause, it follows that the total number in the group at age x, already defined as $\ell_x^{(\tau)}$, is given by

$$\ell_x^{(\tau)} = \sum_{j=1}^{m} \ell_x^{(j)}. \tag{13.6}$$

Several additional relationships follow from these definitions, such as

$$d_x^{(j)} = \ell_x^{(\tau)} \cdot q_x^{(j)}, \tag{13.7a}$$

$$d_x^{(\tau)} = \ell_x^{(\tau)} \cdot q_x^{(\tau)}, \tag{13.7b}$$

$$_n d_x^{(j)} = \ell_x^{(\tau)} \cdot {_n}q_x^{(j)}, \tag{13.7c}$$

$$_n d_x^{(\tau)} = \ell_x^{(\tau)} \cdot {_n}q_x^{(\tau)}, \tag{13.7d}$$

$$_n p_x^{(\tau)} = 1 - {_n}q_x^{(\tau)}, \tag{13.7e}$$

and

$$\ell_{x+n}^{(\tau)} = \ell_x^{(\tau)} \cdot {_n}p_x^{(\tau)}. \tag{13.7f}$$

The reader should clearly understand the logic of each relationship.

13.1.1 THE MULTIPLE-DECREMENT TABLE

The functions involved in a discrete multiple-decrement model are conveniently arranged in a tabular form, analogous to the single-decrement life table presented in Chapter 6, called a *multiple-decrement table*. The construction of a multiple-decrement table from the basic probabilities of failure is illustrated in the following example.

EXAMPLE 13.1

Given the following probabilities of decrement, for each of two decrements at certain ages, construct the full multiple-decrement table. (Note that with two causes of decrement, we would refer to the model as a *double-decrement table*.) Assume an initial group (called the *radix* of the table) of size 1000.

x	$q_x^{(1)}$	$q_x^{(2)}$
45	.011	.100
46	.012	.100
47	.013	.100
48	.014	.100
49	.015	.100
50	.016	.100

SOLUTION

In the completed table below, Columns (1), (2), and (3) contain given values. The entries in Column (4) are found from those in Columns (2) and (3) by Equation (13.1a); those in Column (5) are found from those in Column (4) by Equation (13.2); those in Column (6) are found by Equation (13.7f), along with the radix of $\ell_{45}^{(\tau)} = 1000$; those in Columns (7) and (8) are found by Equation (13.7a).

(1)	(2)	(3)	(4)	(5)	(6)	(7)	(8)
x	$q_x^{(1)}$	$q_x^{(2)}$	$q_x^{(\tau)}$	$p_x^{(\tau)}$	$\ell_x^{(\tau)}$	$d_x^{(1)}$	$d_x^{(2)}$
45	.011	.100	.111	.889	1000.00	11.00	100.00
46	.012	.100	.112	.888	889.00	10.67	88.90
47	.013	.100	.113	.887	789.43	10.26	78.94
48	.014	.100	.114	.886	700.23	9.80	70.02
49	.015	.100	.115	.885	620.40	9.31	62.04
50	.016	.100	.116	.884	549.05	8.78	54.91

❏

EXAMPLE 13.2

Using the double-decrement table developed in Example 13.1, calculate each of the following.

(a) $_3p_{46}^{(\tau)}$

(b) $_2d_{47}^{(2)}$

(c) $_2q_{46}^{(1)}$

(d) $_{2|2}q_{45}^{(1)}$

(e)   The probability that a person in the group at age 46 will leave between ages 48 and 49.

SOLUTION

(a)   We have $_3p_{46}^{(\tau)} = \dfrac{\ell_{49}^{(\tau)}}{\ell_{46}^{(\tau)}} = \dfrac{620.40}{889.00} = .6979.$ Note that this could also be obtained as

$$_3p_{46}^{(\tau)} = p_{46}^{(\tau)} \cdot p_{47}^{(\tau)} \cdot p_{48}^{(\tau)} = .6979.$$

(b) $_2d_{47}^{(2)} = d_{47}^{(2)} + d_{48}^{(2)} = 78.94 + 70.02 = 148.96$

(c) $_2q_{46}^{(1)} = \dfrac{d_{46}^{(1)} + d_{47}^{(1)}}{\ell_{46}^{(\tau)}} = \dfrac{10.67 + 10.26}{889.00} = .02354,$ which could also be obtained as

$$_2q_{46}^{(1)} = q_{46}^{(1)} + p_{46}^{(\tau)} \cdot q_{47}^{(1)} = .02354.$$

(d) $_{2|2}q_{45}^{(1)} = \dfrac{d_{47}^{(1)} + d_{48}^{(1)}}{\ell_{45}^{(\tau)}} = \dfrac{10.26 + 9.80}{1000.00} = .02006$

(e) $_{2|}q_{46}^{(\tau)} = \dfrac{d_{48}^{(1)} + d_{48}^{(2)}}{\ell_{46}^{(\tau)}} = \dfrac{9.80 + 70.20}{889.00} = .08979,$ which could also be obtained as

$$_{2|}q_{46}^{(\tau)} = p_{46}^{(\tau)} \cdot p_{47}^{(\tau)} \cdot q_{48}^{(\tau)} = .08979.$$

❏

13.1.2 RANDOM VARIABLE ANALYSIS

As we have done in several earlier chapters, we can analyze the multiple-decrement model in a stochastic framework. Recall the discrete random variable K_x^* denoting the time interval of failure for an entity of interest with identifying characteristic (x). (Again, without loss of generality, we might assume a person who is age x as our entity of interest.) We now define a second discrete random variable, denoted J_x, which represents the cause of failure for (x). Then $\{K_x^* = k \cap J_x = j\}$ denotes the joint event of (x) failing in the kth interval (say, year) due to the jth cause. For example, the joint event $\{K_x^* = 5 \cap J_x = 1\}$ is that (x) fails between ages $x+4$ and $x+5$ due to Cause 1. The probability of this event is denoted by ${}_{4|}q_x^{(1)}$.

The standard rules of multivariate probability will apply here, and we will be interested in three different probability functions.

The *joint probability function* of K_x^* and J_x is

$$Pr(K_x^* = k \cap J_x = j) = {}_{k-1|}q_x^{(j)} = \frac{d_{x+k-1}^{(j)}}{\ell_x^{(\tau)}}, \tag{13.8}$$

giving the probability that (x) survives all decrements for $k-1$ years and then fails due to Cause j in the kth year.

The *marginal probability function* of K_x^* is

$$Pr(K_x^* = k) = \sum_{j=1}^{m} Pr(K_x^* = k \cap J_x = j) = {}_{k-1|}q_x^{(\tau)} = \frac{d_{x+k-1}^{(1)} + \cdots + d_{x+k-1}^{(m)}}{\ell_x^{(\tau)}}, \tag{13.9}$$

representing the probability that (x) will fail in the kth year due to any cause. From Equation (13.9) we can see that $Pr(K_x^* = k)$ is the sum of the $d^{(j)}$ values in the *row* of the multiple-decrement table corresponding to age $x+k-1$, all divided by $\ell_x^{(\tau)}$.

The *marginal probability function* of J_x is

$$Pr(J_x = j) = \sum_{k=1}^{\infty} Pr(K_x^* = k \cap J_x = j) = \sum_{k=1}^{\infty} \frac{d_{x+k-1}^{(j)}}{\ell_x^{(\tau)}}, \tag{13.10}$$

representing the probability that (x) will eventually fail due to Cause j without restriction as to time of failure. It is the sum of the $d^{(j)}$ values in the *column* of the multiple-decrement table corresponding to Cause j, which might be denoted by $\ell_x^{(j)}$, divided by $\ell_x^{(\tau)}$.

EXAMPLE 13.3

Using the double-decrement table developed in Example 13.1, find (a) $Pr(K_x^*=3 \cap J_x=1)$ and (b) $Pr(K_x^*=4)$ for a person age 46.

SOLUTION

(a) $Pr(K_x^*=3 \cap J_x=1)$ is the probability of failing in the third year due to Cause 1. It is given by

$$_2|q_{46}^{(1)} = \frac{d_{48}^{(1)}}{\ell_{46}^{(\tau)}} = \frac{9.80}{889.00} = .01102.$$

(b) $Pr(K_x^*=4)$ is the probability of failure in the fourth year (i.e., between ages 49 and 50) due to any cause, and is given by

$$_3|q_{46}^{(\tau)} = \frac{d_{49}^{(1)} + d_{49}^{(2)}}{\ell_{46}^{(\tau)}} = \frac{9.31 + 62.04}{889.00} = .08026. \qquad \square$$

13.2 THEORY OF COMPETING RISKS

Before investigating multiple-decrement models in the context of continuous random variables, it is necessary to first discuss the *theory of competing risks*. Suppose we currently have 1000 64-year-old employees. During the next year of age, these employees may leave the company either by death (Cause 1) or retirement (Cause 2). Assume that $q_{64}^{(1)} = .02$ and $q_{64}^{(2)} = .30$.

Assume that employees may retire at any time during the year of age and may die at any time during the year of age. The given probabilities refer to the fractions of employees that we expect to see die and retire during the year, respectively, given that the employees are exposed to the risk of both types of decrement at the same time. If we were to change the retirement rules so that no one could retire before age 65, we would see no retirements during the year and death would be the only decrement possible during the year. That is, there would be no case of *competing risks* during the year.

With death and retirement *both* acting on the employees throughout the year, we expect to observe 20 employees die while employed. The key insight here is to realize that if retirement is removed as a decrement, then we should expect to see *more* than 20 employees die. This is because we have more employees exposed to the risk of dying during the year, since the 300 that otherwise would have retired are staying on the job and thus have a greater chance of dying while employed. In other words, death has more of an opportunity to strike more employees and we will observe more deaths of employees. (We might assume these extra deaths will occur in any case, but after retirement; thus we will not observe those deaths since retirement removes an individual from the group under observation. They have already failed due to Cause 2 by the time death strikes.)

This higher probability of death *in the absence of other decrements* (i.e., in the absence of competing risks) is denoted by $q_x^{\prime(1)}$, and is called the *absolute rate of death*. In general, the *absolute rate of decrement due to Cause j* over the interval $(x, x+n]$ is denoted by ${}_n q_x^{\prime(j)}$.[2] It represents the probability of failing due to Cause *j* in $(x, x+n]$ *if no other causes of decrement were operating*.

But if no other causes of decrement are operating, then we are dealing with a single-decrement model as described in Chapters 5 and 6. Therefore the probability represented by $q_x^{\prime(j)}$ is really the same as the one represented by the simpler q_x in the earlier chapters. For this reason we refer to $q_x^{\prime(j)}$ as the probability of decrement due to Cause *j* in the *associated single-decrement table*. Note that it will always be true that

$$ {}_n q_x^{\prime(j)} \ge {}_n q_x^{(j)}. \tag{13.11} $$

13.3 CONTINUOUS MULTIPLE-DECREMENT MODELS

For the continuous multiple-decrement models, the pair of discrete random variables for failure in the kth time interval, K_x^*, and cause of failure, J_x, are replaced by a set of continuous random variables. Let $T_x^{(j)}$ denote the continuous random variable for the length of time until the entity represented by (x) fails due to Cause *j* in the absence of other decrements. It should be clear that $T_x^{(j)}$ is the same as the T_x time-to-failure random variable defined earlier, but with the single cause of decrement specified as Cause *j*.

Let ${}_t p_x^{\prime(j)} = 1 - {}_t q_x^{\prime(j)}$ denote the probability that (x) will survive for t years (i.e., to age $x+t$) in the absence of other decrements. Since the absence of other decrements creates a single-decrement model, then ${}_t p_x^{\prime(j)}$ has exactly the same meaning as the simpler ${}_t p_x$ from earlier chapters. Also let $\mu_{x+t}^{(j)}$ denote the force of failure due to Cause *j*. Since the force is an *instantaneous* measure, then it is the same whether operating in a single-decrement or a multiple-decrement environment. Thus we do *not* need the separate symbols $\mu_y^{(j)}$ (for force of decrement at age *y* if competing forces *are also operating*) and $\mu_y^{\prime(j)}$ (for the same concept if competing forces *are not operating*). $\mu_y^{(j)}$ and $\mu_y^{\prime(j)}$ would be identical, and the convention is to use $\mu_y^{(j)}$ without the prime.

By analogy with Equation (6.20) we have the relationship

$$ \mu_{x+t}^{(j)} = \frac{-\frac{d}{dt} {}_t p_x^{\prime(j)}}{{}_t p_x^{\prime(j)}}, \tag{13.12a} $$

---

[2] Older texts have referred to $q_x^{\prime(j)}$ as the *pure probability* due to Cause *j*; others use the phrase *absolute probability of decrement* due to Cause *j*.

and the companion relationship

$$_t p_x'^{(j)} = \exp\left(-\int_0^t \mu_{x+s}^{(j)} \, ds\right),$$ (13.12b)

which is the same as that developed in Exercise 6-17 with our augmented notation.

Similarly, if $_t p_x^{(\tau)} = 1 - _t q_x^{(\tau)}$ denotes the probability that (x) will not fail for any cause before age $x+t$ (*i.e.*, that (x) survives against all causes for t years), and $\mu_{x+t}^{(\tau)}$ is the total force of failure at time t, then we have

$$\mu_{x+t}^{(\tau)} = \frac{-\dfrac{d}{dt} \, _t p_x^{(\tau)}}{_t p_x^{(\tau)}}$$ (13.13a)

by analogy with Equation (6.20) and

$$_t p_x^{(\tau)} = \exp\left(-\int_0^t \mu_{x+s}^{(\tau)} \, ds\right)$$ (13.13b)

by analogy with Exercise 6-17.

Finally, by analogy with Equation (5.46), the PDF for the single-decrement time-to-failure random variable $T_x^{(j)}$ is given by

$$f_{x^{(j)}}(t) = _t p_x'^{(j)} \cdot \mu_{x+t}^{(j)},$$ (13.14)

and its CDF is given by

$$F_{x^{(j)}}(t) = Pr\left[T_x^{(j)} \le t\right] = \int_0^t f_{x^{(j)}}(s) \, ds = \int_0^t {_s p_x'^{(j)}} \cdot \mu_{x+s}^{(j)} \, ds.$$ (13.15)

In actuarial notation this is denoted by $_t q_x'^{(j)}$.

If there are m causes of decrement, then the event of survival for length of time t against all causes is the intersection of the m events of survival against each cause separately. If the m causes are independent, then the probability of the intersection event, denoted $_t p_x^{(\tau)}$, is the product of the probabilities of the m separate survival events, each such probability denoted $_t p_x'^{(j)}$, for $j = 1, 2, \dots, m$. Thus we have the important relationship

$$_t p_x^{(\tau)} = \prod_{j=1}^m {_t p_x'^{(j)}}.$$ (13.16)

(See Exercise 13-7 for an alternate derivation of this relationship that does not require the assumption of independence.) From Equations (13.16) and (13.13a) together we can derive another very important result. Starting with Equation (13.13a) we have

$$
\begin{aligned}
\mu_{x+t}^{(\tau)} &= \frac{-\frac{d}{dt}\,_tp_x^{(\tau)}}{\,_tp_x^{(\tau)}} \\[2mm]
&= -\frac{d}{dt}\ln\,_tp_x^{(\tau)} \\[2mm]
&= -\frac{d}{dt}\ln\left[\,_tp_x'^{(1)}\cdot\,_tp_x'^{(2)}\cdot\,\cdots\,\cdot\,_tp_x'^{(m)}\right] \\[2mm]
&= \left(-\frac{d}{dt}\ln\,_tp_x'^{(1)}\right)+\left(-\frac{d}{dt}\ln\,_tp_x'^{(2)}\right)+\cdots+\left(-\frac{d}{dt}\ln\,_tp_x'^{(m)}\right) \\[2mm]
&= \mu_{x+t}^{(1)}+\mu_{x+t}^{(2)}+\cdots+\mu_{x+t}^{(m)}.
\end{aligned}
\tag{13.17}
$$

This result is intuitive as well as analytical. Since the forces are instantaneous measures, the total force of failure is the sum of the cause-specific forces. This result is analogous to the basic addition rule in probability theory in the case of mutually exclusive events. Since the force is instantaneous, the intersection event of failure by two (or more) causes simultaneously is not possible so the probability of this event is zero. Thus the force of the union event is the sum of the forces of the separate cause events making up the union. (See Exercise 13-7 for an alternate derivation of Equation (13.17).)

We now return to the multiple-decrement probability $_tq_x^{(j)}$, defined back in Section 13.1. Recall that the density for (x) failing at time t in the *absence* of other decrements is given by Equation (13.14) as $_tp_x'^{(j)}\cdot\mu_{x+t}^{(j)}$. As explained in Chapter 5, this density is the product of the probability of surviving to time t (which is $_tp_x'^{(j)}$ in the single-decrement environment) times the force of failure at time t for the single decrement that is operating (which is $\mu_{x+t}^{(j)}$). In the multiple-decrement environment, survival to time t must be accomplished against all decrements, so the survival probability is $_tp_x^{(\tau)}$. Then the density for failure at time t due to Cause j in the *presence* of the other decrements is $f_{T,J}(t,j)=\,_tp_x^{(\tau)}\cdot\mu_{x+t}^{(j)}$. From this density it follows that the probability of failure in $(x,x+t]$ due to Cause j in the presence of the other decrements, which we have already denoted by $_tq_x^{(j)}$, is given by

$$
_tq_x^{(j)} = \int_0^t f_{T,J}(s,j)\,ds = \int_0^t {}_sp_x^{(\tau)}\cdot\mu_{x+s}^{(j)}\,ds.
\tag{13.18}
$$

Differentiating both sides of Equation (13.18) yields

$$
\frac{d}{dt}\,_tq_x^{(j)} = \frac{d}{dt}\int_0^t {}_sp_x^{(\tau)}\cdot\mu_{x+s}^{(j)}\,ds = {}_tp_x^{(\tau)}\cdot\mu_{x+t}^{(j)},
$$

so we have

$$\mu_{x+t}^{(j)} = \frac{\frac{d}{dt} \, _tq_x^{(j)}}{_tp_x^{(\tau)}}.$$ (13.19)

Then Equations (13.17) and (13.18) together, along with the familiar result

$$_tq_x^{(\tau)} = \int_0^t \, _sp_x^{(\tau)} \cdot \mu_{x+s}^{(\tau)} \, ds$$ (13.20)

can be used to verify the already-established Equation (13.5b).

EXAMPLE 13.4

If $\mu_{x+t}^{(1)} = .10$ and $\mu_{x+t}^{(2)} = .20$ for all t, find each of (a) $_tp_x^{(\tau)}$, (b) $_tq_x'^{(1)}$, (c) $_tq_x^{(1)}$, and (d) $_\infty q_x^{(1)}$.

SOLUTION

(a) We know $\mu_{x+t}^{(\tau)} = \mu_{x+t}^{(1)} + \mu_{x+t}^{(2)} = .30$. From Equation (13.13b) we have

$$_tp_x^{(\tau)} = \exp\left(-\int_0^t .30 \, ds\right) = e^{-.30t}.$$

(b) This is a single-decrement model probability. From Equation (13.12b) we have

$$_tq_x'^{(1)} = 1 - \, _tp_x'^{(1)} = 1 - \exp\left(-\int_0^t .10 \, ds\right) = 1 - e^{-.10t}.$$

(c) Here we use Equation (13.18) and the result from part (a). We have

$$_tq_x^{(1)} = \int_0^t \, _sp_x^{(\tau)} \cdot \mu_{x+s}^{(1)} \, ds$$

$$= .10 \int_0^t e^{-.30s} \, ds = .10 \left(\frac{e^{-.30s}}{-.30}\bigg|_0^t\right) = \frac{1}{3}(1 - e^{-.30t}).$$

(d) This is the special case of part (c) as $t \to \infty$. We have

$$_\infty q_x^{(1)} = .10 \int_0^\infty e^{-.30s} \, ds = .10 \left(\frac{e^{-.30s}}{-.30}\bigg|_0^\infty\right) = \frac{1}{3},$$

which is also reached by taking the limit as $t \to \infty$ of the answer in part (c). Note that $_\infty q_x^{(j)}$ denotes the probability that (x) will eventually fail due to Cause j with no time restriction as to when failure might occur. ❑

13.4 UNIFORM DISTRIBUTION OF DECREMENTS

Recall the discussion in Section 6.6 regarding the various fractional age assumptions used to determine the numerical values of functions not given directly by the life table itself in the single-decrement model. The same issue arises in the multiple-decrement model: given only the multiple-decrement table presented in Section 13.1.1, only values of $_nq_x^{(j)}$ and $_nq_x^{(\tau)}$ for integral n can be directly determined without making additional assumptions. Furthermore, we cannot establish relationships between the single-decrement probability $_tq_x'^{(j)}$ and the multiple-decrement probability $_tq_x^{(j)}$ without such additional assumptions.

The reader should recognize that the several forces of decrement, $\mu_{x+t}^{(j)}$ for $j=1,2,\ldots,m$, would together define all other functions in the multiple-decrement models. The several $\mu_{x+t}^{(j)}$ sum to $\mu_{x+t}^{(\tau)}$ (see Equation (13.17)), which leads to $_tp_x^{(\tau)}$ and hence $_tq_x^{(\tau)}$ (see Equation (13.13b)), which together lead to $_tq_x^{(j)}$ (see Equation (13.18)) for any t. Being continuous, the function $\mu_y^{(j)}$ defines the pattern of decrement for all y, so no "additional assumptions" are needed. But if all we have is the discrete model of Section 13.1.1, then the additional assumptions are needed.

The multiple-decrement analogy with the single-decrement model described in Section 6.6 will be clear. Here we consider only the uniform distribution assumption of Section 6.6.1, of which there are two subcases. The exponential distribution assumption of Section 6.6.2 is considered in Exercise 13-18.[3]

13.4.1 UNIFORM DISTRIBUTION IN THE MULTIPLE-DECREMENT CONTEXT

We consider first the case where each decrement j is uniformly distributed *in the multiple-decrement context*. That is, each decrement is observed to occur uniformly throughout the year of age when other decrements are also present. In this case we have

$$_tq_x^{(j)} = t \cdot q_x^{(j)}, \tag{13.21}$$

for $0 \le t \le 1$. From this we can derive a relationship between the probability of decrement in the multiple-decrement context, $_tq_x^{(j)}$, and the corresponding probability of decrement in the associated single-decrement table, $_tq_x'^{(j)}$. We begin with

$$_tq_x^{(j)} = t \cdot q_x^{(j)} = \int_0^t {}_sp_x^{(\tau)} \cdot \mu_{x+s}^{(j)} \, ds,$$

from Equation (13.18). Differentiating both sides of this equation with respect to t, using the fundamental theorem of calculus for the right side, we obtain

---

[3] Results based on the hyperbolic assumption of Section 6.6.3 are exceedingly complex at best, and many do not even exist in closed form. They are not considered in this text.

$$q_x^{(j)} = {}_tp_x^{(\tau)} \cdot \mu_{x+t}^{(j)}. \tag{13.22}$$

If each decrement j is uniformly distributed, then it follows that the total decrement is uniformly distributed as well, so we have

$$_tq_x^{(\tau)} = t \cdot q_x^{(\tau)} \tag{13.23}$$

and hence

$$_tp_x^{(\tau)} = 1 - t \cdot q_x^{(\tau)}. \tag{13.24}$$

Taking Equations (13.22) and (13.24) together we have

$$\mu_{x+t}^{(j)} = \frac{q_x^{(j)}}{{}_tp_x^{(\tau)}} = \frac{q_x^{(j)}}{1 - t \cdot q_x^{(\tau)}}. \tag{13.25}$$

Next from Equation (13.12b) we have, for $0 \le t \le 1$,

$$_tp_x'^{(j)} = \exp\left(-\int_0^t \mu_{x+s}^{(j)} \, ds\right) = \exp\left(-\int_0^t \frac{q_x^{(j)}}{1 - s \cdot q_x^{(\tau)}} \, ds\right),$$

when we substitute for $\mu_{x+s}^{(j)}$ using Equation (13.25). Finally, recognizing that $q_x^{(j)}$ and $q_x^{(\tau)}$ are constants, we can integrate to obtain

$$_tp_x'^{(j)} = \exp\left[\frac{q_x^{(j)}}{q_x^{(\tau)}} \cdot \ln\left(1 - t \cdot q_x^{(\tau)}\right)\right] = \left(1 - t \cdot q_x^{(\tau)}\right)^{q_x^{(j)}/q_x^{(\tau)}}. \tag{13.26}$$

Then given the set of $q_x^{(j)}$, and hence $q_x^{(\tau)}$, Equation (13.26) allows us to find values of $_tp_x'^{(j)}$ for all j and for $0 \le t \le 1$.

It is important to note that Equation (13.26) results from assuming that the decrements are uniformly distributed in the multiple-decrement context, so that $_tq_x^{(j)}$ is a linear function of t. A more common assumption, which we explore in Section 13.4.2, is to assume that the individual decrements are uniformly distributed *in the associated single-decrement tables*. That is, we assume that $_tq_x'^{(j)}$ is a linear function of t. This leads to formulas that are generally simpler than those of this section.

EXAMPLE 13.5

If $q_x^{(1)} = .20$ and $q_x^{(2)} = .10$, and both decrements are uniformly distributed over the interval $(x, x+1]$ in the multiple-decrement context, find $q_x'^{(2)}$.

SOLUTION

Using Equation (13.26), with $t=1,$ we have

$$p_x'^{(2)} = \left(1-q_x^{(\tau)}\right)^{q_x^{(2)}/q_x^{(\tau)}} = (.70)^{1/3} = .88790$$

and therefore

$$q_x'^{(2)} = 1-.88790 = .11210. \qquad \square$$

13.4.2 UNIFORM DISTRIBUTION IN THE ASSOCIATED SINGLE-DECREMENT TABLES

This is a more natural assumption than that of uniform distribution in the multiple-decrement context. Here we assume that each decrement would be uniformly distribution *in the absence of other decrements*. Thus we assume

$$_t q_x'^{(j)} = t \cdot q_x'^{(j)}, \tag{13.27}$$

for $0 \le t \le 1,$ which is the same as Equation (6.36) with our augmented notation.

The relationship between probabilities of decrement in the multiple-decrement environment with those in the associated single-decrement tables is simpler under this assumption. Consider first the two-decrement case, where both decrements are uniformly distributed in their associated single-decrement tables. From Equation (6.38) we know that

$$_t p_x'^{(j)} \cdot \mu_{x+t}^{(j)} = q_x'^{(j)}, \tag{13.28}$$

so, using Equation (13.18), we can write $q_x^{(1)}$ as

$$q_x^{(1)} = \int_0^1 {}_t p_x^{(\tau)} \cdot \mu_{x+t}^{(1)} \, dt = \int_0^1 {}_t p_x'^{(1)} \cdot {}_t p_x'^{(2)} \cdot \mu_{x+t}^{(1)} \, dt.$$

Then using Equations (13.27) and (13.28) we have

$$q_x^{(1)} = \int_0^1 \left(1-t\cdot q_x'^{(2)}\right) \cdot q_x'^{(1)} \, dt = q_x'^{(1)}\left(1-\frac{1}{2}\cdot q_x'^{(2)}\right). \tag{13.29a}$$

By symmetry it follows that

$$q_x^{(2)} = q_x'^{(2)}\left(1-\frac{1}{2}\cdot q_x'^{(1)}\right). \tag{13.29b}$$

The reader will be asked to show (see Exercise 13-11) that in the case of three decrements, all of which are uniformly distributed in their associated single-decrement tables, it follows that

$$q_x^{(1)} = q_x'^{(1)}\left[1-\frac{1}{2}\left(q_x'^{(2)}+q_x'^{(3)}\right)+\frac{1}{3}\left(q_x'^{(2)}\cdot q_x'^{(3)}\right)\right]. \tag{13.30}$$

EXAMPLE 13.6

Repeat Example 13.5, but assume both decrements are uniformly distributed in their associated single-decrement tables.

SOLUTION

From Equations (13.29a) and (13.29b) we have

$$q_x^{(1)} = q_x'^{(1)}\left(1 - \frac{1}{2} \cdot q_x'^{(2)}\right) = .20$$

and

$$q_x^{(2)} = q_x'^{(2)}\left(1 - \frac{1}{2} \cdot q_x'^{(1)}\right) = .10.$$

Solving the first equation for $q_x'^{(1)}$ and substituting into the second equation, we obtain

$$q_x'^{(2)}\left(1 - \frac{.20}{2 - q_x'^{(2)}}\right) = .10$$

or

$$q_x'^{(2)}\left(1.8 - q_x'^{(2)}\right) = .20 - .10q_x'^{(2)}.$$

Solving the resulting quadratic produces the result $q_x'^{(2)} = .11184$. ☐

13.5 MISCELLANEOUS EXAMPLES

EXAMPLE 13.7

At Gallinas Elementary School, students exit their grade by one of only two decrements, either by moving away from the community (Cause 1) or by passing on to the next grade (Cause 2). For any grade (x), the probability values are $q_x^{(1)} = .02$ and $q_x^{(2)} = .96$. (Note there is a probability of remaining in grade (i.e., failing) of $p_x^{(\tau)} = .02$.) Decrement 1 (moving) is uniformly distributed throughout the year in its associated single-decrement table, but Decrement 2 (passing) can occur only at the end of the year.

If circumstances change such that students never move away, then what proportion of the students will pass on to the next grade?

SOLUTION

This example illustrates an important point about the relationship between multiple-decrements probabilities (denoted by $q_x^{(j)}$) and the associated single-decrement rates (denoted by $q_x'^{(j)}$). Generally the two measures differ from each other because other decrements *compete* with Decrement j. In this example all of the Decrement 2 activity (passing to the next grade) occurs at year-end, so it does not compete with the Decrement 1 activity (moving away). Consequently the probability and the rate for Decrement 1 are the same, so we have $q_x^{(1)} = q_x'^{(1)} = .02$. However the Decrement 1 activity *does* compete with the Decrement 2 activity by denying some persons the opportunity to experience Decrement 2 at the end of the year, so $q_x^{(2)} = .96 \neq q_x'^{(2)}$. Out of every 100 students beginning the grade, 2 depart due to Decrement 1 during the year and 96 of the 98 remaining at year-end experience Decrement 2, so the rate of experiencing Decrement 2 is $\frac{96}{98} = .9796$. Then if Decrement 1 were eliminated, so that a single-decrement environment resulted, we would have $q_x^{(2)} = q_x'^{(2)} = .9796$. □

13.6 EXERCISES

13.1 Discrete Multiple-Decrement Models

13-1   The following double-decrement table gives probability values for a student at the beginning of each year in a three-year Actuarial Science Graduate School. Some of the entries in the table have been obliterated by tear stains.

Academic Year	Probability of Academic Failure	Probability of Voluntary Withdrawal	Probability of Completing the Year
1	.40	.20	–
2	–	.30	–
3	–	–	.60

It is known that ten times as many students complete Year 2 as fail during Year 3, and the number of students who fail during Year 2 is 40% of the number who complete Year 2. Find the probability that a new student entering the school will voluntarily withdraw before graduation.

13.2 Theory of Competing Risks
13.3 Continuous Multiple-Decrement Models

13-2   Given the following extract from a double-decrement table, find the value of $\ell_{42}^{(\tau)}$.

x	$\ell_x^{(\tau)}$	$q_x^{(1)}$	$q_x^{(2)}$	$q_x'^{(1)}$	$q_x'^{(2)}$
40	2000	.24	.10	.25	y
41	--	--	--	.20	$2y$

13-3   The career of a 50-year-old Professor of Actuarial Science is subject to two decrements. Decrement 1 is mortality, which is governed by a uniform survival distribution with $\omega = 100$, and Decrement 2 is leaving academic employment, which is governed by the HRF $\mu_y^{(2)} = .05$, for all $y \geq 50$. Find the probability that this professor
remains in academic employment for at least five years but less than ten years.

13-4   Let $f_{J|T}(j|t)$ denote the conditional density for Cause j being the cause of decre-
ment, given that t is the time of decrement.

(a) Show that $f_{J|T}(j|t) \;=\; \dfrac{\mu_{x+t}^{(j)}}{\mu_{x+t}^{(\tau)}}.$

(b) Find an expression for $f_{J|T}(1|t)$ in a triple-decrement model, given $\mu_{x+t}^{(1)} = .03$,
    $\mu_{x+t}^{(2)} = .03t$, and $\mu_{x+t}^{(3)} = .03t^2$.

13-5   Given the HRF $\mu_{x+t}^{(1)} = \dfrac{1}{75-t}$, for $0 \leq t < 75$, and $\mu_{x+t}^{(2)} = \dfrac{2}{50-t}$, for $0 \leq t < 50$,
compute each of the following:

(a) $_tp_x'^{(1)}$, $_tp_x'^{(2)}$, and $_tp_x^{(\tau)}$
(b) $f_{T,J}(t,1)$ and $f_{T,J}(t,2)$
(c) $q_x^{(1)}$, $q_x^{(2)}$, and $q_x^{(\tau)}$
(d) $q_x'^{(1)}$ and $q_x'^{(2)}$
(e) $f_J(1)$ and $f_J(2)$
(f) $f_{J|T}(1|1)$ and $f_{J|T}(2|1)$

13-6   A multiple-decrement model with the following properties applies to students entering a certain four-year college:

(i)   1000 students enter college at time $t = 0$.
(ii) Students leave for reasons of failure (Decrement 1) or any other cause (Decre-
      ment 2).
(iii) $\mu_t^{(1)} = \mu$, for $0 \leq t \leq 4$, and $\mu_t^{(2)} = .04$, for $0 \leq t \leq 4$.
(iv) 48 students are expected to leave during the first year for all causes combined.

Calculate the expected number of students to leave during the fourth year due to
failure.

13-7 Use Equations (13.13a), (13.5b), (13.19), (13.13b), and (13.12b), in that order, to derive Equation (13.17) and then Equation (13.16), without assuming independence of
causes.

13.4 Uniform Distribution of Decrements

13-8 Find the value of $q_x^{(1)}$, given $q_x'^{(1)} = .20$, $q_x'^{(2)} = .10$, and decrements are uniformly distributed over $(x, x+1)$ in the multiple-decrement context.

13-9 A company has 1000 employees all age x, who are subject to the decrements death (Decrement 1) and retirement (Decrement 2). Deaths are uniformly distributed over the year of age but retirements can occur only at the midpoint of the year of age. Given that $q_x'^{(1)} = .015$ and $q_x'^{(2)} = .030$, determine the expected number of deaths and retirements during the next year.

13-10 Find the value of $p_x'^{(1)}$, given $q_x^{(1)} = .48$, $q_x^{(2)} = .32$, $q_x^{(3)} = .16$, and each decrement is uniformly distributed over $(x, x+1)$ in the multiple-decrement context.

13-11 Derive Equation (13.30).

13-12 Find the value of $1000 q_x'^{(1)}$, given $q_x^{(1)} = .02$, $q_x^{(2)} = .06$, and each decrement is uniformly distributed over $(x, x+1)$ in its associated single-decrement table.

The following information applies to Exercises 13-13, 13-14, and 13-15.

Students can leave a certain three-year school only for reasons of failure (Decrement 1) or voluntary withdrawal (Decrement 2), where each decrement is uniformly distributed over $(x, x+1)$ in its associated single-decrement table. The following values are given:

x	$q_x'^{(1)}$	$q_x'^{(2)}$	$q_x^{(1)}$	$q_x^{(2)}$
0	.10	.25	–	–
1	.20	.20	–	–
2	.20	.10	–	–

13-13 Calculate the six missing probability values for the table.

13-14 (a) Find the marginal probabilities $p_{J_0}(1)$ and $p_{J_0}(2)$.

      (b) Find the marginal probabilities $p_{K_0}(1)$, $p_{K_0}(2)$, and $p_{K_0}(3)$.

13-15 (a) Given that a person decrements from school in the third year, find the probability that the decrement was a failure.

(b) Given that a student enters Year 2, find the probability of eventually decrementing due to failure.

13-16 A triple-decrement model allows for mortality (Decrement 1), disability (Decrement 2), and withdrawal (Decrement 3). Mortality and disability are uniformly distributed over each year of age in their associated single-decrement tables, but withdrawals can occur only at the end of a year of age. Given the values $q_x'^{(1)} = .01$, $q_x'^{(2)} = .05$, and $q_x'^{(3)} = .10$, find the value of $q_x^{(3)}$.

13-17 Decrement 1 is uniformly distributed over the year of age in its associated single-decrement table with $q_x'^{(1)} = .100$. Decrement 2 always occurs at age $x+.70$ in its associated single-decrement table with $q_x'^{(2)} = .125$. Find the value of $q_x^{(2)}$.

13-18 As an alternative to the uniform distribution assumption of Section 13.4, assume that each decrement in a multiple-decrement model is exponentially distributed, so that $\mu_{x+t}^{(j)} = \mu^{(j)}$ for all j and for $0 \le t \le 1$, where each $\mu^{(j)}$ is a constant.

(a) Show that

$$_tq_x^{(j)} = \,_tq_x^{(\tau)} \cdot \left(\frac{\mu^{(j)}}{\mu^{(\tau)}}\right).$$

(b) Rearrange the relationship in part (a) to show that

$$_tp_x'^{(j)} = \left(1 - \,_tq_x^{(\tau)}\right)^{\,_tq_x^{(j)}/\,_tq_x^{(\tau)}}.$$

(Compare this result with Equation (13.26) in the special case where $t = 1$.)

CHAPTER FOURTEEN

MULTIPLE-DECREMENT MODELS
(APPLICATIONS)

In this chapter we present a number of applications of multiple-decrement theory.

One very important application, which we consider in Section 14.3, arises in connection with regular single-life insurance and annuity contracts, including universal life insurance and deferred variable annuities, when we consider the right of the insured or annuitant to surrender the contract and receive a benefit of some amount when doing so. Surrender of a contract is also referred to as withdrawal from the contract. Accordingly, we will often view such contracts in a double-decrement context, where the two decrements are failure (or death) and withdrawal.

We first consider, in Section 14.1, the theory of actuarial present value in a multiple-decrement environment. From the relevant APVs we can find funding payments and reserves in the same manner as with single-decrement models earlier in the text. A special type of policy value called the asset share is discussed in Section 14.2.

In Section 14.4 we return to the use of multi-state models, introduced earlier, to represent a number of multiple-decrement situations. In Section 14.5 we present a brief overview of defined benefit pension plans.

14.1 ACTUARIAL PRESENT VALUE

In the multiple-decrement environment, the APV of a contingent payment is calculated in much the same way as in the single-decrement case, except that care must be taken if the payment depends on mode of decrement as well as time of decrement. Recall from Equation (7.2) that the APV of a unit payment to a status of interest denoted by (x) paid at the end of the interval of failure is given by

$$A_x = \sum_{k=1}^{\infty} v^k \cdot Pr(K_x^* = k). \tag{14.1}$$

In the multiple-decrement environment, the APV of a unit payment made at the end of the interval of failure if (x) fails due to Decrement j is given by

$$A_x^{(j)} = \sum_{k=1}^{\infty} v^k \cdot Pr(K_x^* = k \cap J_x = j). \tag{14.2}$$

If the time and cause of decrement are independent, this can be written as

$$A_x^{(j)} = \sum_{k=1}^{\infty} v^k \cdot Pr(K_x^* = k) \cdot Pr(J_x = j) \tag{14.3a}$$

or

$$A_x^{(j)} = \sum_{k=1}^{\infty} v^k \cdot {}_{k-1}p_x^{(\tau)} \cdot q_{x+k-1}^{(j)} \tag{14.3b}$$

in actuarial notation. If the benefit is paid at the instant of failure we have

$$\overline{A}_x^{(j)} = \int_0^{\infty} v^t \cdot {}_t p_x^{(\tau)} \cdot \mu_{x+t}^{(j)} \, dt. \tag{14.4}$$

EXAMPLE 14.1

A five-year bond, issued at time 0, faces the decrements of (1) Default, (2) Call (i.e., pre-payment), and (3) Maturity.

The probabilities of decrement by year and cause are shown in the following table:

Year k	Default $q_{k-1}^{(1)}$	Call $q_{k-1}^{(2)}$	Maturity $q_{k-1}^{(3)}$
1	.02	.03	.00
2	.02	.04	.00
3	.02	.05	.00
4	.02	.06	.00
5	.02	.00	.98

A guarantor has contracted to pay 1000 at the end of the year of default if default occurs, and nothing otherwise. Find the APV of this contingent payment contract using an annual interest rate of 6%.

SOLUTION

First we extend the above table to include two additional columns:

k	$q_{k-1}^{(1)}$	$q_{k-1}^{(2)}$	$q_{k-1}^{(3)}$	${}_{k-1}p_0^{(\tau)}$	v^k
1	.02	.03	.00	1.000	.943
2	.02	.04	.00	.950	.890
3	.02	.05	.00	.893	.840
4	.02	.06	.00	.830	.792
5	.02	.00	.98	.764	.747

The APV is given by

$$APV = 1000\sum_{k=1}^{5} v^k \cdot {}_{k-1}p_0^{(\tau)} \cdot q_{k-1}^{(1)}$$

$$= 1000[(.943)(.02) + (.890)(.950)(.02) + (.840)(.893)(.02)$$

$$+ (.792)(.830)(.02) + (.747)(.764)(.02)]$$

$$= 75.33. \qquad \square$$

EXAMPLE 14.2

A whole life insurance with immediate payment of claims pays 1000 at the instant of death by natural causes (NC) or 2000 at the instant of death by accidental causes (AC). Find the APV of the insurance using a force of interest of .05 and constant hazard rates (forces of mortality) $\mu_y^{NC} = .01$ for natural causes and $\mu_y^{AC} = .002$ for accidental causes, for all y.

SOLUTION

We can think of the insurance either as a combination of two single-decrement contingent contracts with APV given by

$$APV = 2000\overline{A}_x^{(AC)} + 1000\overline{A}_x^{(NC)}$$

or as an "all causes" insurance plus an *additional* accidental cause insurance. Using the second approach we have

$$APV = 1000\left(\overline{A}_x + \overline{A}_x^{(AC)}\right)$$

$$= 1000\left[\int_0^\infty v^t \cdot {}_tp_x^{(\tau)} \cdot \mu_{x+t}^{(\tau)} \, dt + \int_0^\infty v^t \cdot {}_tp_x^{(\tau)}\mu_{x+t}^{(AC)} \, dt\right]$$

$$= 1000\int_0^\infty e^{-.05t} \cdot e^{-.012t}(.014) \, dt = 225.81. \qquad \square$$

Benefit premium calculations in the multiple-decrement environment are closely related to those in the single-decrement environment. The key concept to keep in mind is that premiums are paid only as long as the contingent contract is in force, which means that the entity of interest has not yet failed for any cause. The following example illustrates the development of premiums and reserves in a multiple-decrement environment that also includes consideration of expenses. (See Sections 9.6 and 11.4 for the incorporation of expenses in the single-decrement environment.)

EXAMPLE 14.3

Consider a five-year endowment insurance, with gross annual premiums and annual expenses paid at the beginning of each year and benefits paid at the end of the year. The contingent benefit is 1000 for failure (Decrement 1) within the five-year period, or at time $t = 5$ if failure has not previously occurred. A withdrawal benefit (Decrement 2) will be paid in the event of withdrawal from the plan at the end of any of the first four years. All parameter values for the insurance are shown in the following table:

Year k	1	2	3	4	5
Percent-of-Premium Expense	.05	.05	.05	.05	.05
Constant Contract Expense	30	30	30	30	30
Failure Benefit Amount	1000	1000	1000	1000	1000
Withdrawal Benefit Amount	50	100	300	600	0
Endowment Benefit Amount	0	0	0	0	1000
$q^{(1)}_{x+k-1}$	.02	.03	.04	.05	.06
$q^{(2)}_{x+k-1}$	.30	.20	.20	.10	.00
$q^{(\tau)}_{x+k-1}$	.32	.23	.24	.15	.06
$p^{(\tau)}_{x+k-1}$	.68	.77	.76	.85	.94

All cash flows are discounted at annual interest rate 6%.

(a) Find the expense-augmented annual premium using the equivalence principle.
(b) Find the expense-augmented contract reserve $_tV^G$ for $t = 1,2,3,4,5$.

SOLUTION

The APV of the failure benefit is

$$APV^{(1)} = \sum_{k=1}^{5} b_k^{(1)} \cdot v^k \cdot {}_{k-1}p_x^{(\tau)} \cdot q_{x+k-1}^{(1)}$$

$$= 1000\left[\frac{.02}{1.06} + \frac{(.68)(.03)}{(1.06)^2} + \frac{(.68)(.77)(.04)}{(1.06)^3}\right.$$

$$\left. + \frac{(.68)(.77)(.76)(.05)}{(1.06)^4} + \frac{(.68)(.77)(.76)(.85)(.06)}{(1.06)^5}\right]$$

$$= 1000[.01887 + .01816 + .01758 + .01576 + .01517] = 85.538.$$

The APV of the withdrawal benefit is

$$APV^{(2)} = \sum_{k=1}^{5} b_k^{(2)} \cdot v^k \cdot {}_{k-1}p_x^{(\tau)} \cdot q_{x+k-1}^{(2)}$$

$$= \frac{(50)(.30)}{1.06} + \frac{(100)(.68)(.20)}{(1.06)^2}$$

$$+ \frac{(300)(.68)(.77)(.20)}{(1.06)^3} + \frac{(600)(.68)(.77)(.76)(.10)}{(1.06)^4}$$

$$= 14.151 + 12.104 + 26.377 + 18.912 = 71.544.$$

The APV of the endowment benefit is

$$APV^{(3)} = 1000v^5 \cdot {}_5p_x^{(\tau)}$$
$$= \frac{(1000)(.68)(.77)(.76)(.85)(.94)}{(1.06)^5} = 237.591.$$

The APV of the expenses is

$$(30+.05G) \cdot \ddot{a}_{x:\overline{5}|}^{(\tau)} = (30+.05G)\left[1+\frac{.68}{1.06}+\frac{(.68)(.77)}{(1.06)^2}\right.$$
$$\left. +\frac{(.68)(.77)(.76)}{(1.06)^3}+\frac{(.68)(.77)(.76)(.85)}{(1.06)^4}\right]$$
$$= 81.286+.13547G.$$

Finally, the APV of the funding stream itself is

$$G \cdot \ddot{a}_{x:\overline{5}|}^{(\tau)} = 2.70955G.$$

(a) The expense-augmented annual premium by the equivalence principle is then found from
$$2.70955G = 85.538+71.544+237.591+81.286+.13547G,$$
leading to
$$G = \frac{475.959}{2.57408} = 184.90.$$

(b) The expense-augmented reserves are found prospectively by subtracting the APV of future expense-augmented premiums from the APV of future benefits and expenses. The results are shown in the following table, and the calculations are left as an additional exercise for the reader.[1]

k	${}_kV^G$
1	175.60
2	377.30
3	597.80
4	797.80
5	0.00

❑

14.2 ASSET SHARES

In Example 14.3 we combined the multiple-decrement theory developed in Chapter 13 with the expense and gross premium material developed in Section 9.6. We now take this combination even further to develop *projections of the expected accumulation of assets*

---

[1] The complete solution can be found on the ACTEX Publications website.

under a single contingent contract (such as an insurance policy) or for a block of such contracts. The results are known as *projected asset shares*.

Suppose we have a contingent payment contract funded by a level annual contract premium G. The contract pays in the event of the failure (such as death) of a specified entity of interest or in the event of withdrawal from the contingent contract. The payment due in the event of failure in Year k is denoted $b_k^{(1)}$ and the payment due in the event of withdrawal is denoted $b_k^{(2)}$; in either case the benefit is paid at the end of the year. As in Example 14.3, expenses are paid at the beginning of each year and are of both the percent-of-premium and contract constant types.

The projected asset share at duration k, which is the actuarial accumulated value of premiums minus expected benefits and expenses, is denoted by $_kAS$. All notation used in this section is summarized in the following table.

Symbol	Concept
G	Annual contract premium
$b_k^{(1)}$	Benefit paid at end of Year k for failure during Year k
$b_k^{(2)}$	Benefit paid at end of Year k for withdrawal during Year k
r_k	Percent-of-premium expense factor paid at beginning of Year k
e_k	Fixed contract expense paid at beginning of Year k
i	Effective annual rate of interest (presumed constant)
$q_{x+k-1}^{(1)}$	Conditional probability of failure during Year k, given that the contract is still in force at time $k-1$
$q_{x+k-1}^{(2)}$	Conditional probability of withdrawal during Year k, given that the contract is still in force at time $k-1$
$p_{x+k-1}^{(\tau)}$	Conditional probability of the contract staying in force through Year k, given that it is still in force at time $k-1$
$_kAS$	The projected asset share associated with the contract at the end of Year k

We denote the initial asset share at time 0 by $_0AS$, and note that $_0AS$ may or may not equal zero. Successive values of $_kAS$ are then found recursively by expanding the discussion in Section 11.4 to include multiple decrements. For $k=1$ we have

$$\left[_0AS + G(1-r_1) - e_1 \right](1+i) = b_1^{(1)} \cdot q_x^{(1)} + b_1^{(2)} \cdot q_x^{(2)} + {_1AS} \cdot p_x^{(\tau)}, \tag{14.5a}$$

so

$$_1AS = \frac{\left[_0AS + G(1-r_1) - e_1 \right](1+i) - b_1^{(1)} \cdot q_x^{(1)} - b_1^{(2)} \cdot q_x^{(2)}}{p_x^{(\tau)}}. \tag{14.5b}$$

For k in general we have

$$\left[_{k-1}AS + G(1-r_k) - e_k \right](1+i) = b_k^{(1)} \cdot q_{x+k-1}^{(1)} + b_k^{(2)} \cdot q_{x+k-1}^{(2)} + {_kAS} \cdot p_{x+k-1}^{(\tau)} \tag{14.6a}$$

so

$$_k AS = \frac{\left[_{k-1}AS + G(1-r_k) - e_k\right](1+i) - b_k^{(1)} \cdot q_{x+k-1}^{(1)} - b_k^{(2)} \cdot q_{x+k-1}^{(2)}}{p_{x+k-1}^{(\tau)}}.$$ (14.6b)

EXAMPLE 14.4

Consider the five-year endowment insurance described in Example 14.3. If the contract premium is $G = 200.00$ [2] and the initial asset share is $_0AS = 50$, find $_k AS$ for $k = 1, 2, 3, 4, 5$.

SOLUTION

Using the recursive relationship given by Equation (14.6b) the following values are obtained. (The details of the calculations are left to the reader as an exercise.[3])

k	$_k AS$
1	275.90
2	535.10
3	837.90
4	1115.03
5	373.90

❑

The excess (if any) of the assets associated with a contingent contract over the contract liability may be interpreted as an amount of *surplus* generated by that contract. The liability is given by the expense-augmented reserve, and the associated asset value is given by the projected asset share. Then the projected surplus at the end of Year k is given by

$$U_k = {_k AS} - {_k V^G}.$$ (14.7)

EXAMPLE 14.5

Find the surplus U_k, for $k = 1, 2, 3, 4, 5$, for the five-year endowment contract described in Examples 14.3 and 14.4.

SOLUTION

Note that although the projected asset shares are determined using the actual contract premium of 200.00, the reserves are determined using the expense-augmented premium of 184.90, which is the premium necessary to cover the benefits and expenses that constitute the contract liability. The following results are obtained directly from the results of Example 14.3(b) and Example 14.4. Note that $U_0 = 50$ since $_0AS = 50$ and $_0V^G = 0$.

---

[2] The premium might exceed the value calculated in Example 14.3 to reflect considerations of competition and profit.

[3] The complete solution can be found on the ACTEX Publications website.

k	U_k
1	100.30
2	157.80
3	240.10
4	317.23
5	373.90

❏

The projected asset share is calculated using the actual contract premium and projected, or expected, experience regarding interest, mortality, withdrawal, and expenses. As the experience actually unfolds, asset shares can also be calculated using the actual contract premium and actual experience. Asset shares calculated in this way are often called *historical asset shares*.

14.3 NON-FORFEITURE OPTIONS

As we have seen, a long-term insurance contract, such as a whole life or endowment contract, builds up a reserve because the premiums in the early years of the contract exceed the cost of insurance in those years. In the early days of insurance, if the policyholder discontinued the premiums on such a contract the excess premium payment was forfeited to the insurer. The contract reserve was being held for the eventual payment of the face amount in the case of death, but no payment was required to be made in the case of premium cessation. In most modern contracts, however, the policyholder's equity in the contract is not forfeited upon premium default, but instead various *non-forfeiture options* are available to the policyholder. We discuss several of these options in this section.

14.3.1 CASH VALUES

Discontinuation of regular premium payments by the policyholder is referred to as *surrendering* the insurance contract. The amount of the cash value available at each duration of the contract is generally predetermined and printed in the policy. The insurer is required to provide a cash value no less than the legal minimum cash value defined in the U.S. insurance regulation known as the Standard Non-Forfeiture Law.[4] The cash value is likely to be less than the policy reserve in the early years of the contract, but could equal the policy reserve in later years.

Most policies that provide a cash value also permit policyholders to borrow against the equity they have in their policies at a stated interest rate. Then if failure occurs under a contract with an outstanding loan balance, the amount of the indebtedness is deducted from the face amount otherwise payable.

Note that term insurance contracts, which build up very small amounts of policyholder equity, often do not provide cash values.

---

[4] The definition of legal minimum cash values by the Standard Non-Forfeiture Law is beyond the scope of this text.

14.3.2 REDUCED PAID-UP INSURANCE

In lieu of taking the cash value upon surrender of the contract, the policyholder can generally elect to keep the contract in force at a reduced benefit amount with no future premium requirement. Suppose a whole life policy issued at age x is surrendered at duration t, with a cash value of amount $_tCV_x$ available at that time. If the reduced paid-up option is elected, the amount of paid-up whole life insurance available would be

$$RPU = \frac{_tCV_x}{A_{x+t}},\tag{14.8}$$

since the cash value acts as the APV of the future whole life coverage.

In the special case where the cash value equals the NLP reserve, the amount of paid-up insurance is denoted by $_tW_x$ and would be

$$_tW_x = \frac{_tV_x}{A_{x+t}},\tag{14.9}$$

per unit of coverage under the surrendered policy.

If a policy loan of amount L is outstanding at the time of contract surrender, the APV of the reduced paid-up insurance would be $_tCV_x - L$.

14.3.3 EXTENDED TERM INSURANCE

Another option in lieu of taking the cash value is to use it to provide term insurance, of the same face amount as under the surrendered policy, for as long a term as the cash value will provide. Again presuming a whole life policy of unit amount, issued at age x and surrendered at duration t, the length of extended term insurance is the value of n satisfying

$$_tCV_x = A^{\,1}_{x+t:\,\overline{n}|},\tag{14.10}$$

where n would need to be approximated by interpolation in the life table upon which the calculation is based.

An interesting special case arises if an endowment contract is surrendered late in its term with cash value given by $_tCV_{x:\overline{n}|}$, where $t < n$. It is quite possible that the cash value could provide extended term insurance beyond the original maturity date of the endowment, which the insurer might wish not to do. In this case the insurance is extended to the original maturity date, and a reduced pure endowment benefit is paid if survival to that date occurs. The equation of value at duration t would be

$$_tCV_{x:\overline{n}|} = A^{\,1}_{x+t:\,\overline{n-t}|} + PE \cdot {}_{n-t}E_{x+t},\tag{14.11}$$

from which PE can be determined.

14.3.4 APPLICATION TO UNIVERSAL LIFE INSURANCE

Recall the discussion of the account value arising under a universal life insurance contract in Section 11.5. If the contract is surrendered by the policyholder, the account value is released by the insurer. But the account value represents the insured's equity in the contract. If the contract has been in force for a sufficiently long time, the entire account value might be paid as the cash value upon surrender of the contract. If the contract is still in its early years, it is customary to deduct a *surrender charge* from the account value to determine the cash value.

Of course premium cessation can occur without contract surrender. The account value, along with interest on it, continues to provide the face amount death benefit in the standard format of successive one-year term insurance purchases. When the account value is no longer sufficient to provide the insurance coverage, the contract would lapse without value unless special provisions to keep it in force exist.[5]

14.3.5 APPLICATION TO DEFERRED VARIABLE ANNUITIES

In Section 11.6 we saw that if the failure (death) benefit under a deferred variable annuity were the amount of the account value, then the account value accumulates at interest only and there is no cost of insurance. Similarly, if the surrender benefit (cash value) were also the account value, it would accumulate at interest only and its value would not be affected by the rate of contract surrender.

In practice, the cash value does not normally exceed the account value, and will tend to be less than the account value in the early years of the contract. As with universal life insurance, the cash value is defined as the account value less a surrender charge in the early years.

14.4 MULTI-STATE MODEL REPRESENTATION, WITH ILLUSTRATIONS

Recall that a recurring feature of the multi-state model representations presented earlier in the text was that failure was the *only* cause of decrement, so that any state, once left, could never be reentered. In this section we consider several types of multiple-decrement models, some of which will continue to have that property and some will not.

14.4.1 THE GENERAL MULTIPLE-DECREMENT MODEL

As already defined in Chapter 13, the multiple-decrement model considers a group of entities (generally persons), and addresses the activity of persons being decremented from that group due to one of m possible causes. Once decremented from the original group due to Cause j, the decremented person cannot thereafter be decremented by any other cause. That

---

[5] We will discuss such special provisions in Chapter 16.

is, if failure due to Cause j is represented as transition from the initial state to State j, then State j would be an absorbing state.[6] This notion is represented in the following diagram:

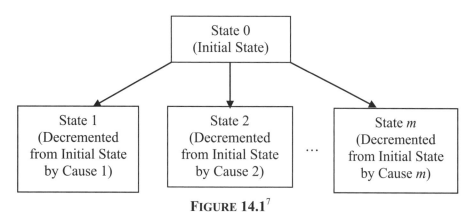

FIGURE 14.1[7]

EXAMPLE 14.6

Analyze Example 14.2 in the multi-state model context.

SOLUTION

The model for this insurance is the general multiple-decrement model with $m = 2$, as shown in Figure 14.2.

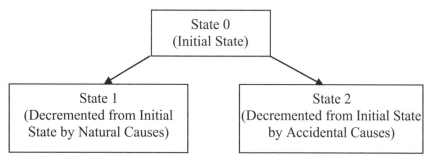

FIGURE 14.2

The insurance pays 1000 at the instant of transition to State 1, or 2000 at the instant of transition to State 2, for a person alive in the initial state at age x at time 0. The APV is calculated exactly as in Example 14.2, except using different notation. ❑

EXAMPLE 14.7

Analyze Example 14.3 in the multi-state model context.

---

[6] In this context we say that there are no *secondary decrements*. In Section 14.4.2 we consider a model with one secondary decrement, in Section 14.4.3 we consider a model with two secondary decrements, and in Section 14.4.4 we consider a model with three secondary decrements.

[7] For this model only, We denote the initial state as State 0, rather than our customary State 1, for the notational convenience of having State j denote the state of failure due to Cause j.

SOLUTION

The model for this insurance is the general multiple-decrement model with $m = 3$, as shown in Figure 14.3. The insurance pays 1000 at the end of the year of transition to State 1, or 1000 at the time of transition to State 3 (which can occur only at time $t = 5$), or a variable amount at the end of the year of transition to State 2. The expense-augmented premium and reserves are calculated exactly as in Example 14.3, except for using different notation.   ❑

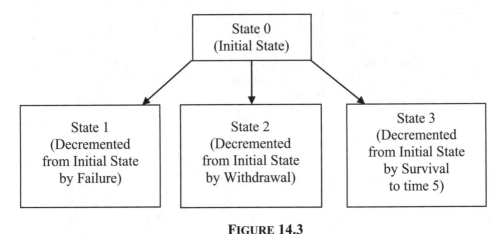

FIGURE 14.3

We can combine the ideas of multiple decrements and multiple lives in the multi-state model context. This is pursued in the following example.

EXAMPLE 14.8

Consider two business partners, denoted by (x) and (y), operating a partnership together. They have an agreement whereby a trust will make a payment to either partner upon retirement from the business, and also make a payment to a named beneficiary upon the death of either partner. Represent this arrangement as a multi-state model.

SOLUTION

The initial state (State 0) finds both partners alive and active in the business. Then let State i be defined as shown in the following table.

i	Definition of State i
1	(x) still active; (y) retired
2	(x) still active; (y) not alive
3	(y) still active; (x) retired
4	(y) still active; (x) not alive
5	(x) and (y) both alive but retired
6	(x) alive but retired; (y) not alive
7	(y) alive but retired; (x) not alive
8	(x) and (y) both not alive

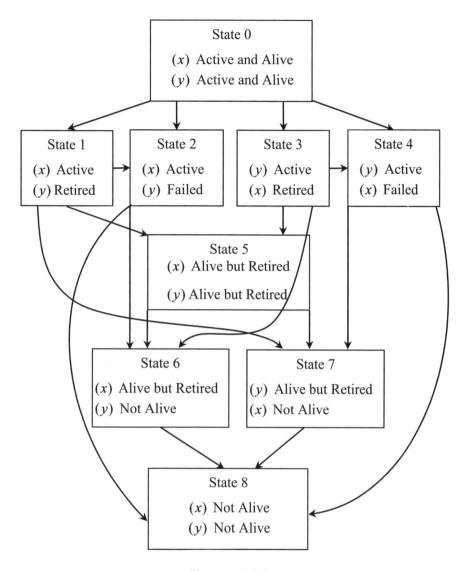

FIGURE 14.4

This nine-state model is represented in Figure 14.4, where the arrows indicate possible transitions between states. (Note that retirement is deemed to be non-reversible, and simultaneous deaths or retirements cannot occur.) Observe how complicated the model becomes with only two lives and two decrements. (See Exercise 14-9.)   ☐

14.4.2 THE TOTAL AND PERMANENT DISABILITY MODEL

In this case we have an insurance contract issued to a healthy person that provides for periodic income if the insured becomes totally and permanently disabled during the term of the contract. As the word "permanent" implies, once insureds have become disabled they remain disabled until death. In the multi-state model context, the coverage is described in Figure 14.5.

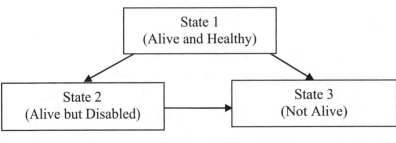

FIGURE 14.5

The contract may provide (a) a lump sum failure benefit (death benefit) for failure while healthy (i.e., upon transition from State 1 to State 3), and/or (b) a similar failure (death) benefit for failure while disabled (i.e., upon transition from State 2 to State 3, as implied by the horizontal arrow in Figure 13.5. (In this case we have an example of a secondary decrement.) Such contracts do not normally pay lump sum benefits upon becoming disabled (i.e., upon transition from State 1 to State 2). Rather, they pay (c) a periodic income to the insured while disabled (i.e., while in State 2). (Note that being decremented from State 2 due to recovery from the disability is not assumed to be possible in this model.)

Consider a healthy person age x being issued such a contract at time 0. The APV for Benefit (a) is a familiar concept, namely

$$^{h}\overline{A}_{x}^{(f)} = \int_{0}^{\infty} v^{r} \cdot {}_{r}p_{x}^{(\tau)} \cdot \mu_{x+r}^{(f)} \, dr \qquad (14.12a)$$

in actuarial notation, where $\mu_{x+r}^{(f)}$ denotes the force of failure for a healthy person. In multi-state model notation we would write

$$^{h}\overline{A}_{x}^{(f)} = \int_{0}^{\infty} v^{r} \cdot {}_{r}p_{11}^{(0)} \cdot \lambda_{13}(r) \, dr, \qquad (14.12b)$$

since the unit benefit for failure while healthy would be payable at the instant of transition from State 1 to State 3.

For Benefit (b), the insured must become disabled first and then fail. (Since recovery is not possible, then failure while disabled is inevitable once disability has occurred.) To develop the APV for a unit failure benefit in this case, suppose disability occurs at time r, which happens with density ${}_{r}p_{x}^{(\tau)} \cdot \mu_{x+r}^{(d)}$, where $\mu_{x+r}^{(d)}$ denotes the force of disability for a healthy person. Conditional on this event occurring, we then have a person in the disabled state at age $x+r$, facing the single decrement of failure. The APV of a unit failure benefit for a person alive but disabled at time r (age $x+r$) is $^{d}\overline{A}_{x+r}$, where the superscript d implies that $^{d}\overline{A}_{x+r}$ is to be calculated using a single-decrement survival model appropriate for a disabled person. We know that

$$^{d}\overline{A}_{x+r} = \int_{0}^{\infty} v^{s} \cdot {}_{s}p_{x+r}^{d} \cdot \mu_{x+r+s}^{d} \, ds \qquad (14.13a)$$

in actuarial notation, or

$$^{d}\overline{A}_{x+r} = \int_{0}^{\infty} v^{s} \cdot {}_{s}p_{22}^{(r)} \cdot \lambda_{23}(s) \; ds \tag{14.13b}$$

in multi-state model notation, since the benefit is paid at the instant of transition from State 2 to State 3. Then the APV at issue of the contract to a healthy person age x at time 0 is

$$^{h}\overline{A}_{x}^{d} = \int_{0}^{\infty} v^{r} \cdot {}_{r}p_{x}^{(\tau)} \cdot \mu_{x+r}^{(d)} \cdot {}^{d}\overline{A}_{x+r} \; dr$$

$$= \int_{0}^{\infty} v^{r} \cdot {}_{r}p_{x}^{(\tau)} \cdot \mu_{x+r}^{(d)} \left(\int_{0}^{\infty} v^{s} \cdot {}_{s}p_{x+r}^{d} \cdot \mu_{x+r+s}^{d} \; ds \right) dr, \tag{14.14a}$$

in actuarial notation, or

$$^{h}\overline{A}_{x}^{d} = \int_{0}^{\infty} v^{r} \cdot {}_{r}p_{11}^{(0)} \cdot \lambda_{12}(r) \left(\int_{0}^{\infty} v^{s} \cdot {}_{s}p_{22}^{(r)} \cdot \lambda_{23}(s) \; ds \right) dr, \tag{14.14b}$$

in multi-state model notation.

For Benefit (c), we again consider that disability occurs at time r, which happens with density ${}_{r}p_{x}^{(\tau)} \cdot \mu_{x+r}^{(d)}$. At that time the APV of a continuous unit income benefit for a disabled person is ${}^{d}\overline{a}_{x+r}$, where again the superscript d implies that ${}^{d}\overline{a}_{x+r}$ is calculated using a survival model appropriate for a disabled person. Then it follows that the APV at issue of the contract for the disability income stream is

$$^{h}\overline{a}_{x}^{d} = \int_{0}^{\infty} v^{r} \cdot {}_{r}p_{x}^{(\tau)} \cdot \mu_{x+r}^{(d)} \cdot {}^{d}\overline{a}_{x+r} \; dr$$

$$= \int_{0}^{\infty} v^{r} \cdot {}_{r}p_{x}^{(\tau)} \cdot \mu_{x+r}^{(d)} \left(\int_{0}^{\infty} v^{s} \cdot {}_{s}p_{x+r}^{d} \; ds \right) dr \tag{14.15a}$$

in actuarial notation, or

$$^{h}\overline{a}_{x}^{d} = \int_{0}^{\infty} v^{r} \cdot {}_{r}p_{11}^{(0)} \cdot \lambda_{12}(r) \left(\int_{0}^{\infty} v^{s} \cdot {}_{s}p_{22}^{(r)} \; ds \right) dr \tag{14.15b}$$

in multi-state model notation.

Note that two models are required in order to determine the several APVs for this contract. The primary model is a double-decrement model for the decrements of failure and disability. The secondary model is a single-decrement model for failure only, but appropriate for a disabled person. The total APV for the contract is the sum of the APVs for Benefits (a), (b), and (c).

EXAMPLE 14.9

Referring to Figure 14.5, consider a healthy person age x at time t, which means the process is in State 1. We wish to consider the probability of this person being alive but disabled at age $x+r$ (time $t+r$), which means the process would be in State 2 at time $t+r$. The multi-state model notation for this probability is ${}_{r}p_{12}^{(t)}$. (There is no standard actuarial symbol for this probability value; other texts[8] have adopted the symbol $_r p_x^{ai}$.) In any case, this probability would be given by

$$_r p_{12}^{(t)} \ = \ _r p_x^{ai} \ = \ \int_0^r {}_s p_x^{(\tau)} \cdot \mu_{x+s}^{(d)} \cdot {}_{r-s} p_{x+s}^d \ ds,$$

in actuarial notation, where $\mu_{x+s}^{(d)}$ denotes the force of disability for a healthy person, subject to a double-decrement model, and $_{r-s} p_{x+s}^d$ denotes the probability of survival from age $x+s$ to age $x+r$ for a disabled person, subject to a single-decrement survival model. We wish to solve the Kolmogorov differential equation to show that

$$_n p_{12}^{(t)} \ = \ \int_0^n {}_s p_x^{(\tau)} \cdot \mu_{x+s}^{(d)} \cdot {}_{n-s} p_{x+s}^d \ ds.$$

SOLUTION

In Equation (3.14a), $i=1$ and $j=2$ so k takes on the values 1 and 3 in the summation. Then we have

$$\frac{d}{dr} {}_r p_{12}^{(t)} \ = \ {}_r p_{11}^{(t)} \cdot \lambda_{12}(t+r) - {}_r p_{12}^{(t)} \cdot \lambda_{21}(t+r) \qquad \text{(at } k=1)$$

$$+ \ {}_r p_{13}^{(t)} \cdot \lambda_{32}(t+r) - {}_r p_{12}^{(t)} \cdot \lambda_{23}(t+r) \qquad \text{(at } k=3)$$

$$= \ {}_r p_{11}^{(t)} \cdot \lambda_{12}(t+r) - {}_r p_{12}^{(t)} \cdot \lambda_{23}(t+r),$$

since $\lambda_{21}(s) = \lambda_{32}(s) = 0$ for all s. Then integrating from $r=0$ to $r=n$ we have

$$\int_0^n d \ {}_r p_{12}^{(t)} \ = \ \int_0^n {}_r p_{11}^{(t)} \cdot \lambda_{12}(t+r) \ dr - \int_0^n {}_r p_{12}^{(t)} \cdot \lambda_{23}(t+r) \ dr.$$

As expected, the left side integrates to $_n p_{12}^{(t)}$, since $_0 p_{12}^{(t)} = 0$. On the right side, $\lambda_{12}(t+r)$ is the force of disability for a healthy person at age $x+r$, subject to a double-decrement model, and is denoted $\mu_{x+r}^{(d)}$ in actuarial notation. $\lambda_{23}(t+r)$ is the force of failure (or mortality) for a disabled person at age $x+r$, subject to a single-decrement survival model, and is denoted μ_{x+r}^d in actuarial notation. Then substituting actuarial notation for $_r p_{11}^{(t)}$, $\lambda_{12}(t+r)$, and $\lambda_{23}(t+r)$, and substituting the integral expression given in the example for $_r p_{12}^{(t)}$, we have

$$_n p_{12}^{(t)} \ = \ \int_0^n {}_r p_x^{(\tau)} \cdot \mu_{x+r}^{(d)} \ dr - \int_0^n \mu_{x+r}^d \left(\int_0^r {}_s p_x^{(\tau)} \cdot \mu_{x+s}^{(d)} \cdot {}_{r-s} p_{x+s}^d \ ds \right) dr.$$

---

[8] See, for example, Section 12.2 of Jordan [15].

Reversing the order of integration in the subtractive term we obtain

$$\int_0^n {}_sp_x^{(\tau)}\cdot\mu_{x+s}^{(d)}\left(\int_s^n {}_{r-s}p_{x+s}^d\cdot\mu_{x+r}^d\ dr\right)ds = \int_0^n {}_sp_x^{(\tau)}\cdot\mu_{x+s}^{(d)}\cdot {}_{n-s}q_{x+s}^d\ ds.$$

Then we finally have

$$_np_{12}^{(t)} = \int_0^n {}_rp_x^{(\tau)}\cdot\mu_{x+r}^{(d)}\ dr - \int_0^n {}_sp_x^{(\tau)}\cdot\mu_{x+s}^{(d)}\cdot {}_{n-s}q_{x+s}^d\ ds$$

$$= \int_0^n\left({}_sp_x^{(\tau)}\cdot\mu_{x+s}^{(d)} - {}_sp_x^{(\tau)}\cdot\mu_{x+s}^{(d)}\cdot {}_{n-s}q_{x+s}^d\right)ds,$$

upon changing r to s in the first integral, and finally

$$_np_{12}^{(t)} = \int_0^n {}_sp_x^{(\tau)}\cdot\mu_{x+s}^{(d)}\left(1 - {}_{n-s}q_{x+s}^d\right)ds$$

$$= \int_0^n {}_sp_x^{(\tau)}\cdot\mu_{x+s}^{(d)}\cdot {}_{n-s}p_{x+s}^d\ ds,$$

as required. ❑

14.4.3 DISABILITY MODEL ALLOWING FOR RECOVERY

In this section we consider the same insurance contract as in Section 14.4.2, except that disability is not presumed to be permanent. Premiums are paid while the insured is healthy, but not while disabled. If the insured becomes disabled, whether by accident or illness, periodic income payments are made. The income payments cease upon either death or recovery from the disability. In the case of recovery, the insured returns to the active state and resumes premium payments. As a multi-state model, the coverage is described by Figure 14.6 in which the possibility of recovery is indicated by the arrow showing possible transition from State 2 back to State 1.

As we shall see, the possibility of recovery complicates our analysis considerably. We resolve this complication by numerically approximating a solution to the Kolmogorov differential equation rather than solving it analytically.

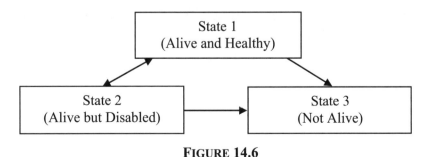

FIGURE 14.6

Whereas the secondary model in Section 14.4.2 was a single-decrement model for failure only, the secondary model in this case is a double-decrement model for the decrements of failure and recovery. In this section we use this new model to value the same three benefits described in Section 14.4.2.

We should first note that Equation (14.12b) is still a correct expression for the APV of Benefit (a). However, when the model allows for reentry to the healthy state, as our new model does, the probability value denoted by $_r p_{11}^{(0)}$ cannot be determined analytically. Recall that $_r p_{11}^{(0)}$ is the probability that a person in State 1 at time 0 will be in State 1 at time r. This event can occur (1) if the person never left State 1 before time r, or (2) if the person had transitioned to State 2 but returned to State 1 before time r, or (3) if the person had moved from State 1 to State 2, and back again, several times before time r. Due to the possibility of unlimited transitions to State 2, and back again to State 1, the probability value $_r p_{11}^{(0)}$ does not have a closed form expression, except in degenerate cases.

To remedy this problem, we use the elementary numerical method from first-year calculus called the linear approximation.[9] Suppose f is a differentiable function, so that the derivative $f'(x)$ exists. From the definition

$$f'(x) = \lim_{\Delta x \to 0} \frac{f(x+\Delta x) - f(x)}{\Delta x}$$

we can say that

$$f(x+\Delta x) \approx f(x) + f'(x) \cdot \Delta x \tag{14.16}$$

for small values of Δx. We can use this method to numerically approximate a solution for $f(x)$, in the differential equation $f'(x) = g(x)$, when $g(x)$ cannot be integrated analytically.

EXAMPLE 14.10

Consider the function $f(x)$ defined by the differential equation

$$\frac{d}{dx} f(x) = 2x + e^x,$$

with the initial condition $f(0) = 3$.

(a) Use the linear approximation method, with the value $\Delta x = .10$, to generate approximate values of $f(1)$ and $f(2)$.

(b) Compare these approximate values to the actual values obtained analytically.

SOLUTION

(a) Using Equation (14.16) with $f(0) = 3$ and $\Delta x = .10$, we have

---

[9] In many texts this is referred to as Euler's method.

$$f(.10) \approx f(0) + f'(0) \cdot \Delta x = 3 + (1)(.10) = 3.10,$$

since $f'(x) = 2x + e^x$ so that $f'(0) = e^0 = 1$. Then, recursively, with $x = .10$, we have

$$f(.20) \approx f(.10) + f'(.10) \cdot \Delta x = 3.10 + (1.305)(.10) = 3.23,$$

since $f'(.10) = 2x + e^x \big|_{x=.10} = 1.305$. Continuing in this recursive manor we reach the results $f(1) \approx 5.53$ and $f(2) \approx 12.87$. (The reader is encouraged to verify these results.)

(b) By integrating both sides of the differential equation from $x = 0$ to $x = n$ we obtain

$$f(x) \big|_0^n = x^2 + e^x \big|_0^n,$$

so that

$$f(n) = f(0) + n^2 + e^n - 1.$$

Then we find

$$f(1) = 3 + 1 + e - 1 = 5.72$$

and

$$f(2) = 3 + 4 + e^2 - 1 = 13.39.$$

This shows that Euler's method provides a reasonable approximation to the solution of this differential equation. ❑

We now consider the Kolmogorov differential equation given by Equation (3.14a). To solve for $_r p_{11}^{(t)}$, we have $i = 1$ and $j = 1$ so k takes on the values 2 and 3 in the summation. Then we have

$$\frac{d}{dr} \, _r p_{11}^{(t)} = \, _r p_{12}^{(t)} \cdot \lambda_{21}(t+r) - \, _r p_{11}^{(t)} \cdot \lambda_{12}(t+r) \qquad \text{(at } k=2\text{)}$$

$$+ \, _r p_{13}^{(t)} \cdot \lambda_{31}(t+r) - \, _r p_{11}^{(t)} \cdot \lambda_{13}(t+r) \quad \text{(at } k=3\text{)}$$

$$= \, _r p_{12}^{(t)} \cdot \lambda_{21}(t+r) - \, _r p_{11}^{(t)} \cdot \left[\lambda_{12}(t+r) + \lambda_{13}(t+r) \right], \qquad (14.17)$$

since only $\lambda_{31}(t+r) = 0$ in this case. To solve for $_r p_{12}^{(t)}$, we have $i = 1$ and $j = 2$ so k takes on the values 1 and 3 in the summation. We have

$$\frac{d}{dr} \, _r p_{12}^{(t)} = \, _r p_{11}^{(t)} \cdot \lambda_{12}(t+r) - \, _r p_{12}^{(t)} \cdot \lambda_{21}(t+r) \qquad \text{(at } k=1\text{)}$$

$$+ \, _r p_{13}^{(t)} \cdot \lambda_{32}(t+r) - \, _r p_{12}^{(t)} \cdot \lambda_{23}(t+r) \quad \text{(at } k=3\text{)}$$

$$= \, _r p_{11}^{(t)} \cdot \lambda_{12}(t+r) - \, _r p_{12}^{(t)} \cdot \left[\lambda_{21}(t+r) + \lambda_{23}(t+r) \right], \qquad (14.18)$$

since only $\lambda_{32}(t+r)=0$ in this case. Since both of Equations (14.17) and (14.18) include both $_r p_{11}^{(t)}$ and $_r p_{12}^{(t)}$, we apply the linear approximation to both equations simultaneously and produce approximate values for both functions.

Consider a healthy person being issued this type of disability coverage at time 0 at age x. The process necessarily begins in State 1 at time 0 so, necessarily, $_0 p_{11}^{(0)} =1$ and $_0 p_{12}^{(0)} = 0$. These are the initial conditions for use in our recursive calculation of values of $_r p_{11}^{(0)}$ and $_r p_{12}^{(0)}$.

Adapting Equation (14.16) to this problem, where $f(x)$ is represented by $_r p_{ij}^{(0)}$, we have

$$_{r+\Delta r} p_{ij}^{(0)} \approx {_r p_{ij}^{(0)}} + \frac{d}{dr} {_r p_{ij}^{(0)}} \cdot \Delta r. \tag{14.19}$$

Then for $i = j = 1$, we substitute the right side of Equation (14.17) for the derivative term in Equation (14.19), obtaining

$$_{r+\Delta r} p_{11}^{(0)} \approx {_r p_{11}^{(0)}} + \Delta r \left\{ {_r p_{12}^{(0)}} \cdot \lambda_{21}(r) - {_r p_{11}^{(0)}} \cdot \left[\lambda_{12}(r) + \lambda_{13}(r) \right] \right\}, \tag{14.20}$$

since $t = 0$. Similarly, for $i = 1$ and $j = 2$, we substitute the right side of Equation (14.18) for the derivative term in Equation (14.19), obtaining

$$_{r+\Delta r} p_{12}^{(0)} \approx {_r p_{12}^{(0)}} + \Delta r \left\{ {_r p_{11}^{(0)}} \cdot \lambda_{12}(r) - {_r p_{12}^{(0)}} \cdot \left[\lambda_{21}(r) + \lambda_{23}(r) \right] \right\}, \tag{14.21}$$

again since $t = 0$. Then by selecting a value for Δr, along with initial values $_0 p_{11}^{(0)} = 1$ and $_0 p_{12}^{(0)} = 0$, we can recursively calculate values of $_r p_{11}^{(0)}$ and $_r p_{12}^{(0)}$ for $r = \Delta r, 2\Delta r, 3\Delta r, \dots$.

EXAMPLE 14.11

Suppose the forces of transition are $\lambda_{12}(s) = .10s + .20$, $\lambda_{13}(s) = .20$, $\lambda_{21}(s) = .50$, and $\lambda_{23}(s) = .125s + .20$, for $0 \leq s \leq 2$ in all cases. Using the value $\Delta r = .10$, calculate the approximate values of $_r p_{11}^{(0)}$ and $_r p_{12}^{(0)}$ for $r = .10, .20, \dots, 2.00$.

SOLUTION

Starting at $r = 0$, and using $\Delta r = .10$, we find

$$_{.10} p_{11}^{(0)} \approx \,_{0} p_{11}^{(0)} + .10 \left\{ _{0} p_{12}^{(0)} \cdot \lambda_{21}(0) - _{0} p_{11}^{(0)} \cdot \left[\lambda_{12}(0) + \lambda_{13}(0) \right] \right\}$$
$$= 1 + .10 \left[0 - (1)(.20 + .20) \right] = .96$$

from Equation (14.20), and

$$_{.10} p_{12}^{(0)} \approx \,_{0} p_{12}^{(0)} + .10 \left\{ _{0} p_{11}^{(0)} \cdot \lambda_{12}(0) - _{0} p_{12}^{(0)} \cdot \left[\lambda_{21}(0) + \lambda_{23}(0) \right] \right\}$$
$$= 0 + .10 \left[(1)(.20 - 0) \right] = .02$$

from Equation (14.21). Continuing in this recursive manner we obtain the values shown in the following table:

r	$_{r} p_{11}^{(0)}$	$_{r} p_{12}^{(0)}$
0.00	1	0
0.10	.960	.020
0.20	.922	.039
0.30	.885	.056
0.40	.850	.072
0.50	.816	.087
0.60	.784	.101
0.70	.753	.114
0.80	.723	.125
0.90	.694	.135
1.00	.667	.144
1.10	.641	.152
1.20	.616	.160
1.30	.592	.166
1.40	.569	.171
1.50	.547	.175
1.60	.525	.179
1.70	.505	.182
1.80	.485	.184
1.90	.466	.185
2.00	.448	.186

Once the values of $_{r} p_{11}^{(0)}$ and $_{r} p_{12}^{(0)}$ have been determined, a number of financial values can be calculated from these $_{r} p_{ij}^{(0)}$ values. This is illustrated in the following example.

EXAMPLE 14.12

A healthy person age x is issued a contract that pays 10,000 at the end of the tenth of the year of death for death while healthy, and 1,000 at the end of each tenth of the year if disabled at that time. Premiums are payable at the beginning of each tenth of the year while healthy.[10] The coverage is for a two-year period only. Assuming a nominal interest rate of $i^{(10)} = .05$, and the transition forces of Example 14.11, find each of the following.

(a) The APV at issue of the death benefit.

(b) The APV at issue of the disability benefit.

(c) The net benefit premium payable each tenth of the year, using the equivalence principle.

SOLUTION

(a) The effective interest rate each tenth of a year is $\frac{i^{(10)}}{10} = .005$. The force of mortality for a healthy person, which is given by $\lambda_{13}(s)$ in this case, is constant at .20, so the probability of death in any tenth of a year is also constant at

$$q = 1 - e^{-\int_0^{.10} .20\, dt} = .01980.$$

Then the APV of the death benefit is

$$APV(a) = 10,000\left(v \cdot q + v^2 \cdot {}_{.10}p_{11}^{(0)} \cdot q + \cdots + v^{20} \cdot {}_{1.90}p_{11}^{(0)} \cdot q\right)$$

$$= 198\left[\frac{1}{1.005} + \frac{{}_{.10}p_{11}^{(0)}}{(1.005)^2} + \cdots + \frac{{}_{1.90}p_{11}^{(0)}}{(1.005)^{20}}\right].$$

Substituting the ${}_r p_{11}^{(0)}$ values calculated in Example 14.11, we obtain the result $APV(a) = 2649.03$, which the reader might verify.

(b) The disability benefit is paid at the end of each tenth of the year if disabled at that time, which means the process is in State 2. The APV of the benefit is

$$APV(b) = 1,000\left[\frac{{}_{.10}p_{12}^{(0)}}{1.005} + \frac{{}_{.20}p_{12}^{(0)}}{(1.005)^2} + \cdots + \frac{{}_{2.00}p_{12}^{(0)}}{(1.005)^{20}}\right].$$

Substituting the ${}_r p_{12}^{(0)}$ values calculated in Example 14.11, we obtain the result $APV(b) = 2472.12$, which the reader might verify.

(c) If the net periodic premium, payable at the beginning of each tenth of the year while healthy, is denoted by P, then the APV of the premium stream is

$$APV(c) = P\left[1 + \frac{{}_{.10}p_{11}^{(0)}}{1.005} + \frac{{}_{.20}p_{11}^{(0)}}{(1.005)^2} + \cdots + \frac{{}_{1.90}p_{11}^{(0)}}{(1.005)^{19}}\right].$$

---

[10] In practice, it would be more natural to pay premiums and disability benefits monthly. The calculations in Example 14.11 would have used $\Delta r = 1/12$ instead of $\Delta r = 1/10$.

Again using the $_r p_{11}^{(0)}$ values from Example 14.11, we find the APV of the premium stream to be $13.44582P$. Then the net premium is

$$P = \frac{APV(a) + APV(b)}{13.44582} = 380.87. \qquad \square$$

Note that the availability of $_r p_{ij}^{(0)}$ values at discrete values of r allows us to calculate discrete APVs directly. If APVs for continuous functions were desired, we would resort to approximate numerical integration, such as the trapezoidal rule or Simpson's rule, using the available discrete values.

The calculation of several other results from the Figure 14.6 model is pursued in the exercises.

The Figure 14.6 model assumes that a person who has recovered from a disability, thereby returning to State 1 from State 2, is then subject to the same forces of transition as other persons in State 1 who have never been disabled. An alternative view is to define a separate state for those who have recovered from a disability. This model is illustrated in Figure 14.7.

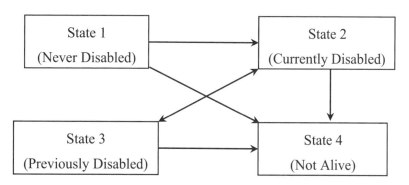

FIGURE 14.7

In this model, transition from State 2 or State 3 back to State 1 is not possible, nor is transition from State 1 to State 3, so $\lambda_{13}(s) = \lambda_{21}(s) = \lambda_{31}(s) = 0$. As always, State 4 is an absorbing state, so $\lambda_{41}(s) = \lambda_{42}(s) = \lambda_{43}(s) = 0$ as well. Note that a previously disabled person could become disabled again, so transition from State 3 to State 2 is possible (i.e., $\lambda_{32}(s) \neq 0$).

The added complexity of this model makes it even more difficult to obtain analytical results, even approximately. This is a good example of where simulation techniques can be useful; this is illustrated in Appendix B (see Example B.11).

14.4.4 CONTINUING CARE RETIREMENT COMMUNITIES

Another model that lends itself to convenient analysis in the multi-state model context is that of a *continuing care retirement community* (CCRC). The CCRC model we consider in this section was proposed by Jones [14].[11] It consists of a set of *individual living units* (ILU) along with two skilled nursing facilities. One healthy retiree lives in each ILU. One nursing facility houses retirees with temporary nursing needs and is referred to as the *temporary nursing facility* (TNF); the other, the *permanent nursing facility* (PNF), houses retirees on a permanent basis. When an individual dies or moves to the PNF, his or her ILU is made available for a new member and we assume it is occupied as soon as it becomes available. While a member is in the TNF, his or her ILU is held vacant. We will predict future occupancy rates at our CCRC by treating it as a homogeneous discrete-time Markov Chain. This is illustrated in Figure 14.8.

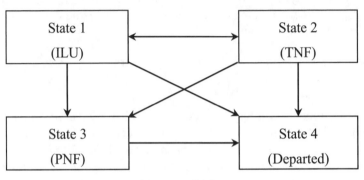

FIGURE 14.8

Residents in State 3 (the PNF) cannot return to either State 1 or State 2, so $\lambda_{31}(s)=\lambda_{32}(s)=0$ for all s. As usual, $\lambda_{41}(s)=\lambda_{42}(s)=\lambda_{43}(s)=0$ as well. Transitions among states are governed by a monthly transition probability matrix given by

$$P = \begin{vmatrix} .94 & .03 & .02 & .01 \\ .50 & .30 & .18 & .02 \\ 0 & 0 & .93 & .07 \\ 0 & 0 & 0 & 1 \end{vmatrix}.$$

Note that the number of possible transitions is greater than under any of the models previously considered. The complexity of the model suggests that analysis of it might best be done by simulation, although several elementary calculations from the model are pursued in Exercises 14-19 and 14-20.

14.4.5 THIELE'S DIFFERENTIAL EQUATION IN THE MULTIPLE-DECREMENT CASE

In this section we illustrate the calculation of reserves in several multiple-decrement situations.

We begin with the simpler disability model of Section 14.4.2, and illustrated in Figure 14.5, where disability is presumed permanent so that return from the disabled to the healthy state is not possible. In Section 14.4.2 we developed the APVs at issue of the contract at age x for each of (a) a unit benefit for death while healthy, (b) a unit benefit for death while disabled,

---

[11] Interested readers should consult this reference for a fuller analysis of the model.

and (c) a unit of continuous income while disabled. These APVs are given by Equations (14.12a), (14.14a), and (14.15a), respectively.

The continuous annuity factor for a healthy life is the familiar

$$\overline{a}_x^{(\tau)} = \int_0^\infty v^r \cdot {}_r p_x^{(\tau)} \, dr. \tag{14.22}$$

Then the continuous annual premium rate for this contract, payable while healthy, is

$$\overline{P} = \frac{APVB}{\overline{a}_x^{(\tau)}}, \tag{14.23}$$

where $APVB$ denotes the sum of the APVs for Benefits (a), (b), and (c).

Expressions for the reserves follow from the APVs and premium rate. There are two different reserves to consider.

If the insured is still healthy at duration t, which is age $x+t$, we determine the *healthy life reserve* at that time, which we denote by ${}_t^h V$. Prospectively the reserve is the total APV of the three benefits, given by the three equations mentioned above with x replaced by $x+t$, minus the APV of future premiums, which is $\overline{P} \cdot \overline{a}_{x+t}^{(\tau)}$.

If the insured is disabled at duration t, we determine the *disabled life reserve* at that time, which we denote by ${}_t^d V$. Since there are no future premiums after disability occurs, the disabled life reserve is simply the APV of the future benefits. The APV of the future unit disability benefit is

$$ {}^d \overline{a}_{x+t} = \int_0^\infty v^s \cdot {}_s p_{x+t}^d \, ds, \tag{14.24}$$

where the superscript d implies that ${}^d \overline{a}_{x+t}$ is calculated using a survival model appropriate for a disabled person. The APV of the future death-while-disabled benefit is given by Equation (14.13a), with r replaced by t.

Since we have precise expressions for both types of reserve under the Section 14.4.2 disability model, they can be calculated without resorting to approximations, provided we are given a parametric double-decrement model for death and disability while healthy, and a parametric single-decrement model for death while disabled.

The disability model of Section 14.4.3, and illustrated in Figure 14.6, is more complicated than the Section 14.4.2 model due to the possibility of recovery from disability back to the healthy state. We saw in Example 14.11 how we might approximate the probabilities of being either healthy or disabled at sequential discrete intervals, and then used these probabilities to calculate APVs in Example 14.12. The APVs and the premium then allow us to calculate both healthy life and disabled life reserves at duration t of the contract, given whichever state applies.

In the case of a fully continuous model, the reserves can be approximated at sequential discrete durations by using Thiele's differential equation adapted to the multiple-decrement case. Again we consider the disability income model of Section 14.4.3, with unit benefits paid at death while either healthy or disabled and a unit income paid continuously while disabled. As mentioned above, we must consider both the fully continuous healthy life reserve, denoted $_t^h\overline{V}$, and the fully continuous disabled life reserve, denoted $_t^d\overline{V}$.

As we did in Chapters 10 and 11, we analyze the derivative of the reserve function as its rate of change, which is made up of its components of change. For the healthy life reserve, the reserve is increasing due to premium payment and interest earnings, and decreasing due to the decrements of death and disability. Then we have

$$\frac{d}{dt}\,_t^h\overline{V} \;=\; \overline{P}+\delta\cdot\,_t^h\overline{V}-\mu_{x+t}^{(f)}\left(1-\,_t^h\overline{V}\right)-\mu_{x+t}^{(d)}\left(_t^d\overline{V}-\,_t^h\overline{V}\right). \tag{14.25}$$

The first three terms in Equation (14.25) are the same as shown in Exercise 10-23, using the superscript (f) to indicate the force of failure (or mortality) while healthy. The unit benefit is paid at failure and the healthy life reserve is released. If disability occurs at age $x+t$, again the healthy life reserve is released. Instead of paying out a fixed amount at disability, the insurer must establish the then APV of future benefits paid while disabled. This APV is the disabled life reserve at that time, $_t^d\overline{V}$.

The rate of change in the disabled life reserve, given by its derivative, will not contain the premium income term. It will have three decremental terms, one for the unit income paid while disabled, one for death while disabled, and one for recovery. We have

$$\frac{d}{dt}\,_t^d\overline{V} \;=\; \delta\cdot\,_t^d\overline{V}-1-\,^d\mu_{x+t}^{(f)}\left(1-\,_t^d\overline{V}\right)-\,^d\mu_{x+t}^{(r)}\left(_t^h\overline{V}-\,_t^d\overline{V}\right), \tag{14.26}$$

where $^d\mu_{x+t}^{(f)}$ and $^d\mu_{x+t}^{(r)}$ denote the forces of failure (mortality) and recovery, respectively, for a disabled life. In the case of either decrement, the disabled life reserve $_t^d\overline{V}$ is released. The unit failure benefit is paid if failure occurs, and the healthy life reserve is established if recovery occurs.

Since each differential equation contains both reserve functions, no closed form solution for them exists. Instead we use Euler's method just as we did to approximate a solution to Kolmogorov's differential equation in Example 14.10, with one important difference. In Example 14.10 the starting values for the recursion were available at time 0, so the recursion moved *forward* in steps of size Δt. In our current problem, the starting values for the recursion are at the end of the term of coverage, so the recursion moves *backward* in steps of size Δt. The end of the term is time $t=n$ for coverage of a fixed term or time $t=\omega-x$ for whole life coverage. (Without loss of generality we can use n in both cases.)

In the earlier case (see Equation (14.16)) we approximated $f'(x)$ as

$$f'(x) \approx \frac{f(x+\Delta x) - f(x)}{\Delta x}.$$

It is equally reasonable to approximate $f'(x)$ as

$$f'(x) \approx \frac{f(x) - f(x-\Delta x)}{\Delta x}.$$

We use this version to accommodate the backward recursion. Then we can rewrite Equation (14.25) as

$$\frac{{}_{t}^{h}\overline{V} - {}_{t-\Delta t}^{h}\overline{V}}{\Delta t} \approx \overline{P} + \delta \cdot {}_{t}^{h}\overline{V} - \mu_{x+t}^{(f)} \left(1 - {}_{t}^{h}\overline{V}\right) - \mu_{x+t}^{(d)} \left({}_{t}^{d}\overline{V} - {}_{t}^{h}\overline{V}\right),$$

or

$${}_{t-\Delta t}^{h}\overline{V} \approx {}_{t}^{h}\overline{V} - \Delta t \left\{ \overline{P} + \delta \cdot {}_{t}^{h}\overline{V} - \mu_{x+t}^{(f)} \left(1 - {}_{t}^{h}\overline{V}\right) - \mu_{x+t}^{(d)} \left({}_{t}^{d}\overline{V} - {}_{t}^{h}\overline{V}\right) \right\}. \qquad (14.27)$$

By similar reasoning we also rewrite Equation (14.26) as

$${}_{t-\Delta t}^{d}\overline{V} \approx {}_{t}^{d}\overline{V} - \Delta t \left\{ \delta \cdot {}_{t}^{d}\overline{V} - 1 - {}^{d}\mu_{x+t}^{(f)} \left(1 - {}_{t}^{d}\overline{V}\right) - {}^{d}\mu_{x+t}^{(r)} \left({}_{t}^{h}\overline{V} - {}_{t}^{d}\overline{V}\right) \right\}. \qquad (14.28)$$

Then using the starting values ${}_{n}^{h}\overline{V} = {}_{n}^{d}\overline{V} = 0$, the force of interest δ, the premium rate $\overline{P}$, the interval size Δt, and the four force functions, we can recursively calculate values of ${}_{t}^{h}\overline{V}$ and ${}_{t}^{d}\overline{V}$ at all desired values of t. If we renotate the force functions in multi-state model notation we have $\mu_{x+t}^{(f)} = \lambda_{13}(t)$, $\mu_{x+t}^{(d)} = \lambda_{12}(t)$, ${}^{d}\mu_{x+t}^{(f)} = \lambda_{23}(t)$, and ${}^{d}\mu_{x+t}^{(r)} = \lambda_{21}(t)$.

EXAMPLE 14.13

Using the force functions of Example 14.11, along with $\Delta t = .10$, $\delta = .04$, and $\overline{P} = .10$, calculate all values of ${}_{t}^{h}\overline{V}$ and ${}_{t}^{d}\overline{V}$ for a two-year term contract.

SOLUTION

We start at $t = 2.00$. Using the given information we have

$$\begin{aligned}
{}_{1.90}^{h}\overline{V} &= {}_{2.00}^{h}\overline{V} - .10\left\{ \overline{P} + \delta \cdot {}_{2.00}^{h}\overline{V} - \lambda_{13}(2) \cdot \left[1 - {}_{2.00}^{h}\overline{V}\right] - \lambda_{12}(2) \cdot \left[{}_{2.00}^{d}\overline{V} - {}_{2.00}^{h}\overline{V}\right] \right\} \\
&= 0 - .10[.10 + (.04)(0) - (.20)(1-0) - (.40)(0-0)] \\
&= -.10(.10 - .20) = .01
\end{aligned}$$

from Equation (14.27), and

$$\begin{aligned}
{}_{1.90}^{d}\overline{V} &= {}_{2.00}^{d}\overline{V} - .10\left\{\delta \cdot {}_{2.00}^{d}\overline{V} - 1 - \lambda_{23}(2)\cdot\left[1 - {}_{2.00}^{d}\overline{V}\right] - \lambda_{21}(2)\cdot\left[{}_{2.00}^{h}\overline{V} - {}_{2.00}^{d}\overline{V}\right]\right\} \\
&= 0 - .10[(.04)(0) - 1 - (.45)(1-0) - (.50)(0-0)] \\
&= -.10(-1-.45) = .145
\end{aligned}$$

from Equation (14.28). Continuing in this recursive manner we obtain the values shown in the following table:

t	${}_{t}^{h}\overline{V}$	${}_{t}^{d}\overline{V}$
2.00	.00000	0.00000
1.90	.01000	0.14500
1.80	.02503	0.27508
1.70	.04393	0.39229
1.60	.06577	0.49837
1.50	.08977	0.59481
1.40	.11529	0.68288
1.30	.14182	0.76366
1.20	.16894	0.83808
1.10	.19630	0.90694
1.00	.22362	0.97092
0.90	.25067	1.03062
0.80	.27727	1.08654
0.70	.30328	1.13913
0.60	.32857	1.18878
0.50	.35305	1.23582
0.40	.37665	1.28057
0.30	.39930	1.32324
0.20	.42097	1.36407
0.10	.44161	1.40327
0.00	.46121	1.44100

Note that ${}_{0}^{d}\overline{V} = 1.44100$ implies a contract issued to an already-disabled person, which would not occur in practice. Otherwise we have ${}_{0}^{d}\overline{V} = 0$. The reserve ${}_{t}^{d}\overline{V}$ is then set up whenever disability occurs. Since there are no premiums while disabled, as the remaining benefit period shortens, the reserve decreases. The positive value of ${}_{0}^{h}\overline{V}$ in this illustration results primarily from the arbitrarily selected $\overline{P} = .10$ being inappropriately small. The value of $\overline{P}$ that makes ${}_{0}^{h}\overline{V} = {}_{2}^{h}\overline{V} = 0$ is $\overline{P} = .4429$; this is the continuous net benefit premium rate.

We can generalize the process described in this section by allowing the benefit payments to be other than unit amount, and by allowing the benefit amounts, the premium, and/or the force of interest to vary with time. We can also introduce expenses and a gross premium, provided the expenses are paid continuously. (See Exercise 14-21.)

We can also generalize the process to more than three states (see Exercise 14-22).

14.5 DEFINED BENEFIT PENSION PLANS

Another major application of multiple decrements is the *defined benefit pension plan* (DB plan), which is a legal promise created by an employer to provide its employees with a defined amount of pension income during retirement.[12]

Although the retirement benefit is the basic benefit provided by a DB plan, it is not uncommon for a plan to also provide some level of benefit upon the death or disability of an employee, as well as upon withdrawal from the plan due to termination of employment before normal (or early) retirement age. Accordingly, a four-decrement table, of the type described in Section 13.1.1, is often used for DB plan calculations.[13] In this section we adopt the letters r, d, i, and w to denote the decrements of retirement, death, disability, and withdrawal, respectively.

As an application of the general multiple-decrement model, the DB plan can be represented as a multi-state model (see Figure 14.1) with $m = 4$, as shown in Figure 14.9.

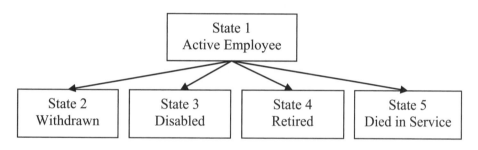

FIGURE 14.9

Note that the arrows are in one direction only. Although it is possible for terminated, disabled, or even retired employees to return to active service, actuarial valuations generally do not anticipate this. If and when a decremented employee does return to active service, the next valuation will reflect the new information.

In the remainder of this section, we focus primarily on the retirement benefit, including the case of retirement earlier than the normal retirement age, and the withdrawal benefit.

14.5.1 NORMAL RETIREMENT BENEFITS

The primary benefit of a DB plan is the *lifetime retirement benefit*, payable starting at the plan's *normal retirement age* (NRA), commonly age 65. The targeted amount of the retirement benefit might be defined as p percent of the employee's projected salary at the time of retirement, and is generally a function of years of service as well. Often the projected average salary over the final, say, three years of employment is used. Then the projected annual benefit, to begin at normal retirement age z, for an employee hired at attained age x, would be

---

[12] An alternative approach, called a *defined contribution plan* (DC plan), obligates the employer only to contribute a defined amount to the plan, rather than guaranteeing a defined benefit.

[13] A multiple-decrement table prepared specifically for use with DB plans is traditionally called a *service table*.

$$PAB_z = .01p \cdot YOS_z \cdot FAS_z, \tag{14.29}$$

where YOS_z denotes the years of service and FAS_z denotes the final average salary at retirement.

The final average salary is estimated by projecting the salary at attained age x to later years by using a set of *salary scale factors*, denoted here by S_k, for $k = x, x+1, \ldots, z-1$. Then if the average is taken over the final three years of employment, the projected final average salary would be

$$FAS_z = \frac{1}{3}\left(\frac{S_{z-3} + S_{z-2} + S_{z-1}}{S_x}\right) \cdot CAS_x, \tag{14.30}$$

where CAS_x denotes the current annual salary at attained age x.

A salary scale could be as simple as a constant percentage increase; for example, setting $S_{20} = 1$ and $S_k = (1.04)^{k-20}$, for $k = 21, 22, \ldots, z-1$, defines a salary scale allowing for a constant annual salary increase of 4%. A more sophisticated salary scale could be derived from a study of salary data.

EXAMPLE 14.14

Consider an employee entering a DB pension plan at age 35, with a current salary of 60,000. The plan guarantees an annual retirement benefit of 2% of final three-year average salary at normal retirement age 65 for each year of service, and uses the 4% constant salary scale model described above. What is the projected annual retirement benefit?

SOLUTION

From Equation (14.30) we find the projected final average salary at age 65 to be

$$
\begin{aligned}
FAS_{65} &= \frac{1}{3}\left(\frac{S_{62} + S_{63} + S_{64}}{S_{35}}\right) \cdot CAS_{35} \\
&= \frac{1}{3}\left(\frac{(1.04)^{42} + (1.04)^{43} + (1.04)^{44}}{(1.04)^{15}}\right) \cdot (60,000) = 180,014.43.
\end{aligned}
$$

Then the projected annual retirement benefit is

$$PAB_{65} = (.02)(30)(180,014.43) = 108,008.66,$$

since we are projecting 30 years of service. ◻

As an alternative to the final average salary method described above, the retirement benefit amount is sometimes based on the employee's projected aggregate career salary. Then for an employee entering a plan at age x, the projected aggregate salary at retirement age z would be

$$PAS_z = \frac{1}{S_x} \cdot \sum_{k=x}^{z-1} S_k \cdot CAS_x. \tag{14.31}$$

Then the projected annual retirement benefit would be defined as

$$PAB_z = .01p \cdot PAS_z. \tag{14.32}$$

Note that years of service are reflected in the aggregate salary, so multiplication by YOS_z is not necessary.

The examples presented thus far refer to an employee at the time of hire. For employees hired in the past, their actual past salaries and service are used to determine their projected benefits. For example, if the final average salary method is used, the benefit for past service is reflected in the YOS_z term and FAS_z is determined from the now-current salary. If the career average salary method is used, the actual total past salaries would be added to the projected future aggregate salary figure before multiplying by .01p to determine the projected annual benefit.

Finally we should note that some plans for hourly workers use a simpler projected annual benefit formula that does not depend on salary, such as one that promises a PAB_z of, say, 600 for each year of service.

With the projected annual benefit to begin at age z now established, we can find the actuarial present value (APV) of the projected benefit, as of attained age x, as

$$APV_x^{NR} = PAB_z \cdot v^{z-x} \cdot {}_{z-x}p_x^{(\tau)} \cdot {}^r\ddot{a}_z^{(12)}. \tag{14.33}$$

In Equation (14.33), ${}_{z-x}p_x^{(\tau)}$ is the survival probability taken from the applicable service table, and ${}^r\ddot{a}_z^{(12)}$ is the APV of the retirement benefits, presumed to be paid monthly, as of age z. The pre-superscript r is used to remind us that the annuity APV is based on survival rates appropriate for retired lives, which might be different from those in the service table.

The annuity factor ${}^r\ddot{a}_z^{(12)}$ in Equation (14.33) suggests that the retirement benefit is paid as a whole life annuity to (z). Alternatively, the form of payment might be life with n years certain (see Example 8.14) or as a joint and last-survivor annuity (see Section 12.2) involving both the retiree and the retiree's spouse. In the latter case, the benefit amount usually decreases if the retiree dies first, but not if the spouse dies first.

If the employee has contributed to the cost of the plan,[14] it is generally provided that if the retiree dies before receiving retirement benefits at least equal to his or her accumulated contributions, then the excess of the accumulated contributions over the retirement benefits paid would be paid to a designated beneficiary. The excess could be paid either in a lump sum (called a *cash refund* arrangement) or by continuing the retirement benefits (called an

---

[14] *Contributory plans* are not very common with private employer DB pension plans today, although they remain popular in plans sponsored by state and local governments.

installment refund arrangement).[15]

14.5.2 EARLY RETIREMENT BENEFITS

It is also customary to provide a retirement benefit to employees who retire earlier than the normal retirement age. A typical rule would allow early retirement at age 55 or after 10 years of service, whichever is later. Note that we distinguish between early retirement and withdrawal, because the benefits associated with the two types of decrement are different.

Suppose an employee is hired at age 25 and terminates employment at age 35. Such employee may be eligible for a withdrawal benefit (see Section 14.5.3), but not a retirement benefit. Conversely, if this person remains in employment to age 55 and terminates then, he or she would qualify for retirement benefits and a withdrawal benefit would not apply. This suggests that at any age k for which $q_k^{(r)} > 0$ (i.e., for which retirement is possible), the service table would show $q_k^{(w)} = 0$.

When an early retirement occurs, the retirement benefit payments might begin immediately, or might be deferred until the NRA. Only salaries and years of service up to the early retirement age (ERA), which we denote by y, would be counted in determining the benefit amount, which is called the *accrued benefit*.

EXAMPLE 14.15

Suppose the employee of Example 14.14 would be eligible for an early retirement benefit if retirement occurs at age 60 or later. Find (a) the projected accrued benefit at early retirement age y, (b) the benefit amount if paid immediately, and (c) the APV of the early retirement benefit.

SOLUTION

(a) Employees tend to retire throughout the year of age, so it is typical to assume retirements in the middle of the year on average. If early retirement is between age y and age $y+1$, the projected final average salary would be determined at age $y+\frac{1}{2}$ as

$$FAS_{y+1/2} = \frac{1}{3}\left(\frac{\frac{1}{2}S_{y-4}+S_{y-3}+S_{y-2}+\frac{1}{2}S_{y-1}}{S_{35}}\right)\cdot CAS_{35},$$

and the projected accrued benefit at age $y+\frac{1}{2}$ would be

$$PAB_{y+1/2} = (.02)\left(y+\frac{1}{2}-35\right)\cdot FAS_{y+1/2},$$

---

[15] Neither cash refund nor installment refund annuities are discussed in this text. The interested reader is referred to Section 17.2 of Bowers, et al. [4].

for $y = 60, 61, 62, 63, 64,$ since there would have been $y + \frac{1}{2} - 35$ years of service.

(b) DB plans generally allow retirement benefits to begin immediately. The accrued benefit amount $PAB_{y+1/2}$ is reduced to reflect that benefits begin earlier and would be expected to continue for more years. Plans often use a simple formula for reducing the benefit, such as a reduction of 5% for each year that retirement precedes the NRA, which approximates the actuarial value of the deferred benefit payable at NRA.[16]

The projected annual retirement benefit payable immediately at age $y + \frac{1}{2}$ will now be $PAB_{y+1/2} \cdot \left[1 - .05\left(65 - y - \frac{1}{2}\right)\right],$ since the accrued benefit at age $y + \frac{1}{2}$ is reduced by 5% for each of $65 - y - \frac{1}{2}$ years.

(c) Then the APV would be

$$APV_{35}^{ER} = \sum_{y=60}^{64} PAB_{y+1/2} \cdot \left[1 - .05\left(65 - y - \frac{1}{2}\right)\right] \cdot v^{y+1/2-35} \cdot {}_{y-35}p_{35}^{(\tau)} \cdot q_y^{(r)} \cdot {}^r\ddot{a}_{y+1/2}^{(12)}, \quad (14.34)$$

since payments begin at age $y + \frac{1}{2}$ rather than at age 65. Note that the survival factor for surviving to age y is taken from the plan's service table, but the annuity factor is taken from a table appropriate for retired persons. ❏

14.5.3 WITHDRAWAL AND OTHER BENEFITS

In the past, employees who quit before NRA or ERA could forfeit all of their accrued pension benefit, but employers today generally pay 100% of such accrued benefits if an employee has at least five years of service. The concept of earning a withdrawal benefit is called *vesting*, and the portion of the accrued benefit taken into account is called the *vesting percentage*.

Some pension plans provide immediate benefits to employees who become disabled while working. Five years of service are often required for this benefit. It is valued similar to early retirement benefits, except that the annuity factor would be based on a life table appropriate for disabled persons. At the very least, a disabled person must receive the vested benefit available to a withdrawing employee (or retiring employee, if eligible).

Pension plans must provide an immediate survivor annuity upon the death of a married employee, if death occurs after the earliest retirement age. The APV formula would be similar to the early retirement APV above, except for the benefit amount, and the annuity factor would be based on a single life table appropriate for the spouse.

---

[16] If the reduction is less than 5% per year, sometimes offered to encourage early retirement, we say that the early retirement benefit has been *subsidized*.

EXAMPLE 14.16

Again consider the DB plan and the employee of Examples 14.14 and 14.15. Find the APV of the withdrawal benefit, assuming the five-year vesting rule.

SOLUTION

Assuming employees take their withdrawal benefit at NRA, the APV at age 35 is

$$APV_{35}^{W} = \sum_{y=40}^{59} PAB_{y+1/2} \cdot v^{30} \cdot {}_{y-35}p_{35}^{(\tau)} \cdot q_{y}^{(w)} \cdot {}_{65-y-1/2}^{w}p_{y+1/2} \cdot {}^{r}\ddot{a}_{65}^{(12)}. \qquad (14.35)$$

The limits on the summation show there is no benefit for withdrawal at any age $y < 40$, nor at any age $y \geq 60$, since termination at those ages is considered early retirement rather than withdrawal. ☐

As an alternative to deferred payments starting at NRA, some DB plans allow a reduced benefit starting at ERA. They may also allow the value of the withdrawal benefit at NRA to be taken as a lump sum.

14.5.4 FUNDING AND RESERVING

The APV of a benefit under a DB pension plan can be interpreted as the net single benefit premium required to fund the eventual benefit. For the plan we have been considering in Examples 14.14 through 14.16, the total APV for our employee hired at age 35 would be the sum of the APVs for each of the decrements.

It is not likely that the benefits would be funded by paying the entire APV_{35}^{T} at the time of hire. Rather the benefits could be funded over the employee's working lifetime. For example, they could be determined by the equivalence principle first encountered in Chapter 9. In pension terminology, the net annual funding payment is called the *normal cost* of the DB plan. Using the equivalence principle, we have

$$NC_{x}^{EAN} = \frac{APV_{x}^{T}}{\ddot{a}_{x:\overline{z-x}|}^{(\tau)}}, \qquad (14.36)$$

where x is the employee's age at entry into the DB plan and z is the normal retirement age. Note that the annuity factor in the denominator is calculated from the plan's service table, so NC_{x} is payable only while the employee is active in the plan. When the normal cost is determined in this way we say that the *entry age normal cost method* (EAN) is being used.

For an employee still active at duration t, the status of the funding plan, which we call the net benefit reserve (see Chapter 10),[17] can be determined prospectively as

---

[17] The term "reserve" is not generally used in pension terminology.

$$_tV_x^T = APV_{x+t}^T - NC_x^{EAN} \cdot \ddot{a}_{x+t:\overline{z-x-t}|}^{(\tau)} \tag{14.37a}$$

or retrospectively as

$$_tV_x^T = NC_x^{EAN} \cdot \ddot{s}_{x:\overline{t}|}^{(\tau)}, \tag{14.37b}$$

if there have been no past benefits as of duration t. (If there could have been past benefits, their actuarial accumulated value would need to be subtracted.)

The reader should recognize that the level normal costs described above are analogous to level net benefit premiums as described in Chapter 9. An alternative to level normal costs would be to fund each year the portion of the eventual benefit that accrues each year. This approach, which is called the *unit credit cost method* (UC), can be seen to be analogous to funding a traditional insurance benefit with a series of one-year term insurance net premiums.

For our sample career average salary plan with a normal retirement benefit of 2% of career average salary for each year of service, the benefit that accrues in the upcoming year is $.02CAS_x$. For the sample final average salary plan, it is $AB_{x+1} - AB_x$, which is larger since it must update the past accruals to the current salary level.[18] This accrual replaces the *PAB* term in each of Equations (14.33) through (14.35) to determine the unit credit normal cost. (The normal cost is just the APV of the current year's accrual.) For example, at any attained age x, the APV of the benefit that accrued between ages x and $x+1$ would be

$$APV_x^{NR} = (AB_{x+1} - AB_x) \cdot v^{z-x} \cdot {}_{z-x}p_x^{(\tau)} \cdot {}^r\ddot{a}_z^{(12)}.^{[19]} \tag{14.38}$$

The total unit credit normal cost, which we denote by NC_x^{UC}, is the sum of the APVs for the several decrements. If it is contributed each year, then the plan is being funded by the unit credit cost method.

If experience is the same as forecasted by the assumptions, then the plan is *fully funded*, which means the plan holds assets equal to the total APV of benefits accrued at the current date. That amount is called the *accrued liability*; it can be determined by calculating the total APV using the accrued benefit instead of using the accrual in the same formulas.[20] However, it is unlikely that experience will be exactly as assumed, so assets may be more or less than the accrued liability under the unit credit cost method. If assets are less than the accrued liability, the plan is *underfunded*. The employer can make an additional contribution to amortize the underfunding over n years, according to funding rules specified in the regulations addressing DB plans.[21]

---

[18] See Exercise 14-26 for a numerical illustration of this.

[19] The reader should carefully note the difference between APV_x^{NR} as defined by Equation (14.38) and the one defined by Equation (14.33). The earlier one is the APV at age x of *all future projected benefits*, whereas the one defined by Equation (14.38) is for the accrued benefit of the current year only.

[20] The unit credit accrued liability is less than the entry age liability (or reserve), because the level entry age normal cost needs to build up a margin for when the increasing cost of benefit accruals exceeds the level normal cost.

[21] Readers specializing in pension plans at a later point in their actuarial education will study these pension regulations in considerable detail.

14.6 EXERCISES

14.1 Actuarial Present Value

14-1 A company hires all new employees at age 25. An employee can leave the company via death while employed (Decrement 1), resignation prior to age 65 (Decrement 2), or retirement at age 65. The company provides the following benefits for its employees:

(a) Employees who retire at age 65 receive continuous retirement income at an annual rate of 500 for each year of employment with the company.

(b) Employees who die while employed receive a one-time death benefit of 200,000 at the precise time of death.

(c) Employees who resign prior to age 65, but survive on to age 65, receive continuous retirement income at an annual rate of 400 for each year of employment with the company (including partial years).

Write expressions involving continuous annuities and/or integrals for the APV at time of hire for each of the three benefits.

14.2 Asset Shares

14-2 Show that

$$_k AS = \left[_{k-1}AS + G(1-r_k) - e_k \right](1+i) - q^{(1)}_{x+k-1} \cdot (b_k^{(1)} - {_k}AS) - q^{(2)}_{x+k-1} \cdot (b_k^{(2)} - {_k}AS).$$

(This relationship shows that the difference between the withdrawal value and the asset share is important to the progression of the asset share values. If the asset share were paid as a withdrawal value, then the asset share values would progress independently of the withdrawal risk.)

14.3 Non-Forfeiture Options

14-3 A whole life contract of face amount 100,000 is issued to (30). The 20th year cash value is 90% of the NLP reserve. The insured has previously borrowed 5,000 against the policy. Using the life table in Appendix A with 6% interest, find the cash value payable for surrender of the contract at the end of its 20th year.

14-4 If the policyholder in Exercise 14-3 elects the reduced paid-up insurance option at the time of surrender instead of taking the cash value, how much reduced paid-up insurance could be purchased?

14-5   Show that

$$_tW_x = 1 - \frac{P_x}{P_{x+t}}.$$

14-6   For a fully continuous whole life policy, the analogous formula to Equation (14.9) for the fully discrete case is

$$_t\overline{W}(\overline{A}_x) = \frac{_t\overline{V}(\overline{A}_x)}{\overline{A}_{x+t}}.$$

Show that

$$\frac{d}{dt}\,_t\overline{W}(\overline{A}_x) = \frac{\overline{P}(\overline{A}_x) - \mu_{x+t}\left[1 - _t\overline{W}(\overline{A}_x)\right]}{\overline{A}_{x+t}}.$$

14-7   A 20-year endowment contract of face amount 100,000 is issued to (40) and surrendered at age 55. The cash value at that time is 60,000. If the extended term insurance option is selected, find the amount of pure endowment payable at age 60 using the life table in Appendix A with 6% interest.

14.4 Multi-State Model Representation, with Illustrations

14-8   (a) Referring to the model in Example 14.7, solve the Kolmogorov differential equation for $_n p_{02}^{(0)}$, the probability that a person issued this insurance at age x at time 0 will have withdrawn from the contract by time n, and translate the result into standard actuarial notation.

(b) Use the data given in Example 14.3 to evaluate this probability at $n = 3$.

14-9   Suppose the model of Example 14.8 involved three partners instead of two. When represented in multi-state form, how many states are in the model (a) if death and retirement continue to be the only decrements, or (b) if disability is also a decrement? (In both cases, let State 0 denote the status of all partners being alive, healthy, and active (not retired).)

14-10 For the model of Figure 14.5, (a) solve the Kolmogorov differential equation for $_n p_{11}^{(t)}$, the probability that a person alive and healthy at time t will still be alive and healthy at time $t + n$, and (b) translate the result into standard actuarial notation.

14-11 Repeat Exercise 14-10 to (a) solve for $_n p_{13}^{(t)}$, the probability that a person alive and healthy at time t will be not alive at time $t + n$, and (b) translate the result into standard actuarial notation.

14-12 Repeat Exercise 14-10 to (a) solve for $_n p_{23}^{(t)}$, the probability that a person alive but disabled at time t will be not alive at time $t + n$, and (b) translate the result into standard actuarial notation.

14-13 The model of Figure 14.6 can arise in many other applications other than disability allowing for recovery. For example, a magazine publisher models all persons who ever subscribed to its magazine as those still subscribing (State 1), those no longer subscribing (State 2), and those former subscribers who are now deceased (State 3). Former subscribers who wish to become active subscribers again are encouraged to do so. The model is viewed as a homogeneous discrete-time Markov Chain, with matrix of annual transition probabilities given by

$$\mathbf{P} = \begin{vmatrix} .65 & .32 & .03 \\ .25 & .72 & .03 \\ 0 & 0 & 1 \end{vmatrix}.$$

Find the probability that a new subscriber at time 0 will be alive but a non-subscriber just after time 3.

14-14 A person is currently employed at time 0, which we call State 1. Let State 2 denote unemployment and State 3 denote deceased. The transition forces between states are as follows:

(i) $\lambda_{12}(s) = .20 + .0002s^2$

(ii) $\lambda_{13}(s) = \lambda_{23}(s) = .05$

(iii) $\lambda_{21}(s) = .08 - .04s$

(iv) $\lambda_{31}(s) = \lambda_{32}(s) = 0$

(a) Draw the transition state diagram for this model.

(b) Using one-year time-steps ($\Delta r = 1$) to approximate the solutions to the Kolmogorov differential equation, estimate $_r p_{11}^{(0)}$ and $_r p_{12}^{(0)}$ for $r = 1, 2, \ldots, 20$.

(c) Use half-year time-steps to estimate the same functions for $r = 0.5, 1.0, \ldots, 10.0$, and compare the results for $_{10} p_{11}^{(0)}$ and $_{10} p_{12}^{(0)}$ to those obtained in part (b). Which result should be closer to the true solution?

(d) Use tenth-year time-steps to estimate the same functions for $r = 0.1, 0.2, \ldots, 10.0$, and compare the results for $_{10} p_{11}^{(0)}$ and $_{10} p_{12}^{(0)}$ to those obtained in parts (b) and (c).

14-15 Referring to Exercise 14-14, a 20-year insurance contract is issued that pays 1400 at the end of each month that the person is unemployed.

(a) For this contract, what is the natural time-step to use to approximate a solution to the Kolmogorov differential equation?

(b) Assuming a nominal interest rate of $i^{(12)} = .04,$ find the APV at issue of the unemployment benefit.

14-16 Immediately after the contract of Exercise 14-15 is issued, the person becomes disabled, so the company issuing the contract must adjust its reserve to reflect the changed APV of the contract. Find the APV of the unemployment insurance for a person who is currently unemployed at time 0.

14-17 For the insurance of Exercise 14-15, suppose the insured is required to pay a level premium at the beginning of each month that she is employed. Find the net benefit premium P.

14-18 Suppose the insurance of Exercise 14-15 also pays 50,000 at the end of the month of death if the insured is unemployed at time of death. Find the APV for this contract.

14-19 For the model of Section 14.4.4, as illustrated in Figure 14.8, find the probability that a person in State 1 (ILU) at time 0 will be in State 1 at the end of the third month.

14-20 Repeat Exercise 14-19, this time for the probability that a person in State 1 at time 0 will be in State 3 at the end of the third month.

14-21 Generalize the Thiele differential equations, given by Equations (14.25) and (14.26), to allow the benefits, premiums, and force of interest to vary with time, and to allow for percent-of-premium and continuous fixed expenses.

14-22 The most general case considers that we have m distinct states, with premium paid continuously at rate $\bar{G}_t^{(i)}$ while in State i (with $\bar{G}_t^{(i)} = 0$ for some values of i), percent-of-premium expense rate $r_t^{(i)}$ at time t if in State i, fixed expense payable continuously at rate $\bar{e}_t^{(i)}$ at time t if in State i, benefit paid continuously at rate $\bar{b}_t^{(i)}$ if in State i at time t, single-sum benefit of amount $b_t^{(ij)}$ paid for transition from State i to State j at time t, and interest credited to the reserves at force of interest δ_t at time t regardless of state. Let $_t\bar{V}^{(i)}$ denote the reserve at time t if the process is in State i. State the general form of Thiele's differential equation in this general case.

14.5 Defined Benefit Pension Plans

14-23 Consider a newly hired employee age 30, earning 100,000 in the first year of employment. Regular salary increases are assumed to be 4% per year; in addition, employees are assumed to receive merit increases of 6% at each of their first three employment anniversaries. The pension benefit formula is 1% of the final five-year average salary per year of service.

    (a)   Find the final five-year average salary.

    (b)   Find the projected pension benefit at age 65.

    (c)   Find the employee's replacement ratio, defined as the pension benefit divided by the final year's salary.

    (d)   What would a 1% career average benefit be as a percentage of this final five-year average benefit?

14-24 Consider a worker taking early retirement at age 55 under a plan where the NRA is 65, and the early retirement benefit is the actuarial equivalent of the benefit at NRA. The equivalence is determined at interest rate 6% and the life table shown in Appendix A.

    (a)   Find the age 55 early retirement reduction factor.

    (b)   What is the informal "5% per year early" factor described in Example 14.15(b)?

14-25 Consider a newly hired employee age 51. The salary at hire is 100,000 and is projected to increase by 4% per year. Vesting occurs after five years of service, and no benefits will be paid before that time. The normal retirement age is 65, and is mandatory at that time so $q_{65}^{(r)} = 1$; the retirement benefit is 1% of final three-year average salary per year of service. The employee is eligible for early retirement at age 61, with a 3% reduction per year early. The withdrawal benefit is the then accrued benefit otherwise payable at NRA. The disability benefit is the then accrued benefit payable immediately, without reduction, if the employee has at least five years of service. The death benefit requires ten years of service, and is set at 50% of the then accrued benefit, reduced as for early retirement. Assume the surviving beneficiary is three years younger than the employee.

Write the APV formulas for each of (a) normal retirement, (b) early retirement, (c) withdrawal, (d) disability, and (e) death. Assume early retirement, withdrawal, disability, or death occur half way through the year of age, on average.

14-26 Assume the employee of Exercise 14-25 is now exact age 56, with a salary of 150,000 in the year from age 55 to age 56 and a salary of 156,000 in the year from age 56 to age 57. Determine each of the following:

    (a)   The benefit accrual for the year from age 56 to age 57.

    (b)   The unit credit normal cost.

    (c)   The accrued liability under the unit credit cost method.

PART THREE

MODELS FOR
INTEREST RATE RISKS

For all of the values calculated thus far in the text, we have assumed a fixed interest rate to apply. In the chapters contained in this part, we relax that assumption and consider the effect of variable interest rates. This notion is described in detail in Chapter 15.

When an insurer makes a contractual promise to pay certain benefits, and calculates a premium rate to fund those benefits, it assumes that the reserve funds it holds will earn a certain rate of investment return. If they fail to earn the assumed rate, this works to the insurer's financial disadvantage. In this case we say that the insurer assumes the *interest rate risk*, or the *investment risk*. This is a characteristic of the traditional insurance and annuity contracts considered in Part Two of the text.

In Chapters 16 and 17 we present a class of modern insurance and annuity contracts, respectively. In both cases the applicable interest rates might be allowed to vary according to certain external conditions. Due to the influence of the external conditions, these insurance and annuity products are often referred to as *interest-sensitive* products.

We will also see that, in certain cases, the interest rate risk can be transferred, in whole or in part, from the insurer to the insured or annuitant.

CHAPTER FIFTEEN

MODELS WITH VARIABLE INTEREST RATES

Thus far in the text, when calculating the actuarial present value (APV) for contingent payment models, including insurance products, we have treated time until failure and mode of failure as random variables. But we have always assumed that a single interest rate was valid throughout the life of the model, however long that might be. It can be risky to assume that interest rates will remain constant at today's rates. Indeed some insurance companies around the world have experienced severe losses as a result of pricing products at interest rates that proved to be too optimistic.

In this chapter we address contingent payment models using interest rates that vary with time. Sections 15.1 and 15.2 address models with deterministic contingent payment amounts evaluated using non-deterministic interest rates. The term structure of interest rates and implied forward rates of interest are introduced in Sections 15.3 and 15.4.

The treatment of topics in Chapter 15 follows a heuristic approach. To simplify the discussion in Sections 15.1 and 15.2, we make the assumption that the market consists only of *one-period securities*. For our discussion of interest rates, the only securities available for investment are one-period bonds that pay a single coupon plus principal at the end of the period. This assumption enables us to introduce features of interest rate variability without having to deal with issues such as a term structure or partial-period payments. In addition, there is no distinction (in the absence of default) between the interest rate of a bond and the rate of return on that bond. In Sections 15.3 and 15.4 we broaden the discussion to include multi-period bonds, including those with partial-period payments (coupons). This will enable us to develop the term structure of spot interest rates along with implied forward rates of interest.

15.1 ACTUARIAL PRESENT VALUES USING VARIABLE INTEREST RATES

Interest rates in the United States have varied substantially over time. Table 15.1 shows sample one-year U.S. Treasury interest rates between 1962 and 2009.[1] This table gives a good indication of just how variable interest rates can be over time. In this section, we discuss one method for incorporating this variability into calculating the actuarial present value for contingent payment models. This method involves the construction of *interest rate scenarios* for the future. An interest rate scenario is a possible future path for interest rates. For example, Table 15.2 shows three illustrative interest rate scenarios for one-year interest rates in the first five years of a contingent contract. Each row represents a different scenario for the one-year interest rate in each year over the next five years. The pre-subscript j on the interest rate symbol

---

[1] Source: www.ustreas.gov.

indicates the scenario from which that rate was taken. For example, $_3i_3 = .04$ means that the interest rate in the third interest rate scenario in the third year is 4%.

TABLE 15.1

Year	Rate	Year	Rate	Year	Rate
1962	3.10%	1978	8.34%	1994	5.32%
1963	3.36	1979	10.65	1995	5.94
1964	3.85	1980	12.00	1996	5.52
1965	4.15	1981	14.80	1997	5.63
1966	5.20	1982	12.27	1998	5.05
1967	4.88	1983	9.58	1999	5.08
1968	5.69	1984	10.91	2000	6.11
1969	7.12	1985	8.42	2001	3.49
1970	6.90	1986	6.45	2002	2.00
1971	4.89	1987	6.77	2003	1.24
1972	4.95	1988	7.65	2004	1.31
1973	7.32	1989	8.53	2005	2.79
1974	8.20	1990	7.89	2006	4.38
1975	6.78	1991	5.86	2007	5.00
1976	5.88	1992	3.89	2008	3.17
1977	6.08	1993	3.43	2009	0.40

TABLE 15.2

Scenario j	$_ji_1$	$_ji_2$	$_ji_3$	$_ji_4$	$_ji_5$
1	6%	7%	8%	9%	10%
2	6	6	6	6	6
3	6	5	4	3	2

EXAMPLE 15.1

For each of the three interest rate scenarios in Table 15.2, find the actuarial present value of a five-year pure endowment issued at age $x = 65$ for amount $1000. The mortality rates for each year of age are $q_{65} = .03$, $q_{66} = .04$, $q_{67} = .05$, $q_{68} = .06$, and $q_{69} = .07$.

SOLUTION

In each scenario, the APV is

$$1000\,_5E_{65} = 1000(_jv^5 \cdot {}_5p_{65}),$$

where $_jv^5$ represents five years of discounting at interest rates given by Scenario j. Regardless of the chosen scenario,

$$_5p_{65} = (.97)(.96)(.95)(.94)(.93) = .7734.$$

We can find $_1v^5$, for example, as

$$_1v^5 = \left(\frac{1}{1.06}\right)\left(\frac{1}{1.07}\right)\left(\frac{1}{1.08}\right)\left(\frac{1}{1.09}\right)\left(\frac{1}{1.10}\right) = .6809,$$

so the APV under Scenario 1 is $(1000)(.7734)(.6809) = 526.61$. Under Scenarios 2 and 3 the APV's are 577.93 and 635.97, respectively. (The reader should verify these results as an exercise.) □

We can imagine that an insurer who has priced a pure endowment contract assuming level interest rates of 6% (Scenario 2) will be unhappy if it chooses to invest the net single premium in one-year bonds, and the interest rates then emerge similarly to Scenario 3.[2]

EXAMPLE 15.2

Using the same mortality and interest assumptions as in Example 15.1, find the actuarial present value for a five-year term insurance of unit amount issued at age $x = 65$, with benefit paid at the end of the year of failure. Find a separate APV for each of the three scenarios.

SOLUTION

We adapt Equation (7.8) to find the actuarial present value for the five-year term insurance under Scenario j, and we denote this APV by $_jA^1_{65:\overline{5}|}$.

TABLE 15.3

t	Year t Rate	$_1v^t$	$_{t-1|}q_{65}$	$_1v^t \cdot {}_{t-1|}q_{65}$
1	.06	.9434	.0300	.0283
2	.07	.8817	.0388	.0342
3	.08	.8164	.0466	.0380
4	.09	.7490	.0531	.0398
5	.10	.6809	.0582	.0396
$_1A^1_{65:\overline{5}|}$				.1799

---

[2] In practice, the situation is more complicated than that presented here, because the insurer will generally try to invest in securities with a maturity similar to that of the product from which the net single premium arose. In this case the insurer will only have to worry about current interest rates for bond cash flows requiring reinvestment. However, for some very long-term contracts such as whole life contingent annuities, whole life insurance, or long term care insurance, this problem can be serious.

The results of the calculation for Scenario 1 are shown in Table 15.3 in spreadsheet form. Note how the term v^k in Equation (7.8), which assumes a constant interest rate, is generalized to $_jv^k = \prod_{t=1}^{k}(1+ _ji_t)^{-1}$ in the case of the jth variable interest rate scenario. The APV under Scenario 1 is $_1A^1_{65:\overline{5}|} = .1799.$ (The reader should repeat the steps depicted in Table 15.3 under Scenarios 2 and 3 to verify that $_2A^1_{65:\overline{5}|} = .1875$ and $_3A^1_{65:\overline{5}|} = .1958.$) Note that the APV is higher for the lower interest rate scenarios. ❐

15.2 DETERMINISTIC INTEREST RATE SCENARIOS

Interest rate scenarios used in actuarial analysis are of two distinct types. *Deterministic scenarios*, described in this section, are determined *a priori* and are often used to "stress" a product's profitability in the event future interest rates are unfavorable. Scenarios of this type are sometimes prescribed by regulatory agencies to provide a test of sensitivity to interest rates that is common across products and companies. *Stochastic scenarios* are scenarios that are created using a stochastic interest rate simulator based on an assumed probability distribution for future interest rates.

We address the deterministic scenarios in this section by studying a sample regulatory policy designed to test the interest sensitivity of insurance products. If a product "fails" the interest sensitivity test, the company selling the product must hold additional capital as contingent funds for adverse changes in interest rates. Although the example here is fictional, similar deterministic scenarios are performed in some jurisdictions as part of cash flow testing of products for interest sensitivity.

EXAMPLE 15.3

An annuity company sells the following two products:

(a) A five-year annual payment temporary immediate annuity

(b) A five-year pure endowment

The national regulatory authority requires the following two-step interest rate test in order to determine if the annuity company must hold additional capital:

(1) The net single premium (NSP) for each product is calculated under three deterministic interest rate scenarios:

(i)   Rates remain level at the current rate.
(ii) Rates rise 1% per year until they reach twice the current rate, and then remain level in succeeding years.
(iii) Rates fall 1% per year until they reach one-half the current rate, and then remain level in succeeding years.

(2) If the NSP under the falling interest rate scenario is 5% or more above the NSP in the level rate case, the company must hold additional capital.

If the probability of death in any given year remains constant at $q_x = .02$ and the current interest rate is 6%, determine whether this annuity company must hold additional capital for either product.

SOLUTION

(a) For the five-year temporary immediate annuity, we first calculate the NSP (or APV) in the level rate case, using Equation (8.21). We obtain

$$_l a_{x:\overline{5}|} = \sum_{t=1}^{5} {}_l v^t \cdot {}_t p_x = \sum_{t=1}^{5} \left(\frac{1}{1.06}\right)^t \cdot (.98)^t = 3.9756,$$

where the pre-subscript l denotes the level interest rate case. For the falling interest rate case, denoted by the pre-subscript f, the NSP is given by

$$_f a_{x:\overline{5}|} = \sum_{t=1}^{5} {}_f v^t \cdot {}_t p_x = \sum_{t=1}^{5} {}_f v^t \cdot (.98)^t.$$

The calculation is summarized in Table 15.4 on the following page. The reader should repeat the steps depicted in Table 15.4 to calculate the APV under the rising interest rate scenario, obtaining the value $_r a_{x:\overline{5}|} = 3.8461$. Since the falling interest rate scenario does not produce an APV more than 5% greater than under the level rate case, the annuity company does not need to hold additional reserves for its five-year temporary immediate annuity product.

TABLE 15.4

t	Year t Rate	$_f v^t$	$_t p_x$	$_f v^t \cdot {}_t p_x$
1	.06	.9434	.9800	.9245
2	.05	.8985	.9604	.8629
3	.04	.8639	.9412	.8131
4	.03	.8388	.9224	.7737
5	.03	.8143	.9039	.7360
	$_f a_{x:\overline{5}|}$			**4.1102**

(b) For the five-year pure endowment, we again calculate first the APV in the level interest case, obtaining

$$_l A_{x:\overline{5}|}^{\ 1} = {}_l v^5 \cdot {}_5 p_x = \left(\frac{1}{1.06}\right)^5 \cdot (.98)^5 = .6755.$$

Under the falling interest rate scenario, we have $_f v^5 = .8143$ (from Table 15.4) along with the value $_5 p_x = (.98)^5 = .9039$, so the APV for the five-year pure endowment is $(.8143)(.9039) = .7361$. The ratio of the falling rate APV to the level rate APV is $\frac{.7361}{.6755} = 1.0897$.

Since the falling rate APV is more that 5% above the level rate APV, the annuity company is required to hold additional capital for each five-year pure endowment product that it sells. ◻

15.3   SPOT INTEREST RATES AND THE TERM STRUCTURE OF INTEREST RATES

We now drop the assumption made in Sections 15.1 and 15.2 that the market consists only of one-period securities, and move to a more realistic set of investment products. We assume that it is possible to buy interest-bearing securities of varying maturities. Also, we assume that some of these interest-bearing securities make periodic interest payments every six months and make an interest and principal payment at maturity. For the sake of simplicity, we assume that all of these securities are risk-free (i.e., they are certain to pay interest and principal with no chance of default), and we refer to all of them as *bonds*. Bonds with periodic interest payments are called *coupon bonds* whereas bonds with no periodic payments and a single payment at maturity are called *zero-coupon bonds*. There is a large market in United States Treasury securities fitting these descriptions.

Table 15.5 shows available interest rates for coupon-bearing treasury securities of varying maturities on a particular date.[3]

TABLE 15.5

Maturity (in years)	Nominal Annual Yield for Coupon-bearing Bonds ($i^{(2)}$)
0.5	2.44%
1.0	2.60
1.5	2.76
2.0	2.93

This table suggests that on the day in question, we could expect to purchase a treasury security with a maturity of six months at a yield of 2.44%.[4] In other words, for an investment of $1000, we would expect to receive $1012.20 in six months. Note that the coupon payment, made in addition to the principal, is half the stated yield. A one-year bond purchased the same day would pay $13 in six months and $1013 at the end of one year.

---

[3] Source: Daily Treasury Yield Curve Rates at www.ustreas.gov; 1.5 year yield is interpolated.

[4] In reality, such a security with exact yield and maturity dates may not be available on that day.

Similarly, a two-year bond would entitle the purchaser to three semi-annual payments of $14.65 and a final payment of $1014.65.

The first important feature of this table is that bonds with differing maturities offer differing rates of interest. The extra yield for longer-term bonds reflects the loss of liquidity that investors suffer by committing their money for a longer period of time, and can be thought of as a type of *liquidity premium*. Differences in yield also reflect market expectations for what the future short-term rates of interest will be. On occasion, expectations for lower short-term rates in the future will offset the liquidity premium and longer maturities will have lower yields than shorter maturities.

A second important feature of the table is that there is an implied set of zero-coupon bond interest rates for each maturity listed in the table, which can be derived from the coupon-bearing bond yields using a method called *bootstrapping*. First, the zero-coupon bond yield for a maturity of six-months must equal that of the coupon-bearing bond, since both consists of only a single payment at that maturity. Therefore the nominal annual yield, convertible semiannually, for a six-month zero-coupon bond, denoted $z_{0.5}$, is $z_{0.5} = 2.440\%$, or 1.220% as an effective semiannual rate.

To calculate the yield for a zero-coupon bond which matures in one year, we use the six-month zero-coupon rate to value the six-month coupon payment and the original price of the bond to determine the implied one-year zero-coupon rate. For example, the one-year bond described above pays $13 in six months and $1013 in one year for the price of $1000. Therefore the implied one-year zero-coupon yield, denoted $z_{1.0}$, must satisfy

$$1000 = \frac{13}{1.01220} + \frac{1013}{\left(1+\frac{z_{1.0}}{2}\right)^2},$$

where $.01220$ is effective semiannual and $z_{1.0}$ is nominal annual, convertible semiannually. From this we obtain $z_{1.0} = 2.601\%$. Similarly, $z_{1.5}$ must satisfy

$$1000 = \frac{13.80}{1.01220} + \frac{13.80}{\left(1+\frac{.02601}{2}\right)^2} + \frac{1013.80}{\left(1+\frac{z_{1.5}}{2}\right)^3}.$$

(The reader should note that the one-year zero-coupon rate was used for that maturity, rather than the one-year coupon-bearing rate.) From this we obtain $z_{1.5} = 2.763\%$. Finally, using

$$1000 = \frac{14.65}{1.01220} + \frac{14.65}{\left(1+\frac{.02601}{2}\right)^2} + \frac{14.65}{\left(1+\frac{.02763}{2}\right)^3} + \frac{1014.65}{\left(1+\frac{z_{2.0}}{2}\right)^4},$$

we determine that $z_{2.0} = 2.936\%$. In summary, the bootstrap method produces the results shown in Table 15.6.

Table 15.6

Maturity (in years)	Nominal Annual Yield for Coupon-bearing Bonds	Nominal Annual Yield for Zero-coupon Bonds
0.5	2.44%	2.440%
1.0	2.60	2.601
1.5	2.76	2.763
2.0	2.93	2.936

Regarding Table 15.6, the dependence of available yields on years to maturity is referred to as the *term structure of interest rates*. The associated zero-coupon bond rates are often referred to as *spot rates*. Once a set of spot rates has been obtained, it is easy to value any set of cash flows, whether or not those cash flows are uniform.

Example 15.4

To finance the construction of an auditorium, a college has agreed to make the following payments at the following maturity times:

Payment	$200,000	$50,000	$50,000	$100,000
Maturity	Today	6 months	12 months	24 months

Using the term structure of interest rates in Table 15.6, calculate the net present value of these payments.

Solution

We directly find

$$NPV = 200,000 + \frac{50,000}{1.01220} + \frac{50,000}{\left(1+\frac{.02601}{2}\right)^2} + \frac{100,000}{\left(1+\frac{.02936}{2}\right)^4} = 392,459.12. \qquad \square$$

Example 15.5

A client age 60 purchases a five-year term life insurance policy that will pay $1,000,000 at the end of the year of death. The client will fund the policy with level annual premiums, and the insurance company has the ability to lock in appropriate forward rates of interest on those premiums. Using the information in Table 15.7, calculate the net level annual premium for the policy.

Table 15.7

Maturity (in years)	Annual Yield for Zero-coupon Bonds	x	q_x
1.0	3.0%	60	.02
2.0	4.0	61	.03
3.0	5.0	62	.04
4.0	6.0	63	.05
5.0	7.0	64	.06

SOLUTION

The most straightforward solution to this problem is to calculate the APV of the premium payments and set it equal to the APV of the insurance death benefit, using the equivalence principle. For a level annual premium, P, the APV of premium is

$$P \cdot \ddot{a}_{60:\overline{5}|} = P(1 + vp_{60} + v^2\,_2p_{60} + v^3\,_3p_{60} + v^4\,_4p_{60}),$$

where each v^t value is calculated using the t-year spot rate. Using this and the mortality rates shown above, we have

$$P \cdot \ddot{a}_{60:\overline{5}|} = P\left[1 + \frac{.98}{1.03} + \frac{(.98)(.97)}{(1.04)^2} + \frac{(.98)(.97)(.96)}{(1.05)^3} + \frac{(.98)(.97)(.96)(.95)}{(1.06)^4}\right].$$

From this we find the APV of the premiums to be $4.3054P$. The APV of the death benefit is

$$A_{60:\overline{5}|}^1 = vq_{60} + v^2 p_{60} \cdot q_{61} + v^3\,_2p_{60} \cdot q_{62} + v^4\,_3p_{60} \cdot q_{63} + v^5\,_4p_{60} \cdot q_{64},$$

where, again, spot interest rates are used. (As an exercise, the reader should verify that $A_{60:\overline{5}|}^1 = .1527$.) Then the net level premium is

$$P = \frac{(1,000,000)(.1527)}{4.3054} = 35,467.09. \qquad \square$$

15.4 FORWARD INTEREST RATES

For this section, we assume a financial environment in which investors can buy and sell zero-coupon bonds that pay interest at current spot rates in any dollar amount and with no transaction costs. In such an environment, current spot rates imply another set of interest rates that can be locked in today for future deposits. For example, suppose an investor simultaneously undertakes the following pair of transactions:

Transaction A: Buy a $1000 par value two-year zero-coupon bond paying 2.96% interest.

Transaction B: Sell a $1000 par value one-year zero-coupon bond paying 2.62% interest.

With this pair of transactions, the investor has a net cash flow of zero today. In one year he must pay principal and interest on the one-year bond, and in two years he will receive principal and interest on the two-year bond. The resulting net cash flows experienced by the investor are shown in Table 15.8.

TABLE 15.8

Time (in years)	Net Cash Flow
0	$ 0.00
1	− 1026.20
2	1060.08

These are the same cash flows that would be experienced by an investor who agrees one year in advance to invest $1026.20 in a zero-coupon bond at 3.30% interest (except for some small round-off error). Therefore by purchasing and selling securities of differing maturities today, an investor can "lock in" a return on an investment one or more periods from now. In the current example, we say that the 3.30% interest rate obtained for an investment one year from now is the *one-year forward one-year rate*, since the interest rate obtained is for an investment one year from now (i.e., one year forward) and is obtained for a one-year security. When a similar set of transactions is implemented to lock in a rate n years from now on a k-year zero coupon bond, the resulting rate is called the *n-year forward k-year rate*. We denote this rate by $f_{n,k}$.

EXAMPLE 15.6

Using the yields in Table 15.9, find all possible forward rates for forward securities with maturities of one, two, three, and four years.

TABLE 15.9

Maturity (in years)	Annual Yield for Zero-coupon Bonds
1.0	3.0%
2.0	4.0
3.0	5.0
4.0	6.0
5.0	7.0

SOLUTION

We show here the calculations for $f_{1,4}$ and $f_{2,2}$. (Calculations for other forward rates are similar, and are left to the reader as Exercise 15-12.) $f_{1,4}$ is the only forward four-year rate that can be calculated from the rates in the table. This rate is most easily calculated using the logic that an investor obtains the same total return *either* by buying a five-year zero-coupon bond, *or* by investing in a one-year bond and then investing the proceeds for four years at the one-year forward four-year rate. That is,

$$(1+z_5)^5 = (1+z_1)^1 \cdot (1+f_{1,4})^4. \tag{15.1}$$

In this case we have

$$(1.07)^5 = (1.03)^1 \cdot (1+f_{1,4})^4,$$

from which we find $f_{1,4} = 8.024\%$. Similarly, $f_{2,2}$ must satisfy

$$(1+z_4)^4 = (1+z_2)^2 \cdot (1+f_{2,2})^2, \tag{15.2}$$

from which we find $f_{2,2} = 8.038\%$. All of the forward rates, rounded to four decimal places, are shown in Table 15.10. ❑

TABLE 15.10

n	$f_{n,1}$	$f_{n,2}$	$f_{n,3}$	$f_{n,4}$
1.0	5.01%	6.01%	7.02%	8.02%
2.0	7.03	8.04	9.05	–
3.0	9.06	10.07	–	–
4.0	11.10	–	–	–

EXAMPLE 15.7

A five-year pure endowment contract issued to a person age 60 is funded with level annual premiums and has a maturity benefit of $10,000. Premiums are payable at the beginning of each year, and the benefit is payable at the end of the fifth year. Table 15.11 shows mortality rates for a 60-year-old and forward rates that are currently available. Use this information to calculate the net level annual premium for the pure endowment. Note that $f_{0,5} = z_5$.

TABLE 15.11

y	$f_{y,5-y}$	x	q_x
0	4.0%	60	.02
1	5.0	61	.03
2	6.0	62	.04
3	7.0	63	.05
4	8.0	64	.06

SOLUTION

Since we are given forward rates, it will be easiest to determine the level annual premium retrospectively. The premiums must accumulate with interest and survivorship to total $10,000 at the end of the fifth year. That is,

$$10,000 = P \cdot \ddot{s}_{60:\overline{5}|} = P\left(\frac{1}{_5E_{60}} + \frac{1}{_4E_{61}} + \frac{1}{_3E_{62}} + \frac{1}{_2E_{63}} + \frac{1}{_1E_{64}} \right),$$

where, for example,

$$_3E_{62} = \frac{_3p_{62}}{(1+f_{2,3})^3} = \frac{(.96)(.95)(.94)}{(1.06)^3} = .7198.$$

Similar calculations produce

$$10,000 = P \cdot \ddot{s}_{60:\overline{5}|} = P\left(\frac{1}{.6698} + \frac{1}{.6841} + \frac{1}{.7198} + \frac{1}{.7800} + \frac{1}{.8704}\right),$$

from which we find $P = 1476.02$.

Note that we could also have found the net level annual premium prospectively by first converting the forward rates to current spot rates. We first note that $z_5 = f_{0,5} = 4.0\%$. Then to calculate z_n for $n < 5$, we use the relationship

$$(1+z_n)^n \cdot (1+f_{n,5-n})^{5-n} = (1+z_5)^5. \tag{15.3}$$

The resulting spot rates, rounded to four decimal places, are shown in Table 15.12. (The reader should verify that they are correct.)

TABLE 15.12

n	z_n
1	0.094%
2	1.071
3	2.049
4	3.023
5	4.000

Then prospectively we have

$$10,000_5 E_{60} = P \cdot \ddot{a}_{60:\overline{5}|} = P(1 + v \cdot {}_1p_{60} + v^2 \cdot {}_2p_{60} + v^3 \cdot {}_3p_{60} + v^4 \cdot {}_4p_{60}).$$

The left side of this equation evaluates to

$$10,000v^5 \cdot {}_5p_{60} = \frac{(10,000)(.98)(.97)(.96)(.95)(.94)}{(1.04)^5} = 6698.13,$$

where the five-year spot rate has been used. For the right side of the equation, each v^n is calculated using the corresponding spot rate z_n. From this we find $\ddot{a}_{60:\overline{5}|} = 4.53795$, from which we again find

$$P = \frac{6698.13}{4.53795} = 1476.02. \qquad \square$$

15.5 AN EXAMPLE WITH SIMULATED RATES OF RETURN

This text does not deal explicitly with stochastically generated rates of return. However, the following examples illustrate the use of simulation models regarding the total return on a portfolio of investments. Each of the examples in this section deals with the following scenario:

A large corporation would like to self-insure its employees' annual dental expenses. The company would like to maintain sufficient assets to be reasonably sure of paying the first $2,000,000 in expenses each year and will reinsure aggregate losses above that amount. All assets are to be invested in one-year corporate bonds yielding 6% annual interest. Bonds may be purchased in increments of $1000.

EXAMPLE 15.8

We first make the simple assumption that the portfolio earns a 6% total return during the year. In this case, what dollar amount of bonds will be sufficient to pay the first $2,000,000 of claims?

SOLUTION

The initial investment must be at least $P = \dfrac{2,000,000}{1.06} = 1,886,792.45$, so $\$1,887,000$ of bond value, or 1887 bonds, must be purchased at the beginning of the year. ☐

EXAMPLE 15.9

We now assume that each bond has a 4% chance of default during the year. If a bond defaults, the bond's value at the end of the year will be uniformly distributed between $0 and $1000. In this case, what number of bonds should be purchased to have an expected value of at least $2,000,000 at the end of the year? We assume the bonds in the portfolio are all independent with regard to frequency and severity of default.

SOLUTION

The probability of not defaulting is .96, in which case the year-end bond value is $1060. In the case of default, the expected bond value is $500. Therefore each bond's expected value at yearend is $(.96)(1060) + (.04)(500) = 1037.60$, so the total number of bonds to be purchased is $\dfrac{2,000,000}{1037.60} = 1928.$ ☐

EXAMPLE 15.10

Suppose the corporation purchases the 1928 bonds suggested in Example 15.9. Since the value of each bond at yearend is uncertain, the corporation's assets may exceed or fall short of the $2,000,000 needed at yearend. We now simulate the return on the 1928 bonds to determine each of the following:

(a) First we generate 20 simulated year-end portfolio values.[5]

(b) Use the 20 runs to estimate the probability that the insurer has funds in excess of $2,000,000 at year end.

(c) Use the 20 runs to estimate the 15th percentile of the fund value at yearend.

SOLUTION

(a) A uniform random number u is drawn from $[0,1)$ for each bond to determine whether that bond defaults during the year. If $.96 \leq u < 1$, we assume that bond has defaulted. For each defaulted bond, a second random draw from $[0,1)$ is multiplied by 1000 to simulate the bond's year-end value. Thus every bond ends the year with a value between $0 and $1060. Our results for 1928 simulated bond values are summarized in Table 15.13.[6]

TABLE 15.13

Run Number	Simulated Number of Defaults	Simulated Year-end Portfolio Value
1	71	2,007,013
2	83	1,996,821
3	76	1,999,596
4	88	1,999,620
5	74	2,004,403
6	101	1,985,824
7	88	1,996,517
8	66	2,006,397
9	81	2,001,682
10	84	1,998,392
11	70	2,009,449
12	69	2,006,524
13	76	2,000,335
14	74	2,001,262
15	86	1,993,844
16	86	1,996,388
17	71	2,005,363
18	84	2,000,393
19	83	1,996,413
20	63	2,004,851

---

[5] In practice, a much larger number of simulated portfolio values would be generated.

[6] The number of defaulted bonds is binomially distributed, with standard deviation $\sqrt{(1928)(.96)(.04)} = 8.60$. The value of a defaulted bond is uniformly distributed over $[0, 1000]$, producing a standard deviation of

$$\sqrt{\frac{(1000)^2}{12}} = 288.68.$$ Consequently, we can expect considerable variation in simulated results.

(b) Using Table 15.13, we see that eleven simulations produced year-end portfolio values in excess of $2,000,000, so we estimate the probability of having the year-end value be above that number as 55%. (Parametrically, we can determine that the actual probability is 50%.)

(c) To estimate the 15th percentile, we could assume that the three lowest year-end portfolio values correspond to the bottom 15 percent of returns. This suggests a 15th percentile year-end value of $1,996,388. ❑

15.6 TRANSFERRING THE INTEREST RATE RISK

The overriding theme of this text is that persons facing financial risks can be relieved of those risks by paying an insurer to assume them. From the insurer's perspective, there are three primary risks associated with a contract of life insurance, namely those of expenses, mortality, and interest.

The insurer charges for the expenses of doing business by increasing the benefit (net) premiums to reach the contract (gross) premiums actually paid. If operational expenses turn out to be less than assumed in setting the contract premiums, the insurer makes a profit on the expense element. If the opposite turns out to be the case, then the insurer loses money on the expense element. Generally insurers are fairly good at charging for their expenses, so the *expense risk* is not very great.

For many years the view was held that the major risk to the insurer was the *mortality risk*. If failures occurred earlier than, or at greater rates than, as predicted by the underlying survival model, the insurer suffered losses on the mortality element under life insurance contracts. Under annuities, the opposite would be true; the insurer would suffer a loss if mortality was lighter (i.e., if annuitants lived longer) than as predicted by the survival model.

By assuming that the lifetimes of different policyholders are independent, the insurer can *diversify* the mortality risk over the collection of policyholders. Some will fail earlier and some later, so that the aggregate risk can be better predicted. In light of this, we refer to the mortality risk as a *diversifiable risk*. (This concept was illustrated in Section 9.3.)

When the insurer selects an interest rate for the premium calculation, it is assuming that it will be able to earn that rate on its invested assets backing the insurance or annuity contracts. If it earns interest on its assets at a greater rate than that assumed, it makes a profit on the interest element. On the other hand, the insurer faces an *interest rate risk* that earned rates will fall below assumed rates and it will therefore suffer a loss on the interest element. This has been a problem for many insurers in recent years.

If an interest loss occurs, due to falling interest rates in the investment marketplace, it will occur on all contracts alike. For this reason we refer to the interest rate risk as a *non-diversifiable risk*.

Although the insurer cannot diversify the interest rate risk across the collection of policyholders, it is possible for the insurer to *transfer* part or all of that risk back to the insured. When this is done under a life insurance or annuity contract, we say that the policyholder is participating in the interest rate risk.[7]

In this text we explore how this is accomplished under universal life insurance and variable annuity contracts. The basic features of these two types of contracts were explored in Sections 11.5, 11.6, and 14.3.4. In the next two chapters, we discuss this key feature of interest rate risk transfer from the insurer to the insured.

15.7 EXERCISES

15.1 Actuarial Present Values Using Variable Interest Rates

15-1 Complete Example 15.1 for Scenarios 2 and 3.

15-2 Complete Example 15.2 for Scenarios 2 and 3.

15.2 Deterministic Interest Rate Scenarios

15-3 (a) Complete part (a) of Example 15.3 for the rising interest rate scenario.

(b) Complete part (b) of Example 15.3 for the rising interest rate scenario.

15-4 A company sells insurance in a country where only one-year bonds are available as investments to back its business. Our task is to compare the interest sensitivity of the following three products in this environment.

(i) A 5-year immediate annuity-certain, where payments are made regardless of survival status.

(ii) A 5-year immediate life annuity.

(iii) A single premium 5-year term insurance contract.

The applicable failure rates are $q_x = .10, q_{x+1} = .15, q_{x+2} = .20, q_{x+3} = .25,$ and $q_{x+4} = .30.$

(a) Assuming today's interest rate is 7%, calculate the actuarial present value for each of the three products using each of the following two interest rate scenarios:

(1) Increasing: rates rise by 1% each year, but do not exceed 11% in any year.

(2) Decreasing: rates fall by 1% each year, but do not fall below 3% in any year.

(b) Which of the products is least interest sensitive in this environment? Explain.

---

[7] Another strategy available to an insurer to reduce interest rate risk is *hedging*.

15-5   For the same country and interest scenarios as in Exercise 15-4, we wish to evaluate the following two similar products:

   (1) Single premium 10-year term insurance of face amount $1000, with benefit paid at the end of the year of failure.
   (2) Annual premium 10-year term insurance of face amount $1000, with benefit paid at the end of the year of failure. The level annual premiums are paid at the beginning of each year.

   (a) For both products, assume $q_x = .05$ for all years. Calculate the benefit premium for each product, assuming rates remain level over the life of the product.

   (b) Calculate the actuarial present value of the gain for each product under the increasing and decreasing scenarios. (Note that the premium was chosen so that the actuarial present value in each case is zero in the event of level rates.)

   (c) In terms of interest risk, which payment scheme appears less risky for the insurance company? Explain.

15.3 Spot Interest Rates and the Term Structure of Interest Rates

15-6   Verify that $A^1_{60:\overline{5}|} = .1527$ in Example 15.5.

15-7   Use the nominal annual coupon yields in the table below to calculate the corresponding zero-coupon yields of the same maturities. (In both cases the nominal annual yield rates are convertible semiannually.)

Maturity (in years)	Nominal Annual Yield for Coupon-bearing Bonds	Nominal Annual Yield for Zero-coupon Bonds
0.5	2.0%	
1.0	4.0	
1.5	6.0	
2.0	8.0	

15-8   Use the annual coupon yields in the table below to calculate the corresponding zero-coupon yields of the same maturities. (For this exercise, we assume annual-payment coupon bonds rather than semiannual-payment coupon bonds.) How does the solution compare to that of Exercise 15-7?

Maturity (in years)	Annual Yield for Coupon-bearing Bonds	Annual Yield for Zero-coupon Bonds
1	2.0%	
2	4.0	
3	6.0	
4	8.0	

15-9   Use the annual zero-coupon yields in the table below to calculate the corresponding yields for annual-payment coupon bonds of the same maturities. (We assume here that coupon bonds pay coupons annually rather than semiannually.)

Maturity (in years)	Annual Yield for Coupon-bearing Bonds	Annual Yield for Zero-coupon Bonds
1		2.0%
2		4.0
3		6.0
4		8.0

15-10   Assume the following zero-coupon rates and calculate the implied yields for coupon bonds with equivalent maturities. (In both cases the nominal annual yield rates are convertible semiannually.)

Maturity (in years)	Nominal Annual Yield for Coupon-bearing Bonds	Nominal Annual Yield for Zero-coupon Bonds
0.5		2.0%
1.0		4.0
1.5		6.0
2.0		8.0

15-11   The regents of Fantastic University provide a four-year scholarship for one incoming freshman who plans to major in actuarial science. Current tuition at Fantastic is $26,000 per year and tuition is expected to increase 8% per year over the next four years. The first annual tuition payment is due today. Each year we assume a 25% chance that the scholarship recipient will change majors or drop out of school; either event cancels future scholarship payments. Using the table of yields from Exercise 15-9, calculate the actuarial present value of this scholarship.

15.4 Forward Interest Rates

15-12   Complete Example 15.6 by verifying the $f_{n,k}$ values shown in Table 15.10.

15-13   Verify the spot rate values shown in Table 15.12.

15-14   Using the n-year forward one-year rates in the following table, find all determinable spot rates.

n	$f_{n,1}$
0	4.0%
1	5.0
2	6.0
3	7.0
4	8.0

15-15 Using the n-year forward one-year rates from Exercise 15-14, find all available forward rates.

15-16 In connection with taking over a client's retirement account, the client agrees to invest $300,000 of that account with your firm for three years, starting two years from now.

(a) According to the interest rates in Exercise 15-15, what rate of interest can be locked in for the investment period?

(b) What spot-rate transactions should be entered into today in order to lock in the yield found in part (a)? Include the term and principal amount of the two transactions.

15-17 Due to the demise of a distant relative, you will receive $25,000 in one year that you would like to invest at that time for two years.

(a) According to the rates in Exercise 15-15, what rate can be locked in for the investment period?

(b) What transactions should be entered into today in order to lock in the rate from part (a)? Include the terms and principal amounts of the two transactions.

15-18 Calculate all forward rates that can be inferred from the annual coupon-bearing bond yield rates in the following table.

Maturity (in years)	Annual Yield Rates for Coupon-bearing Bonds
1	2.0%
2	4.0
3	6.0
4	8.0

CHAPTER SIXTEEN

UNIVERSAL LIFE INSURANCE

The mechanics of this popular insurance product were briefly described in Sections 11.5 and 14.3.4. In this chapter we considerably expand our description of universal life insurance.

16.1 BASIC ASPECTS

There are three fundamental aspects of the universal life insurance product, namely (a) extensive policyholder choice, (b) policyholder participation in the interest rate risk, and (c) secondary guaranteed features of the coverage. We discuss each of these basic aspects in the following three subsections.

16.1.1 POLICYHOLDER CHOICE

A basic characteristic of universal life insurance is that a great degree of flexibility is available to the policyholder.

As mentioned in Section 11.5, we refer to the payments made by the policyholder as contributions, rather than premiums, because they need not be fixed at any one amount and can be stopped and restarted at the policyholder's option.

The policyholder has a degree of choice regarding the balance between death benefit coverage and savings accumulation, with the caveat that a minimum amount of insurance coverage may be required by the tax laws to prevent the contract from becoming one of investment only, which has a less favorable tax status. For example, the minimum insurance amount might be defined as a specified percentage, such as 150%, of the cash value of the contract.

The amount of the death benefit could be defined as the fixed face amount of the policy only (as described in Section 11.5.2), or as the face amount plus the account value (as described in Section 11.5.1). In either case, the amount of death benefit coverage is provided by a sequence of one-year (or shorter period) term insurances. In the case of a fixed benefit, the term insurance is for the net amount at risk.[1] Another possibility is to define the death benefit as the face amount plus a return of all contributions made, up to a maximum cap.

Other policyholder choices include the option to borrow against the equity in the contract, pledge the account value as collateral on a loan from an outside lender, take a partial

---

[1] As noted earlier, different insurers may use different definitions of net amount at risk. A common definition is the excess of the face amount over the prior account value plus current net contribution.

withdrawal of the account value, or surrender the contract entirely for its cash value. If the contract is surrendered during its early years, say within the first ten to fifteen years, a *surrender charge* is likely to be deducted from the account value to determine the cash value available to the surrendering policyholder. Any outstanding loan balance would also be deducted to reach the cash surrender value actually paid.

EXAMPLE 16.1

A universal life insurance contract with fixed death benefit of 100,000 has an account value of 4000 on April 30. A contribution of 1000 is made on May 1. The annual credited interest rate is 4.5%, the percent of contribution expense rate is 4.0%, the monthly administrative expense charge is 40, and the monthly mortality rate is .0001. The surrender charge at this duration of the contract is 10 per 1000 of face amount. There is no outstanding loan balance. Calculate, as of May 31, each of (a) the account value, (b) the cash value, and (c) the cash surrender value.

SOLUTION

(a) Using the common definition of net amount at risk as the excess of face amount over the prior account value plus net contribution, we find the NAR for May to be

$$NAR = 100,000 - [4000 + 1000(1-.04)] = 95,040.$$

Then the account value on May 31 is

$$AV = [4000 + 1000(1-.04) - 40 - (.0001)(95,040)] \cdot (1.045)^{1/12}$$
$$= (4000 + 960 - 40 - 9.504) \cdot (1.045)^{1/12} = 4928.54.$$

(b) The surrender charge is 10 per 1000 of face amount, which is $(10)(100) = 1000$, so the available cash value is

$$CV = AV - SC = 4928.54 - 1000.00 = 3928.54.$$

(c) Because there is no outstanding loan balance, the actual cash surrender value is also 3928.54. ❑

16.1.2 INTEREST RATE RISK

If the interest rate credited on the account value is guaranteed by the insurer, then the insurer bears the risk that the associated assets might not earn that guarantee rate. If marketplace rates were to fall below the guaranteed credited rate, policyholders could take advantage to the contribution flexibility allowed in these contracts, make relatively large contributions, earn the higher guaranteed rate, and then surrender their contracts when market rates increase, all to the insurer's disadvantage.

A common feature of modern universal life contracts is that the net contributions are invested in *separate investment accounts*, and the rates earned on these accounts are used to accumulate the contract account values. Then if market rates fall, the interest earned on the account values falls as well. The interest rate risk has been transferred to the insured from the insurer. Contracts with this feature are referred to as *variable universal life insurance* (VUL). The death benefit continues to be provided by sequential one-period term insurances. The other features of cash and loan values are also available as long as the account value remains positive.

A separate investment account is not established for each individual VUL contract, of course. Rather the net contributions made under a collection of similar contracts would be pooled and invested in the various separate accounts, which would likely have different investment philosophies. Each individual contract would own a number of units, or shares, in the various separate accounts, and the account value would then be the product of the unit value and the number of units owned.

EXAMPLE 16.2

A VUL contract has 100 units invested in Fund A, with unit value 20, and 200 units invested in Fund B, with unit value 10. A contribution of 1000 is made.

(a) How many units are purchased if the entire contribution is allocated to Fund A?

(b) If the market value of Fund A increases by 20%, what is the account value of the contract?

SOLUTION

(a) The Fund A unit value is 20, so a deposit of 1000 will purchase 50 units.

(b) The new unit value in Fund A is $(20)(1.20) = 24$, and the contract now owns 150 units in Fund A and 200 units in Fund B. Then the account value is

$$(150)(24) + (200)(10) = 5600.00. \qquad \square$$

A special version of investment in a separate account is investment in a mutual fund directly tied to some published stock index, such as the S&P 500. Then interest is credited to the universal life contract at rates being earned by the index fund. This version is discussed further in Section 16.2.

16.1.3 SECONDARY GUARANTEES

The version of universal life described thus far, with the interest rate risk transferred to the policyholder, might be considered the most basic form. Account values grow according to actually earned rates, and no reserve needs to be held since the death benefit is provided by sequential one-interval term insurances. In practice, universal life contracts may contain *secondary guarantees*, which provide for a minimum guaranteed cash value, death benefit, and/or maturity value regardless of the performance of the underlying investments. An example would be a guarantee that the contract will stay in force at the original schedule of benefits, as long as a specified contribution is made, even if such contribution would have been insufficient in the absence of the guarantee.

Another example is the case where the insurer guarantees a minimum credited interest rate, if it is higher than the actually earned rate. In this case there is a sharing of the interest rate risk between the insured and the insurer.

Secondary guarantees embody a cost to the insurer and must therefore be funded and reserved. These topics are more advanced than the basic features we have considered thus far, and are pursued further in Sections 16.3 (for pricing) and 16.4 (for reserving).

16.2 INDEXED UNIVERSAL LIFE INSURANCE

Also known as *equity-indexed universal life* (EIUL), interest is credited to this contract at a rate that depends on some published stock index, such as the S&P 500 (currently the most popular), the Dow Jones Industrial Average, or the Europe, Australia and Far East (EAFE) Index. (In some cases an average or other combination of several indices might be used, such as 75% of the highest, 25% of the second highest, and 0% of the lowest.) The appeal of such contracts is the potential for strong growth in value from growth in the equity market without direct participation in equity trading. The contract guarantees a minimum credited rate, providing some protection against loss of funds.

Once the underlying index and the length of the indexing period are chosen, an indexing method is selected. The *annual point-to-point indexing method* defines the index growth rate as

$$i_P = \frac{Final\ Index\ Closing\ Value}{Initial\ Index\ Closing\ Value} - 1, \qquad (16.1)$$

and the *monthly average indexing method* defines the index growth rate as

$$i_{MA} = \frac{\frac{1}{12}\sum Monthly\ Index\ Closing\ Values}{Initial\ Index\ Closing\ Value} - 1. \qquad (16.2)$$

The monthly method would ease some of the volatility that might be produced by the point-to-point method.

Once the indexing method is chosen, there are several other factors that are considered in setting the index-based credited interest rate.

(1) The *participation rate* is the percentage of the raw index growth rate that enters the calculation of the credited rate.

(2) The *index floor* is the minimum rate to be credited. It is usually set at 0%, but could be set higher.

(3) The *index margin* is a fixed reduction in the index growth rate. It can be applied either before or after the participation rate, but cannot reduce the credited rate below the index floor.

(4) The *index cap* is the maximum credited rate that can apply in any period. As with the index margin, it can serve to set the credited rate lower than the actual index growth rate.

The mechanics of the process of setting the credited rate, given the index growth rate, are illustrated in the following two examples.

EXAMPLE 16.3

Consider an EIUL contract using the annual point-to-point indexing method, with a 10% index cap, a 1% index floor, and a 110% participation rate. Given the index values shown in Column (2) of Table 16.1 below, calculate the credited interest rates shown in Column (5).

SOLUTION

TABLE 16.1

Year	Index Closing Value	Index Growth Rate (Before Participation)	Index Growth Rate (After Participation)	Credited Interest Rate
(1)	(2)	(3)	(4)	(5)
0	1000			
1	1050	5.00%	5.50%	5.50%
2	1200	14.29	15.72	10.00
3	1100	− 8.33	− 9.16	1.00
4	950	− 13.64	− 15.00	1.00
5	1060	11.58	12.74	10.00
6	1150	8.49	9.34	9.34

The index growth rate (before participation) in Column (3) for Year t is the ratio of the index value for Year t to the index value for Year $t-1$. The adjusted rates in Column (4) are those in Column (3) times 1.10. The final credited rates in Column (5) are the Column (4) rates adjusted for the 10% cap or the 1% floor. ❑

EXAMPLE 16.4

Suppose the EIUL contract of Example 16.3 used the monthly average indexing method instead. Given the monthly index closing values shown in Table 16.2, calculate the credited interest rate.

Table 16.2

Month	Index Closing Value
0	1000
1	1020
2	1100
3	1150
4	1080
5	1040
6	960
7	1030
8	1000
9	1070
10	1150
11	1200
12	1150

Solution

The index growth rate is

$$i_{MA} = \frac{\frac{1}{12}(1020 + 1100 + \cdots + 1150)}{1000} - 1 = .07917.$$

Neither the 10% cap nor the 1% floor will apply, so the credited interest rate is 7.92%. ❑

16.3   Pricing Considerations

In this section we discuss the important assumptions involved in pricing universal life insurance products. These considerations apply to all three of basic universal life, variable universal life, and indexed universal life contracts.

16.3.1   Mortality

The *mortality rates* used to determine the cost of insurance are generally in select and ultimate form (see Section 6.7), with a select period of at least 15 years. They are estimated from the insurer's own past experience, or possibly from the experience of several similar insurers combined.

The rates based on past experience are generally then adjusted upward to reflect the effects of any *anti-selection* anticipated to be more severe than that contained in past experience. Anti-selection occurs when a portion of a group of insured lives elects to lapse their policies for various reasons. Those who lapse tend to be healthier than those who persist, so the level of mortality to be expected from the remaining insured lives is greater than that expected from the original total group.

16.3.2 LAPSE

The *lapse rates* assumed in pricing universal life contracts generally vary only by duration since issue, but could also vary by issue age as well (i.e., select and ultimate). They could also vary by such factors as contribution frequency, policy size, product type, or amount of insurance coverage.

Surrender charges may be deducted from the account value when the contract is totally surrendered or possibly also when only a part of the account value is withdrawn. An exception to the latter case occurs if the contract specifically allows a portion of its value to be withdrawn without penalty.

Considering mortality and withdrawal together, we see that our universal life insurance products are priced according to a double-decrement model (see Chapter 13). Letting $q_x^{(d)}$ and $q_x^{(w)}$ denote the probabilities of death and withdrawal, respectively, we recall that the probability of not being decremented from the group of lives between ages x and $x+1$ is

$$p_x^{(\tau)} = 1 - q_x^{(\tau)} = 1 - q_x^{(d)} - q_x^{(w)}. \tag{16.3}$$

For simplicity, an insurer's pricing actuary might assume that lapse can occur only at the end of the policy year. In that case, mortality is the only decrement during the year, so the probability of surviving to the end of the year is $1 - q_x^{(d)}$.[2] Given survival to the end of the year, the probability of withdrawing is then $q_x^{(w)}$ so the probability of surviving into the next year in this case is

$$p_x^{(\tau)} = (1 - q_x^{(d)})(1 - q_x^{(w)}). \tag{16.4}$$

EXAMPLE 16.5

Consider a UL contract with face amount 100,000 issued at age x. The contributions, mortality rates, and withdrawal rates are shown in Table 16.3 for the first five years.

TABLE 16.3

Year t	Contribution	$q_{[x]+t-1}^{(d)}$	$q_{[x]+t-1}^{(w)}$
1	20,000	.001	.02
2	25,000	.002	.02
3	25,000	.003	.03
4	30,000	.004	.04
5	20,000	.005	.05

Assume that withdrawals occur only at the end of the policy year. Calculate each of the following:

---

[2] In the notation and terminology of Chapter 13, we say that $q_x^{(d)} = q_x'^{(d)}$; the probability and rate of mortality are the same when withdrawal does not operate.

(a) The persistency rate for policy year t.

(b) The survival rate to the end of policy year t.

SOLUTION

(a) From Equation (16.4), the persistency rate for policy year t is

$$p_{[x]+t-1}^{(\tau)} = \left(1 - q_{[x]+t-1}^{(d)}\right)\left(1 - q_{[x]+t-1}^{(w)}\right).$$

Then for $t = 1,2,3,4,5$, we have the following results:

$$p_{[x]}^{(\tau)} = (.999)(.98) = .97902$$

$$p_{[x]+1}^{(\tau)} = (.998)(.98) = .97804$$

$$p_{[x]+2}^{(\tau)} = (.997)(.97) = .96709$$

$$p_{[x]+3}^{(\tau)} = (.996)(.96) = .95616$$

$$p_{[x]+4}^{(\tau)} = (.995)(.95) = .94525$$

(b) The survival rate to the end of year t is

$$_t p_{[x]}^{(\tau)} = p_{[x]}^{(\tau)} \cdot p_{[x]+1}^{(\tau)} \cdot \cdots \cdot p_{[x]+t-1}^{(\tau)},$$

so we directly have $p_{[x]}^{(\tau)} = .97902$, $_2 p_{[x]}^{(\tau)} = .95752$, $_3 p_{[x]}^{(\tau)} = .92601$, $_4 p_{[x]}^{(\tau)} = .88541$, and $_5 p_{[x]}^{(\tau)} = .83694$ □

16.3.3 EXPENSES

For the purpose of pricing these contracts, the *expense assumptions* are derived from an analysis of the insurer's incurred expenses.[3] These include the following:

(1) *Acquisition expenses*, which are those related to acquiring new business. They can be expressed as percent of contribution or face amount, or as a fixed amount per policy, and are usually incurred in the first year only.

(2) *Commission expenses*, which are those paid to sales agents plus other sales expenses. The first year expense is higher and renewal year expenses are lower.

(3) *Maintenance expenses*, which are those of contribution billing and collecting, contribution tax payment, policy record maintenance, accounting, valuation, pricing, and other policyholder services. They can be expressed as any of percent of contribution, percent of face amount, or a fixed amount per policy.

---

[3] See Section 9.6.

16.3.4 INVESTMENT INCOME

The insurer earns *investment income* on the assets backing the policy account value that are already invested at the start of a contract year, as well as the net cash flow during the year.

An alternative approach is to base investment income on the *cumulative cash flow*, which ignores capital contributions and distributions. Negative cumulative cash flows accumulate negative interest in the early policy years. The method is often used by mutual insurers who have no shareholders and therefore no outside source of capital. It is also used to calculate asset shares (see Section 14.2).

16.3.5 PRICING FOR SECONDARY GUARANTEES

There are two methods in use to provide the secondary guarantees.

The *stipulated premium method* provides that a defined premium, if paid on a regular basis, will guarantee the death benefit for the duration of the contract. Furthermore, if the policyholder pays less than that required to maintain the guarantee for a temporary period, a *premium catch-up provision* gives the policyholder the right to make up past premium deficiencies, in which case the guarantee is reinstated.

EXAMPLE 16.6

A UL contract is issued with a cumulative premium catch-up provision in which the lifetime coverage is guaranteed as long as the stipulated premium of 10,000 is paid each year. Assume the policy is in force at the end of ten years, with cumulative contributions paid of 90,000. What must the policyholder do at this time to maintain the lifetime guarantee?

SOLUTION

The cumulative paid contribution is 10,000 short of the amount required to maintain the guarantee, but the shortfall can be rectified under the catch-up provision. The policyholder must pay 20,000 at this time, representing a 10,000 catch-up premium plus the 10,000 stipulated premium required for the next year.　　　　　　　　　　　　　　　　□

The *shadow fund method* has become the more popular design in recent years. Under it a "shadow" account value is maintained based on credited interest rates higher than the contract's guaranteed minimum, and cost of insurance (COI) rates lower than the contract's guaranteed maximum. As long as the shadow fund remains positive, the death benefit secondary guarantee remains in place. Note that the shadow account value is not available to the policyholder; its only purpose is to maintain the death benefit.

EXAMPLE 16.7

Consider a UL contract exhibiting the values shown in Table 16.4.

TABLE 16.4

Contract Year	Contract Account Value	Surrender Charge	Cash Value	Shadow Account Value
1	1000	900	100	1100
2	800	800	0	900
3	400	600	0	700
4	100	400	0	500
5	0	200	0	200
6	0	100	0	0

At what point does the contract lapse (a) if there were no secondary guarantee, or (b) under the shadow fund method of providing a secondary guarantee?

SOLUTION

(a) With no secondary guarantee, the contract would lapse by the end of the fifth year where the account value becomes zero.

(b) Under the shadow fund secondary guarantee, the contract remains in force until the end of the sixth year where the shadow fund becomes zero. (Note that the shadow account exceeds the contract account, as expected, since it is based on higher interest and lower mortality and expense charges.) ❑

If the shadow account value falls negative, it can be reestablished to a positive position by making additional contributions. This is a similar catch-up provision to that mentioned under the stipulated premium method above. If the shadow fund becomes too deeply negative, however, the amount required to bring it back to a positive position might become prohibitively large.

16.4 RESERVING CONSIDERATIONS

In light of their special contract features, the valuation approaches used for universal life insurance contracts differ considerably from those used for traditional life insurance (see Chapters 10 and 11). In this section we describe the reserving approaches, separately for basic UL, VUL, IUL, and secondary guarantees.

16.4.1 BASIC UNIVERSAL LIFE

In addition to the flexibility in both the amount and timing of future contributions, future death benefits are also unknown if they depend on the contributions made or the underlying account value. Therefore the prospective reserve method discussed in Chapters 10 and 11 cannot be used here.

In 1983 the NAIC promulgated a model regulation to define a *minimum reserving standard* for UL products, which presumes a hypothetical premium and incorporates the actual policy performance. The process is summarized in the following steps:

(1) At policy issue, a *guaranteed maturity premium* (GMP) is calculated as the level gross premium sufficient to endow the policy at its maturity date. The GMP is based on the policy guarantees of premium loads, interest rates, and expense and mortality charges.

(2) Also at policy issue, a sequence of *guaranteed maturity funds* (GMF) is calculated based on the roll forward of the GMP and the policy guarantees.

(3) At the valuation date, the actual account value is determined by the account value roll forward process.

(4) At the valuation date, the ratio of the actual account value to the GMF is calculated as

$$r_t = \frac{AV_t}{GMF_t},$$ (16.5)

subject to a maximum value of 1.00.

(5) At the valuation date, the greater of the account value or the GMF is projected forward based on the GMP and the policy guarantees, producing a sequence of guaranteed death benefits (GDB) and a sequence of guaranteed maturity benefits (GMB).

(6) At the valuation date, the present value of the projected future benefits $(PVFB)_t$ and the present value of the future GMP stream $(PVFP)_t$ are calculated using valuation assumptions. Then the *pre-floor CRVM reserve* is defined as

$$_tV^{\text{pre-floor CRVM}} = r_t \cdot \left[(PVFB)_t - (PVFP)_t \right],$$ (16.6)

where r_t is defined in Step (4) above.

(7) The *CRVM reserve floor* is defined as the greater of (a) the half-month term reserve based on minimum valuation mortality and interest, or (b) the cash surrender value at time t (CSV_t).

(8) Then the final CRVM reserve is the greater of the pre-floor CRVM reserve defined in Step (6) or the CRVM reserve floor defined in Step (7).[4]

EXAMPLE 16.8

Consider a UL contract of 100,000 face amount, with a 4% of contribution expense rate, a 3% guaranteed interest rate, a 5% current interest rate, and a GMP of 14.49 per 1000 of face

---

[4] The regulation also defines *alternative minimum reserves* (AMR). First the valuation net premium is calculated at policy issue based on the GMP and the policy guarantees. Then if the GMP is less than the valuation net premium, the reserve held should be the greater of (a) the reserve calculated using the actual method and assumptions of the policy and the valuation net premium, or (b) the reserve calculated using the actual method but with minimum valuation assumptions and the GMP.

amount. At the end of the ninth policy year, the account value is 57.60 per 1000 of face amount and the GMF is 140.40 per 1000 of face amount. At the beginning of the tenth policy year, the guaranteed policy charge is 11.80 per 1000 of face amount and the current policy charge is 10.76 per 1000 of face amount. No contribution is received for the tenth policy year, there is no outstanding loan on the contract, and there is no surrender charge for surrender in the tenth policy year. Calculate each of the following at the end of the tenth year:

(a) The cash value.

(b) The GMF.

(c) The value of r_{10}.

(d) The pre-floor CRVM reserve, given that $(PVFB)_{10} - (PFVP)_{10}$ is 70 per 1000 of face amount.

SOLUTION

(a) At the end of the tenth year, the account value per 1000 of face amount is

$$AV_{10} = (57.60 - 10.76)(1.05) = 49.182,$$

since there is no tenth year contribution. Then the total account value would be $(49.182)(100) = 4918.20.$ There is no surrender charge, so the cash value is also 4918.20.

(b) The GMF accumulates using the GMP and the guaranteed charges and interest rate. Then per 1000 of face amount we have

$$GMF_{10} = [140.40 + 14.49(1 - .04) - 11.80] \cdot (1.03) = 146.7857.$$

The total value of GMF_{10} is $(146.7857)(100) = 14,678.57.$

(c) From Equation (16.5) we have

$$r_{10} = \frac{AV_{10}}{GMF_{10}} = \frac{4,918.20}{14,678.57} = .33506.$$

(d) From Equation (16.6) we have

$$_{10}V^{pre\text{-}floor\ CRVM} = r_{10} \cdot [(PVFB)_{10} - (PVFP)_{10}]$$

$$= (.33506)(70) = 23.4542$$

per 1000 of face amount, or 2345.42 in total. ❑

16.4.2 VARIABLE UNIVERSAL LIFE

The NAIC regulation mentioned above specifically exempts VUL products, since its prospective techniques would be inappropriate because the future investment performance is not guaranteed. The model regulation simply states that the reserves should be established using actuarial procedures that recognize the variable nature of the provided benefits. However, if a VUL product offers a general account investment option, with its more predictable interest rates, then the reserve is determined in the same manner as for a basic UL product.

In the case of flexible premium VUL, we distinguish between front-end loaded and back-end loaded products. For fully front-end loaded VUL products, the policy's cash value can serve as a sufficient reserve in the absence of future guarantees. For back-end loaded products, the reserve is typically the type defined by the UL regulation, with the interest rate used to project future benefits taken as one of (a) the long-term guaranteed rate in the fixed account, (b) the net valuation rate, (c) the rate used to calculate guideline level premiums, or (d) the policy loan rate. The reserve for a back-end loaded product should be no less than the cash value.

Under the *New York Life Design*, the death benefit at any time is the original face amount times the ratio of the actual account value to the tabular account value which has been calculated using the assumed interest rate (AIR). Then the reserves are identical to those of a non-variable policy with the same current death benefit, issue age, and duration.

Under the *Equitable Design*, any net investment earnings over the AIR are used to purchase variable paid-up additions at net rates using the AIR. If net investment earnings are less than the AIR, *negative* paid-up additions are purchased. Then the reserves are equal to tabular reserves calculated for a non-variable policy of the same face amount, issue age, and duration. Reserves for the paid-up additions are equal to those for similar non-variable paid-up additions.

16.4.3 INDEXED UNIVERSAL LIFE

The valuation standards for IUL contracts are specified in NAIC Actuarial Guideline 36 (AG 36), which is available from the NAIC or from the American Academy of Actuaries, with the intent of showing that the computational methods comply with the Standard Valuation Law and the UL regulation mentioned earlier. There are three types of compu-tational methods, as follows:

(1) The *implied guaranteed rate* (IGR) *method*, which requires insurers to satisfy the *hedged-as-required* criteria.[5] These criteria set forth a strenuous constraint requiring exact, or nearly exact, hedging, as well as an indexed interest-crediting term of not more than one year.

(2) The *CRVM with updated market value* (CRVM/UMV) *method* must be used if the contract has an indexed interest-crediting term of more than one year, or if the renewal

---

[5] This refers to the option replication strategy to offset the liability positions. (The reader will study hedging strategies elsewhere in his or her actuarial education process.)

participation rate guarantee gives an implied guaranteed rate greater than the maximum valuation rate. This method can be volatile when market conditions change.

(3) The *CRVM with updated average market value* (CRVM/UAMV) *method* is a hybrid of the other two, designed for an insurer who qualifies for the first method above but does not wish to satisfy the hedged-as-required criteria.

In this text we consider further only the CRVM/UMV method, described below. It applies the UL regulation to IUL contracts by requiring a number of calculations at issue of the contract and at the valuation date.

The issue date calculations are as follows:

(1) An *implied guaranteed interest rate* for the duration of the initial term, which is the guaranteed rate plus the *accumulated option cost* expressed as a percentage of the policy value to which the indexed benefit is applied.[6] In turn, the accumulated option cost is the amount needed to provide the index-based benefit in excess of any other interest rate guarantee, accumulated to the end of the initial term at the appropriate maximum valuation rate.

(2) An implied guaranteed rate for the period after the initial term.

(3) The GMP, GMF, and valuation net premium based on the implied guaranteed rate.

The valuation date calculations are as follows:

(1) The implied guaranteed rate for the remainder of the current period, using the option cost based on the market conditions at the valuation date.

(2) The implied guaranteed rate for the period following the current period, based on the option cost on the valuation date.

(3) A re-projection of future guaranteed benefits based on the implied guaranteed rate on the valuation date.

(4) The present value of the re-projected future guaranteed benefits.

Note that the GMP, GMF, and valuation net premium remain the same as calculated at issue.

EXAMPLE 16.9

Consider an IUL contract using the annual point-to-point indexing method, with a 10% current index cap, a 3% minimum guaranteed index cap, a 0% guaranteed index floor, and a 100% participation rate. The option cost at issue, expressed as a percent of the policy value to which the index benefit is applied, is 5% for a 10% index cap and 2% for a 3% index cap. The valuation rate is 4%. Find the implied guaranteed interest rate for (a) the initial term and (b) the period beyond the initial term.

---

[6] The option cost for the underlying liability guarantee can be valued by an option valuation tool such as the Black-Scholes projection method.

SOLUTION

(a) For the initial term, the implied guaranteed interest rate is the guaranteed floor rate plus the option cost accumulated for one year at the valuation rate, producing

$$.00 + .05(1.04) = .052,$$

or 5.2%.

(b) For the period beyond the initial term, the option cost percentage is 2%, rather than 5%, because the 3% index cap applies, producing

$$.00 + .02(1.04) = .0208,$$

or 2.08%. ❑

16.4.4 CONTRACTS WITH SECONDARY GUARANTEES

UL products with secondary guarantees have gained in popularity compared with traditional whole life insurance. The UL products offer the same guarantees of premium level and death benefit as do traditional products, but at much lower cost. The trade-off is that the guaranteed cash value may likely be lower under secondary guarantee UL, but many consumers are content to accept a lower cash value in exchange for a lower premium that is permanently guaranteed. In light of the lower cash value, regulators and many industry people have expressed concern regarding the adequacy of the reserves for the secondary guarantees under UL policies. In response, the NAIC promulgated Actuarial Guideline 38 (AG 38) to address the calculation of such reserves.

AG 38 reserves are calculated in nine steps:

(1) The *minimum gross premium* required to satisfy the secondary guarantees is derived at issue of the contract; the value of this premium will depend on whether the stipulated premium method or the shadow fund method (see Section 16.3.5) is in use. Its calculation uses the policy charges and credited interest rate guaranteed in the contract.

(2) The basic and deficiency reserves for the secondary guarantees are calculated using the minimum gross premium described in Step (1).

(3) The amount of actual contributions made in excess of the minimum gross premiums is determined, again with the process depending on whether the stipulated premium method or the shadow fund method is used.

(4) At the valuation date, a determination is made regarding amounts needed to fully fund the secondary guarantee.

   (a) Under the shadow fund method, this would be the amount of the shadow fund account needed to fully fund the guarantee.

   (b) Under contracts not using the shadow fund method, this would be the amount of cumulative premiums paid in excess of the required level such that no future premiums are required to fully fund the guarantee.

Special rules apply to policies for which the secondary guarantee cannot be fully funded in advance. Here a *prefunding ratio*, r, which cannot exceed 1.00, is calculated that measures the level of prefunding for the secondary guarantee, and is eventually used in the calculation of reserves. It is defined as

$$r = \frac{Excess\ Payment}{Net\ Single\ Premium\ Required\ to\ Fully\ Fund\ the\ Guarantee}. \tag{16.7}$$

(5) At the valuation date, the net single premium for the secondary guarantee coverage for the remainder of the secondary guarantee period is computed.

(6) A *net amount of additional premiums* is determined by multiplying the prefunding ratio described in Step (4) times the difference between the net single premium of Step (5) and the basic plus deficiency (if any) reserve of Step (2).

(7) A *reduced deficiency reserve* is determined by multiplying the deficiency reserve (if any) by the complement of the prefunding ratio from Step (4).

(8) Then the actual reserve is the lesser of (a) the net single premium of Step (5), or (b) the amount in Step (6) plus the basic and deficiency (if any) reserve from Step (2). This result might be reduced by applicable policy surrender charges.

(9) An *increased basic reserve* is computed by subtracting the reduced deficiency reserve of Step (7) from the reserve computed in Step (8), which then becomes the basic reserve.

EXAMPLE 16.10

Consider a UL contract with secondary guarantee provided by the shadow fund method. As of time t the shadow fund balance is 60,000, the net single premium required to fully fund the guarantee is 100,000, the valuation net premium is 150,000, the applicable surrender charge is 5,000, and the basic reserve is 10,000. There is no deficiency reserve. Calculate the AG38 reserve for this contract.

SOLUTION

The excess premium paid is the shadow fund balance of 60,000. From Equation (16.7) we find the prefunding ratio to be

$$r = \frac{60,000}{100,000} = .60.$$

The net amount of additional premium, as defined in Step (6) above, is

$$r \cdot (Valuation\ NSP - Basic\ and\ Deficiency\ Reserve) = .60(150,000-10,000) = 84,000.$$

Since there is no deficiency reserve, there is also no reduced deficiency reserve. Then the actual reserve, as defined in Step (8) above, is found by adding the basic and deficiency reserve of 10,000 to the *smaller* of the valuation net premium of 150,000 or the net amount of additional premium from Step (6), minus the applicable surrender charge. In this case we have

$$10,000 + 84,000 - 5,000 = 89,000.$$

Since the reduced deficiency reserve is zero, then the final AG38 reserve is the amount calculated in Step (8), which is 89,000. ❐

16.5 EXERCISES

16.1 Basic Aspects

16-1 A universal life insurance contract of face amount 100,000 has an account value of 4000 on April 30. A premium payment of 1000 is made on May 1 and another of 500 is made on May 15. The annual credited interest rate is 5.0%, the percent of premium expense rate is 4.0%, the monthly administrative charge is 40, and the monthly mortality rate is .0001. The surrender charge at this duration of the contract is 10 per 1000 of face amount. There is an outstanding loan balance of 700. Policy charges are taken at the beginning of the month, and interest is credited at the end of the month. Calculate each of the following as of May 31.

(a) The account value

(b) The cash value

(c) The cash surrender value

16-2 At time t a variable UL contract has 100 units invested in Fund A, with unit value 20, and 200 units invested in Fund B, with unit value 10. The market value of Fund A is 10,000,000 and that of Fund B is 5,000,000. From time t to time $t+1$ Fund A increases by 20% and Fund B decreases by 10%.

(a) Find the unit value of Fund A and Fund B at time $t+1$.

(b) Find the market value of Fund A and Fund B at time $t+1$.

(c) A premium payment of 2000 is made at time t, allocated equally to Funds A and B. Find the account value of the contract at time $t+1$.

16.2 Indexed Universal Life Insurance

16-3 An equity-indexed UL contract of face amount 100,000 uses the annual point-to-point indexing method, with a 10% index cap, a 1% index floor, a 100% participation rate, a 4% premium expense rate, and an annual administrative charge of 50. A premium of 1000 is paid at the beginning of each year, policy charges are deducted at the beginning of each year, and interest is credited at the end of each year. The following values apply over the next three years:

Year	Index Closing Value	Cost of Insurance per 1000 of Amount at Risk	Surrender Charge per 1000 of Face Amount
0	1000		
1	1080	2.0	5.00
2	1200	3.0	4.00
3	1100	4.0	3.00

(a)   Find the credited interest rate for the contract at the end of each of the next three years.

(b)   Find the cash value of the contract at the end of each of the next three years.

16.3 Pricing Considerations

16-4 Consider the UL contract of face amount 100,000 issued to (x) with contributions, mortality rates, and withdrawal rates as described in Example 16.5.

(a) Assuming 5% annual interest rate, calculate the actuarial present value of the premiums.

(b) Suppose the contract pays the face amount as a pure endowment benefit upon survival to the end of five years. Find the actuarial present value of the pure endowment benefit.

16-5 Suppose the contract described in Example 16.5 and Exercise 16-4 incurs the following expenses:

(i)   Commissions of 80% in first year and 5% in renewal years.
(ii)   Sales expense of 110% of first year commission.
(iii)   Acquisition expense of 50% of first year premium plus 100 per policy.
(iv)   Annual maintenance expense of .20% of face amount plus 50 per policy.
(v)   Claim settlement expense of 100 per policy.

Calculate the actuarial present value of expenses at policy issue.

16.4 Reserving Consideration

16-6 Consider the UL contract described in Example 16.8, and assume a contribution of 1000 at the beginning of the tenth policy year. (All other details of the contract remain the same.) Calculate each of (a) the cash value, (b) the GMF, and (c) the value of r_{10} at the end of the tenth year.

16-7 An equity-linked UL contract uses the annual point-to-point indexing method, with a 70% current participation rate, a 50% guaranteed participation rate, no index cap, and a 0% guaranteed index floor. The option cost at issue, as a percent of the policy value to which the index benefit is applied, is 7% for a 100% participation rate. The valuation interest rate is 4%. Calculate (a) the implied guaranteed interest rate for the initial term, and (b) the implied guaranteed interest rate for the guarantees beyond the current term.

16-8 Refer to Example 16.10, and recalculate the AG38 reserve assuming a deficiency reserve of 5000.

CHAPTER SEVENTEEN

DEFERRED VARIABLE ANNUITIES

In this chapter we expand on our introductory description of deferred variable annuities, contained in Sections 11.6 and 14.3.5, to present many additional aspects of these contracts.

17.1 BACKGROUND

When the annuitant reaches a chosen retirement age, the deferred annuity is converted from its accumulation phase to its payout phase, with the account value at that time acting as the APV of the future annuity payments. The account value, in essence, is used to purchase an immediate annuity at retirement. Similarly, a person seeking retirement income could purchase an immediate annuity with a single premium provided by personal funds accumulated over the years via other investments. Since the mathematics is the same, in this chapter we consider the direct purchase of a *single premium immediate annuity* (SPIA) and the conversion of an *annual premium deferred annuity* (APDA) to payout status as similar operations.

We consider the basic, or prototype, deferred variable annuity model to be as described in Section 11.6 and illustrated by Equation (11.28). As long as the death and withdrawal benefits during the deferred period are equal to, or less than, the account value, then the account value is simple the accumulation of the net contributions with interest and is independent of assumed or actual mortality and withdrawal rates.

A basic feature of the model suggested by Equation (11.28) is that the interest rate credited on the account value can vary considerable over the deferred period. This is in contrast to our discussion of deferred annuities in Chapter 8 where the interest rate was assumed constant in both the deferred and payout periods.

Furthermore, if the assets backing the account value are invested in a separate account, and the rate credited on the account value is the same as that earned on the separate account, then the interest rate risk has been transferred from the insurer to the annuitant. This model is further discussed in Section 17.2.2 below.

The properties mentioned above, however, such as death and withdrawal benefits capped at the account value and total transfer of the interest rate risk to the annuitant, are seldom found in practice. That is, the prototype model seldom holds. Variations from the prototype model include such things as (a) minimum guaranteed interest rates during the accumulation period, (b) guaranteed minimum death benefits, (c) guaranteed minimum withdrawal benefits, and/or (d) guaranteed minimum accumulated value at retirement (which in turn would provide a guaranteed minimum retirement income). These variations create contracts which are hybrids between the prototype model, wherein the insurer bears nearly no risk at all, and the traditional annuity of Chapter 8, wherein the insurer bears all of the risk.

A word of warning regarding terminology should be mentioned here. All of the annuity contracts throughout this chapter could be called *variable* annuities in the sense that the applicable interest rates *vary* over the years of the contracts. In practice, insurers tend to reserve the adjective "variable" to apply only in the case of separate investment accounts, with its associated transfer of the interest rate risk to the annuitant. In the remainder of the chapter, we will respect this industry use of the term but also keep in mind that all of the annuity contracts allow for variation in the applicable interest rates.

17.2 DEFERRED ANNUITY PRODUCTS

Depending on how the contract funds earn interest during the accumulation phase, there are three types of annuities, namely (1) *fixed*, (2) *variable*, and (3) *equity-indexed*.

(1)   The fixed annuity guarantees a minimum interest rate during the accumulation phase, and fixed payout rates during the payout period.

(2)   The variable annuity allows the contract holder to choose the investment options for the funds accumulating under the contract. Then when the contract is annuitized (i.e., converted to an immediate annuity) at the end of the accumulation period, the payout rates will also depend on the performance of the invested funds.

(3)   The equity-indexed annuity is essentially a fixed annuity with credited interest rates linked to a stock or equity index. The value of the annuity depends on the performance of the index to which it is linked.

The variable annuity and equity-indexed annuity have been gaining popularity in recent decades.

In this section we present, for each of the three deferred annuity types, their basic features and mechanics. Pricing and reserving considerations are presented in Sections 17.4 and 17.5, respectively.

17.2.1 FIXED DEFERRED ANNUITY

During the accumulation period of a fixed deferred annuity, each deposit, less any applicable charges, earns interest at a rate set at issue of the contract. This rate can be adjusted later, but a minimum interest rate is guaranteed for the entire accumulation period.

Various kinds of charges or fees can be imposed on the annuity, either as *front-end loads* or *back-end loads*. A front-end load might be a percent of premium, or a one-time charge deducted at issue of the contract. Alternatively, such fees might be spread over a number of years including possibly the entire life of the contract. More commonly the fixed deferred annuity is back-loaded, whereby a charge is assessed if the contract value is withdrawn or the contract is surrendered during the surrender charge period. Surrender charges are presented in more detail in later sections.

The *minimum guaranteed interest rate* should never be less than the statutory rate prescribed by insurance law. As of this writing, this rate is set equal to the five-year Constant Maturity Treasury (CMT) Rate, less 1.25%, but not to be less than 1.00%. In practice, the five-year CMT rate reported by the Federal Reserve as of the last business day of November of the prior calendar year, rounded to the nearest .0005, is used to set the minimum guaranteed interest rate.

The initial guaranteed interest rate applies during an initial guarantee period, usually of length three to ten years. At the end of the guarantee period, the contract holder can choose to surrender the contract without surrender charge, or to renew it for another guarantee period, which may or may not be the same length as the initial guarantee period. The rate current on the renewal date will then apply during the renewal guarantee period, and will not be less than the minimum guaranteed rate at that time.

A non-guaranteed bonus interest amount is sometimes credited during the first contract year in order to attract new business.

Interest is generally credited to the contract funds on a daily basis. If the guaranteed rate is denoted by i, the fund is accumulated each day by a factor of $(1+i)^{1/365}$.

EXAMPLE 17.1

A company offers a fixed deferred annuity product with initial guaranteed annual interest rate of 5% and initial guarantee period of five years. The minimum guaranteed interest rate is 3%. There is no interest bonus and no contract charges except a surrender charge. A client purchases this product on 1/1/10 with a deposit of $10,000. If there are no withdrawals before 12/31/15, find the *minimum* fund value for this annuity on that date.

SOLUTION

The deposit earns 5% interest during the initial guarantee period of five years, so the fund value is

$$10,000(1.05)^5 = 12,762.82$$

on 12/31/14. We do not know the renewal guaranteed rate, but we know it cannot be less than 3%. Therefore the *minimum* fund value on 12/31/15 will be

$$(12,762.82)(1.03) = 13,145.70. \qquad \square$$

If the contract holder wishes to withdraw part or all of the fund value from a contract that is back-loaded, a *surrender charge*, expressed as a percentage of the fund value or possibly of the deposit, may be applied. Usually a surrender charge is applied only for surrender within the first seven to ten years of the contract. The amount of the charge is greater for earlier surrender, perhaps 10% for surrender in the first contract year, and grading down to no charge at the end of the surrender charge period. Some contracts specify a small amount, expressed as a percentage of the contract value, that can be withdrawn free of surrender charges.

When a contract is surrendered, the net amount obtained by the contract holder after the deduction of any surrender charge is called the *cash surrender value* (or simply *cash value*) of the contract.

EXAMPLE 17.2

Suppose the client in Example 17.1 decides to surrender the contract on 12/31/12. If the surrender charge is 3% of the contract value for surrender within the first five contract years, find the cash surrender value on 12/31/12.

SOLUTION

The contract value on 12/31/12 is

$$10,000(1.05)^3 = 11,576.25,$$

and the surrender charge is $(.03)(11,576.25) = 347.29,$ so the cash surrender value is

$$11,576.25 - 347.29 = 11,228.96 \qquad \square$$

A company selling fixed deferred annuities bears a level of interest rate risk, in that rising interest rates reduce the market value of the assets supporting the fixed annuity liability. If the contract is surrendered, these depressed assets are sold at a loss in order to pay the cash surrender value. The interest rate risk can be shifted to the contract holder via a *modified guaranteed annuity*, which includes a *market value adjustment* applied to the cash surrender value to reflect the current market value of the supporting assets. These contracts are sometimes called *market value adjusted annuities*, or MVA annuities. (They are not discussed further in this text.)

17.2.2 VARIABLE DEFERRED ANNUITY

Unlike a fixed deferred annuity, the variable annuity does not offer a minimum guaranteed interest rate. Instead, various investment options, referred to as *separate accounts* (or *sub-accounts*), are given to the contract holder by the insurer at issue of the variable annuity contract. The investment options might be mutual funds or other segregated portfolios managed by investment fund managers. In any case, the interest earned on the deferred variable annuity will depend on the performance of the associated stock or bond market.[1] Because the separate accounts are managed by professional fund managers, an *investment advisory fee* (IAF) is deducted from the investment income and paid to the fund manager.[2]

---

[1] In many cases a fixed sub-account is also offered, which functions similarly to the fixed deferred annuity of Section 17.2.1.

[2] Some contracts refer to the IAF as an *advisory expense fee*, *advisory investment fee*, or *investment management fee*. We use investment advisory fee (IAF) throughout this chapter.

In practice the sub-account fund of a particular contract will be pooled with other assets and invested in some mutual fund. To avoid the need to distinguish between an individual contract's sub-account and the associated mutual fund in which is it invested, we will assume here that each sub-account constitutes its own investment entity.

The expenses incurred by the insurer are covered by various charges and fees, of which the following are examples:

(1)   A one-time contract fee charged at issue.

(2)   Percentage charge deducted from each premium or deposit.

(3)   Transaction fees associated with certain transactions.

(4)   Premium tax charge, when levied by certain states.

(5)   Daily, monthly, or annual administrative charge (discussed in more detail later).

(6)   Mortality and expense (M&E) charge, expressed as a percentage of the contract value. (This is the most common charge under a variable annuity.)

Often the IAF and the M&E charge are deducted from the fund value on a daily basis. Note that if several separate accounts are involved under one variable annuity contract, the charges would be deducted from the fund values proportionally.

EXAMPLE 17.3

A deferred variable annuity contract has a daily administrative charge at annual rate .15%, and an M&E charge at annual rate 1.25%. There is only one separate account and no other charges. What is the daily expense charge for this contract as a percent of fund value?

SOLUTION

The combined annual rate is 1.40%, so the effective daily rate is

$$(1.014)^{1/365} - 1 = .00381\%.$$ ❑

Next we consider the calculation of the variable annuity fund value, which is considerably more complex than for the fixed annuity of the previous section. One contract might involve several sub-accounts, so the value of the contract is the sum of the values over all sub-accounts. The investment of the contract in each sub-account is expressed in terms of *accumulation units*, so the daily value of each sub-account is found by multiplying the number of accumulation units by the *accumulation unit value* (AUV) on that day.[3] When a deposit is made to a sub-account, the deposit amount, minus any expense charges deducted directly from the deposit, is divided by the AUV for that sub-account on that day to determine the number of accumulation units purchased.

The daily *net investment rate* (NIR) for each sub-account is calculated by adding the net investment income (such as bond interest or stock dividends), plus capital gains (minus losses), both realized and unrealized, subtracting the applicable investment advisory fee, and

---

[3] This use of units is similar to mutual fund investments.

dividing by the sub-account's fund value at the beginning of the day. Then the daily *net investment factor* is $NIF = 1 + NIR$.

We can put the preceding words into symbols to show the relationships more clearly. Since all calculations are done on a daily basis, we subscript each symbol with t to denote the value on day t. Except for the overall contract value, all calculations are done separately for sub-account n. The important notation is defined in Table 17.1.

TABLE 17.1

Symbol	Meaning on Day t for Sub-Account n
$FV_t(n)$	Fund Value
$AUV_t(n)$	Accumulation Unit Value
$AU_t(n)$	Number of Accumulation Units
$NIF_t(n)$	Net Investment Factor
$NII_t(n)$	Net Investment Income
$RCG_t(n)$	Realized Capital Gains (Losses)
$UCG_t(n)$	Unrealized Capital Gains (Losses)

As mentioned earlier, an investment advisory fee (IAF), expressed as a percentage of the fund value, is deducted from the investment income. (The amount of this fee is typically from 0.5% to 2.5% as an annual rate, but is deducted on a daily basis.) In addition to the IAF (which is deducted directly from investment income), there would likely be other expense charges deducted from the sub-account fund value on a daily basis.

If we let $IAF(n)$ denote the investment advisory fee rate for sub-account n, as an annual rate, then the investment advisory fee for that sub-account for day t would be

$$IAF_t(n) = FV_{t-1}(n) \cdot \left[\left(1 + IAF(n) \right)^{1/365} - 1 \right]. \tag{17.1}$$

The net investment rate for day t is then determined as

$$NIF_t(n) = \frac{NII_t(n) - IAF_t(n) + RCG_t(n) + UCG_t(n)}{FV_{t-1}(n)}, \tag{17.2}$$

and the net investment factor is

$$NIF_t(n) = 1 + NIR_t(n). \tag{17.3}$$

Then the sub-account fund value is updated by

$$FV_t(n) = FV_{t-1}(n) \cdot NIF_t(n) - EXP_t(n), \tag{17.4}$$

where $EXP_t(n)$ denotes expense charges deducted directly from the fund value. Finally, the overall contract account value on day t is

$$AV_t = \sum_n FV_t(n).$$

(17.5)

EXAMPLE 17.4

Suppose the variable annuity of Example 17.3 has three sub-accounts instead of one. A client purchases a contract on 12/1/10 with a $100,000 deposit, and allocates 35% to sub-account A, whose unit value is 35 at that time. The investment advisory fee is 1%, as an annual rate. There is no investment income nor realized capital gain or loss that day, but the fund goes up by 2% because of underlying market gains. Calculate the fund value and unit value for 12/2/10 for sub-account A.

SOLUTION

From Example 17.3 we know the combined daily expense charge is .00381%, so the expense charge amount for sub-account A for the first day is

$$EXP_1(A) = (100,000)(.35)(.0000381) = 1.33350.$$

The deposit purchases 1000 units, and the initial sub-account value is 35,000. By Equation (17.1), the first day's investment advisory fee is $35,000\left[(1.01)^{1/365} - 1\right] = .95415$. The underlying market gain produces an unrealized capital gain of $(35,000)(.02) = 700.00$. By Equations (17.2) and (17.3), the net investment factor for the first day for sub-account A is

$$NIF_1(A) = 1 + \frac{700 - .95415}{35,000} = 1.01997274.$$

Then by Equation (17.4), the updated sub-account fund value is

$$FV_1(A) = (35,000)(1.01997274) - 1.33350 = 35,697.71,$$

and the updated unit value is $AUV_1(A) = 35.69771$. ❑

Finally, we note that a variable annuity contract is subject to surrender charges upon partial withdrawal of funds or full surrender of the contract. The surrender charges, and resulting cash surrender value, are calculated in the same way as for fixed deferred annuities.

17.2.3 EQUITY-INDEXED DEFERRED ANNUITY

This special type of annuity is generally considered to be a hybrid of the fixed and variable annuities already discussed. It generally offers a minimum guaranteed interest rate designed to satisfy the Standard Non-Forfeiture Law (SNFL). The rate earned on the contract fund, as the name implies, is linked to a common stock index, such as the Standard and Poor 500 (SP500) or the Dow Jones Industrial Average (DJIA). The minimum guaranteed rate provides the contract holder with a degree of protection against bad market performance.

The interest actually earned on the account will depend on the performance of the index as well as the indexing method in use.

Most companies do not charge explicit front-end loads or fees with this product, but rather cover their expenses by the *interest spread* that is built into the indexing formula. In this section we describe the common indexing methods and the subsequent fund value calculations. The calculation of surrender charges and cash surrender values is similar to that presented for fixed deferred annuities in Section 17.2.1.

An important concept associated with this product is the *minimum guaranteed value* (MGV), which is prescribed by the Standard Non-Forfeiture Law. At the time of this writing, the SNFL requirements are as follows:

(1)   First take the current five-year CMT rate, round it to the nearest .0005, and reduce it by 1.25%, but with the resulting rate to be not less than 1.00%.

(2)   Then take the lesser of the rate described in Step (1) or 3%.

(3)   Then accumulate all gross considerations (premiums) paid under the contract at the rate from Step (2).

(4)   Then the MGV for a deferred equity-indexed annuity is 87.5% of the accumulated value from Step (3).

Usually the company will reset the rate each year, to apply to new contracts issued in the coming year, using the CMT rate as of November 30 of the prior year.[4]

EXAMPLE 17.5

A single-premium equity-indexed deferred annuity is issued on 1/1/05. The constant maturity treasury (CMT) rate on 11/30/04 is 3.72%. Find the minimum guaranteed interest rate for this contract.

SOLUTION

The CMT rate is .0372 which is rounded to .0370. Then we reduce it by .0125 to reach .0245. Since this is less than 3%, the defined minimum guaranteed interest rate is .0245, or 2.45%. ❑

The calculation of the MGV will be illustrated in several examples later in this section.

There are two common indexing methods used to determine investment return in relation to changes in the chosen index, called the *point-to-point indexing method* and the *average indexing method*. Before describing these two methods, we first wish to define some important terms.

The *index period*, usually ranging from seven to ten years, is the time period over which the index-based interest is credited. At the end of the index period, the contract holder is usually given the option of choosing another index period or leaving the fund in a fixed account.

---

[4] The five-year CMT rate can be found on the Federal Reserve website at www.federalreserve.gov/releases/h15/.

The *participation rate* determines how much of the increase in the value of the index will be applied to increase the account. For example, if the participation rate is 80% and the index grows by 10%, then the indexed account will grow by 8%. The participation rate is set at issue of the contract, and can be changed after the initial index period.

The *cap rate* sets a ceiling on the index-based interest rate. For example, if the contract has a cap rate of 6% and the calculated index-based interest rate is 8%, then the credited rate on the account is 6%. If the calculated index-based rate is 4.6%, that will also be the credited rate on the account.

The *index spread* is the amount deducted from the initially-calculated index-based interest rate. The spread can be reset each year, but will never be set to allow the resulting index-based interest rate to be negative.

The *floor* is the minimum possible index-based interest rate. It is often set at 0%, but could be set higher. It serves as a minimum guarantee for the index-based account value, guaranteeing that the account value will never be less than the initial fund value allocated to the index-based account.

We now consider the two most common indexing methods. The point-to-point method calculates the credited interest rate using the performance of the index for the term of the calculation. Letting i_p denote the index-based credited rate using this method we have

$$i_P = \frac{Index\ value\ on\ closing\ day\ of\ index\ period}{Index\ value\ on\ initial\ day\ of\ index\ period} - 1.$$

$$(17.6)$$

The average method, as the name implies, calculates the credited interest rate using the average (daily or monthly) performance of the index over the calculation period. For example, if i_{MA} denotes the index-based credited rate using the monthly average method we have

$$i_{MA} = \frac{\frac{1}{12n}[Sum\ of\ index\ values\ on\ last\ day\ of\ each\ month\ during\ index\ period]}{Index\ value\ on\ initial\ day\ of\ index\ period} - 1,$$

$$(17.7)$$

where n is the number of years in the calculation period. Either indexing method could be used in conjunction with a cap rate, index spread, and/or participation rate, and usually is subject to a floor return of at least 0%.

A concept called *annual ratcheting* (or *annual reset*) is often used in calculating the index-based credited rate. Under this concept, interest earned each year is locked in so that gain will not be offset by a future loss. In this case, the index-based credited rate is calculated each year using the beginning index value and the closing index value each contract year.

The indexing methods are illustrated in the following three examples.

EXAMPLE 17.6

Consider a $10,000 single-premium equity-indexed deferred annuity issued on 1/1/05, using the SP500 index and an index period of five years. The contract uses the point-to-point indexing method with no annual ratcheting, an 8% cap rate, an 80% participation rate (PR), and 0% spread and floor. The minimum guaranteed interest rate for this contract was found to be 2.45% in Example 17.5. Calculate the MGV and indexed account values for the first five years of the contract.

SOLUTION

The calculated values are shown in Table 17.2.

TABLE 17.2

Time Period	Minimum Guaranteed Value	SP500 Value[5]	Index-Based Interest Rate (Before PR)	Index-Based Interest Rate (After PR)	Indexed Account Value
(1)	(2)	(3)	(4)	(5)	(6)
0	10,000	1181.27			10,000
1	8,964	1248.29	5.67%	4.54%	10,454
2	9,184	1418.30	20.07	8.00	10,800
3	9,409	1468.36	24.30	8.00	10,800
4	9,640	903.25	−23.54	0.00	10,000
5	9,876	1115.10	− 5.60	0.00	10,000

Recall that the minimum guaranteed value is 87.5% of the accumulated value as defined earlier in this section. Then in this example we have

$$(MGV)_t = (10,000)(.875)(1.0245)^t,$$

and the reader can verify the values shown in Column (2). Using the point-to-point indexing method, the index-based interest rate at time t, before applying the participation rate, is found as $\frac{(SP500)_t}{(SP500)_0} - 1$, and the reader can verify the values shown in Column (4).[6] After applying the 80% participation rate, and considering the 8% cap rate and the 0% floor, we reach the final index-based interest rates at time t shown in Column (5), which the reader should verify.[7] Finally, the indexed account values shown in Column (6) are the accumulated values of the single premium using the rates shown in Column (5). Note the effect of no annual ratcheting; the early gains are wiped out by the decline in the SP500 value in the later years. ◻

---

[5] SP500 index values can be found on any of several financial websites, such as www.finance.yahoo.com/q/hp?s=%5EGSPC+Historical+Prices.

[6] Note that these rates, as well as those in Column (5), are *cumulative* from time 0 to time t, so each rate has a different effective period.

[7] Likewise, each rate in Column (5) is effective over the interval from time 0 to time t.

EXAMPLE 17.7

Now we impose the annual ratcheting feature on the contract of Example 17.6, with all other features remaining the same. (Note that the minimum guaranteed values will not change, and are therefore omitted from our results.) Again we wish to determine the indexed account values.

SOLUTION

The calculated values are shown in Table 17.3.

TABLE 17.3

Time Period	SP500 Value	Index-Based Interest Rate (Before PR)	Index-Based Interest Rate (After PR)	Indexed Account Value
(1)	(2)	(3)	(4)	(5)
0	1181.27			10,000
1	1248.29	5.67%	4.54%	10,454
2	1418.30	13.62	8.00	11,290
3	1468.36	3.53	2.82	11,609
4	903.25	− 38.49	0.00	11,609
5	1115.10	23.45	8.00	12,537

This time the point-to-point indexing method produces *annual* index-based interest rates (before applying the participation rate) using $\frac{(SP500)_t}{(SP500)_{t-1}} - 1$, and the reader should verify the values shown in Column (3). After applying the 80% participation rate, and considering the 8% cap rate and the 0% floor, we reach the final index-based annual interest rates shown in Column (4), which the reader should verify. Finally, the indexed account values shown in Column (5) are the accumulated values of the single premium using the Column (4) annual rates. Note that they are never less than the MGVs shown in Column (2) of Table 17.2.   ❏

EXAMPLE 17.8

Again consider the contract of Examples 17.6 and 17.7, using annual ratcheting, but this time with no cap rate, 100% participation rate, 2% spread, and 0% floor. Again we wish to determine the indexed account values, this time using the monthly average indexing method.

SOLUTION

The calculated values are shown in Table 17.4 on the following page. The average monthly SP500 values in Column (2) were calculated using month-end values during the year, and they imply the annual rates (before spread) shown in Column (3). This time the participation rate is 100%, but there is a spread reduction of 2%. Since no cap rate applies, the resulting rates shown in Column (4) can exceed 8% but the 0% floor prevents them from being negative. Then the indexed account values in Column (5) follow from the annual interest rates of Column (4).

Table 17.4

Time Period	Average Monthly SP500 Value	Index-Based Interest Rate (Before Spread)	Index-Based Interest Rate (After Spread)	Indexed Account Value
(1)	(2)	(3)	(4)	(5)
0	1181.27			10,000
1	1207.77	2.24%	0.24%	10,024
2	1318.31	9.15	7.15	10,741
3	1478.10	12.12	10.12	11,828
4	1215.22	−17.78	0.00	11,828
5	948.52	−21.95	0.00	11,828

17.2.4 The Payout Phase of a Deferred Annuity

At the maturity date of the deferred annuity contract, the accumulation phase is completed and annuity payments begin.[8] This is called the *payout phase* of the annuity. The accumulated value at the maturity date is the actuarial present value of the future payments.

The contract holder usually can choose from among several payout options, including an annuity certain or a life contingent annuity, with or without a number of certain payments. The frequency of the payments could be annual or m times per year. The APVs of these annuity functions were presented in Chapter 8.

Often the contract holder elects to receive the payments on a last-survivor basis with another person, commonly the contract holder's spouse, again with or without a term certain. The details of such multi-life annuities were described in Chapter 12.

In the cases described above, the payment would be a fixed amount for the duration of the payout phase. Alternatively, a variable payment amount might be elected. In this case the first payment would be calculated using an interest rate prevailing at the maturity date, and subsequent payments could be higher or lower depending on the interest rate prevailing at the time of payment. The details of this are presented in Section 17.3.2.

Example 17.9

A deferred annuity contract matures with an accumulated value of $120,000. The annuitant is 85 years old and elects a life annuity with no certain period so as to maximize the annual payment. The insurer's life table produces $\ddot{a}_{85} = 7.8950$ calculated at 5% interest. Determine the annual annuity payment.

Solution

The fixed life annuity payment is $P = \dfrac{120,000}{7.8950} = 15,199.49.$

---

[8] Not all contracts reach their maturity date, as many are surrendered for their cash value prior to maturity.

17.2.5 GUARANTEED MINIMUM DEATH BENEFIT

If the contract holder dies during the accumulation phase of a variable deferred annuity, the contract value is paid to a designated beneficiary. Because the contract value could fall to a very low level during a period of poor financial market performance, the deferred annuity might include a *guaranteed minimum death benefit* (GMDB) rider. In this case the death benefit paid would be the larger of the contract value or the GMDB amount.

There are two common death benefit options in use. The *return of premium* option provides a death benefit of the larger of the contract value or the sum of premiums paid less any withdrawals that have been taken. The *annual step-up* option resets the GMDB at the end of each contract year to be the largest of (a) the contract value, (b) the prior GMDB, or (c) the GMDB under the return of premium option. The effect of this is that the GMDB could be greater than under the return of premium option since favorable investment performance would have been locked in. If additional deposits were made to the contract between the last step-up (i.e., the end of the prior contract year) and the date of death, those deposits would be added to the GMDB as well.

EXAMPLE 17.10

A variable annuity contract is purchased on 1/1/07 with a deposit of $50,000. On 12/31/07 the contract value is $53,000. The contract holder makes a second deposit of $10,000 on 6/30/08. Due to a falling market, the contract value on 12/31/08 has dropped to $59,000. The contract holder dies on 4/5/09, at which time the contract value is $61,000. No withdrawals were taken from the contract. What is the GMDB under the return of premium option?

SOLUTION

The contract value of $61,000 exceeds the $60,000 total of premiums paid, which is the GMDB, so the death benefit actually paid is $61,000. (The GMDB under this contract, using the annual step-up option, is considered in Exercise 17-7.) ◻

Usually the return of premium option is offered at no cost to the contract holder. On the other hand, the annual step-up option, which provides a greater benefit, carries a cost that is calculated in the same way as the M&E charge described earlier.

17.2.6 GUARANTEED MINIMUM INCOME BENEFIT

Because the contract value at maturity could be disappointingly small due to a falling market, producing a disappointingly small annuity payment, variable annuities offer a *guaranteed minimum income benefit* (GMIB) rider. The rider provides a guaranteed minimum accumulation value at maturity, which is called the *guaranteed benefit base*. The guaranteed benefit base is calculated simply by accumulating all deposits to the contract at a specified compound annual interest rate, such as 5%. Then the guaranteed minimum income payment is found by dividing the guaranteed benefit base by the appropriate annuity factor at maturity.

Of course if the actual contract value at maturity exceeds the guaranteed benefit base, the contract value is used to calculate the annuity payments.

The cost of the GMIB rider is reflected in a charge deducted from the contract value, usually expressed as a percentage of the contract value or as a percentage of the greater of the contract value or the guaranteed benefit base. It is deducted in the same way as the M&E charge described earlier.

EXAMPLE 17.11

A variable annuity is purchased on 1/1/00 with a deposit of $50,000. On 12/31/07 the contract value is $63,000. On 6/30/08 the contract holder makes another deposit of $10,000. Due to a declining market, the contract value drops to $70,500 on 12/31/09. The contract holder retires on 1/1/10. If a GMIB rider, guaranteeing 5% compound annual interest, was purchased at issue for a fee of .75% of contract value, calculate the guaranteed benefit base.

SOLUTION

The guaranteed benefit base is the accumulation of the deposits at 5% effective annual rate, producing

$$50,000(1.05)^{10} + 10,000(1.05)^{1.5} = 81,444.73 + 10,759.30 = 92,204.03.$$

Because this amount exceeds the 1/1/10 contract value of $70,500.00, it is used to calculate the annuity income payment. ❒

17.2.7 MISCELLANEOUS CONSIDERATIONS

In recent years, two other riders on deferred variable annuities have become available.

The *guaranteed minimum accumulation benefit* (GMAB) rider defines a guaranteed benefit base to be the sum of all premiums paid. (It differs from the GMIB rider in that it allows the accumulated value to be taken as a lump sum rather than as periodic annuity payments.) Then if a falling market produces a contract value at maturity that is less than the sum of deposits to the contract, the contract holder can take the sum of deposits instead of the contract value at maturity as a lump sum settlement.

The *guaranteed minimum withdrawal benefit* (GMWB) rider is similar to the GMAB rider, except that it applies earlier than the maturity date. It locks in investment gains during the term of the contract, allowing them to be taken as partial withdrawals once the policy holder reaches a certain age.

Both the GMAB rider and the GMWB rider are expensive, especially during a period of depressed markets. The company will deduct a charge from the contract value to cover the cost of the riders in the same way as for the GMIB charge. Furthermore, there may be some restrictions imposed on the contract holder's choices of investment options when these riders are purchased with the annuity contract.

17.3 IMMEDIATE ANNUITY PRODUCTS

Unlike the deferred annuity described in Section 17.2, under an *immediate annuity* there is no accumulation period. Here a lump sum, or single premium, is paid to an insurer in return for a sequence of payments usually beginning one month after the single deposit is made. No explicit charges or fees are imposed; rather the insurer's expenses are covered in setting the income payment.

17.3.1 FIXED IMMEDIATE ANNUITY

With a *fixed immediate annuity* the payment is fixed and guaranteed, and is based on the insurer's annuity factor at the attained age of the contract holder at issue. This calculation is the same as that made at the end of the accumulation phase, and the beginning of the payout phase, of a deferred annuity. The payment options described earlier for deferred annuities would usually be available in the immediate annuity case as well.

EXAMPLE 17.12

An 85-year-old investor, with a certificate of deposit maturing for $105,000.00, wishes to purchase a single premium fixed immediate annuity payable for life with five years certain. Using the life table in Appendix A, with 6% annual interest, calculate the annual annuity payment.

SOLUTION

The immediate annuity factor is

$$a_{\overline{85:5}} = a_{\overline{5}} + {}_5E_{85} \cdot a_{90} = a_{\overline{5}} + v^5 \cdot {}_5p_{85}(\ddot{a}_{90}-1)$$

$$= 4.21236 + (.74726)(.57561)\left(\frac{1-.75282}{.06/1.06} - 1\right)$$

$$= 4.21236 + (.74726)(.57561)(3.36685) = 5.66054.$$

Then the guaranteed annual payment is

$$P = \frac{105,000}{5.66054} = 18,549.46. \qquad \square$$

17.3.2 VARIABLE IMMEDIATE ANNUITY

The *variable immediate annuity* will offer the same payment options as in the fixed case. The initial payment, which we denote by P_1, is calculated as in the fixed case, dividing the deposit by the insurer's annuity factor at the attained age. The interest rate used in the annuity factor to determine the initial payment is called the *assumed interest rate* (AIR).

Subsequent payments might then be more or less than the initial payment, depending on the investment performance of the associated separate accounts. Similar to the use of accumulation units during the accumulation phase of a deferred annuity, here we use *payment units* and *payment unit values* (also called *annuity unit values*). Then the initial payment divided by the payment unit value at that time gives the (fixed) number of annuity payment units. That is,

$$APU = \frac{P_1}{PUV_1}. \tag{17.8}$$

As before, the *net investment return* (NIR_t) is calculated each period from the performance of the associated separate accounts, and the *net investment factor* (NIF_t) is defined as $NIF_t = 1 + NIR_t$. Then the payment unit value is updated as

$$PUV_t = PUV_{t-1}\left(\frac{NIF_t}{1+AIR}\right), \tag{17.9}$$

and the payment at time t is

$$P_t = (APU)(PUV_t). \tag{17.10}$$

Using Equation (17.9) to substitute for PUV_t in Equation (17.10), we have

$$P_t = (APU)(PUV_{t-1})\left(\frac{NIF_t}{1+AIR}\right) = P_{t-1}\left(\frac{NIF_t}{1+AIR}\right). \tag{17.11}$$

EXAMPLE 17.13

Suppose the investor in Example 17.12 purchases a variable immediate annuity instead, choosing the life option with no term certain. The annuity factor is $a_{85} = 8$, based on an AIR of 3%. The unit value at the time of purchase is $PUV_1 = 7.234$. The net investment factors for the first two contract years are $NIF_1 = 1.048$ and $NIF_2 = 1.006$. Calculate the number of annuity payment units and the first, second, and third annual annuity payment amounts.

SOLUTION

The initial payment is $P_1 = \frac{105,000}{8} = 13,125.00$, so the number of payment units is

$$APU = \frac{P_1}{PUV_1} = \frac{13,125.00}{7.234} = 1814.35.$$

Then the second payment is

$$P_2 = P_1\left(\frac{NIF_1}{1+AIR}\right) = 13,125.00\left(\frac{1.048}{1.03}\right) = 13,354.37,$$

and the third payment is

$$P_3 = P_2\left(\frac{NIF_2}{1+AIR}\right) = 13,354.37\left(\frac{1.006}{1.03}\right) = 13,043.20. \qquad \square$$

Note how the payment decreases whenever NIF_t is less than $1 + AIR$. Some insurers will offer a *minimum income guarantee*, which is charged for by reducing the payment amount.

17.4 PRICING CONSIDERATIONS

An insurer needs to consider a number of factors in selecting the structure of charges and fees used in pricing a variable annuity product. The resulting product needs to be profitable, so all expenses need to be covered, while remaining competitive in the marketplace.

17.4.1 VARIABLE DEFERRED ANNUITY

Even if a guaranteed minimum death benefit (GMDB) rider is attached to a variable annuity contract, if the funds perform well, so that the GMDB does not come into play, then the company will not have to pay a death benefit in excess of the account value. Then there is no mortality risk and no cost of insurance under the contract. On the other hand, if the death benefit amount exceeds the contract value there will be an extra cost to the company, so that a GMDB fee will need to be charged.

Profit to the insurer from a variable deferred annuity contract arises primarily from investment income being greater than the amount required to be credited to the contract. This can be particularly lucrative at the later durations of a contract, so it is very important to the insurer that the contract be kept in force for as long as possible. In light of this, the *lapse* (or *persistency*) assumptions are very important. Often we find that a contract needs to stay in force for ten, or even more, years in order to be profitable for the insurer. This explains why surrender charges are generally assessed for surrender during the first ten years.

Commissions are generally paid to sales agents as a percentage of the premiums (or deposits), and are generally higher in the first year than in subsequent years. If a contract is surrendered at an early duration, some insurers use a commission chargeback to recoup some of the early commission expense.

The assumption of investment return under these contracts is the most unpredictable of the assumptions. Many insurers use stochastic simulation to predict returns on the various separate accounts supporting variable annuity contracts. The details of these complicated models are beyond the scope of this introductory text.

17.4.2 VARIABLE IMMEDIATE ANNUITY

In Section 17.4.1 we saw that the mortality experience during the deferred period does not have a significant effect on profitability, since the death benefit is generally the contract value.

Under an immediate annuity with a life contingent payout option, however, adverse mortality experience can have a significant impact on profitability. Consequently the mortality assumption is very important. Insurers will generally start with a life table based on a recent experience study, and add a margin for conservatism and future mortality improvements. This often takes the form of a *projection scale factor*, expressed as an annual rate of improvement in survival rates. This is illustrated in the following example.

EXAMPLE 17.14

Consider the following set of survival probabilities for an 85-year-old person:

t	$_t p_{85}$	t	$_t p_{85}$	t	$_t p_{85}$
1	.979	6	.792	11	.437
2	.953	7	.735	12	.344
3	.922	8	.671	13	.244
4	.885	9	.600	14	.124
5	.842	10	.522	15	.000

At interest rate $i = .05$, the APV of a life annuity-due is $\ddot{a}_{85} = 7.895$. Recalculate $\ddot{a}_{85}$ by assuming a mortality improvement projection scale factor of .50% per year for the first ten years only.

SOLUTION

The projection scale factor is applied by setting

$$q^*_{x+t} = (1-.005)^t \cdot q_{x+t},$$

for $t = 1, 2, \cdots, 10,$ and

$$q^*_{x+t} = (1-.005)^{10} \cdot q_{x+t},$$

for $t \geq 10.$ The projected (improved) survival rates, denoted by $_t p^*_{85}$, are as shown in the following table:

t	$_t p^*_{85}$	t	$_t p^*_{85}$	t	$_t p^*_{85}$
1	.9790	6	.7949	11	.4503
2	.9531	7	.7394	12	.3596
3	.9224	8	.6772	13	.2697
4	.8860	9	.6084	14	.1445
5	.8438	10	.5328	15	.0098

At interest rate $i = .05$, the value of $\ddot{a}_{85}$ based on the projected (improved) survival rates is $\ddot{a}^*_{85} = 7.963.$ ❑

In order to attract business from persons with impaired health conditions, substandard mortality rates might be used in the pricing factors. The higher mortality rates for the substandard class produce larger annuity payments.

Lapse rates are not important in pricing immediate annuities, since once payments begin the contract cannot be surrendered for a cash value.

As with the variable deferred annuity, the assumed investment return is an extremely important pricing assumption for a variable immediate annuity.

17.5 RESERVING CONSIDERATIONS

The NLP terminal reserve for a deferred annuity was presented in Section 10.1.6. As an alternative to holding the NLP reserve, insurers in the United States might hold the statutory minimum reserve given by the *Commissioners Annuity Reserve Valuation Method* (CARVM).

17.5.1 DEFERRED ANNUITY RESERVE

The reserve would be calculated by the basic prospective definition. The CARVM reserve is calculated by the following steps:

(1)   Project the fund value to the end of each contract year.

(2)   Project the guaranteed benefits, using the projected fund values, to the end of each contract year.

(3)   Calculate the APV of the guaranteed benefits minus the APV of future contract premiums.

(4)   Then the CARVM reserve is defined to be the greatest of the results obtained in Step (3).

The fund values are projected using the guaranteed interest rate, and the APVs are calculated using the valuation interest rate prescribed by the regulators. The details of this calculation are illustrated in the following example.

EXAMPLE 17.15

Consider a $10,000 single premium deferred annuity, with surrender charges of 10% in the first year, 8% in the second year, $\cdots$, 2% in the fifth year, and 0% in all years thereafter. Assume the death benefit is equal to the cash surrender value and there are no other charges or fees. The guaranteed interest rate is 5.5% in the first year, and 2.5% in all years thereafter, and the valuation rate is 5%. Calculate the initial reserve at time 0, immediately after issue of the contract.

SOLUTION

The death benefit is the same as the cash surrender value, so mortality can be ignored. Furthermore, being a single-premium contract, there are no future premiums, so the subtractive term in Step (3) is zero. The projected fund values in Step (1), using 5.5% in the first year and 2.5% in all subsequent years, are shown in the second column of the table on the following page. The projected cash surrender values are the projected fund values, reduced by the surrender charge. They are the *only* guaranteed benefits under the contract, and are shown in the third column of the table. The present values of the guaranteed benefits, using the valuation rate of 5%, are shown in the fourth column.

t	Projected Fund Value at End of Year t	Guaranteed Cash Value at End of Year t	APV at $t=0$ of Guaranteed Cash Value
1	$10,000(1.055) = 10,550$	$(.90)(10,550) = 9,495$	$9,495v = 9,043$
2	$10,550(1.025) = 10,814$	$(.92)(10,814) = 9,949$	$9,949v^2 = 9,024$
3	$10,814(1.025) = 11,084$	$(.94)(11,084) = 10,419$	$10,419v^3 = 9,000$
4	$11,084(1.025) = 11,361$	$(.96)(11,361) = 10,907$	$10,907v^4 = 8,973$
5	$11,361(1.025) = 11,645$	$(.98)(11,645) = 11,412$	$11,412v^5 = 8,942$
6	$11,645(1.025) = 11,936$	$11,936$	$11,936v^6 = 8,907$
7	$11,936(1.025) = 12,235$	$12,235$	$12,235v^7 = 8,695$

Note that surrender *immediately* after issue, i.e., at time 0^+, would impose a 10% surrender charge producing a cash surrender value of 9,000 and an APV at $t = 0$ of 9,000 as well. The initial CARVM reserve is the largest value in the fourth column, which is 9,043. ❐

17.5.2 IMMEDIATE ANNUITY RESERVE

An immediate annuity has no surrender value (i.e., the contract is *irrevocable*), so the reserve is simply the APV of future annuity payments using the valuation interest rate and life table. For example, an insurer's assumptions might produce an annual annuity payment of $1,267 under a $10,000 single premium immediate annuity, so the APV of future payments at issue, *using the insurer's pricing assumptions*, would be $10,000. The APV of future payments at issue, *using the valuation assumptions*, however, might be, say, $10,805.16. Then the initial reserve at time $t = 0$ would be $10,805.16 rather than $10,000.00.

17.5.3 RESERVING FOR A GUARANTEED MINIMUM DEATH BENEFIT

Recall our discussion of the GMDB rider in Section 17.2.5. The presence of such a guaranteed benefit adds importance to the calculation of the reserve for the contract. The regulators have provided guidance on reserving for such contracts in Actuarial Guideline XXXIV,[9] which suggests the following steps in calculating the statutory reserve for a GMDB attached to a variable annuity contract.

(1)   At the valuation date, *assuming no GMDB*, project the fund value using the assumed crediting rate, which is the valuation interest rate, less any asset-based charges, and determine a benefit stream based on this projection.

(2)   At the valuation date, project the fund value including the GMDB, assuming an immediate drop in the fund value at the valuation date followed by recovery at a specified rate. The drop and recovery rates are specified in Guideline XXXIV, and vary by asset class. Then determine the stream of GMDBs and the resulting net amounts at risk (NAR). The NAR is the excess of the GMDB over the reduced account value.

(3)   Calculate the *integrated reserve*, which includes the GMDB from Step (2) and the other benefits from Step (1). The integrated reserve is defined to be the maximum present value of the future integrated benefit streams.

---

[9] Actuarial Guideline XXXIV can be found on the website of the American Academy of Actuaries, www.actuary.org.

(4)   Calculate the *separate account reserve*, assuming no GMDB. The separate account reserve is the maximum present value of the integrated benefit streams.

(5)   Then the GMDB reserve is the excess of the integrated reserve over the separate account reserve. This reserve is held in the general account.

17.5.4 RESERVING FOR A GUARANTEED MINIMUM INCOME BENEFIT

Actuarial Guideline XXXIX[10] provides guidance on the calculation of the statutory reserve for a GMIB attached to a variable annuity. It suggests the following steps:

(1)   Calculate the aggregate reserve for the contracts assuming no revenue or benefit associated with a GMIB.

(2)   Then the GMIB reserve is equal to the aggregate GMIB charges, from the date of issue to the valuation date, for all contracts eligible for the guaranteed benefits. If there are no explicit charges for the GMIB, a charge should be imputed.

With the recent emergence of the concept of principle-based reserving (see page 347), many insurers have adopted a stochastic simulation approach to calculating reserves for contracts containing GMIB riders. The details of this approach are beyond the scope of this textbook.[11]

17.6 EXERCISES

17.1 Background
17.2 Deferred Annuity Products

17-1   Referring to Example 17.4, suppose the contract holder allocates 20% of the deposit to sub-account B and 45% to sub-account C. The investment advisory fees for these two funds are 0.8% and 0.5%, respectively, and the fund values went up by 1.2% and 4.0%, respectively. Calculate the total account value at the end of the first day.

17-2   Continuing with Exercise 17-1, suppose the contract holder surrenders the contract for its cash value during the second contract year. The surrender charges are 10% of account value in the first year, 8% in the second year, and so on, grading down to 0% in the sixth and subsequent years. The fund values at the time of surrender are $37,000 for sub-account A, $19,000 for sub-account B, and $53,000 for sub-account C. Calculate the cash surrender value paid to the contract holder.

17-3   As an alternative to Equations (17.2), (17.3), and (17.4), we could define $NIR_t(n)$ to include the non-IAF expenses in its numerator rather than deducting them from the updated fund value. Rework Example 17.4 to show that, under this definition of $NIR_t(n)$, the same value of $FV_1(n)$ will result, and that $AUV_1(A) = AUV_0(A) \cdot NIF_1(A)$.

---

[10]See Footnote 5.

[11] Actuarial Guidelines XXXIV and XXXIX have recently been replaced by the new Actuarial Guideline XLIII; it is not discussed in this text.

17-4   A $10,000 deposit purchases a single-premium equity-indexed annuity on 1/1/2008, using the SP500 index with an index period of six years. The contract uses the point-to-point indexing method with no annual ratcheting. The CMT rate on 11/30/07 is 3.41%. Calculate the minimum guaranteed interest rate for this contract.

17-5   Assume that the contract described in Exercise 17-4 has a 7% cap rate, an 80% participation rate, and a 0% index spread and floor. Using the minimum guaranteed interest rate determined in Exercise 17-4, calculate the minimum guaranteed values and the indexed account values at the end of each of the first three years. (The SP500 values on 1/1/05 through 1/1/10 are given in Table 17.2. The SP500 value on 1/1/11 is 1257.64.)

17-6   Suppose the contract described in Exercise 17-4 does use annual ratcheting, along with a 7% cap rate, an 80% participation rate, a 1% index spread, and a 0% floor. Calculate the indexed account values at the end of each of the first three years.

17-7   Referring to Example 17.10, calculate the guaranteed minimum death benefit under the annual step-up option.

17-8   Referring to Example 17.3, assume the annual step-up option is available for determining the GMDB and is charged for at annual rate 0.75%. Calculate the effective daily expense percentage if this option is elected.

17-9   Referring to Example 17.3, assume a GMIB rider is available for purchase at annual rate 0.60% of the contract value. Calculate the effective daily expense percentage if both the GMIB rider and the annual step-up GMDB option are elected.

17.3 Immediate Annuity Products

17-10   A variable deferred annuity is purchased on 1/1/2000 with a deposit of $50,000. The contract includes a return-of-premium GMAB rider, and a seven-year surrender charge schedule. On 12/31/2007 the contract value is $63,000. On 6/30/2008 the contract holder makes another deposit of $10,000. On 12/31/2009 the contract value is $70,500. The contract holder retires on 1/1/2010 and elects to take the value of the contract as a lump sum. Determine the lump sum payment to the contract holder.

17-11   Referring to Example 17.12, calculate the monthly annuity payment if the investor selects a monthly payment option with no payments certain. (Use the Appendix A table and the UDD assumption to approximate the monthly annuity factor.)

17-12 Show that the investment performance of the associated separate account is reflected in the payment amount when the AIR method is used with a five-year certain annuity-due.

17.4 Pricing Considerations

17-13 Referring to Examples 17.12 and 17.14, recalculate the annual payment presuming a .50% projection scale factor for future mortality improvement for the first ten years only.

17-14 A variable deferred annuity contract is issued at age 88 for a deposit of 1000. The contract contains a GMDB rider, and must begin annuity payments at age 90 (so the GMDB does not apply after that age). The GMDB fee is charged at the beginning of the contract year, and any death benefit is paid at the end of the year. There are no other contract fees. Assume that $q_{88} = .10$, $q_{89} = .15$, and $i = 0$. Due to a declining equities market, the account value experiences a 10% decrease in value each year. Using the equivalence principle, calculate the GMDB fee as a percentage of the account value.

17.5 Reserving Considerations

17-15 Referring to Example 17.15, calculate the reserve at $t = 3$, assuming a fund value at that time of $11,150.

17-16 A deferred annuity is purchased with a single deposit of 1000. The valuation interest rate is 4.0%. The guaranteed interest rate is 4.5% in the first three contract years and 2.5% thereafter. The death benefit is equal to the cash surrender value. The following schedule of surrender charges, as a percentage of account value, applies:

Contract Year of Surrender	1	2	3	4	5	6	7	8+
Surrender Charge	7%	6%	5%	4%	3%	2%	1%	0%

Calculate the CARVM reserve at issue for this contract.

APPENDIX A

USING MICROSOFT EXCEL AND VISUAL BASIC MACROS TO COMPUTE ACTUARIAL FUNCTIONS

As mentioned in Chapter 6, the basic representation of the tabular survival model is in terms of the values of ℓ_x. All other functions, such as d_x, p_x, q_x, A_x, $_nE_x$, and so on, can be derived from ℓ_x. In this appendix, we present some examples that use Microsoft Excel and Visual Basic macros to make the computations easier and more efficient.

A.1 DOWNLOADING THE BASIC LIFE TABLE FROM THE ACTEX WEBSITE

On the ACTEX website, the 1989-91 U.S. Life Table (for female lives) is posted to serve as an example for these calculations. The table is in Microsoft Excel files. You can download the table directly to your own computer to work on the calculations.

There are two ways to access the life table:

1. Go to actexmadriver.com/client/client_pages/actex_downlods2.cfm.

   There you will see the Illustrative Life Table Microsoft Excel (.xls) under *Models for Quantifying Risk* in the Free Downloads section.

2. Alternatively, you can go to the main page of our website at actexmadriver.com.

   Click on Free Downloads under Services on the left side. Then click on the link for ACTEX Textbooks, and you will find the same Illustrative Life Table.

A.2 USING EXCEL SPREADSHEETS TO CALCULATE d_x, p_x, AND q_x

A.2.1 REVIEW OF FORMULAS

Consider first the simple formula $d_x = \ell_x - \ell_{x+1}$. Since ℓ_x represents the size of the cohort group at age x, and ℓ_{x+1} represents the number of them still surviving at age $x+1$, then clearly d_x gives the number who fail (or die) between ages x and $x+1$.

EXAMPLE A.1

From the Illustrative Life Table on the ACTEX website, find the number who fails between ages 5 and 6.

SOLUTION

At age 5,

$$d_5 = \ell_5 - \ell_6$$
$$= 99,006 - 98,983 = 23.$$ ❑

Next consider the survival probability $P_x = \dfrac{\ell_{x+1}}{\ell_x}$, where p_x denotes the conditional probability of surviving to age $x+1$, given alive at age x.

EXAMPLE A.2

From the Illustrative Life Table on the ACTEX website, find the probability of surviving to age 6, given alive at age 5.

SOLUTION

We have

$$p_5 = \frac{\ell_6}{\ell_5} = \frac{98,983}{99,006} = .99977.$$ ❑

Next consider $q_x = \dfrac{d_x}{\ell_x} = \dfrac{\ell_x - \ell_{x+1}}{\ell_x} = 1 - p_x$, where q_x gives the conditional probability of failure before age $x+1$, given alive at age x.

EXAMPLE A.3

From the Illustrative Life Table, find the probability of failure before age 6, given alive at age 5.

SOLUTION

This time

$$q_5 = \frac{d_5}{\ell_5} = \frac{23}{99,006} = .00023 = 1 - p_5.$$ ❑

A.2.2 USING MICROSOFT EXCEL TO DO THE ABOVE CALCULATIONS

The above calculations can be made very easily and efficiently by using the formulas and functions in Microsoft Excel. Consider the calculation of d_0 shown in the following spreadsheet.

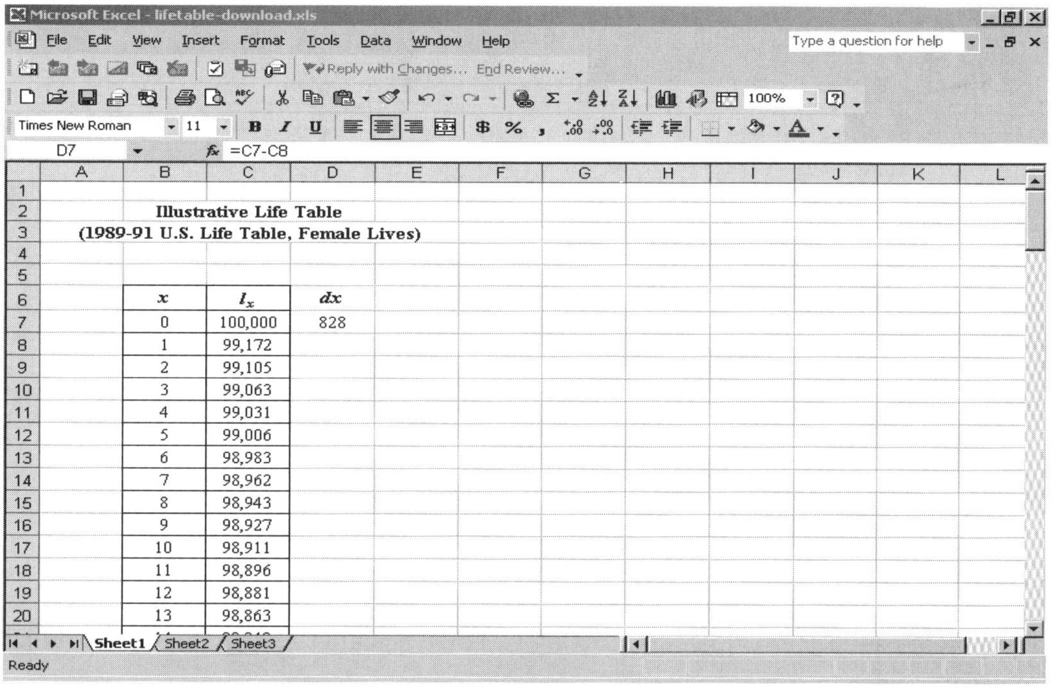

FIGURE A.1

To calculate

$$d_0 = \ell_0 - \ell_1$$
$$= 100,000 - 99,172 = 828,$$

we take the following steps:

1. Click on the cell (D7) where you want to enter a formula.
2. Type an equal sign $(=)$ to begin the formula.
3. Type the formula $(= C7 - C8)$, and then press the **Enter** key.
4. The result of the calculation appears in the cell $(d_0 = 828)$.

For the calculation of $d_1, d_2, ...$, we need the same formula, in relationship to the location into which it is to be typed. There are a number of ways to perform this operation. One way is to use the short cut **Fill Down**.

1. Select the cell that has the original formula (D7).
2. Hold the **Shift** key down and click on the last cell in the series that needs the formula, which is D117 for the Illustrative Life Table.
3. Under the **Edit** menu, go down to **Fill** and over to **Down**.

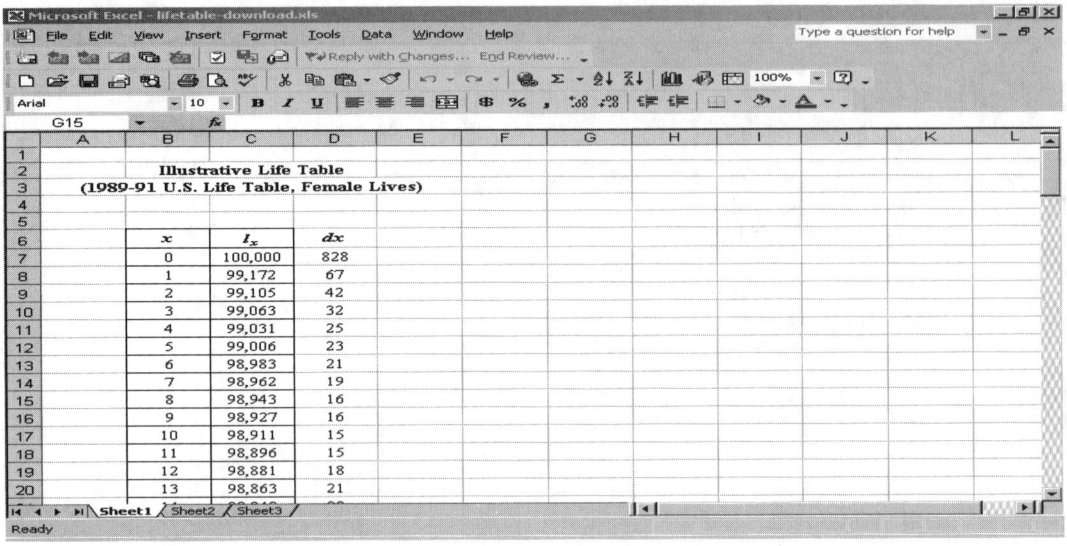

Illustrative Life Table
(1989-91 U.S. Life Table, Female Lives)

x	l_x	dx
0	100,000	828
1	99,172	67
2	99,105	42
3	99,063	32
4	99,031	25
5	99,006	23
6	98,983	21
7	98,962	19
8	98,943	16
9	98,927	16
10	98,911	15
11	98,896	15
12	98,881	18
13	98,863	21

FIGURE A.2

The equation pasted into D8 would be (C8 – C9), the equation pasted into D9 would be (C9 – C10), and so on.

Alternatively, we can use the **Auto Fill Options** button to do the copying of formulas.

1. Position the mouse over the bottom right corner of the cell (mouse changes to +).
2. Drag the mouse + over the cells you want to include in the series.

The calculations of p_x and q_x can be done in a similar way using Microsoft Excel, and are left to the reader as exercises.

A.3 CALCULATING A_x USING VISUAL BASIC MACROS

Although most simple computations can be made using formulas and built-in functions in Excel, Visual Basic macros can make the complicated computations easier and more efficient. For example, consider the discrete whole life insurance APV, denoted by A_x, and given by

$$A_x = \sum_{k=0}^{w-x-1} v^{k+1} \cdot {}_{k|}q_x = \sum_{k=0}^{w-x-1} v^{k+1} \cdot \frac{d_{x+k}}{\ell_x}. \tag{A.1}$$

We can still use the Excel spreadsheet to calculate A_x, but we will find that using Visual Basic macros will simplify the computations. We use the following Visual Basic code to calculate A_x:

```
Private Sub CalculateAx()
    Dim r As Double, v As Double
    Dim I As Integer, K As Integer
    Dim OffsetV As Integer
    Dim Ax As Double
```

'We assume that the interest rate is 6%. (This can be changed.)[1]

r = .06

'v is the discount rate corresponding to the given interest rate r.

v = 1 / (1 + r)

'Offset V defines the vertical position of the starting cell A_0 within the Excel spreadsheet.

```
OffsetV = 7
Sheet1.Cells(OffsetV - 1, 7) = "Ax"
For I = 0 To 110
Ax = 0
    For K = 0 To 111 - I - 1
    Ax = Ax + v ^ (K+1) * Sheet1.Cells(I + K + OffsetV, 4) / Sheet1.Cells(I+OffsetV, 3)
    Next K
    Sheet1.Cells(I + OffsetV, 7) = Ax
Next I
End Sub
```

(Note that to make the Visual Basic code more understandable, we followed the formulas in a straightforward manner. However, the computation can be made more efficient, and the interested reader might try other ways to write the program.)

The result of the computation of A_x is depicted in the following spreadsheet.

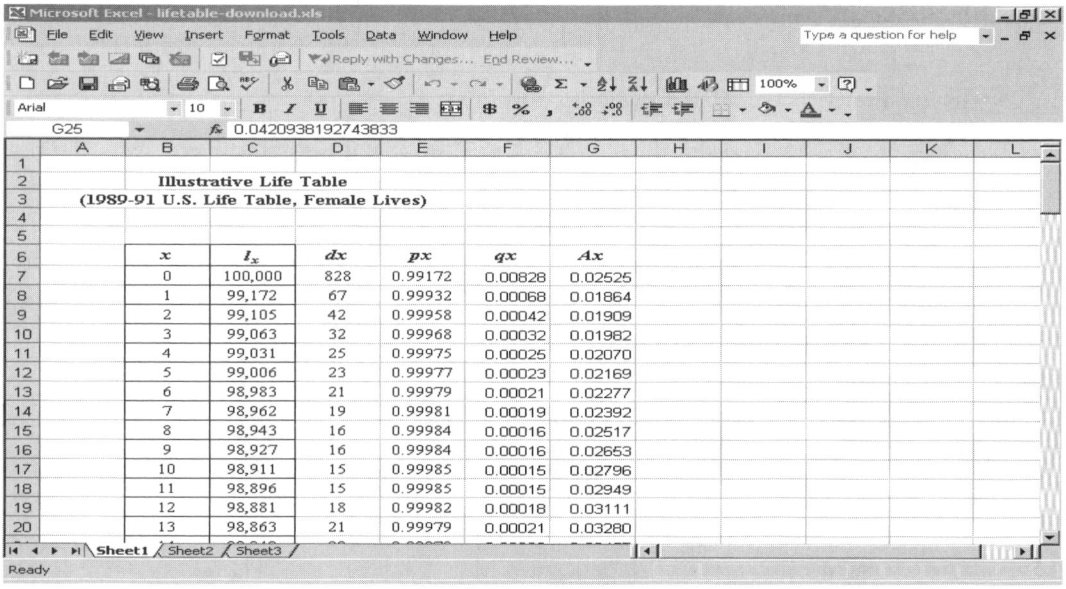

x	l_x	dx	px	qx	Ax
0	100,000	828	0.99172	0.00828	0.02525
1	99,172	67	0.99932	0.00068	0.01864
2	99,105	42	0.99958	0.00042	0.01909
3	99,063	32	0.99968	0.00032	0.01982
4	99,031	25	0.99975	0.00025	0.02070
5	99,006	23	0.99977	0.00023	0.02169
6	98,983	21	0.99979	0.00021	0.02277
7	98,962	19	0.99981	0.00019	0.02392
8	98,943	16	0.99984	0.00016	0.02517
9	98,927	16	0.99984	0.00016	0.02653
10	98,911	15	0.99985	0.00015	0.02796
11	98,896	15	0.99985	0.00015	0.02949
12	98,881	18	0.99982	0.00018	0.03111
13	98,863	21	0.99979	0.00021	0.03280

Illustrative Life Table
(1989-91 U.S. Life Table, Female Lives)

FIGURE A.3

---

[1] Lines that begin with the symbol (') are comments, but not commands in the program.

A.4 CALCULATING $_nE_x$ USING MICROSOFT EXCEL

Throughout the text we have seen that the n-year pure endowment function $_nE_x = v^n \cdot {_np_x}$ is very important in the calculation of other functions, such as

$$A^1_{x:\overline{n}|} = A_x - {_nE_x} \cdot A_{x+n}. \qquad (A.2)$$

Given the age (x) and the number of years n, $_nE_x$ can easily be computed using ℓ_x, ℓ_{x+n}, and the discount rate v.

EXAMPLE A.4

Given the Illustrative Life Table and the interest rate $i = .06$, find $_5E_{45}$.

SOLUTION

Since $i = .06$, then $v = \dfrac{1}{1+i} = .9434$. Then

$$_5E_{45} = v^5 \cdot {_5p_{45}} = v^5 \cdot \frac{\ell_{50}}{\ell_{45}} = .73724. \qquad \square$$

To compute $_5E_{45}$ in Microsoft Excel, we can do the following:

1. Type interest rate $i = .06$ as input in the cell (I3).

2. The discount rate v is calculated using the formula $v = \dfrac{1}{1+i}$.

    Click on the cell (I4), type the formula $(=1/(1+\$I\$3))$, and press the **Enter** key; the result 94.34% then appears in the cell (I4).

3. To calculate $_5E_{45}$, click on the cell (I47) where we want to enter the formula, type the formula $(=\$I\$4 \wedge 5 * C57/C52)$, and press the **Enter** key, to get the value of $_5E_{45}$ $(= .73724)$ in the cell (I47).

The computation of $_5E_{45}$ is depicted in the following spreadsheet:

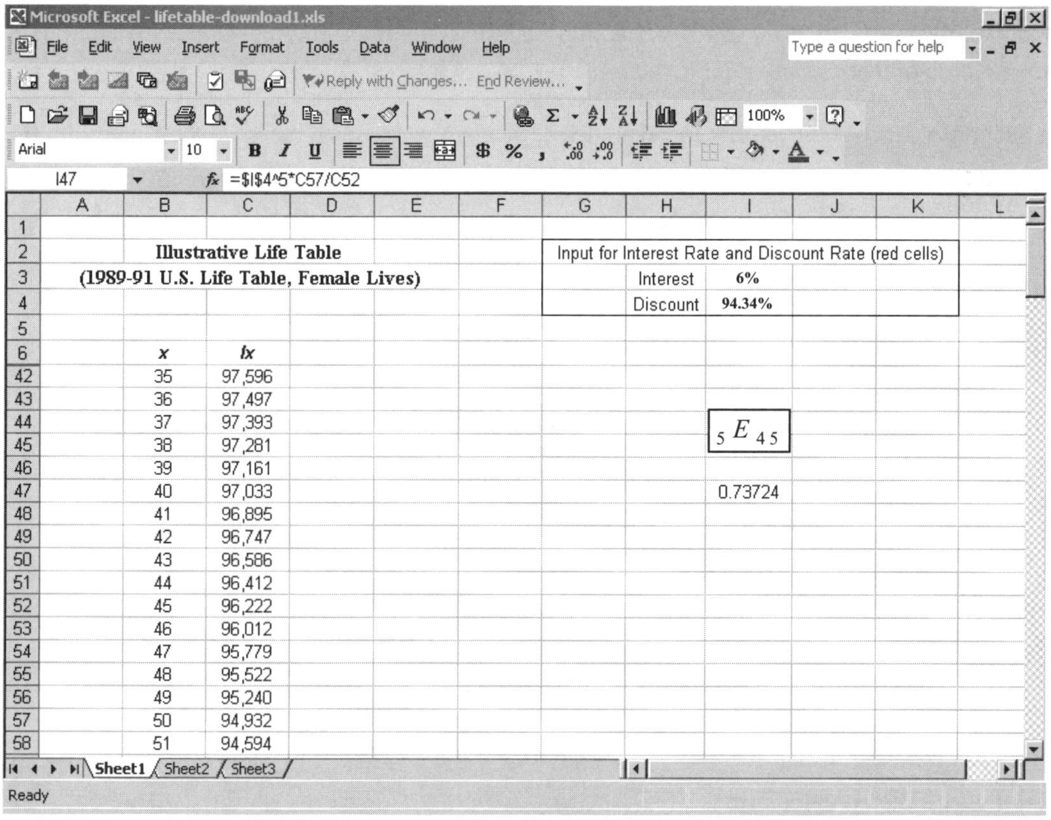

FIGURE A.4

Using an interest rate of 6%, the following table illustrates selected values of $_nE_x$.

TABLE A.1

x	$n=5$	$n=10$	$n=15$	$n=20$	$n=25$
5	.747	.557	.416	.310	.231
25	.745	.554	.412	.305	.225
45	.737	.539	.389	.276	.190
65	.690	.455	.279	.151	.065
85	.430	.127	.023	.002	.000

The reader should choose several combinations of n and x and practice the calculation of $_nE_x$.

A.5 CALCULATING SECOND MOMENTS AND VARIANCES

Recall from Chapter 7 that ^2A_x is the same kind of function as A_x, except that it is calculated at a force of interest that is double the force of interest used to calculate A_x. That is, if interest rate i is used to calculate A_x, then ^2A_x is calculated at rate $i' = (1+i)^2 - 1$, not $i' = 2i$. For example, if $i = .06$, then $i' = .1236$. It is important to remember that ^2A_x is calculated at double the force of interest, not double the effective rate of interest.

In Section A.3, we showed how to calculate A_x using Visual Basic macros. After doubling the force of interest, we can use the same method to compute ^2A_x, being careful to put the values in the right positions. Then the variance of the present value random variable Z_x is given by

$$Var(Z_x) = {}^2A_x - A_x^2. \tag{A.3}$$

EXAMPLE A.5

Given the 1989-91 U.S. Life Table on the ACTEX website, and interest rate $i = .06$, find the variance of Z_{30} from the values shown in Table A.2.

SOLUTION

From Table A.2 we find $A_{30} = .07570$ and $^2A_{30} = .01489$. Then

$$Var(Z_{30}) = {}^2A_{30} - A_{30}^2 = .01489 - (.07570)^2 = .00916. \qquad \square$$

Table A.2, shown on pages 591-593, depicts the 1989-91 U.S Life Table (for female lives), with the completed calculations of d_x, p_x, q_x, A_x, and ^2A_x, where A_x and ^2A_x are calculated at interest rate 6%. The reader could practice his or her programming skills by reproducing the entire table.

A.6 CALCULATING JOINT-LIFE STATUS FUNCTIONS

For a joint-life status assuming independence of the individual lifetimes, the survival distribution function is

$$_tp_{xy} = {}_tp_x \cdot {}_tp_y. \tag{A.4}$$

EXAMPLE A.6

Given the Illustrative Life Table, calculate the value of $_5p_{40:50}$.

SOLUTION

We have

$$_5p_{40:50} = {}_5p_{40} \cdot {}_5p_{50} = \frac{\ell_{45}}{\ell_{40}} \cdot \frac{\ell_{55}}{\ell_{50}} = \frac{96,222}{97,033} \cdot \frac{92,881}{94,932} = .9702. \qquad \square$$

For the calculation of A_{xy}, we can use the formula connecting insurance and annuity functions, which is

$$A_{xy} = 1 - d \cdot \ddot{a}_{xy}, \tag{A.5}$$

since the calculation of $\ddot{a}_{xy}$ is easier to make than is the calculation of A_{xy}. Recall that

$$\ddot{a}_{xy} = \sum_{t=0}^{\infty} v^t \cdot {}_tp_x \cdot {}_tp_y, \qquad (A.6)$$

which can be done using either Microsoft Excel or Visual Basic macros.

EXAMPLE A.7

Given the Illustrative Life Table and interest rate $i = .06$, calculate the value of $A_{80:85}$.

SOLUTION

First we find

$$\ddot{a}_{80:85} = \sum_{t=0}^{\infty} v^t \cdot {}_tp_{80} \cdot {}_tp_{85} = 4.450419$$

and then

$$A_{80:85} = 1 - d \cdot \ddot{a}_{80:85} = 1 - \frac{.06}{1.06} \times 4.450419 = .74809. \qquad \square$$

The above computation can be carried out using Microsoft Excel or Visual Basic macros. Here we give the Visual Basic code as an example. The reader is encouraged to do the calculation himself or herself using the Excel spreadsheet.

```
Private Sub Calculate_Axy()
    Dim r As Double, v As Double, d As Double
    Dim J As Integer
    Dim x As Integer, y As Integer
    Dim axy As Double, A_xy As Double
    Dim tpx As Double, tpy As Double
    Dim OffsetV As Integer

    'The interest rate is assumed to be 6%. (This can be changed.)

    r = .06

    'The discount factor v and the effective discount rate d can be calculated.

    v = 1 / (1 + r)
    d = r * v

    'x and y define the ages for a two-life joint status.

    x = 80
    y = 85

    'OffsetV defines the vertical position of the starting cell of ℓ₀ in the spreadsheet.
    OffsetV = 7
    axy = 0
    For J = 0 To 111 - y
```

```
    tpx = Sheet2.Cells(J + OffsetV + x, 3) / Sheet2.Cells(OffsetV + x, 3)
    tpy = Sheet2.Cells(J + OffsetV + y, 3) / Sheet2.Cells(OffsetV + y, 3)
    axy = axy + v ^ J * tpx * tpy
    Next J
    Sheet2.Cells(11, 6) = axy
    A_xy = 1 - d * axy
    Sheet2.Cells(16, 6) = A_xy
End Sub
```

The results of the above program are depicted in the following spreadsheet:

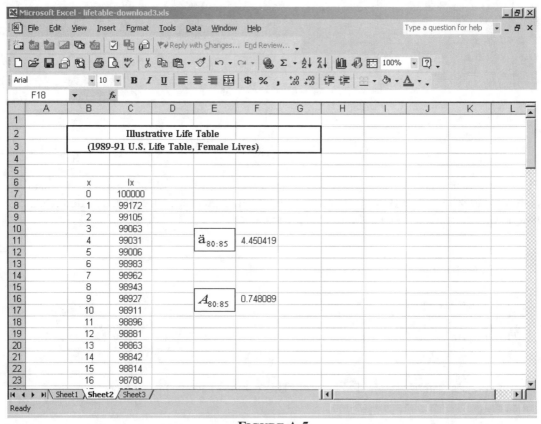

FIGURE A.5

We emphasize that A_x and $_nE_x$ are the basic functions to be understood. Then all the other functions, such as term insurance, annuities, reserves, and so on, can be derived from A_x and $_nE_x$.

TABLE A.2

1989-91 U.S. Life Table (for female lives)					
x	ℓ_x	d_x	p_x	q_x	A_x	^2A_x
0	100,000	828	.99172	.00828	.02525	.01015
1	99,172	67	.99932	.00068	.01864	.00315
2	99,105	42	.99958	.00042	.01909	.00286
3	99,063	32	.99968	.00032	.01982	.00279
4	99,031	25	.99975	.00025	.02070	.00282
5	99,006	23	.99977	.00023	.02169	.00291
6	98,983	21	.99979	.00021	.02277	.00304
7	98,962	19	.99981	.00019	.02392	.00321
8	98,943	16	.99984	.00016	.02517	.00341
9	98,927	16	.99984	.00016	.02653	.00367
10	98,911	15	.99985	.00015	.02796	.00396
11	98,896	15	.99985	.00015	.02949	.00430
12	98,881	18	.99982	.00018	.03111	.00468
13	98,863	21	.99979	.00021	.03280	.00508
14	98,842	28	.99972	.00028	.03457	.00550
15	98,814	34	.99966	.00034	.03637	.00590
16	98,780	40	.99960	.00040	.03822	.00628
17	98,740	45	.99954	.00046	.04012	.00666
18	98,695	48	.99951	.00049	.04209	.00703
19	98,647	50	.99949	.00051	.04416	.00741
20	98,597	51	.99948	.00052	.04632	.00783
21	98,546	54	.99945	.00055	.04861	.00828
22	98,492	54	.99945	.00055	.05100	.00876
23	98,438	56	.99943	.00057	.05355	.00930
24	98,382	57	.99942	.00058	.05622	.00989
25	98,325	58	.99941	.00059	.05905	.01053
26	98,267	59	.99940	.00060	.06204	.01125
27	98,208	61	.99938	.00062	.06520	.01205
28	98,147	65	.99934	.00066	.06853	.01293
29	98,082	69	.99930	.00070	.07203	.01387
30	98,013	74	.99924	.00076	.07570	.01489
31	97,939	79	.99919	.00081	.07955	.01599
32	97,860	83	.99915	.00085	.08359	.01717
33	97,777	88	.99910	.00090	.08783	.01846
34	97,689	93	.99905	.00095	.09228	.01986
35	97,596	99	.99899	.00101	.09696	.02139
36	97,497	104	.99893	.00107	.10186	.02304
37	97,393	112	.99885	.00115	.10702	.02485
38	97,281	120	.99877	.00123	.11242	.02680
39	97,161	128	.99868	.00132	.11808	.02891
40	97,033	138	.99858	.00142	.12401	.03121

1989-91 U.S. Life Table (for female lives)

x	ℓ_x	d_x	p_x	q_x	A_x	^2A_x
41	96,895	148	.99847	.00153	.13021	.03370
42	96,747	161	.99834	.00166	.13671	.03639
43	96,586	174	.99820	.00180	.14349	.03929
44	96,412	190	.99803	.00197	.15056	.04242
45	96,222	210	.99782	.00218	.15794	.04578
46	96,012	233	.99757	.00243	.16559	.04936
47	95,779	257	.99732	.00268	.17352	.05317
48	95,522	282	.99705	.00295	.18174	.05721
49	95,240	308	.99677	.00323	.19025	.06151
50	94,932	338	.99644	.00356	.19908	.06609
51	94,594	372	.99607	.00393	.20820	.07095
52	94,222	409	.99566	.00434	.21762	.07609
53	93,813	446	.99525	.00475	.22732	.08151
54	93,367	486	.99479	.00521	.23734	.08724
55	92,881	526	.99434	.00566	.24766	.09331
56	92,355	571	.99382	.00618	.25832	.09974
57	91,784	621	.99323	.00677	.26930	.10655
58	91,163	680	.99254	.00746	.28059	.11372
59	90,483	741	.99181	.00819	.29215	.12122
60	89,742	803	.99105	.00895	.30398	.12907
61	88,939	864	.99029	.00971	.31610	.13730
62	88,075	929	.98945	.01055	.32854	.14598
63	87,146	999	.98854	.01146	.34130	.15511
64	86,147	1,072	.98756	.01244	.35438	.16471
65	85,075	1,146	.98653	.01347	.36778	.17480
66	83,929	1,222	.98544	.01456	.38151	.18543
67	82,707	1,302	.98426	.01574	.39560	.19665
68	81,405	1,391	.98291	.01709	.41005	.20850
69	80,014	1,492	.98135	.01865	.42483	.22095
70	78,522	1,603	.97959	.02041	.43987	.23398
71	76,919	1,722	.97761	.02239	.45514	.24754
72	75,197	1,847	.97544	.02456	.47060	.26160
73	73,350	1,972	.97312	.02688	.48621	.27616
74	71,378	2,091	.97071	.02929	.50200	.29124
75	69,287	2,205	.96818	.03182	.51800	.30693
76	67,082	2,318	.96545	.03455	.53425	.32333
77	64,764	2,443	.96228	.03772	.55079	.34051
78	62,321	2,588	.95847	.04153	.56752	.35839
79	59,733	2,747	.95401	.04599	.58431	.37681
80	56,986	2,909	.94895	.05105	.60102	.39559

1989-91 U.S. Life Table (for female lives)

x	ℓ_x	d_x	p_x	q_x	A_x	^2A_x
81	54,077	3,061	.94340	.05660	.61756	.41460
82	51,016	3,196	.93735	.06265	.63389	.43379
83	47,820	3,308	.93082	.06918	.64999	.45315
84	44,512	3,397	.92368	.07632	.66588	.47268
85	41,115	3,472	.91555	.08445	.68153	.49236
86	37,643	3,530	.90622	.09378	.69682	.51201
87	34,113	3,540	.89623	.10377	.71158	.53135
88	30,573	3,498	.88559	.11441	.72582	.55036
89	27,075	3,409	.87409	.12591	.73957	.56909
90	23,666	3,294	.86081	.13919	.75282	.58749
91	20,372	3,141	.84582	.15418	.76533	.60514
92	17,231	2,921	.83048	.16952	.77684	.62159
93	14,310	2,638	.81565	.18435	.78742	.63686
94	11,672	2,326	.80072	.19928	.79729	.65129
95	9,346	2,007	.78526	.21474	.80659	.66504
96	7,339	1,698	.76863	.23137	.81533	.67812
97	5,641	1,398	.75217	.24783	.82338	.69028
98	4,243	1,119	.73627	.26373	.83087	.70166
99	3,124	873	.72055	.27945	.83799	.71258
100	2,251	667	.70369	.29631	.84494	.72335
101	1,584	498	.68561	.31439	.85170	.73391
102	1,086	361	.66759	.33241	.85823	.74420
103	725	256	.64690	.35310	.86476	.75461
104	469	176	.62473	.37527	.87115	.76485
105	293	116	.60410	.39590	.87743	.77493
106	177	74	.58192	.41808	.88424	.78597
107	103	46	.55340	.44660	.89225	.79915
108	57	27	.52632	.47368	.90203	.81554
109	30	15	.50000	.50000	.91670	.84105
110	15	15	.00000	1.00000	.94340	.89000

APPENDIX B

SIMULATION ILLUSTRATIONS

As mentioned in the Preface, various illustrations of applications of stochastic simulation to the analysis of actuarial models are presented in this appendix, all in the format of examples. The early illustrations are quite elementary, but will grow in complexity as the topic unfolds.

B.1 ILLUSTRATIONS INVOLVING SINGLE-LIFE MODELS

When a survival model has been adopted, whether in parametric or tabular form, actuarial values can be calculated directly from that model with no need for resorting to methods of simulation. In such cases, simulation could be used to estimate an already-known quantity. The examples in this section are all of that nature. We present them merely to illustrate the mechanics of the simulation process.

EXAMPLE B.1

Suppose the CDF of the age-at-failure random variable has the value $F_0(20) = .15$. As our first example of the use of simulation, we show how to "estimate" the value of $S_0(20)$.

SOLUTION

We generate a random number, denoted u, from the interval $[0, 1)$, and consider a hypothetical entity age 0. If $0 \le u < .15$ we consider that the entity failed before (or at) age 20, and if $.15 \le u < 1$ we consider that the entity survived beyond age 20.

If we repeat this process n times, and count the number of survivors, denoted s, we have simulated a plausible outcome of a binomial random variable with parameters n and $p = .85$. We would then expect the ratio $\frac{s}{n}$ to be close to .85. (Our performance of this simulation produced $s = 79$ survivors in a set of $n = 100$ trials, which would "estimate" the known value $p = .85$ as $\hat{p} = .79$.)

We could then repeat the performance many times, say m times, using n trials in each performance, producing m values of s. If we denote these outcomes by $s_1, s_2, \cdots, s_m$, and then determine the mean of this data as

$$\bar{s} = \frac{1}{m}\left[s_1 + s_2 + \cdots + s_m\right],$$

we can view $\bar{s}$ as an estimate of $E[S] = .85n$. (Our performance was repeated $m = 1000$ times, with $n = 100$ trials in each performance, producing a value of $\bar{s} = 81.625$.) ❏

EXAMPLE B.2

Let T_0 denote the age-at-failure random variable for a particular mechanical device, where T_0 has an exponential distribution with mean 7. We wish to simulate a plausible data set of exact failure times for a sample of these devices.

SOLUTION

We generate a random number u, with $0 \le u < 1$, and interpret it as a value of the CDF of T_0. Then we solve the equation $1 - e^{-t/7} = u$ for

$$t = -7 \cdot \ln(1-u),$$

and regard the value of t as an observed failure time for such a device. ❏

EXAMPLE B.3

Suppose the age-at-failure random variable T_0 has a continuous uniform distribution with $\omega = 50$. Then for an entity known to have survived to time $t = 40$, the continuous time-to-failure random variable T_{40} has a uniform distribution over $(0, 10]$, so that $F_{40}(t) = \frac{t}{10}$, for $0 < t \le 10$. Then it follows that

$$Pr(K_{40}^* = k) = Pr(k-1 < T_{40} \le k)$$
$$= F_{40}(k) - F_{40}(k-1) = \frac{1}{10},$$

for $k = 1, 2, \cdots, 10$. We use simulation to "estimate" the known value $Pr(K_{40}^* = k) = .10$.

SOLUTION

We generate a random number u, where $0 \le u < 1$, and interpret it as a value of $F_{40}(t) = \frac{t}{10}$. If $0 \le u < .10$, we deem that Entity (40) failed in $(40, 41]$, which we denote by $k = 1$; if $.10 \le u < .20$, we deem that Entity (40) failed in $(41, 42]$, which we denote by $k = 2$; $\cdots$; if $.90 \le u < 1.00$, we deem that Entity (40) failed in $(49, 50]$, which we denote by $k = 10$.

We repeat this process $n = 1000$ times, and record the number of results, denoted n_k, which implied failure in the kth interval, for $k = 1, 2, \ldots, 10$. (Note that $\sum_{k=1}^{10} n_k = 1000$.) Then the ratio $\frac{n_k}{n}$ is a simulated estimate of the known probability value $Pr(K_{40}^* = k) = .10$. ❏

EXAMPLE B.4

From Table 6.1a we know that

$$p_3 = \frac{\ell_4}{\ell_3} = \frac{97,082}{97,160} = .99920.$$

How would we estimate the value of p_3 using simulation?

SOLUTION

We generate a five-decimal-place random number u, where $0 \le u < 1$, and consider an entity age 3. If $0 \le u < .99920$ we deem the entity to have survived to age 4. We repeat the process n times, and count the number, s, of deemed survivors. Then $\frac{s}{n}$ is a simulated value of the known $p_3 = .99920$. (We ran this process $n = 1000$ times and found $u < .99920$ each time, obtaining the estimate $\hat{p}_3 = 1.00000$.) ❑

EXAMPLE B.5

From Table 6.1a we can determine the values of $_k p_0$, for $k = 1,2,3,4$. From these we can calculate

$$e_{0:\overline{4}|} = \sum_{k=1}^{4} {}_k p_0$$

$$= 3.8809.$$

How would we estimate the value of $e_{0:\overline{4}|}$ using simulation?

SOLUTION

First we calculate the values of $F_0(t)$, for $t = 0,1,2,3,4$, obtaining the following:

t	0	1	2	3	4
$F_0(t)$	.00000	.02592	.02741	.02840	.02918

We then generate a five-decimal-place random number u_1, where $0 \le u_1 < 1$, and consider hypothetical Person 1. If $0 \le u_1 < .02592$, we deem that Person 1 failed in $(0,1]$ and therefore survived $k_1 = 0$ whole years; if $.02592 \le u_1 < .02741$, we deem that Person 1 failed in $(1,2]$ and therefore survived $k_1 = 1$ whole year; if $.02741 \le u_1 < .02840$, we deem that Person 1 failed in $(2,3]$ and therefore survived $k_1 = 2$ whole years; if $.02840 \le u_1 < .02918$, we deem that Person 1 failed in $(3,4]$ and therefore survived $k_1 = 3$ whole years; and if $.02918 \le u_1 < 1$, we deem that Person 1 survived to age 4 and therefore survived $k_1 = 4$

whole years in the age interval $(0, 4]$. We repeat the process n times and record each simulated value of k_i, for $i = 1, 2, \cdots, n$. Then our simulated estimate of $e_{0:\overline{4}|}$ is found as

$$\hat{e}_{0:\overline{4}|} = \frac{1}{n} \cdot \sum_{i=1}^{n} k_i. \qquad \square$$

EXAMPLE B.6

Consider the model described in Example 7.1. How would we use simulation to approximate the known value of $E[Z] = 9.73094$, as determined in part (a) of Example 7.1?

SOLUTION

We generate a random number u_i, where $0 \le u_i < 1$. If $0 \le u_i < .20$, we deem that failure (of the detergent supply) occurred in the first week, so the present value of payment would be $z_i = \frac{10}{1.01} = 9.90099$. If $.20 \le u_i < .50$, we deem that failure occurred in the second week, so the present value of payment would be $z_i = \frac{10}{(1.01)^2} = 9.80296$. The five possible values of z_i are as follows:

u_i	Week of Failure	Value of z_i
$[0, .20)$	1	9.90099
$[.20, .50)$	2	9.80296
$[.50, .70)$	3	9.70591
$[.70, .85)$	4	9.60980
$[.85, 1.00)$	5	9.51466

If we run $n = 1000$ trials of this simulation, and record each value of z_i, we could then approximate the value of $E[Z] = 9.73094$ by

$$\overline{z} = \frac{1}{1000} \sum_{i=1}^{1000} z_i.$$

(Our simulated estimate of $E[Z] = 9.73094$, using 1000 trials, turned out to be $\overline{z} = 9.31216$.)

$\square$

EXAMPLE B.7

Consider the life table values of Example 8.1, which imply the probability function $q_{95} = .30$, $_{1|}q_{95} = .30$, $_{2|}q_{95} = .20$, $_{3|}q_{95} = .16$, and $_{4|}q_{95} = .04$. Let us use simulation to estimate the known value of $a_{95} = 1.2352$ found in Example 8.1.

SOLUTION

We generate a random number u_i from the $U[0,1)$ distribution. If $0 \le u_i < .30$, we deem that failure occurs before age 96, so no annuity payment is made and the present value of payment is $y_i = 0$. If $.30 \le u_i < .60$, we deem that failure occurs between ages 96 and 97, so one payment is made and the present value of payment is $y_i = a_{\overline{1}|} = .95238$. The possible values of y_i are as follows:

u_i	Number of Payments	Value of y_i
$[0, .30)$	0	.00000
$[.30, .60)$	1	.95238
$[.60, .80)$	2	1.85941
$[.80, .96)$	3	2.72325
$[.96, 1.00)$	4	3.54595

If we run $n = 1000$ trials of this simulation, and record each value of y_i, we could then approximate the known value of $a_{95} = 1.2352$ determined in Example 8.1 by

$$\bar{y} = \frac{1}{1000} \sum_{i=1}^{1000} y_i.$$

(Our simulated estimate of $a_{95} = 1.2352$, using 1000 trials, turned out to be $\bar{y} = 1.3944$.) ❏

EXAMPLE B.8

We now reconsider Example 10.13, again assuming that $i = .06$ interest will be earned on the reserve fund each year and the net level benefit premium is .16902. Using the values of q_x, for $x = 50, 51, 52, 53, 54$, from the table in Appendix A, we simulate the survival experience to test the adequacy of the NLP reserve fund and hence of the premium.

SOLUTION

Using $q_{50} = .00356$, we simulate the survival of Person i by generating a random number u_i, where $0 \le u_i < 1$. If $0 \le u_i < .00356$, we deem that Person i fails before age 51 and otherwise we deem that Person i survives to age 51. This is then repeated to simulate the number of failures before age 51 and therefore the number of survivors to age 51. Then the process is repeated for the survivors at age 51, using $q_{51} = .00393$, and so on, using $q_{52} = .00434$, $q_{53} = .00475$, and $q_{54} = .00521$. Starting with an initial group of 1000 contracts, our first simulation produced a reserve fund at time 5 of 976.21 and 978 survivors. Under this simulation, the reserve fund was deficient by 1.79. Then the entire simulation process was repeated 10,000 times, producing an excessive reserve fund 5223 times and a deficient reserve fund 4777 times, so we can conclude that the benefit reserve fund, and hence the premium, will be adequate with probability .5223. The average reserve fund was 978.46, which is very close to the 978.40 result in Example 10.13, as expected.

It is not surprising that the simulated probability of premium adequacy turns out to be in the area of 50%, because this test for premium adequacy has been done on a net basis. That is, the premium being tested is the exact amount, on an expected value basis, to cover the promised benefits. In practice, an insurer would rather find that the probability of contract premium adequacy is more like, say, 80%. This would be achieved by increasing the premium with a loading (or margin) for adverse experience. We revisit this idea in Example B.9.   ❐

EXAMPLE B.9

Returning to Example 9.7, let $x=100$ and calculate the value of G using the life table in Appendix A. Then test this value of G for adequacy by simulating the survival experience after age 100 using $\ell_{100}=2251$, the q_x values in the Appendix A life table, and $i=.06$. (The gross premium is adequate if an excessive aggregate fund remains at time 11 (age 111).)

SOLUTION

From Appendix A we find $A_{100}=.84494$, which implies that

$$\ddot{a}_{100} = \frac{1-A_{100}}{d} = \frac{1-.84494}{.056604} = 2.73938.$$

Then from Example 9.7 we find

$$G = \frac{(1020)(.84494)+8+(2)(2.73938)}{(.90)(2.73938)-.65} = 482.15.$$

If the 2251 failures after age 100 were distributed over the next eleven years *exactly as stated in the life table*, the fund at time 11, after paying the failure benefits and expenses for the 15 failures in the 11th year, would be precisely zero. Our first simulation imagined greater longevity than that shown in the table, and produced an aggregate fund at time 11 of 3274.85, indicating that the gross premium was more than adequate. We ran the simulation 1000 times, producing an excessive aggregate fund 503 times. From this we conclude that a gross premium of 482.15 will be adequate with probability .503.

As suggested in Example B.8, simulation could be used to determine a gross premium with a particular probability of adequacy. We could arbitrarily increase our gross premium to, say, 500.00 and repeat the simulation to estimate the probability of premium adequacy. By trial and error, a premium amount could be determined such that its probability of adequacy met the predetermined target.   ❐

B.2 AN ILLUSTRATION INVOLVING MULTIPLE LIVES

EXAMPLE B.10

A married couple purchases a ten-year term life insurance policy that also contains a pure endowment benefit payable at the end of the term if either spouse survives to that time. At issue of the contract the wife is 80 years old and the husband is 82 years old. While both are alive, their survival probabilities are given by the respective gender-specific 1990 U.S. Life Table.

If the wife dies first, the husband's mortality rates are assumed to be greater than those in the table during each of the three years following the wife's death, specifically at 130% of the table rate during the first year, 120% during the second year, and 110% during the third year. After those three years, the rates are assumed to be the same as the table rates.

If the husband dies first, the wife's mortality rates are similarly assumed to be greater than the table rates during each of the three years following the husband's death, specifically 115% of the table rate during the first year, 110% during the second year, and 105% during the third year. After those three years, the rates are assumed to be the same as the table rates.

We wish to use simulation to estimate the probability that the endowment benefit will be paid (i.e., that at least one spouse will survive the ten-year period).

SOLUTION

The two future lifetimes are not independent, since the survival rates for each spouse depend on the survival status of the other. (To simplify the process, we assume that death occurs at the end of a contract year.)

We generate a random number u_1, where $0 \leq u_1 < 1$. If $0 \leq u_1 < q_{80}^F$, we deem that the wife dies in the first year, and otherwise that she survives. We similarly compare a second random number u_2 with the value of q_{82}^M to deem the failure or survival of the husband in the first year. If and when our simulation indicates a failure, we then increase the table rates for the next three years for the surviving spouse. In this manner we can predict whether or not the endowment benefit will be paid.

We performed this simulation 10,000 times and found that at least one spouse survived the ten-year period 5,179 times. From this we estimate the probability of paying the endowment benefit to be .5179, or slightly less than 52%. ❏

B.3 ILLUSTRATIONS INVOLVING MULTI-STATE MODELS

EXAMPLE B.11

Consider the Figure 14.7 model as a homogeneous discrete-time Markov Chain (see Section 3.1), with monthly transition probability matrix given by

$$\mathbf{P} = \begin{vmatrix} .98 & .01 & 0 & .01 \\ 0 & .57 & .40 & .03 \\ 0 & .03 & .95 & .02 \\ 0 & 0 & 0 & 1 \end{vmatrix}.$$

Consider a healthy person in State 1 at time 0. We wish to simulate the person's condition at time 5.

SOLUTION

Since our person begins in State 1, we deem that he remains in State 1 over the next month if $0 \leq u < .98$; transitions to State 2 if $.98 \leq u < .99$; or transitions to State 4 if $.99 \leq u < 1.00$. Suppose we draw the sequence of random values $\{.843, .561, .983, .791, .038\}$ from the uniform distribution over $[0,1)$. The value $u_1 = .843 < .98$, so the person remains in State 1 over the first month. The value $u_2 = .561 < .98$, so the person remains in State 1 over the second month as well. The value $u_3 = .983 \geq .98$, so the person is deemed to transition to State 2.

Once in State 2, the person remains there if $0 \leq u < .57$; transitions to State 3 if $.57 \leq u < .97$; or transitions to State 4 if $.97 \leq u < 1.00$. The value $u_4 = .791$ satisfies $.57 \leq u_4 < .97$, so we deem that our person transitions to State 3.

Once in State 3, the person transitions back to State 2 if $0 \leq u < .03$; remains in State 3 if $.03 \leq u < .98$; or transitions to State 4 if $.98 \leq u < 1.00$. The value $u_5 = .038$ satisfies $.03 \leq u_5 < .98$, so we deem that our person remains in State 3. This is his condition at time 5.

◻

EXAMPLE B.12

Consider the model of Figure 14.8. For a resident in an ILU at time 0, we wish to simulate the resident's status within the CCRC at the end of each month for the next year. We use, in order, the following sequence of random values from the uniform distribution over $[0, 1)$:

$$\{.254, .941, .557, .661, .905, .594, .118, .091, .002, .615, .963, .887\}$$

SOLUTION

As the reader should by now understand, a person in State 1 is deemed to remain in State 1 if $0 \leq u < .94$; to transition to State 2 if $.94 \leq u < .97$; to transition to State 3 if $.97 \leq u < .99$; and to transition to State 4 if $.99 \leq u < 1.00$. A similar set of rules, taken from the second row of the matrix $\mathbf{P}$, will apply to a person in State 2, and similarly for State 3. The following table shows the state of residence at the end of each month for a person in State 1 at time 0, simulated by the given set of random values.

End of Month	Random Value	State of Residence
1	.254	1
2	.941	2
3	.557	2
4	.661	2
5	.905	3
6	.594	3
7	.118	3
8	.091	3
9	.002	3
10	.615	4
11	.963	4
12	.887	4

It is coincidental that this person moved strictly upward in numbered states without ever returning from State 2 to State 1. A different set of random values would likely produce a different simulated outcome. ❏

EXAMPLE B.13

Suppose our CCRC has 100 independent living units, and begins operation at time 0 with all such units occupied, and no residents in either the TNF or the PNF. We wish to simulate the distribution of these original 100 residents among the four possible states at the end of each month for the next six months.

SOLUTION

The results will necessarily vary with the set of random values used. The random value u_i for $i = 1, 2, \ldots, 100$, is used to imply the state status of Person i at the end of the first month, as explained in Example 13.21. Our simulation predicted 94 persons still in State 1, 1 person in State 2, 3 persons in State 3, and 2 persons in State 4. Then a second set of 100 random values was used to simulate each person's state status at time 2 (in months), recognizing the state status at time 1, and so on. Our simulation produced the results shown in the following table.

End of Month	State 1	State 2	State 3	State 4
1	94	1	3	2
2	89	3	3	5
3	85	6	4	5
4	81	5	8	6
5	76	7	10	7
6	70	3	15	12

Since we are modeling a closed group, the sum across each row will be 100. The number in State 4 at successive month ends can never decrease, of course, but the month-end numbers in the other states could either increase or decrease.

B.4 ILLUSTRATIONS INVOLVING SIMULATED INTEREST RATES

We have chosen to present this notion within the body of the text itself (see Section 15.5).

ANSWERS TO THE EXERCISES

CHAPTER 5

5-1   (a) $e^{-(at+bt^2/2)}$

       (b) $(a+bt)\cdot e^{-(at+bt^2/2)}$

       (c) $b^{-1/2} - ab^{-1}$

5-2 $45\sqrt{2}$

5-3   Because $\lim_{t \to \infty} S_0(t) = e^{-1/r} \neq 0$

5-4   (a) No

       (b) Yes

       (c) Yes

5-5 $\dfrac{1}{3}$

5-7   .60199

5-8   (a) Constant

       (b) Decreasing

       (c) Increasing

5-9   38.99

5-11   588

5-12 $\dfrac{1}{6000}$

5-13   .59049

5-14   7

5-15   5.249

5-16   40

5-17   15.4822

5-18   (a) .60

(b) 5

(c) $\frac{1}{20-t}$

5-20 $\max[t \ni X(t)=1]$ or $\min[t \ni X(t)=2]$

5-21 $\max[t \ni X(t)=1]$ or $\min[t \ni X(t)=2]$

5-22   (a) $\int_0^n {}_rp_{11}^{(t)} \cdot \lambda_{12}(t+r)\, dr$

(b) $\int_0^n {}_rp_x \mu_{x+r}\, dr$

5-23 $\int_0^\infty {}_rp_{11}^{(0)}\, dr$

5-24 $e^{-n\lambda}$

5-25 $1-e^{-n\lambda}$

CHAPTER 6

6-1   (a) $S_0(x)$: 1.00, .90, .72, .432, .1296, 0.00

(b)

x	ℓ_x	d_x
0	10,000	1,000
1	9,000	1,800
2	7,200	2,880
3	4,320	3,024
4	1,296	1,296
5	0	—

(c) $\omega = 5$, the first age for which $S_0(x) = 0$

6-2   (a) 5680

(b) .52

(c) .144

(d) 1.00

6-3   (a) $S_0(x) - S_0(x+1) \;\; = \;\; \dfrac{\ell_x - \ell_{x+1}}{\ell_0} \;\; = \;\; \dfrac{d_x}{\ell_0}$

6-4   (a) 90

        (b) .20

        (c) $\dfrac{5}{24}$

6-5   2081.61

6-6   (a) $-\,{}_tp_x\mu_{x+t}$

        (b) $\,{}_tp_x(\mu_x - \mu_{x+t})$

6-7   .001275

6-8   .20094

6-9   (a) $(64-.80x)^{-2/3}/15$

        (b) 60

        (c) 514.286

6-10   133.33

6-11   .15

6-12   7.50;   8.03572

6-13   108

6-14   15.59852

6-19   (a) $1-p$

        (b) $\begin{vmatrix} p & 1-p \\ 0 & 1 \end{vmatrix}$

        (c) $(p^n, 1-p^n)$

6-20 $\dfrac{p}{1-p}$

6-21   All are correct

6-22   .80

6-23   1.4547

6-24   .0782

6-26   .0078431; .0078905; .0079061; .0079218

6-27   2.78084

6-28   (a) 25.10
        (b) 25.09682

6-29   278.85

6-30   .56767

6-35   150,000

6-36   .01029

6-37   .45886

CHAPTER 7

7-3   −.19686

7-4   .54

7-7   .05486

7-8   5.188

7-9   831.84

7-10   555.27

7-13   .81014

7-14   .30

7-15   .99950

7-16   (a) $\bar{Z}^1_{x:\overline{n}|} = \begin{cases} v^{T_x} & \text{for } T_x \leq n \\ 0 & \text{for } T_x > n \end{cases}$

(b) $E[\overline{Z}^1_{x:\overline{n}|}] = \overline{A}^1_{x:\overline{n}|} = \int_0^n v^t \cdot {}_tp_x\mu_{x+t} \, dt$

$\quad E[\overline{Z}^{1}_{x:\overline{n}|}{}^2] = {}^2\overline{A}^1_{x:\overline{n}|} = \int_0^n (v')^t \cdot {}_tp_x\mu_{x+t} \, dt$

7-17 (a) $\quad {}_n|\overline{Z}_x = \begin{cases} 0 & \text{for } T_x \le n \\ v^{T_x} & \text{for } T_x > n \end{cases}$

(b) $E[{}_n|\overline{Z}_x] = {}_n|\overline{A}_x = \int_n^\infty v^t \cdot {}_tp_x\mu_{x+t} \, dt$

$\quad E[{}_n|\overline{Z}_x^{\,2}] = {}^2{}_n|\overline{A}_x = \int_n^\infty (v')^t \cdot {}_tp_x\mu_{x+t} \, dt$

7-18 Probability mass of $\frac{2}{7}$ at 0

7-19 .044

7-20 $\dfrac{\lambda}{\lambda+2\delta} - \left(\dfrac{\lambda}{\lambda+\delta}\right)^2$

7-21 $\dfrac{\lambda}{\lambda+\delta} \cdot e^{-(\lambda+\delta)n}$

7-22 .35714

7-24 .03825

7-25 (b) 3.80957

7-26 837.24

7-27 (a) $\frac{1}{7}$

(b) .61339

(c) .01816

7-28 .17973

7-29 .11359

7-30 .21787

7-32 (a) $v^n \cdot {}_np_{11}^{(0)}$

(b) $\displaystyle\sum_{t=0}^{n-1} v^{t+1} \cdot {}_tp_{11}^{(0)} \cdot p_{12}^{(t)}$

(c) $\displaystyle\sum_{t=n}^{\infty} v^{t+1} \cdot {}_t p_{11}^{(0)} \cdot p_{12}^{(t)}$

7-33 (a) $\displaystyle\int_0^n v^r \cdot {}_r p_{11}^{(0)} \cdot \lambda_1(r)\, dr$

(b) $\displaystyle\int_n^{\infty} v^r \cdot {}_r p_{11}^{(0)} \cdot \lambda_1(r)\, dr$

7-34 (a) $\displaystyle\sum_{k=1}^{\infty} k \cdot v^k \cdot {}_{k-1} p_{11}^{(0)} \cdot p_{12}^{(k-1)}$

(b) $\displaystyle\sum_{k=1}^{n} k \cdot v^k \cdot {}_{k-1} p_{11}^{(0)} \cdot p_{12}^{(k-1)}$

(c) $\displaystyle\int_0^{\infty} r \cdot v^r \cdot {}_r p_{11}^{(0)} \cdot \lambda_1(r)\, dr$

(d) $\displaystyle\int_0^n (n-r) \cdot v^r \cdot {}_r p_{11}^{(0)} \cdot \lambda_1(r)\, dr$

CHAPTER 8

8-4   106

8-7   .17719

8-8   150,000

8-13   .65

8-14   .02

8-15   .46600

8-18   4.59

8-26   2.2186

8-27   .26039

8-32   .81058

8-33   1.49032

8-47   .60

8-48   5.78534

8-50　(a) $\displaystyle\sum_{k=1}^{\infty} v^k \cdot {}_k p_{11}^{(0)}$

　　　(b) $\displaystyle\sum_{k=0}^{n-1} v^k \cdot {}_k p_{11}^{(0)}$, where ${}_0 p_{11}^{(0)} = 1$

　　　(c) $\displaystyle\sum_{k=n+1}^{\infty} v^k \cdot {}_k p_{11}^{(0)}$

　　　(d) $\displaystyle\int_0^n v^r \cdot {}_r p_{11}^{(0)} \, dr$

CHAPTER 9

9-4　　33.06

9-5　　434.71

9-6　　154.62

9-7　　7272.73

9-10　−.25449

9-11　.43200

9-12　36.77077

9-13　.02188

9-14　.00360

9-15　12.77

9-18　.70215

9-19　1.1025

9-20　.04

9-21　.22787

9-23　$\left(\dfrac{P+\delta l}{P+\delta}\right)^{\lambda/\delta}$

9-24　.20130

9-25　955.07

9-26   .06701

CHAPTER 10

10-1   (a) $_t^h V_{x:\overline{n}|}^1 = \begin{cases} A_{x+t:\overline{n-t}|}^{\,\,1} - {_h}P_{x:\overline{n}|}^1 \cdot \ddot{a}_{x+t:\overline{h-t}|} & \text{for } t < h \\ A_{x+t:\overline{n-t}|}^{\,\,1} & \text{for } t \geq h \end{cases}$

   (b) $_t^h V_{x:\overline{n}|} = \begin{cases} A_{x+t:\overline{n-t}|} - {_h}P_{x:\overline{n}|} \cdot \ddot{a}_{x+t:\overline{h-t}|} & \text{for } t < h \\ A_{x+t:\overline{n-t}|} & \text{for } t \geq h \end{cases}$

10-2 $_t^h V(_n|A_x) = \begin{cases} _{n-t}|A_{x+t} - {_h}P(_n|A_x) \cdot \ddot{a}_{x+t:\overline{h-t}|} & \text{for } t < h \\ _{n-t}|A_{x+t} & \text{for } h \leq t < n \\ A_{x+t} & \text{for } t \geq n \end{cases}$

10-3   .27273

10-4   (a) $P_{x:\overline{n}|}^1 \cdot \ddot{s}_{x:\overline{t}|} - {_t}k_x$ (b) $P_{x:\overline{n}|} \cdot \ddot{s}_{x:\overline{t}|} - {_t}k_x$

   (c) $P_{x:\overline{n}|}^{\,\,\,1} \cdot \ddot{s}_{x:\overline{t}|}$ (There is no accumulated cost of insurance because there is no benefit payable in $(x, x+t]$.)

   (d) $_h P_x \cdot \ddot{s}_{x:\overline{h}|} \cdot \frac{1}{_{t-h}E_{x+h}} - {_t}k_x$

10-6   330.38

10-7   1180.00

10-8   (a) $_t L_{x:\overline{n}|} = Z_{x+t:\overline{n-t}|} - P_{x:\overline{n}|} \cdot \ddot{Y}_{x+t:\overline{n-t}|}$, where

$$Z_{x+t:\overline{n-t}|} = \begin{cases} v^{K_x-t} & \text{for } K_x \leq n \\ v^{n-t} & \text{for } K_x > n \end{cases}$$

   and

$$\ddot{Y}_{x+t:\overline{n-t}|} = \begin{cases} \ddot{a}_{\overline{K_x-t}|} & \text{for } K_x \leq n \\ \ddot{a}_{\overline{n-t}|} & \text{for } K_x > n \end{cases}$$

   (b) $A_{x+t:\overline{n-t}|} - P_{x:\overline{n}|} \cdot \ddot{a}_{x+t:\overline{n-t}|}$ (c) $\left(1 + \frac{P_{x:\overline{n}|}}{d}\right)^2 \cdot \left(^2 A_{x+t:\overline{n-t}|} - A_{x+t:\overline{n-t}|}^2\right)$

10-9   .83

10-12   1.39730

10-13   .025

10-14   .979

10-15   .03312

10-16   9.82254

10-17   8.75630

10-20   .40

10-21   22.22

10-22   .07516

10-23   0; all continuous contingent functions based on the exponential distribution are constants with respect to age, so future premiums are always adequate to fund future benefits and no reserve is ever needed (prospective view) and no reserve ever accumulates (retrospective view).

10-25   .17352

10-26   .06036

10-27 $\displaystyle \sum_{k=0}^{\infty} v^{k+1} \cdot {}_k p_{11}^{(20)} \cdot p_{12}^{(20+k)} - \frac{\displaystyle \sum_{k=0}^{\infty} v^{k+1} \cdot {}_k p_{11}^{(0)} \cdot p_{12}^{(k)}}{\displaystyle \sum_{k=0}^{\infty} v^k \cdot {}_k p_{11}^{(0)}} \cdot \sum_{k=0}^{\infty} v^k \cdot {}_k p_{11}^{(20)}$

10-28 $\displaystyle \sum_{k=0}^{9} v^{k+1} \cdot {}_k p_{11}^{(10)} \cdot p_{12}^{(10+k)} - \frac{\displaystyle \sum_{k=0}^{19} v^{k+1} \cdot {}_k p_{11}^{(0)} \cdot p_{12}^{(k)}}{\displaystyle \sum_{k=0}^{19} v^k \cdot {}_k p_{11}^{(0)}} \cdot \sum_{k=0}^{9} v^k \cdot {}_k p_{11}^{(10)}$

CHAPTER 11

11-7 $\displaystyle \sum_{k=0}^{t-1} P_{k+1} \cdot \frac{1}{{}_{t-k}E_{x+k}} - \sum_{k=1}^{t} b_k \cdot \frac{(1+i)^{t-k} \cdot {}_{k-1|}q_x}{{}_t p_x}$

11-8   9.41107

11-9   528.14

11-10   .50152

11-11   799.00

11-13   (a) .21500   (b) .75000

11-16 $\dfrac{d}{dt}\, {}_t\overline{V} = \overline{G}_t(1-r_t) - \overline{e}_t + \delta \cdot {}_t\overline{V} - \mu_{x+t}(b_t - {}_t\overline{V})$

11-17   2,489.89;   2,479.75;   2,469.59

11-18   1,107.20;   5,676.06;   10,382.10;   15,229.06;   20,221.79

11-19   2,141.67

CHAPTER 12

12-2   .08384

12-3   .51017

12-4   3.54167

12-5   100

12-6 $\dfrac{1}{12}$

12-7   (b) and (c)

12-9   .99725

12-10   100

12-11   .54545

12-12   1.07692

12-13   10.10

12-14   .05

12-15   .18000

12-16   .02222

12-17   14

12-18   (a) $\displaystyle\int_0^n v^r \cdot {}_r p_{11}^{(0)}\, dr$

(b) $\dfrac{\sum\limits_{k=0}^{\infty} v^{k+1} \cdot {}_k p_{11}^{(0)} \left(p_{12}^{(k)} + p_{13}^{(k)} \right)}{\sum\limits_{k=0}^{\infty} v^k \cdot {}_k p_{11}^{(0)}}$

(c) $\sum\limits_{k=0}^{n-1} v^{k+1} \cdot {}_k p_{11}^{(0)} \left(p_{12}^{(k)} + p_{13}^{(k)} \right) + v^n \cdot {}_n p_{11}^{(0)}$

(d) $\dfrac{\int_0^n v^r \cdot {}_r p_{11}^{(0)} \left(\lambda_{12}(r) + \lambda_{13}(r) \right) dr}{\int_0^n v^r \cdot {}_r p_{11}^{(0)} \, dr}$

12-19 $\sum\limits_{k=1}^{\infty} v^k \cdot {}_k p_{13}^{(0)}$

12-20 (a) $\displaystyle\int_0^{\infty} v^r \cdot {}_r p_{11}^{(0)} \cdot \lambda_{13}(r) \, dr$

(b) $\displaystyle\int_0^{\infty} v^r \cdot {}_r p_{11}^{(0)} \cdot \lambda_{12}(r) \, dr$

(c) $\displaystyle\int_0^{\infty} v^r \cdot {}_r p_{12}^{(0)} \cdot \lambda_{24}(r) \, dr$

(d) $\displaystyle\int_0^{\infty} v^r \cdot {}_r p_{13}^{(0)} \cdot \lambda_{34}(r) \, dr$

12-21 (a) $\displaystyle\int_0^{\infty} v^r \left({}_r p_{11}^{(0)} + {}_r p_{12}^{(0)} + {}_r p_{13}^{(0)} \right) dr$

(b) $\sum\limits_{k=0}^{n-1} v^k \left({}_k p_{11}^{(0)} + {}_k p_{12}^{(0)} + {}_k p_{13}^{(0)} \right)$

(c) $\sum\limits_{k=0}^{n-1} v^{k+1} \left({}_k p_{12}^{(0)} \cdot p_{24}^{(k)} + {}_k p_{13}^{(0)} \cdot p_{34}^{(k)} \right)$

(d) $\displaystyle\int_n^{\infty} v^r \left({}_r p_{12}^{(0)} \cdot \lambda_{24}(r) + {}_r p_{13}^{(0)} \cdot \lambda_{34}(r) \right) dr$

12-22 ${}_n P_{xy}$

12-23 (a) ${}_n P_x$

(b) ${}_n q_x$

12-25 $(1+t)^{-1}$

12-26 .46667

12-27 .16667

12-28 $(1+3n)^{-1}$

12-29 $\dfrac{2n^2(2+3n)}{(1+n)(1+2n)(1+3n)}$

12-30 .03922

12-31 .73609

Chapter 13

13-1 .38

13-2 802.56

13-3 .2157

13-4 (b) $\dfrac{1}{1+t+t^2}$

13-5 (a) $\dfrac{75-t}{75}$, for $0 \le t < 75$

   $\left(\dfrac{50-t}{50}\right)^2$, for $0 \le t < 50$

   $\dfrac{(75-t)(50-t)^2}{187,500}$, for $0 \le t < 50$; 0 for $t \ge 50$

   (b) $\dfrac{(50-t)^2}{187,500}$; $\dfrac{(50-t)(75-t)}{93,750}$

   (c) .01307; .03934; .05241

   (d) .01333; .03960

   (e) $\dfrac{2}{9}$; $\dfrac{7}{9}$

   (f) .24873; .75127

13-6 7.7373

13-8 .19020

13-9 14.775; 29.775

13-10 .20

13-12 20.625

13-13

x	$q_x^{(1)}$	$q_x^{(2)}$
0	.0875	.2375
1	.1800	.1800
2	.1900	.0900

13-14 (a) .29108; .39788   (b)   .32500; .24300; .12096

13-15 (a) .67857   (b)   .30160

13-16 .09405

13-17 .11625

CHAPTER 14

14-1 (a) $20,000\left(v^{40}\cdot{}_{40}p_{25}^{(\tau)}\cdot\bar{a}_{65}\right)$

(b) $200,000\int_0^{40}v^t\cdot{}_tp_{25}^{(\tau)}\cdot\mu_{25+t}^{(1)}\,dt$

(c) $400\int_0^{40}t\cdot v^t\cdot{}_tp_{25}^{(\tau)}\cdot\mu_{25+t}^{(2)}\cdot{}_{40-t|}\bar{a}_{25+t}\,dt$

14-3 7,013.63

14-4 35,230.21

14-7 82,711.91

14-8 (a) $\int_0^n{}_rp_{00}^{(0)}\cdot\lambda_{02}(r)\,dr = \int_0^n{}_rp_x^{(\tau)}\cdot\mu_{x+r}^{(2)}\,dr$ (b) .54072

14-9 (a) 27   (b) 64

14-10 (a) $\exp\left\{-\int_0^n\left[\lambda_{12}(t+r)+\lambda_{13}(t+r)\right]dr\right\}$

(b) ${}_np_x^{(\tau)}=\exp\left(-\int_0^n\mu_{x+r}^{(\tau)}\,dr\right)$

14-11 (a) $\int_0^n\left[{}_rp_{11}^{(t)}\cdot\lambda_{13}(t+r)+{}_rp_{12}^{(t)}\cdot\lambda_{23}(t+r)\right]dr$

(b) ${}_nq_x^{(f)}=\int_0^n\left({}_rp_x^{(\tau)}\cdot\mu_{x+r}^{(f)}+\mu_{x+r}^d\int_0^r{}_sp_x^{(\tau)}\cdot\mu_{x+s}^{(d)}\,ds\right)dr$

14-12   (a) $\int_0^n {}_r p_{22}^{(t)} \cdot \lambda_{23}(t+r)\, dr$ (b) ${}_n q_x^d = \int_0^n {}_r p_x^d \cdot \mu_{x+r}^d\, dr$

14-13   .47645

14-14   (a) The diagram is the same as in Figure 14.6.

(b)

r	${}_r p_{11}^{(0)}$	${}_r p_{12}^{(0)}$	r	${}_r p_{11}^{(0)}$	${}_r p_{12}^{(0)}$
1	.750	.200	11	.374	.195
2	.714	.188	12	.341	.199
3	.671	.187	13	.310	.203
4	.629	.186	14	.279	.209
5	.588	.185	15	.248	.215
6	.550	.186	16	.218	.222
7	.512	.186	17	.188	.230
8	.476	.188	18	.158	.240
9	.441	.189	19	.127	.250
10	.407	.192	20	.096	.262

(c) .409; .193
   These results are closer to the true solution than those of part (a).

(d) .412; .194

14-15   (a) $\Delta r = \frac{1}{12}$
       (b) 43,825

14-16   58,415

14-17   543.90

14-18   6507

14-19   .863283

14-20   .064472

14-21 $\dfrac{d}{dt}\, {}_t^h\overline{V} = \overline{G}_t(1-r_t) - \overline{e}_t + \delta_t \cdot {}_t^h\overline{V} - \mu_{x+t}^{(f)}\left(b_t^{(f)} - {}_t^h\overline{V}\right) - \mu_{x+t}^{(d)}\left({}_t^d\overline{V} - {}_t^h\overline{V}\right)$

and $\dfrac{d}{dt}\, {}_t^d\overline{V} = \delta_t \cdot {}_t^d\overline{V} - \overline{b}_t^{(d)} - {}^d\mu_{x+t}^{(f)}\left(b_t^{(f)} - {}_t^d\overline{V}\right) - {}^d\mu_{x+t}^{(r)}\left({}_t^h\overline{V} - {}_t^d\overline{V}\right)$, where $\overline{b}_t^{(d)}$ is

the rate of continuous disability income and $b_t^{(f)}$ is the amount of failure benefit at time t, assumed to be the same whether healthy or disabled.

14-22 $\dfrac{d}{dt}\, {}_t\overline{V}^{(i)} = \overline{G}_t^{(i)}\left(1-r_t^{(i)}\right) - \overline{e}_t^{(i)} + \delta_t \cdot {}_t\overline{V}^{(i)} - \overline{b}_t^{(i)} - \sum_{j \neq i} \lambda_{ij}(t) \cdot \left(b_t^{(ij)} + {}_t\overline{V}^{(j)} - {}_t\overline{V}^{(i)}\right)$

14-23 (a) 418,458.16

(b) 146,460.46

(c) 32.41%

(d) 59.62%

14-24 (a) .42981

(b) .50

14-25 (a) $APV_{51}^{NR} = PAB_{65} \cdot v^{14} \cdot {}_{14}p_{51}^{(\tau)} \cdot {}^r\ddot{a}_{65}^{(12)}$, where $PAB_{65} = 22,425.92$

(b) $APV_{51}^{ER} = \sum_{y=61}^{64} \left[1 - .03\left(65 - y - \tfrac{1}{2}\right) \right] \cdot PAB_{y+1/2} \cdot v^{y+1/2-51} \cdot {}_{y-51}p_{51}^{(\tau)} \cdot q_y^{(r)} \cdot {}^r\ddot{a}_{y+1/2}^{(12)},$

where

$$PAB_{y+1/2} = .01\left(y + \tfrac{1}{2} - 51\right)(100,000) \cdot \frac{1}{3}\left(\frac{\tfrac{1}{2}S_{y-3} + S_{y-2} + S_{y-1} + \tfrac{1}{2}S_y}{S_{51}}\right)$$

(c) $APV_{51}^{W} = \sum_{y=56}^{60} PAB_{y+1/2} \cdot v^{14} \cdot {}_{y-51}p_{51}^{(\tau)} \cdot q_y^{(w)} \, {}_{65-y-1/2}^{w}p_{y+1/2} \cdot {}^r\ddot{a}_{65}^{(12)}$

(d) $APV_{51}^{I} = \sum_{y=56}^{64} PAB_{y+1/2} \cdot v^{y+1/2-51} \cdot {}_{y-51}p_{51}^{(\tau)} \cdot q_y^{(i)} \cdot {}^i\ddot{a}_{y+1/2}^{(12)}$

(e) $APV_{51}^{D} = \sum_{y=61}^{64} .50\left[1 - .03\left(65 - y - \tfrac{1}{2}\right)\right]$

$\cdot PAB_{y+1/2} \cdot v^{y+1/2-51} \cdot {}_{y-51}p_{51}^{(\tau)} \cdot q_y^{(d)} \cdot {}^r\ddot{a}_{y+1/2-3}^{(12)}$

14-26 (a) 1860

(b) The APV for each benefit is calculated the same as in Exercise 14-25, except that PAB_{65} in part (a) and $PAB_{y+1/2}$ in parts (b)-(e) are all replaced by the benefit accrual 1860. The unit credit normal cost is the sum of these five APVs.

(c) The APV for each benefit is calculated the same as in part (b), except that the 1860 benefit accrual is replaced by the 7500 accrued benefit. The accrued liability is the sum of these five APVs.

CHAPTER 15

15-1 577.93; 635.97

15-2 .1875; .1958

15-3 (a) 3.8461

(b) .6155

15-4 (a)

Interest Rate Scenario	Annuity Certain	Life Annuity	Term Insurance
Increasing	3.97	2.53	.53
Decreasing	4.25	2.65	.57

     (b) The life annuity

15-5 (a) 289.84; 46.73
     (b) Increasing: 23.74; 6.10
         Decreasing: −29.25; −7.96
     (c) The annual premium product

15-7   2.0%; 4.020%; 6.082%; 8.211%

15-8   2.0%; 4.041%; 6.169%; 8.447%

15-9   2.0%; 3.960%; 5.844%; 7.615%

15-10 2.0%; 3.980%; 5.921%; 7.804%

15-11 74,020

15-14

n	1	2	3	4	5
z_n	4.000%	4.499%	4.997%	5.494%	5.991%

15-15

n	$f_{n,1}$	$f_{n,2}$	$f_{n,3}$	$f_{n,4}$	$f_{n,5}$
0	4.00%	4.499%	4.997%	5.494%	5.991%
1	5.00	5.499	5.997	6.494	--
2	6.00	6.499	6.997	--	--
3	7.00	7.499	--	--	--
4	8.00	--	--	--	--

15-16 (a) 6.997%
     (b) Sell a 2-year zero-coupon bond and buy a 5-year zero-coupon bond, each of face amount 274,724.24.

15-17 (a) 5.499%
     (b) Sell a 1-year zero-coupon bond and buy a 3-year zero-coupon bond, each of face amount 24,038.46.

15-18

n	$f_{n,1}$	$f_{n,2}$	$f_{n,3}$
1	6.12%	8.32%	10.685%
2	10.56	13.04	--
3	15.58	--	--

CHAPTER 16

16-1 (a) 5411.49
(b) 4411.49
(c) 3711.49

16-2 (a) 24; 9
(b) 12,000,000; 4,500,000
(c) 6300

16-3 (a) 8.0%; 10.0%; 1.0%
(b) 268.87; 1122.47; 1762.82

16-4 (a) 103,588.72
(b) 65,576.44

16-5 49,027.33

16-6 (a) 5926.20
(b) 14,678.57
(c) .40373

16-7 (a) 5.096%
(b) 3.640%

16-8 93,000

CHAPTER 17

17-1 102,734.39

17-2 100,280.00

17-4 2.15%

17-5
Date	Minimum Guaranteed Value	Indexed Account Value
12/31/08	8,938.13	10,000
12/31/09	9,130.29	10,000
12/31/10	9,326.60	10,000

17-6
Date	Indexed Account Value
12/31/08	10,000
12/31/09	10,700
12/31/10	11,449

17-7 63,000

17-8   .00583%

17-9   .00743%

17-10   70,500

17-11   1723.65

17-13   18,376.28

17-14   2.40%

17-15   9053.88

17-16   963.77

BIBLIOGRAPHY

1. Balducci, G., "Costruzione e critica della tavola di mortalita," *Gior. degli Economisti e Riv. Di Statis.*, 55 (1917), 455.

2. _____, Correspondence, *JIA*, LII (1921), 184.

3. Batten, R.W., *Mortality Table Construction*. Englewood Cliffs: Prentice-Hall, Inc., 1978.

4. Bowers, N.L., et al., *Actuarial Mathematics* (Second Edition). Schaumburg: Society of Actuaries, 1997.

5. Box, G.E.P. and M.E. Muller, "A Note on the Generation of Random Normal Deviates," *Annals of Mathematical Statistics*, Vol. 29, No. 2 (1958), 610.

6. Broverman, S.A., *Mathematics of Investment and Credit* (Fifth Edition). Winsted: ACTEX Publications, 2010.

7. Brown, R.L., *Introduction to the Mathematics of Demography* (Third Edition). Winsted: ACTEX Publications, 1997.

8. Dickson, D.C.M., M.R. Hardy, and H.R. Waters, *Actuarial Mathematics for Life Contingent Risks*. Cambridge: Cambridge University Press, 2009.

9. Dobson, R.H., "Mortality and Morbidity Tables," Society of Actuaries Study Note 7BA-111-83, 1983.

10. Gompertz, B., "On the Nature of the Function Expressive of the Law of Human Mortality," *Phil. Trans.*, Royal Society of London, 1825.

11. Halley, E., "An Estimate of the Degrees of the Mortality of Mankind, Drawn from Various Tables of Births and Funerals at the City of Breslau," 1693.

12. Hassett, M.J. and D.G. Stewart, *Probability for Risk Management* (Second Edition). Winsted: ACTEX Publications, 2006.

13. Herzog, T.N. and G. Lord, *Applications of Monte Carlo Methods to Finance and Insurance*. Winsted: ACTEX Publications, 2002.

14. Jones, B.L., "A Stochastic Model for CCRC's," *ARCH*, 1955.1.

15. Jordan, C.W., *Life Contingencies* (Second Edition). Chicago: Society of Actuaries, 1967.

16. Kellison, S.G., *The Theory of Interest* (Third Edition). New York: McGraw Hill Irwin, 2009.

17. Kellison, S.G. and R.L. London, *Risk Models and Their Estimation*. Winsted: ACTEX Publications, 2011.

18. Klugman, S.A., H.H. Panjer, and G.E. Willmot, *Loss Models*: *From Data to Decisions* (Third Edition). Hoboken: John Wiley & Sons, 2008.

19. Knuth, D.E., *The Art of Computer Programming*, Vol. 2 (Third Edition). Reading: Addison-Wesley, 1997.

20. Lehmer, D.H., "Mathematical Models in Large-Scale Computing Units," *Annals of the Computation Laboratory of Harvard University*, 26: *Proceedings of 2nd Symposium on Large-scale Digital Calculating Machinery* (September 13-16, 1949). Cambridge: Harvard University Press, 1951.

21. Lewis, P.A.W., A.S. Goodman, and J.M. Miller, "A Pseudo-random Number Generator for the System/360," *IBM Systems Journal*, Vol. 8 (1969), 136.

22. London, D., *Survival Models and Their Estimation* (Third Edition). Winsted: ACTEX Publications, 1997.

23. Makeham, W.M., "On the Law of Mortality, and the Construction of Annuity Tables," *JIA*, VIII (1860).

24. Mereu, J.A., "Some Observations on Actuarial Approximations," *TSA*, XIII (1961), 87.

25. Ross, S.M., *A First Course in Probability* (Sixth Edition). Old Tappen: Prentice-Hall, 2001.

26. _____, *Introduction to Probability Models* (Eighth Edition). San Diego: Academic Press, 2003.

27. Woolhouse, W.S.B., "On an Improved Theory of Annuities and Assurances," *JIA*, XV (1869).

INDEX